PHOENIX

PHOENIX

The Life of Norman Bethune

Roderick Stewart and Sharon Stewart

McGill-Queen's University Press   Montreal & Kingston • London • Ithaca

© Roderick Stewart and Sharon Stewart 2011

ISBN 978-0-7735-3819-1

Legal deposit second quarter 2011
Bibliothèque nationale du Québec

Printed in Canada on acid-free paper that is 100% ancient forest free
(100% post-consumer recycled), processed chlorine free.

This book has been published with the help of a grant from the Canadian Federation for the Humanities and Social Sciences, through the Aid to Scholarly Publications Program, using funds provided by the Social Sciences and Humanities
Research Council of Canada.

McGill-Queen's University Press acknowledges the support of the Canada Council
for the Arts for our publishing program. We also acknowledge the financial support
of the Government of Canada through the Canada Book Fund for our publishing
activities.

Library and Archives Canada Cataloguing in Publication

Stewart, Roderick, 1934–
Phoenix : the life of Norman Bethune / Roderick Stewart and Sharon Stewart.

Includes bibliographical references and index.
ISBN 978-0-7735-3819-1

1. Bethune, Norman, 1890–1939. 2. Surgeons–Canada–Biography.
3. Surgeons–China–Biography. I. Stewart, Sharon II. Title.

R464.B4S754 2011   617.092   C2010-907159-X

This book was designed and typeset by studio oneonone in Sabon 10/14.5

Contents

Acknowledgments

Information used in the writing of *Phoenix* came from a multitude of individuals. Several among them merit special thanks for their significant contributions to our knowledge of Bethune and his achievements. They include Giovanna Badia, Library, Royal Victoria Hospital, Montreal, QC; George Bolotenko, Library and Archives Canada, Ottawa, ON; Min-sun Chen, Lakehead University, Thunder Bay, ON; Margaret Cooper, Sault St Marie, ON; Scott Davidson, Bethune Memorial House, Gravenhurst, ON; Diana Dodd, Mettlach, Germany; Dong Chun, Beijing, China; Mary Margaret Johnston-Miller, Library and Archives Canada, Ottawa; Ji Junmei, Norman Bethune International Peace Hospital, Shijiazhuang, China; Cameron Knight, Richmond Hill Public Library, Richmond Hill, ON; Elizabeth Lamont, Library, Royal Victoria Hospital, Montreal; Kenneth Lewis, Lodeve, France; Jesus Majada Neila, Arroyo de Miel, Spain; Angel Mendía, Pamplona, Spain; Laura Meyer, Victoria, BC; Qi Ming, Bethune Medical College, Shijiazhuang, China; Pamela Miller, Osler Library of Medicine, McGill University, Montreal; Dr Larry Stephenson, Wayne State University, Detroit, MI; Dr Grant Stewart, Vancouver, BC, James Sturgis, Tunbridge Wells, England; Guy Tessier, Library and Archives Canada, Ottawa; Zhang Yesheng, Beijing, China.

For their invaluable assistance as interpreters of documentation in Chinese, we thank the following: Ling Chen, Nee Lee, Jane Lu, Greg Whincup, David Zhang, Kun Zhang, Lesley Zuo.

Should there be an inadvertent omission in the following list of persons who provided much of the information used to write *Phoenix*, we apologize profoundly. They include: Ellen Adams, Dr Helen Alsop, Irene Amsden, Robert Anger, G. David Anderson, Paul G. Anderson, Susan Anderson, Andres Arenas Gomez, Kim Arnold, Ken Arnson, Barbara Attebery, James Bacque, Mary Balfour, Paul Banfield, Judy Bates, Rosalyn Fraad Baxandall, Dr Jacques Beaudoin, Denise Beaugrand-Champagne, Pierre Beaulieu,

Heather Bethune, Stewart Boden, Michael Boland, Mark Bowden, Matt Bray, Estelle Brisson, Moises Broggi, Kevin Brown, Claudette Bue, Ronald H. Bulatoff, Stacie D.A. Burke, Jose-Ramon Navaro Carballo, Morag Carnie, Liette Casola, Joan Cavanagh, Chen Yuen, Christine Clark, John Clarke, Michelle Cousineau, Merrianne Couture, Tina Craig, Mark Dallas, Deng Lilan, Barbara Dent, Paulette Dozois, Jim Dukes, Richard Durack, Linda Facey, Oliver Fairclough, John Fairley, Rosemary Le Faive, Victor Falkenheim, William Feindel, Mike Filey, Meredith Fitzpatrick, Ryan S. Flahive, David Ford, Marion and Cyril Fry, Fred and Styn Furness, Anne Goddard, Frances Geddes, Dan German, David Goodman, Susan Gosling, Michael Gnarowski, Sonya Grypma, Diana Hall, Dr Lesley Hall, Paul Hambleton, Larry Hannant, Phoebe Harkins, Stephanie Harlick, Peter Harris, John Harrison, Dr Gerd Hartmann, Wendy and Gordon Hawksley, John E. Haynes, Carolyn Hein, Roger Hollywood, Bridgett Howlett, Kate Hughes, James Hunter, Kate Jacob, Jon James, Marianne Jettmar, Betty Kalmanash, Brecque Keith, Steven Kerr, Marjorie W. Kehoe, Harvey Klehr, Edward Korvin, James Labosier, Andrée Lavoie, William W. LeFevre, Jean-François Leclerc, Margaret A. Lee, Loren Lerner, Allan Levine, Hannah Liang, Liang Hongyuan, Feng Lin, Shirley Lindemann, Joan Lindley, Claude Lord, Eric v. d. Luft, Fiona Lundy, Bernard Lutz, Ma Baoru, Loryl MacDonald, Michael MacDonald, Iain Mackenzie, Stephen MacKinnon, Norma MacLeod, Hugh P. MacMillan, Diana Madgin, Gail Malmgreen, John Manley, Rhea Marcellus, Carrie Marsh, Jean Mason, Brian Massachaele, Jose María Massons, Steven McArthur, David and Diana MacFadyen, Linda McKnight, Rosie McLure, Joan McTavish, Rob McTavish, Nada Mehes-Rovenelli, Jean Pierre Morissette, James Morrison, Myron Momryk, Dr Sean Moore, Jean Morrison (Thunder Bay, ON), Jean Morrison (Montreal), Dr David Mulder, Indren Mutukistna, Peter Nelson, Naomi L. Nelson, Tom Newnham, David Nicolson, Victoria North, Colin Olds, John O'Leary, Ani Orchanian-Cheff, Lea Osborne, Bruno Pacheco, Laurel Parson, Ian Penney, Dr Peter Pinkerton, David Pitcher, Margarita Pitt, Anita Ponsford, Felicity Pope, Jim Powell, Lutzen Riedstra, Natalie Riegler, Martha Riley, Susan Rishworth, Andrea Robbins, Mary Rossiter, Bill Russell, Matthew Ruttan, Caroline Schmidt, Paul Schmidt, Peter Dale Scott, Anne Scotton, Dr Andrew Seeley, Arlene Shaner, Manfred Skopec, Philip Skroska, Donald Smith, J. Earl Smith, Zoe Stansell, Marcia Stentz, Rick Stow, Mark Suggit, Delores Sui, Adam Symansky, Dave Tackenberg, John Tagg, Sophie Tellier, Guy Tessier, Alex Thompson, Dr Tom Treasure, Esther Trépanier, Bogusia Trojan, Lucy Viedma, Wang Siqiang, Leon Warmski, Garron Wells, Kristi Wermager, Lonnie Weatherby, Wei Hongyun, Merrily Weisbord, Lynne Westerby, Anne Wheeldon, Allison

Whitney, Les Whitney, Laura Wicks, Chuck Wilcox, Jill Wilmott, Bill Willmott, Dale Wilson, Wu Zhuqing, Yang Xuelun, Dan Zelenyj, Pat Zimmer, Mark Zuehlke, Zou Zhengrong, and Zuo Ling.

We would also like to thank Maureen Garvie for her careful editing of the manuscript.

The authors have made every effort to identify, credit appropriately, and obtain publication rights from copyright holders of illustrations in this book. Notice of any errors or omissions in this regard will be gratefully received and corrections made in any subsequent editions.

Preface

The Bethune Trail

My involvement with Norman Bethune began in a classroom in the autumn of 1969. Searching for something to stimulate the interest of my senior students in the history of Canada in the 1930s, I had decided to show them the documentary film *Bethune*. I knew little more about the man than they did – only that he had something to do with China. We were all stirred by the film, and a group of students followed me back to my office afterward, peppering me with questions that I was for the most part unable to answer. My curiosity piqued, I set about trying to learn more. I read the only then existing biography of Bethune, Ted Allan and Sydney Gordon's *The Scalpel, the Sword* (1952), but although it was well written, it was undocumented and left me with many questions unanswered. And so I decided to do some research myself. Little did I know that my life's work was about to unfold before me.

At that time Bethune had only been dead for thirty years; many people who had known him well were still alive and had vivid memories of him that they were willing to share. During the next four years I located more than two hundred such people, including members of Bethune's family, university classmates, students he had taught, patients he had treated, medical colleagues, political associates, military comrades, friends, and lovers. Some I corresponded with, but most I travelled to meet and interview, in Canada, the United States, Mexico, England, and Spain. It was also my great good fortune to be able to go to China in 1972, even though the country was still in the throes of the Great Proletarian Cultural Revolution. My hosts, the China People's Association for Friendship with Foreign Countries and the China Medical Association, provided me with a superb interpreter, Chen Lomin, and arranged interviews in several cities with people who had known Bethune. As a result of this research, my biography *Bethune* was published in 1973, and in 1974 I also wrote a second, brief biography, *Norman Bethune*, which was intended for secondary-school students.

But my involvement with the man did not end there. Not long after the publication of *Bethune,* Parks Canada asked me to act as its advisor on Bethune's life for its project of restoring to period the house in Gravenhurst in which he had been born. In this role I was able to do further research into Bethune's career, returning to the countries I had visited earlier. This led to the publication in 1977 of *The Mind of Norman Bethune*; in this third book I compiled some of Bethune's writings and a large number of photographs of him, and wrote connecting text. In that same year the Canadian Broadcasting Corporation purchased the rights to my original biography to produce their telefilm *Bethune*. Also, through contacts in China gained in the course of my research trips there, I was invited to teach English as a foreign language at the Sichuan Foreign Language Institute. During the year I spent living in Chongqing with my family, I was invited by the Canadian Embassy in Beijing to join a small delegation of Canadians who had arrived in China to participate in ceremonies marking the fortieth anniversary of Bethune's death. My wife, Sharon, and I subsequently spent a year teaching in Harbin, in China's far north, in 1983.

By this time I was convinced that the Bethune vein in my life had been mined out, but I was to be proved wrong. At the end of the final year of my teaching career in June 1999, the publisher of *The Mind of Norman Bethune* and *Norman Bethune* asked me to revise both books, and new editions were published three years later. The new round of research I conducted for these revisions revealed that much fresh information was now available about Bethune's life. One source was books and articles published since I had completed my original research. Another was highly relevant archival material that had only recently been made available to researchers. In addition I was able to access the memoirs of two persons who had worked closely with Bethune, one in Spain, the other in China, and also discovered diverse sources of letters and reports written by Bethune in China. So great was the amount of new material that I abandoned my original plan to revise *Bethune* and decided to write a completely new biography.

At this point Sharon agreed to join me as co-author. Trained in historical research, a professional editor and published author, she had been assisting me in my research and had helped me revise my earlier books. We decided to go to China to look for more information on Bethune's life and achievements there. To this end we approached Ji Junmei of the Norman Bethune International Peace Hospital in Shijiazhuang, which is the main Chinese repository of documentation on Bethune. She invited us to Shijiazhuang to carry out research in April 2005. We were accompanied to Shijiazhuang from Beijing by Dong Chun, a daughter of Dong Yueqian, one of Bethune's interpreters, and Zhang Yesheng, a former medical student of Bethune and the pre-eminent Chinese authority on his work in China. Together we spent ten days in the remote mountainous region southwest of Beijing where Bethune had worked, retracing some of the routes he had followed in 1938 and 1939. During the writing of this book we maintained frequent contact with Zhang Yesheng about details of Bethune's life and work in China.

Back in Canada, we travelled to most of the places where Bethune had lived during his youth. In the autumn of 2005 we visited Owen Sound, then drove west along the northern shore of Lake Huron to Blind River and on to Sault St Marie, before returning east to end our journey at Gravenhurst. We visited the houses in which Bethune had lived and the schools and churches he had attended and also saw for ourselves some of the wilderness of forests, rivers, and lakes that was so dear to his heart.

In 2006 we went to Spain. In Madrid we located the building that housed Bethune's blood transfusion headquarters, followed routes he had taken to deliver blood to hospitals, visited the Ciudad Universitaría where he ventured in the midst of the most intense fighting in November 1936, and the Gran Vía Hotel where he had stayed in the early days after his arrival in Spain and was nearly arrested as a supposed fascist fifth columnist. In Salamanca we attended a Bethune symposium at the city's venerable university, then went south to Málaga. We drove part of the winding coastal route where Bethune and two companions struggled to aid panic-stricken refugees fleeing fascist military units in February 1937, and we met Jesús Majada Neila, the leading Spanish scholar on Bethune's work in Spain. He is the latest, but far from the least, of all those who have helped us so much over the years. Without their aid we could not have written such a detailed account of Bethune's life – and it is a tale worth telling.

The trail has been a long one, and sometimes we have asked each other, "Is there life after Bethune?" Only time will tell.

RODERICK STEWART AND SHARON STEWART
Richmond Hill, ON
May 2010

PHOENIX

A Pain in the Neck

Childhood and Early Youth, 1890–1907

In 1935 Norman Bethune wrote to a woman he loved, "I come of a race of men violent, unstable, of passionate convictions and wrong-headedness, intolerant, yet with it all a vision of truth and a drive to carry them on to it even though it leads, as it has done in my family, to their own destruction."[1] It was his credo, summing up his character as he saw it and the sense of destiny that lay at the core of his being. Descended from distinguished and often colourful ancestors, he revelled in the family history as a personal fairytale; from his youth onward he believed that he was exceptional, and destined like his forebears to achieve notable things.

The Bethune saga was part of the family culture. The name itself, young Norman was told, originated in the province of Artois on the northwestern border of France and first appeared in recorded documents in the ninth century.[2] In the fourteenth century a Béthune had crossed the North Sea to begin a new life in Scotland, and for the next three centuries some of his descendants prospered as high-ranking clergy; others became renowned practitioners of medicine, hereditary physicians to the clan Macdonald in the Isle of Skye. The Bethunes could even claim a heraldic badge: the head of a snarling otter above a shield, with the motto "Debonnaire."[3]

In the latter part of the eighteenth century the Bethune thread became woven into the tapestry of North America. Soon after emigrating to North Carolina, the Reverend John Bethune (1751–1815) was caught up in the American Revolution, joined a loyalist regiment, and was captured and imprisoned by the rebels. On his release he headed north to British-occupied territory, founding Montreal's first Presbyterian congregation and then another in Williamstown in what is now Ontario.[4] His descendants distinguished themselves as noted clergymen, respected educators, and successful medical practitioners in Toronto and Montreal.[5] Many of them also made a lot of money in business.

But there were wild cards among the Bethunes too. For instance, Norman's great-grandfather Angus (1783–58), eldest son of the Reverend John Bethune, had left the security of Williamstown for the hard, dangerous life of a fur trader. He was at first employed by the North West Company and made two fur-trading trips to Canton between 1814 and 1816 on behalf of his employers, during which his adventures included "trading for silks, gold lace, and artificial flowers; eating gulls' eggs and young sea lions and dealing in exotic empires with Russian and Spanish governors, Hawaiian royalty, and officials of the Emperor of China."[6] After helping to negotiate the takeover of the North West Company by the Hudson's Bay Company, Angus had risen to a well-paid position as a chief factor, and married Louisa McKenzie, the daughter of a Scottish trader and a full-blooded Woodland Cree. So the blood of "Miss Green Blanket" ran in Norman's veins too.[7]

The boy's hero, however, was his grandfather Norman Bethune (1822–92), who studied medicine and surgery in Toronto and then won further distinction in London and Edinburgh, qualifying as a fellow in the colleges of surgery of both capitals. He had built a thriving surgical practice in Toronto and had been a professor of surgery in Trinity College. Respected for his professional skills, he was also a gifted artist and achieved a certain reputation for his accomplished drawings and the literary quality of his writing.

Such was the family history, and young Norman took it deeply to heart, committing himself to hold high the name of Bethune. He would make it his personal quest to perform daring deeds: it was only a question of what kind of dragon he would slay. However, what his parents did not dwell on was a darker side to the Bethune story, which had most recently appeared in the life of the boy's grandfather, Norman. Brilliant doctor though he was, he had two fatal flaws: he was incompetent in managing money and he abused alcohol. Because of these failings, his wife had left him, taking their four daughters and older son, Angus, back to Edinburgh to live with her brother. Only Malcolm Nicolson (1857–1932), the younger son, remained with his father. The following year, when Norman Bethune received word that his wife had died of tuberculosis of the lungs, he persuaded his sister-in-law to care for the children in Edinburgh. As his drinking increased, his financial means dwindled, and he reneged on his promise to pay for his children's support. His outraged sister-in-law went so far as to launch a lawsuit against him. Meanwhile his surgical practice declined, and he lost his university appointment.

In this situation, Malcolm Bethune found it impossible to continue to live with his father. In his early twenties he left home to work his way around the world. But not long after he set out, the plan went awry. After quarrelling with the captain of the ship he was on, he was put ashore, destitute, in Australia. Unable to get work, he underwent a long period of misery and finally had to swallow his pride and write home for help. He eventually received some money from his father, part of a bequest from Malcolm's fur-trader grandfather Angus, which allowed him to make his way back to Canada. It was at this time that he met Elizabeth Ann Goodwin (1852–1948), who had emigrated from England. How and where the two met is not known precisely, although a family story says it was in Hawaii, where Malcolm had supposedly stopped on his way home to look into investing in orange groves and where Elizabeth was a missionary.[8] They may have found each other sympathetic in part because they shared a mutual misfortune, a father who was unable to control his drinking.[9] Elizabeth's horror of alcohol went even deeper than Malcolm's, for it had also ruined the lives of two of her brothers.[10] As solace for her family troubles, she had become a fervent Christian evangelist. A strong-willed woman with a proselytizing nature, she soon converted Malcolm, who became a born-again Christian. And it was no lip-service conversion: he had indeed undergone a profound religious experience. In later years he often spoke of how, shaken to the depths of his soul by a conviction of his personal sin and guilt, he had abased himself spiritually before his Creator. Then, embracing Christ as his saviour, he had felt a rapturous sense of peace.

Malcolm proposed marriage to Elizabeth, but she replied that she would accept only if he vowed to renounce the pursuit of money and worldly pleasures and pledge himself to a life of service to God. And so the globe-trotting vagabond agreed to become a Christian evangelist and dedicated himself to leading other souls along the holy path he himself had recently discovered.[11] To carry out this commitment, he decided to follow in the footsteps of his great-great-grandfather John Bethune: he would be a Presbyterian minister. In September 1884 he entered the University of Toronto to obtain the academic qualifications for admission to Knox College, where two years later he began to study theology.

In April 1887, near the end of his first year at Knox College, he and Elizabeth were married, and the following May their first child, Janet Louise, was born. Two years later, after completing his religious studies, Malcolm Bethune answered the call of the congregation of Knox Presbyterian Church in the town of Gravenhurst, 150 kilometres north of Toronto. On the edge of the Muskoka District, the town of about two thousand was an important centre in the thriving logging industry in the 1880s. Known as "Sawdust

City," Gravenhurst boasted seventeen mills within its municipal boundaries. Logs from the thick forests surrounding Lake Muskoka were towed across the lake to be rough-milled there before being shipped out by train.

The Bethunes moved into the golden-yellow clapboard manse on John Street, two short blocks from the church. Almost one in every three citizens of Gravenhurst was Presbyterian, so a new pastor and his wife were objects of avid curiosity and gossip. On Monday, 10 June 1889, a large crowd gathered to greet them and look them over. Most agreed that the tall, serious-looking gentleman with the heavy moustache seemed like an ideal minister and his smiling wife the perfect helpmate. After a series of welcoming addresses, Malcolm rose to thank the congregation for their warm wishes and to express "his intense desire that they might grow in holiness and Christian character under his ministry."[12]

The congregation soon learned exactly what their new minister meant. Believing as he did in fundamentalist evangelism, he set out to oppose a liberalizing trend that had been growing in Protestant circles. God, he believed, was everywhere, saw everything, and rewarded or punished every individual act. Therefore, as God's servant, his minister had a sacred obligation to draw attention to sinful acts and to criticize sinners openly and firmly. Those who were lax in their religious observances in everyday life he condemned as "Sunday Christians." Even worse were those who did not strictly observe the Sabbath: for him, Sunday was a day on which no form of activity beyond rest and worship might be pursued. Good Christians must not indulge in any "amusements," a term that included playing sports, reading novels, dancing, and playing cards and games of chance. In his fervour, he even waged a strenuous but losing campaign to stop trains from running on Sundays.

However, the greatest evil of all, in Malcolm Bethune's eyes, was the drinking of alcohol. Again and again he denounced the practice from the pulpit, saying that it was the greatest scourge, the most pernicious evil that tempted God-fearing Christians. Both he and his wife belonged to temperance organizations, and he preached fiery sermons against drink. During a campaign for a plebiscite on the liquor question, he left his congregation temporarily to go on a speaking tour to encourage people to vote against the sale of alcohol.[13] Most Presbyterians at the time rejected alcohol, but Malcolm's opposition to it was deeply personal, rooted in its disastrous effect on his father. The new minister soon gained a reputation as a powerful speaker, not only in his own pulpit but at revival sessions held in churches, public halls, and summer camp meetings. He would make impassioned pleas, urging his listeners to open their hearts, give up their sinful ways, and take the path he had followed through humiliation and exaltation to God. Newspaper reports praised him: in one, he was described as "a fearless and outspoken preacher [who] never fails to attract large congregations."[14]

But Malcolm also had his critics. People noticed that he often found it difficult to accept others' opinions, especially on questions of the interpretation of God's word, an area where he regarded his views as incontrovertible. Others were taken aback by his practice of launching thunderbolts from the pulpit. "I cannot understand why people come to church to sleep!" he once exclaimed in the middle of a sermon, having noticed a church elder nodding off.[15] His forthrightness, inflexibility, and intensity would eventually turn some of his flock against him. Impatient and with a temper that he controlled only by considerable effort, he felt the physical effects of his temperament and showed it. "He will wear fast and weary as he wears," a fellow clergyman commented perceptively.[16]

While the Presbyterians of Gravenhurst were discovering just what kind of preacher they had called to the pulpit, the Bethunes were expecting an addition to their family. Near the end of their first winter in the Gravenhurst manse, on Tuesday, 4 March 1890, Elizabeth sent for the family physician a few doors up the street.[17] Within minutes Dr Cornell and the midwife who regularly assisted him in deliveries arrived at the manse, and later that day Elizabeth Bethune gave birth to her first son. They named him after her father, Henry, and Malcolm's father, Norman; all his life he would prefer to be called Norman.[18]

A healthy baby, he had wisps of light brown hair on a rather large head and a nose that showed a promise of becoming rather long. His alert blue eyes were slightly crossed, which gave him an intent look that in maturity would become a piercing gaze.[19] From the moment he began to crawl, his parents realized he would bear watching. Hyperactive, highly intelligent, and insatiably curious, he explored every nook and cranny of the house and yard the moment his parents' backs were turned. Gazing eagerly about, he would notice something, examine it intently, then drop it and move on as fast as he could go. It was a pattern of attention that would prove to be lifelong.

From the beginning he was the kind of child to whom things happened. When he was less than a year old, his nurse lost hold of the handle of his carriage, which careered down a steep hill, struck a fence, and overturned. With the good luck on which he would later come to rely, Norman emerged unharmed.[20] Two years later, on a sultry August day in 1892, a tornado roared down on Elizabeth as she stood with Norman by a lake, his new baby brother, Malcolm Goodwin, in her arms. Seizing Norman's hand, she dashed toward a shanty at the end of the wharf. They were barely inside when the wind ripped the building from its foundations and flung it and its occupants ten metres out into the lake. Norman's hand was yanked from his mother's, and he disappeared into the churning water. Clinging to the baby, Elizabeth made her way to shore screaming for help. Fortunately several campers on the beach saw Norman bob to the surface and rushed to rescue him.[21]

On the eve of Norman's third birthday, his father decided to leave Gravenhurst to answer the call of the congregation of Knox Church in the village of Beaverton some sixty kilometres to the south on the eastern shore of Lake Simcoe. There is no evidence of any complaint against him by the Gravenhurst congregation, but Malcolm had certainly rubbed some members the wrong way, and there may have been a tacit agreement that he move on. Why he chose Beaverton, a much smaller municipality than Gravenhurst, is not clear. It certainly was not money that attracted him, for the annual stipend of $850 offered in Beaverton was slightly less than what he had received in Gravenhurst in 1892.[22] This was the first of a series of moves during Norman's early life that would eventually create in him a deep-seated feeling that he never really belonged anywhere. Always the outsider, he would seek to define himself by opposition to much that he encountered, trying to impress others with his own point of view. This ingrained contrarian attitude became one of his defining characteristics.

But the boy was delighted by this first move because, behind the wooden-frame manse high on a hill overlooking the village and the lake, stretched four wooded acres of land belonging to the church. And at the back of the house was a stable that housed the horse and canopied four-wheel buggy that Malcolm used to travel to Gamebridge, a tiny community ten kilometres to the north, to minister to a second, smaller congregation. Norman loved nature and animals, especially dogs and horses, and at Beaverton he spent hours exploring the woods and hanging about the stable. One day his father found him unconscious just outside the stable door, a bloody gash in his forehead; presumably he had been kicked by the horse.[23] But this mishap did not affect the boy's fascination with the animal. In the earliest-known photograph of the family, Norman's sister and brother are seated in the buggy, their mother standing beside them. Malcolm is in front, holding a harness strap. On the horse's back, head cocked, sits Norman.

The move to Beaverton did nothing to relieve the stress Malcolm imposed on himself. By the spring of 1895 he was beginning to "wear fast," showing signs of extreme mental fatigue. Hoping that a break from duties and a change of scenery might help, he and Elizabeth decided to spend the summer visiting relatives in Great Britain. He left in early June, and several weeks later the family followed on the ss *Vancouver*.

Here was a whole new world for five-year-old Norman to explore, and it did not take him long to get into trouble. The voyage was barely underway when Elizabeth was horrified to see a steward approaching with the limp body of her son in his arms. "Here is your dead boy, Mrs Bethune," the man announced dramatically. Tearing about at top speed, Norman had tripped on some coils of rope and fallen, striking his head on the deck. Luckily, the "dead boy" soon revived, but the ship's doctor put him to bed in the infirmary until he was past danger. And there he stayed, protesting, for most of the voyage.[24]

The family spent a pleasant summer in the United Kingdom, but the change did Malcolm Bethune no good. At the beginning of November, suffering from "an enlarged heart and overwork," he was urged by his congregation to give up his duties for six months.[25] It was agreed that he should do nothing but rest and read from his growing library of books on theology and philosophy. But by late winter, with no change in his health, he decided that he would not be fit to return to pastoral work at the end of his leave and felt he owed it to his congregation to allow them to find a replacement.

Shortly after Norman's sixth birthday, in April 1896, Malcolm submitted his resignation and moved the family to Toronto. It was the city where he had grown up and still had some friends, but in choosing it he was likely thinking of his children. With Janet about to enter third grade and Norman first grade, being near a good school would be important, and Toronto, with its population of 200,000, offered plenty of choices. The family first settled at 136 Robert Street, but before the school year was out they had moved to 217 Pape Avenue – their fourth home in six years.

Little is known of the Bethunes' three years in Toronto, except for one dramatic incident. On a bright summer morning Norman slipped out of the house, telling no one where he was going. For much of the day the eight-year-old boy explored the city, wandering all the way across its northern edge before turning back. Meanwhile his parents frantically searched his usual haunts and canvassed every neighbour in an effort to find him. When he had not returned by evening, they reported their son missing to the police. Just as the last light was fading, Norman walked nonchalantly into the house and announced he had been from one side of the city to the other, a distance of about ten kilometres. And, he added plaintively, he had had nothing to eat since breakfast. His father exploded and in a voice of thunder told the culprit that he and Elizabeth had been beside themselves with anxiety for hours and that the police were combing the streets for him. Did he not realize how wickedly he had behaved? He was to go directly to his room without supper and stay there until morning. Disappointed that no one had praised his adventure, Norman trotted off to bed.[26]

During the time in Toronto the family continued to struggle financially. Although his health remained poor, Malcolm began searching for another congregation soon after they settled in the city, but not until the end of the third year in Toronto did he find one. The call came at last from Knox Church in the town of Aylmer, about 250 kilometres southwest of Toronto, and from Chalmers Church in the nearby village of Springfield. Aylmer was a stop on the Grand Trunk Railway line and a commercial centre for the rich agricultural area that surrounded it; with a population of about 2,200, it was slightly larger than Gravenhurst. After nearly four years without a salary, Malcolm Bethune welcomed the financial relief of the new posting, even though the annual stipend was only $400, less than half of what Gravenhurst had paid him ten years earlier.[27]

A few days after Norman's ninth birthday in March 1899, the Bethunes left Toronto for Aylmer by train. The small town must have seemed dull to the boy after the bustle of the city, and as a minister's son and an outsider he would once again have to prove himself to his peers. He set out to dominate every new situation; eager to attract attention, he revelled in taking dares, and the bolder the challenge, the better he liked it. In his second summer in Aylmer, he and a group of school friends competed against each other chasing and netting butterflies. While others hung back, Norman climbed the tallest trees, risking his neck by venturing out on the thinnest branches to capture his specimens; he ended the season with the best collection.[28] His enjoyment of derring-do seemed based on an instinctive belief that nothing bad would happen to him. Though in later life he rationalized this as a sense of family and personal destiny, it seems to have been part of his makeup from the beginning.

The following winter he again proved his boldness. He was skating with a group of boys on a frozen pond when one of them fell through the ice. The others scrambled for shore, but Norman went to the aid of the floundering boy. Crawling on hands and knees across nearly ten metres of treacherous ice, he clutched the boy's outstretched hand and managed to pull him from the water. But toward shore the ice gave way, and both boys fell in. Rescuers soon reached them, but Norman stayed in the water until the other boy was pulled to safety.[29]

Now ten years old, strong and wiry, Norman was a good athlete. His favourite sports were swimming and running, and he also participated in team sports. He was intensely competitive; winning was very important to him. Already he seemed to equate failure with humiliation and loss of self-worth, and this spurred him on. In his first year in Aylmer he was promoted into the fifth year of elementary school, standing twenty-first in a class of twenty-four.[30] In his later studies he would earn respectable grades in most subjects, except foreign languages. Like his grandfather before him, he was gifted in art – he loved to sketch – and he also enjoyed reading.[31] He had a nimble, intuitive mind, and while others pondered, he would leap to conclusions. Intensely self-absorbed, he failed to notice that not everyone agreed with him; like his father, opposition to his opinion only made him more stubbornly convinced that he was right. And there was another distinctive pattern in the way his mind worked, an echo of his baby curiosity. Caught up in some new interest, he would drop everything else, often exasperating his parents or friends by forgetting errands, arriving home late, or missing meetings. Then, just as suddenly, he would completely lose interest in the subject and fly to a new attraction.

His character was also shaped by a strong sense of justice, an outcome of his religious upbringing. In August 1900 the family rented a cottage near Port Burwell, a short distance from Aylmer on Lake Erie. On arrival they were told that the lawn surrounding the building was out of bounds unless they paid $5 in additional rent. Forbidden to romp on the grass, Norman was outraged. The owner had no right to impose such a condition, he protested, and railed against his father for submitting to what he considered to be robbery.[32]

During these years Norman's relationships with his family settled into life-long patterns. He never got on well with his younger brother, Malcolm Goodwin, a much more placid boy. As a middle child, Norman may have resented the arrival of a younger brother to claim his mother's attention. Even in later years, whenever his brother's name was mentioned, he would respond, "Oh, that Malcolm, brrrr!"[33] However, Norman and his sister, Janet, were natural allies, and she supported him in various pranks and projects. One summer Sunday after church, he talked her into helping him rearrange the furniture. Their parents returned home to find the manse's living room turned upside-down.[34] Brother and sister also began a campaign to convince their parents to call them by different names. Norman hated being called Henry, and hoped at least to be called Harry, and Janet wanted to be called Jean. When their parents rejected their ideas, they lobbied in vain for Norman and Juna.[35] Norman had to wait until later in life to rid himself of the hated Henry.

Between father and son a deep-rooted conflict developed. Many confrontations resulted from Malcolm's determination that his children, and Norman in particular, not become "Sunday Christians." He required them to accept faith as an everyday matter that took precedence over all interests, shaping their deportment and regulating their activities. Elizabeth belonged to various congregational organizations, and she and Malcolm held business meetings and social gatherings in the manse. On such occasions the children had to be on their best behaviour. They were also expected to join youth groups, run errands on church business, and on occasion deliver baskets of food to needy families. But for Norman, Sunday observance was the worst of all the restrictions on his freedom. First he had to attend Sunday school, and as he grew older, church service too. In the afternoon his mother gathered the children in the living room and read to them from the Bible or inspirational Christian literature such as Bunyan's *Pilgrim's Progress*. Then she sent them to their rooms to read and meditate. The only reading allowed was of a religious nature, and to ensure this, she locked all newspapers and magazines away. The children were never allowed to leave the manse on Sunday, unless on a church-related activity. Their mother even prepared the Sunday meals on Saturday so as to avoid working on the Sabbath, the day of the Lord.[36]

For most children of ministers at that time, particularly evangelicals, these were normal restrictions, but Norman found them unbearable. He longed to be free to choose his own reading material or to go swimming or take solitary walks in the woods. The more his parents attempted to constrain him, the more he broke the rules. Confounded by his rebelliousness, they resorted to punishing him. For his part, Norman could not understand his parents' deep anger at his misbehaviour. To add to his perplexity, after receiving a tongue-lashing from his father and being sent to his room, he would often hear a knock on his door at night and Malcolm would enter, kneel by the bed, and apologize for having lost his temper. Bewildered and embarrassed by this turnabout, Norman lost respect for his father.

So he took his punishment when he had to but continued to stand up for his rights. His rebellious nature and easily triggered temper led to frequent bitter arguments with his father. And from the beginning, there was one part of his father's religious training that he utterly refused to accept. On occasion his father would order him down on his knees to eat a handful of earth. This, he explained, was to teach him humility, so that he could be born again. Norman refused: humility was not part of his nature. This struggle did not end with his youth, and in some ways he never recovered from the harm inflicted on his young ego by his father's overbearing ways. As late as 1929 he wrote, "Father and I had our usual hate together."[37] Their duel shaped his lifelong opposition to authority and deeply affected his personal relationships. In later life he told friends that in his childhood he had not felt important enough.[38] He would act out to get the attention he craved, and no one – professional superior, friend, lover, or wife – would ever be allowed to gain emotional ascendancy over him.

Elizabeth Bethune was an even stricter disciplinarian than her husband, and Norman and his siblings feared her wrath more than that of their father. Unlike her husband, she never raised her voice when chastising her children. Instead, she would fix culprits with a penetrating stare, freezing them to the spot. Then she would mete out punishment, often sending them to their room to memorize a long scriptural passage. Norman in particular became thoroughly acquainted with the St James version of the Bible.[39] Fearful that his stubborn nature would lead him to stray from the true faith, his mother took special pains with him, placing religious tracts under his pillow and inside books he was reading. Only years later, when he was at university, did he dare to strike back. Discovering a tract inside his copy of Darwin's *The Origin of Species*, he playfully tucked the tome under his mother's pillow. She was not amused and burned the book.[40] Despite her strictness, Norman always loved her and was eager to please her. It was she who encouraged him to express the family ideals of service and duty to humanity in a career in medicine. In the first year of his life she had placed some of his grandfather's surgical instruments near his cradle, and when he was growing up she presented them to him along with a brass nameplate bearing the inscription "Dr Norman Bethune." This he proudly tacked to his bedroom door.[41]

Although he struggled against the restrictions of his parents' religious beliefs, Norman did not reject Christian teachings. Someone who knew him during his early teens remembered him as "lively, intensely religious, and at times vehemently rebellious."[42] While he remained at home, he attended church services, and even much later in life, after he abandoned his faith in Christianity, he would still be motivated by concepts taught by his parents. He assimilated their belief that the world contained only two forces, good and evil, and he internalized the obligation of the evangelical to crusade against evil. This black-and-white view of the world and the belief that he had a duty to destroy evil never left him; neither did his parents' teaching that it was one's duty to assist the sick, the needy, and the underprivileged. The need to serve became as ingrained in his character as his rebelliousness: they were the twin poles of his being and would remain so throughout his life.

As Norman was nearing the end of the fifth grade, his father became involved in a controversy that forced the family to move yet again. It was related to "amusements," the pastimes that Malcolm Bethune so often preached against. What particular form of amusement triggered his wrath on this occasion is not known, but after he had denounced it from the pulpit, members of the congregation continued to misbehave. His response was drastic. During a Sunday morning service he announced that for him to continue preaching to the congregation on this subject would be "like casting pearls before swine." Offended, several members of his flock later approached him, demanding he withdraw his remark. He refused, telling them he would prefer to resign as their preacher, which he did. Later, cooler but resolute, he offered to withdraw his remark but not his resignation. At a presbytery meeting called to investigate the conflict, he explained his conduct: "I have simply tried to elevate the congregation to the ideal set by the Master and failing to succeed, I desire to resign."[43]

So in early July 1900 Malcolm took the family back to Toronto, renting a house at 132 Yorkville Avenue. On 2 September Norman entered Grade Six at Winchester Street Public School, moving two weeks later to Jesse Ketchum Public School on Davenport Road. No records of his studies survive, but a family anecdote shows he was already giving thought to a career in medicine. His mother arrived home one day to find him in front of the coal stove, malodorous steam rising from a large pot. Inside it, to her horror, she discovered a dead dog that Norman had carried home, skinned and was now boiling to strip the flesh from the skeleton. He explained that he wanted to study the creature's anatomy.[44]

Most of his pastimes were less original. He loved physical activity, particularly if it involved risk-taking, and was always looking for opportunity to test himself. Downhill sledding was a favourite sport, and one day after he and his friends had made several descents of lesser hills, he announced he was going to challenge the steepest slope in the Rosedale ravine. Careering down, he lost control of his sled and crashed into a tree. One metal runner pierced the calf and thigh of his left leg, causing serious wounds that left two long scars when they healed.[45]

Another adventure occurred during a summer holiday. Watching his father, a strong swimmer, make a long swim across an inlet in Georgian Bay, Norman decided he could do it too. The following day he set out, as usual telling no one what he was up to. However, his father saw him swim away from the shore and followed in a rowboat. Part way across the inlet Norman began to flounder, and his father rescued him just as he was going under. Nothing daunted, the boy vowed to attempt the swim again the following summer. That time he made it.[46]

Meanwhile, Malcolm's abrupt departure from the church at Aylmer had wrecked the family's finances, for no new congregation had called him to their pulpit. To bring in a little money, Elizabeth began taking in boarders, and Norman got an after-school job selling newspapers. However, as had been the case with his grandfather, money always slipped through his fingers, and whatever he earned he spent or gave away.[47]

Two years later, as Norman was about to enter his eighth and final year of elementary school, Malcolm was still without an income. In desperation he turned to the home mission field. This was made up of small congregations in remote, lightly populated areas that were unable to pay a minister and relied on support from the presbytery and the national church. The mission field was shunned by many ministers because the congregations were distant from urban centres, living conditions were often barely adequate, and the pay was much less than in other areas of the ministry. But Malcolm had no choice. He was appointed to minister to the congregation of the First Presbyterian Church in Massey Station on the North Channel of Lake Huron. He was also to preach in another church in Walford, and in a third in The Mine. These tiny communities were more than six hundred kilometres northwest of Toronto, in the southern fringe of the thickly forested area known as the Algoma District. This thinly populated area was in the early stages of an economic boom, caused primarily by American demand for Canadian timber. Almost every municipality on the Canadian Pacific Railway line between Sudbury and Sault Ste Marie had a lumber mill. The largest of these communities, Blind River, had a population of just under two thousand and boasted several sawmills.

The Bethunes arrived in Blind River in September 1903. They had chosen to live there because the town had a high school, which would allow Janet to continue her education. The drawback was that Malcolm would be 75 kilometres away by rail from his congregations in and around Massey Station. Each Sunday he took the early train for the hour-and-a-half trip eastward to preach in Massey Station, Walford, and The Mine.[48] For the first six months he was away from home every Sunday and occasionally on Monday as well. This inconvenient arrangement ended in the spring of 1904 when the congregation of St Andrew's Presbyterian Church in Blind River asked him to be their pastor.

In Blind River the Bethunes lived in the former Baptist parsonage on Centre Avenue. The two-and-a-half storey building with white clapboard siding was one of the largest in the community. From the parsonage Norman and Janet had a short walk down Michigan Street to attend the newly opened three-room school. The "high school" was a single room in the building's second floor, where students from the eighth grade onward were taught. Norman and Janet joined fifteen others who were being taught all subjects by the school principal.

After living in Toronto, Malcolm and Elizabeth Bethune must have seen Blind River as a terrible comedown. But Norman was fascinated by the busy little village, where cows wandered along the narrow unpaved streets and bears sometimes ventured into town. The aroma of wood smoke hung heavy in the air, and the saws of the lumber mills screeched from morning to night. During the frigid winters the little community was often snowbound for days. Many of the residents were single men attracted by work in the lumber trade, who lived in hastily thrown up tar-paper shacks. Rootless and lonely, they spent much of their spare time brawling in bars; the most popular of these, located in the Blind River Hotel, was known as the "Bucket of Blood."[49]

Norman made the most of his new surroundings. It was a tough community, and he soon learned to handle his fists.[50] His love of the outdoors dated from his Beaverton days, and it would deepen during the next two years of his life, for the physical setting of Blind River was wilder and grander than anything he had yet seen. The shores of Lake Huron were carpeted with dense forests of white pine, and the swiftly flowing Mississagi River carved its way south through the rocky cliffs of the Canadian Shield near the town in cascades of white-water rapids. Norman learned to paddle a canoe on the river's lower reaches, and he soon mastered another popular local sport: log-rolling. At the boom camp at the mouth of the river, thousands of logs were assembled after having been floated down from the hinterland. On holidays, large crowds would gather to cheer on champions of rival logging camps. Two competitors would spring onto opposite ends of a huge pine log, spinning it by running on it in their spiked boots, stopping and starting to try to throw each other off into the water. Thrilled by this test of skill and strength, Norman began to practise log-rolling on his own and soon became adept.

The wilderness was his refuge, and he needed one, for his conflict with his father was growing ever more intense. Things had gone better over the winter with Malcolm away at Massey Station on Sundays, but once he began preaching at St Andrew's and was at home more, he and Norman began quarrelling again. To avoid these confrontations, Norman took to leaving home Friday nights to spend weekends with a friend.[51]

Despite changing schools so often, he managed to do well academically. In June 1904 he took the train to Sault Ste Marie to sit for a series of eleven provincial examinations that would allow him to enter Form One, the first year of high school. Two weeks later he eagerly scanned the list of the seventy-six successful examination candidates in the *Sault Star* and discovered his name ranked fourteenth in the entire Algoma District.[52] But his success created fresh problems for the family, because the tiny high school in Blind River did not offer the science courses he would need to enter medical school. He would have to attend a larger high school, and the closest was in the bustling lumber and steel centre of Sault Ste Marie, 150 kilometres to the west. So the family made yet another move, the seventh in eleven years. The life Norman had made for himself in Blind River would have to be left behind.

The Bethunes moved to Sault Ste Marie in August and rented a roomy two-and-a-half storey house of grey concrete brick set on a spacious lot at 55 Woodward Avenue. It was only a ten-minute walk to the high school, which occupied several rooms on the second floor of the Beck Block, above a plumbing and tinsmith business. Two teachers taught all subjects to fifty students. Norman must have put his mind to his studies, because at the end of the year he obtained an honours standing and was promoted to Form Two.[53] Meanwhile he had taken a part-time job at the local branch of the Young Men's Christian Association, which rented accommodation to young men and also offered a reading room. What Norman's job was is not known, but he may have worked as a room clerk or in the reading room.

Once again he had to prove himself in a new situation, and the only way he knew was to assert himself and go his own way. This brought about more confrontations with his father. Fortunately, Malcolm intended to continue preaching to the congregation of his church in Blind River, so he had to return to the routine of taking the train every Sunday. Taxing though this was for him, his absence on Sundays must have been a relief to Norman. The boy was not so close to the big woods as he had been at Blind River, but whenever he could, he would escape to the shores of Lake Superior. He loved swimming there, in the largest and coldest of the Great Lakes, and diving after turtles. Armed with a trident, he would paddle his canoe near the mouths of streams feeding the lake to spear the huge sturgeon that came there to spawn. In the winter he would drag an ice-hut far out on the lake's frozen surface to fish through a hole by lantern light for herring, perch, and pickerel.[54]

But bad luck continued to dog the family, for no sooner had they settled down in Sault Ste Marie than trouble erupted between Malcolm Bethune and his congregation in Blind River. In February 1905 the church elders announced their decision to become independent of the Home Mission Board and choose their own minister. They planned to invite applications from other Presbyterian clergyman.[55] Malcolm treated this decision as a snub, and only seven months after taking the family to Sault Ste Marie he resigned from St Andrew's. One month later on Sunday, 26 March, he preached his farewell sermon in Blind River.[56] As before, his ministry had ended on a sour note: there was no farewell party with gifts as in Beaverton, and the local newspaper did not print the customary words of praise for a departing minister.

Once again unable to support his family, Malcolm had already urged the Home Mission Board to find him a new appointment as soon as possible.

Fortunately, there was a vacancy in the rural congregations of Johnstone and Caven in the Presbytery of Owen Sound, on the south shore of Georgian Bay. He accepted the position.[57] When he disembarked from the steamer that had brought him from Sault Ste Marie, he was driven twenty kilometres north of Owen Sound to a building known as the Livingstone farmhouse, the only residence available for the new minister.[58] He preached his first sermon on 16 April and for the next ten weeks, until his children finished school and the family could join him, he lived alone in the isolated farmhouse.

Elizabeth and the children followed him to Owen Sound in late June. The town itself looked lively enough, but even the ebullient Norman must have been taken aback when he saw his new home. On a dusty side road, surrounded by broad fields, the old house had no indoor plumbing or central heating. It was without electricity as well, as this service did not reach many rural areas around Owen Sound until many years later. The only redeeming feature of the place was the sweeping view over the sound and Georgian Bay beyond. Norman must have been relieved to hear that he and his brother were to board in town in September and attend school until his father could find accommodation there.[59] In early October the family moved into a two-storey red brick house on the Division Street hill, only a few blocks from the high school. But this stay too was brief. Worn out by long journeys among his three widely separated congregations, Malcolm gratefully accepted a call from the newly formed congregation of St Paul's in the hamlet of Brooke on Owen Sound's outskirts.[60] And the family moved yet again, to a house on Standish Avenue, their tenth residence in fourteen years.

With a population of just over ten thousand, Owen Sound was larger than any other community they had lived in since leaving Toronto. The wheat trade was booming in the early years of the twentieth century, and the town had become the receiving centre for grain from the prairies carried by ship across Lake Huron. The town was prospering, and its population was growing. When Norman entered the Owen Sound Collegiate and Vocational Institute in September 1905, work was nearing completion on a six-classroom addition to the school. With a staff of ten teachers, all of them specialists in their subjects, the collegiate provided a higher quality of education than he had ever had.[61]

It did not take him long to make his mark. In his first year he was elected class representative on the student executive, and he was a keen player on the school basketball team.[62] He also joined a Bible class, which must have warmed the cockles of his much-tried parents' hearts.[63] In his spare time he carried out various scientific experiments at home and built up an impressive collection of insects, capturing some of his best specimens by scaling the town's streetlight standards.[64] Although there are no detailed school records of his marks, the University of Toronto later admitted him on the basis of an honours standing granted on receiving his Junior Matriculation certificate from the Collegiate in 1907.[65] His graduation with honours was remarkable because, busy with his extracurricular activities and hobbies, he apparently spent little time on his studies.

Despite his father's new position, family finances were still shaky, so once again Elizabeth decided to take in a boarder. Norman and his younger brother had to share a bedroom, and this proved disastrous. Norman resented the loss of his privacy, and the brothers frequently clashed.[66] After some of their fights Norman would storm out of the house and stay away for hours.[67]

So there was probably relief as well as regret in the family when Norman left home shortly after graduation in June 1907. As his mother lamented long afterwards, "He was my bad boy. He was a pain in the neck when he was home and a pain in the heart when he was away."[68]

Tempering

Work and War, September 1907–February 1919

Given his family's chronic lack of money, the young Norman Bethune knew that he had to find work if he wanted to attend university, because he would have to pay his tuition fees and most of his living expenses himself. He spent the summer working as a busboy on passenger ships on the Owen Sound–Port Arthur route. His sister, who kept his money for him, recalled that he often quarrelled with the ship's crew while asserting his rights and independence.[1]

When the tourist season ended in September, he headed to the Algoma District, the area he had fallen in love with during the years in Blind River and Sault Ste Marie. There he found work in construction camps between September 1907 and December 1908, likely building railways.[2] He soon discovered that bush work was tough. The men worked six days a week, ten hours a day, and lived in log bunkhouses in a fug of sweat and tobacco smoke. At night they slept on straw mattresses, huddling under coarse woollen blankets. Many of them were immigrants, for the most part poorly educated and unable to speak much English. For the seventeen-year-old son of a preacher, the rough language and the stress of communal life with older men in a small bunkhouse must have come as a shock. He had to prove himself all over again, and in a more difficult situation than he had ever faced before. But he rose to the challenge. Though only of medium height, he was broad-shouldered and well built, fast on his feet and good with his fists; he did not look for fights, but if challenged, he never backed down, no matter the size of his opponent.[3] Camp life toughened him, and he learned to enjoy roughing it and being with "the boys." The ruggedly masculine work suited him, and he loved living in the forests near lakes where he could swim and fish, revelling in this first taste of real freedom. Likely it was at this point that he developed an abrasive rudeness, amounting at times to crudity, which he would deliberately use later in life as a weapon to punish those who offended him.

During the summer of 1908 he worked on the lake boats again and then returned to construction work in Algoma in the autumn. Just before Christmas his sister Janet heard an insistent rapping at the back door of the Bethune house in Owen Sound. Opening it, she faced a seedy-looking bearded fellow in shoddy working clothes, his hat pulled low over his eyes. He demanded food in a gruff voice, and she began to close the door. Then the man chuckled and said, "Juna, don't you recognize me?"[4] Fortunately for family peace and harmony, Bethune stayed only a few days. Unable to find other work that winter, he had accepted a teaching assignment in Edgeley, a small village in Vaughan Township northwest of Toronto.

On Monday morning, 4 January 1909, he faced his first class. His task was to teach all the subjects in each of the eight elementary grades. The school was a single-room brick building, nine by fifteen metres, packed to bursting with nearly a hundred farm boys and girls ranging in age from six to the mid-teens. In the centre of the room were rows of desks, at each of which sat two pupils; others, squeezed together on benches lining the side walls, had to use their laps as writing surfaces. A wood stove occupied a corner near the door, and at the other end of the room stood the teacher's desk on a raised platform in front of the slate blackboard.

There was a buzz of surprise when the pupils got their first look at their new teacher, who was informally dressed in an open-necked shirt instead of the high wingback collar and jacket and tie that were standard for male teachers in those days.[5] "My name is Mr Bethune. B-E-T-H-U-N-E." He wrote it on the blackboard. Then, much as his father was wont to do from the pulpit, he crisply laid down a set of rules, making it clear that he expected them to be obeyed. Some of the older boys were burly fellows with moustaches, only a year or two younger than their eighteen-year-old teacher, and they were provoked by his air of command. After a few days of his iron rule, three of them decided to test him and began to act up. Until moments before dismissal time Bethune ignored them. Then he summoned the rowdies to the front of the room and lined them up against the blackboard facing the class. Getting out a long black leather strap, he ordered them to turn their palms upward and moved along the line walloping each outstretched hand.

This produced a brief effect, but several days later two older boys again began to act up, and when Bethune ordered them to stop, they defied him. Jumping down from his platform, he grabbed one of the boys' shoulders and shoved him into his seat, hard. He started toward the other, who quickly retreated to his place. The following morning he found the word "Spittoon" crudely splattered in red paint across the school fence, but aside from this mute protest, nothing else happened for several days. Then, as he was leaving school late one afternoon, he was set upon outside the school gate by a hulking fellow who threw a punch at him. Bethune dodged and landed a punch of his own, following it up with a rain of blows that knocked the man to the ground. Standing over him with cocked fists, Bethune challenged him to get up and fight, but his opponent grabbed his cap and fled. Bethune's trouncing of the boys' champion marked the end of his problems with discipline. When the school year came to an end and he left Edgeley, he had earned $269, minus the cost of his room and board. Added to the sums he had earned on the lake ships and in construction work, it was enough to allow him to begin his university studies.[6]

At the beginning of October 1909, Bethune enrolled in the University of Toronto. However, he was unable to enter the Faculty of Medicine, because to do so he required either Greek or German, and although these subjects had been offered at the Owen Sound Collegiate, he had taken neither. So he entered the Physiological and Biochemical Course and chose to study German to meet his language requirement. But he did not do well in his studies. His best grade was a B in English, and although he managed to pass his science and mathematics courses, he failed not only the required German but French and Latin as well. It is not known how he spent the following summer, but he may have worked in logging camps again. Back in Toronto in September 1910, he wrote his supplemental examinations, but again the results were discouraging. He passed French this time, but again failed Latin and German.[7]

His second year at university went little better than the first. This time he opted to study scientific German too, no doubt hoping that it might be easier to grasp than literary German. But when he learned his results in May 1911, his grade in German was an abysmal 10 per cent. After this second frustrating failure, he must have spent the summer fretting about whether or not he could make up the language course he needed. In September he sat for three supplemental examinations. He failed literary German yet again, but managed to pass Latin and scientific German, which would have allowed him to enter the Faculty of Medicine in October.

But he did not, and the likely reason for this is lack of money. He had already used up most of his savings, and his father could not help him, being once again without an income. Having resigned from or otherwise lost several more congregations in the intervening years,[8] Malcolm Bethune had moved the family to Toronto. The plan was that Norman would live at home while in medical school, and Elizabeth would again operate a boarding house. Malcolm expected to earn small amounts from filling in for ministers on holiday and in this way hoped the family could make ends meet. In November 1910 they had bought a large, semi-detached, three-storey house at 19 Harbord Street near the university campus, probably using money from a bequest recently received from the estate of Malcolm's grandfather, Angus Bethune.[9] The second floor had bedrooms for the family, and the floor above had space to accomodate four boarders, who would take their meals with the family in the first-floor dining room.

Even with his lodging taken care of, Norman still needed money for tuition and textbooks. Working for another year before entering medical school may have seemed the only answer, and there were other reasons to delay his return to university. He had lived away from home for more than three years before moving in with the family again in November 1910 and likely missed his independence. Because the boarders required the extra bedrooms, he again had to share a room with his brother, and the thought of doing so for the rest of his years in medical school did not appeal to him. He was also restless after two years of struggling with course work and ready for a change of scene. So when he saw a chance to return to his beloved Algoma District, he decided to put off entering medical school. The opportunity was provided by the Reading Camp Association, today known as Frontier College, which provided education to workers in remote camps. It offered Bethune an assignment as labourer-teacher in the Algoma District. The job was a perfect fit with his passion for the wilderness and must also have appealed to his deeply rooted sense that it was his duty to help others.

On the morning of 12 October 1911 he took the train north to Sudbury. With him went two big boxes of books and magazines. After a brief stopover, he continued west by rail to the village of Whitefish. The rest of the trip, a distance of fifteen kilometres, was by wagon on a narrow road that wound through the woods along the northern shoreline of Lake Panache to its western end and then turned south to Martin's Camp, one of five on the lake owned by the Victoria Harbour Lumber Company.[10] Bethune presented his letter of introduction to the foreman, R. Robinson, who explained the camp routine and then took him to the Reading Room, a small log building that would serve as both Bethune's living quarters and a library/classroom. In his first report to the Reading Camp Association, he would write that he spent the first week "laying in a supply of wood, plastering and arranging the comforts of an effete civilization in conformity with the strict mission-style furnishings of my bungalow."[11]

Then he started to work. His first job was as a "swamper," the lowest rank in the bush work hierarchy; he joined a gang repairing and levelling the main road along which timber would be hauled after snow fell. His enthusiasm and his ability to learn quickly must have impressed the foreman, because he soon gave Bethune more demanding assignments. He worked next as an axeman, blazing a trail by chopping gashes in the trees to be felled later by sawmen; he then joined a group of skidders, who dragged felled timber along the ice-covered roads. It had been three years since Bethune had worked in the bush, and although in a report to the secretary of the Reading Camp Association in Toronto he claimed that he was used to roughing it, he at first found the sixty-hour week punishing. Confessing that the work of the first three weeks had produced "blisters and fully developed symptoms of a kink in my vertebral column," he added in his optimistic way, "however, I enjoy it, and am sure I shall like it immensely later on."[12]

His work in the bush was only part of his duties, for in the evenings he became a teacher-librarian. He gave classes to his fellow workers in English, Canadian history and geography, arithmetic, letter writing, and hygiene, and he also managed a small library of books and magazines. Disappointed by its scanty holdings, he wrote to the secretary of the Reading Camp Association requesting copies of the *Illustrated London News* and offered to pay for a subscription to the *Saturday Evening Post*, one of the men's favourite magazines. He also asked for a dictionary and some booklets in German, French, Polish, and Hungarian for use in teaching English. As well, he needed "a few Bibles and … a dozen paper-covered Alexander's Hymn books, used by the revivalist committee, containing '*Where is My Wandering Boy Tonight?*' and all those kinds of songs, you know." Then he added: "This is not a joke."[13] In an attempt to reduce the boredom of camp life, he also led the men in group singing, and he conducted religious services on Sundays. He was no doubt amused that, like his father, he was now ministering to a flock.

As he had predicted, once he had toughened up he began to enjoy the whole experience. He loved being back in the Canadian North and felt deep satisfaction at proving himself as good a lumberman as any other man. He was also enthusiastic about the mission of the Reading Camp Association and his own role in it. On New Year's Eve, more than two months after arriving at the camp, he wrote to the association that all was going well. Still worried about the dozen or so men in the camp who could not speak English, he said that it was "extremely desirable that they know something at least about the language when they leave the camp in the spring," and asked for more language instruction books. In the same letter he also described using his skills as a paramedic, perhaps for the first time, stating that he was about to leave camp with a fellow worker "who had his leg broken yesterday – a simple fracture of the tibia. Administered first-aid-splints etc. Will haul him to Whitefish & telegraph for ambulance to meet the train to Sudbury."[14]

Enjoying outdoor life and looking out for his fellow workers, he was in his element. A photograph taken six weeks later shows him posed front and centre among a group of loggers, all older than he. Hands on hips, his hat cocked at a rakish angle, he is clearly in charge of the situation.

When the camp broke up for the season in mid-March, he sent a telegram to the Reading Camp Association asking for a railway pass to allow him to return to Toronto. Discovering that it could not at once pay him the entire sum of $100 owed to him for his five months' work, he stayed at home for a short time and then set off on a trip to the western United States.[15] After travelling through Michigan and Minnesota, he ran out of funds in Fort William, Ontario; on 4 July he sent a telegram to the Reading Camp Association with the urgent message, "Kindly telegraph at once $55.00 balance due."[16] Twelve days later he was in Winnipeg, where he had found a job with a local newspaper, *The Telegram*, as a cub reporter.[17] But after only a few days he quit, perhaps feeling too confined by working at a desk and wearing a shirt and tie. Longing for the outdoors, he asked the Reading Camp Association for an assignment as instructor in a railway or construction camp so he could "get out in the open again for the next three months."[18] But no positions were available, so by the beginning of October he was back in Toronto, ready to return to university.[19]

On 3 October 1912 he finally registered in the Faculty of Medicine, two days late for the beginning of the session. Because he had picked up one course in mathematics and two in science during his previous two years, he was allowed to enter the second year of medicine, but with the proviso that he take a first-year course in embryology.[20] Free at last of daunting language courses, he ended the year with a creditable 70 per cent average. Sometime after the end of examinations in May 1913, he went back to the North, this time to join a work gang for the National Transcontinental Railway.

When he returned in September for his third year of medical school, Bethune had to find lodgings in Toronto because the family had moved to the Niagara region, his father having found a posting with congregations in Blackheath and East Seneca. Bethune took a job in a restaurant near the university to supplement his limited savings and pay for his room and board. On his own in the city for the first time, he began to drink alcohol.[21] On his visits to his family, he insisted on bringing liquor, flaunting his new habit before his sternly abstemious parents. Surprisingly, they eventually agreed that he could drink, on condition that he do it in the bathroom. Over the next few months the long hours he spent on his job allowed him to make ends meet but cut into his study time. In May 1914 his academic average had slipped to 66 per cent. But the dash and decisiveness of clinical surgery strongly appealed to him, and in that course he achieved a grade of 85.

What he did to earn money over the summer of 1914 is not known, but by the beginning of August he was in Toronto, and his attention, like that of most people, was focused on the rapid unfolding of events in Europe. The assassination of the Austrian archduke Franz Ferdinand by a Serbian nationalist had led to the Austro-Hungarian invasion of Serbia on 28 July. On 2 August the ominous news that Germany had declared war on Serbia's ally, Russia, reached Toronto. Outside the offices of each of the six daily newspapers, crowds gathered, waiting for bulletins. On 3 August, German troops marched into neutral Belgium on their way to France. The next evening Bethune joined the huge throngs of people in downtown Toronto waiting for news. Shortly after seven o'clock, banners began to appear outside newspaper offices announcing that Great Britain had declared war on Germany. Bethune stood among the cheering crowds while men threw their hats into the air and others broke into "Rule Britannia" and "God Save the King."[22] Soon hastily assembled marching bands arrived and led the way to the armouries on University Avenue, where the militia regiment headquarters had thrown open its doors to sign up volunteers. Proud of his British heritage and carried away by the thrill of adventure, Bethune was one of the hundreds of men who rushed to form long lines there that evening. According to the Bethune family story, he was the eighth man in Toronto to enrol.[23]

Called up at the beginning of September, he left Toronto by train for Valcartier, Quebec, where the Canadian Expeditionary Force was assembling. On 8 September he passed his medical examination and seventeen days later signed the Attestation Paper, the formal commitment to enlist.[24] Because of his medical training, he was assigned to the Second Field Ambulance of the Canadian Army Medical Corps, and on 4 October he boarded the ss *Cassandra* at Quebec City; the ship crossed the Atlantic in a thirty-two vessel convoy bound for England.

There Bethune and his fellow recruits lived in tents on Salisbury Plain southeast of London while they went through basic training. It was a wretched experience: double the normal amount of rain fell, and they slogged about under leaden skies.[25] The enlisted men slept on the sodden ground and had no choice but to wear wet clothing, hoping it would dry on the few rainless days. Meanwhile they performed mind-deadening rounds of drill carried out in a sea of mud. Bored, miserable, and itching for action, Bethune complained long and loud. A fellow recruit claimed that his antics ensured that everyone in the unit was well aware of his presence. On one occasion he insisted on testing a new ambulance issued to the unit. He revved it up, then careered off at high speed; rounding a corner too fast, he lost control. The resulting crack-up destroyed the ambulance, but Bethune emerged unharmed.[26]

In early February 1915 he got to see action at last. The British High Command ordered the First Canadian Division to join British forces in France and Belgium. On 9 February, Bethune's unit boarded a troop ship on the south coast of England for the trip across the English Channel. By early March they had been moved into position on the Western Front, a line that stretched from the English Channel to Switzerland, a distance of more than seven hundred kilometres. They were based on the outskirts of the town of Ypres, northeast of the Belgian city of Lille. To the left of the Canadians were French territorial troops from Senegal and Algeria; on their right was the British Second Army. Facing them in their portion of the line was the German Fourth Army.

For several weeks there was little action. Then, on 21 April, German heavy artillery suddenly began an intense bombardment of the French trenches, continuing without let-up through the night and into the following afternoon. In the lull that followed the shelling, soldiers in the French sector of the line looked out across No Man's Land and saw a yellowish-green cloud drifting toward them close to the ground, carried by a light wind. As the cloud reached them, many of the French troops began to writhe in agony, choking to death on their own vomit; others staggered from the trenches, trying in vain to escape the enveloping shroud of death. Survivors ran pell-mell toward the rear, and within minutes a huge gap yawned in the Allied lines. The cloud was deadly chlorine gas, used in warfare for the first time at Ypres.

As the Germans advanced, the British commander ordered Canadian troops to move northward at top speed. This was the beginning of the Second Battle of Ypres, and the Canadians' first test of strength. Rushing into the area vacated by the French, with many of them pressing urine-soaked pieces of cloth to their mouths in an attempt to neutralize the effects of the poisonous gas, the Canadians threw themselves against the numerically superior Germans and halted their advance. Their action prevented a major enemy breakthrough.[27]

As the battle continued, Canadian wounded were carried back in a steady stream to the main dressing station at Vlamertinghe. For ten days Bethune had been assigned to a mobile laboratory at No. 1 Hospital, but on 26 April, the sixth day of the battle, he received orders to report to No. 2 General Hospital. His new assignment was extremely dangerous. He was part of a team of stretcher-bearers summoned to the forward trenches, often under enemy fire, to administer first aid and then transport the wounded over shell-pocked terrain to a regimental aid post two kilometres to the rear. Snatching only brief periods of rest for the next three days, Bethune's team ferried the

wounded to safety. However, on 29 April, his luck ran out. A piece of shrapnel tore through his left leg below the knee, and he fell to the ground, twisting
in pain.

His mates carried him to the regimental aid post and then to Vlamertinghe, where his wound was treated and he received an anti-tetanus shot
before being moved the following day to a casualty clearing station. From
there he was transferred to the British Hospital Ship *St Andrew*, which sailed
to Dover. After nearly three months of convalescence in No. 1 Eastern General Hospital in Cambridge, he was released on furlough on 23 July. He spent
the time in London, staying at the Union Jack Club across from Waterloo
Station.[28] His time on the town was brief, for his furlough lasted only a week.
On 2 August he reported for duty at Shorncliffe, and after nine days he was
sent to a special hospital for Canadians in the historic village of Monk's
Horton near the coastal town of Folkestone in Kent. There he remained for
two months, until the decision was made to declare him medically unfit
and to allow him to return to Canada to complete his medical studies. On 1
November he arrived in Quebec City on board the ss *Scandinavian*. Two days
later he received his discharge papers, which described his military character
as "exemplary."

Back in Toronto, he returned to medical school in a special accelerated program created by the medical faculty at the Canadian governmnent's request
to qualify young doctors to enter the armed services.[29] As usual he did his
best to make an impression. By this time he had recovered from his wound,
though he still had a limp, which at least one fellow student felt he rather exaggerated.[30] Having been stationed near the French town of Béthune, he now
insisted that everyone pronounce his name "Bay-tune" as it was in French.[31]
According to a classmate, "He made himself known in the class, by being a
bit odd, a bit peculiar. Everybody knew that Bethune was in the class."[32] Another classmate recalled him as a "good student, [who] dressed well and always seemed to have other things on his mind besides medicine ... He had a
reputation for being a distinct individualist, and most of us felt we did not
know him really well ... We felt he was a bit of an enigma."[33] Bethune made
no close friends, and his sister Janet remembered that he did not attend dances
or other social functions while he was studying.[34] His fourth year ended in
April 1916; fifth-year classes began immediately and continued until December. Bethune did well academically, averaging 70 per cent for the two classes.
In the late afternoon of 11 December 1916, eighty-four students gathered in
Convocation Hall on the University of Toronto campus for a special graduation ceremony. Among them were Bethune and forty-six classmates who received the degree of Bachelor of Medicine.[35] In the University of Toronto

yearbook for 1917 the caption under his photograph read, "Death predicted, but date uncertain, will probably live again."[36]

Though he always told anyone willing to listen that every healthy Canadian male belonged in uniform, Bethune seemed in no hurry to re-enter the army now that his medical training was completed. Tired of lectures and labs, he was eager to practise medicine. His chance came when Dr James Robertson and his son Lorne, two doctors from Stratford, Ontario, contacted the Faculty of Medicine for the name of a promising young graduate who might be willing to manage their joint practice while they were away on holiday from mid-February to the end of April. Learning that Bethune might be interested, they approached him. Bethune accepted.

Sometime after Christmas he left Toronto to visit friends in the Algoma District. Back briefly in Toronto in February before going on to Stratford, he was stopped on the street by a woman demanding to know why a healthy young man like him was walking down the street in civilian dress. Why wasn't he in uniform, serving his country as thousands of patriotic men were doing? With a stern glance she slipped a white feather, a symbol of cowardice, into his lapel buttonhole and marched away. Bethune's first reaction was likely anger, for he had been among the first to volunteer and do his part. But, stung by her rebuke, he decided that as soon as he finished his obligation to the Robertsons in Stratford, he would join the Royal Navy.[37]

He must have carried out his first professional duties to the Robertsons' satisfaction, because two years later they would ask him back to replace them for a second time. After the two doctors returned to Stratford, Bethune left by train for Toronto on Monday, 23 April.[38] On the following Thursday he was in Ottawa completing his enlistment papers at the Royal Navy recruitment centre.[39] Less than a month later, on 25 May, he arrived at the Royal Naval Hospital in Chatham, England, where he underwent training until early August. It appears that he did not relish navy discipline, for Royal Navy records reveal that on two occasions during this brief period he had run-ins with superior officers. In one of them he "incurred 'severe displeasure' [for] indiscreet remarks made in public." His habit of speaking his mind was clearly not considered a military virtue.

Three weeks later he was on his way to the John Brown Limited shipyard on the Clyde River near Glasgow to join the crew of HMS *Pegasus* with the rank of temporary surgeon-lieutenant. The *Pegasus,* originally built as a ferry, was in the final days of remodelling to become one of the three first aircraft carriers in the Royal Navy. Two days after Bethune's arrival, he and his fellow crew members stood at attention on the deck as Commander W.D. Phipps raised the Royal Ensign to signal commissioning of the ship. After several days of testing on the Clyde, *Pegasus* joined the fleet in Scapa Flow on 23 August 1917. Serving as part of the Flying Squadron of the fleet, it patrolled the North Sea between the Firth of Forth and Scapa Flow for the next fifteen months. The ship joined the Grand Fleet for exercises from time to time but did not take part in any naval engagement with the enemy. Its only moment of danger came in May 1918, when it suffered slight damage in a collision with HMS *Oakley* in thick fog in the Firth of Forth. No one aboard the *Pegasus* was injured.

So Bethune had no opportunity to test his skills on battle casualties. But another challenge came soon enough. In early October 1918 he diagnosed several crew members with a severe form of influenza and consigned them to the sick bay. In the following days the contagion spread quickly. Eventually, 107 of the crew of 207 came down with the illness; thirty-four were bedridden.[40] Among the sick was Bethune, who had contracted the disease from his patients. On 28 October when the *Pegasus* was at Scapa Flow unloading its planes, Commander Phipps arranged for a surgeon to come aboard to replace Bethune, who was too weak to perform a scheduled hernia operation. Despite his worsening condition, Bethune continued to tend the seamen stricken with influenza, who lay in beds in the hangar that was being used as an emergency sick bay. Five days later, on 2 November, he collapsed; he remained in sick bay until 7 November, when he was transferred to the hospital ship HMS *China*. By this time he was suffering from bronchial pneumonia as well as influenza and was desperately ill for the following eighteen days. On 25 November he was sent forty kilometres south of Edinburgh to Peebles, a quiet town in the Moorfoot Hills in the rugged Scottish Uplands. There his condition gradually began to improve, and on 16 December he was discharged, with orders to rest until called for a subsequent medical examination. In January he was declared medically fit and allowed to return to duty. However, his long convalescence had given him time to think things over, and he now submitted his request to leave the navy. He was demobilized three weeks later on 9 February 1919.

Bethune now stood on the threshold of life. In the rough-and-tumble of the Canadian woods, he had already proved that he could live as a man among men, and despite his nearly three years of military service he had still managed to qualify in his chosen profession. He had experienced the World War in all its horror and would never forget it. Years later, at a low point in his life, he would write, "[I am] too much the product of my generation to conceive my situation as tragic – there has been no tragedy since the war."[41] And he always treasured a small lead statuette of a French *poilhu* as memento of his experiences. Unlike countless others who had been killed or physically or emotionally crippled in the conflict, he had escaped with no more than a scar on his leg from the wound received at Ypres. The deadly Spanish influenza, the greatest pandemic in modern history, had struck him down, but he had survived that too. Like a phoenix he had emerged from the fire and wanted only the chance to spread his wings.

✢ 3 ✢

Vanity Fair

London, 1919–1924

A new world now opened before Bethune. He had no intention of immediately returning home to Canada, for he had always hoped to follow in his grandfather's footsteps and qualify in surgery in England. Now, through a stroke of good luck, he had a chance to do so. Possibly through Royal Navy connections, he was offered a surgical internship in London's famous Hospital for Sick Children in Great Ormond Street.[1] On 1 February 1919, eight days before his official demobilization from the Royal Navy, he began a six-month appointment as a house surgeon.

Bethune had had his first glimpse of London on his furlough in August 1915, and he had also visited Edinburgh on various occasions when his ship was moored at Rosyth, a few kilometres away. Although he loved the solitude of the Canadian woods, the noise and bustle of these two great cities with their fine buildings and rich cultural life appealed to a different side of his nature, and with chameleon quickness he adapted to his new surroundings. Before the war his favourite garb had been bright flannel shirts, trousers with suspenders, and work boots, but now he began to dress the part of the debonair man-about-town in made-to-measure-suits, polished shoes, and bowler hat.

After four and a half years of war and deprivation, London throbbed with life. Having had his own brush with death, Bethune was caught up in the city's celebratory mood. Free at last from commanding officers, far away from disapproving parents, he plunged into life with gusto. A fellow Canadian intern at the Hospital for Sick Children, Dr Graham Ross, remembered that he was determined "to get the best out of everything in life that he wanted ... he seemed to breeze into the place rather like a breath of fresh air from the sea, and one was impressed at the time by his ... confidence, in his outlook on the world. One felt that he had no worries, that the world was his oyster ... and that he was there to get it."[2]

Through family connections Bethune was introduced to London social life, and his young cousins, Janet and Alexandra Paterson, swept him into their circle of fashionable friends.[3] He learned to wear white tie and tails, and with a pretty cousin on each arm, attended the theatre, Russian ballet, and concerts.[4] But he soon realized that his greatest passion was going to art galleries and exhibitions. Like his grandfather Norman, he had always been good at art, but he had never studied it, concentrating instead on the subjects he would need to enter medical school. Now in London this long-dormant interest sprang to life. He began to read books about art and to delve into aesthetic theory. But he was learning about more than art – he was learning how to *be*, discovering in himself a sensuous appreciation of many aspects of life, from the feel of rich fabrics to the scent of sophisticated perfumes.[5] His education had been both shallow and narrow, and now, as the world began to open before him, he experienced an intense joie de vivre. It was likely at this time that he read Walter Pater's *The Renaissance: Studies in Art and Literature*. In its conclusion Bethune encountered a world view that he instantly made his own: he would quote it for the rest of his life. Pater wrote, "Not the fruit of experience, but experience itself, is the end … To burn always with this hard, gem-like flame, to maintain this ecstasy, is success in life."[6]

These words became Bethune's mantra, the perfect expression of the flamboyant personal style he set about creating. Inspired by Pater's credo, he would try to live his own life as an artistic creation, painted in bold strokes. However, he wished not only to burn but to be seen to be burning. Intensely narcissistic, he would later go so far as to write, "As far as I am concerned, I am the only person alive in the world. Other people – men & women, are to me canvas, interesting, animated 'things' – but not more important or not readily distinguishable from rocks, trees, wind, rain, sun & water."[7] Yet he would spend the rest of his life seeking the reflection of himself in the eyes of others, his showy self-confidence cross-cut by an insecurity that he himself may never have fully recognized. Its origins lay in his childhood as an outsider and in his struggle against his father to defend his identity. But his experiences in England contributed to it too. His well-off English cousins had welcomed him, but they lived in a style far beyond anything that his family in Canada had ever known. He had had to find his footing quickly in an alien social milieu. Might it have been hinted, ever so delicately, that his manners could stand a little polish, that his flat Canadian accent was a touch uncouth? Certainly his colleagues at the Hospital for Sick Children made it clear to him that he was marked by his "colonial" origins, that he could never "pass" as an Englishman.[8] This feeling of exclusion was humiliating to him and contributed to the resentment he would always display toward wealth and social privilege. And so he began to build himself a glittering carapace, becoming adept at acting a part, using charm or vulgarity as the mood took him to draw the attention he so desperately needed.[9] His narrow gaze was challenging – he would sum someone up after a moment's intense scrutiny, and his most damning appraisal was, "He belongs to the herd."[10] Few people would get through his defences – only patients, those who were wounded either physically or emotionally and, always, children.

In his eager quest for experience, Bethune made contact with artists in London's Chelsea district, falling in easily with the bohemian lifestyle of the art community. He admired the artists' unconventional behaviour, dress, and speech, contrasting this with the rigid restrictions of military life and the narrow views of the middle-class people he worked with at the Hospital for Sick Children. Most of his colleagues there he found stiff and boringly discreet, willing conformists to stuffy professional and social conventions. They soon formed opinions about him too. They approved his focus on his work – he seldom engaged in small talk while on duty – but his manner was commented on. One doctor, with a touch of condescension, described him as "very unorthodox, even for a Canadian … a trifle bumptious and slapdash [but also] refreshing and amusing."[11]

In his sunny moods Bethune could be whimsical and humorous. Learning that a member of the staff had been promoted, he dashed out, still in his white coat, and returned with a bottle of champagne under each arm, his contribution to a celebratory dinner. Reports of his bohemian lifestyle soon began making the rounds of hospital gossip. The upwardly mobile doctors, too prim to party much themselves, were shocked at how often he spent his evenings and early mornings revelling with his artist friends.[12] His flair for drama was also viewed with suspicion. Dr Ross described him as a "natural actor" and said he never knew whether Bethune was acting or being sincere.[13] Certainly he craved an audience; able to talk fluently on almost any subject, he made himself the centre of attention at social gatherings. But at times he simply enjoyed being a pain in the neck. He would introduce a subject and launch into an argument intended to provoke. Then, having annoyed his listeners sufficiently, he would burst into laughter, enjoying their chagrin when they realized he had been fooling them.

As Ross put it, Bethune "stirred the place up a bit."[14] Not all his performances were playful, however. He loved to mock attitudes or individuals he disliked, and nothing made him bristle more than someone putting on airs. In the rigidly stratified English society of the 1920s, he found many targets. Determined not to be treated as an inferior from the colonies, he was often aggressive, using his rapier-sharp tongue to put pompous individuals in their place. Some found this amusing, but many more did not.

His contract at the Hospital for Sick Children expired at the end of July 1919, and although he was gaining valuable professional experience and enjoying himself in London, he decided to leave England for a time. He had not seen his parents in more than two years, but perhaps more important was his realization that even if he renewed his contract or found another hospital position, his income would still be too little to support his taste for fine clothing and expensive restaurants. And so he had corresponded with the Robertsons in Stratford, Ontario, and agreed to tend their medical practices while they went on holiday, as he had done two years before.

Returning to Canada in early September, he visited his parents and then took the train to Stratford. For the next two months he lived in the Robertsons' stately Victorian house on Albert Street. With its two large cast-iron dogs flanking the steps to the front entrance, "The Elms" was a local landmark, and Dr James Robertson's practice was the most successful in the area. Bethune knew he was being trusted with considerable responsibility and lived up to it. The patients he treated told the Robertsons' nurse-receptionist, Ruth Patton, that they highly approved of him. Patton found him "devoted to his profession" and said he gave "as much attention if not more to the humblest patient than he would to one perhaps more important."[15] She also noted wryly that he was "broke as usual. Money meant nothing to him except to spend."[16]

As an attractive and eligible bachelor, Bethune was much sought after and became a social lion at gatherings, never lacking female companions. He took delight in shocking the locals. One girl reported that he arrived on her doorstep wearing a powder-blue suit, vivid red tie, and yellow shoes and that he thoroughly enjoyed the effect his outré outfit created when they arrived at a dance.[17] But despite his unconventional ways, a group of men approached him near the end of his stay to point out that Dr James Robertson was soon to retire and Stratford would welcome a talented young doctor. They offered financial support to allow him to set up a practice in the city.[18] Bethune politely declined. After the bright lights of London, the low lights of Stratford did not appeal.

In the last week of November 1919, he moved on from Stratford to Ingersoll, Ontario, to manage the practice of Dr Ralph Williams while he went on a winter holiday.[19] Careering around town visiting patients in Williams's Model T, Bethune soon became a well-known figure.[20] People liked his easy manner and air of confidence. One female patient, rather smitten, recalled, "I walked in Dr Williams' office and there was a serious, cocky, no-nonsense doctor dressed in a beautiful hand-knit sweater, tweed trousers, argyle socks of red plaid and heavy oxfords. I can still see him with feet on the desk in a relaxed position as if he didn't care."[21] Bethune soon began to romance Marion Thomas, the pretty daughter of the town's most successful businessman. The two spent many evenings together, and Marion sometimes went with him on calls in outlying districts.[22] But Bethune had to move on, and near the end of January, with Dr Williams soon to return, he invited patients and neighbours and their children to the house for a farewell party of sandwiches, cake, and milk. He also left a cheeky parting token for Dr Williams – a large collection of empty gin bottles in the bathtub.[23]

Lacking the money to set himself up in practice in a situation he fancied, Bethune decided to try military life again. Having already served in the army and the navy, it was probably inevitable that he would now join the newly formed Canadian Air Force. In fact, he was among the first to sign up.[24] He may have got the idea from his time aboard HMS *Pegasus,* where he had served with RAF pilots who flew the seaplanes carried on the ship. His commanding officer's notations on Bethune's Royal Navy service record indicate that he had examined pilots to determine the effect of flight on their physical condition.[25] He probably hoped to carry out similar investigations in the CAF. The dash and excitement of this newest branch of the military services would also have appealed to him.

Information about his ten-month stint in the CAF is sketchy.[26] In the aftermath of the war, cost-cutting was the order of the day in the military; Bethune, like other air force personnel taken on in 1920, would have been offered a provisional appointment and been on duty only periodically.[27] The first training season began on 7 June when Squadron Leader F.G. Pinder, sixteen officers, and thirty-five airmen of Number 1 Wing arrived at Camp Borden, north of Toronto.[28] Bethune, with the rank of flight-lieutenant, was the unit's medical officer.[29] He managed to persuade his superiors that studying the physiological effect of flights upon pilots was essential. On an undated postcard which he entitled "The Compleat Aviator," there is a photograph of him in a heavily padded uniform, wearing goggles. On it he wrote: "Dear Mother – This is a picture of me just before I went up for a 'flip' the other morning to test a pilot's blood pressure, pulse & respiration at different heights up to 10,000 feet. Even so dressed I was cold! Love to all. Yours affectionately, Norman."[30] Soon, however, finding he was spending most of his time on the ground in administrative tasks, he grew restless. Perhaps, too, he felt the pull of his original goal to become a surgeon. He asked for a leave of absence without pay, and on 23 October 1920 served his last day in the CAF.[31]

As soon as he could tidy up his affairs and say goodbye to his parents, he returned to England. By mid-November 1920 he was in London where he saw friends before hurrying north to Edinburgh. His intention was to enrol in classes at the Royal Infirmary to prepare for the January examinations to qualify as a Fellow of the Royal College of Surgeons (Edinburgh). But he arrived too late and learned that the next classes would not be offered until the following summer. He would have to return to London to find work.

At this point fate stepped in. Before he had left for Edinburgh, a London friend had arranged an introduction to a Scottish girl there, and she had offered to take Bethune as her escort to a dinner party. In impeccable evening dress, a white carnation in his buttonhole, he went to pick her up, only to discover she was under quarantine with measles.[32] But she had asked a friend to accompany him instead. Years later, that friend, Frances Eleanor Campbell Penney (1892–1964), described her first reaction to him: he was "sufficiently presentable, distinguished, ugly, a man of the world – an unhappy one, presumably rich ... He was not putting on an act for anyone but himself. His dinner conversation was good. He pleased my hostess. My duty was done."[33] Typically, Bethune's reaction was more intense. He was smitten with Frances Penney, and as always when he wanted something, he went after it. Scottish custom required an aspiring suitor to hover in the background until the girl's family deigned to extend him an invitation, but Bethune brushed convention aside. Immediately after their first meeting he swept Frances off to dinner at a fashionable Edinburgh restaurant where he ordered a lavish meal and plied her with champagne.[34]

Frances Penney came from an upper-middle-class Edinburgh family. Her father, Joseph Campbell Penney (1851–1920), had been a prominent Edinburgh lawyer. Her mother, Margaret Gourlay, was the daughter of a wealthy Dundee shipbuilding family. Born in 1892, Frances was their first child and only daughter. Educated by a governess and then at Lansdowne House School, she had gone on to finishing schools in Dresden and Paris.[35] She spoke French, was well read in English, French, and Russian literature, and knew a good deal about art and theatre. She was also strikingly good-looking, with a porcelain complexion, thick chestnut hair, and long-lashed velvet brown eyes under dark eyebrows. Of medium height and slight build, she carried herself well and dressed stylishly. Perhaps her most distinctive quality was her voice: there was a husky throb in it that gave it a pathetic note. But beneath her elegant exterior she was shy and uncertain, her diffidence the result of her relationship with her domineering mother, a noted beauty who preferred her five sons and was highly critical of her daughter.[36] By contrast, Frances's father, whom she adored, had been fond of her and had always given her a generous allowance.[37] But the young woman had no idea how to manage it, and her finances were always strained.[38]

With his keen ability to sum people up, Bethune likely sensed the painful inner uncertainty beneath Frances's poised exterior. That may have been part of her attraction: all his life he was most able to express tenderness toward those who were in some way vulnerable. However, he said it was Frances's lilting Edinburgh accent that appealed to him: "It was love at first *sound*," he later wrote.[39] Soon after their first date, Frances persuaded her mother to invite him to tea. Mrs Penney suspected the young "colonial" of being as much interested in her daughter's social status and wealth as in her beauty, and her heart sank when she met Bethune. She later said that he was exactly the kind of man that her daughter was likely to fall for and she felt helpless to stop this from happening.[40] As for his wanting money, Frances soon discovered for herself that Bethune was not rich, as she had at first thought. A few days after the tea party, he telephoned to say that he had to return to London at once. She gathered that his sudden departure was caused by lack of money, so she mailed him a cheque – and he cashed it. But from London the following week he sent her a silver urn worth a good deal more than the amount she had lent him.[41]

Bethune had found a position as house surgeon in the West London Hospital in Hammersmith. On 1 April 1921 he began a six-month contract at an annual salary of £50.[42] Although he continued to write to Penney, he also became involved with another woman. She was Isabelle Rosalind Humphreys-Owen (1885–1965), the third child of Sir Edward Elias Sassoon, a member of the wealthy family of Iraqi origin that had extensive business holdings in India and China.[43] Isabelle had been privately educated and at the age of twenty-two had married into another moneyed family, the Humphreys-Owens of Montgomeryshire in Wales. Her husband, Arthur Erskine Owen Humphreys-Owen, was a successful lawyer, and they had two children. He went to France in 1914, where he served with the rank of major with the British Expeditionary Force. Meanwhile, wishing to do something socially useful, his wife trained as a physiotherapist and near the end of the war began to practise in London. At about the same time Arthur Humphreys-Owen was invalided home. He had been wounded in France and was apparently suffering from shell shock. Tragedy soon followed. Sometime in 1919 he left the Sassoon residence at 7 Draycott Place in Chelsea just after tea and was never seen again.[44]

In October 1920 Isabelle Humphreys-Owen entered King's College in London. At the age of thirty-five, she had decided to become a surgeon.[45] There is no way of knowing exactly how she and Bethune met, or when, but it appears to have been after his return to London from Edinburgh in early 1921. Though medicine was a link, their relationship may well have begun with a shared interest in art, and they likely met in Chelsea artistic circles where Bethune had many friends. Humphreys-Owen, a poised, clever woman with dark hair and large brown eyes, became one of them.

This friendship with a wealthy woman must have seemed a godsend for Bethune, who was racking his brains to come up with a way to supplement his meagre income. On his prowls through secondhand shops in Chelsea he had seen piles of dusty paintings stacked in corners, and, ever the optimist, had speculated that there might be an Old Master among them. So he began a shop-to-shop search, and whenever he came across a promising canvas, he would dash off to the National Gallery to have it appraised. Despite his lack of training in art, he was a quick study, and from his gallery visits, contacts with artists, and voracious reading he developed a keen sense of artistic style. He never found his Old Master, but he gained much insight into the marketing of paintings and objets d'art. He realized that these could be bought at very low prices in Spain and Portugal and sold for a great deal more in London. He became convinced that if he went on buying trips to the continent and sold his purchases in art shops in London, he could turn a tidy profit.[46] But he lacked the money to cover his travelling expenses and the costs of purchases abroad.

He discussed his problem with Humphreys-Owen. It is possible that he convinced her that his scheme was commercially viable, but more likely she merely wanted to please this attractive man who, though a bit brash, was overflowing with enthusiasm and confidence. At any rate she offered to put up the capital to allow him to start his venture, and he agreed to accept her aid on a business basis: he would borrow the money he needed and repay it. But their relationship went beyond the cash nexus, and on some of his trips to the continent, she went along. She and Bethune had become lovers.[47]

Meanwhile he continued with his hospital duties, but his goal was still to obtain a fellowship at the Royal College in Edinburgh. When his contract with the West London Hospital expired at the end of September, he returned to Edinburgh and on 11 October bought the ticket that allowed him to attend classes in the Royal Infirmary until the end of December.[48] In early January 1922 he sat for a series of examinations, and four months later, back in London, learned that he had been successful and was now a fellow of the Royal College of Surgeons of Edinburgh.[49]

However, he had already decided to undertake a further professional qualification: a fellowship in the Royal College of Surgeons of England. As a first step, in the first week of February he enrolled in a special course in physiology with Professor John Frazer in St Mary's Medical School in London.[50] To support himself while he studied, he found a position as assistant medical officer at the North-Western Fever Hospital on Lawn Road in the Camden section of London.[51] He was living in the Duchess of Connaught Hostel at 14 Bedford Place in Bloomsbury, a recently opened residence for visiting Canadians.[52]

Despite his affair with the Sassoon heiress, he had continued to write to Frances Penney from London, and when he returned to Edinburgh in October to prepare for his fellowship examinations, he had resumed his courtship. Back in London again in early 1922, he wrote urging her to come to London. His appeal made her think about her options. She already knew London well, having worked there during the war years in the British army pension bureau, but she had returned to Edinburgh when her father had become ill in 1919. After his death in 1920 her mother had insisted that, as the only daughter, it was her duty to remain at home. Although she was then twenty-eight years old and longing to live her own life, she had agreed. Now she decided to make the break: she came to London and found a position as a volunteer social worker.[53] The day after she began her duties, a co-worker told her that a strange man had been asking for her. Puzzled, she went to the main reception room where she came face to face with a scruffily dressed fellow, who held out his hand and begged for food. His voice gave him away, and she knew at once that it was Bethune.[54]

Now that they were free to see one another as they pleased, Bethune began to press Frances for a more intimate relationship. Over-protected at home, she had learned nothing about sex. Although she had had a suitor at one time, she had never kissed him on the lips, believing that such intimacy would make her pregnant. Only when she later discussed the facts of life with an Edinburgh physician did she learn the truth.[55] Now, in London, it did not take Bethune long to overcome her worries about passionate kissing. Impatient for more, he began coaxing her to go away with him for a weekend in the country. At first she refused, but he persisted and at last she reluctantly agreed. But Bethune's lovemaking was of the rough-and-ready sort. Insensitive to Frances's inexperience he made no attempt at foreplay and simply thrust himself on her. Overcome by fear and shame, she froze, and afterwards lamented that love was nothing after all. Bethune accused her of humiliating him.[56]

Somehow their relationship survived the disastrous tryst. But having only just escaped from the tyranny of her mother, Frances now found herself under the sway of another controlling personality. Bethune called her "Tyke," meaning "bum," or sometimes "Rabbit." Although he admired her class and breeding, he tried to reshape her according to his own ideas – he was always looking, he told her, for someone "to wear his silver garment." He insisted on helping her choose her clothes and sometimes even applied her makeup.[57] If he did not like a hat she was wearing, he would snatch it off her head and toss it away; once when she left for a break from their relationship, he mailed her three "inconsiderable" hats – which he had charged to her London account. He was, she later recalled, "a perfect autocrat." On a holiday on the coast of France he took a dislike to a knitted dress she was wearing and told her to walk into the North Sea. Stung by his criticism, she did so, much to his surprise.[58]

Bethune eventually told her about Isabelle Humphreys-Owen, but he led her to believe that the relationship was strictly a business arrangement. Nevertheless Frances worried, comparing herself with the wealthy older woman and feeling inferior.[59] Then, in the late spring of 1923, on the eve of a holiday visit to friends in northern England, she somehow discovered that a garnet ring Bethune had given her, telling her it was a family heirloom, was actually a gift that Humphreys-Owen had bought for him in Barcelona during one of their trips to the Continent together.[60] Furious at his deception, she threw the ring away and stormed off to Yorkshire. Bethune began to realize that however exquisite it was to have two attractive women in love with him, he risked losing both.

Marrying Humphreys-Owen was not an option, because even if she would have considered such a thing, she was not free. Four years had passed since her husband had vanished, but although various search efforts had produced no results, there remained the faint chance that he might reappear.[61] Though she was clearly very fond of the attractive and highly unusual Bethune, she had always seen to it that their affair was conducted discreetly. For his part Bethune returned her affection, but he found her strong willed and domineering, perhaps too much like his mother.[62] He must have worried too about the debt he owed her, which he had no way of repaying. Buying and selling art had not turned out to be as profitable as he had hoped, and now it was interfering with his attempt to prepare for his English fellowship.

The crisis with Frances Penney had come on the eve of the examinations for which he had been preparing for more than a year. Word reached him that Frances had come down with a bad case of scarlet fever, and he made an impulsive decision. Throwing up his examinations, he caught a train to Harrogate in Yorkshire where she was under quarantine, and rushed to her bedside. He told her that he loved her but had little money and was thinking of returning to Canada. However, she told him that she had recently come into a legacy of £1,250.[63] This would be more than enough to support them for a while, should they choose to marry. Caught up in the thrill of their reunion, they decided to take the plunge.

Frances knew very well that Bethune was unpredictable and quixotic, but that only added to the thrill of her love for him. And marriage offered her the chance to break free from the stifling family life she had known for most of her thirty-one years. For his part Bethune loved her and recognized her longing to escape. The romantic role of the knight-errant carrying the damsel off to a happier life appealed strongly to him, and Frances, well-bred and intelligent, would be an ideal wife for an up-and-coming surgeon. The marriage would also provide at least a temporary solution to his financial difficulties, for the tiny salary he was receiving as an assistant medical officer at the Fever Hospital had never been enough to allow him to live well in London.

As soon as Frances recovered, they began to make arrangements. The forthcoming wedding was announced in the *Times*, and Monday, 13 August, was the chosen day. Still in mourning for her father, Frances wore a black frock for her wedding and was upset because she broke a mirror that morning, which she considered a bad omen. When the wedding party arrived at the registry office in the St Giles district of London, the clerk who was to perform the ceremony insisted on dashing home to fetch a proper collar more appropriate for marrying a lady and gentleman. And so they were wed. After signing the registry book, Bethune turned to Frances and said, "Now I can make your life a misery, but I will never bore you. It is a promise."[64] It was one he would keep. They then went to a nearby photography studio for a wedding portrait, but Bethune was too impatient to wait for the image to be properly "fixed." In a quirk of foreshadowing the picture would soon fade, leaving Frances with nothing but "a sheet of blackness."[65]

The wedding party moved on to a pub for a drink. With them was the groomsman, Clifford Ellingworth, a lanky Australian doctor. One drink led to another until the bride and groom had to support Ellingworth as they made their way to Victoria Station. They had planned to catch the boat train for Paris but missed it, so Bethune bought tickets for the next train to leave the station, which happened to connect with Guernsey in the Channel Islands. As the train inched forward, the couple disentangled themselves from Ellingworth. His last words to Frances were, "He really *is* fond of you." She found the remark "unreassuringly reassuring."[66]

It was not long before doubts about her choice of a husband began to creep in.[67] Bethune had always tried to dominate her, and this behaviour continued. In Guernsey they went for a long walk in the hills. Reaching the edge of a narrow but deep chasm, one they could easily have walked around, Bethune insisted on jumping across. When Frances hung back, he said, "I would sooner see you dead than funk that." She leaped and landed safely but never forgot the incident, saying many years later that his cold words had made something die inside her. She chided herself for it, feeling she should have been stronger. But she had remembered a story from her childhood about a lady who asked her knight to retrieve a glove she had deliberately thrown into a den of lions to test his valour. He braved the lions and presented the lady with the glove, but then rode off, leaving her behind. Frances said nothing to Bethune at the time, but he must have sensed her resentment, for he later warned her, "Always look at me through half-closed eyes."[68]

Several days later, a minor disagreement between them escalated into a full-scale row. Finally Bethune shouted that he had nothing more to say and was going for a swim. Frances silently pointed to the window, for a tempest was raging outside. Ignoring her, he put on his bathing suit and headed for the angry sea. Furious, but now also frightened, she snatched up a coat and followed him. He plunged through several waves; suddenly the undertow seized him and he disappeared. She caught one more glimpse of him before he vanished under the walls of black water battering the coast. Moments later, by sheer luck, a wave hurled him closer to the beach and he managed to stagger ashore. Falling face down on the sand, he lay still, then, gasping for breath, got to his knees. More time passed before he could stand. Frances later said that she saw something in his eyes that she had never seen before: fear and shame. Without a word they returned to the hotel to dress for dinner. In the dining room Bethune ordered a bottle of Imperial Tokay. Raising their glasses of golden wine, they looked at each other and burst into laughter.[69]

Bethune had planned their honeymoon as a working holiday and arranged that during their tour of the Continent he would undertake short stints of surgical training. From Guernsey they went to Paris where for several weeks he spent part of each day in a brief course at the Hôtel Dieu; the rest of the time the couple spent sightseeing, visiting art galleries, dining, and dancing.[70] From Paris they went to Rome and north to Florence, Padua, and Verona, indulging Bethune's passion for art. Between hurried early morning breakfasts and late evening dinners, he led them on a whirlwind tour of historic sights, museums, cathedrals, and art galleries. In London he had preferred the sensuously rich style of seventeenth-century Baroque art, and in Rome had made a point of seeing the works of some of the great masters of that period including Caravaggio and Carracci. But in Padua he encountered the work of the medieval Florentine painter Giotto and was overwhelmed by the calmness and serenity of his frescoes. He began to question his earlier aesthetic judgment, a process, Frances said, that made him extremely prickly. Much of the rest of their time in Padua they spent studying other works of the great Italian master.[71]

From Italy they hurried on to Switzerland and then to Austria, where Bethune had made arrangements to spend six months training in medicine and surgery in Vienna.[72] Isabelle Humphreys-Owen was visiting her sister there, and it was not long before Bethune went to see her. It seems that he had informed her of his marriage only after the fact, because their encounter was brief and bitter. She rejected his attempt to greet her with a kiss and charged him with misleading her, of wanting only her money and not her love. Bethune assured her that he would find a way to pay what he owed her, by that time a sum that must have amounted to several thousand dollars, but she proudly refused his offer, saying the matter was closed. Bethune returned crestfallen to his wife.[73]

But life was good for the newlyweds in Vienna. When Bethune was free from his hospital duties, they enjoyed themselves, spending freely. They ate and drank well, attended concerts, and visited Vienna's many galleries. At last they realized that they only had enough money to pay their expenses for a few days more, and Frances cabled her London bank, asking that funds be sent immediately. Bethune went out to collect the return wire and on his way back dropped into an art shop he knew and happened to notice an exquisite porcelain statuette. His instinct told him it was a find. When his wife greeted him at the door of their room, he sheepishly handed her the package, holding out his other hand with the few *schillings* of change. Tearing off the wrapping, she took one look at the statuette and threw it at him. It struck a wall and shattered. Repenting her action, she went down on her knees and began to collect the pieces, telling Bethune to find some glue. Mumbling apologies, he bent to help her, and as so often after their quarrels, they looked at each other and began to laugh. Checking their finances, they decided to splurge on a last night on the town.[74]

Next morning they had to face the fact that the honeymoon was over. Frances wired her bank for more money, and they soon returned to London. During their continental romp they had gone through most of her legacy and now had little left to live on. In the early spring of 1924 Bethune tried but failed to find a suitable position in a hospital, and they realized that the pittance that he could earn and the small amount left of the legacy could not support their lifestyle. His priority now had to be to make more money, and this meant giving up his goal of obtaining an English FRCS qualification. Although he still yearned to follow in his grandfather's footsteps, doing so would mean beginning again the long process of preparing for the examinations. It was a luxury he could no longer afford.

London was a dead end. Despite the glitter of the life he had led there, Bethune had rarely felt comfortable in a society in which his accent and place of birth marked him as an alien. He had been made to feel an outsider in British society, and this had stung his pride.[75] He knew in his heart that, lacking sufficient social connections, his chances of succeeding there were slim, simply because of who he was. The more he thought about it, the more he was sure that going home to Canada was the right thing to do. With his ability and qualifications he was certain he could easily establish himself there and make a good income. Full of fresh enthusiasm, he set out his plan to his wife: they would go to Canada, and with the last of her money he would set himself up in practice and make their fortune. At first she rejected the idea, having no wish to leave London for what was to her a distant colony, but at last she gave in. For Bethune there was no alternative: the flight had been fabulous while it lasted, but now he had come down to earth.

✦ 4 ✦

The Slough of Despond

Detroit and Saranac Lake, 1924–1927

Eager now to begin life afresh in the New World, Bethune booked reservations aboard the ss *Adania*, which sailed from Southampton on 27 June 1924. In Montreal he and Frances boarded the train to Toronto, where his brother picked them up and drove them around the western end of Lake Ontario to the town of Grimsby where Bethune's parents were living in retirement. The senior Bethunes greeted their son's bride warmly, and at first all went well. But the atmosphere soon chilled. Bethune had warned Frances about her new in-laws' intense religiosity, but she had never experienced anything like it. It was not long before Elizabeth Bethune, whom Frances later described as "a hellion," started sneaking religious tracts into the novels she was reading, and Malcolm began insisting that she and his son must each eat a handful of dirt to learn humility.[1] As soon as he could, Bethune told his parents he had to begin his search for a place to set up a private practice, and the newlyweds left Grimsby behind.

Bethune knew that an urban practice would offer him the best chance of quick financial success. But now that he was back in Canada, he began to yearn for the North. Perhaps hoping to convince his wife that they could settle in some northern town, he took her on a short trip into the Algoma District and Quebec. The wilderness may indeed have enchanted her, but it is more likely that she felt panic at the thought of living so far from what she regarded as civilization. Years later, referring to one of the places they visited, Bethune wrote to her, "Do you remember Rouyn in 1923? [*sic*] It's now a mining town – not of 3 buildings – but of 20,000 people. We could have been wealthy, but oh what a life of poverty."[2]

Giving up the idea of carving out a practice in the wilderness, Bethune decided to try his luck in the United States, so at the end of their Algoma trip they went to Rochester, Minnesota, staying there for part of the summer while Bethune observed various surgical procedures at the renowned Mayo Clinic.[3]

He was considering whether he should study brain surgery; however, they were running out of money and he realized that specialization would have to wait. So after a brief visit with his sister, Janet, and her husband in Stratford, Ontario, he decided to try his luck in Detroit.[4] The idea may have come from Albert Robert Ernest Coleman, an Englishman he had met during his service in the Royal Navy and with whom he had kept in touch. Coleman had emigrated to the United States where he found a job with the Bell Telephone Company in Detroit. In writing to Bethune, Coleman may well have touted the opportunity to be found in the booming city. Detroit, nicknamed "Motor City, USA," was growing rapidly. Its population had increased by more than 50 per cent since the beginning of the World War, and it was now the fourth largest urban centre in the United States, a noisy, congested metropolis sprawling along the north bank of the Detroit River.[5]

The Bethunes arrived in Detroit in early October 1924. They rented a large high-ceilinged apartment at 411 Selden Street, not far north of the downtown, in a declining residential area where small commercial shops were replacing houses. Originally it had been a largely German and Greek community but was now home to many African-Americans and Mexicans drawn north by employment opportunities in motor-related industries. The neighbourhood had a seamy side, having witnessed dramatic shoot-outs between the dominant Purple Gang and its rivals in a struggle for control of the illicit liquor trade.

Bethune applied for the right to practise medicine, and after passing an examination, received his State of Michigan medical licence in the first week of December 1924.[6] Confident of instant success, he opened a spacious seventh-floor office in the General Necessities Building downtown. But few patients appeared, and after a few weeks, unable to pay the rent, he had to give up the office and use part of the Selden Street apartment as his consulting room. The change attracted more patients but brought in little money, for many who came were too poor to pay Bethune's fees. Some could only offer goods in exchange for treatment, and others simply promised to pay and never returned. But at least Bethune encountered an interesting variety of cases. His first patient was a female victim of an attempted strangulation; her assailant had tried to throttle her using her petticoat.[7] Other patients were local prostitutes. Looking out the window and seeing one of them sauntering up and down Selden Street, Bethune would say, "There's Peggy, working for us."[8]

Frances Bethune became more and more unhappy. Preoccupied with building his practice and struggling to make ends meet, her husband ignored her distress at living in the rough Selden Street neighbourhood and dealing with the patients who came from it. The small waiting room in their apartment was crowded with prostitutes, working-class poor, and immigrants able to speak only a few words of English. Despite her experience as a social worker in Edinburgh and London, Frances did not want such people to become the mainstay of Bethune's practice. She also hated having the refrigerator filled with medicines and their only saucepan being used to boil up instruments. Desperately homesick, she loathed Detroit and quoted Oscar Wilde's aphorism that "America is the only country that went from barbarism to decadence without civilization in between."[9] On this subject Bethune did at least empathize with her feelings, for he too had little good to say of Detroit. "How dirty this place is!" he wrote. "Awfully squalid – terribly so. The people look vulgar and brutal … I do wish they didn't but they do."[10] But on those same people his income depended.

When he was away, Frances sat in their apartment and brooded. She felt that their marriage had gone wrong and that she was partly to blame for her predicament. She had been warned – her mother had been opposed to Bethune's courtship and angered by her daughter's insistence on marrying him. If she were to leave him, it would be terribly hard to go home and face her mother's wrath, so she felt she had nowhere to go. Most of her money had been spent on Bethune's needs and whims, and she now resented this. They were barely getting by financially and she was alone and friendless. Then one day Bethune brought A.R.E. Coleman home to meet her. Tall, blond, handsome, and best of all, an Englishman, he immediately appealed to Frances, starved as she was for contact with home and things European. Half-seriously, she warned Bethune not to bring R.E., as they called him, around too often, as he was the sort of man she could fall in love with.[11]

Meanwhile Bethune was beginning to make professional progress. He knew that prescribing for colds or sore backs would never make him rich, even with patients able to pay his fees. Surgery was far more lucrative, but to practise his craft he needed the use of an operating theatre, and that meant he had to join a hospital staff. Through a doctor he had met, he obtained an interview with Eugene Osius, a resident surgeon at the Harper Hospital, a highly respected medical institution dating from the Civil War era. Armed with his extensive curriculum vitae and laying on the charm, Bethune impressed Dr Osius, who agreed to present his credentials to the hospital superintendent.[12] A short time later Bethune was accepted as voluntary assistant in the Outpatients' Department. The position carried no salary but gave him operating privileges. Harper had many prominent Detroit doctors on its staff, and Bethune counted on being introduced to some of them, sure that he could convince them to send him patients who needed surgery.

His next step was to send a letter of introduction to Dean Walter Mac-Craken of the Detroit College of Medicine. Like Osius, MacCraken was attracted by Bethune's resumé and granted his request for an interview. At the end of their meeting, MacCraken offered Bethune a position on the faculty. He recognized that Bethune's credentials entitled him to teach a course in surgery but told him that the only vacancy at the time was a part-time one in prescription writing. The course, which consisted of twelve weekly sessions, paid a salary of $50 per month. Bethune quickly accepted the job.

One of his students, Edward Kupka, remembered the first day that Bethune appeared before his class, wearing a sports jacket, open-necked shirt, flannel slacks, and casual shoes. Lighting his pipe, he drew slowly on it several times as he surveyed his audience and then announced, "This course is a deadly bore, but I must teach it to you."[13] After pausing to gauge the effect of his words, he launched into an "impassioned lecture on the practice of medicine as a modern priestly craft."[14] He lectured in an exaggerated Oxford accent with a touch of Cockney, using a "mixture of ethics, history, exhortation, [and] anecdotes, delivered in a dramatic way and with humour." Refusing to conform to the usual academic procedure, he announced that he would give a pass to everyone and refused to keep attendance. Despite this casual approach, he managed to get across the basics of prescription writing.[15]

Most medical school professors at this time dressed formally and kept their distance from their students, so Bethune's relaxed manner in the classroom stood out. He chain-smoked while he lectured and let his students do the same. He even provided cigarettes.[16] And the camaraderie did not end at the lecture-hall door. He invited students to accompany him on Saturday nights to local speakeasies, where he cheerfully bought rounds of beer and joined in the mixture of serious and ribald talk that went on till closing. He also loaned students small sums of money and helped them to find part-time employment to pay for their college expenses.[17] Students enjoyed his often bawdy sense of humour. In a class in which he had asked them to write prescriptions on the blackboard, one student wrote "anus" (rather than "anise") water. Asked how the potion tasted and smelled, the student replied, "Fine." Bethune said dryly, "I suggest to you, Mr Schlaefer, that it would taste and smell fecal." The howls of laughter that greeted his remark went on so long that he had to dismiss the class.[18] On another occasion he warned students, "If you write a prescription for a suppository for a woman, be sure to tell her where to put it; otherwise, she'll put in her vagina."[19] Bethune's teaching style may have been unconventional, but it did not keep Dean Mac-Craken from giving him another appointment. In 1926 he assigned Bethune to act as a demonstrator in clinical surgery to groups of four students in St Mary's Hospital, across the street from the Detroit College of Medicine. This brought in the same monthly amount that he received for teaching prescription writing.[20]

Chameleon that he was, Bethune acted a very different role with colleagues than he did with students. With other doctors he did his best to appear as the American idea of an Englishman: he spoke in clipped tones, held himself erect, and affected a carefully trimmed mustache, bowler hat and cane, and ascot and gloves.[21] His courtly manners and the lustre of his Edinburgh FRCS allowed him to cut a swath through the local medical community. He began receiving invitations to dinner parties and other social engagements, where the well-bred and aloof Frances and the dynamic Norman made a striking couple. As usual, he managed to make himself the centre of attention wherever he went.

Word spread that a promising new surgeon was in town, and physicians throughout the city began to send patients to Bethune. He became extremely busy, and money began to flow in. So early in 1926 the Bethunes found an apartment in a more desirable location just north of the city on the Detroit River overlooking Belle Isle. Alden Park Manor was a new apartment complex at 8100 Jefferson Avenue. They chose a luxurious furnished suite on the fourth floor of the Charing Cross building. Despite their mountain of debts, Bethune spent his first big fee on an expensive Florentine mirror, which he proudly attached to the wall above the bedroom dresser. With his next payment he purchased a "fairy tale chandelier."[22] Despite such extravagance, he soon paid their debts. He then began to decorate their apartment with art and fine furnishings, putting his eye for beautiful things to good use in junk shops and running up huge bills at upscale department stores. Among the treasures he brought home were a Chinese chair and an ornate table made for the King of Rome, the son of Napoleon I. Frances did her part by sewing green velvet curtains and chintz covers for their chairs and sofas. They lined the apartment walls with hundreds of books. Bethune had a habit of tucking money into them, so whenever cash was needed, they had to search frantically among favourite authors from Flaubert to Marcus Aurelius.[23]

In little more than a year, despite a rocky beginning, Bethune had arrived. He bought a car, joined a golf club, and indulged his and his wife's tastes for imported clothing and dinners at fine restaurants. To pay for such luxuries he charged high fees where he could; among those whose purses he lightened were not only affluent citizens but certain prostitutes whom he knew were paid handsomely for their services. His approach to fees was always flexible. For example, after performing on Edward Kupka's father an operation for which the standard fee was between $30 and $35, Bethune asked for $75. The student protested that the amount was more than his father, a small merchant, had expected. Bethune replied, "Well, make it $50." When Kupka told him that he had brought only $30 with him, Bethune settled for that.[24]

But although he charged well-off people to the hilt, he asked nothing from patients who could not afford to pay. Worshipping Bethune as a hero and eager to be his acolyte, Kupka persuaded him to let him accompany him on some of his emergency house calls. On one of these they attended a pregnant woman living with other Mexican immigrants in a disused railway car; the husband had rushed to Bethune's office when his wife went into labour. Bethune followed him to the railway car, and though the delivery was difficult, he and Kupka brought the baby into the world. When the grateful father confessed he had little money, Bethune patted him on the shoulder and assured him that he wanted nothing for his services.[25] But on other occasions his compassion gave way to impatience, and then he could be abrupt and unpleasant. One day he was using a sigmoidoscope to make a rectal examination, and the patient, an elderly African-American, complained several times that Bethune was hurting him. Exasperated, Bethune ordered him out of the office, and when the door closed, turned to Kupka and muttered, "Damn old nigger." A similar situation occurred when he was rough in his treatment of a patient suffering from gonorrhea.[26]

For the most part, however, he showed a deep concern for his patients. Throughout his medical career he would appear at any time of the day or night to look in on patients on whom he had operated, even when his visits conflicted with hospital routines. This annoyed the nursing staff but delighted his patients. He also often reacted emotionally when he lost a patient, feeling genuine sorrow for the loss of life and a humiliating sense of his own failure. On one occasion, during an operation at Harper Hospital in 1926, the patient began to bleed; her damaged arteries later became infected, and one of her legs had to be amputated. Bethune was deeply upset, and at a Harper staff meeting he got up and said that he might have made an error in his surgery that caused the bleeding. His fellow doctors were taken aback, for few surgeons care to focus attention on their mistakes. After the meeting, the superintendent questioned Dr Osius, who had assisted at the operation. He assured the superintendent that the loss of the limb was not Bethune's fault.[27]

But despite Bethune's growing professional success and the comfortable lifestyle he could now provide, his marriage continued to fray. Frances still loved him and missed him when he was away, but they quarrelled furiously when they were together. A spat might begin about anything – the decision to come to Detroit, Bethune's long hours, or his use of so much space in the refrigerator to store medicines – but time after time every argument turned on money – *her* money that he had used for his own purposes. Their frequent conflicts complicated their deeply troubled sexual relationship. Sex had never been easy between them, and some years later Bethune would write to Frances telling her to consult a physician about her hymen, claiming that he could no longer stand their "unnatural union."[28]

Bethune began to spend more evenings away from home. He also began to drink heavily, and this made him more irascible. The sharpness of their quarrels escalated until even when sober he would launch into furious outbursts against Frances. To provoke her he would spit in the bathtub, which she abhorred, and defy her standards of gentlemanly conduct by refusing to bathe before changing into evening dress.[29] She also believed that Bethune spent time with female friends who were hostile to her.[30]

Not all of Bethune's moods were angry: he sometimes plunged into depression. Frances later said that when he hated himself, he slashed at things and didn't want her to love him.[31] By the early autumn of 1925, little more than two years after they married, she felt she could take no more. Needing a long break to think things over, she went to Nova Scotia to stay with Kathleen McColl, a childhood friend who had immigrated there.[32] While she was away Bethune wrote to her:

> I am missing you frightfully but paradoxically, wouldn't miss missing you for worlds. So please stay away a little longer. Of course when you do return you must bear with fortitude the accumulated affection of these ages … Yes, I am able to share with you your delight in being back once more on Canadian (for want of a better) soil. I think with you that we simply must move. At times this place overpowers even my stout spirit and what it must do to your soul my darling I can only conjecture with feelings of mingled despair and admiration. Patience and fortitude: these rather old-fashioned virtues have stood you in good stead. Any other women I have known, would have chucked the whole business long ago … My poor dear I only wish that I was able to make Detroit a possible place for both of us. But the more I see of it the more I long to escape.[33]

After several weeks in Nova Scotia, Frances received some money from her mother to allow her to visit her brother Frederick, then living in Oregon. From there she went on to San Francisco to spend Christmas with friends.[34] In the early part of 1926 she decided to give her marriage another try and returned to Detroit. But the relationship only grew worse. Bethune was now busier than ever, earning more money but working longer hours. The surgery he performed at the Harper Hospital brought him a good income, but he kept the Selden Street apartment and maintained office hours there. He was also often out at night on emergency calls. He had little time for social life – or any life other than his work. So Frances soon left again, this time to spend a few weeks in Montreal with Norah Hume Wright, a classmate from her year in a Paris finishing school.[35]

She was back home again when Bethune came down with influenza in September. He seemed to recover but then woke in the middle of the night bathed in perspiration. The following day he felt short of breath and lethargic, and after a week his condition was unchanged. He called on a colleague, Dr Herbert Rich, who gave him a complete medical examination on 14 September and took a specimen of his sputum. As a doctor, Bethune knew very well what the test was for, and the results of the laboratory analysis confirmed his worst fears: he had tuberculosis. Rich told him that it appeared that he had contracted the disease as early as that April. Bethune's mind raced, trying to think how he could have become infected, and he remembered a consultation in the early spring when a patient later diagnosed with tuberculosis had coughed in his face.

Rich advised Bethune to consult Dr J. Burns Amberson, a specialist in tuberculosis cases. Amberson saw Bethune without delay and ordered a chest x-ray, which confirmed the diagnosis. Bethune had developed pulmonary tuberculosis, with the disease moderately advanced in the left lung and minimal in the right. Dr Amberson assured him that his symptoms were not too severe and that with proper care in a sanatorium he was likely to recover.[36] Knowing that his condition would worsen without treatment, Bethune said he was ready to begin it. He agreed at once to Amberson's suggestion that he go to the Trudeau Sanatorium in Saranac Lake, New York. However, when Amberson called Trudeau, he discovered that there were no vacancies. His second choice was Calydor Sanatorium, which by coincidence was located in Gravenhurst, Bethune's birthplace. Bethune accepted this suggestion but asked to have his name put on the Trudeau waiting list.

Stunned by this sudden reversal of fortune, he broke the news to his wife. Both knew that the diagnosis probably meant disaster for their failing marriage. Although the doctors had given Bethune considerable hope, there was no guarantee that treatment in a sanatorium would cure him. Even if it did, there was no way of knowing how long the process would take. In the meantime, where would he find the money to provide for Frances, pay his debts, and cover the cost of his medical treatment? Worried that his disease was contagious, she insisted on boiling his dishes and was chary of kissing him.[37]

He was angered by this and they began to quarrel again. She told him that the only solution now was for her to return to her mother in Edinburgh, although she hated to do it for it would be an admission of failure and she dreaded having to face her mother's wrath.

After a few miserable days, Bethune set off by train for Gravenhurst. Raging against the illness that had disrupted his professional life and wrecked his marriage, he arrived at Calydor on 1 October 1926. Being the helpless victim of an insidious disease felt like failure to him, and although he had sought treatment quickly, he was not emotionally ready to comply with it. This he made clear from his first day at Calydor.[38] The accepted treatment for tuberculosis at the sanatorium was enforced bed rest, which Bethune regarded as a form of imprisonment and fiercely resisted. This would have come as no surprise to Dr D.W. Crombie, Calydor's assistant director, who had known Bethune in London in 1923 and was well acquainted with his hyperactive nature.

Confined to bed against his will, Bethune had time to dwell upon his troubles. His biggest worry was how to provide financial support for his wife. On the day he arrived at Calydor, he wrote to her: "But darling, you're all I've got in the world I care a rap about and for you I will do anything – and the first thing is to make you financially free from worry and that way you are sufficient unto yourself to conquer dragons. I do hate your coming combat in Edinburgh – the useless explanations, sexplanations ... Our marriage has been wonderful for me. If I had to go over it again I would still want *you* for *my* side, my darling ... Keep a *stiff* upper lip – we, you and I will beat them yet. The thought of you to fight for makes me strong. Goodbye, goodbye darling, Beth."[39]

He added a postscript the following morning: "My dear girl, don't worry or fuss. You can tell your people that I took your money, wasted it and left you stranded, and beyond calling you a fool for your action and I knave for mine what's to be said? *You* have done nothing wrong except to have consigned yourself and your money to a man who did not appreciate the one and was careless of the other. *But let me get up! Get well first and I will repay.*"[40]

Such words of encouragement did little to help Frances. She had now come round to thinking that returning to Edinburgh was not the right thing to do. Haunted by fear of facing her mother, she became depressed, and in one of her letters to Bethune from Detroit confessed she had considered suicide. He replied, "I wept over one of the letters you wrote me – darling, don't go home if you feel so bad about it but come to Toronto and get a job so at least we can be near each other."[41] Wanting to escape from Detroit, uncertain about rejoining Bethune, and dreading the humiliation of returning to Edinburgh, she returned to her friend Kathleen McColl in Nova Scotia. From there she went to Montreal to stay again with Norah Hume Wright. In this way she spent part of the winter of 1926–27.

For Bethune, whose own despair had deepened since his arrival in Calydor, Frances's decision not to go back to Edinburgh was the only good news he had received. No less alone than Frances, he wrote several times to his faithful former student Edward Kupka. Telling him that he expected to have to stay in bed for a second month, Bethune added, "I am forced to regard the situation, if not with grimness, then at least with a shrug of my shoulders for an entirely farcical and futile world – myself as an entirely farcical, futile figure in it. Unable to force [sic] back on the merciful but mysterious ways of a Hidden Purpose in life, and having entirely abandoned the anthropological idea of God, there is but little comfort in the conception of a Vital Force, [and] one is reduced to the consolation of similar sufferers and one's friends become elevated to the altar like a ceborum [sic]."[42]

Three weeks later Bethune was delighted to hear that a space had been found for him in the Trudeau Sanatorium, the best in North America. If he could be cured anywhere, he believed, it would be there. On 7 December he went from Calydor to Byron Sanatorium near London, Ontario, for several days of rest and examination, then stopped for a brief visit with his parents in Hamilton. On 14 December he left by train for Saranac Lake. By 1926 the Trudeau Sanatorium was world famous.[43] From an original one-room cottage it had grown into a large institution spread over several hectares on the pine-covered slopes of Mount Pisgah, just outside the resort town of Saranac Lake. The staff of 200 could accommodate 160 patients in two infirmaries and 28 cottages; there was also a library, laboratory, medical and reception pavilion, therapy workshop, nurses' home, chapel, and post office. Admission was restricted to patients "in the first stages of pulmonary tuberculosis and free from serous complications."[44] At a cost of $15 weekly for room, board, and medical treatment, they could remain for six months. Sometimes patients who wanted to extend their stay and who were able to persuade other patients to share their cottage were allowed to remain on the grounds as ex-patients.

Dr Trudeau, the sanatorium's founder, and his successors, most of whom had suffered from tuberculosis themselves, felt that the disease could not be entirely cured but only arrested. Their aim was to teach their patients how to live with it. They believed that rest prevented the spread of tubercular growth; patients were therefore permitted some mild exercise but only after a mandatory period of bed rest. Even after they were allowed to walk about and live in the sanatorium's cottages, they were subject to a 10 PM curfew enforced by a nurse patrol.

On Saturday, 16 December 1926, Bethune was admitted to the sanatorium, and after a complete physical examination, tests, and chest x-rays, was sent to Ludington Infirmary to spend the required month in bed. Determined to take control of the situation, he put on a running performance that soon made him the best-known patient in the infirmary. Sometimes he feigned anger and yelled at the student nurses; at other times, with a devilish gleam in his eye, he would entertain them with wildly colourful stories, insisting they were true. The young women found him eccentric but amusing and attractive.[45] The older nurses, less susceptible to his charm, made certain that he obeyed the rules. It was to be the only time he did so during his stay at Trudeau.

At the end of the first stage of his treatment, he moved on 14 January 1927 into Robbins Cottage to join four other patients, three of them medical doctors. With two, Lincoln Fisher and John Barnwell, he formed lasting friendships. From the beginning he tested his cottage-mates, telling them tall tales about his past and his experiences in a manner that dared them to disbelieve him.[46] After what he regarded as a month of detention under guard, he was itching to enjoy his physical freedom and defy authority. He began by working out a plan to break curfew and escape at night into the town. Patients were allowed to leave the grounds only three nights a month, and they were supposed to be back in their beds with lights out by curfew. This did not suit Bethune's plans, so he came up with a ruse to fool the nurse patrol. He stuffed Barnwell's snow suit with blankets and pillows and placed the dummy, covered with a blanket, in the bed nearest the window where the nurses would see it and think the patients were sleeping. Timing their departure to avoid the patrol, the truants slipped through the shadows to the gate and sneaked past the watchman. Once at a safe distance, they sauntered down the road, ending up at Brook's Tavern, their favourite among the town's twelve speakeasies. Bethune set about winning over the nurses, and planned a party for them at the tavern. When they arrived, they found the room decked with pine and spruce boughs. Bethune greeted them with a sweeping bow, then from under the table produced a large box of bottles of French wine. To cheers from the nurses and his cottage-mates, he announced that he had arranged for it to be smuggled in from Montreal.[47]

Yet despite the camaraderie of the cottage and the success of his pranks, Bethune's mood often swung toward depression, for he was still fretting about his major preoccupation: money. He was haunted by the need to pay his debts and support his wife. After Frances had gone to Nova Scotia, he had sold his car and given up the Charing Cross apartment; he arranged for a Dr Newfield to manage his practice in his absence in return for a small percentage of Newfield's earnings. He was also receiving a monthly payment of

$150 from an insurance policy he had happened to take out shortly before he was diagnosed with tuberculosis.[48] But this small income was not enough to meet his obligations. Sometime during this period Frances paid a visit to him at Trudeau. They may have argued about money again, for Bethune could not help feeling burdened by her dependence on him. One of his cottage-mates recalled that during her visit Bethune treated her coldly, almost cruelly.[49]

In the end, although he knew he was far from cured, Bethune decided that he had no option but to return to Detroit to resume his practice and teaching. He left Trudeau on 24 March and, after a day with his parents in Hamilton, arrived in Detroit two days later. That night he wrote to his wife, begging her to come back to him:

> Do you remember the nice room with its … parapets of books? – oh you must & not all your memories are bitter, are they dear? … I know you don't want me to love you but I do. I don't care what you say or do to me – I love you more than I ever have. I've had a *perfect* 6 months away from you and enjoyed every minute of it – that's a terrible thing, I know, but it's true, and because of it I love you a thousand times more. Now I want to see you. Now I think I can talk with you and understand you and *you* me, perhaps. I would like to see you tonight and hold your hand for an hour in a garden. Tomorrow I start work … I will be careful with myself for you depend on me – I don't worry now like I used to about your depending on me – I like it now.[50]

But such professions of love were not all he had written to her. There had been furious letters and bitter ones, many to do with money.[51] Several weeks later Frances told him that she had decided to end their marriage and return to Edinburgh. Her terms were stiff: she demanded $25,000 to be paid in installments of $100 per month, and $1,500 in cash. Her lawyer filed the suit on 4 June 1927, and Bethune did not contest it. He had arranged to sell his practice to a young Detroit physician, Joseph Wruble, for $5,000, and from this he paid his wife the lump sum she had asked for.[52] On 9 June he received a court summons outlining her demands and also a receipt for the $1,500.[53]

He had now lost his wife and his practice, and the sting of this double failure plunged him deeper into depression. Not surprisingly, his health took a turn for the worse, and he began to have trouble catching his breath. Realizing that he had been foolish to leave Trudeau, he resigned from his teaching position in Detroit in July and returned to Saranac Lake. The prospect of another month in bed must have tried his nerves, but his spirits rose when many patients welcomed him back, eager to see what mischief the well-known troublemaker would get up to next. Back on stage, the wicked gleam reappeared in his eye, and he did his best to push black thoughts to the back of his mind. One of his pet performances was a daily tea ceremony. Won over by his charm, the head nurse of Ludington, Elsie Thorn, told her staff that he must have his daily "Canadian cup of tea"; this the morning duty nurse carried to his bedside using an elegant silver tea service he had brought from Detroit.[54] He had also brought along his top hat and cane, and when no nurses were about he would cock the hat on his head, slip out of bed, and sashay down the ward twirling the cane. Peals of laughter from the other patients would bring a nurse scurrying in to find a grinning Bethune slipping back under the covers. He also enjoyed teasing the nurses who made rounds taking each patient's temperature. He had learned to shake the thermometer in a certain way, causing the mercury to shoot up well above normal body temperature. When the nurse had her back tuned, Bethune would whip the thermometer from under his tongue, flick his wrist and put it back. He took great delight in the astonishment on the nurses' faces when they read the temperature and their annoyance when he confessed what he had done.[55]

Released from Ludington in August, he moved into Lea Cottage. "The Shack," as Bethune and his cottage-mates called it, was actually two buildings linked by a passage in which the toilet was located. Clad in brown clapboard, the cottages had high slanting roofs. Bethune settled in, but one of his new companions later recalled that he was "abrupt in speech and a bit distant until you got to know him; you didn't get to know him right away … [he seemed] preoccupied." Dr Louis Davidson, another fellow patient, said he was "aloof except under the influence of liquor."[56] All of Bethune's former cronies had left Trudeau, but John Barnwell, who was soon to join the Trudeau medical staff, was living near the sanatorium grounds, and he regularly came over to spend the evening with Bethune and the others. They often played a card game called Russian Bank. Squeezing into the tiny bathroom and covering the window with a blanket, they competed fiercely long after the ten-o'clock curfew. Other nights they dodged the nurse patrol and walked into town for an evening of carousing at Brook's Tavern.[57]

It was not long before Bethune thought up another project. Struck by how much talent existed among the various patients, he came up with a plan for a "Trudeau University," in which the patients would supply the staff. Many people he canvassed about his idea were sceptical; however, John Barnwell got him an invitation to appear before the Saranac Lake Medical Society, an organization made up of several of the leading members of the staff of Trudeau Sanatorium and local physicians. Unfortunately, Bethune drank too much at the dinner before the meeting and botched his presentation, dooming his project.[58]

Despite such distractions and the relative freedom of Lea Cottage, Bethune still chafed at having to put in the required periods of rest. Avoiding all forms of exertion was against his nature, and even though he knew the restrictions were for the good of his health, he became irritable. He told a friend that being forced to do nothing was one of the most trying experiences of his life.[59] Yet he would later claim that the mandatory inactivity had changed his outlook. "It is only the dull and unimaginative who can lie in a bed in a sanatorium for six months or a year and fail to rise a better and finer person," he would write in an article published in 1932. "Life should be enriched and not impoverished by this retreat from the world."[60]

To some extent he was also influenced by the nineteenth-century romantic myth that tuberculosis was an ennobling disease. The writers he most admired, D.H. Lawrence and Katherine Mansfield, both suffered from tuberculosis, and he felt that his own intellectual and spiritual life had been deepened by his illness. "T.B. has an effect on the brain," he told a friend years later. "It makes you think faster. You become more aware of things." He was convinced that TB had developed his sensitivity and his artistic sense.[61] But at the time this positive view of the effects of his illness did not console him. Dark thoughts plagued him as he lay on his cot, and he suffered from chronic insomnia which began to wear him down. Haunted by the rise and fall of his fortunes, he relived his struggle to qualify as a surgeon, his marriage to a woman of means, and his success in the Detroit medical community. It had all come to nothing, and in his blackest moments he feared that this time he had burnt himself out and would never arise from the ashes.

By early September nearly two months had passed since his return to Trudeau, but there was no sign that his health had improved. For the first time he began to think that he might not recover. In discussions at night in Lea Cottage, he referred again and again to "the black wings of death" hovering over him and the others. He morbidly described their days at Trudeau as part of a sentence imposed on them, saying they were all following a dance of death.[62] To a few people he even talked of suicide. One night he and Louis Davidson picked up a bottle of whisky from a local bootlegger and walked down to nearby Lake Flower. After Bethune had drunk most of the bottle's contents, he plunged into the water and swam about for several minutes. When he came out, he said to Davidson, "Look, Louis, every one of us ought to jump in the lake; we're no damn good to ourselves or to anyone else."[63] Another time he told John Barnwell that he had worked out an effective way of committing suicide. After rowing a boat to the middle of Lake Flower, he would inject himself with a large dose of morphine, slip over the side of the boat, and begin to swim. Within a few strokes he would lose consciousness and sink below the surface.[64]

His depression may have been deepened by another aspect of his character – the feeling of predestination instilled by his Calvinistic upbringing.[65] He had long since lost his Christian faith, yet he continued to believe that his life followed a predestined course. In a letter to his ex-wife in 1929, he would write, "I ... feel my life's rhythm is a determined and predestined irregular one, so I accept it."[66] He had always thought that, like his ancestors, he would accomplish great things, but now he struggled against a growing dread that in some mysterious way he was predestined not for achievement but for death.

Yet his individualistic nature rebelled against waiting passively to die. The rest cure was clearly not working, and he began to look for some other form of treatment. Researching tuberculosis in the sanitorium's medical library, he came across a recently published book, *The Surgery of Pulmonary Tuberculosis*, by Dr John Alexander, a professor of surgery at the University of Michigan.[67] One procedure, called artificial pneumothorax, caught Bethune's attention. It required a hollow needle to be inserted between the ribs; through this, air was pumped into the chest cavity around the lung. The air pressure temporarily collapsed the lung, allowing the diseased part to rest, which in time would enable it to heal. This process of collapsing part of the lung, called compression, was a known form of treatment at Trudeau, but even though Dr Trudeau had credited the technique with having prolonged his own life for several years, his more conservative successors preferred the method of bed rest.

Bethune instantly pinned his hopes on this treatment. Book in hand, he marched off to see Dr Fred Heise, head of the medical staff, and demanded that the pneumothorax procedure be performed on him. Heise refused, saying it was too risky. Bethune immediately appealed to the highest medical authority, Dr Lawrason Brown, but Brown too considered the procedure too dangerous. However, Bethune insisted, and in the end Brown reluctantly agreed to let him appear at a medical staff meeting to make his case. At the meeting Bethune listened with growing impatience while Brown detailed the risks involved in the procedure, the most dangerous of which was the possibility of puncturing the lung. Then Bethune got up and unbuttoned his shirt. Baring his chest, he announced, "Gentlemen, I welcome the risk."[68] Brown gave in, and told Bethune that he would authorize a staff physician to perform a pneumothorax procedure on him later in the week. Energized by his joust with authority, Bethune returned to Lea Cottage and bragged to his cottage-mates about his success. He soon realized that they found his description of the procedure frightening and regarded his decision to undergo it as foolhardy, if brave.

One of the cottagers then told Bethune that an envelope had arrived for him. Bethune opened it to find a telegram from Frances, informing him that the court had granted her a divorce. Turning his back on the others, he walked outside, stunned by the irony that the news had arrived just when he had found a treatment that might lead to his recovery. When the shock wore off, he telephoned the Western Union office in town and sent a telegram to Frances, congratulating her on her divorce and proposing that they get married again.[69]

Spurred on by the energy from his decision to risk the pneumothorax procedure, Bethune now decided to act on another idea. During a discussion with some of his fellow patients, they had talked about the unpredictable nature of life, and someone mentioned *The Rake's Progress*, a series of engravings in which the eighteenth-century English artist William Hogarth depicted the decline of a young Englishman as he sank into debauchery and immorality, imprisonment and death. Bethune had begun to paint a little during his time in Detroit, and he now mentioned the idea of creating a mural to outline the life of a person afflicted with tuberculosis. His cottage-mates urged him to do it.[70] The morning after he telegraphed Frances, he went into town and bought chalk crayons; from a local laundry he got a roll of light-brown wrapping paper about 1.5 metres wide. Precariously balanced on a chair placed atop a reading table, he began to tack the paper to the moulding that ran along both sides of the cottage below the roof. The day afterward, he began to draw.

On Thursday morning he walked down to the children's infirmary, where Dr Earle Warren performed the pneumothorax procedure on his left lung. It was a harrowing experience. When Dr Warren inserted the needle between his ribs, Bethune felt a stabbing pain that continued as air was pumped through the tube into his chest cavity. When the procedure was finished, Dr Warren warned him that he must rest. Gasping for breath, Bethune struggled up the slope to Lea Cottage. But after only a brief rest, he returned to his drawing. Wheezing and coughing, a sputum cup in one hand and a piece of chalk in the other, he worked on the mural through the rest of the day.

To avoid keeping everyone awake with his coughing that night, Bethune volunteered to sleep on the veranda. Dr Alfred Blalock, a fellow patient, offered to take his cot outside as well.[71] Neither got much sleep, and at about three o'clock Bethune began to cough convulsively. The coughing became so intense that Blalock feared Bethune might not survive the night.[72] At daybreak

Bethune agreed to go to the infirmary. There he underwent a fluoroscopic examination which showed that, as the doctors had warned, his lung had been punctured. Instead of the intended partial collapse, the entire lung had ceased functioning. To allow it to resume operation, Dr Warren removed a considerable amount of air from Bethune's chest cavity, and the agony of the past twenty hours eased. Bethune again marched back up the hill and, although he was still in pain, went on with his drawing.

The mural, which Bethune called *The T.B.'s Progress,* extended nearly twenty metres along the wall of Lea Cottage. An allegorical dramatization of Bethune's life and death, it consisted of nine panels, one more than in Hogarth's work, with a descriptive verse at the bottom of each. Its style incorporated some of the techniques of the medieval frescoes Bethune had so admired in Italy, but was also influenced by impressionism and expressionism.[73] In the first panel the tubercle bacillus, in the form of a red pterodactyl, attacks Bethune in the womb. In the next he watches from the arms of a beautiful female angel while other angels weep as they read his future on a scroll unrolled by the Angel of Fate.

His life story unfolds on the rest of the panels. After surviving various childhood diseases, and full of confidence despite the deadly pterodactyl hovering above him, he enters into early manhood, sailing across the Sea of Adolescence on a galleon named *Youth at the Prow and Pleasure at the Helm.*[74] Almost at once he is lured off course by the Sirens of Fame, Wealth, Love, and Art and seeks the Castle of Heart's Desire perched on a rocky cliff. He makes his way to the heights and is about to enter the castle when he is attacked by a swarm of bats, representing tuberculosis, and plunges into the Abyss of Despair toward the red river of hemorrhage. As he falls, he realizes that the castle is not real but only the facade of a Hollywood set.

Lying hopelessly diseased at the bottom of the chasm, he observes another castle, this one flying a Red Cross flag symbolizing the Trudeau Sanatorium. After another steep climb he enters it, taking shelter from the attacking bats. However, still unable to learn his lesson, he yields to the Siren of Spurious Fame, who lures him back to the city where he is again attacked by tuberculosis bats. Summoning his remaining strength, he sets out for Arizona in the hope of recovery in the dry desert climate. On the way the Angel of Death overtakes him, and in the final panel she holds Bethune in her arms as she stands above a graveyard containing his tombstone and those of his six cottage-mates. Beneath this macabre scene Bethune wrote the following verse:

Sweet Death, thou kindest angel of them all,
In thy soft arms, at last, O let me fall;

Bright stars are out, long gone the burning sun
My little act is over and the tiresome play is done.

After consulting his cottage-mates, Bethune added a projected date of death for each of them on the tombstones, choosing 1932 as the year of his own demise.[75]

When Bethune had first entered Trudeau, his mother, who had been alarmed by his drinking in Detroit and scandalized by the failure of his marriage, told him that his illness was God's punishment for his sinful ways. "God sees all," she had warned him.[76] Although at the time Bethune likely dismissed her comment as religious claptrap, her warning must have affected him. For what the murals show is his belief that he had surrendered to temptations that distracted him from the noble achievements of which he had dreamed. In doing so, he had thrown his life away, and he now feared he might pay the ultimate price for his folly. *The T.B.'s Progress* was his confession of his sins; it was also his obituary.[77]

But now a new thought occurred to him. Doomed he might be, but what if he could cheat the Angel of Death for the five years that he had predicted were left to him? Might he not yet manage to do some good in the world? As he was putting the finishing touches to his drawings, another doctor, who was also a patient, dropped by. Depressed, he complained to Bethune that even if he recovered from tuberculosis, he faced an uphill struggle to regain what he had lost. Gazing down at him from the tabletop, Bethune confessed that, as his drawings showed, he had allowed selfishness and avarice to rule his own life. But pursuing wealth, he said, was not the true purpose of practising medicine. "Now, in whatever time is left to me," he added, "I'm going to look around until I find something I can do for the human race, something great, and I am going to do it before I die."[78]

Bethune Memorial House, Gravenhurst. The house in which Bethune was born is now a national historic site. Courtesy BMH

The Bethune family at Beaverton. Young Henry Norman takes the lead in the family photograph. Courtesy BMH

Malcolm Nicolson
Bethune. A globe-trotting
vagabond in his youth,
Bethune's father was
born again and became
an evangelist minister.
Courtesy BMH

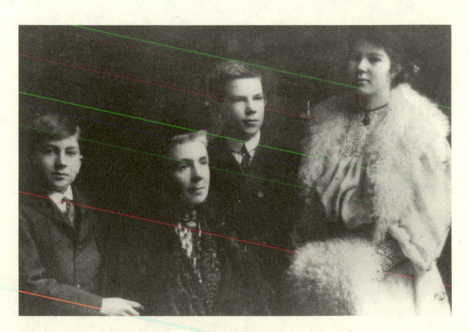

Elizabeth Ann Bethune and her children. Malcolm Goodwin (left), Henry Norman,
and Janet Louise feared their mother's cool discipline far more than their father's
anger. Courtesy BMH

High-school days. Busy with sports and hobbies, Henry Norman (middle right)
spent little time on his studies. Courtesy BMH

With loggers at Whitefish, Ontario. Posted to the north woods by the Reading Camp Association, Bethune relished the outdoor work and his role of mentor to the other loggers. Courtesy BMH

Graduate in medicine, University of Toronto, 1916. Among Bethune's fellow graduates was Dr Frederick Banting, later the co-discoverer of insulin. Courtesy BMH

Surgeon-lieutenant in the Royal Navy. Always seeking new experiences, Bethune served in the army, navy, and air force. Courtesy BMH

Intern at London's Hospital for Sick Children. Bethune (back row, second from right) always felt an outsider among his colleagues at Great Ormond Street who made it clear that he could never "pass" as an Englishman. Courtesy BMH

Man about town. During his years in London, Bethune transformed himself into an art expert and developed a taste for the finer things in life. Courtesy BMH

Frances Campbell Penney.
Twice married to Penney
and twice divorced,
Bethune remained
obsessed with her as
long as he lived.
Courtesy BMH

Isabelle Humphreys-Owen.
The Sassoon heiress financed
Bethune's art expeditions,
and their relationship deepened into an affair. Painting
by Dolf Van Roy. Courtesy
of the National Library
of Wales PG4590

A model "Englishman" in Detroit. Among his American colleagues at the Harper Hospital Bethune played the part of an idealized English-man. Frances Bethune kept this photograph at her bedside until her death. Courtesy BMH

At Lea Cottage, Trudeau Sanatorium. Bethune with (from left to right) Lincoln Fisher, John Barnwell, Alfred Blalock, and Nan Li. Courtesy BMH

In the arms of the Angel of Death. In this final panel of the mural he drew at Lea Cottage, Bethune depicted himself dead of tuberculosis. He predicted that 1932 would be the year of his demise. Courtesy BMH

Born Again

Ray Brook and Montreal, 1927–1931

What happened next was extraordinary, even for Bethune. Still recovering from the nearly disastrous pneumothorax procedure, he had every reason to be pessimistic about his health. Yet as if completing the mural and putting a period to his own life had been some kind of catharsis, his black mood vanished and he rebounded. He was in much less pain now, and on Sunday he persuaded nurse Elsie Thorn to go with him to a Halloween masquerade party in town at the home of one of the staff doctors. Each day he felt better, and a week after the pneumothorax procedure he even sneaked off to join a deer hunt.[1]

Bethune knew that one treatment was not enough to cure him. Air pumped into the chest cavity was gradually absorbed and would have to be replaced to ensure that the diseased area of the lung remained collapsed. So throughout November and into early December, he received more pneumothorax procedures, called refills, every week to ten days.[2] The results were dramatic, and Bethune began to recover so rapidly that on 10 December, just over six weeks after his first pneumothorax, he was able to leave the Trudeau Sanatorium. He weighed fifteen pounds more than he had on admission, his pulse rate had improved, and his sputum was no longer positive; the cavity in his right lung had disappeared and the one in his left lung had been stabilized. He was considered fit and able to resume normal activities. The doctors told him that if he continued to receive refills for some time, he could eventually be entirely free of the disease.

Like his father before him, though in a different sense, Bethune had been born again, and he intended to keep his vow to do something for humanity. He decided to enter the field of tubercular medicine, hoping to make a discovery that would lead to the eradication of the "white plague," as the disease was called. In those days before the advent of streptomycin, tuberculosis was a deadly disease that killed many people and incapacitated many more. In the

Province of Quebec, where Bethune would eventually work, the mortality rate of tuberculosis was the highest in Canada – almost three thousand Quebecois died of the disease in 1925 alone.[3] The Canadian pioneer in the surgical treatment of tuberculosis was Dr Edward Archibald of the Royal Victoria Hospital in Montreal, who had been a patient at Trudeau some years before. Bethune had met him when Archibald had visited the sanatorium, and he now decided that a position with Archibald would be the ideal way to begin his new career. He sent him a copy of his curriculum vitae and a letter explaining his interest in training under him. Archibald replied that he would consider taking Bethune on if he would get further training in bacteriology and recommended that he study at the New York State Hospital for Incipient Tuberculosis at Ray Brook, only a short distance east of Saranac Lake.[4] Bethune then approached the medical director and chief medical officer of Ray Brook, Dr Harry A. Bray, a fellow Canadian, and Bray agreed to find a place for him.

Carrying several pieces of expensive English luggage stuffed with fine clothing and a hatbox containing his top hat, Bethune attracted instant attention when he breezed into Ray Brook just before Christmas of 1927. He was given a residence room in the hospital and told he would receive a monthly honorarium of $100 provided by Dr Bray. He was to attend staff meetings, and because there was no surgeon at the sanatorium, he would also be asked to perform preliminary surgical consultations.[5] However, he was allowed to spend most of his time in the laboratory, where he worked under the direction of Dr David T. Smith. As he always did with a new interest, he plunged into his work. The laboratory director later noted that Bethune picked up more knowledge in three months "than most graduate students learn in three years."[6] Bethune's enthusiasm proved contagious, and Dr Smith and his colleague Dr Julius L. Wilson decided to resume work on a project they had earlier abandoned. Under their guidance Bethune reassembled the data and completed the project, a study of pseudo-tuberculosis in rats. The three of them summarized their findings in a paper that would be published in a learned journal in 1930.[7]

Bethune and Bray got on well at first but Bray's authoritarian teaching methods soon began to grate on Bethune's nerves. Bray's Sunday morning routine was to show visiting medical students or young staff members x-rays of patients and then grill them about how to interpret them. The questions were complex, and Bray's condescending manner humiliated anyone who could not answer to his satisfaction. One Sunday he directed a question to Bethune. Unable to answer, Bethune went on the attack, firing one question after another back at Bray. Embarrassed and angry, the chief gathered up the x-rays and walked away. Several weeks later, at a medical conference in Montreal, Dr Archibald asked Dr Smith how he was getting on with Bethune. He was curious, he explained, because he had written a letter to Bray asking for his appraisal of him, and Bray had replied that Bethune was uncooperative and insubordinate. Smith then explained how Bethune had embarrassed Bray in front of the staff. Archibald burst out laughing and said, "I'll take him!"[8]

Bethune soon settled into his new life. At the end of each workday, as long as there was snow on the ground, he would ski over Mount Baker to Saranac Lake to spend the evening with friends, usually returning by midnight. John Barnwell, who had been appointed to the staff of the Trudeau Sanatorium, was living just outside the grounds in a run-down shack that Bethune called "John's Cottage." There a group gathered around a wood stove most evenings to drink, talk, and listen to records on an old gramophone that Barnwell had bought in town. Bethune's favourite tunes were "Hallelujah, I'm a Bum" and on the flip side, "Lonesome Road"; these he played endlessly, singing along loudly and off-key.

He also socialized at Ray Brook. With the notable exception of Dr Bray, he got along well with most of the other staff members, several of whom also knew John Barnwell. They seem to have been amused by Bethune's irrepressible spirits and madcap antics. One night, after a Saranac Lake Medical Society Meeting, Bethune, thoroughly drunk, insisted on riding home through a blizzard on the roof of a colleague's car, the driver inching along as Bethune repeatedly slid down over the windshield and skittered back up onto the roof.[9] But he was not always so frolicsome, for although alcohol made him more sociable, it often unleashed his temper and made him quarrelsome. Once, in the midst of a dispute with Dan Gallery, a local doctor, he seized a knife and cut a slit in Gallery's rug.[10]

Even when not drunk, Bethune could be unkind. When John Barnwell learned that Bethune was making a brief trip to New York City and would be very near where Barnwell's sister Lucy was visiting, he asked him to call on her, because she was worried about his health and he wanted her to know how well he was. On Bethune's return, Barnwell asked eagerly about his sister, but Bethune said that the house in which she was staying looked pretentious, and he had not bothered to visit her.[11] As one less-than-admiring contemporary of Bethune's at Ray Brook put it, "He was not a nice man. He was a hard man."[12]

In late March 1928 Bethune completed his basic training in bacteriology at Ray Brook and went north to Montreal to join Archibald's staff at McGill University.[13] McGill was the pre-eminent medical faculty in Canada and

Archibald its leading thoracic surgeon. He took Bethune on in his Thoracic-Pulmonary Service to train him in the techniques of chest surgery and allowed him to begin tubercular research in the McGill laboratories. Pleased with his progress, Archibald appointed Bethune to the Department of Surgery and Physiology on 1 July.

In terms of Bethune's later career, it is important to note that in addition to surgical techniques he likely learned the basics of blood transfusion from Archibald, who along with a few other army doctors had used whole blood from donors to transfuse wounded soldiers at treatment stations near the front during World War I.[14] One technique Archibald and others had used was to extract blood from a donor and then add a small amount of sodium citrate to prevent clotting before injecting the blood into a vein in a recipient's arm. Depending upon the circumstances, Archibald also used a more common procedure, called arm-to-arm or direct transfusion, which was performed with the patient and a donor with the matching blood type lying on adjoining surgical tables. Blood extracted from a vein in the arm of the donor flowed directly through a tube into a glass cannula sewn into the arm of the patient.[15] It is reasonable to speculate that Bethune learned to perform such direct transfusions at the Royal Victoria, because he later introduced them at another hospital.[16] Because of his connection with Archibald, it seems likely that he would also have known about the preservation of blood using sodium citrate.

Caught up as he was in such technical and surgical advances, Bethune's spirits were high. And he received good news about his health too. Regular x-rays examinations in Montreal showed that he was progressing well. His right lung remained completely healthy, and regular pneumothorax refills kept his left lung in a stable condition. Every day he made the twenty-five minute walk from his apartment at 1221 St Mark Street along Sherbrooke Street and up McTavish Street to the hospital and back again in the early afternoon. From three to five he rested.[17] By keeping up this routine of exercise and rest, he hoped he would eventually be able to do without refill treatments, even though he had learned to do these himself, to the astonishment of onlookers. Meanwhile Dr Ronald Christie, a McGill colleague, examined him frequently and measured his lung capacity. He pronounced him physically fit.[18]

Bethune's position at McGill was ideal in all ways but one: it initially provided no income. Archibald lacked the money to pay Bethune a salary and had taken him on as an unpaid voluntary assistant.[19] Shortly after his arrival in Montreal, Bethune had to explain to Archibald that he could not live on his insurance disability income alone and might have to go elsewhere to find a paying position. Archibald then turned to Percy P. Cowans, a wealthy friend, who set up a scholarship at McGill from which Bethune would receive $1,500 per year. Almost overnight, his income had nearly doubled.[20]

This windfall allowed him to set about regaining his ex-wife, who had returned to Edinburgh after their divorce. He had never accepted losing her and was sure that he could win her back. He realized that as a first step he had to keep up the $100 monthly alimony payments he had agreed to, so he began sending her cheques in the autumn of 1928. With them he enclosed letters describing his work and life in Montreal. For several months Frances cashed his cheques but did not reply to his letters. But when at last she did, he began to woo her in earnest, and toward the end of the year he made a direct appeal: "If it were not for my doubts I would say at once – 'Come here. Marry me. Why should we be separate who love each other?' I can be happy with you – but you not with me. I was thinking that if you came here this winter – we could meet just as friends, living apart. In any case, whether you marry me or not, that is, I am sure, *our* only way ... I miss you dreadfully but I don't want to snatch at you ever again. I want you to be just Frances Penney – the Frances Penney I knew in Edinburgh – self-contained and undistorted. Goodbye, darling, for the present, you are ever in my thoughts. Your affectionate lover, Beth."[21]

But she did not reply, because although she loved him she knew his instability only too well, and distrusted him. Realizing he had been too bold, Bethune approached her again, more cautiously. In a brief early January letter containing an alimony payment, he concluded, "I wish you were here. I am glad you are relatively happy and well, at least more so than when you lived with my petulant irritability. God bless you, Beth."[22] As time passed, she softened, and in one letter even confessed that she had dreamed of him. In his reply he asked, "And did we love each other in your dream – were we in each other's arms again?"[23]

Despite the professional advantages of his position at the Royal Victoria and his new hope of luring Frances to Montreal, Bethune was already growing restless. He had always seen the Royal Victoria appointment as no more than a basic training position, which he intended to leave at the first opportunity, and had told colleagues that having got the position he intended to use it as "a mailing address."[24] In a letter to Frances he had mentioned that after a year Archibald would be able to place him somewhere. But he must have had some doubts about this, because in the same letter he said that he was thinking of two possibilities for the following year. One was to search for a position in an English sanatorium, and the other was to pursue a tentative offer from a hospital in Shanghai.[25] However, by January 1929 he had apparently lost interest in England and China and had begun to consider the United States where, he told Frances, he was going to look for a job later in the year. A few weeks later he had even fixed a date for leaving. "This is a lovely town," he wrote to a friend. "It's a pity I can't stay but I leave in June – on again – God knows where, not that it matters."[26] But whatever plans he had for June fell through, perhaps because he wanted to continue working on an involved research project that he had begun and which required a year to complete.[27]

In the autumn of 1929, Frances at last gave in to his pleas and agreed to join him in Montreal. She was miserable in Edinburgh, for her mother kept reminding her that she had brought all her troubles on herself by insisting on marrying Bethune. Her chances of finding a good job were slim because of her limited work experience, and at the age of thirty-six it was late to begin training for an occupation. Socially, her age and the stigma of being a divor-cée made it unlikely that she would marry again. Perhaps accepting that the devil she knew was better than no one at all, she agreed to return to Bethune.

Their second marriage took place within days of her arrival in Montreal. With deliberate irony, Bethune chose 11 November 1929, the eleventh anni-versary of the armistice that ended World War I, as their wedding day. As wit-nesses they called on two old friends, Dr Graham Ross, who had interned with Bethune in the Hospital for Sick Children in London, and Norah Hume Wright, with whom Frances had stayed in Montreal during the stormy times in their first marriage. To the amusement of the about-to-be-wed couple, the minister insisted on prefacing the ceremony with a twenty-minute homily on the gravity of marriage. Barely able to contain themselves until they were safely out of the church, they howled with laughter as they clambered into the back seat of Dr Ross's car.[28]

Yet despite their hilarity they knew that their relationship was fragile, so they were careful with each other, trying hard to avoid the errors of the past. For several months all went well, and Frances was beginning to believe that she had been wrong to worry about her husband's erratic ways, for he seemed a changed man. They did not quarrel, and he no longer spent his evenings at the hospital or carousing with friends. He now returned early from work and stayed home with her after dinner. He also helped her adjust to her new surroundings, taking her around Montreal and proudly intro-ducing her to his friends and colleagues. She liked the city and the agreeable people she met at dinner parties and other social events. Many of them thought her charming, although there were others who found her "shallow, naïve, humourless and vindictive."[29] In time, she accepted Bethune's sug-gestion that she might enjoy working, and found a job as a sales clerk in

Ogilvy's, an upscale department store that offered many expensive British-made products.

In early 1930 Frances discovered that she was pregnant. Her reaction was not entirely joyful, because she had never wanted to have children that would be raised as "little Canadians." She also could not help wondering what sort of father the mercurial Bethune would make.[30] But he was thrilled. He had always been fascinated by children and during his time at the Hospital for Sick Children in London had thought of specializing in children's medicine; throughout his professional life he had showed the greatest care for his young patients. Now the thought of having a child of his own lifted his spirits and made him look even more eagerly toward the future. He was sure, too, that a child would strengthen his relationship with his wife.

Meanwhile, despite his restlessness, his professional life had been going well. As had been the case everywhere else he had worked, his distinctive personality had impressed itself on the staff of the Royal Victoria Hospital. Dr Wendell MacLeod, in those days a medical student at McGill, remembered the dashing figure Bethune cut, a jaunty beret perched on his head, a colourful scarf around his throat, and his stylish wife on his arm.[31] Bethune's enthusiasm for his work also attracted attention. In the hospital dining room an attentive group often gathered to watch him sketching diagrams on the wallpaper as ideas came to him. Dr Archibald, rather bemused by his new assistant, compared Bethune's brain to a St Catherine's wheel, saying that it threw out sparks in all directions. Bethune was "full of hunches," he wrote, but added that he had to reject many of his ideas "because they lacked solid foundation in knowledge of the human material."[32]

Others also recognized that Bethune's ideas were sometimes flawed by the lack of detailed knowledge or analysis. On one occasion he decided to write a definitive monograph on the physical signs of tuberculosis, an area in which he had little training. After he completed it, he asked Dr Ronald Christie for a criticism. Christie recalled: "I sat down and it took me about half and hour to read it. I scribbled in the margin all the way down, 'not proved,' 'unknown,' 'hypothesis' and so on. I went over it with him and he said, 'Ronald, you are absolutely right.' He got up in his theatrical way and he tore this manuscript in small bits, chucked it in the wastepaper basket and said, 'Now let's go and have a drink.' That is the last I heard of it and he had spent weeks on it."[33] Dr Arthur Vineberg, another of Bethune's colleagues, noticed the same pattern, saying, "He had a superficial inquiring mind; like a child, he would see something else before digging deep and move on."[34] But sometimes Bethune's flashes of insight were sound, and he produced a series of research projects and published papers that added to his reputation and to knowledge in his field. Deeply involved in his research, he often remained in the laboratory long after his colleagues left. His focus was at times so intense that he would miss meetings and arrive late for operations.[35]

Socially, Bethune's record at the Royal Victoria was mixed. He enjoyed provoking a good argument and, as always, loved to play the devil's advocate. Better read and more interested in matters outside medicine and surgery than most of his colleagues, he managed to sound authoritative even on subjects about which he knew little. However, his liking for verbal fireworks sometimes outraged his senior colleagues. Focused on finding answers to a problem, he would challenge every concept and opinion, especially those of his superiors. The more traditional the procedure, the more critical he was of it. His bold manner was often seen as offensive, irreverent, and disrespectful. Some staff members believed that his criticisms were directed against them personally, or against highly respected colleagues such as Dr Archibald.

But if Bethune's iconoclastic manner antagonized some of his colleagues, it stimulated the students in a course on diagnosis and surgery that he and Archibald taught.[36] They liked his informal manner, for unlike other professors, Bethune would sit and draw them around him, chatting with them rather than lecturing. His explanations were lively and concise, often touched with bawdy humour. Students felt challenged by his insistence that they question all theories and practices no matter how hallowed they were by tradition. To force students to think for themselves, he would make patently false statements, parading them as truth and then praising those who dared to disagree with him. In the conservative atmosphere of a great university where most students accepted the teachings of their professors without question, those Bethune taught found his approach highly unusual. One of them, remembering his classroom manner and his reputation around the hospital, described him as "a brilliant screwball."[37]

Despite his unconventional behaviour, Bethune's work had been rated as "extremely satisfactory" in the Royal Victoria Hospital annual report of December 1929. One reason for this was the quality and amount of his research, for he had published four articles that year alone.[38] He owed his impressive output partly to the free hand that Archibald had given him to develop his own research projects. In addition to learning thoracic surgery by assisting Archibald, he spent many hours in the laboratory and in the animal house in the Department of Physiology where he performed experimental surgery. In one case he conducted a series of experiments in which he introduced maggots into the diseased lungs of a patient to clean out dead tissue. In another he blew talc into the lung cavity to stabilize one lung while surgery was being performed on the other. Known as pleural *poudrage*, this procedure was highly praised by Archibald and was soon widely adopted by thoracic surgeons.[39] Bethune also experimented on himself. On one occasion, curious to discover how blood was absorbed in the lung, he had blood inserted into his good lung though a catheter and then had a series of x-rays taken.[40]

He was also keenly involved in developing improved surgical instruments. Frustrated when an instrument did not function as he expected it to, he would sometimes hurl it across the operating room. But afterwards he would think about the problem and discuss it with an Australian technician named Masters, who had been a gun-maker in World War I.[41] Bethune would produce a flurry of suggested alterations, many of them impractical, and Masters would provide technical advice. Gradually Bethune would work out a different shape or some other alteration that he sensed would create a superior instrument, and Masters would then take on the task of forging it. If the new instrument did not perform as Bethune had hoped during an operation, he would reject it and begin again. Most of the instruments he designed went through many mutations before he considered them successful. John Barnwell later remarked, "On our visits to the Royal Victoria you literally stumbled over instruments which Bethune had designed but became impatient with and designed anew."[42]

Bethune's first invention was an improved pneumothorax apparatus that he designed shortly after his arrival in Montreal. This attracted the attention of the George P. Pilling Company, a highly respected Philadelphia manufacturer of surgical instruments. In 1930 a surgeon told Henry N. Pilling, the company president, that Bethune's apparatus was superior to the one made by his company; Pilling examined it and agreed. He approached Bethune, who decided to allow Pilling to manufacture his model. During their meeting Bethune sketched some of the surgical instruments that he was redesigning; Pilling was impressed and asked Bethune to send him samples. Two years later illustrations of various instruments designed by Bethune would fill more than a page in the Pilling catalogue. As long as he remained in Montreal, he continued to develop instruments, many of which Pilling manufactured. Perhaps the best known of these, the Bethune Rib Shears, was adapted from a pair of shoemaker's shears.[43] Another of his innovations, a set of special silver ligatures, was made for him by Henry Birks & Sons, a well-known Canadian jewellery company.[44]

An instinctive believer in technological change, Bethune became convinced that the invention of x-rays had made obsolete the use of a stethoscope to diagnose physical signs of pulmonary tuberculosis, and became a bit of a crank on the subject. He scathingly referred to doctors who did not agree with his opinion as "the fellows with the stethoscopes," and while instruct-ing students at McGill he would brandish a stethoscope and say, "If you are called to see a chest case, leave this at home."[45] During one of Dr Archibald's weekly rounds of the surgical wards, an assistant used his stethoscope to listen to a patient's chest and diagnose his condition. Archibald then asked, "What about you, Norman?"

"I don't know," snapped Bethune. "I don't want to listen to his chest. Give me an x-ray of it, and I'll give you my diagnosis."[46] Bethune also went public in his campaign against the use of stethoscopes to diagnose pulmonary tuberculosis. In a speech to the Canadian Progress Club of Montreal about the rapidly growing incidence of tuberculosis in the city, he warned, "The use of the stethoscope without x-ray examination in discovering tuberculosis is nothing more than a farce."[47]

Deeply involved in his research and inventions, successful in the operat-ing room and in the classroom, Bethune was still not wholly content. He had never forgotten his vow to do something great for humanity and still be-lieved that his best hope of doing that was as a thoracic surgeon. But having turned his back on private practice, he badly needed to find a paid hospital position. Archibald had told him that none was available at the Royal Victoria, and in any case Bethune did not want to go on being an assistant surgeon. Confident that he had learned all he needed to know, he was eager to head his own thoracic surgery department, but in 1930 there were few such openings in North America.[48] Meanwhile he was worried about losing his current income. He had no idea how long the Cowans scholarship would last, and he knew that his insurance payments would continue only as long as an annual medical examination proved that he was still suffering from tuberculosis.

However, despite his hope that he could leave the Royal Victoria and find a position elsewhere, Bethune realized that Frances was only beginning to adjust to Montreal and that a move might upset her. As it turned out, in the early spring of 1930 he received two new appointments, one after the other. On 20 March Archibald appointed him his clinical assistant in surgery at the Royal Victoria, and although this was not a salaried position, Archibald per-suaded Percy Cowans to guarantee that Bethune would still be paid $1,500 a year.[49] Archibald also recommended him for an appointment at Sainte Anne de Bellevue Veterans Hospital, and Bethune was named consultant in tuber-culosis there at a salary of $25 a week.[50]

Now just past his fortieth birthday, Bethune seemed to have successfully welded the shards of his life back together. In little more than two years he had regained his health and his wife and was on the road to success as a thoracic surgeon. But only weeks later, he suffered a bitter blow. Frances miscarried, and although the loss was a disappointment to her, it devastated Bethune, undermining his emotional balance. Still grieving, he happened to see a large rag doll in a department store window and bought it and brought it home. They named the doll Alice, perhaps after Lewis Carroll's heroine in *Alice in Wonderland*, a book of which Bethune was fond. Dressed in baby clothes, Alice became the symbol of the child Bethune feared they would never have. Raging against his disappointment, he began to find fault with Frances again and reverted to his old ways, losing his temper and bullying her. She fought back, and they began to re-enact the scenes that had destroyed their first marriage.

Bethune started drinking heavily and staying out at night. When he was home, he often deliberately tried to provoke Frances, sometimes storing parts of human cadavers in the refrigerator.[51] On one occasion, they had just sat down to dinner when Bethune seized the tablecloth and jerked it, scattering food and dishes.[52] He would end their arguments by stalking out of the apartment, returning drunk many hours later. He now frequently spent his evenings playing bridge or poker with some of the younger doctors or other acquaintances.

Fred Taylor, an artist friend who played cards with him, recalled:

When I first met Beth I was drawn to him by his keen intelligence, forceful personality and intensity, but quite quickly I came to regard him as a menace and to actually resent him ... He was a bad drinker, that is, as he drank he became increasingly irascible and difficult ... Bethune loved [to play poker] ... in a somewhat domineering manner ... And so it frequently fell to my lot to cope with him when he had been drinking and was exhibiting the least favourable aspects of himself. He picked arguments and insulted people everywhere we went and got into many more or less serious squabbles. Beth knew that I had been the Canadian Intercollegiate Heavyweight Boxing champion and as I was a good deal bigger than he was, he was careful never to pick on me. But it devolved upon me to get him out of a good many fights, some of them quite nasty, and to get him home.[53]

On one such occasion the two men were playing poker in Verdun. The game ended when Bethune provoked a fight. He and Taylor had to flee, hotly pursued by the other players. The chase continued by car through downtown Montreal. Unable to shake off their pursuers, Bethune stopped the car in front of the Ritz Hotel on Sherbrooke Street, and he and Taylor ran for the

McGill University campus, where they hid until the irate card-players gave up.[54] Tiring of such hijinks, Taylor came to resent having to play the role of protector and eventually dropped Bethune.

Before the end of the year the intensity of their quarrelling made it obvious to Bethune and Frances that their marriage had failed again. In desperation she turned to his friend Coleman, to whom she had been so attracted during their stay in Detroit and who had recently settled in Montreal.[55] Coleman was now thirty-two; handsome and possessed of an easy charm and relaxed manner, he fancied himself a lady's man.[56] When Frances told him that her marriage was on the verge of collapse, he invited her to move in with him if she decided to leave Bethune. In the early spring of 1931 she joined Coleman in his apartment at 3480 Chemin de la Côte de Neiges. Bethune did not try to stop her.

He resumed his bachelor ways. Busy in the operating room and the laboratory on weekdays, he spent his evenings playing cards or drinking at bars, usually with acquaintances from the hospital. On winter weekends he often joined friends to go north to the Laurentians to ski. He began to date nurses again, as he had done before Frances's return in the autumn of 1929, and it soon became common knowledge in the Royal Victoria that a nurse who found herself alone in a room with Dr Bethune should expect that his focus of interest would not always be professional.[57] A friend later said that he had "the sort of charm that is so often associated with the cocky, wilful, self-consciously 'naughty' type, the charm that can so effortlessly disarm latent opposition and flatten the ladies right and left."[58] Well aware of his reputation, Bethune made the most of it. He always arrived at the hospital with crisply pressed trousers, polished shoes and a flower in his lapel. On ward rounds he insisted on a freshly starched and spotless white coat.[59]

However, this did not prevent him from making his rounds dressed as a lumberjack on one occasion, probably on a dare. When his mood was on the upswing, his gaiety and vitality made him almost irresistible. He would turn his narrow gaze on a woman, making her feel she was the whole object of his attention. Eileen Flanagan, a student nurse, found him "dynamic and attractive," and another woman recalled, "Even to go shopping with Beth was somehow a memorable and exciting experience. It was not only his gaiety; he was able to invest everything he did – every object that interested him – with a sort of heightened reality. It was not just enthusiasm, but something more … vivid."[60] One former lady-friend put his appeal even more strongly: "When Bethune turned on his charm, women would turn to jelly and their heels became rounded."[61]

He continued to dine out and attend parties but made a difficult guest, going out of his way to mock the comfortable bourgeois values of many of the people he knew in Montreal. Part of his rancour may have come from his old resentment of having restrictions put on how he could behave. Another source may have been his belief in his aristocratic descent, which he bragged about to his friends. Dr Aubrey Geddes, who would share a flat with him, re-called, "He was proud of what he called his aristocratic lineage, fond of talk-ing about the Bethunes of France who date back to William the Conqueror and before. And he often quoted the line of the Four Marys – 'Mary Queen of Scots, Mary Bethune, Mary Seddon, Mary Carmichael and me.' And he always claimed lineage from Mary Bethune."[62] Despite his pretensions, wealth and privilege always antagonized him. Yet although he criticized the stuffiness and narrow selfishness of the upper classes, Frances said he was envious of his rich Montreal relatives.[63]

An inveterate challenger of medical traditions, Bethune also never missed an opportunity to attack conventional social mores. During one dinner-party in a wealthy Montreal home he ridiculed the fetish of body cleanliness, suggesting that the animal odours of human bodies were stimulating and pleasant. One woman asked him anxiously, "But ... if we didn't bathe, how could we remain clean?" Leaning across the table, Bethune suggested, "Oh, I don't know ... we might just lick each other clean."[64] His eagerness to shock people could lead him to be cruel. At another black-tie party he ap-peared with a prostitute on his arm. He paraded her before the astonished guests, stating her profession and telling them that he had picked her up in the streets. Then he led her to the buffet where he supplied her with food and drink. After she had eaten, he announced, "Now, ladies and gentlemen, I shall return her whence she has come – the streets and degradation."[65]

He was also not above mocking his friends. In mid-June 1931 he received a letter from Dr Edward Kupka, his former student in Detroit, informing him that he was about to be married and intended to come to Montreal on his honeymoon. When the newlyweds arrived, Bethune greeted them effu-sively and over Kupka's protests insisted on throwing a party to celebrate their marriage. He arranged for a formal banquet in the dining room of Kupka's hotel, to which he invited a dozen colleagues. The champagne flowed freely, and at the end of the evening Bethune presented the astonished Kupka with the very large bill for the affair. Later, during a carriage-ride up Mount Royal, he drunkenly fondled Kupka's wife. Kupka had always hero-worshipped Bethune, but this was going too far. The couple shook Bethune off and returned to their hotel. However, the following day, persuaded by his wife that he should not bear a grudge, Kupka made up with Bethune and was foolish enough to offer him the use of his brand-new car while he and his wife went to New York by train. This was rather asking to be kicked, and Bethune was happy to oblige: when Kupka got his car back ten days later, it was filthy and dented and the odometer showed that Bethune had driven it 2,500 kilometres.[66]

Shortly after this escapade, Bethune asked Frances to come back to him. She had fled from his temperamental outbursts and domineering ways, but when they had met occasionally over the past few months, he had sensed that she questioned her decision to leave him. She felt trapped between her attraction to Coleman and her yearning for Bethune. She was also uneasy about "living in sin" while her husband was only a few blocks away. So when Bethune told her he still loved her, she decided to return to him. But they had learned nothing and forgotten nothing: they began to quarrel bitterly again, and soon realized that they simply could not go on together.

This time Bethune decided he would be the one to leave – not only his wife but Montreal too. He felt he had gone as far as he could go at the Royal Victoria Hospital and his relationship with Dr Archibald had frayed considerably. Several months after beginning his training under him, Bethune had described his chief to Frances as "the outstanding figure in chest surgery in America and a most charming fellow."[67] Archibald in turn had referred to Bethune in glowing terms as "invaluable [and] a very promising young man."[68] However, by 1931 the two surgeons' professional honeymoon was over.

Although personal and temperamental differences contributed to the breach between them, there was more to it than that. Bethune's chief criticized his failure to undertake remedial study in areas in which he lacked knowledge, a condition agreed upon between them when Bethune became one of Archibald's assistants.[69] Archibald was still impressed by the quickness of Bethune's mind but criticized his tendency to concentrate his reading of medical literature on areas related to inventions.[70] But his greatest concern was Bethune's surgery. The basic lung operation he had taught him to perform was the thoracoplasty, the purpose of which was to collapse the diseased part of a lung in order to rest it. In cases where adhesions joining the lung to the chest wall prevented the use of pneumothorax, surgeons partially collapsed the lung by removing ribs around the diseased area. But the operation could be dangerous: the patient might lose too much blood or die from being kept under anaesthetic too long. For these reasons, surgeons needed to move quickly. When Bethune began to operate independently of Archibald, he became noted for his dexterity and speed. At the beginning of an operation he would point to the clock and when he had finished would have his assistants note the time again. He was always disappointed when he took longer than he believed necessary. Colleagues recognized his skill, but some suggested that his preoccupation with speed was showy and could lead to carelessness.[71]

Archibald later described Bethune's operating technique as "quick but rough, not careful, far from neat, and just a little dangerous."[72] He maintained that the fixation on technique and speed caused Bethune to ignore the physical condition of his candidates for surgery. His evidence was that Bethune's patients suffered more post-operative trauma than those of other surgeons and more of them died. Some simply did not have the stamina to survive surgery. He believed that Bethune lacked judgment in choosing cases for surgery and considered this his greatest flaw as a surgeon.[73] But when Archibald reproached him for taking risks, Bethune reacted angrily, saying that it was his interest in the patient that made him focus on technique and speed. Many of those on whom he operated had little chance of survival anyway. Surgery was their last hope, even if the odds were against them. He argued that most surgeons, keen to keep their operating records spotless, would not take on the cases he did.

At least one fellow doctor at the Royal Victoria supported Bethune, saying, "Norman was what I would consider an excellent operator and … exhibited sound surgical judgment … His philosophy was that every open case of T.B. was responsible for at least ten more. He therefore felt that high-risk procedures were justified in the endeavour to convert every open case of T.B … He was a very impulsive individual in both his professional and social activities. His opinions were quickly made, probably without complete knowledge of the particular situation but peculiarly enough [he] was usually right. This impulsive attitude frequently annoyed Dr Archibald and his confrères."[74]

Bethune's erratic personal behaviour at the Royal Vic had shaped his professional reputation just as much as had his surgical record. Immersed in one research project or another, he was often late for operations, and Archibald reprimanded him for this. On one occasion Bethune had begun an operation visibly upset about something that had happened earlier. Suddenly, without warning or explanation, he put down the scalpel and walked out of the operating room. Fortunately for the patient, the nurses hastily summoned the resident doctor on duty who completed the operation.[75] Like many others on staff, Archibald found such self-preoccupation, as well as Bethune's impatience and fits of temper, offensive.

For all these reasons Bethune had worn out his welcome with Archibald. So when he asked for a leave of absence for several months, his chief quickly agreed. Smarting from the failure of his second marriage to Frances, feeling he had reached a dead end at the Royal Victoria, Bethune was eager to turn his back on Montreal.

The Hill of Difficulty

Travels and Montreal,
September 1931–November 1933

Bethune's plan was to go to Arizona, where some of the most highly regarded sanatoriums in the United States were located. He intended to visit as many of them as he could to learn about new developments in the treatment of tuberculosis and hoped that by introducing himself and the instruments he had designed to the leading medical men in the American Southwest, he might find a job. His health could benefit too: exposure to the desert climate might speed the healing of the small cavity remaining in his left lung, for which he was continuing to take pneumothorax treatments.[1]

His first stop on what his friend John Barnwell later described as his "barnstorming trip" was Ann Arbor, Michigan, in late September 1931.[2] There he visited Barnwell, now on the staff of the University of Michigan medical school, and was introduced to Dr John Alexander, author of *The Surgery of Pulmonary Tuberculosis*, the book that had inspired Bethune to undergo the pneumothorax procedure. In October he headed to Arizona, where he made the small city of Prescott his base for the next two months. Prescott was the location of Pamsetgaaf, a sanatorium for tuberculars operated by Dr John Flinn, an expatriate Nova Scotian.[3] Flinn had invited Bethune to visit Pamsetgaaf because of his association with Archibald, his research publications, and his growing reputation as an inventor of instruments, particularly his pneumothorax apparatus.

Flinn asked Bethune to examine some patients, one of them the Hollywood actress Renée Adorée, famous at the time for her starring role in the 1925 movie *The Big Parade*. Bethune concluded that a phrenicectomy might improve Adorée's condition. In this type of operation the surgeon removes a portion of the phrenic nerve that causes the diaphragm to rise, partially compressing the lung. The incision is made near the base of the neck. The actress at first refused the operation, fearing that the disfigurement might ruin her career, but Bethune promised that he would find a way to conceal the scar. To prepare for the operation he removed several beads from her favourite necklace and replaced them with a narrow slotted silver bar. Fastening the necklace around her neck, he then he traced a thin line onto her skin through the slot. During the operation he made the incision along the line he had traced. Afterwards, with the beads back in place, the scar was hidden. "Strange to say, this seems to fill the female breast with the most profound gratitude," he later wrote in an article entitled "A Phrenicectomy Necklace," published in a medical journal. The article's appearance led to mutterings by some members of the medical community who, as Bethune expected, considered such cosmetic concerns frivolous and even unprofessional.[4]

From late October onward, Bethune moved about Arizona visiting other sanatoriums and clinics and speaking to medical groups on the treatment of tuberculosis and the function of his surgical instruments. From Phoenix he flew south to Tucson, where he accepted the invitation of Charles A. Thomas of the Thomas Davis Clinic to be his guest for a week at the Old Pueblo Club, one of the oldest and most exclusive in the Southwest.[5] He seems to have enjoyed himself thoroughly, because when Dr Thomas went to settle Bethune's bill after he had left, he was startled to find that in addition to the charges for his room and meals, his guest had run up an extraordinary bar bill of $108.[6]

Meanwhile, Bethune had driven north to spend several days in Grand Canyon National Park, which he described in a letter to Frances as "a tremendous super-Switzerland – quite the most amazing sight I have ever beheld."[7] Throughout his travels he had still been communicating with his estranged wife. Frances sent him his monthly cheques from the insurance company, and after depositing them in his account in a Prescott bank, he remitted money to her regularly to cover her rent and other expenses. This exchange of mail allowed them to carry on their conflict at long distance. In one letter Frances told him that Coleman still wanted to marry her; when Bethune did not protest she wrote again, saying that it was clear that he thought she should accept Coleman's proposal. Bethune's response was ambiguous. "I have no desire to force you into marriage with R.E.," he wrote back, and then in his best passive-aggressive style he went on, "Believe me, I will never force you to do anything your heart is opposed to, ever again. I love you and always will, however much you may hurt or wound me – and now all that is left for me to show you I love you is to help you to gain what you want. I can do that best by keeping you supplied with money … But I do think, my dear, the honourable thing is that if you are not going to marry

R.E. is to tell me so." He told her that he would not obtain a divorce, but at the end of the letter he reversed himself, saying, "I can go direct to Reno in December if you wish to marry R.E. but I must know at once."[8]

Although he tried to appear indifferent to his wife's affair with Coleman, his pride had clearly been wounded. In some of their earlier quarrels he had punished her by refusing to grant a divorce when she demanded one, but when she complained about Coleman he would reverse his tactics and urge her to marry him. In his heart of hearts he knew that he and Frances were incompatible and could not live together, yet he remained obsessed with her and on some deep level could not let her go.

Then, suddenly, everything changed. While his wife pondered his latest letter, he plunged into a new romance. In early December he went to Phoenix to give a paper at a convention of the Medical and Surgical Association of the Southwest.[9] There he met Dr J. Mott Rawlings, the son of a prominent physician from El Paso, Texas. Taking a liking to Bethune, Rawlings invited him to visit his father's clinic. Bethune accepted and after returning to Prescott to wind up his affairs at Pamsetgaaf, he went to El Paso. He spent several days there and met Rawlings's young wife, Laura. Bethune's charm had its usual effect, and he and Laura Rawlings were instantly attracted to each other. She invited him to spend Christmas with them after he returned from a visit he had planned in Louisville, Kentucky.

The purpose of the Louisville trip was to see Dr Lincoln Fisher, one of Bethune's former cottage-mates at Trudeau. Fisher had become a surgeon on the staff of the Waverly Hills Sanatorium and an instructor in the University of Louisville Medical School. When he learned of Bethune's plans to visit Arizona sanatoriums, he had urged him to come to Louisville at the end of his tour. Bethune arrived at the Fishers' home toting a heavy suitcase, which turned out to be full of bottles of Habanero rum. Because Prohibition was still in force, he had paid to have the rum smuggled across the border into El Paso from Juarez, Mexico. To make room for it in his suitcase, he claimed, he had given his dress suit, robe, and pyjamas to a hotel bellboy. Despite much rum drinking over the next four days, he assisted Fisher in several operations at the University Hospital and showed off some of his surgical instruments to Fisher and his colleagues.[10]

During one of Bethune's evenings with the Fishers, he began to discuss the use of the pneumothorax procedure to collapse or compress the infected portion of the lung of a patient afflicted with pulmonary tuberculosis. Since experiencing the dramatic improvement in his own health during his final month at Trudeau, this had become his pet subject, and he believed that through collapse therapy thousands of tubercular patients could be given, as he had, a new lease on life. Yet the technique was seldom used, because the medical community was committed to rest as the only therapy for tuberculars. Never one to pass by a windmill he could tilt at, Bethune had embarked on a campaign to spread the gospel of compression therapy wherever he went.

He told the Fishers that he had been thinking about writing a credo that would summarize his belief in collapse therapy. When Inez Fisher asked for details, Bethune picked up a pen and began to write. Fuelled by many sips of rum, he dashed off a draft.[11] Later, when he reached Ann Arbor, he would read what he had written to John Barnwell, who happened to be living in an Episcopal Church rectory he had rented. Sitting at the rector's desk, the Episcopal Prayer Book open on his lap at the Apostle's Creed, Bethune made final revisions. Then, using a pen and brushes, he copied the credo onto a sheepskin, framed it and presented it to Barnwell. Entitled "The Compressionist's Creed," it praised the leading scientists in the search for a cure for tuberculosis, including those who had developed collapse therapy. The following is a version he used to illustrate a Christmas card he sent out in 1935.[12]

I believe in Trudeau, the mighty father of the American Sanatorium, maker of a heaven on earth for the tuberculous; and in Artificial Pneumothorax; which was conceived by Carson; born of the labors of Forlanini: suffered under Pompous Pride and Prejudice; was criticized by the Cranks whose patients are dead and buried; thousands now well, even in the third stage, rose again from their bed; ascending into the Heaven of Medicine's Immortals, they sit on the right hand of Hippocrates our Father; from thence they do judge those pthisiotherapists quick to collapse cavities or dead on their job.

I believe in Bodington, Brehmer, Koch and Brauer, in Murphy, Friedrich, Wilms, Sauerbruch, Stuertz and Jacobeus, in the unforgiveness of the sins of omission in Collapse Therapy, in the resurrection of a healthy body from a diseased one and long life for the tuberculous with care everlasting.

Amen.

From Louisville Bethune went back to El Paso where he spent several days over Christmas with the Rawlings.[13] His stay, though brief, proved eventful because on New Year's Eve he wrote the following letter to Frances from Mobile, Alabama:

Frances dear –

… If you remember, you begged me not to force you to marry R.E. and my reply that I would do nothing to put you in such a position against your own desires. I also wrote you that since you apparently did not at this time want to marry R.E. and since I had no inclination to marry again myself, that I would not divorce you, but we would be separated only. Well, my dear, the unexpected has happened as usual. I have fallen in love and want to marry this girl that I feel sure I can be happy with. It was love at first sight with both of us. She is a most charming American, 26, the granddaughter of a famous Alabama physician who Osler has written about in his 'Alabama Student'. Her name was Zarna Bassett Boynton and she is now married to a Dr Mott Rawlings of El Paso, Texas. We have told her husband we love each other and she is going to divorce him. I will go ahead with our divorce as soon as I can raise the money necessary.

Darling, let us give up trying to reconcile our irreconcilable natures. As you have said so often "Breakfast, dinner and bed are not for us two." Our only kinship is a "spiritual affinity" and this, alas, is not enough at our time of life and age. We have never been at ease with each other such as you and R.E. feel in each other's company and such as Bassett and I feel together. Instead of torturing ourselves with mutual recriminations let us quietly acknowledge the fact and live apart as friends – true friends. We can and will. The affection I feel for you and have felt for you in the past is unique – I can never feel it again for any one – I am not sure I want to.

You will love Bassett. You are both much the same – the same qualities in you attracted her to me in the first place – her lovely spirit and mind with the soul of a poet.

Will you write her?

Mrs. J. Mott Rawlings

714 Baltimore St., El Paso.

Texas

… Since I love and am loved I have lost all the bitterness I felt towards you, darling, and my heart is filled with the warmest affection and regard.

Your friend,

Beth[14]

That same evening he caught a flight to Detroit and from there went by train to Ann Arbor to visit John Barnwell again. He also wished to consult Dr John Alexander, head of the Department of Surgery at the University of Michigan medical school, about his own health. Tired of having to take small pneumothorax refills, which he had been doing for four years, he wanted to know if Dr Alexander would recommend a phrenicectomy, which could allow him to stop taking the refill treatments. After examining Bethune, Alexander agreed to operate. However, during the procedure Alexander was unable to find the accessory fibres around the nerve and had to pull the nerve out in order to excise the necessary portion. Bethune suffered excruciating pain; he himself had always pulled out the nerve while performing phrenicectomies but vowed never to do so again. He remained as a patient for a few days at the University Hospital, teasing the nurses and wowing them with his purple silk pyjamas.[15]

The other reason for Bethune's trip to Michigan was to learn specialized aspects of tubercular treatment. Dr Archibald had arranged this with various Michigan colleagues, including Dr Alexander. After recovering from the phrenicectomy, Bethune stayed in Ann Arbor for a time, observing Alexander perform various forms of surgery. From there he went to Grace Hospital in Detroit to study bronchoscopy and esophagoscopy, two types of internal examinations conducted at that time by passing a lighted hollow metal tube through the patient's mouth. He studied these techniques under the direction of Dr William A. Hudson, chief of Thoracic Surgery.[16] During his stay in Michigan, Bethune was also planning an article that he intended to write about his pet subject of collapse therapy.

Meanwhile, he was preoccupied with his new love. In order to marry Laura Rawlings, he first had to divorce his wife but he lacked the money to do so. From Detroit, eager and amorous, he wrote to John Barnwell in Ann Arbor pleading for help: "Write, telephone, telegraph. Immediately set all underground forces to work. I simply must make more money. Love to all, Beth."[17] He also asked Frances for a loan to allow him to go to Reno to arrange a divorce. She agreed but not long after receiving the money from her Bethune discovered in early February that Laura Rawlings was having second thoughts and had decided to postpone their impulsive marriage plans. As his training session with Dr Hudson had now run its course, Bethune decided to return to Montreal. John Barnwell offered to drive him back, suggesting that on the way they could attend a medical meeting in Syracuse and then go to Saranac Lake for a nostalgic visit before heading north to Canada.

Just before they left, Bethune received his monthly insurance cheque from Frances; enclosed was a letter in which she told him that she was pregnant by Coleman. Bethune told Barnwell nothing about this, but his friend noticed that something was wrong, for Bethune brooded all the way to Saranac Lake. On their way out of town he asked if he could drive and once behind the wheel he put his foot to the floor. What followed was a hair-raising two-hour race along the narrow winding road through the Adirondack Mountains, with Bethune maintaining a grim silence all the way. Screeching to a halt in front of the apartment building in Montreal, he jumped out of the car and bounded up the stairs to the top floor. He banged on the door and his wife opened it – and screamed. She had thought that he was in Nevada getting a divorce.

Frances explained that she had at first been happy when she learned of her pregnancy, but then discovered that although Coleman said he loved her he did not want to become a father. She had come to believe that rushing into marriage with him would lead to disaster and had decided not to bear the child. Now that Bethune was there, she begged him to perform an abortion. Bethune protested but finally agreed. Even with Barnwell's help there were problems, and Frances had a difficult time, but the operation was successful.[18]

His protective instincts aroused, Bethune decided that Frances should not be left on her own, so he decided to move in with her for a time. As usual they began to quarrel; this time the conflict was not about Bethune's behaviour but about Coleman's. Bethune had told himself that his wife had taken up with R.E. only to spite him, but now he came to believe that she truly loved Coleman after all, though R.E.'s reluctance to become a father had hurt her. So he began to put pressure on her to get a divorce and marry Coleman. No doubt he was also thinking about Laura Rawlings, who he hoped would still decide to come to him in the end. But Frances, torn between the unpredictable Bethune whom she loved but could not live with and the more conventional Coleman, simply could not make up her mind what to do. The three were trapped in an impasse from which there seemed no way out.

No doubt to Bethune's relief, a temporary escape for him turned up. In mid-April, 1932, he received a telephone call from Dr Edward J. (Pat) O'Brien, chief of Thoracic Surgery at Herman Kiefer Hospital in Detroit. O'Brien had broken his back in an automobile accident and would be laid up for months. Having known Bethune since his arrival in Detroit in the mid-twenties and liking the quality of his work, O'Brien asked if he would take over his duties during his convalescence. In addition to his position in the large Detroit hospital, O'Brien was chief of Surgery at three other hospitals outside Detroit: the Saginaw County Tuberculosis Hospital, the American Legion Hospital in Battle Creek, and the William. H. Maybury Sanatorium in Northville.[19] Bethune knew a splendid opportunity when he saw one, for however brief the appointment might be, it meant recognition of his professional achievements and might possibly lead to another position. It was also a chance to escape from the thorny situation with Frances. He accepted immediately and agreed to arrive on 29 April to perform the operations scheduled on that day for Dr O'Brien.

However, as he was about to leave, Bethune received a letter from Laura Rawlings, who was on a trip north to visit relatives. She had arranged to come to Montreal – on the very day that Bethune had planned to leave for Detroit. Unable to contact her to put off her arrival, Bethune telegraphed O'Brien to say that he would be unable to come to Detroit until the following week.[20] Laura Rawlings's ostensible reason for visiting Montreal was to visit the Osler Library of the History of Medicine at McGill, because Dr William Osler had once written an article in praise of her grandfather. But the real reason for her trip was to tell Bethune that she had finally decided not to break up her marriage for him. Bethune later explained that they had decided that the hurt that they would inflict on Rawlings's husband was too high a price to pay for their happiness; however, this lofty scruple had apparently not bothered the two of them in the first place. The more likely explanation is that Laura Rawlings, having thought things over, had simply got cold feet.[21]

Hastily packing his belongings, Bethune now left for Detroit. He faced a demanding assignment, for O'Brien had many different duties in the four institutions where he was employed. In each of them Bethune had to work with a different operating team and use facilities that varied in quality. But he measured up to the challenge. He was acquainted with some of the doctors from his former years in Detroit, and relied on his charm to establish good relations with the staff of each hospital. The job suited his love of action for he was often on the move, dashing out of Kiefer Hospital in downtown Detroit to drive 130 kilometres northwest to the County Tuberculosis Hospital in Saginaw City, or 200 kilometres west to the American Legion Hospital in Battle Creek. He found it exhilarating.

His new colleagues quickly noted Bethune's unusual character, more flamboyant even than that of their chief, the colourful Pat O'Brien. Bethune made it clear from the beginning that though wholly committed to performing well in the operating theatre he was no less intent on enjoying himself outside it. O'Brien had arranged for him to stay at the Maybury Sanatorium in Northville, fifty kilometres west of downtown Detroit, where he had a room in the staff quarters and could take his meals. After Bethune had been there for some time, the other doctors would amuse themselves at breakfast by trying to guess how heavily he had been drinking the night before. A glance out the window at the parking lot told the tale. If Bethune's car was in one of the designated spots, they knew he had drunk relatively little, but when it was straddling the sidewalk in front of the building, they knew that he had partied late.[22] As usual, Bethune made a splash at social gatherings, showing off his knowledge of many subjects beyond the narrow limits of medicine. He also won the attention of some of the doctors' wives, which did not endear him to their husbands. According to one, "he made lewd suggestions to the faculty wives whilst dancing with them at the various faculty parties."[23]

Opinions of his professional performance varied. Dr Bruce Douglas, medical director of Herman Kiefer Hospital, summed up what many thought, saying, "He was erratic as a surgeon, he was erratic in judgment."[24] However, his colleagues recognized his ability. His dexterity with instruments was impressive, and he flew through thoracoplasties or phrenicetomies faster even than Dr O'Brien, who was widely noted for his speed. But some felt that Bethune took chances too often, with a resulting loss of life, and though he always showed regret when a patient died, he did not seem to care what others thought of his mortality rate. However, his critics did admit that in many cases he took on, the disease was so far advanced that surgery offered the only hope. There were many such cases at the time in Kiefer and its sister institution, Maybury. Many of the patients in both hospitals were charity cases who, because they were poor, had often sought medical help only when it was too late.[25]

However as the weeks passed, the mortality rate of Bethune's patients began to worry his colleagues. O'Brien had enjoyed an extremely low mortality rate in the several months before his accident, and this magnified the contrast between the two surgeons. Dr Douglas said it was partly "the luck of the draw" but that "things went sour" after Bethune took over for O'Brien.[26] The climax came when Bethune lost a patient during a phrenicectomy. He cut into an artery and blood began to gush out. Instead of packing the wound, he attempted to clamp off the severed blood vessel, but this only increased the size of the tear, and the blood kept flowing. Realizing his error, he tried to pack the wound, but the patient died. Without a word to his assistant, Bethune walked out of the operating theatre, and the following day a colleague happened upon him dead drunk in the street.[27] Shortly after that incident O'Brien returned prematurely from his convalescence, and in early August 1932 Bethune went back to Montreal.

Busy though he had been in Michigan, the matter of his wife and Coleman had never been far from his mind. No sooner had he settled in Detroit than he wrote to Coleman asking to discuss the situation. Receiving no answer, Bethune wrote again in a more aggressive tone. He charged Coleman with having taken advantage of Frances and demanded that he come to Detroit to discuss how to put things right. When this second letter was ignored too,

Bethune lost his temper. He contacted his wife and told her to tell Coleman that he would murder him if he did not respond. This threat fetched Coleman, who soon showed up in Detroit. Bethune told him that his moral obligation as a gentleman was to marry Frances. Coleman insisted he was in love with her and would be happy to marry her if she would have him.[28]

Bethune then put pressure on Frances to marry Coleman. But first she had to obtain a divorce, which was extremely difficult to do in Quebec at the time. Under Quebec law, adultery was the only acceptable grounds, and to win the case the appellant had to present clear evidence of the infidelity of the guilty spouse to a committee of the Canadian Senate. Coleman persuaded Bethune and Frances that she should sue for divorce, and Bethune agreed to provide the evidence. A private detective was hired to follow him, with comic-opera results. Bethune had agreed to be "caught" in a compromising situation with a companion in a Toronto hotel room, but the set-up fell through. In an angry outburst in a letter to Frances from Detroit on 10 July, he summarized the folly of the proceedings so far and threatened to get a Mexican divorce on his own, which presumably would have been valid for him in Michigan but not for her in Montreal. Even though he had been the one who had been pressuring her to marry Coleman, he added, with what to her must have seemed a maddening lack of consistency, "I can see now that your mind is made up. Well, so be it. Beth."[29] A few weeks later, back in Montreal, he wrote to John Barnwell in Ann Arbor, "I am sorry I came back and disturbed Frances' peace of mind, however … I can see no other way out except to go through with it. I feel that I will destroy not only myself but any one intimately connected with me."[30]

Bethune described the Toronto fiasco to Harold Beament, an artist friend. Beament had contacts in the legal community and persuaded Bethune to use the services of an Ottawa legal firm with experience in arranging divorces. The lawyers told Bethune that he should be the one to sue. With the agreement of Frances and Coleman, another comic-opera performance was staged after Bethune's return from Detroit, this time in a Montreal hotel room. At an agreed time, accompanied by his friend Louis Huot and a photographer, Bethune knocked on the hotel room door, then burst in. Frances and Coleman were in bed, affecting looks of shock as the photographer went to work. Then Bethune opened a bottle of champagne, and they all gaily toasted the hoped-for success of their efforts.

Yet despite such camaraderie, Bethune remained deeply conflicted about the dissolution of his marriage, perhaps the more so because his own amour with Laura Rawlings had fallen through. He had asked Huot to act as a witness, but instead of thanking him afterwards, he reproached him, saying,

"You are coming between me and the woman I really love in a positive and definitive way."[31] His next move was to suggest a ménage à trois, inviting Coleman to come and live with him and Frances in their apartment. It was only a matter of months before the divorce would be granted, he argued, so why should the two of them wait for a legal document to allow them to live together? He would sleep in the second bedroom until he could move to his own apartment. Of course this gambit, seemingly offered in a spirit of friendly collusion, put him in a position to supervise what Coleman and Frances were doing. With good reason she disliked the idea but at last gave in to Bethune's urging.[32]

Meanwhile, Bethune had returned to the Royal Victoria and as usual was fretting about money. He had not received funds from the Cowans scholarship fund for more than a year.[33] His only current sources of income were his monthly disability insurance cheque and the consulting fee he would receive when he resumed his weekly visit to the Ste Anne de Bellevue Hospital.[34] His need to leave the Royal Victoria and find a salaried hospital position was more urgent than ever, because his relationship with Archibald was increasingly strained. The staid, cautious Archibald and the fiery Bethune had never seen eye to eye on medical matters; Bethune had once startled his chief at a social event by saying, "Oh, what's the use? I will never manage to explain anything to you. The trouble is that, by nature, you shoot butterflies with a shotgun and I like to hunt elephants with a bow and arrow!"[35] Small wonder that Archibald referred to his volatile assistant as "a stormy petrel."[36] However, despite their professional disagreements and Bethune's eccentricities, Archibald had tolerated him much longer than many chiefs of surgery would have done because he recognized his abilities. He had invited Bethune to his home on several occasions, ignoring his off-colour language and bad manners even though these so offended Archibald's wife that she begged her husband never to invite Bethune again.[37] In 1931 Archibald had granted Bethune the leave he wanted and arranged for him to receive supplemental training in Michigan. And as late as April 1932 he paid tribute to Bethune's contributions to the field of tubercular research and surgery by recommending he be made a member of the American Association for Thoracic Surgery, the foremost professional organization of chest surgeons in North America.[38]

But not long after Bethune's return from Detroit, Archibald's patience ran out. It happened after two operations performed before a visiting group of surgeons in the main operating theatre in the Royal Victoria. Archibald performed the first operation, taking more than the usual time required. Then it was Bethune's turn; he was to operate with Dr Arthur Vineberg, another protégé of Archibald, as his assistant. Vineberg recalled that Bethune, impatient with Archibald's slowness and keen to display his own skill, said, "'Come on, Arthur, we will show them how good we are' ... and out came three ribs." But several minutes after the opening incision, Vineberg began to worry about the speed with which Bethune was working and said anxiously, "Norman, this guy is going to bleed to death." "No," Bethune replied, "sixteen minutes from skin to skin." He completed the operation in a very short time, but complications and bleeding followed, and the patient died.[39]

This time Bethune had gone too far, and Archibald decided that he had to get rid of him. Although the evidence is unclear, doctors at the Royal Victoria believed that Bethune was asked to resign.[40] Years later, after Bethune's death, Archibald summed up his feelings: "I never really liked him; our outlook on life was too dissimilar ... He was definitely abnormal but not 'mental' ... He was an egocentric. His vision was keen but narrow. He wore blinkers. He trod on many toes, quite often without knowing it or without caring if he did know it. He had a superiority complex and he was entirely amoral."[41] Another colleague at the Royal Victoria, C.A. McIntosh, put it more succinctly, saying simply. "He didn't fit in here."[42]

But Bethune's luck held, and at the critical moment another appointment turned up. Back in February 1932, Archibald had been contacted by Dr G.E. Migneault, surgeon-in-chief of the Hôpital du Sacré Coeur in the village of Cartierville, just north of Montreal. Sacré Coeur was an 850-bed Roman Catholic hospital for the chronically ill and incurables, and Dr Migneault wished to establish a chest clinic there. He asked Archibald if he would be willing to perform a limited number of thoracic operations at Sacré Coeur. Archibald had replied that he was too busy at the Royal Victoria and too old to take on an added responsibility; perhaps seeing a way to get rid of his prickly assistant, however, he suggested that Migneault consider inviting Bethune to take the position.

Migneault had reported the idea to the religious administration of the hospital, but Archbishop Villeneuve warned the mother superior of Sacré Coeur, Sister Fabiola, that Bethune was not a suitable candidate as he had learned that he led "*une vie de bohème*."[43] No one else qualified was found, and several months later, Dr Migneault again proposed Bethune for the job. In late November, Sister Fabiola finally decided to accept him on the condition that he agree to train an assistant. Negotiations dragged on, but on 29 January 1933 Bethune was appointed head of Pulmonary Surgery and Bronchoscopy at Sacré Coeur.[44]

The following day he performed his first operation there. He wrote to John Barnwell on the last day of the month, "Ten miles from Montreal – French Canadian and Catholic. Twelve hundred dollars a year, one day a

week, so the strain is less strained. I cauterized some adhesions there yesterday and the chorus of oh's and ah's from the nuns rose like a chant at the high
altar. My title is 'Chef dans le Service de Chirugie Pulmonaire et de Bron-
choscopie.' I'm going to have a nice big white cap made with 'Chef' marked
in front. Really, I'm delighted."[45] He had good reason to be pleased, for the
position meant a substantial increase in his income, and although Sacré
Coeur was not as prestigious a hospital as the Royal Victoria, the appointment represented recognition of his professional worth. His responsibilities
would increase with time, and he would come to see Sacré Coeur as the beginning of a new phase of his professional achievement.

Meanwhile, the drama of the destruction of his marriage was still playing
out. Leaving his apartment to Frances and Coleman, he had taken a rented
room. From there he wrote a brief note to his now ex-wife: "Frances darling
– I enclose a letter of Millar, Horne & Hanna, the official hangman [sic].
Well, they may think they have done the job but how surprised the Senator
& Horne would be to know that all their mumblings and posturings have left
the 2 principals – like 2 naughty, reprimanded boys – sniggling [sic] behind
their backs. God bless you. I love you. Beth"[46] His declaration of love was
calculated, for he had not been joking when he had once told Coleman, "I
do not give away my wife. I only lend her." Although Bethune had had to
accept that he and Frances could not live happily together, he was still unwilling to let her go.

His letter, with its loving salutation and closing, revived all her doubts
and fears. She had sought a divorce at Bethune's urging, yet now he was
declaring that he continued to love her. She became distraught, and to make
matters worse, Coleman's superior at the Bell Telephone Company learned
from office gossip that he was living with a woman to whom he was not
married and told Coleman he was extremely displeased.[47] Fearful of losing his job, Coleman said that he and Frances had only been awaiting the
divorce and were about to wed. He put pressure on her to go through with
the marriage, which took place in a simple ceremony on 11 May 1933 at
Erskine Presbyterian Church in Westmount.[48]

Frances regretted the marriage almost at once. Still in love with Bethune,
she told her new husband that by remaining with him she was living in sin.
Worn out by the stress of the past year, she spiralled into an emotional breakdown, and only after a stay in a Montreal hospital did she begin to recover.[49]
Learning of her illness, Bethune too plunged into depression. Needing to lash
out at something, he chose the doll-child Alice, the symbol of his failed, child-
less marriage. He had taken Alice with him when he left Frances; as a "child"
of divorce, she was to spend six months a year with each of them. He had

written letters to Frances on the doll's behalf and even had Alice's portrait painted by the artist Jori Smith. Now he set Alice on fire in his rented room and somehow allowed the flames to spread; by the time he managed to extinguish the blaze, it had destroyed most of his books and his clothing.[50] He showed up the following day at Sacré Coeur wearing a shabby suit and a pair of old shoes, one with a sole flapping loose. After explaining what had happened to Dr Georges Cousineau, his anaesthetist, he complained that he had absolutely no money to buy new clothes. Cousineau immediately set out to collect fees owed to Bethune by a few private patients and managed to raise three hundred dollars. But the day after Cousineau gave it to him, Bethune showed up at the hospital broke again and asked to borrow five dollars. He had bought some clothes with the money raised and spent the rest.[51]

His misery over the loss of Frances seemed to have driven Bethune to the brink of a breakdown. Friends now noted that his social behaviour was becoming ever more abrasive, to the point of aggressive rudeness. His former student and friend Dr Wendell MacLeod ruefully acknowledged, "He did some atrocious things, no question." It was alleged that he bedded other men's wives, drank to excess, and made crude remarks to patients and colleagues.[52] His compulsive need for attention drove him to extremes. Entering a party at a private residence where his host was entertaining the other guests with a story, he broke in, shouting, "Hey fellow! This is Beth – I am here!" When the group continued to ignore him, he took a poinsettia plant from the windowsill, set it on the floor, and urinated in it.[53] On another occasion he and Dr Ronald Christie were invited to a musical evening at the home of a wealthy Montreal family. When the concert ended, the host came up and asked Bethune whether he had enjoyed the music. "Yes!" he replied. "It reminded me of the back and forth thrust of warm sex." An embarrassed Christie later asked him why on earth he had said such a thing. Bethune replied, "They had it coming to them."[54]

Yet he could be charming. His colleagues noted his mood swings, as did others who knew him well. His ex-wife, who knew him best, described him as a delayed adolescent, and one political contact commented that his character was not integrated, that he was "a man of extremes."[55] Another political colleague made the same point: "As I got to know him it seemed there were two sides to his make-up – a gentleness, a warm, patient concern – and sometimes an impatience that could turn quickly to terrible anger."[56] Given Bethune's self-focus, his compulsion to act out, his mood swings, his chronic irritability and erratic behaviour, it is impossible not to wonder whether he suffered from what today would be called a borderline mood or personality disorder. One possibility is cyclothymia, a mild form of bipolar disorder.

Throughout the course of his life he certainly exhibited some though not all of its paradigm of symptoms, including irritable outbursts, elated and depressive moods, repeated conjugal or romantic failures, shifts in interests or future plans, alcohol abuse, and financial extravagance.[57] Such speculation offers only one possible angle of insight into his dynamic but irascible personality, to which many people were attracted throughout his life but which even more disliked.

For months after the fire that ruined his room, Bethune regressed to living almost from hand to mouth, depending on the hospitality of friends and acquaintances. He stayed for a few weeks at Cousineau's home in Cartierville and, without asking permission, set about painting a mural on the walls of one of the rooms. Fortunately, Madame Cousineau, who dabbled in art herself, quite liked the effect.[58] However, Bethune preferred to live in downtown Montreal, so he accepted the offer of a room from Louise Vézina, a nurse at the Royal Victoria. When Bethune explained his circumstances, she assured him that her parents, Mr and Mrs Louis Guadagni, with whom she was living, would welcome him. For the next several months he lived with the Guadagnis while carrying on a torrid affair with their daughter, who was separated from her husband.[59] It was she who decided to end the relationship. This was partly as a result of Bethune taking her to meet his ex-wife: Vézina was the first of several women whom he would parade before Frances over the next three years, ostensibly seeking her friendly approval of his taste but perhaps also demonstrating to her his sexual prowess. Bethune told Vézina that he now felt only platonic friendship for Frances, but she believed he was still deeply attached to his ex-wife and concluded that her own relationship with him was simply sexual. Moreover, she felt Bethune lacked skill as a lover and was also "more than a bit of a ham."[60] Meanwhile she had become interested in John Pitt, an acquaintance of Bethune, and decided to go out with him instead. Bethune did not take the news well. He stormed out of the Guadagni residence without even arranging for a place to stay.[61]

With nowhere to go, he decided to set up a tent in a corner of the grounds of Sacré Coeur. He attended the hospital most mornings and would walk through the woods and turn up at the nursing station of Sister Joseph Leon, his main nursing assistant and the only anglophone on the operating staff. She would bring him breakfast from the kitchen – an egg, toast, and orange juice.[62] He lived this way for part of the summer of 1933, until the hospital administration discovered he was entertaining women in the tent and insisted he find accommodation elsewhere. For the next several months he rented an inexpensive cottage on the bank of the Rivière des Prairies not far from the hospital. There he received visitors, sometimes in the nude, and drank and partied.[63] He likely enjoyed the contrast between his *vie de bohème* and the prim surroundings of the hospital: at the age of forty-three he was living the life of an undergraduate. But his appointment at Sacré Coeur was literally all he had left – his personal life had gone up in flames and he had been thoroughly singed.

✣ 7 ✣

Awakenings

Montreal, Autumn 1933–November 1935

At the Hôpital du Sacré Coeur, Bethune held a position of full authority for the first time, and he revelled in it. He would remain there for nearly four years, and during this time he would do much for the hospital. He performed the first person-to-person blood transfusion done at Sacré Coeur and continued to perform transfusions throughout his time there.[1] As part of his agreement with Sister Fabiola, the mother superior, he trained not only Georges Deshaies as a thoracic surgeon but also a second doctor, Gerard Rolland. Until his departure in 1936, he and his two assistants maintained a rigorous weekly operating schedule.[2]

The medical staff at Sacré Coeur soon realized that their new chief of thoracic surgery was unlike any other doctor they had met. His impact on the monastic order and quiet of the hospital was like that of a hurricane. Except for scheduled operations, he often appeared without notice. Preoccupied, always in a hurry, he would summon Sister Joseph to interpret for him and then sweep off to carry out some task. His rapid movements and unpredictable temper kept his operating-room staff on their toes. If an instrument did not perform as expected, he would curse and hurl it across the room; if a nurse was a second slow in placing an instrument in his hand, he would bark at her. Pushing himself to ever greater speed during a thoracoplasty, he would sometimes toss the patient's excised ribs over his shoulder.[3]

His assistants breathed sighs of relief when he left at the end of an operation, but they were in awe of his surgical skills, and he must have found this deeply gratifying.[4] Their only criticism was that he did not maintain a proper standard of asepsis. While operating he sometimes did not wear gloves, insisting that they reduced his digital sensitivity, and in his haste he often refused to wait for clean instruments. On ward rounds he frequently neglected to wash his hands as he went from patient to patient.[5] And as always, the mortality rate among his patients was very high. Perhaps in recognition of this, he arranged to visit abattoirs in east-end Montreal where he and Deshaies honed their operating techniques and tried out innovative surgical procedures on the carcasses of pigs and calves.[6]

In contrast to his tenseness during operations, Bethune had a relaxed bedside manner. Perched on the edge of a patient's bed, he would outline the steps he would follow during an operation, building up the patient's confidence, and he was prepared to go to considerable lengths to calm those who were upset. One agitated man complained of stomach pains, insisting they were caused by a frog he had swallowed. The next day Bethune arrived at his bedside with a frog in his pocket. He ordered that the patient be given an enema, then slipped the frog into the pan. He showed it to the patient, whose pains then vanished. Bethune speculated that the patient would probably come up with yet more *outré* symptoms but had been given at least some temporary relief.[7]

Bethune often appeared on the thoracic ward late in the evening to examine patients he had visited earlier. Whenever he lost a patient, particularly a child, he remained disconsolate for days.[8] A friend later speculated that this tender commitment to his young patients may have been an effect of his frustrated desire for children of his own.[9] It also reflected his profound commitment to saving lives, every bit as intense as his parents' crusade to save souls.

Although nominally a Protestant and unable to speak more than a few words of French – he told his friend George Holt that he refused to learn the language – Bethune was accepted without question by the Catholic sisters of the hospital. Nearly fifty years after his death, Sister Joseph Leon remembered very well his temper, his carelessness about asepsis, his impatience and unpredictability, yet admitted that if he had asked her, she would have followed him to the end, even to China. She said that, unlike any other doctor she had ever known, he had showed an almost obsessive concern for his patients.[10]

During these same years Bethune became better known in international medical circles through the articles he published in medical journals and also through the increasing use by North American surgeons of the "Bethune" instruments manufactured by the George Pilling Company. In Boston in June 1934 he was elected to the five-man executive council of the American Association for Thoracic Surgery (AATS). To be chosen for this position after only two years as a member of the organization was impressive, and by association the status of Hôpital du Sacré Coeur was enhanced. However, his professional achievements were to some extent overshadowed by his eccentric behaviour at professional gatherings, where his unconventional dress and deliberate attempts to provoke the medical establishment created as much discussion as the papers he gave.[11]

But Bethune had more on his mind than his duties at Sacré Coeur and professional advancement. Having come to believe that surgical excellence was not enough in itself to combat tuberculosis, he was thinking seriously about the social origins of the disease, a concept that had first crossed his mind at the Trudeau Sanatorium. In a medical paper he wrote in 1932, he quoted a remark by Dr Trudeau, the sanatorium's founder: "There is a rich man's tuberculosis and a poor man's tuberculosis ... The rich man recovers and the poor man dies." And Bethune had added, "We, as a people can get rid of tuberculosis, when once we make up our minds it is worth while to spend enough money to do so."[12] By looking beyond the narrow bounds of surgery, he hoped to find a way to attack the root causes of the "white plague." So in the late autumn of 1933 he began a campaign to increase public knowledge of the symptoms of tuberculosis and the existing methods of treatment. Quick to understand the reach of radio as a mass medium, he wrote a fifteen-minute radio play, *The Patient's Dilemma*, which he submitted to the Canadian Tuberculosis Association in December 1933.[13] He also began to search for opportunities to speak publicly about his belief that, among the leading causes of death in Canada, tuberculosis was the easiest to eradicate. In April 1934 he accepted an invitation from the Canadian Progress Club of Montreal to appear as guest speaker, casting his speech in the form of an investigation into the death of John Bunyan, an imaginary victim of tuberculosis. Examined by a doctor who used only a stethoscope, the patient was misdiagnosed and became progressively more ill. A second doctor, using an x-ray machine, discovered that Bunyan had pulmonary tuberculosis and sent him to a sanatorium. However, in an advanced stage of the disease, Bunyan was released too soon from the crowded institution and returned home, where he infected his wife and child before dying.

The root cause of Bunyan's tuberculosis, Bethune said, was the fact that he and his family – including his grandmother, an active carrier of tuberculosis germs – had been living for twenty years in a dirty, congested tenement house. Bethune summed up his case, laying the blame for Bunyan's death on the landlord who permitted such terrible living conditions to exist, then on Bunyan himself for not having sought treatment sooner. He also condemned the first doctor who relied on the stethoscope, the second doctor who, though he diagnosed the disease using x-ray, had failed to examine the other members of Bunyan's family, the sanatorium officials for having released the patient prematurely, and the government for having allowed a man who was

50 per cent handicapped and a danger to both his family and society to return to his home and his work.

He then listed suggestions on how to prevent such deaths. The first step, he said, was to mount an extensive publicity campaign to inform the public of the menace of tuberculosis in Montreal and the Province of Quebec, where the disease took twice as many lives as elsewhere in Canada.[14] Medical students should also receive more information concerning the disease. To ensure early detection, all schoolchildren should receive regular chest x-rays, and all nurses, nursemaids, and food handlers in Montreal should receive thorough physical examinations. All known active tubercular cases should be segregated. Finally, a halfway house between sanatoriums and industry should be established where partly cured tubercular patients could be given light work while they recovered fully.[15]

Bethune's "case study" captured the interest of his audience, who gave him a polite round of applause. But he knew very well that without the active participation of government, the only agency with the capital and the necessary powers to implement his ideas, nothing would be done. And government action was far too radical a policy for the lawyers and businessmen in his audience. What is interesting is that, not long before, Bethune had shared their point of view. Despite his iconoclasm and many anti-establishment views, he had never before been attracted to the political left. To the limited extent that he had any interest in politics, he was conservative and even revealed a certain enthusiasm for the social and organizational aspects of fascism. Probably because of the bitter experience of his generation in the World War, he went so far as to profess admiration for Adolf Hitler. "Someone's got to rule that country [Germany] and keep it under control," he told his friend Arthur Vineberg.[16] Even as late as 1933 he had taken a firm anti-worker stand in an argument with George Holt over a management-labour dispute. Around the same time he had disapproved of a friend's fiancée, saying she was "too socialistic."[17] Despite the crowds of unemployed men drifting along the streets of Montreal, he was slow to recognize the devastating impact on Canadian society of the Great Depression, then in its fifth year.

However, his work at the Hôpital du Sacré Coeur gave Bethune new insight into social conditions. The hospital drew most of its patients from Roman Catholic working-class neighbourhoods, and by 1933 nearly two out of every five heads of household there were out of work and unable to pay for medical treatment.[18] The friends Bethune made in Montreal artistic circles also helped to open his eyes to the widespread poverty in the city and throughout Canada. Many of these friends were left-wing liberals or socialists, and a very few were communists. As he talked with them at various social events, the discussion often turned to the Depression. All condemned the failure of governments at all levels to take some form of action to reduce unemployment and bring relief to the poor.

As Bethune's consciousness of social and economic conditions in Montreal grew, he began to develop an interest in politics. In early 1934 he attended a meeting of the Montreal branch of the League for Social Reconstruction (LSR). Founded in 1931 by a group of left-wing intellectuals highly critical of unregulated capitalism, the LSR advocated a managed economy in which a democratically elected government would play the leading role.[19] Bethune continued to attend LSR meetings, and at one of them he met George Mooney, the director of a branch of the Young Men's Christian Association (YMCA). The two became friends, and Bethune visited Mooney's office in the working-class suburb of Verdun. He listened as Mooney described the misery caused by massive unemployment there. One of the worst effects, Mooney said, was the inability of many of his YMCA members to pay for the medical treatment they needed. As he listed the cases of various people who needed care but could not afford it, Bethune interrupted, offering to set up a free consulting clinic in Mooney's office. He said he could arrive on Saturday at noon and spend an hour examining sick people from the neighbourhood. Mooney readily agreed, and Bethune opened his clinic in the autumn of 1934.

His association with Montreal artists had also reawakened his interest in painting. Despite some brief instruction in art in Detroit, *The T.B.'s Progress* was the only piece of art he had created. In Montreal in early 1931 he had turned up at the studio of Adam Sheriff-Scott, a commercial artist and respected teacher, to inquire about lessons. The studio was not far from the Royal Victoria Hospital, and Bethune began attending one of Sherriff-Scott's small evening classes. He showed up for several months, preferring to work alone and seldom asking for advice; eventually he stopped attending.[20] He was also visiting art galleries as he had done in London a decade earlier and had begun to buy canvases, becoming a familiar figure at exhibitions. Even during the Depression the arts were thriving in Montreal, and Bethune attended many social events where actors and artists mingled with the public.[21]

Inspired by the company he was keeping, he was now painting whenever he could. In a conversation about the upcoming Annual Spring Exhibition of the Art Association of Montreal in 1935, an artist friend sceptically remarked that the works accepted for the show were always those of well-known painters. Bethune immediately contradicted him, saying that *he* could paint a canvas that the judges would approve. His friend scoffed, challenging him to try, and Bethune accepted the dare. In just two afternoons, his preferred time to paint, he produced an oil canvas showing a surgeon and assistants grouped around a patient in an empty amphitheatre. His *Night Emergency* was accepted for the show and was awarded a prize.[22] However, this success did not motivate him to work harder at developing his painting technique. As a friend noted, having proved his point, Bethune turned his mind to other things.[23] Yet his painting, like the poetry and stories he occasionally wrote, was fundamental to his view of himself. He often said he was an artist, and that he felt the same way when he was operating as he did when he was painting.[24]

By this time Bethune had found himself a more conventional place to live. In the late autumn of 1933, cold weather had driven him from his riverside cottage, and he had begun sharing an apartment in downtown Montreal with Dr Aubrey Geddes, a colleague from the Royal Victoria Hospital.[25] Bethune settled in and began adding his own distinctive touches. Some visitors to the apartment were shocked, as he no doubt hoped they would be, by his choice of art. He hung a painting of a beautiful nude over his bed and pictures of fornication and vaginas graced the bathroom walls.[26] His visitors were usually artist and writer friends, many of them women, so Geddes had ample opportunity to observe Bethune's prowess with the opposite sex. "He had an extraordinary attraction to women," Geddes recalled. "They loved to listen to him talk and they liked to follow him around. I don't think I ever knew anyone who attracted women to him more like a magnet than he did. One brilliant woman, I recall, and a very beautiful woman … said, 'I saw him but once and he was the most aggressively male creature I have ever encountered.'"[27] With their guests, Bethune and Geddes spent evenings discussing matters trivial and serious over glasses of beer or port, exchanging witty sallies. One night someone suggested that they ought to keep a record of their *bons mots*, so they began writing them on one wall of the large living room. Before Bethune left in early 1935, the wall was covered.[28]

Meanwhile, despite his professional success and awakening social consciousness, Bethune had still had not recovered from losing his wife. As often as they had squabbled and parted – she would later claim to have left more often than he – one or the other had always returned. He once explained to her what brought him back: "I mean to me, you are steadfastly set, so stable … You are *my rock* … I drift and change and you are always the same mind. So I come back to you for security and peace."[29] Clinging to this security, he had continued to see her now and then after her marriage. Inevitably, her new husband resented this and found a way to get back at the man he saw as his rival. Coleman had learned that Bethune was still receiving his monthly disability payment of $150 because he had persuaded a colleague to send the company an annual report that falsely stated he had still not recovered from his tuberculosis. Coleman decided to notify the company.[30] In January 1934 Bethune received his last monthly cheque, and one month later the company terminated the policy.[31]

Perhaps suspecting Coleman's role in the matter, Bethune wrote to Frances in mid-February 1934 pledging not to see her again and recognizing the folly of his attempts over the years to change her to suit his own idea of what she should be:

Frances – Thank you for your letter. I see your confusion of mind, body and soul and since, within the past 3 months, my ideas have clarified, today I think I may be able to put into words what I believe to be the truth.

Truthfully and sincerely I believe I want nothing more from you. Not I as a man, physically nor as a soul – spiritually. I believe we have had all the profitable commerce between us that is possible, and nothing more is to be gained by prolongation of our relationship. It never at any time completely satisfied either of us – let us make no more attempts. I regret nothing of the past that has happened between us except one thing – my essential masculine stupidity on the non-recognition of reality – and my fumbling attempts to change a fantasy into a fact.

Forgive me, if you can. I am truly sorry for the unhappiness I have caused you. I was like a clumsy and furious gardener, hacking away at a tree, a living tree, in an attempt to make it conform to a preconceived and fantastic design of his own. I tried to bend you, to re-make you, not recognizing you as you are, but only with the sort of genetic, stupid male idea of you as woman. Any woman – and not as *a* woman, a special kind of woman called Frances Campbell Penney. I know now you must be taken only as you are. You are not to be changed. Either a man must take you as you are or he will destroy both you and himself in the attempt to change you. Well, I am not going to do that. Because of my love for you, I am not going to do that. I believe you must be left alone and then you will flower in peace and quiet and give peace and quietness to those about you. But no persuasion, no aggression of others, and on your part, most important, no attempt to change yourself to please another. There would be no need for us to part completely if R.E. would abandon his suspicions – suspicions of both you and I. I am not the cause of the disharmony between you two. I am no rival. He has nothing to fear from me. He has only to fear himself. He said at your marriage he accepted the idea of the spiritual relationship between you and I. He must accept it, or it will destroy him. He must accept what you and I have been to each other in the past. It does him no harm. Only egotism forbids acceptance of this.

And you must spend your life acting in the true, internal, deep compulsion of your own spirit. You must give up trying to conform to another's idea of you. Do as I do – if I can say that – be yourself and *don't try to please people*. For you that only results in self-mutilation. If they do not accept you as you are – remove yourself, let them go – or go yourself. Only live with those who respect the spiritual and physical necessities of your nature. The tragedy of it all is this – that between the two of us – R.E. and myself – two men who protest they love you – we have torn you, violated you and will, if we persist in our present course, distort or destroy one of the sweetest natures that God ever made. Well, I will do my part – I will leave you alone.

I accept gratefully what you once gave me, and now ask you nothing more. That is the only way I can show I love you. I can do nothing for you except leave you alone, entirely. We must die to each other. For peace between you and R.E. you and I must die to each other. Let us remember it only as a dream.

Good-bye, my sweet Frances. I loved you once and to prove it, I will leave you now. Let us part. Good-bye.

Beth

P.S. Show this letter to R.E. I have written it as truthfully and sincerely as I am able. A truthful and sincere soul would accept it as such.[32]

Despite this dramatic declaration, Bethune never quite gave Frances up. Still resentful of Coleman, he wrote again several months later, reproaching the couple for talking about him to others behind his back and claiming that their "chatter" had done him "irreparable harm in Montreal."[33] But despite his testy outburst, he and Frances went on meeting occasionally and exchanging letters. To the end of his time in Montreal he always referred to her as his wife whenever they went somewhere together.[34]

Bethune was now emotionally adrift, although he did not lack female companionship. He had begun an affair with Dr Margaret Cameron, a colleague at the Royal Victoria Hospital.[35] However, this relationship does not seem to have been serious, at least on his part, for just a few weeks after he had vowed to give up seeing Frances, he became involved in a new romance. At a house party in Westmount a friend introduced him to Elizabeth Hurcomb, an attractive woman in her late twenties. Hurcomb was married but separated from her husband. Bethune suggested they leave the party so they could talk, and they drove up Mount Royal to a site overlooking the city. There they talked for several hours, and Hurcomb told him about her struggle to free herself from her unhappy marriage. Bethune listened with an air of deep sympathy and called her the next day. Their relationship soon developed into a love affair, and for the next several weeks they saw each other often. On several occasions Bethune drove her into the country to allow her to spend the weekend with her daughter, who was living with Hurcomb's mother in the Gatineau Hills.

The impulsive Bethune felt he had found another "rock." Soon after their first meeting he told Hurcomb that he had gone out with several women in the year after his divorce, but she was the first that he wanted to marry. He said he was unhappy at Sacré Coeur and wanted to leave Montreal. Would she go with him? She longed to accept his proposal but was worried about her ongoing divorce proceedings. He offered to drive her to Mexico right away to obtain a divorce, saying that once they were married, they could return for her daughter. However, Hurcomb's lawyer warned her that a Mexican divorce would not be recognized in Canada, and her mother refused to look after her daughter if she married Bethune, whom she disliked. Hurcomb told Bethune that they must wait until she could resolve her difficulties, but she sensed an urgency in him, a need for immediate action.[36]

Indeed, Bethune's attention soon turned elsewhere. At the end of May 1934, two months after meeting Hurcomb, he decided to attend the three-day annual convention of the American Association for Thoracic Surgery in Boston. He planned to drive there several days in advance, possibly to visit the clinic of Dr Richard H. Overholt in the hope of finding a new position.[37] He invited Margaret Cameron to come down to join him and arranged for them to share a room in the upscale Statler Hotel, the convention venue.[38] But first he went to stay with his artist friend, George Holt, in Boston. Through Holt and his wife, Bethune was introduced to a young woman named Harriet Hammond. In her mid-twenties, intelligent, and extremely pretty, she appealed instantly to him, and he invited her to meet him for lunch at the Statler. Even though he was expecting Cameron to arrive at the same hotel, he managed to keep his date with Hammond and promised to stay in touch with her.[39] The culmination of his hectic weekend came on Sunday morning when he discovered he had run up a hotel bill of $125 that he could not pay. In desperation he phoned a colleague, Dr Gavin Miller, pleading, "I've spent all Maggie's money and I haven't any of my own left." Although short of cash himself, Miller found the means to bail him out.[40]

Shortly after his return to Montreal, Bethune suffered a partial or complete collapse of his left lung. This was likely the result of a tiny area on the surface of the lung rupturing, causing air to leak out into the space between the lung and the inside chest wall. Such a collapse did not necessarily indicate the presence of active tuberculosis, as Bethune wrote to John Barnwell: "I had a spontaneous traumatic pneumo in my 'bad' side. Entirely OK now, no blowing up of the smouldering embers, no stirring or growls from the tigers, nor rattle from the dead snakes and dragons. I guess they're all dead."[41] "Traumatic" in this case meant it was related to a traumatic event such as a blow to the chest or falling and striking his chest. He recovered quickly but had to remain in bed until the end of June and so was unable to pursue his most recent romance.

In July he accepted a friend's offer of a cottage in Cape Cod, where he stayed until early August. It was conveniently near where Harriet Hammond lived with her parents, and Bethune saw her often; on more than one occasion he was the family's house guest. However, Hammond's parents, like those of most of his other amours, were suspicious of Bethune, perhaps because he was so much older than their daughter, and warned her to be cautious in her relationship with him. He returned to Montreal, and despite her parents' warnings, Hammond visited him there in September en route to the West Coast by train. Bethune showed her around Sacré Coeur, then took her for a picnic in the countryside. Choosing a romantic spot under a shady tree, he spread a blanket for her to sit on and picked her a bouquet of wildflowers, saying that he preferred them to florists' flowers, which he despised as artificial. He had laid on an ample lunch, and after they had eaten and were sipping their wine, he proposed. As with Hurcomb before her, he wanted a quick marriage. But perhaps because of her parents' warnings, Hammond sensed his instability and put him off, saying that she did not yet know him well enough to make a commitment for life. The following day she caught her train for Oregon. Another "rock" had slipped Bethune's attempts to moor his drifting barque.[42]

In January 1935 he quarrelled with Aubrey Geddes, his flat-mate. Geddes, a stickler for honesty, had apparently learned of Bethune's insurance scam, and there also seems to have been a disagreement over a woman. An acquaintance who knew them both said that Geddes threw Bethune bodily out of the apartment, adding that he was "a genius, but a scalawag."[43] Bethune then moved to 3437 Peel Street in Westmount, renting a large bed-sitting room on the second floor of the four-storey building. He took his meals with the other five boarders.[44]

At about the same time, George Mooney invited him to hear Maurice Hindus, an American journalist who had recently returned from the Soviet Union, speak at a Canadian Club luncheon meeting. Like many others on the political left, Mooney was curious about the Soviet communist experiment and eager to hear what Hindus, a widely recognized authority on the USSR, had to say. In his address Hindus claimed that in certain respects Soviet medicine was more advanced than that in North America. At this Bethune became angry: the statements were irresponsible, he muttered to Mooney, who did his best to calm his friend down, fearing he might jump up and challenge the speaker. After the speech Mooney suggested that the only way Bethune could find out whether Hindus was right or wrong was to visit the USSR. Bethune replied that he would go there as soon as he could.[45]

The opportunity arrived shortly. Learning that the Fifteenth International Congress of Physiologists would be held during the second week in August in Leningrad and Moscow, Bethune obtained his passport in May 1935. He intended to see for himself how the Soviet medical system operated, but he also wanted a break from Montreal and so decided to extend his itinerary by three weeks to include visits to England, France, and Germany. His only problem was how to finance the trip, for despite his various sources of income, he was as always short of funds. Everything hung in the balance until the last moment. Days before his planned departure, he managed to raise the money by selling his car.[46]

At the beginning of July he had gone to New York to attend meetings of the five-man executive council of the American Association for Thoracic Surgery to which he had been elected the previous year. Returning to Montreal, he learned about a vacant position for a thoracic surgeon in an important hospital in New York and sent off a letter of application. On the eve of taking the train to Quebec City to board the *Empress of Britain*, he also posted a letter to Dr John Alexander, president of the AATS, informing him of his application for the New York appointment and asking for his support.[47] Once again he was hoping to put Montreal behind him.

What happened over the next few weeks made him change his mind. On board ship he found that Marian Scott (1906–93), a Montreal painter, was a fellow passenger. She was the wife of Frank R. Scott, a professor of law at McGill and a founder of the League for Social Reconstruction and the Cooperative Commonwealth Federation (CCF), a Canadian social democratic political party. Bethune had met Frank Scott at League meetings and had also met Marian several months earlier at a weekly "salon" at the residence of the artist John Lyman. However, Bethune had arrived late and extremely drunk and remembered little of their encounter.[48] Now, at sea emotionally as well as literally, he was immediately drawn to her. Though not conventionally pretty, Marian Scott was small and graceful, with a strongly modelled face and a gentle, well-bred manner. As when he first met Frances Penney, Bethune found the latter quality irresistible. Scott was aware that women were fascinated by him and had heard him called a black sheep in the circles in which she and her husband moved. But she was attracted by his "fine intimidating grin." His exuberance and vitality appealed to her too: "You could feel it even in the way he walked," she recalled years later.[49] They spent many hours in each other's company, strolling the deck and often dining together, along with her six-year-old son, Peter. Bethune read her poetry by William Blake, and they talked about their common interest in art. This led to wide-ranging discussions on many subjects including politics. Scott's concern for the misery caused by the Depression and her knowledge of left-wing ideas impressed Bethune. He recognized that she was far more politically literate than he and was struck by the extent of her reading of Marx, about whom she was more enthusiastic than was her husband.[50]

In time Bethune also learned that there were more than political differences between Frank and Marian Scott. A condition of their marriage in 1928 had been that as creative individuals – Frank Scott was a poet as well as a lawyer, academic, and political activist – they would enjoy freedom in the way they managed their lives, including their choice of friends of the opposite sex.[51] Not long into their marriage Scott realized that her husband, whose political activities kept him out of the house many evenings and also made it necessary for him to travel across the country, had begun to carry on a series of affairs. Trying valiantly to live up to the terms of her marriage, she once said, "Creative minds need a variety of experiences ... especially men," and noted in her diary that "man is both faithful and polygamous." Such rationalizations notwithstanding, her husband's philandering had hurt her deeply.[52]

Bethune sensed her unhappiness: here was another vulnerable soul to save, someone on whom to lavish his latent tenderness. His volatile emotions kindled, he soon told her he loved her. He nicknamed her "Pony," apparently a reference to her graceful gait. Although she did not wish to leave her husband, she saw no harm in a flirtation that must have been balm to her wounded feelings. So she responded to Bethune's advances, but eventually warned him that she was not interested in anything more than a shipboard romance. He flew into a rage, ungallantly telling her that she was the kind of woman he would not take the trouble to cross the street to see.[53]

Yet despite his annoyance at her refusal to plunge into an affair, he pursued her after they arrived in England. Knowing that she was staying with her aunt in Ecclestone Square but not knowing her aunt's surname or the number of the house, he had a handbill printed and posted it in the area. It read: "Lost. In the neighbourhood of Ecclestone Square on July 17th, a Canadian-bred Pony, accompanied by foal. Stands about five and half hands high, white face gentle disposition. Was the companion of a small boy who is inconsolable over his loss. Any information received leading to her recovery will be handsomely rewarded. Address – Beth c/o Canada House."[54]

From London he continued on to France and Germany and then the Soviet Union where he spent the week of 9–16 August at the International Physiological Congress. In fact he almost ignored the congress and spent most of the week visiting hospitals and clinics discussing medical matters with various officials. Determined to make the most of his experience, he spent his time, as he later said, "swimming in the Neva, walking about unhindered in the streets, looking into windows, making the rounds of the picture galleries and markets and shops – a combination of Walter Winchell, Peeping Tom and an Innocent Abroad."[55]

On the return voyage to Canada, Bethune and Marian Scott met again. No doubt to Bethune's annoyance, her husband was travelling back to Canada with her, and this scotched any hope of renewed romance. But despite Frank Scott's presence, Bethune's feelings for Marian Scott deepened on the return journey. He was passionately in love again, though he feared that she would not leave her husband for him. On 31 August, back in Montreal, he wrote her a letter full of longing in which he veered between saying she should reject their love to pleading with her to come to him:

Pony,

It is pleasant to sit and think that you are near me, close beside me, only a few streets away. I am very conscious of your presence and happy because of it – yet sad too, darling, because of the knowledge that you and I are bound together, to work out some part of our lives together – for good or for evil – we seem to be bound.

Perhaps this is a presumption of my part – but I think not. And if your glance, your touch, your hands & lips are not mistaken, unreal or misread – you feel it too.

Do you remember the girl in *Farewell to Arms* saying with that mysterious foresight of love 'Let us be good to each other. We are to have such a strange life together.' And her lover comforts her sad heart as best he may, not knowing or understanding. But she knew the dark paths ahead.

Well, my sweet, I know it too.

Let me persuade you to stop now.

Go back. Put away this small child of our love you are holding so quietly and tenderly in your cupped hands – now, when it can be put away without agony & tears – before it has grown in stature & strength & threatens to destroy all you hold precious in life – your home, your husband, your child. And I say this because I am persuaded there is something fatal and doomed and pre-destined about myself. (& I know it.)

But again I think – no. Let us go on into the future together – heads up & with a smile on our lips. If we are true to ourselves, the future may not be happy (O Pony I'm afraid, so afraid for you) – but no real harm or injury can touch us – nothing can come from without to destroy us. This is the way I try to persuade myself & you.

Dare we risk it?

It is because I love you I write like this, so darkly, lest I injure you with my love & do you a harm. In the name of love & life instead of bedecking you with jewels I load you with chains.

Beth your sad lover

With the letter he enclosed a poem:

To Pony

Hands clasped
Look, see us stand, with eager upturned faces
Lit by the rising sun of our new love,
Whose gentle light touches so tenderly
Eyelids and mouth.

O, my sweet, I am afraid
That soon, perhaps, his mounting rays
Now roseate and kind
Will, in the high noon of passionate desire,
Strike down, with shafts of molten fire
Our bared, defenceless heads,
And neath those blazing beams, we languish and despair
Too eager then his course should run

Into the west and harm us once again
In the cool shade of well-remembered trees,
Alone and separate.

Dare we hold high our unprotected heads
Or, warmed by the memory of other dawns
Behind us, smile gently, part & go our ways,
Across the waste land of the years
Carefree and undisturbed.

Or stay instead and unafrighted, cry
Come light of love and life, shine down,
STRIKE, if strike you must
But warm us first, 'twas better so to die
Beneath your fierce flames than perish in the shade,
Cold and alone.

Perhaps a miracle as happened once, should come again
That golden globe were made to stand
And never sink and never leave the land
Desolate and dark.
But stay, suspended overhead,
High, serene and clear
Perpetuate.[56]

There is no doubt that Marian Scott was as smitten with Bethune as he was with her; both recognized that they shared a yearning for something neither had yet found in life. Compared to her husband's self-contained aloofness, Bethune's impulsive warmth and vitality strongly appealed to her. The two also shared a deep interest in art. On 9 September she addressed Bethune in her journal, saying, "You, a complicated unsatisfied creature, recognize me a complicated unsatisfied creature – recognize each other and know that because we are what we are we need each other." But there was more to it than that, for she obviously found Bethune sexually exciting. On September 10 she wrote, "he was quicksilver in my blood," and would later describe him as "a tiger of sweetness, of fierceness and delight."[57] Yet she continued to refuse to commit herself fully to him. She was still in love with her husband, and they were a well-known couple in Montreal political and artistic circles. The breakup of their marriage would have caused a scandal that would have harmed them both and seriously affected their son. She was well aware that Frank Scott did not much care for Bethune, for there was an element of sexual rivalry between the two men. Her son, Peter Dale Scott, later said, "My father liked to be the male in the room. Bethune also was the commanding male."[58]

The question remains: why, especially given her husband's many infidelities, did Marian Scott did not take simply take Bethune as a lover while maintaining her marriage? The reasons for this were deeply personal. Despite the liberal social views she professed, she may have been held back by her conventional upbringing. But of far more importance was her desire to become a first-rate painter; at this point in her life her whole being was focused on this goal. She was drawn to Bethune's intensity, seeing her exchange of ideas with him as a way of energizing her creative self, but she believed that a love affair with him would threaten her ability to concentrate and hence her development as an artist. On 16 September she wrote unhappily in her journal, "Were you disappointed by a lack in me when I answered your letter & poem that way? It would have been so easy to answer so differently, but that would only have meant ultimate destruction." And again, "My wanting to hear from B. is real and my not wanting him to be so important is real."[59]

Over the next weeks and months Bethune persisted, inviting her to tea, sending her notes and whimsical gifts – a wooden spoon ("Isn't he a lovely spoon?"), a little model horse ("It *must* have been a pony sometime"). He also plied her with telegrams, signing one "The Sick Rose" in memory of Blake's poem, which he had read to her on board ship; another repeated a pet phrase of his, "Oh my, oh my, oh my!"[60] But "the policeman of her will," as Scott called it, held her back. On 19 October she wrote, "I have not written to B. I might have gone to see him today but I chose the right course – infrequent seeing. I think it is possible with him, if it is not, well, I will do without altogether. I live most fully while I paint." And in her journal she wrote a poem with the first line "The apple that was not eaten."[61]

Despite the pangs of a love that, if not unrequited, remained unconsummated, Bethune continued to live hard. Lacking deep personal roots and with "boredom biting at his heels," as Marian Scott put it, he kept up the hectic pace of a man half his age.[62] He burnished his image of the carefree bachelor, tooling about town in a yellow Ford roadster he had bought, nattily dressed in tweeds and a green pork-pie hat. One of those who knew him best at this time was Fritz Brandtner, a painter with an interest in progressive social reform.[63] The two men first met in 1934 when Bethune and a group of artists dropped into Brandtner's studio with a bottle of wine. Bethune did not like one of Brandtner's paintings and as usual said so – loudly. When Brandtner stood his ground, Bethune went off and consulted several books on art. Returning the next day he admitted, "You are absolutely right." Thus began what became a close friendship. Bethune often visited Brandtner and his wife, Mieze, and felt free to take liberties with whatever painting Brantner happened to be working on, picking up a brush and changing a detail here and there to suit his taste.[64] He and Brandtner became drinking companions and went out on the town together. From late autumn of 1935 until the spring of 1936, they were neighbours too, because Bethune rented a studio apartment above the Brandtners' at 1255 Fort Street.

Bethune had the walls of his new flat painted bright red, adding splashes of vivid colour – yellow and green and his favourite gentian blue – in the furnishings and cushions. The drapes were orange velvet.[65] As Brandtner discovered, his habits were as unusual as his taste in décor. He liked to sit on the floor, keeping a velvet cushion for the purpose, and padded about the apartment barefoot. His clothing he left where he dropped it, and he never cleaned the flat, expecting his friends, who were free to drop in at any time, to do it for him. When people did come, he might answer the door in an old patched dressing gown, or even in the nude, and if the guests bored him, he simply ignored them – or left.[66]

He loved to give and receive little presents and was quite possessive about his belongings. When a silver cocktail shaker was stolen from his apartment, which he had carelessly left unlocked, he was outraged, and Brandtner had to talk him out of searching the neighbourhood for it. He would readily give something away if a friend admired it, but after a few days might ask for it back, saying it was only "a gift for lend." Perhaps with this in mind, Brandtner designed a book plate for Bethune that read, "This book belongs to Norman Bethune and his friends." But heaven help the friend who did not read fast enough and failed to return the book promptly.[67]

Always busy, he forgot to eat and would "tear along" for lengthy periods until he suddenly realized that he was ravenous. Then he would eat hugely. He often cooked large hunks of meat – ham, beef, a leg of lamb – and wolfed them down cold over several days, along with the vitamin pills he loved to take.[68] Still unsated after dining in a fancy restaurant with Brandtner, he would go off to a greasy spoon and stuff himself on tripe and onions. Yet he was picky about restaurant fare; he might declare it was no good, then pay up and leave, or, as he did on one occasion, simply overturn the table. After making a scene somewhere, he sometimes asked Brandtner the next day why he hadn't stopped him. "No one could," was Brandtner's comment.

During their drinking bouts they often went slumming in dives, but Bethune also loved to frequent fancy bars. Seeing an acquaintance he did not like, he would say, "Excuse me, but I have to say something nasty to someone." He would then proceed to skewer the victim's complacency before returning to his friends. He and Brandtner sometimes drank into the wee hours of the morning; Brandtner would suggest that Bethune had better get some sleep before showing up at the hospital, but instead he would drive around for a couple of hours, breathing in the cold air. Arriving at Sacré Coeur, he would straighten his shoulders, put on a formal and correct expression, and march to the operating room.[69]

Still dogged by insomnia, he often painted far into the night, sometimes appearing at Brandtner's door at 2 or 3 AM to demand paints. Afterward, he would plunge into sleep for hours to catch up. Critical of his paintings, he might labour long over a canvas and then pitch it out the window. One of his creations showed a tiny naked man crawling among looming female breasts. This curious image seems to reveal that he felt both attracted to and threatened by the female and suggests an insecurity beneath his showy sexuality and the multiplicity of his amorous conquests. He would in fact later talk to a colleague in Spain about "his long history of unsatisfactory sexual relationships."[70] Marian Scott, who saw the painting, said he was angry because it did not express his meaning well enough.[71] In the end he slashed the canvas to pieces with a knife.

Despite his new love and the distractions of his hyperactive lifestyle, Bethune was still mulling over how to continue his crusade against tuberculosis. Given his closeness to Brandtner, it was natural that in the autumn of 1935 he had begun to discuss with his friend his scheme for the development of a "half-way house" to rehabilitate released tubercular patients. He had introduced the idea to the Canadian Progress Club the year before, but what he had seen of the treatment of tubercular patients in the USSR had revived his enthusiasm for the project. His plan was to set up light industries that would employ former patients, allowing them to regain their strength before finding more physically demanding work.

Caught up in Bethune's enthusiasm, Brandtner agreed to design a model of what he and Bethune would later name "The Tubercular City." It included not only industries but residences for the former patients and their families, medical clinics, shops, a theatre, and other community amenities. The two men spent many evenings refining the model. As his enthusiasm for the project grew, Bethune invited friends and colleagues to examine and comment on it, and on one occasion gave a lecture on his ideas. However, although those he consulted praised the aims of the plan, most dismissed it as too idealistic: where did he think he could find the necessary venture capital in the midst of the Depression? Only government had the funds required, and elected officials would never support such a patently socialistic scheme. Bethune reacted angrily to the criticism but then became despondent. After nearly six hectic weeks of designing, promoting, and defending his concept, he abruptly abandoned it without a word to Brandtner.[72]

During the same period he had also been considering a more profound commitment. On the return voyage from England, Bethune had shared with Marian Scott his enthusiasm for what he had seen in the Soviet Union. Deeply interested as always in the welfare of children, he told her how impressed he had been by the apparent health and happiness of the children he saw on the streets and in the nursery schools he visited.[73] Even more significantly, what he had seen in hospitals in the Soviet Union had confirmed many of his ideas about the necessary role of the state in providing health care, especially in the treatment of tuberculosis. He was returning convinced that the Soviets were ahead of Canada in this and other fields of medicine, with a renewed determination to campaign for government support to eradicate tuberculosis. His admiration of the Soviet medical system had also piqued his curiosity about Marxism, and during the voyage he eagerly attended meetings of a youth study group analyzing Marxist thought.[74]

Once back in Canada, he was brimming over with eagerness to discuss his Soviet Union trip, although as he pointed out, he was as usual playing the role of contrarian: "My expressions have not been entirely complimentary in some quarters (depending of course on my audience! – enthusiastic to the reactionaries, minimizing to the radical)."[75] One person particularly interested in his impressions was Louis Kon, a Russian immigrant who had founded the Montreal branch of the Friends of the Soviet Union (FSU), a propaganda organization established by the Communist International (Comintern) in the late 1920s.[76] Its purpose was to promote interest in and support of the USSR worldwide. Like Kon, many of the members of the Montreal branch were European immigrants, and most were workers. Kon recognized the prestige the organization might gain by adding someone of Bethune's professional stature to its membership, especially if he could be persuaded to accept the position of chairman.

In early October, Kon and the members of the FSU executive committee spoke to Bethune, offering him the position for the following year. Kon repeated the offer in a subsequent letter. Bethune replied, making it clear that he had not yet decided whether his admiration for the basic aims of Marxism was more important than what he saw as the regrettable lack of democratic freedoms under Soviet communism. He was still actively trying to reach a conclusion, he told Kon, and when he did, he would respond to the offer.[77] Unbeknownst to him, his enthusiasm for the USSR had been noted by others besides Kon: from October 1935 onward, he was under surveillance by the RCMP.[78]

Soon after his meeting with Kon, he took to his bed[79] with what he considered a mild case of jaundice. However, when Georges Deshaies visited and took his temperature, it had risen to nearly 39 degress Celsius. Deshaies told Bethune he had a serious case of hepatitis and urged him to enter Sacré Coeur for treatment. Bethune refused at first but finally gave in. For nearly three weeks he occupied a private room at the hospital.[80] Though his illness was not life-threatening, his recovery was complicated by the passions of love and politics. The enforced bed-rest gave him plenty of time to brood about Marian Scott and to consider the consequences to his professional life of accepting Kon's offer.

There was little to lift his spirits. On his return from Europe, a letter from Dr John Alexander had informed him that the New York position he had applied for had been filled.[81] And Marian Scott, while admitting her fondness for him, was still unwilling to become his lover. From Sacré Coeur he sent her a whimsical watercolour showing himself, bright yellow with jaundice, in bed reading Marx. Visiting him at Cartierville, she found him depressed.[82] He had long conversations with her and other friends about his political perplexity, for although the afterglow of enthusiasm from his Soviet trip still warmed him, he was torn over how deeply he was attracted to communism.

He had no doubts about the philosophical basis of Marxism. Many of its values were identical to those taught to him by his parents. Like evangelical Christians, communists were committed to uprooting the evil and corrupt base of society in order to build a world in which poverty and suffering would disappear and equality would replace privilege. In Soviet officials and the communists he knew in Montreal he recognized an intensity of belief and a dedication mirroring that of his parents and other evangelicals of his youth. The impatience of communists with the status quo and their eagerness to bring about sweeping change spoke to the values imbued in Bethune early in life. "I know I'm always in a hurry," he had once said of himself, "but I come by this trait honestly. My father was a Presbyterian minister who joined the Moody and Sankey evangelical movement. Their slogan was 'the world for Christ in one generation,' and that is my slogan, whether people like it or not."[83] So dedicating himself to the cause of bringing about "the world for Marx" in his lifetime was in harmony with his deepest impulses.

The fact that communists, unlike evangelical Christians, were willing to use violence to achieve their ends held a definite attraction. In contrast to the social democrats of the CCF, Bethune wrote to Marian Scott, communists recognized "the absolute inevitability of the use of force and force alone as the only true persuader. Moneyed people will *never* give up money and power until subjugated by physical forces stronger than they possess."[84] This incisive, surgical aspect of communism appealed to his impatient nature and his tendency to move instantly from thought to action. In the same letter to Scott he wrote, "Yet I feel a tremendous impulse *to do, to act*. I hate to be thought one of the intelligentsia who talk and talk and talk and behind their words you feel their hearts are cold and it's only an intellectual conundrum. A game."[85]

But he saw flaws in communism as it was practised in the Soviet Union, and he had listed them in his letter of 20 October to Kon. The most important for him was the lack of democratic freedoms. That significant weakness, he told Kon, offended "my strong feeling of individualism – the right of a man to walk alone, if that's his nature – my dislike of crowds and regimentation."[86] Another drawback to committing himself to the cause was that in Canada it was illegal to be a Communist Party member. The federal government had arrested and tried Tim Buck, leader of the Communist Party of Canada, and four of his colleagues under Section 98 of the Criminal Code of Canada. Found guilty, they had been imprisoned in Kingston Penitentiary in 1931. The Roman Catholic Church in Quebec, Bethune's employer, was fervently anti-communist, and he knew it would be risky to identify himself publicly with a communist-leaning organization such as the FSU. Undoubtedly, to do so would lose him his position at the Hôpital du Sacré Coeur. "If I felt as strongly and as purely towards communism as perhaps I should," he had written to Kon, "such jeopardization of my means of livelihood would not be an obstacle in any way. But the ironic and ludicrous picture of a half-hearted convert, reluctantly being burnt at the stake for his half-hearted, feeble convictions, rises in my mind. So it all hinges on this – I am not ready as yet to throw in my lot with you."[87]

In spite of this decision, he was quite willing to outline his impressions of his Soviet trip at one of the FSU's regular meetings, and ten days later he appeared as the advertised speaker at a public meeting in Strathcona Hall. After describing some of the aspects of Soviet life that appealed to him, he repeated what he had explained to Kon. Despite his acceptance of what he described as "the religious and spiritual aspects of Marxism," his commitment to democracy and his belief in freedom of speech and individualism had convinced him that the Soviet style of communism was not desirable for Canada. "There are things I can say under this system that I cannot say under the communist system," he stated, adding that although he admired the Russian people and what they had achieved, he did not believe that Russian communism would be the final answer. And he concluded his speech with the telling remark, "We all sighed with relief as the train sped out of the country."[88]

But he wavered during the first part of November about his decision to reject communism. He knew it was prudent to protect his professional position and his livelihood, but he felt that he had backed away from a challenge. This rankled: for possibly the first time in his life, *he had not dared*.

Meanwhile his love for Marian Scott still tormented him. On 6 November he wrote a tender letter to her about an operation he had performed on Yvette Patrice, a little girl of ten: "6 P.M. My child is well. It was a very beautiful operation. I felt very happy doing it. The entire right lung was removed – the first time this has been done – in a child of 10 – in Canada & the 45th operation of its kind ever done in the world. Isn't that nice? Yes, I will sleep deep tonight – last night was a 'nuit blanche' – not whether I could do it but whether I should. I decided I must at 4 a.m., slept till 7, felt refreshed & 'tight' and went at it like a canvas – my picture full in my mind. Good night, my sweet. Beth.[89]

On 18 November Marian Scott went out to Sacré Coeur and spent several hours with him. The visit marked a turning point in their relationship. It is likely that she once again rejected deeper intimacy with him and told him she had decided to see him less frequently, for her journal entry for that day is a poem that begins "Goodbye Beth" and ends "Goodbye warmth of being together."[90] Four days later Bethune wrote a reply to a letter he had received from her that day. "The tyranny of old love is holding you back," he reproached her. Then, rallying his self-esteem, he went on, "I was sad, yet glad when you left on Monday. I saw you as a wall closing in again on me – a loving wall! – & I raised my head, restless. Oh, God, I said to myself, must I go thru [sic] it all again – the ecstasy & agony of love." And he proudly told her that he did not need her. The letter concluded:

You are the *first* woman in the world I have met about whom I have felt *no doubt* that we could live together, physically & mentally & spiritually mated. This has never happened to me before & is important …

I am glad now we did not take each other physically. For me it would have meant that I would not have left you, as I am leaving you now – so nobly! so generously! so sweetly! No. I should have behaved with most unseemly vigour, & lack of manners, shouts and clamours. And for you, it was as well too. You have now the exquisite sense of virtue preserved, of moral rectitude which is so sustaining. You are still a faithful wife. And if you had, what then – for a thirst appeased, a hunger satisfied, but with your conflict, your essential problem unchanged, so for you no serenity, no peace, no quietness of soul. And because I would know this instantly, neither for me either, serenity, peace or quietness. Yes. I understand you, my own, my darling. The great question – "what do you do with your old loves"?

Well, Pony, my sweet, all this is to say I love you, I want you & I respect you.

I am here if I can be of any use to you at any time. And that's all one man·can say to a woman. *Au revoir*.
Beth[91]

Along with the letter he sent as a memento a self-portrait in oils, and in an ironic postscript said that if Frank Scott did not want her to hang it in the house, she should send it back. But he could not maintain his pose of detachment for long. On 10 December he sent another note pleading, "Oh, Pony, Pony – it was false. I do need you."[92]

For Bethune the past two years had been a time of profound awakenings. He had become passionately aware of the social causes of tuberculosis and had decided that only through political action could social conditions be altered so that the roots of the disease could be attacked and the wider suffering caused by the Great Depression be addressed. His visit to the Soviet Union had deepened this belief and impressed him with the superiority of socialized medicine over private; as a result he was wrestling with the idea of committing himself to communism. He was forty-five now, and despite his professional achievements, he knew he had not yet done something great for the human race as he had vowed. Frustrated in love, increasingly restive at Sacré Coeur, he had reached the end of another cycle. In the end it may have been emotion that pushed him to act, for it was sometime during the turmoil of his relationship with Marian Scott in November 1935 that he applied for membership in the Communist Party of Canada.[93] It was a leap of faith, and the most important decision of his life.

❖ 8 ❖

True Believer

Montreal, December 1935–October 1936

Joining the Communist Party provided Bethune with a core belief that he may have hungered for unconsciously. He had long since rejected formal Christianity, but many of the precepts of the faith of his parents were bred in his bones: his deep sense of personal predestination, the concept of the struggle of good against evil, and the moral obligation to serve the poor and helpless. Now he had found a "modern religion," as he called it, that answered all his needs. From now on he would devote himself with evangelistic fervour to Marxism, whose founder he described as "one of the true religious leaders of the world" and whom he compared favourably to Christ.[1] and he felt honour bound to embrace his new faith wholly, whatever the cost.[2] Having seen how his father's tenaciously held beliefs had made him unpopular and led to harrowing periods of unemployment, Bethune was aware of what the consequences of acting on his convictions might be. But he was willing to risk as much and more. His identification with the communist cause was emotional and passionate rather than reasoned and logical.

As well as feeding his hunger for faith, his conversion served other psychological needs. Joining an illegal organization was a kind of dare, which likely held a strong appeal for him and no doubt gratified his perennial desire to shock. And there was another aspect. In his letter of 21 November to Marian Scott, he had proudly described himself as "a solitary, loving privacy, my own satisfactory aloneness."[3] But the truth was that he had never been able to strike roots anywhere, and now in his middle years, despite his demanding work and hectic social life, he was often lonely. One acquaintance remembered how he would phone people late at night to talk at random about whatever was on his mind – anything from a class in Marxist theory he had attended to a beautiful woman he had seen in the street.[4] He made friends easily but just as easily dropped or lost them when his moods or interests changed. Few of his acquaintances dated back more than several years, John Barnwell, Lincoln Fisher, and Edward Kupka being notable exceptions. Now, committed to working with others for a cause he believed in, he said it was wonderful to be with people who were moving in the same direction.[5] In September 1935 Marian Scott had perceptively written of him, "You must find some centre of interest which is all important around which the focus of life may be gathered. This centre, once found, other virtues may be built about it ... You say all you want is an arm chair. Actually these conditions would not satisfy you – you will always crave experience, romantic adventure, growth and change, excitement, even struggle."[6] In communism Bethune felt he had found such a centre of interest, an opportunity for growth and change.

He had pondered long before deciding to join the CPC, and the local party leadership had been cautious about granting him membership. Party members at that time were largely working-class, mostly European immigrants. So Bethune was a big catch, a valuable addition to the tiny handful of anglophone professionals and white-collar workers in the party. However, the leadership realized that admitting him posed a risk, for how could party discipline be imposed on such a notably unconventional character? To protect both him and his potential value to the party, it was agreed that only a few leading cadres would know of his membership. And because of his temperament and his outspokenness, they decided to place him not in a "closed" party cell but in a study group examining basic Marxist philosophy. The group was open to the public and not formally associated with the Communist Party.[7]

Bethune enjoyed his study of Marxist philosophy and was captivated by the concept of the dialectic, the idea that history was a process of change propelled by contradiction (between thesis and antithesis, which in turn produced synthesis). For him medicine was a dialectical science, and he noted the parallel between the dialectic and his own contrarian approach to existence, musing, "Funny, I've been practicing dialectics all my life without knowing it."[8] He was also deeply impressed by the theme developed in the group's discussions of international solidarity against fascism.

The other part of his assignment as a party member was to carry out a project he had already begun thinking about and which the party approved. This was an outgrowth of his earlier concern about the care of post-tubercular patients and his realization that the only way to eradicate the disease was through improved social conditions and health care. He now set out to find an answer to a problem that the Depression had created for patients and doctors throughout Canada. In the 1930s a large part of the population could not afford needed medical care, with the result that the sick went without treatment and many doctors were unable to earn a decent income. Having given the matter thought, Bethune decided that a comparative study of health and medical systems in various European countries might provide answers. After doing some preliminary research during the first week of December, he invited three medical practitioners to his Fort Street apartment to discuss his idea. They were Dr Wendell MacLeod, a former student of his at the McGill medical school, Dr H.E. (Hy) Shister, a cardiologist and colleague, and a registered nurse, Libbie Park, whom he had met after his address to the Friends of the Soviet Union on 30 October and saw socially from time to time afterwards. All three agreed to participate in the study, and each selected a country to research; Bethune chose both Great Britain and the Soviet Union. The four also agreed to invite other health care and social workers to join them.

Eventually the group totalled sixteen, with an average of ten turning up at the twice-monthly meetings held on a rotating basis at members' homes. It was not until the spring of 1936 that they named their organization the Montreal Group for the Security of the People's Health (MGSPH).⁹ Though Bethune would soon speak publicly of the need for "socialized medicine," by which he meant government control of health care and of the salaries of medical practitioners, he accepted the majority opinion that the group limit itself to advocating that the government should introduce some form of universal health insurance. Bethune much enjoyed the get-togethers and became friends with some of the other members. After meetings he would take Libbie Park and another woman home, the top down on his roadster, loudly carolling popular songs like "Moonlight and Roses" as they drove through the bourgeois bastions of Montreal West.¹⁰

Meanwhile, filled with the fervour of the new convert, "washed in the blood of Marx,"¹¹ Bethune was yearning to preach the "good news" of communism, no matter what the risks. Despite party orders to be discreet, he came close to going too far in an address he gave shortly before Christmas 1935. He and three other Montreal doctors had been invited to provide a brief summary of their analyses of the Soviet medical system based on their observations during the International Physiological Congress in the USSR the previous August. They spoke on 20 December to the Montreal Medico-Chirugical Society, an organization of physicians and surgeons. Bethune chose to speak last, and in contrast to the three other doctors whose remarks were directly on topic, he barely mentioned the congress and said nothing at all of Russian medicine. Instead, using the title "Reflections on Return from *Through the Looking Glass,*" he delivered a eulogy of the Soviet Union. By drawing a parallel between the topsy-turvy land of Lewis Carroll's Alice and contemporary Soviet Russia, he said, it would be easy to write an article called *Malice in Blunderland*. But that, he pointed out, would say more about the writer's point of view than about the actual situation. He then compared the emergence of the young Soviet Union to the act of human birth, quoting Isadora Duncan's description of her experience of motherhood: "There I lay, a fountain spouting blood, milk and tears." He went on, "Creation is not and never has been a genteel gesture. It is rude, violent and revolutionary." He concluded, "It is the passionate belief of Communists that the degrading poverty and misery of modern life is not the will of god but the wilfulness of man.[12] But to those courageous hearts who believe in the unlimited future of man, his divine destiny which lies in his own hands to make of it what he will, Russia presents today the most exciting spectacle of the evolutionary, emergent and heroic spirit of man which has appeared on this earth since the Reformation. To deny this is to deny our faith in man – and that is the unforgivable sin, the final apostasy."[13]

Several weeks after his speech, he went to Memphis, Tennessee, where he had been invited to address the Mid-South Assembly, a convention of nurse-anaesthesists. After describing the use of a new form of anaesthesia in thoracic surgery, he launched into an impassioned plea for the introduction of socialized medicine in the United States. Doctors, like military personnel, should receive salaries according to ability, not fees for services provided, he said: "True, we would never make much money, but persons should not enter the profession to get rich."[14] The heading over the photograph of Bethune and three members of the Mid-South Assembly in the *Memphis Commercial Appeal* was "Surgeon Startles Medical Assembly." As usual, he had managed to shock the maximum number of people in the minimum amount of time.

Not long after, he took on the Canadian medical profession as well. The occasion was a symposium held on 17 April 1936 by the Montreal Medico-Chirurgical Society on the subject of medical economics. Using a similar approach to that of his address to the Progress Club in 1934, he played the role of the prosecutor of a legal case with the title of *The People versus the Doctors*, in which his audience was to play the role of both defendant and judge. He began by stating that the Depression had created a predicament for people seeking medical care and a dilemma for doctors eager to exercise their professional skills. Citing data from recent American studies, he pointed out that four out of ten people had not visited a doctor or dentist during the previous year. At the same time, more than three out of ten doctors had received inadequate incomes under the fee-for-service system because many people could not pay for medical services. He declared that the system must be changed, that fee-for-service, private charity, and philanthropic institutions as means of improving social welfare were inequitable, degrading, inefficient, and anachronistic, and he demanded that government assume the responsibility for providing health care for all citizens. The best way to do this would be to introduce a system of socialized medicine and abolish or restrict private medical practice.

"Let us take the profit, the private economic profit, out of medicine," he urged, "and purify our profession of rapacious individualism. Let us make it disgraceful to enrich ourselves at the expense of the miseries of our fellow-men." He continued, "The contest in the world today is between two kinds of men: those who believe in the old jungle individualism, and those who believe in cooperative efforts for the securing of a better life for all." He proposed that all medical and social service organizations form a "great army ... to make a collectivized attack on disease." Their first step would be to design and present to the government "a complete, comprehensive program of a planned medical service for all the people." In his summary of the case of *The People Versus the Doctors*, he left no doubt upon whose shoulders the blame should fall if his recommendations were not adopted. "The people are ready for socialized medicine," he insisted. "The obstructionists to the people's health security lie within the profession itself."[15] The speech was not well received by his colleagues; according to one account, the Montreal Medico-Chirurgical Society executive later held a special meeting at which he was drummed out of the organization.[16]

Having bearded the medical lions in their den on the matter of socialized medicine, Bethune attacked the professional establishment from another angle. During the nearly twelve years in which he had practised surgery, he had become more and more outraged to see many surgeons maintaining their reputations by accepting only cases in which there was little danger of losing the patient, then boasting of their success rates in published articles. He had always believed it was a surgeon's duty to take risky cases. Such patients might die on the operating table, but without surgery their death was guaranteed.

Bethune was still a member of the executive committee of the American Association for Thoracic Surgery, and this gave him a springboard for launching his criticism of his colleagues. One of his roles was to assist in preparing the program for the association's annual convention, scheduled for early May 1936 in Rochester, Minnesota. Writing to Richard Meade, a thoracic surgeon from Philadelphia who shared the program responsibilities with him, Bethune discussed his intention of addressing the convention, saying that the title of his paper would be "Some Errors in Technique and Mistakes in Judgment Made in the Course of 1,000 Thoracic Surgical

Operations." He added, "That should startle them!" His letter continued, "I'm getting very tired (and envious) of successful brilliant results so I have collected '25 howlers' of my own & would want others to join me at the public confessional for the benefit of the young."[17]

Bethune arrived in Rochester in his roadster on 4 May. His appearance was calculated to shock the more staid: he wore a sport jacket, old trousers, and an open-necked black shirt that looked as though it had not been washed in some time. Across his chest he had pinned a broad red ribbon like a European order of honour.[18] He amused some of the younger doctors by showing them that his grip contained nothing more than a large telephone directory and his shaving equipment. He enjoyed travelling light, he explained, but because hotels were suspicious of people without luggage, he used this ruse to get a room.

Most members of the program committee had objected to the topic Bethune had chosen for his speech and as a compromise, they decided to place his presentation at the end of a day when many doctors would be attending other functions. Some of those who did hear the speech found it interesting but felt that in writing it Bethune had drawn considerably on his imagination. And his hope that the address would appear in the *Journal of Thoracic Surgery* was dashed; Dr Ewarts Graham, his fellow executive committee member and editor of the journal, decided not to publish it even though he had earlier published other articles by Bethune.

Meanwhile, Bethune's love life remained as dialectical as his politics. He continued to yearn for Marian Scott and to see her occasionally, as he did his ex-wife. He wrote notes to Scott inviting her to tea and rang her up now and then. On 22 March they had happened to meet somewhere, as she records in her journal: "Beth. The shock of our meeting again driving words away. The spontaneous enfolding of arms but nothing to do – escape out into the rain driving fast and exposed so that the rain cut us like arrows which we answered with laughter – mist so that we were on top of the world and nothing below us. The well-remembered room and talk and seeing that released us from our bodies and we were separate and free."[19] The meeting seems to have rekindled their romance. Over the next weeks Bethune contacted Scott more often, coming to see her, inviting her to have tea or to attend meetings with him. He also wrote poetry to her, which he sent to her, along with a short story called "Encounter." This whimsical piece, full of rhetorical flourishes, described a meeting between a drunken man, his head reeling from an argument over communism, and a dog.[20]

Although Scott clung to her decision not to become Bethune's lover, her journals make it clear that she was still deeply involved with him, hoping against hope that they could work out some kind of relationship that would allow them to share their thoughts and ideas and energize each other. Watching Bethune, loving him, she saw a man who, even given his new-found faith in communism, was still struggling to make sense of his life. In January 1936 she had observed, "B. feels the only way to escape from the monotony of day-by-day – from the mundane is by violence – by excess." In March she wrote, "B. is tired of most things in life – the spark has gone out of most things so that most of his emotion has seeped back to its most primitive source. 'There is nothing but this!' he cries." And in April, "I think you want to live greatly & that is why you sometimes do a lot of silly things."[21]

This second intense phase of their relationship would continue on and off until early June. On 10 May, Scott wrote, "He wired to me to keep tomorrow afternoon ... I would so like to prove to him – and to myself that there can be a worthwhile relationship between a man and a woman without the sexual consummation." And on 4 June, "I need him as a stimulus. *I need him*." But she continued to worry about being distracted from giving all of her energies to painting. Then on 8 June she wrote, "And we both say it is ended. Yet in your letter you reluctantly showed how I come upon you. So tonight your disappointment is my disappointment. And I think of you with the old bright warmth & remember our flowering nearness." Months later she would write sadly, "He does not want what I want and I do not want what he wants." And later still, after he had left for Spain, "My feelings for F. [her husband] make certain things impossible," and "loving with the body is not the only way."[22] Perhaps in the end she had come to understand more about Bethune than he knew about himself, for many years later she would say in an interview, "The women Beth slept with he fought with."[23]

Frustrated in his desire for Scott, Bethune had already become involved in a love affair with the Montreal poet Margaret Day.[24] She was a young teacher who like him had travelled to Russia to see the truth of the Revolution for herself. Attending Bethune's speech on 30 October 1935 about his trip to Russia, she had immediately fallen in love with him. That night she had written him an impassioned letter saying she would like him to make love to her; too timid to send it, she later destroyed it. Then, by chance, Bethune appeared as a guest at her Marxist study group, probably sometime in January 1936. Introducing herself to him as the sister of a former patient of his, the star-struck young woman accepted his offer to drive her home. "I was looking for trouble, and I found it," she later said. They went instead to Bethune's apartment and she spent the night with him. When she told him of the love letter she had not had the nerve to send, he exclaimed, "Why didn't you send it? We've wasted the past three months!" Day, who had expected no more than a one-night stand, was astonished. "My dream was only once. I wasn't aiming higher than that."

The affair soon turned stormy and was complicated by Bethune's heavy drinking. He told Day that he wanted to marry her and have a child, but like so many other women before her, she feared his instability. His erratic behaviour confirmed her doubts: one night during a quarrel he deliberately drove his car into a tree. Neither of them was injured, but the car suffered considerable damage. With Day, Bethune showed his shadow side, far different from the self he revealed to Marian Scott. "He was a destroyer," Day later said. "He was not right in his mind; he was an alcoholic, twice divorced. I have seen him fall drunk on the bed at three A.M. when he had to operate at nine that morning."[25]

Despite his tempestuous love life and his political commitments, Bethune still managed to find time to paint. He also kept up contacts with members of the artistic community and continued to buy paintings. On occasion he could be devastatingly frank with artists. Jori Smith, who had painted a portrait of the doll-child Alice, once took him to meet a young artist named Allan Harrison, also a Communist Party member. Preoccupied and eager to go elsewhere, Bethune glanced at the artist's work, said, "Harrison, you paint shit," and went on his way. Some days later he tried to make amends, returning to compliment Harrison and buy a painting from him.[26]

Around the same time he found a way to link his fascination with art with his fondness for children. From Fritz Brandtner he learned of an art education program for children in Toronto under the direction of Arthur Lismer at the Art Gallery of Ontario. Lismer, a member of the Group of Seven, called his program "the Saturday Morning Classes." He patterned it on a Viennese art school founded by Dr Franz Cizek, who believed that if children were encouraged to feel free to express themselves through art, they could discover their creative selves. The concept appealed strongly to Bethune. He contacted Pegi Nicol, a Toronto artist introduced to him by Marian Scott, asking her to make arrangements for him to meet Lismer and learn more about the program. Nicol agreed and invited Bethune and Brandtner to stay with her during their visit.

Several days later the two men set off in Bethune's roadster. In manic mode, Bethune raced along the highway, taking corners on two wheels, and they made record time to Toronto. There they met Nicol and two of her friends, who took them to a hotel bar. After several bottles of beer, Nicol suggested going to see her friend and fellow-artist Paraskeva Clark. They arrived to find the Clarks and their guests in evening dress in the midst of dinner. Bethune swaggered into the room, tossed his hat in a corner, and demanded loudly, "Is there any beer?" Then he marched into the kitchen and opened the refrigerator.

Only momentarily taken aback, Paraskeva and her husband, Philip, welcomed Bethune and Brandtner. Beer bottle in hand, Bethune entered the living room, to which the dinner guests had retreated, and sat down on a coffee table, knocking over a vase of flowers. Pretending to ignore such uncouth behaviour, one of the guests picked up a book and opened it, but Bethune reached over and snatched it from the man's hands; wetting his thumb and flicking through the pages, he tossed it into the empty fireplace. He then rolled up his shirt sleeve to show off his anchor and serpent tattoo, a memento of his Royal Navy days. A row began, in which some of the guests, believing him to be a roughneck off the streets, tried to bait him. He responded with a tongue-lashing that left them open-mouthed. In the ensuing silence Nicol coaxed Bethune and Brandtner to leave. Paraskeva Clark, however, was amused by the performance. The next day, learning that Bethune and Brandnter had already visited the Lismer school and returned to Montreal, she told Nichol she was disappointed; she had hoped that Bethune might have stayed "so we could get the whole town wakened up."[27]

Bethune returned to Montreal intent on setting up something similar to Lismer's classes. He and Brandtner hoped to reach out to disadvantaged children in the poorer sections of the city, offering them a brief escape from the drabness and deprivation of their lives. Expressing themselves artistically in bright colours, Bethune thought, might help to prepare them emotionally for the difficulties they faced in life.[28] Brandtner agreed to direct the classes, to be held in Bethune's apartment. Realizing he would need more space, Bethune began searching for a new flat and found one in March. It was located at 1154 Beaver Hall Square on the third floor of a building overlooking the downtown and beyond it, the St Lawrence River; it had earlier been used as a studio by Jori Smith, her husband, and another artist.[29]

Before taking possession Bethune persuaded the landlord to let him make renovations to create a large room where art classes could be held. He had a big window built into the east side of the apartment to allow morning sunlight to flood the studio room. Beside it was his bedroom with another window looking out on the square. The kitchen and bathroom and a living room with a fireplace were on the west side. In contrast to the exuberant colour scheme of the Fort Street apartment, he had the walls painted off-white; the living-room rug and upholstery were in his favourite gentian blue. Pegi Nicol later contributed a mural in harmonizing colours, and paintings covered the walls of every room, even the stairwell. Bethune was proud of his new home, yet when his working day was done, despite the bustle of meetings and his round of parties and visits, he found himself lonely there. He was the only person living in the building, and he missed having Brandtner downstairs.[30]

The children's art classes began in May and were held on Saturday mornings. As Bethune had intended, most of the children came from poorer sections of the city. He eventually chose the name Children's Creative Art Centre (CCAC) for his program. Though an average of a dozen children attended, there were often more, the crowd spilling over into the bedroom. The object of the classes was not to provide instruction in art but to encourage the children to express themselves freely. To open eyes and ears to sights and sounds unfamiliar to many of them, Brandtner and Bethune took them on Saturdays to places in the city where many of the children had never been – the harbour, parks, art galleries and museums. Here they stopped to sketch; on their return they were given large sheets of wrapping paper and paints and found a space on the floor where they attempted to portray their impressions of what they had seen and felt during their outing. Brandtner, joined after several weeks by Marian Scott, remained on hand to answer questions and provide encouragement. Bethune often arrived with cookies and milk and stayed to observe and talk to the children. He got on well with them, and they responded to his interest. The school attracted considerable attention in Montreal, and the children's expressive paintings were exhibited at several public showings.[31]

However, Bethune's main preoccupation at this time was the MGSPH. He had never intended that the project be limited merely to research and discussion – he wanted action. The calling of a provincial election in Quebec for 17 August 1936 spurred the group to more intense activity; they were determined to make health care an issue in the election campaign, hoping to inspire debate that might lead to real progress. They began to summarize the results of more than six months' work with the aim of making the results public.

Near the end of July they put forward a series of proposals for the reform of health care in Quebec. These were grouped in two sections, municipal and provincial. The municipal section consisted of three different plans to be tried in three Quebec municipalities of similar size. In the first, salaried health workers would provide medical care for the entire population, with all costs borne by the municipal and provincial governments. In the second, all wage-earners would pay compulsory health insurance, and in the third, voluntary health insurance would be offered. The provincial section called for unemployed workers throughout the province to receive free medical treatment, to be paid for by the provincial government; doctors would bill the government on a fee-for-service basis. With the exception of the first municipal plan, which was universal and would rely on government financing, the term "socialized medicine" hardly applied to their proposals, because the members of the study group remained convinced that any such plan would be doomed to failure. Bethune reluctantly agreed with them.

To save time and money, the group mimeographed typed copies of the proposals and sent them with a letter calling for a public meeting to medical, social service, and labour organizations and public health officials in Montreal. The meeting took place, but the turnout was poor. Disappointed but still hopeful, the group sent out a second mailing with an elaborated version of their proposals. Oddly, neither version was translated into French, nor were francophone medical organizations invited to participate. With only a week remaining before the election, the group sent the revised proposals to many of the previous recipients as well as to all candidates in Montreal ridings and to all civic politicians.

Maurice Duplessis, the leader of the Union Nationale, publicly acknowledged receiving the proposals, and Adélard Godbout, the incumbent Liberal premier of Quebec, apparently did so privately.[32] This, plus a few references to the proposals in the English-language press, at first raised the MGSPH's hopes. But the ideas seem to have been ignored by the general public, professional and union organizations, and most politicians. As weeks passed after the election with no public response and no hoped-for debate on the issue of health-care reform, Bethune and the other MGSPH members realized that their work had been in vain.

For Bethune this result must have been devastating. Ever since his epiphany while painting the murals at the Trudeau Sanatorium, he had dedicated himself to fighting tuberculosis. For him it was not enough to deal surgically with the ravages of the disease; he had hoped to find a way to eradicate it and believed it was possible to do so. Now his attempt to cut to the real root of the menace of tuberculosis, inadequate health care, had been frustrated by ignorance, apathy, and professional prejudice. He had failed in the mission he had set himself.

Emotionally he was at loose ends as well. His affair with Margaret Day continued to be tempestuous, and he was also still thinking about Marian Scott. On 13 August he had written to her wistfully, "Is the water still cool & dark, the sands still curving white, And are you still so beautiful? I long for you – being none of all these."[33] Frances Coleman remained a part of his life too, and Libbie Park recalled how possessive he was of her. They appeared together at a supper party to raise funds for the Canadian League against War and Fascism. Frances stood out, dressed in a black velvet gown with red roses at the V of its plunging neckline, and Bethune danced with no one else all evening.[34]

Thwarted in his mission to do something great for humanity, unhappy in love, he chafed under the restraints of the life he was living. Montreal felt like a dead end, and even his passionate faith in communism did him little good in the abstract, for his restless energy needed a practical outlet. Casting about for a cause to give meaning and direction to his life, he found it in Spain. On 18 July 1936 the Spanish chief of staff, General Francisco Franco, had led a military uprising intended to topple the democratically elected Popular Front government of the country. The conflict that followed rapidly escalated into civil war. Franco's supporters, known as the Nationalists, included most members of the armed services, the Roman Catholic hierarchy, the moneyed interests, and the Falange, the Spanish fascist organization. Rallying in defence of the government were the Loyalists or Republicans, a loosely linked coalition of anarchist, socialist, and communist organizations representing the majority of Spanish agricultural and urban workers.

By way of the Comintern, news of the reaction of Moscow to the Spanish conflict quickly reached the CPC headquarters in Toronto. The fear was that a fascist offensive was threatening to sweep Europe. As early as 1 August, while Bethune was still struggling to bring out the MGSPH material, the CPC had published an editorial in the *Daily Clarion* appealing to its members and all anti-fascists for a "big mass movement ... of the Canadian working men and women to help our Spanish brothers and sisters."[35] Bethune's attention became riveted on this developing conflict. Here was a new "disease" to crusade against, for had not fascism, which he had once felt had some redeeming features, proved itself to be a political epidemic that threatened democracy everywhere and might lead to another world war? On his daily visits to Sacré Coeur, he got into discussions about the Spanish Civil War that sometimes turned into arguments. No less rapidly than the CPC, the Roman Catholic hierarchy in Quebec had made its position clear: it was in absolute support of the Spanish Nationalists. In all parish churches as well as church-operated institutions such as Sacré Coeur, the focus was on reports by the pro-Nationalist media of the burning of Spanish churches and of atrocities committed against nuns and priests by Republican sympathizers or, as they were frequently described, "reds." Open in his support for the republic, Bethune shocked some of his co-workers and the Catholic hospital administrators. After nearly four years of extremely cordial relations, the issue of Spain began to turn the authorities at Sacré Coeur against him.

By early September, Bethune had become obsessed with Spain. He scoured the pages of the English-language Montreal newspapers, the communist *Daily Clarion*, and the leftist weekly the *New Commonwealth* for news of the progress of Franco's Army of Africa as it advanced toward Madrid. With friends both inside and outside the party, he shared his fear of a Republican defeat, saying, "It is in Spain that the real issues of our time are going to be fought out. It is there that democracy will either die or survive."[36] He decided he must go to Spain to see things for himself. It was the same irresistible impulse "to do, to act" that had launched him into the CPC only months earlier.

His affair with Margaret Day began to disintegrate under the intensity of his focus on Spain. He still wanted to marry her and have a child but, given the circumstances, she continued to refuse. Then she became pregnant. Bethune was delighted, but knowing that he wanted to go to Spain, she refused to have the baby. She begged him to perform an abortion and, fearing she might find an unqualified abortionist instead, he reluctantly agreed. For him it must have been a bitter disappointment, another lost child. But Day was relieved.[37]

At loose ends now that the MGSPH had failed, Bethune accepted an invitation from John Barnwell to drive to Ann Arbor in September to give a talk at a medical meeting. To Barnwell's dismay he arrived with his luggage stuffed with propaganda and at the meeting proceeded to give a pro-communist oration instead of the expected medical speech. Barnwell and his friends were embarrassed.[38] Back in Montreal, Bethune continued to focus on Spain but did not know what role he might be able to play there. Broke as usual, he approached a friend, Percy Newman, a CCF member sympathetic to the Loyalist cause. "I'd like to go over there," Bethune said. "What do you think? Can you lend me $200?"[39] When Newman could not come up with the money, Bethune wrote to the Red Cross offering his services if the organization was planning to send aid to Spain. The curt response was, "The Canadian Red Cross Society is not raising a unit for service in Spain and has not, I think, any intention whatsoever of doing so."[40]

Bethune's dismay gave way to elation when he read a front page story in the *New Commonwealth* describing plans for a medical unit to be sent to Spain. He immediately telegraphed Graham Spry, the editor of the newspaper and author of the article, offering to join the unit and saying that he would drive to Toronto the next day to discuss the matter. But when he arrived at the *New Commonwealth* offices, Spry confessed that the organization he had named "The Spanish Hospital and Medical Aid Committee" did not exist. He explained that as a pacifist he was horrified by the war and appalled by the apparent lack of public concern about it; he had written the article hoping to stir up some kind of support. He had certainly succeeded in stirring up Bethune. Disappointed to find the committee did not yet exist, he talked eagerly to Spry about creating some such organization and mentioned that he was meeting later that day with A.A. MacLeod, a prominent member of the CPC who had just returned from Spain.[41]

At their meeting, MacLeod was pleased to learn of Bethune's keen interest in going to Spain, and they discussed what he might be able to do there. A sticking point was his unwillingness to stay in Spain for a long period of time. MacLeod argued that the war would not end soon, and that to be truly useful Bethune could not go merely as a visitor but would have to commit himself totally, without a limit on his length of service. Bethune objected that it would mean giving up his position at Sacré Coeur and therefore his source of income, a step he was not prepared to take.[42]

The two men talked into the early hours of the morning and met again that afternoon. MacLeod then changed his line of argument. As one of the small group of officials who had decided to offer Bethune CPC membership, MacLeod had learned a great deal about him. He knew that, after eight years in Montreal, Bethune was eager for change, and that the recent failure of the MGSPH effort had been a blow to him. He also believed that Bethune's dislike of the pro-Franco atmosphere of Sacré Coeur would soon force him to go elsewhere, so he shrewdly decided to appeal to Bethune's restless nature and love of adventure. He reminded him that the war had become the focal point of global interest. Reporters from around the world were making their way to Madrid, and the Spanish Civil War was already being depicted as the climactic struggle between the two major ideological forces of the era, communism and fascism. Going to Spain, he said, would do more than serve a political cause. Bethune would be able to save lives and would doubtless gain recognition for his achievements. He would also experience the supreme exhilaration of serving a noble cause in the midst of a war. It was an opportunity that he would be a fool to miss.[43]

This argument struck home. Bethune had come to see himself as being mired in Montreal, no more than a "big frog in a small pond," as he had once complained to his ex-wife. His crusade against tuberculosis had reached a dead end, and he was unsure of where next to direct his energies. MacLeod's words roused his old sense of destiny: might not Spain, with the world watching, be the place where he would at last do something for the human race? Interrupting MacLeod, he said that he had changed his mind: he would resign from Sacré Coeur immediately and go to Spain.[44] Neither he nor MacLeod had a clear idea of how he would offer his services, but they were sure that a surgeon would be needed.

Meanwhile, spurred by Bethune's mentioning that he would be talking to a CPC representative, Spry had gone into action. As well as being the editor and publisher of the *New Commonwealth*, he was the vice-president of the Ontario CCF, and as soon as Bethune left he had made a series of telephone calls to CCF members in Toronto and Montreal, urging them to take the lead in forming a committee to send Bethune to Spain. The decision was made quickly, dictated by political as well as humanitarian motives: the CCF wanted credit for being the first political party to take steps to provide medical aid to Spain and was determined to act before its rival the CPC did.[45] Within days an organization called the Committee to Aid Spanish Democracy (CASD) was beginning to operate. However, although the CCF took the lead, the CPC and other groups were also represented within the CASD.[46] Inspired by a common goal and despite their mutual hostility, the CCF and CPC worked closely during the following weeks to raise money for the medical supplies Bethune would take with him. By good luck they did not have to pay for his sea passage. Elizabeth Smart, the daughter of a friend of Spry, had decided not to continue her studies in Europe that autumn, and when she learned from Marian Scott that Bethune planned to go to Spain, she offered Spry the return portion of her steamship ticket.[47]

Bethune began winding up his affairs. For a man of his age and professional stature, there was remarkably little to do. He began by sending letters of resignation to the three hospitals with which he was connected.[48] The doctors and nursing sisters of Sacré Coeur who had worked under his direction for nearly four years arranged a farewell luncheon. It was an emotional affair in which they paid their respects to him for his significant contributions to the hospital. Touched by their tributes, Bethune gave a speech explaining only that he was embarking on a humanitarian mission.[49] Afterwards he took Georges Deshaies, his assistant surgeon, aside and told him his actual destination.

He spent the next few days saying goodbye to various friends and acquaintances and basked in their admiration of his courage in plunging into the war in Spain. Leaving a gathering of Montreal little theatre members called together to bid him farewell, he paused dramatically at the door and said, "Goodbye. Remember, it is easier for us who go than for those who stay behind."[50] His leave-taking to Marian Scott was jaunty. "Goodbye Pony," he wrote, "the world has been a fine place to live in because of you."[51]

But she wrote in her journal, "And so I watched you leave. And I was left alone on the rind of the earth. I knew the anguish of the cave man that knew no way of speech."[52]

The parting from Margaret Day was difficult. Insisting that she wished to make a clean break with him, she asked Bethune not to write to her. "I never regretted a moment [of our affair]," she told him. "But we'll never meet again."[53] And then there was Frances Coleman, whom Bethune still regarded as his most important obligation even though she was still married to R.E. Just before leaving Montreal, he made out a will in which he left her his few possessions, including the furniture in his Beaver Hall Square apartment as well as control of the apartment lease. He also gave her power of attorney and control of his bank account.[54] His beloved yellow roadster he sold to Hy Shister for $300 on condition that Shister pay for it by making monthly payments of $25 to Frances over the following year. Bethune had already moved in with the Shisters to allow Fritz Brandtner and his wife to occupy his apartment and continue the Children's Creative Art Centre. To cover the centre's operating expenses, he pledged a payment of $25 for each of the following four months.

Meanwhile, he was closely following the worsening situation in Spain. On Saturday, 17 October, Franco's army launched an attack on the town of Illescas, thirty kilometres southwest of Madrid; it was the last Republican barrier between the Nationalist forces and the capital. Bethune turned to poetry to express his feelings. "Red Moon" would be published nine months later in the *Canadian Forum*.[55]

And this same pallid moon tonight,
Which rides so quietly, clear and high,
The mirror of our pale and troubled gaze,
Raised to the cool Canadian sky.

Above the shattered Spanish mountain tops
Last night, rose low and wild and red,
Reflecting back from her illumined shield
The blood bespattered faces of the dead,

To that pale disc, we raise our clenchèd fists,
And to those nameless dead our vows renew,
"Comrades, who fought for freedom and the future world,
Who died for us, we will remember you."

The CASD chose the occasion of a huge rally in the Mutual Street Arena in Toronto on Wednesday, 21 October 1936, to publicly announce Bethune's medical mission. The focus of the meeting was a Spanish delegation sent by the Republican government to make a North American speaking tour to counter Nationalist propaganda. The delegation was made up of Isabel de Palencia, the Spanish ambassador to Sweden; Marcelino Domingo, a former Spanish minister of education; and Father Luis Sarasola, a Basque Roman Catholic priest. Despite pouring rain, the arena was filled, hundreds of people standing.[56] Many held placards or banners and wore red, yellow, and purple streamers, the colours of the Spanish flag. A band in red blazers played pop tunes, but at a signal from A.A. MacLeod, the meeting's chairman, it struck up the "Internationale." The audience rose to its feet cheering as the three Spaniards, followed by Bethune and several CASD officials, made their way to the platform. The Spaniards spoke in turn for nearly two hours, vividly describing the bitter struggle being waged in their country, the crowd frequently interrupting their speeches with applause. The final speaker, Isabel de Palencia, concluded: "*When* we win, not *if* we win, we shall have won because there is unity in my country. And this," she cried, raising her clenched fist, "is their symbol. We know that we are helped by the support, material and moral, of all the nations of the world. For this, to you, my Canadians, I give my thanks."

The crowd rose, cheering wildly, fists clenched above their heads. When the applause ended, MacLeod announced that the CASD had made arrangements to send a medical mission to Spain, and pointing to Bethune, said he would lead it. To thunderous applause, MacLeod called for donations towards the necessary medical supplies, and people pushed to the platform to give money. The representatives of labour unions and other organizations presented cheques. The largest donor was the CPC, which handed over a cheque for $1,000.[57]

MacLeod then introduced Bethune as "Canada's ambassador to Spain," and Bethune spoke briefly. "I stand here as a believer in democracy and as a humanitarian in the traditional role of the doctor to minister to those who need us," he told the crowd. He stressed the need for medicines, and their cost: for example, he hoped to take 1.5 million units of insulin to Spain, and this alone would cost $2,500. "Just remember," he concluded, "more people are going to die of plague and tetanus in the coming siege of Madrid than will ever be killed by the enemy." As he returned to his seat, Marcelino Domingo clasped him in a Spanish *abrazo*.

The Spanish delegation was scheduled to speak in the Mount Royal Arena in Montreal on Friday night. On the morning of Thursday, 22 October, religious and political groups in Montreal sprang into action. The Roman Catholic diocese of Montreal charged that Father Sarasola was an apostate whose opinions regarding the situation in Spain were contrary to those of the pope and the bishops of Spain and warned Catholics not to listen to him.[58] The statement received wide coverage in French-language newspapers and radio stations, and *La Presse,* the most popular French-language Montreal daily, refused to run a paid advertisement for the Friday night rally. Meanwhile right-wing political elements accused the Spaniards of being communists and threatened to break up the meeting by force. The Montreal City Council and the chief of police discussed banning the meeting to avoid rioting and damage. However, they feared that doing so would lead to left-wing retaliation at a huge rally on Sunday night organized by the Roman Catholic diocese of Montreal; a crowd of 100,000 was expected to attend. In the end the council decided not to act.

On Friday morning MacLeod and other CASD representatives tried but failed to convince diocesan officials that they were wrong about Father Sarasola. Later, several hundred students from the University of Montreal chanting *"A bas les communistes!"* forced their way into City Hall, where they warned officials that they would use violence to break up the meeting at the Mount Royal Arena unless the city council banned it. Following an emergency session, the council gave orders to the chief of police to bar the doors of the arena that evening. Learning of the ban, CASD officials scrambled to find another location, and that afternoon rented an auditorium in the Victoria Hall in neighbouring Westmount. But by mid-afternoon the Westmount chief of police informed them that he would not allow the meeting to take place. The CASD then rented a small meeting room in the Mount Royal Hotel.

By 8 PM a hostile crowd of 2,500 had gathered at the arena. Many were armed with canes and sticks, some were singing, and others shouted anticommunist slogans. Convinced by the police that the auditorium would stay closed, the mob began to disperse. But having heard that the Spanish delegation might speak instead at the Victoria Hall, a group of more than three hundred marched there. Later, learning that the "the communists" were meeting at the Mount Royal Hotel, they set off in that direction. At 8:30 the nearly one hundred people who had come to hear the Spanish delegation were taking their seats in Salon D of the hotel. Frank Scott, the meeting's chairman, announced that Bethune would speak after the three Spaniards had outlined current conditions in Spain. But at 9:15 the hotel manager appeared, saying that the police had warned him that two mobs were making their way to the hotel; he asked Scott to end the meeting in fifteen minutes. Angry murmurs sped through the audience as the meeting continued.

At 9:30 PM the management cut the electricity, plunging the room into darkness. Scott was able to maintain order and to convince the audience that the safety of the Spanish guests must be their first concern. A group of men escorted the three Spaniards to their rooms in the nearby Windsor Hotel, and the audience dispersed. Several newspaper reporters then approached Scott and Bethune for comments. Bethune criticized city officials for their meek submission to fascist threats and the overt restriction of free speech. He had hoped that the scheduled rally in the Mount Royal Arena could match the $4,000 donated in Toronto. He added angrily, "The Montreal authorities are responsible for the deaths of 1000 innocent women and children by their refusal to give a hearing to the Spanish delegates."[59]

As Bethune made his way back to the Shisters' home, Montreal police continued to disperse the mob. The following morning, 24 October, he left for Quebec City to board the *Empress of Britain,* carrying medical supplies including surgical instruments, anti-toxins and serums, and blood transfusion apparatus. A Canadian Press reporter interviewed him as he was about to go up the gangplank. The reporter commented that recent news reports suggested Franco's forces might take Madrid before Bethune reached Spain. Bethune replied: "Whether or not Madrid falls before the invading forces, I will complete my mission."[60]

Frank Scott later said of Bethune, "The Canadian Communist Party was too small [for him]. He needed some great dramatic attraction where he felt his particular qualities could be put to use."[61] Spain offered that broader stage. While in Toronto, Bethune had visited the studio of the artist Charles Comfort; on a piece of paper he had sketched the Spanish flag and written, "Viva Espana. Long live the revolution." Half playfully, half-seriously, he added his own epitaph for future reference: "Born a bourgoise [*sic*], died a communist."[62] With his Marxist colours nailed proudly to his mast, he was setting sail for the unknown.

At Ray Brook. Even after his bout with tuberculosis Bethune remained an inveterate smoker. Courtesy BMH

The Royal Victoria Hospital, Montreal. Bethune spent the years from 1928 to 1932 learning and practising thoracic surgery at the Royal Vic. Courtesy BMH

Dr Edward Archibald. Bethune's mentor in thoracic surgery admired his brilliance but criticized what he considered to be Bethune's "just a little dangerous" method of operating. Courtesy BMH

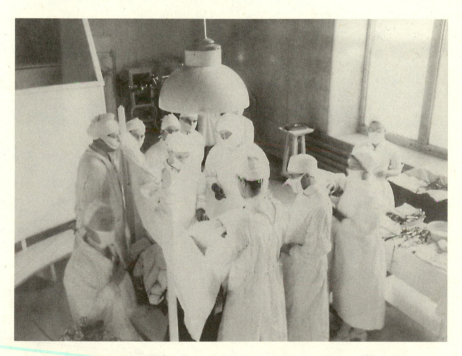

Assistant thoracic surgeon. The speedy and impatient Bethune (back row, centre) deplored Archibald's cautious operating style. Courtesy BMH

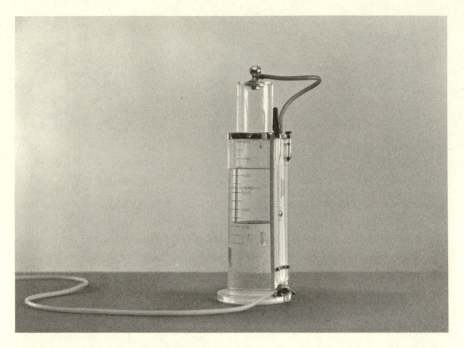

Bethune Pneumothorax Apparatus. Bethune's apparatus came with an attached foot pump. NFB/LAC PA-160618; reproduced by permission

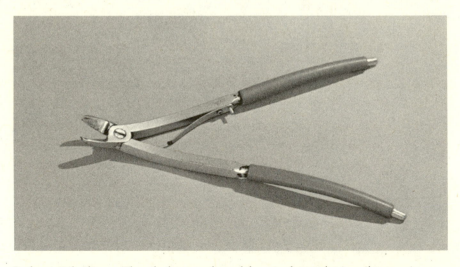

Bethune Rib Shears. The rib shears, adapted from a shoemaker's nail cutter, is the only one of Bethune's instruments still used today. NFB/LAC PA-160723; reproduced by permission

Night Emergency, 1935. This canvas, painted by Bethune on a dare, was accepted for the Annual Spring Exhibition of the Art Association of Montreal and awarded a prize. Courtesy Royal Victoria Hospital

Christmas card, 1935. Bethune's holiday greeting promoted his pet pneumothorax treatment and included his Compressionist's Creed. LAC E010788158; reproduced by permission

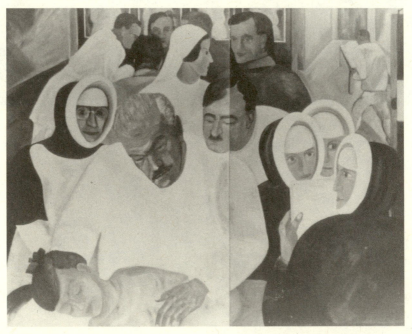

Surgeon at Sacré Coeur. Fritz Brandtner's painting commemorates Bethune's first operation at Sacré Coeur. Courtesy BMH/Fritz Brandtner estate

ANESTHETISTS HEAR DR. NORMAN BETHUNE

Surgeon Discusses New Method At Convention Here

Surgeon Startles Medical Assembly

Intravenous evipal anesthesia, developed in Germany five years ago, is the most pleasant anesthetic for thoracic surgery, Dr. Norman Bethune, chief surgeon of the Sacred Heart Hospital at Montreal, told the Mid-South Post Graduate Nurse Anesthetists' Assembly in convention session yesterday.

"The fast induction of the dissolved white crystals in the veins makes the anesthesia especially effective with fractures, dislocations, abdominal operations and amputations," he said. "If a patient begins to count when the anesthetic is being given, he will be asleep before he can count to 15 at a moderate speed."

The effects of the anesthesia wears off in a half hour, according to Dr. Bethune, and there is no masking, no struggling and no ill effects afterwards.

Other speakers on yesterday's program were Miss Emma Easterling, Vicksburg, Miss, who spoke on "Preparation of the Patient for Anesthesia"; Dr. Gilbert J. Thomas, Minneapolis, "Choice of Anesthetics in Surgery for Kidney and Prostatic Diseases"; Dr. Frederick A. Coller, Ann Harbor, Mich., "Water Losses by Surgical Patients in Relation to the Anesthetist"; Miss Blanche G. Petty, Little Rock, "The Patient's Viewpoint"; Dr. R. H. Jaffe, Chicago, "The Anemias with Special Reference to Their Significance in Anesthesia"; and Dr. C. R. Crutchfield, Nashville, "Spinal Anesthesia."

Mrs. Jennie Houser, chief anesthetist at the General Hospital, was named president of the Tennessee State Anesthetists' Association early last night to succeed Mrs. Louise Gilbertson, of Memphis. Mrs. Gertrude Alexander Troster, with the Crisler Clinic was elected vice president; and Jean O'Brien, of Campbell's Clinic, secretary-treasurer. The directors, all of Memphis, are Jewel Fink, Eleanor Burkhead, Irene Dixon, Pauline McClelland, Alice Little, Mrs. Lucy Gaffney, Bessie Caldwell and Grace Skinner.

Today's session will be featured by the election of officers of the Mid-South Assembly of Anesthetists, and addresses by Miss Grace Skinner, Memphis; Mrs. Gertrude Alexander Troster, Memphis; Miss Margaret A. Price, New Orleans; Dr. Claude S. Beck, Cleveland; and Dr. C. R. Straatsma, New York. Sessions are held at the Peabody.

UNPAID TAX STATUS

(Continued From Page One)

killed the authority by which the tax was impounded and hence released the grower from any tax which had accumulated.

"Frees R," Says Author

Senator Russell of Georgia

Photo caption: Dr. Norman Bethune, the Montreal surgeon who startled the Mid-South Medical Assembly with his proposed socialized medicine, is shown on the left. Next to him, from left to right, are Dr. C. H. Sanford, Memphis, chairman of the program committee; Dr. C. R. Crutchfield, Nashville, incoming president, and Dr. H. King Wade, Hot Springs, retiring president.

SURGEON ADVOCATES

(Continued on Page Three)

operation because we have hundreds who can not pay anything. If medicine was socialized as it is in Russia, the doctors could be paid by a tax on everyone. They would receive salaries commensurate with their ability, as officers in the army and navy. True, we never would make much money, but persons should not enter the profession to get rich."

Dr. Bethune pleaded for a re-examination by medical men of their position under the present economic system.

Elementary Obligation

"There is little hope for a great improvement of the health of the people until the practice of medicine is liberated from its debasing aspects of private profit and taken as an elementary obligation of the state," he said.

He said that the government was "exploiting the medical profession by its non or reduced payments in taking care of the chronic unemployed or unemployable," and asked that the profession become more politically minded in realizing the inseparability of health and economic security.

"Let us abandon our so-called splendid scientific isolation and grasp the realities of the present social crisis. A change is coming and already the craft of Aesculapius is beginning to feel beneath it the great nurse and movement of the

Ickes Refuses to Pose With Talmadge

SPRINGFIELD, Ill., Feb. 12—Photographers seeking to make a picture of Secretary Ickes and Governor Talmadge shaking hands at Abraham Lincoln's tomb fared 50 per cent today.

Talmadge, critic of the New Deal, agreed to pose with the Roosevelt cabinet member, but Ickes replied emphatically:

"I will not."

only right in one out of three. He termed the tuberculin test as "old stuff."

"with a fluoroscope I can tell in 60 seconds whether a person has tuberculosis," he said. It is an X-ray device with which a physician can detect lung cavities without the necessity of a photograph.

Dr. Bethune admits that his scheme for fighting tuberculosis would require a large sum. "But think of the money being spent on the dole and many of those on relief have tuberculosis. The lower you go in the social scale the more tuberculosis you will find. The disease now is costing this country $300,000,000 a year."

Proposes a Clinic

For Memphis, he would have a clinic with equipment costing $12,500; $48,000 more a year for technicians' salaries and supplies; sanatoriums with 2,000 beds, $5,200,000; yearly cost for an estimated 2,000 patients, $1,778,500, plus $50,000 a

FOUR ESCAPE DEATH AS PLANE CRASHES

Desert Wind Forces Ship Down In New Mexico

ALBUQUERQUE, N. M., Feb. 12—(AP)—A private cabin biplane, caught in a stiff desert wind, was demolished today in a forced landing in which the four occupants were shaken and injured, one critically.

A veteran New Mexico flier said it was a "miracle" B. C. Skinner, owner and pilot, and his three companions were not killed. Buffeted by the wind over Enchanted Mesa 50 miles west of Albuquerque, they landed at Acomita.

Miss Vivien Skinner, 22-year-old daughter of the pilot, Dunedin, Fla., manufacturing company official, suffered internal injuries and fractures. L. B. Keller, 34, employed by Skinner, and his niece, Miss Beatrice Keller, 22, and the pilot were badly shaken and bruised. They were flown here by Maj. A. D. Smith, division superintendent of the Transcontinental and Western Air Line, after 'an emergency radio call from the Acomita field. All were taken to a hospital.

"We struck a bad squall over Acoma (famous 'sky city' of the Pueblo Indian tribe)." Skinner said.

Making headlines in Memphis: Bethune electrified the Mid-South Medical Assembly by proposing socialized medicine. Courtesy BMH

Frances Bethune Coleman. Bethune's ex-wife eventually divorced her second husband, A.R.E. Coleman, and returned to Scotland. Courtesy BMH

Marian Dale Scott. The Montreal artist's love affair with Bethune was deeply felt but remained platonic. Reproduced by permission of the Art Gallery of Ontario/George Youssef

Recuperating from jaundice. In this watercolour he sent to Marian Scott from Cartierville, Bethune coloured himself bright yellow. LAC C-142809; reproduced by permission

Self-portrait, 1935. Bethune sent this painting as a gift to Marian Scott, along with a note stating that if her husband didn't want her to hang it in their house, she should return it. Courtesy BMH

Bethune's apartment in Beaver Hall Square. Bethune added a large window to his new apartment to allow plenty of light for painting. Courtesy BMH

Margaret Day Surrey. Bethune's former lover married the artist
Philip Surrey in 1938. LAC E010788157; reproduced by permission

Session of the Children's
Creative Art Centre. The
group met every Saturday
in Bethune's apartment.
Some of the children's
paintings later won awards
in Paris. Courtesy BMH

Blood

Madrid, November 1936–January 1937

Arriving in Madrid, the geographical and political heart of Spain, Bethune found himself in a city under siege. While he had been crossing the Atlantic, Nationalist forces had overrun the last Republican defence posts thirty kilometres southwest of the city and reached its western outskirts. German Junker 52 bombers then launched the first of a series of heavy air raids on Madrid. Their targets were not military. The aim of the daily bombing, inspired in part by the professional curiosity of Franco's German advisers to determine its effect, was to terrorize the civilian population. Meanwhile, a well-equipped and battle-hardened Nationalist force of nearly twenty thousand had begun taking up positions along the left bank of the Manzanares River on the city's western edge. Under the command of General Emilio Mola, the Army of Africa had a nucleus of Foreign Legion and Moroccan troops. Madrileños dreaded their arrival, for the legionnaires' motto was "*Viva la muerte!*" (Long live death), and panicked rumours circulated of the Moors' stealth and ferocity.

Facing the Nationalists on the right bank of the river was a hastily formed force made up mainly of militia groups belonging to the two most powerful unions, the socialist Unión General de Trabajadores (UGT) and the anarchist Confederación Nacional del Trabajo (CNT). The well-disciplined Fifth Regiment formed by the Communist Party was also there. Though the defending force of almost thirty thousand was larger than the Army of Africa, few of the defenders had received military training. *Milicianos* (militia men) were members of units formed by their own occupational group, such as railway or construction workers, teachers, graphic artists, or barbers. Most of the officer class of the Spanish army had gone over to the Nationalists, so there were few officers left to organize and command them. Even worse, there was a serious lack of weapons and ammunition.

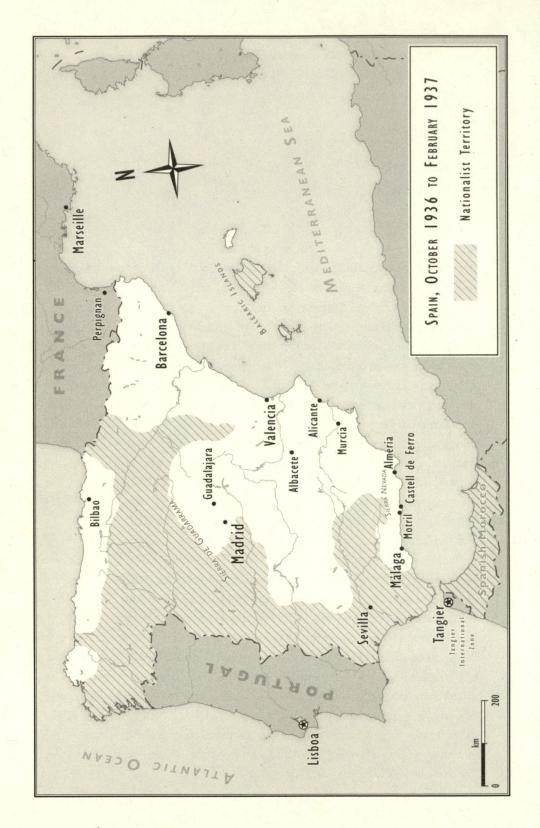

Spain, October 1936 to February 1937

Nationalist Territory

MEDITERRANEAN SEA

FRANCE

Marseille

Perpignan

Barcelona

BALEARIC ISLANDS

Valencia

Alicante

Guadalajara

Murcia

Albacete

Almería

SIERRA NEVADA

Castell de Ferro

SIERRA DE GUADARRAMA

Motril

Bilbao

Madrid

Málaga

Spanish Morocco

Sevilla

PORTUGAL

Tangier

Tangier International Zone

ATLANTIC OCEAN

Lisboa

km
0
200

The Nationalists boasted that once Franco gave the order for the all-out attack, Madrid would fall in a matter of days, and this was accepted as likely by most foreign observers, including members of the diplomatic corps and international journalists. When a reporter asked General Mola which of his four army columns would lead the attack on Madrid, he responded that, in addition to his regular troops, he was also relying on a "fifth column" inside the city.[1] To the people of Madrid, the message was clear and terrifying: there were among them an unknown number of Nationalist sympathizers who would commit sabotage or murder to weaken the city's defences and aid the attackers. The more than eight thousand fascists held in various Madrid prisons were already known, but the wave of fear inspired by Mola's remark led to attempts to root out the fifth column. More known and suspected fascists were arrested in the last days of October, and on the pretext of being transferred to other prisons, some were led from their cells, driven to secluded locations, and executed.[2]

Such was the tense situation in which Bethune found himself after a journey of ten days. His ship had stopped briefly in Southampton before continuing to France where it docked at Cherbourg. Taking a train to Paris on the morning of Friday, 30 October, he had found a hotel room and made his way to the Spanish Embassy on the Avenue George V. There he met with the ambassador, Luis Araquistain, and produced a letter written by the Reverend Benjamin Spence identifying him as a representative of the CASD. Then he handed over an envelope containing $1,000 in American Express money orders. This sum, he explained, had been collected by the CASD for whatever purpose was desired by Spanish medical authorities.[3] In response, Araquistain had a member of his staff prepare a *salvo conducto* (safe conduct) for Bethune to allow him to enter Spain.

Bethune had then dashed out to buy additional anti-tetanus vaccine and surgical instruments. Over the weekend, as he waited for the first available flight to Madrid, he kept in telephone contact with Matthew Halton, a Canadian journalist in London who was filing stories on Spain for the *Toronto Star*.[4] On Monday, 2 November, during his final telephone conversation with Halton before his plane took off, Bethune mentioned that a fellow passenger was André Malraux, the French novelist, who was going to serve in the España Squadron, an international air force that had already been in action against Nationalist forces since the early days of the war.[5]

Bethune's flight stopped at Toulouse, Barcelona, and Alicante before reaching Madrid.[6] From the airport he took a taxi to the Avenida Gran Vía, the main east-west artery of the city, where two hotels that had become the favourites of the resident foreign press were located. One was La Florida and the other, several blocks to the east, was the Gran Vía, where Bethune found a room. Across the street was the city's tallest building, the Telefónica; the Foreign Press Office, which censored all stories cabled by the foreign press, was located on its fifth floor.

Less than twenty-four hours after his arrival, Bethune found out for himself just how pervasive was the psychology of fear in the city. El Bar Chicote in the Hotel Gran Via was the favourite watering-hole for international journalists and other foreigners attracted to the conflict in Spain. It was here that Bethune would later make the acquaintance of such luminaries as John Dos Passos and Ernest Hemingway (not surprisingly, Bethune and Hemingway did not hit it off).[7] In the bar Bethune struck up a conversation with Ilsa Kulcsar, an Austrian journalist. Saying that it would be easier to talk away from the crowd, he persuaded her to go for a walk. When they returned to the hotel, Kulcsar excused herself, saying she had work to do, and Bethune went back to the bar. As he was talking to another journalist, he noticed a *miliciano* watching him intently.

A short time later Bethune again left the hotel and strolled along the Gran Vía, followed at a distance by the *miliciano*. When he paused to look into a store window, the man confronted him, addressing him in rapid Spanish of which Bethune could not understand a single word. The man placed one hand in his jacket and motioned to the hotel entrance. Thinking he might have a gun, Bethune decided not to argue and returned to the hotel, the *miliciano* close on his heels. In the lobby Bethune saw a concierge who had spoken to him earlier in English, and he asked him what the agitated *miliciano* wanted. The *miliciano* thought Bethune was a fascist, the concierge explained: his long trench coat, suit and tie, porkpie hat, pencil moustache, and military bearing all fitted the part. Besides, the *miliciano* insisted, he had heard Bethune say the word "fascist" in the bar. The concierge and *miliciano* began to argue, and Bethune slipped upstairs to his room. Minutes later there was a knock at the door. Opening it, he was confronted by a man holding a briefcase, flanked by five *milicianos*, one of them his pursuer. Identifying himself in English as a policeman, the man asked Bethune for his papers. After carefully examining his British passport and the *salvo conducto* provided by Araquistain, the policeman returned them and left without comment.

Less than a minute later, there was another knock and Bethune braced himself for more trouble. But this time the caller was a tall, sandy-haired man in his thirties who identified himself as Henning Sorensen (1901–86). Before leaving Canada, Bethune had been told that Sorensen, a Montrealer who had gone to Spain in early October, would meet him in Madrid. Digging in his suitcase for a letter he had brought from Canada for him, Bethune described the events of the past half-hour. Then the door flew open, and the policeman and his five-man escort burst into the room. The policeman snatched the envelope from Sorensen's hand, ripped it open and began to read the letter. Beginning with the salutation, "Darling," it was an emotional lament from Sorensen's lonely girlfriend back in Montreal. Sorensen, who spoke Spanish, explained to the policeman what the letter was about. The policeman returned it, mumbled an apology, and ushered his visibly disappointed comrades out of the room.[8]

Born and educated in Copenhagen, Sorensen had come to Canada in 1929. He spoke several languages, and this had allowed him to find translation work with the Sun Life Insurance Company of Montreal. As the Depression deepened, his concern for the plight of the unemployed had led him to become interested in socialist ideas. Eventually he joined one of the several Marxist study groups covertly formed by Sun Life employees.[9] He had followed the outbreak of the conflict in Spain and, believing as Bethune did that its outcome would decide the struggle between communism and fascism, had decided to do something to aid the Loyalist cause.[10]

In mid-September he quit his job and bought a ticket on a Polish steamer sailing for Copenhagen the following week. His hope was that his knowledge of Spanish and French would enable him to obtain press credentials from the Copenhagen socialist newspaper *Socialdemokraten* to which he could send reports from Spain. Learning of Sorensen's plans, Graham Spry and Frank Scott had visited him on the eve of his departure. They explained their plan to form a committee to send medical assistance to Spain and told him they needed reliable information on developments there. They proposed that he act as an accredited correspondent of the *New Commonwealth* and the *Canadian Forum*, and Sorensen accepted.[11]

He now explained to Bethune the developments that had led to the wave of fear and suspicion that gripped Madrid. Though the incident with the *miliciano* had ended in comic-opera fashion, it revealed the degree of paranoia provoked by fear of fifth columnists. Disgusted to hear he resembled the fascists he had come to fight, Bethune immediately shaved off his moustache and took off his jacket and tie.[12] From that point on he wore sweaters, often a yellow turtleneck, under his trench coat. Apparently realizing for the first time that his inability to speak Spanish was a serious disadvantage, he set about convincing Sorensen to give up his journalistic ambitions temporarily and become his interpreter. Sorensen soon fell under the sway of Bethune's magnetism. Believing that he had come on a mission of mercy to help the Spanish people and needed his aid, he agreed to work with him. In any case, the idealistic Sorensen had already become deeply disillusioned with the members of the press he had met. Referring to them as hard-drinking "scoundrels and prostitutes," he complained that they were insensitive to the scenes of misery and death they reported.[13] Bethune told Sorensen that with his help he would offer his services as a surgeon to the Spanish medical authorities.

However, a full-scale enemy assault was expected any minute; loudspeakers on the roofs were playing the "Internationale" continuously, and foreigners were being told to go to their respective embassies. Thus the two men had to separate temporarily, Bethune to spend the night at the British embassy and Sorensen at the Danish embassy.[14] The following morning Sorensen suggested that Bethune should speak directly to the chiefs of surgery at the largest hospitals, so they went first to the Palace Hotel, which had been converted into Hospital No. 1 in the early days of the war. There they waited for several hours while a stream of wounded arrived from the front. At last Bethune managed to speak to a surgeon, but the best he could get from him was an offer to contact him at a later date. Bethune and Sorensen would visit several more hospitals that day, but at each of them Bethune was told that chest surgeons were not needed. In all of the hospitals Sorensen sensed an unspoken but deeply felt objection: Bethune's usefulness was limited because he could not speak Spanish.

Even more extensive bombing of the city now began. German and Italian aircraft attacked all residential areas with the sole exception of the upper-middle class district of Salamanca, the home of many fascist sympathizers. Madrid became the first city in history to undergo systematic daily aerial attack, and Bethune later found vivid words to describe the horror he witnessed:

Standing in a doorway as these huge machines flew slowly overhead, each one heavily loaded with bombs, I glanced up and down the streets. People hurried to "refugios"; a hush fell over the city – it was a hunted animal crouched down in the grass, quiet and apprehensive. There is no escape, so be still. Then in the dead silence of the streets the songs of birds came startlingly clear in the bright winter air ... If the building you happen to be in is hit, you will be killed or wounded. If it is not hit, you will not be killed or wounded. One place is really as good as another.

After the bombs fall – and you can see them falling like great black pears – there is a thunderous roar. Clouds of dust and explosive fumes fill the air, whole sides of houses fall into the street. From heaps of huddled clothes on the cobblestones blood begins to flow – these were once live women and children.

Many are buried alive in the ruins. One hears their cries – they cannot be reached. Burst water and gas mains add to the danger. Ambulances arrive. The blackened and crumpled bodies of the still-alive are carried away.[15]

Bethune and Sorenson trudged from hospital to hospital with the shrill screams of sirens dinning in their ears. They passed through streets where buildings were aflame or had been reduced to smouldering rubble. In the Avenida Castellana they had to throw themselves to the ground, narrowly escaping injury as a bomb exploded nearby. Through it all trucks moved slowly through the streets, their loudspeakers blaring the Loyalist slogan "*No pasarán!*" (They shall not pass).[16]

Witnessing this onslaught on helpless civilians, Bethune raged at not being able to find a place where his training could be of use. The following day he tried again. He and Sorensen visited Hospital No. 5 near the working-class district of Cuatro Caminos in northwest Madrid. They were unable to meet Dr Juan Planelles, the hospital's administrator and director of health services for Madrid. However, they were introduced to Tina Modotti, one of Planelles's assistants. She was an agent of the Socorro Rojo Internacional (International Red Help), a Communist organization that had assumed responsibility for health services in the areas under Republican control. She mentioned that she was also the partner of Carlos Contreras, the political commissar of the Communist Fifth Regiment and an important functionary in the International Brigades (IB), a volunteer force organized by the Comintern.[17] Made up of men from many countries who were arriving in Spain to aid the Loyalists, the Brigades had begun to take shape in the middle of October.

Modotti's words gave Bethune a new idea, and that evening he told Sorensen he was going to approach Contreras to ask for a place as a surgeon in the Brigades. But when they went the next day to see Contreras at the headquarters of the Fifth Regiment, he was disappointed again. Contreras snapped, "We're defending Madrid. I'm too busy. Come back tonight. There's a bus leaving for the front." Eager to at least see some of the fighting, Bethune arrived with Sorensen that evening, only to learn that the bus was going instead to the Brigades headquarters in Albacete, southeast of Madrid. They took it anyway, and arrived there at 4 AM on Saturday, 7 November.

After a brief sleep they were introduced to Dr Pierre Rouquès, a Frenchman who was setting up a base hospital for the Brigades. Rouquès told Bethune that he would welcome him as a member of his staff. He invited him and Sorensen to accompany him on an inspection, saying that during the drive they could discuss the role that Bethune might be able to play. They set out before dawn on Sunday morning in Roquès's car, arriving nearly eight hours later at 1B headquarters in Vicálvaro on the eastern outskirts of Madrid. However, Bethune had grown more and more impatient with Roquès, who had made several wrong turns in the road, and whose answers to his questions were vague. "I can't work with that bastard," he growled to Sorensen. "He doesn't know what he's doing."[18]

At Vilcálvaro they had lunch with several Brigades officers and caught up with the latest developments. There they learned that the Republican prime minister and his council had left Madrid and retreated to Valencia, granting authority to General José Miaja to take control of the city's defence forces. Miaja had then formed a Junta de Defensa (defence council), composed of representatives from the unions and political parties, which had issued orders to the various militia units facing the Nationalists along the banks of the Manzanares River. Early on Saturday morning the Army of Africa had launched the long-expected attack. Its major thrust was directed at the Casa de Campo, a heavily treed area, once the royal hunting grounds, that the Republican government had converted into a public park. To the surprise of the attackers, the militia units, which had been retreating for more than a month, did not give way despite heavy losses, and by nightfall on Saturday there had been little change in the position of each side. The Nationalists had renewed their attack on Sunday morning. Meanwhile Miaja had ordered General Emilio Kléber to lead the XI International Brigade out of Vicálvaro to reinforce Loyalist forces at the Casa de Campo.

This news electrified Bethune. The battle was now well into its second day, and he knew that doctors must be desperately needed. He was sure he would find a place to serve under General Kléber, so he and Sorensen headed back to Madrid. The defenders had once again managed to stop the enemy advance, but before dawn on 9 November, Bethune and Sorensen were awakened by the boom of artillery little more than two kilometres away. Kléber had set up his headquarters in the area of the Ciudad Universitaria (University City), the sprawling campus of the University of Madrid high above the right bank of the Manzanares near the north end of the Casa de Campo.[19]

Trying to locate the general, Bethune and Sorensen took cover in a building with XI International Brigade soldiers who crouched below the open windows, taking quick aim and firing before ducking the answering hail of bullets from the enemy thirty-five metres away. Keen to see the fight, Bethune paced from window to window ignoring the bullets whining around him and the shouts of the others to get down. Sorensen was awed by his supreme confidence that he would not be hit.[20] When they finally got to see General

Kléber, they found him to be outgoing, talkative, and best of all, fluent in English. Bethune took an immediate liking to Kléber, who offered him a position as a front-line surgeon. His only caveat was that Bethune would have to obtain the approval of Dr Fritz Fraenkel, chief of the medical services of the XI International Brigade. But Bethune's hopes were dashed once again: after waiting impatiently for two days, he learned that Dr Fraenkel had refused to accept him.[21]

A frustrated Bethune now gave up on offering his services as a surgeon. It had never occurred to him that he would be rejected without explanation, and it was a humiliating end to his dramatic and public journey to fight fascism. To give up and go home would be embarrassing, so he began casting about for something he could do. He never considered joining the International Brigades as a soldier, for despite his rhetoric about the need for violence to achieve political ends, he was a saviour of lives, not a fighter.[22] At this critical point he remembered that Dr Rouquès had said that the Brigades desperately needed ambulances, and that these could be bought in Valencia.

Bethune now seized upon the idea. He sent a cable to the CASD requesting that $3,000 be wired to him immediately and that another $1,000 be transferred to a bank in Valencia.[23] On the same day, in a postcard to Marian Scott, he wrote, "Going to Valenzia [sic] to buy ambulance. No doctors needed but medical supplies."[24] However, he and Sorensen had to wait for a ride to Albacete, from where they could catch a train to Valencia. On the morning of 14 November they were still in Madrid, part of a crowd absorbed in watching the largest aerial battle over the city since Soviet fighter planes had arrived a week earlier. The conflict between fourteen Italian Fiats and thirteen Soviet planes had stopped traffic, and people were cheering on the Soviet planes, shouting, "*Son nuestros, son nuestros!*" (They're ours, they're ours!). Caught up in the excitement, Bethune kept exclaiming, "Oh boy, oh boy, what a dogfight!"[25]

Arriving in Albacete, he and Sorensen spent the night and then took the train for Valencia. During the early part of the journey Bethune brooded, saying little. Then he burst out, "Henning, I've got it!" Marrying his new focus on ambulances with his previous experience performing blood transfusions, he had come up with an idea. During their visits to Spanish hospitals he had seen many wounded *milicianos* being brought in on stretchers in a state of shock. His experience as a stretcher-bearer during World War I had taught him that soldiers who bled a great deal went into shock and died, while those who were treated before losing too much blood often survived. Even some of those who had lost a great deal of blood sometimes revived if they received a transfusion, he told Sorensen. However, during World War I there had been few transfusion facilities near the front, and the process required specially trained doctors as well as donors whose blood type matched that of each of the wounded. Although direct transfusion was a useful method, it had serious limitations because the distance that separated the wounded in battle area from transfusion facilities caused much loss of life. He had been pondering these problems, he said, and had come up with an idea. Why not rush whole blood to the wounded in refrigerated ambulances? The blood could be typed and extracted from donors in advance, stored in bottles, and preserved by adding sodium citrate; it could then be transferred by ambulance to hospitals or casualty clearing stations where the wounded were arriving during a battle.[26]

By coincidence, a service similar to the one that Bethune was now planning already existed in Spain. Set up by Dr Frederic Duran i Jordà in Barcelona, it had begun to operate in September 1936, delivering blood by refrigerated truck and train to the Aragon Front west of the city. However, in October Franco had made Madrid his main target, and conflict on the Aragon Front came to a virtual standstill. Few outside the Aragon Front, including officials of the Socorro Rojo Internacional in Madrid, knew of Duran i Jordà and his work, so it is almost certain that Bethune too was unaware of it.[27]

He likely realized that setting up a mobile blood transfusion service might have other advantages beyond succouring the wounded. If he had joined a Spanish hospital team or found a posting with the XI International Brigade, he would have been serving as an anonymous member of a group. Reports of his performance as a surgeon in either situation would not have been particularly newsworthy in Canada. On the other hand, if the CASD could point to an independent Canadian organization operating near the front lines in Spain, Canadians would be much more likely to donate funds to support it; a service to deliver life-giving blood to the desperately wounded would surely have enormous public appeal. There was a Scottish ambulance unit and also an English hospital unit in Madrid, Bethune told Sorensen: why should there not be a Canadian blood transfusion unit? And surely the thought crossed his mind that if he could persuade the authorities to grant him permission to head such a unit, he would have the independence of action that he always craved.

Although Sorensen was caught up at once in Bethune's enthusiasm, he told him there was no hope of establishing such a service without the backing of the Socorro Rojo Internacional. So the day after they arrived in Valencia, they went to the organization headquarters. With Sorensen interpreting, Bethune outlined his plan to several officials. The conservative doctors among them were deeply sceptical. They pointed out that while Bethune's idea might have merit, it had to be tested, and wartime conditions were hardly appropriate for medical experimentation.[28] Bethune pressed his ideas, arguing that to save lives they could not wait until there were ideal conditions, and now was the time to take a chance. Finally the officials admitted that his plan might work – but what about the cost of setting up and maintaining such an operation? They had no money to spare to pay for laboratory equipment, refrigerators, various types of blood transfusion apparatus, a specially equipped vehicle to transport the bottled blood, and the salaries for various medical and support staff personnel. Bethune confidently assured them that the entire operation would be financed with money sent from Canada. Convinced at last that the blood transfusion service would be financially self-sustaining, the Spanish officials consented to Bethune's plan and offered to provide a location in Madrid out of which he could operate.

Sorensen was taken aback at Bethune's promise that all funds for the blood transfusion service would come from Canada, for Bethune certainly had no clear idea of costs and he had given his word to the Spaniards without consulting the CASD. When Sorensen raised the question during their return trip to Madrid, Bethune replied that the CASD simply could not refuse. Back in Madrid he sent a cable to the CASD informing them of the commitment that he had made on their behalf for the establishment of a blood transfusion service. He added that he was now en route to Paris to purchase equipment and needed more money at once. His confidence was justified, because the same day, apparently without question, the CASD chairman, Benjamin Spence, authorized the sending of another American Express money order to Bethune in Paris. The amount of $2,000 was added to $3,000 sent earlier in the week.[29] In another letter Bethune wrote excitedly, "A real snappy service can be set up with special badges for donors, stars for each donation ... it's a beautiful idea ... and Canadian!"[30]

On Saturday, 21 November, Bethune and Sorensen flew to Paris, where they began visiting medical supply companies to purchase equipment. But despite Sorensen's assistance as interpreter, Bethune soon became frustrated by the language barrier. The next day he told Sorensen that he was going to London where he would have no difficulty locating the required supplies. Sorensen was to remain in Paris until summoned. Having lived in London for several years, Bethune knew exactly where to find the most recent papers on research in hematology, and he may have contacted doctors there who he knew might be able to provide him with advice on the project he was about to launch.[31] There he also set about finding a vehicle to be used to deliver bottled blood, and for this purpose he bought a wood-panelled Ford station wagon. (Because of the light tone of the wood, the Spaniards would fondly refer to the vehicle as *la rubia*, the blonde.) He had installed in the interior a kerosene-operated refrigerator, a sterilizer, a gas-operated autoclave, a kerosene-run incubator, and a distilled-water still. Even with all this equipment there would still be enough space for storing bottles of blood.

Because he and Sorensen would be driving the new vehicle through France en route to Spain, Bethune went to the French Embassy in London to ask for a *laisser-passer*, hoping to avoid paying duty on the ambulance and its contents. However, France was one of the signatories of the Non-Intervention Agreement by which European nations had pledged their neutrality in the Spanish conflict, so Bethune's request was refused. A French official conceded that if he were able to provide assurance from the Canadian high commissioner, Vincent Massey, that he was a bona-fide physician, he would authorize a *laisser-passer*.

At Canada House, Massey agreed to look into the matter as quickly as possible and asked Bethune to return. However, after investigating in response to Massey's cable, the Canadian government refused to cooperate.[32] On Monday, 30 November, Bethune returned to Canada House only to be informed by Lester B. Pearson, then first secretary of the Department of External Affairs and attached to the High Commissioner's Office at the time, of the Canadian government's decision. Desperate to salvage something from his efforts, Bethune persuaded Pearson to provide him with a letter of introduction on Canada House stationery. However, the letter was not enough to convince the official at the French embassy, who told Bethune that he would have to pay duty on his vehicle and the medical supplies that he was taking into France.

Meanwhile, Bethune had found another volunteer. On Sunday 29 November, he had called on Cluny Dale, Marian Scott's brother, who lived in London. Dale offered to introduce him to Hazen Sise, another Montrealer who was deeply interested in the conflict in Spain. Dale telephoned Sise and suggested that he take Bethune out for dinner that night and then go on to the Royal Albert Hall to attend a rally in support of Republican Spain. Just after 6 PM Sise answered the doorbell of his Chelsea apartment. On the doorstep stood a ramrod-straight figure. "I'm Norman Bethune," the visitor announced. Then he marched upstairs to Sise's studio and plunged straightaway into a description of wartime conditions in Madrid. Despite the brutal aerial bombardment and the attempt of the Army of Africa to break through the city's western defences, he told Sise, the heroic Madrileños had not wavered. Bethune's description of the suffering of the civilian population and his own visceral response to it had an electric effect on Sise, and before Bethune had finished, he blurted out, "My gosh, I would like to go with you!" Later, after leaving the Royal Albert Hall, Sise said to him, "I'm quite serious about this. I would like to go back with you. I've been so immensely concerned for months about what is going on there." Bethune replied that he would have to obtain the permission of the CASD and promised to cable Benjamin Spence in the morning.[33]

The day before, Bethune had also cabled Sorensen in Paris; he arrived in London on Monday, and Bethune brought him up to date on the events of the past week.[34] Meanwhile, the CASD had immediately cabled their approval for Sise to enter what Bethune had begun to call "the unit." After introducing the two men, Bethune explained that he had bought all of the necessary supplies except for a few items they could purchase in Paris. A final task before they left was to pick up the new uniforms he had ordered. Rather than purchase standard ones, Bethune had designed his own. Made in imitation of the *mono azul*, a garment worn by *milicianos*, they were cloth-belted, light-blue coveralls with a zipper running from crotch to neck.[35] On the chest pocket beneath a red cross was the word "Canada."[36]

With Bethune at the wheel, the three set off at dawn on the drive from London to Folkestone, where they boarded a ferry to cross the Channel to France. At French customs in Boulogne, Bethune, to his chagrin, had to pay the equivalent of $1,200 in duty on the Ford and the medical supplies. On the way to Paris he refused to consult a map, insisting that he didn't need one, and they soon got lost; only after wandering about for some time did he get them back on the right route.[37] During their brief stay in Paris they made the rounds of medical supply houses for equipment that Bethune had been unable to find in London. Bethune next visited the Spanish Embassy, where he obtained a *salvo conducto* for Sise and papers to allow the Ford to enter Spain. He also gave money to the ambassador to be used to purchase anti-tetanus serum.[38]

Just before they left Paris they fastened to the side of the station wagon a canvas sign bearing the words "Service canadien de transfusion." As they drove it through the Rhone valley, it attracted the attention of workers along the highway, who saluted them with clenched fists. On Tuesday, 8 December, they passed through Spanish customs at the town of Port Bou, a few kilometres south of Perpignan. After the nearly five-hour run south to Barcelona, they stopped overnight while mechanics repaired a problem that had developed in the Ford. When they picked up the vehicle the following morning, the manager of the garage refused Bethune's offer of payment and wished them good luck on their twelve-hour journey south to Valencia, which was now the Republican capital.

At the headquarters of the Socorro Rojo Internacional in Valencia, Bethune met with the officials who had agreed to back his blood transfusion service and outlined the plan that he had worked out in detail after his research in London. Discussions continued until late Friday, when he, Sise, and Sorensen left on the drive northwest to Madrid. The Socorro Rojo had already selected quarters for the unit in the Salamanca district, on the east side of Madrid several blocks north of the Parqué del Buen Retiro. Inhabited by middle and upper-middle class Madrileños, Salamanca had so far been spared from the daily aerial and artillery attacks on the city that had begun on 16 November. The headquarters of the Socorro Rojo Internacional was located on the third floor of a seven-storey building at Principe de Vergara 36. On the floor below was a luxurious eleven-room apartment seized from a lawyer who had acted as legal counsel to the German Embassy.[39] This now became the quarters of the Instituto canadiense de transfusión de sangre (Canadian Blood Transfusion Institute), the name chosen by Bethune for the unit. The Socorro Rojo Internacional also agreed to provide the Instituto with several Spanish doctors and nurses and some lab technicians.

Bethune and the others examined the apartment, and on 14 December they moved in their various pieces of equipment. An elevator and a flight of broad, winding steps led to the second floor and a glass door that opened onto a large foyer panelled in green damask. Bethune had chosen this as a reception and waiting room. On the right off the foyer was a large room where they set up most of their equipment: two operating tables on which blood donors would lie, a refrigerator to store the blood, and an autoclave to sterilize bottles and instruments. On the left off the foyer was the library, with shelves holding more than eight thousand books lining three walls. This became the administrative centre. To the right off the library was a den and to the left a bedroom, which Bethune decided would be his. Directly off the foyer was a long hall, with three bathrooms on one side and bedrooms used by Sise, Sorensen, the cook, a maid, and the doorman on the other. At the end of the hall was the kitchen.

It is important to note that an arm-to-arm blood transfusion service was already operating at the Faculty of Medicine of the University of Madrid. Bethune's plan was to set up a system, which he later described as a glorified milk-delivery service, to collect blood from donors at the Instituto and deliver it on call to hospitals and casualty clearing stations near the front lines. When required, his team could also perform transfusions there. To find donors, he organized radio and newspaper appeals stating that the Instituto would open on 19 December. He was very nervous about whether the Madrileños would respond, knowing that without donors the Instituto could do nothing. But he counted on the dramatic appeal of a service to replenish the blood of the wounded and on the heroic spirit of the Loyalists.[40] Peering out the window on that Saturday morning, he was delighted to see a long line extending around the block. For the next several days the members of the Instituto registered donors without taking blood. After learning the name, address, and blood type of each person and receiving a pledge that the individual had never been afflicted with syphilis or hepatitis, they explained that each would be notified when to arrive to donate blood. Soon after the unit opened, they were able to test for various diseases with their own laboratory, which was set up by an American technician named Celia Greenspan.[41]

Bethune realized that how much blood should be collected would be determined by the demand. He would have to persuade officials in the five Madrid hospitals, which had qualified staff and facilities to give transfusions, that his innovative method of delivering whole donated blood would work.[42] He was also uncertain of how long the blood could be preserved after sodium citrate was added; his research indicated that a safe limit was less than two weeks, although there was a possibility that it could last longer. Only experience would provide the answer. There was also an unforeseen technical hitch at the outset. When Celia Greenspan opened the refrigerator to examine the first lot of blood that had been donated, she found that all seven bottles had frozen overnight.[43] Bethune had to buy a refrigerator operated by butane gas to replace the kerosene-operated one they had brought from London.[44]

In ten hectic days following their arrival in Madrid, Bethune and his team had managed to set up their quarters and attract and register many potential donors. The chaotic situation in besieged Madrid left him free to operate as he saw fit, and he made the most of the opportunity. Energized by the drama of the situation, he was in his element. On Christmas Eve he gave the first of several radio talks that were beamed to North America on the shortwave station EAQ. The final sentences revealed his elation and his millenarian optimism: "What Spain does today, what you Spaniards do tomorrow, will decide the future of the world for the next hundred years. If you are defeated the world will fall back into the new dark ages of Fascism – if you are successful, as we are confident you will be successful, we will go forward into the glories of the new golden age of economic and political democracy.

Remember we Canadian workers are with you. We have come here as into the opening battle of the world revolution. Your fight is our fight. Your victory is our victory. Ask us how we can help you. You will find us ready to respond. *Salud*."[45] Giving these radio talks was an adventure in itself. Sise later recalled how he and Bethune drove through the darkened streets of Madrid to broadcast at 2 AM from the cellar of a building off the Avenida Gran Vía. There, in a small room, its high windows barricaded with mattresses against bomb blasts, they spoke into microphones, wondering whether anyone was listening.[46]

The plan was to begin collecting blood after Christmas. So after Bethune gave his first broadcast, he, Sise, and Sorensen drove into the Guadarrama Mountains northwest of the city to inspect several hospitals. At one of them Bethune made the most of an opportunity to visit a fortified outpost at the front. Travelling with an officer in an armoured car, they climbed high into the mountains and arrived at an abandoned sanatorium where an alpine battalion was stationed. The commandant and some of the other soldiers, all in their twenties, had brought their wives to the post to celebrate the holiday. They received the Canadians warmly and invited them to join the party. Despite the snow covering the ground, the day was mild and the afternoon sun bright. A table and chairs were brought outside, and while the women set out food and wine, a soldier produced a guitar and began to play. After lunch their hosts took them back to the hospital but returned on Christmas Day to guide them to the headquarters of a nearby ski battalion. From there they gazed down on El Escorial, the magnificent sixteenth-century palace built by King Philip II, now being used as a hospital. Bethune and the others went skiing on borrowed equipment, and later that afternoon drove down to visit the hospital. The experiences exhilarated Bethune, who regarded the Loyalist fighters as ideal representations of the people he had come from Canada to support. "They have a wonderful morale up there," he later told Fredrick Griffin of the *Star Weekly*. "They have real discipline. All comrades, of course, good proletarians, but they snap to attention and salute their officers."[47]

He returned to Madrid in high spirits, absolutely certain now that in committing himself to communism he had made the right decision. He believed that the movement he had joined would sweep the world, root out the greedy and corrupt, and establish peace, justice, and prosperity for all. And he himself was at the forefront of events, doing something to aid suffering humanity. It seemed to him that in Spain a new world was dawning before his eyes. In his second radio talk on EAQ on 29 December, he referred to the conversion of the Palace Hotel into a military hospital that was now serving the common people: "Its operating room … with tremendous crystal chandeliers and glittering gold mirrors, has eight tables side by side, each staffed by two doctors, an anaesthetist and nurse. Here some of the most famous surgeons of Spain, the equal, to say the least, of any country in the world, are at work. Each on his own specialty. This first one is a famous brain surgeon who is now exploring a wound of the head. He once received $5000.00 for a similar operation in private practice; now he does it gladly for his $1.00 a day. Next to him a great abdominal surgeon is sewing up carefully multiple perforations of the intestine … This is his 20th operation today. He is tired and weary but his love of his countrymen, his pride in his art is as high as ever."[48]

Bethune had told Frances long before that a doctor should ideally offer his services freely to all, and, like a medieval monk, should be fed, clothed, and housed through acts of charity. Seeing doctors motivated by the need to serve rather than the lure of fee for service seemed the confirmation of everything he had argued for in the past. On Christmas Eve he had sent an open letter to members of the Canadian medical profession via the CASD. In it he had written: "I am undertaking this work as a doctor and a humanitarian … We doctors cannot stand aside and view the present tragic situation of millions of desperate people without physicians and adequate medical aid with the detachment of any political opinion. To come to the relief of human suffering is the historic and traditional role of the medical profession. Our duty is plain and inescapable. There are at present hospital and ambulance units in Spain from England, Scotland, France and Scandinavian countries. Canada should be and must be represented. It will be. May I urge you to join with me in this non-political humanitarian effort?"[49]

The Instituto canadiense de transfusión de sangre was ready to begin collecting and delivering blood after Christmas, but already there were tensions within the unit, most of them relating to outsiders. From the beginning Bethune had encouraged members of the foreign press to visit the Instituto. With his instinct for public relations he knew that international coverage of the setting-up of the transfusion service would draw attention to the Republican struggle against the besieging fascist forces. Back in Canada this would help raise funds to support his work. During his first weeks in Madrid he had met most of the foreign newsmen in the city at the bar in the Gran Vía Hotel. Knowing they shared his love of drink, he kept an ample supply of alcohol at the Instituto, so even after they had written their stories about the unit, some journalists continued to make social visits. Knowledge of the Canadian blood transfusion service also spread throughout the small foreign community in Madrid. Officials from legations and from the International

Brigades, among others, soon learned that the door of the Instituto was always open to those wanting to enjoy a drink, a chat, and a brief escape from the danger that surrounded them daily.

However, not all members of the unit were comfortable with Bethune's open-door policy. Celia Greenspan, who was never able to adapt to Bethune's helter-skelter ways, wrote to her husband in Valencia, "This place is getting to me. It's used as general meeting place ... and as a club."[50] Sorensen was even more critical, and Bethune's failure to carefully screen all visitors alarmed him. One night at the end of a party at the Instituto, Bethune escorted one of the guests, a Scandinavian journalist, back to her residence. On his return he strutted into the dining room where the staff was eating a typically late Spanish dinner. "I know two people who just had a good fuck," he boasted. Far from being amused, Sorensen reminded him of the rumour that Felix Schlayer, the Norwegian consul, was offering protection to fifth columnists in the Norwegian Legation.[51] Bethune should be more careful about his social contacts, he said.

Sorensen was also upset by Bethune's habit of treating the Instituto as a hotel, inviting guests for extended stays. During the first two weeks of its operation, several individuals moved in. One who stayed for several weeks was Claud Cockburn, writing under the name Frank Pitcairn for the London communist newspaper *The Daily Worker*.[52] Another was the English scientist J.B.S. Haldane, who arrived in late December and stayed for two weeks.[53] Haldane in turn brought another guest, Vera Elkan, a South African photographer living in England who had come to Spain to make a film on the International Brigades.[54] An attractive young woman, she immediately appealed to Bethune, who invited her to stay at the Instituto until she found other accommodation. Shortly after she arrived, he invited her to have a pre-dinner cocktail. While Sorensen mixed the drinks, Bethune sat beside her and asked to look at her hand. Taking it gently in his, he gazed intently at the lines on her palm then looked up, smiling, and said, "You are a nice person." As if on cue, Elkan murmured, "May I sleep with you tonight?" Bethune did not hesitate to offer her a warm bed, and until she left in January she frequently accompanied him as he delivered blood to field hospitals and casualty clearing stations.[55]

Another woman who arrived in late December was Kajsa Rothman (1900–69), a Swede. Tall, blond, and sexually uninhibited, the thirty-three year old Rothman had worked as a nursemaid for a French family and as a marathon dancer. After arriving in Spain in early 1936, she had established a travel agency in Barcelona. She was the daughter of a former part-owner of the *Karlstad-tidningen*, a liberal Swedish newspaper, to which she sent articles on the Spanish Civil War; she also contributed to Radio Madrid's Swedish broadcasts.[56] Her reason for visiting the Instituto, she told Bethune, was that she wanted to write a book about him. They retired to his bedroom almost immediately after her arrival and remained there for the better part of two days. When Bethune emerged to tend to Instituto business, he said that Rothman was a journalist who was conducting an in-depth interview with him. Then, with a lewd grin, he added, "or vice versa."[57] He made no attempt to be discreet about the liaison. One morning in early January, Celia Greenspan knocked on his door with papers for him to check. When he told her to come in, she found him and Rothman in bed together, naked. Embarrassed, Greenspan said that she would return later, but Bethune insisted on dealing with the papers there and then.[58] Rothman would stay on in the Instituto until March, performing various administrative tasks in addition to her role as lover.

This open-house policy and Bethune's naiveté in assuming that everyone who visited the Instituto was politically reliable eventually spurred Sorensen to act. He had taken an instant dislike to Rothman, and other minor incidents had disturbed him.[59] In January 1937 someone complained to the director of the Socorro Rojo Internacional about lack of security at the Instituto, and it is likely that this person was Sorensen. Shortly after the complaint was made, police officers entered the Instituto and took all the foreigners into custody. Bethune, Sorensen, and Sise as well as Haldane, Rothman, and an Austrian named Hurturg were arrested. All except Rothman and Hurturg were released after they were identified by the director of the Socoro Rojo Internacional. Rothman was detained for some time but then set free. Hurturg was not so lucky – he was executed as a spy.[60]

However, despite the security problem, the Instituto functioned well. The unit began to collect blood after Christmas, calling on the donors who had registered the previous week. After receiving the assurance that the donor had fasted, a necessity to eliminate contaminating fats from the blood, and that he or she did not have syphilis, a 500 cc donation was extracted.[61] Through a tube, it flowed into a bottle to which was added a small amount of sodium citrate. The type of blood, donor's name, and date of the extraction were recorded on a label fixed to the bottle. The blood was then placed in a refrigerator and chilled to between 2 and 4 degrees Celsius. Donors at first received a chit to purchase a small amount of food; later each was given a tin of bully beef instead and offered a shot of brandy.[62]

The delivery of blood began near the end of the last week in December, but it was not until early January that the unit administered their first transfusion. Shortly before 3 AM on 3 January, they received a telephone call urging them to come immediately to the small village of Fuencarral on the northern outskirts of Madrid. Bethune roused Sorensen and their guard, picked up his bag of instruments and several bottles of blood from the refrigerator, and headed downstairs to the Ford. Driving through the pitch-dark streets without lights, stopped every few blocks by armed militia guards who demanded to hear the current password, they at last reached their destination. It was a former ducal palace that had been turned into a hospital and detachment centre for a unit of Assault Guards. Following a guard through a series of long halls hung with ornate tapestries, they entered the former chapel of the duke and duchess, now being used as an operating room. Where the altar had stood was an operating table on which lay a severely wounded soldier, clearly in a state of shock. A bullet entering his left thigh had ruptured his femoral artery, causing heavy bleeding. Bethune could barely feel the man's pulse and realized there was no time to test for blood type. He asked Sorensen, whose blood was Type IV, the universal type, to act as a donor. Sorensen pulled off his coat, rolled up his sleeve, and lay on a second table. With Sorensen's blood flowing into his vein, colour gradually crept into the soldier's cheeks and he began to stir. After they returned to the Instituto, Bethune recorded the man's name, the date and the location of the transfusion, and added, "Immediate improvement. Recovery. No reaction."[63]

In a letter written a week later to Benjamin Spence, chairman of the CASD, Bethune described the work done by the unit:

Our night work is very eerie! We get a phone call for blood. Snatch up our packed bag, take 2 bottles (each 500 cc) – one of group IV and one of group II blood – out of the refrigerator and with our armed guard off we go through the absolutely pitch dark streets and the guns and machine guns and rifle shots sound like as if they were in the next block, although they are really half a mile away. Without lights we drive, stop at the hospital and with a search light in our hands find our way into the cellar principally. All the operating rooms in the hospitals have been moved into the basement to avoid falling shrapnel, bricks and stones coming through the operating room ceiling.

Our bag contains a completely sterilized box of instruments, towels etc. so we can start work at once. The man is lying most frequently on a stretcher so we kneel down beside him, prick the finger and on a slide put 1 drop each of Serum type II and type III. If his red blood cells are agglutinated by II and not by III – he is a type III. If agglutinated by II he is a III, if by both he is a type I, if neither, he is a group IV.

So now we know what blood he can take safely. If I, III or IV he gets our bottle of blood group IV (the universal blood). If he is a II he gets blood group II. He could also take IV but as these "Universal Donors" are about only 45% of the people, we must use II's when we can. Then the proper blood is warmed in a pan of water and we are ready to start. The man is usually as white as the paper, mostly shocked, with an imperceptible pulse. He may be exsanguinated also and not so much shocked, but usually is both shocked and exsanguinated. We now inject novo-caine over the vein in the bend of the elbow, cut down and find the vein and insert a small glass Canula, then run the blood in. The change in most cases is spectacular. We give him always 500 cc of preserved blood and sometimes more and follow it up with saline of 5% glucose solution. The pulse can now be felt and his pale lips have some color.

Yesterday, we did three transfusions – this is about the average daily, besides the blood we leave at hospitals for them to use themselves. We collect ½ to ¾ gallon daily, mix it with Sodium Citrate (3.8%) and keep it just above freezing in the refrigerator in sterile milk and wine bottles. This blood will keep for about a week …

Well, this is a grand country and great people. The wounded are wonderful.

After I had given a transfusion to a French soldier who had lost his arm, he raised the other to me as I left the room in the Casualty Clearing Station, and with his raised clenched fist exclaimed "*Viva la Revolution*" [*sic*]. The next boy to him was a Spaniard – a medical student, shot through the liver and stomach. When I had given him a transfusion and asked him how he felt – he said "It is nothing" – *Nada*! He recovered. So did the Frenchman.

Transfusion work should be given in Casualty Clearing Stations when they come out of the operating room of the 1st hospital behind the lines and *before* they are sent back to rear hospitals. But as Madrid is the front line, our work is mostly here although we go out 25 kilometers to other parts of the line.[64]

In his letter to Spence, Bethune described the experience of his unit as "a very hectic ten days."[65] The Instituto had undergone a baptism of fire. Hoping to prevent supplies from entering the city, Franco's forces made a concentrated strike at the highway leading out of the northwest corner of Madrid. The offensive caught the Republicans off guard, but they fought back doggedly and when the attack ended in the second week of January, the Nationalist gain was minimal. The performance of the unit during this brief but intense campaign proved that it not only worked but worked well. Although there is no doubt that Duran i Jordà's service on the Aragon Front was the first mobile blood transfusion service in Spain, the heavy action on the Madrid Front meant that Bethune's Instituto would in fact deliver blood to far more casualty stations.

In the midst of a besieged city fighting to survive, Bethune's vision and will had in a matter of weeks created a functioning service from nothing and proved that, despite the primitive equipment available, it could be successful in delivering much-needed blood to the wounded.[66] Despite his freewheeling ways, which led to a certain amount of disorganization and various tensions within the Instituto staff, it was a magnificent accomplishment. But far from being content, Bethune was spurred on by the exhilaration of his success: he was already planning to achieve more.

✤ 10 ✤

The Path with Lions

Madrid, Valencia, Almería,
January–February 1937

Ever the "quickener," the activist, Bethune had little interest in the day-to-day details of running the Instituto. Elated by its performance under the pressure of battle, he now wanted to expand its scope. This had been his intention from the beginning, as is revealed in a letter he had written to Benjamin Spence before Christmas: "We have plans to branch out and give the service up in the Guadarrama Mountains up to a distance of 100 miles from the City later and might need another car but this won't be for several months yet."[1] Only three weeks later, he decided that he should create a service to supply forces in all of Republican Spain with blood. In the relative calm that followed the early January campaign, there was much speculation in Madrid about where Franco's forces would strike next. Bethune sensed that the next battlefront might be the southeast coast where Republican forces had a tenuous hold on the city of Málaga, and that blood would be urgently needed there.

In early January he approached officials of the Socorro Rojo Internacional in Madrid, suggesting that other units like the Instituto should be set up throughout Republican Spain. They replied that the scope of his plan placed it far beyond their jurisdiction. The situation had changed, and they no longer had the authority of two months earlier when they had allowed him to create the Instituto. They had assumed responsibility for the care of military casualties then only because most medical personnel in the Sanidad Militar (the army medical bureau) had gone over to Franco in the early days of the Nationalist uprising. But the government in Valencia had now consolidated all military power in the Republican zone, and a unified army under central command was quickly taking shape. Part of that development was a reconstituted Sanidad Militar, and the Socorro Rojo officials told Bethune that he would have to present his proposal to officials in that army department.

So on Monday, 11 January 1937, he and Sorensen left Madrid in the Ford for Valencia. At the headquarters of the Sanidad Militar at Avenida Colón 86, they were directed to the office of Colonel Cerrada. He was one of few army medical personnel who had remained loyal to the Republic, and now had the title of head doctor.[2] With Sorensen interpreting, Bethune outlined his scheme for a unified blood transfusion service to cover all sectors in the Republican zone. Cerrada agreed in principle but drew Bethune's attention to two problems. The first was financial: where would the money come from? Bethune's response was instant. He was certain that the same source that was funding the Instituto, the CASD, would be willing to provide financial support for the expanded plan. Cerrada then went on to a second problem. Dr Frederic Duran i Jordà had already established the Barcelona Blood Transfusion Service, and no plans for a unified service to cover all of Republican Spain could be made without his cooperation.[3]

It seems more than likely that by this time Bethune knew about Duran i Jordà's work, having learned about it sometime after taking possession of the apartment on Principe de Vergara in December.[4] Realizing that without Duran i Jordà's participation, Cerrada would not support his plans for a unified transfusion service, Bethune said that he would go to Barcelona at once to meet the Catalan doctor. The following day, after a twelve-hour drive, he and Sorensen reached Barcelona and found rooms in the Hotel Continental in the Rambla Catalunya. In the morning they went to Hospital No. 18 to see Duran i Jordà. After showing Bethune his facilities and discussing with him their respective techniques of collecting and storing blood, the doctor listened to Bethune's plan for a uniform service throughout the Republican sector. He was prepared to accept the idea, with certain modifications. The major change, as Bethune later informed Sise in a letter, was to make Barcelona, not Madrid, the collection and distribution centre. "We propose to start a 'shuttle' service from Barcelona to Valencia, Madrid and Cordova [sic] with distributing centres at these other points," he wrote.[5] Bethune was clearly not in a position to argue. Duran i Jordà was an expert hematologist, which Bethune was not, and the Catalan's blood transfusion service had been first in the field. It was also obvious that Duran i Jordà's facilities and equipment were more sophisticated than those in the Instituto, and that he had developed a method for collecting and storing blood in packaged pressure ampoules, which Bethune recognized was superior to the use of bottles by his unit in Madrid.[6] So he accepted Duran i Jordà's conditions. A tentative agreement was reached, and Bethune handed over 3,000 pesetas to be used for the purchase of equipment.[7]

After examining Duran i Jordà's refrigerated railway car and two large refrigerated trucks, Bethune decided to buy a similar truck and have it outfitted with refrigerators, which he was able to buy in Barcelona. When he was unable to find a truck that met his requirements, he and Sorensen took the train to Marseille on 16 January to look for one. Several days later they found a 2.5 ton Renault, which Bethune bought. Their task accomplished, Bethune, whose mind was never strictly on business, suggested to Sorensen that they celebrate by visiting a "decent" brothel. A taxi driver deposited them at the Club des Femmes, where the madam paraded a number of women before them. Bethune at once chose a tall, Scandinavian-looking blonde and headed upstairs. Sorensen followed and enjoyed himself with his choice. When he went downstairs, he found Bethune, his sexual mission already accomplished, impatient to leave.[8]

Bethune telegraphed Sise in Madrid to meet him and Sorensen in Barcelona. There Sise ran into Stephen Spender, a young English poet he had met in London. On assignment to *The Daily Worker*, Spender and his friend Tom Worsley had just arrived in Spain.[9] Worsley, a former teacher and freelance writer, was eager to make some kind of contribution to the Republican cause. Sise mentioned that there might be a role for him with the forthcoming expansion of the blood delivery service, and suggested that he come to the Hotel Continental on Friday night when Bethune was expected to return.

On 22 January Sise introduced Worsley to Bethune. As they drank whiskey that Bethune had brought back from France, he told Worsley that he needed another driver for the new unit. He urged him to come back in the morning to try driving the big Renault and decide whether to take on the job. The next morning Worsley joined Bethune, Sise, and Sorensen on a visit to examine Duran i Jordà's two refrigerated trucks and discuss refitting the Renault in a similar fashion. They spent several hours with Duran i Jordà and worked out a plan for the conversion of their vehicle. Enthusiastic about what he had seen, Worsley agreed to join the unit as an assistant driver to Sise.

Bethune was eager to get final approval of the new service from Colonel Cerrada in Valencia. Unfortunately Sorensen could not go along to translate, for he had come down with what Bethune diagnosed as bronchitis; Bethune prescribed medicine for him and told him to take to his bed. Leaving Sise to oversee the conversion of the truck at the General Motors plant in Barcelona, Bethune left in the Ford late Sunday morning. In Valencia he took a room in the Victoria, an upscale hotel a few blocks from the headquarters of the Sanidad Militar. At a meeting with Colonel Cerrada the next day, he described the purchase and refitting of the Renault and outlined the result of his discussions with Duran i Jordà. Cerrada replied that he and his superiors recognized the need for a unified blood service but now realized that it would require considerably more money than the budget of the Sanidad Militar could support. Bethune said he was certain that the required amount to fund such an important project could be raised in Canada. They discussed the costs of the various aspects of his proposal, and Bethune made an offer. In addition to covering the salaries of the three Canadians, the CASD would pay for all equipment for the maintenance of the Madrid operation and also make a substantial contribution toward the cost of the distribution centre in Valencia.[10] In return the Sanidad Militar would be expected to pay the salaries of the Spanish personnel. Cerrada agreed to draw up a contract to indicate clearly the mutual responsibilities of the CASD and the Sanidad Militar, but he warned Bethune that it would have to be approved by the war ministry.

Certain that this was only a matter of form, Bethune left Valencia, convinced that the new operation was a virtual *fait accompli*. He drove to Madrid, arriving on Wednesday, 27 January, and immediately sent the CASD a cable listing the amounts of money he had received from them and informing them of the purchase of the Renault in Marseille. He also discussed the outcome of his meeting with Cerrada: "Our new plan enthusiastically accepted by Valencia government. Will cover all fronts. The scheme is to transfer sealed ampules [sic] by blood refrigeration train from collection centre at Barcelona to ... Valencia. From thence to ten selected front-line points three thousand kilometers apart. This is first time in history such long distance covered. Also maintaining original organization working perfectly on Madrid front."

He also responded rather testily to the CASD's frequent demands for more information from him. "Reason for silence either nothing new or censor forbids. For Lenin's sake be reasonable," he wrote. "Working eighteen hours day. Can't be war correspondent and doctor too. Sent you three letters from France."[11]

But despite Bethune's boast, the Instituto was not "working perfectly." During his two-and-a-half week absence, various latent difficulties had developed into full-blown problems, and he had to stay in Madrid for four days to sort things out. The most important issue was that the Instituto's Spanish personnel were not being paid. Intent on his new project and busy in Barcelona and Marseille, Bethune had forgotten to allocate money for their salaries. He apologized for the oversight and assured the unhappy staff that a new plan of organization would guarantee regular income for them. They grudgingly accepted his promise.

A more serious problem was the lack of system in the operation of the Instituto. Celia Greenspan had quickly noted this flaw after joining the unit in December. Improvising as he went along, Bethune had not created an organizational structure or procedural guidelines, and his frequent absences compounded the problem. When he was there, he was nominally in charge, but during his absences there was no clear chain of authority. Even when he was present, his impatience with details and indifference to organizational trivia irritated the staff, who were at times not sure how best to carry out their duties. Greenspan, who came to see Bethune as "part adventurer, part humanitarian," felt that in some ways his erratic comings and goings actually complicated matters; left to themselves, the staff might have been able to work out a system to make the Instituto function more smoothly.[12]

Keen to make progress on the unified blood delivery service, Bethune set out again for Valencia on the last day of January. But the next day he learned to his chagrin that Cerrada had still not received government approval for the agreement they had reached the previous week. Cerrada also brought up another matter: in the very near future, all health facilities and personnel in the Republican sector, including the Instituto, would be placed under the exclusive control of the Sanidad Militar. Cerrada made the point that the only change would be the title of the unit, which would become the Instituto hispano-canadiense de transfusión de sangre. Bethune would remain in charge with the honorary rank of *comandante* (major), and Sorensen and Sise would become captains. Cerrada ended the meeting by promising to check again with his government superiors on the agreement. He told Bethune to come back on Saturday, 6 February, when he expected to have confirmation.

Despite Cerrada's words of assurance, Bethune knew that the proposed change in the overseeing of the Instituto would be fundamental. His transfusion service had operated with complete autonomy for two months, and he had hoped that the unified service would function in the same way. After his meeting with Cerrada, he knew this would not be the case: from now he would become responsible to the Sanidad Militar.[13] The thought of serving in an army bureaucracy cannot have been appealing to him, but he was still determined to expand the blood service along the lines he had suggested to Cerrada. So convinced was he that he would have his way that after his meeting with Cerrada he sent another cable to the CASD claiming that all had been arranged as he wished:

We have succeeded in unifying all remaining Spanish transfusion units under us. We are serving 100 hospital and casualty clearing stations in the front lines of Madrid and 100 kilometres from the front of the Sector del Centro.

The new name of the Canadian Medical Unit is Instituto Hispano-canadiense de Transfusion de Sangre. I have been appointed director-in-chief as a grateful tribute to Canadian workers and have been given the military rank of comandante. Sise and Sorensen have been appointed captains ...

This is the first unified blood transfusion service in army and medical history. Plans are well under way to supply the entire Spanish anti-fascist army with preserved blood. Your institute is now operating on a 1000 kilometre front ...

Madrid is the centre of gravity of the world. All are well and happy. No pasarán!

Salud Camaradas and Compañeros.[14]

This cable caused considerable consternation when it reached the CASD. Bethune's announcement of broader responsibilities clearly meant that in the future he would be requesting even greater financial support than he had been receiving. Chairman Benjamin Spence convened a meeting to discuss action on the matter. On 8 February the CASD decided to send someone to Spain, ostensibly to help Bethune but actually to check into his handling of various matters. It was announced in the *Daily Clarion* that a "medical man" was being sent. However, the person chosen was in fact Allen May, a Toronto newspaperman who left for Spain later in the month. His mission was to make a thorough report on the activities and finances of the Instituto.[15]

Meanwhile Bethune had sent a telegram to Sorensen in Barcelona announcing the change in status of the Instituto and the conferring of honorary ranks on him and Sise.[16] He told Sorensen to come to Valencia with Sise and Worsley, bringing several ampoules of blood from Duran i Jordà's hospital. However, Sorensen's bronchitis had worsened and he was unable to make the trip. On the advice of a Spanish doctor who feared that he might have tuberculosis, he was admitted to a hospital. Two days later on 5 February, Sise and Worsley reached Valencia in the Renault, which Sise had had refitted with refrigerators and other equipment at the General Motors plant in Barcelona.[17]

They found Bethune in a buoyant mood. He told them about the cable he had sent to the CASD, saying he was sure that he would receive final approval of his plan from the Sanidad Militar at his meeting with Cerrada the following morning. Afterwards, he added, they would leave Valencia and drive south along the coastal road to the city of Málaga, which was at the southern limit of Republican control and the most distant point where blood would be supplied from Barcelona. In that way he could determine the quality of the roads, inspect hospitals along the route, and explain the coming of the new transfusion service; they could also deliver bottles of blood, should they be needed. It would be a good way to try out Duran i Jordà's pressurized ampoules of blood and test the refitted Renault on a route that it would follow in the future.[18]

Bethune's meeting with Cerrada had been scheduled for 10 AM on 6 February, but at noon he, Sise, and Worsley were still cooling their heels outside the headquarters of the Sanidad Militar. Losing patience, Bethune tramped up to Cerrada's second-floor office, only to retreat crestfallen a short time later. He told Sise and Worsley that Cerrada claimed the government had still not decided about his plan for an expanded blood service. Although Cerrada had not admitted it, Bethune sensed that the real problem was that the Spaniards were reluctant to give a foreigner control over the proposed expansion of the service. He may also have realized that Duran i Jordà would not accept serving under a man whose qualifications in hematology were inferior to his own. It is possible as well that Bethune, impatient of bureaucratic bungling and extremely frustrated by the delay, had managed to offend Cerrada and complicate matters further.

Disappointed though he was, Bethune still wanted to make the trip to Málaga, and an encounter in the hotel that evening made him even more determined. Like the Hotel Gran Vía and the Hotel Florida in Madrid, the Hotel Victoria in Valencia was a gathering place for members of the international press. After dinner, Bethune, Sise, and Worsley were sitting in the hotel lounge discussing their upcoming trip with several correspondents when Claud Cockburn, the *Daily Worker* correspondent who had been their guest at the Instituto, approached the group. Bethune invited him up to his room for a drink. He explained his reasons for going to Málaga and laid a map of Spain on the floor, asking for Cockburn's advice on routes. He also wanted Cockburn's assessment of the military situation in the south. Cockburn confessed that the little that he had heard indicated that the Republican position there had weakened considerably.

Bethune knew the background of the conflict in the south. Málaga, a city of 100,000, was in the centre of a thirty-kilometre wide sliver of Republican territory lying between the Mediterranean and the Sierra Nevada and ending a few kilometres north of Gibraltar. The areas to the west and to the north of the mountains were held by the Nationalists. The only land route out of the cul-de-sac was a narrow road that wound along the rugged sea coast to the port of Almería, nearly two hundred kilometres to the east of Málaga. Franco's decision to concentrate on taking Madrid had left the area around Málaga as a relative backwater in the war so far. But in mid-January an offensive led by the Nationalist Army of the South and assisted by a detachment of nearly ten thousand Italian Black Shirts had broken through at several points along the periphery of the Republican territory. During the next ten days these units had moved toward Málaga.

What neither Bethune nor Cockburn knew on the evening of 6 February was that disaster had already ensued. Despite the earlier arrival of crowds of refugees driven into the city by the advance of the enemy, Republican military authorities in Málaga had ignored the danger of their position until the previous day. Then, on Friday, 5 February, five Nationalist warships had appeared to the west of Málaga and begun to shell Republican forces along the coastline. The poorly equipped and badly organized militia units immediately began to flee toward the city, followed only a few kilometres behind by Nationalist troops. On Saturday, as the awareness of the imminent arrival of the enemy spread throughout the city, the military authorities under the command of Colonel José Villalba dithered about what to do. Communist and anarchist militia leaders held hastily convened meetings at which they accused the authorities of treachery. Only the governor of the province acted decisively: in mid-afternoon, without informing anyone, he abandoned Málaga to its fate.

Cockburn had told Bethune that he did not believe that Málaga would fall, adding, "There's no place in Spain hotter right now." Sise chimed in excitedly, "Madrid was the hot spot in November; we were there. Now Málaga, and we'll be there!" Bethune's enthusiasm also kindled – Málaga was the place to be. He announced that they would leave Valencia early the following day.[19] On Sunday morning, 7 February, packed and anxious to get started, he drove Sise and Worsley to pick up the Renault, which was being repaired. But the vehicle was still awaiting a necessary part. A mechanic explained that one could be fabricated within a short period of time, but the task proved more difficult than expected and they had to wait the entire day. It was early evening before Sise arrived at the Hotel Victoria with the Renault, but Bethune insisted they must start right away. He would drive the Ford, and Sise and Worsley the Renault.

By the time they left at 9 PM, the Nationalist assault on Málaga had begun. That morning the city had come under intense fire from warships in the bay and from bombers and from land forces ranged to the north and west. The attackers faced little resistance from ineptly organized militia units that received no direction from their leaders. More concerned about their personal safety than about the defence of the city, the military command had abandoned Málaga that afternoon, slipping away in cars without notifying anyone. Even before the departure of their leaders, many *milicianos* had already begun to rush to the highway leading east to Almería. Behind them came wave after wave of terror-stricken civilians.

Since the outbreak of the war in July, the people of Málaga had lived in fear of the arrival of Nationalist troops, especially the Moors. Their dread had been inspired by the repeated vicious threats made by the Nationalist commander-in-chief, General Queipo de Llano, in his nightly chat broadcasts on Radio Sevilla. "The first sentence that we shall pronounce in Málaga is the death sentence," Queipo warned. Speaking of the Republicans, he charged: "It is true that they are swine and we are gentlemen. They are assassins who open the bellies of women, burn children at their mothers' knees and do things of which we would not be capable … Idiots … Soon you will have your just deserts, although you may hide below the ground, because I will drag you out of there, swine, cowards."[20] Six months of such intimidation had had a chilling effect on the Loyalist populace. Except for the tiny cadre of covert Franco supporters who eagerly awaited the arrival of Nationalist troops, most Malagueñans fled the city in terror. The refugees who had been living in the streets since arriving several days before were the first to go. Neighbour imitated neighbour, and whole families soon joined the throng moving toward the only escape route, the coastal highway to the east. The fortunate few left by car, but the majority were on foot. Before nightfall on 7 February all the streets connected to the highway were clogged with *milicianos* and civilians; they spilled onto the road leaving only a narrow space for the few remaining cars, trucks, and an occasional bus to pass.

While this was happening, Bethune and his companions had run into a raging sandstorm two hundred kilometres out of Valencia. Driving became so hazardous that they decided to stop in the seaport town of Alicante. It was now 2 AM, but they managed to find rooms at a small hotel. In the morning, 8 February, after refuelling their vehicles, they went to tour the local hospital. Bethune's excitement kindled when the commandant told him that he had received an unconfirmed report that Málaga had fallen, and they hurried back to the vehicles. However, Sise discovered that a part of the dynamo that powered the refrigeration unit had broken, and he urged Bethune to wait to have the part repaired. Bethune insisted they had to push on to Málaga at once. At 10:30 AM they were on the road to Murcia, eighty-five kilometres to the southwest.

As Bethune and his companions were touring the hospital in Alicante, the first fugitives from Málaga reached the seaside village of Torre del Mar, twenty-five kilometres to the east of the city. In the lead were militia cavalry, then infantry, many men accompanied by their wives and children. Following some distance behind came civilians, entire families with children and grandparents. A few had mounted mules or rode in donkey carts piled with household goods – a mattress, some pots and pans, a few prized possessions. But most were on foot carrying no more than a bundle of clothing or a suitcase; a lucky few had baskets of food. Already they were overcome by fatigue, and the roadside was strewn with items that had become too heavy to carry.

At a few minutes past 8 AM the first attack on the refugees began. Near Rincon de La Victoria, ten kilometres out of Málaga, two Nationalist fighter planes banked out of the clouds; swooping low above the human flood, they opened fire with their machine guns. People shrieked in terror and threw themselves face down on the road, parents trying to shield their children with their bodies. Some people jumped into roadside ditches, others panicked and ran back and forth, easy targets for the pilots to strafe. The second attack took place two hours later some distance farther to the east and came from the sea. The Nationalist cruiser *Canarias,* accompanied by a destroyer, began to shell the multitude on the Málaga road. It was at a spot where the highway was flanked by a steep rocky cliff on the landward side and a precipice that fell more than thirty metres to the sea on the other. There was no escape for the terrified fugitives. Some were blown apart by the shells and others were crushed under large boulders dislodged from the cliff by the shelling. The gunners were well aware that their targets were not military: so close were the warships to the shore that the fugitives could clearly see the sailors jumping up and down with glee after scoring a direct hit on a mule-drawn cart or a bus.[21] The sole purpose of the attack was to slaughter civilians who supported the Republican cause.

From 8 February to 10 February the shelling continued throughout daylight hours and was sometimes synchronized with air attacks. Even at night the ships' crews used powerful searchlights to locate their victims along the road and spray them with machine-gun fire. Following the assault of the naval and air forces, a unit of Italian Black Shirts pursed the refugees, and by late on the night of 10 February these troops had arrived a few kilometres west of the town of Motril, the halfway point between Málaga and Almería. At the same moment, Loyalist reinforcements were entering Motril from the east where, shamed by the initial flight of their forces, the Republican military command had decided to make a stand against the enemy.

Bethune and his companions had arrived in Murcia on the afternoon of Monday, February 8. After checking in at a hotel, Bethune went to the local hospital to inspect it and discuss his blood transfusion scheme with the military-medical authorities. His inspections continued the following day. At dawn on Wednesday morning, they left in the Renault on the next leg of the journey to Almería, more than two hundred kilometres away. Deciding it was not necessary to continue with two vehicles, Bethune had made arrangements to leave the Ford in Murcia until their return. In Almería he went directly to the local hospital, where officials of the Socorro Rojo Internacional told him that rumours of the fall of Málaga were true. Confirmed reports of sea and air attacks on fleeing refugees also indicated that enemy troops were moving rapidly along the coastal highway behind them, heading toward Motril.

Galvanized by the news, Bethune said they must go on at once, for doctors would be needed. They left Almería at 3:30 that afternoon with Bethune at the wheel of the Renault.[22] After only a few kilometres they began to see small groups moving slowly along the roadside, entire families with mules heavily burdened with family goods. At first the groups were separated by distances of nearly a hundred metres, but soon the gap narrowed until there was an unbroken line that gradually widened as people spilled out on to the highway, forcing Bethune to drive closer to the right-hand edge of the road. These were the first refugees on foot who were nearing the end of their two hundred kilometre trek from Málaga.

About fifteen kilometres out of Almería the road veered inland, rising steeply to the crest of a hill before descending to a vast plain. As they reached the summit, Bethune suddenly slammed on the brakes, and he and his companions got out and stared down at the spectacle below them. As far as their eyes could see, a distance of some twenty kilometres, a broad black column of refugees from Málaga snaked toward them across the plain, following the road. Bethune and the others got back into the truck, and he drove on, keeping his hand on the horn as the masses parted around them. The fugitives were covered with dust and many were barefoot; some had rags tied around their feet, but most had no protection against the sharp stones of the road. Mothers held babies in their arms and fathers plodded along with children draped across their shoulders. Hungry and thirsty, they struggled forward under the blazing afternoon sun; many had not eaten since leaving Málaga days before. Soon Bethune saw a troop of cavalry approaching, followed by larger and larger groups of *milicianos*, their uniforms dirty and torn, their eyes downcast as they silently shuffled along. He and the others estimated that more than three thousand men passed them. He pulled to a halt, hoping to question the civilians, but no one would stop. A few pointed back along the road, uttering the word "*Fascistas!*" but they kept on moving toward the hoped for haven of Almería.

With the human stream flowing around them, Bethune stood in the road beside the Renault debating what to do. Sise reminded him that they had no weapons to defend themselves, and Worsley said that if they met an advance unit of the Italian Black Shirts, they would be easy targets as they tried to turn the big Renault around on a highway crowded with refugees. But Bethune pointed to the inscription on the side of the Renault which read "Servicio canadiense de transfusion de sangre al frente" (Canadian Blood Transfusion Service at the Front). "See that, boys?" he said. "Service at the front. To the front we go."[23] He clambered back into the Renault and started the engine. Sise and Worsley got in and they set off again.

At first they were numbed into silence by their growing awareness of the extent of the tragedy that they were witnessing. Then they began to draw each others' attention to the plight of individuals – people staggering under heavy burdens and forced to the side of the moving throng; elderly persons who had given up and collapsed at the road's edge. But it was the plight of the children that moved Bethune most. Through much of the distance, muttering and cursing, he had tried to keep a count of the children under ten years of age and those who were shoeless, their feet swollen or wrapped in bloodied rags. They numbered in the thousands.[24]

Near nightfall, still nearly twenty kilometres short of Motril, Bethune suddenly stopped the Renault and told the others that they should forget about trying to find wounded who needed transfusions. He had decided to turn the vehicle around, fill it with children, and drive them to Almería. As soon as he opened the back doors, the throng of refugees massed around him. Aware that a miraculous opportunity was presenting itself, the mute, suffering people came to life, shouting, crying, reaching out, begging for a place in the vehicle. Bethune tried to accept only children but was unable to separate them from their mothers; nor was he able to reject two women in the late stage of pregnancy. In a matter of minutes the Renault was crammed with nearly forty women and children. Bethune slammed the doors. Turning to Sise, he told him to drive the refugees to Almería as fast as he could, then return to pick up him and Worsley. Meanwhile they would join the crowd moving toward Almería.

For about an hour Bethune and Worsley tramped along the road in the midst of the weary flood. Bethune began to tire, so they tried unsuccessfully to sleep for a while under some palm trees, then resumed the march again. Around midnight Bethune noticed a stable near the road; inside they found enough straw for a makeshift bed, and Bethune fell asleep immediately. Worsley was unable to tolerate the stench of the dung-covered floor and joined a group gathered outside around a fire. Several hours later he and

Bethune returned to the road. Just before dawn they saw the headlights of the approaching Renault. From the point where Sise had left them on Wednesday night, they had walked seventeen kilometres.[25]

Sise reported that Almería was in chaos, and that no provision had been made to feed or shelter the refugees crowding into the city. After taking the women and children to the Socorro Rojo hospital, he had refuelled the Renault and made his way slowly back along the clogged highway. He had not slept and was obviously exhausted. Bethune quickly decided to fill the vehicle with another load of refugees. He told Worsley to drive to the hospital in Almería. Sise would then go to the hotel to sleep, and Worsley would drive back to find Bethune.

Just one figure more now among the many thousands, Bethune trudged along the coastal road. A short distance east of the village of Castell de Ferro he heard the sound of aircraft. In the clear afternoon sky he saw three Italian Fiat fighter planes attacking two small Republican bombers; smoke suddenly trailed from the engine of one of the fleeing planes which went into an uncontrolled dive and hit the water.[26] Bethune ran down the rocky hillside to the beach, where a small crowd was gathering on the shore. Militia men had already waded into the shallow water to help the crew of the downed aircraft. Two crew members were unharmed, but five others, seriously injured, lay stretched on the sand. Bethune used one of the few Spanish words he knew, "*médico*," to identify himself and rapidly examined the wounded, two of them bleeding badly. Wading out to the plane, he ripped out some wires to use as tourniquets to stop the hemorrhaging. Then he led the way as militia men carried the wounded up the hill to the highway. Somehow he commandeered a truck, and with the wounded inside and Bethune standing on the running board, the vehicle headed for Almería, more than eighty kilometres away.

It was not long before Bethune saw the Renault approaching. He flagged Worsley down and quickly explained what had happened, telling him to return to the spot where they had spent part of Wednesday night in the stable, fill the truck with refugees, and return to Almería. Worsley followed Bethune's instructions, but on his return the Renault broke down and he had to spend most of the night on the road until early Friday morning when a truck towed him and his load into the city. Meanwhile, Bethune continued on to Almería with the wounded airmen. Without medical instruments he could do little for them, and before they reached the city in the early evening, the co-pilot died. In the Socorro Rojo Hospital in Almería, surgeons had to amputate one arm of another crew member. In the same hospital Bethune subsequently performed transfusions on other members of the crew using blood brought in the Renault from Barcelona. Unfortunately, the men died, whether as a result of their wounds, or as Sise suspected, from the blood itself, which had probably deteriorated during the several trips the truck had taken over the rugged coastal road.[27]

Later, Bethune joined Sise at a sanatorium on the outskirts of Almería where he had taken a load of children. To his fury he found that they were hungry and nothing was being done to feed them. He charged into the kitchen, seized some big saucepans and put them on the stove. Cursing all the while and issuing orders in English that were incomprehensible to the Spanish staff, he commandeered all the milk and bread he could find, heated the milk, and crumbled the bread into it. Then he and Sise fed the children and put them to bed. In the morning they found the formerly wan and exhausted children running about playing, "as lively as crickets."[28]

Bethune, Sise, and Worsley now encountered Adrian Phillips, a representative of the International Red Cross. When Bethune discovered that Phillips had no idea of the calamity that had been going on for the past five days and showed no interest in taking any steps to find food and medical supplies for the refugees, he insisted that Phillips drive along the Málaga road to see for himself the scope of the disaster. Phillips reluctantly agreed to do so and also to take Sise in his car. Wishing to record the tragedy occurring on the Málaga road for posterity, Sise asked to be dropped off along the way so that he could spend several hours taking photographs. It was agreed that when the repairs to the Renault were completed, Bethune and Worsley would drive out and pick him up.

By 7 PM on 12 February the Renault was still being repaired. As Bethune and Worsley stood watching the mechanic, the lights suddenly went out and a siren sounded. Seconds later the ground shook and a series of explosions rent the air. As a shower of stone, metal, and glass rained down on them, Bethune pulled Worsley to the floor, yelling at him to cover his head. The deafening bombardment continued for several minutes, then stopped. After a few seconds of silence, they began to hear screams. Raising their heads, they found everything suffused by a reddish-orange glow. From the doorway they could see buildings a block away engulfed in flames. Bethune yanked Worsley's arm and started to run toward the burning buildings. Pushing his way through the crowds of terrified, stunned people, he kept shouting "*Médico! Médico!*" Ahead of them a bomb had destroyed a house. Screaming people covered with blood were trapped beneath jagged pieces of masonry, shattered timber, and a tangle of electrical wires. For the next six hours Bethune worked with others to aid the victims of the bombing. The savage incendiary attack had been carried out by a squad of the German Condor

Legion. Though their bombs did some slight damage to a Republican cruiser in the harbour, their principal target had been the helpless refugees jammed into the city.

Bethune returned to the hotel at 2 AM to sleep. Later that morning, with the Renault repaired, he and Worsley drove west on the Málaga road again. In the early afternoon they picked up Sise some fifty kilometres west of Almería and continued along the road to Motril, meeting fewer and fewer refugees until, rounding a bend, they found the road ahead of them clear for as far as they could see. They drove on a few more kilometres before realizing that they had passed the last refugee from Málaga. Worsley and Sise urged Bethune to turn around, but he was determined to reach Motril where, he argued, there must be refugees in need of medical treatment. They continued to a point about fifteen kilometres from Motril where a military barrier was erected across the road. There an officer turned them back, insisting medical personnel in Motril were attending to those who needed care. Only then did Bethune permit Worsley to turn the Renault around. Catching up with the last refugees, they stopped, filled the vehicle with women and children, and made their way back to Almería, pulling up in front of the hospital just before midnight. It was their last load of refugees. Bethune, Sise, and Worsley had witnessed one of the greatest atrocities of the Spanish Civil War and were the only foreigners who did anything to help the refugees on the Málaga road.

That night Bethune could not sleep. He was furious because of rumours he had heard in Almería that, as elsewhere during the Civil War, disputes had broken out in Málaga between local communists and anarchists. This dissension among left-wing elements had worsened the situation there, contributing to the demoralization and rout of the population from the city and the disaster on the road to Almería. Later, in Valencia, he would fume that there were "about a million of these anarchist bastards that we will have to put up against the wall and shoot."[29] The horrors of the Málaga road and the bombardment of Almería replayed themselves in his mind. The fascists' savage treatment of helpless human beings, particularly children, evoked sheer rage in him, and he burned to express his revulsion. He fired off telegrams to various press organizations informing them of what had happened. Then he sat down and wrote an impassioned account of the three days that he and his companions had spent in their efforts to assist the refugees from Málaga, and described the aerial attack:

And now comes the final barbarism. Not content with bombing and shelling this procession of unarmed peasants on this long road, on the evening of the 12th when the little seaport of Almeria was completely filled with refugees, its population swollen to double its size, when forty thousand exhausted people had reached a haven of what they thought was safety, we were heavily bombed by German and Italian fascist air planes. The siren alarm sounded thirty seconds before the first bomb fell. These planes made no effort to hit the government battleship in the harbor or bomb the barracks. They deliberately dropped ten great bombs in the very centre of the town where on the main street were sleeping huddled together on the pavement so closely that a car could pass only with difficulty, the exhausted refugees. After the planes had passed I picked up in my arms three dead children from the pavement in front of the Provincial Committee for the Evacuation of Refugees where they had been standing in a great queue waiting for a cupful of preserved milk and a handful of dry bread, the only food some of them had for days. The street was a shambles of the dead and dying, lit only by the orange glare of burning buildings. In the darkness the moans of the wounded children, shrieks of agonized mothers, the curses of the men rose in a massed cry higher and higher to a pitch of intolerable intensity. One's body felt as heavy as the dead themselves, but empty and hollow, and in one's brain burned a bright flame of hate. That night were murdered fifty civilians and an additional fifty were wounded. There were two soldiers killed.

Bethune called this account "The Crime on the Road: Málaga to Almería," and with a selection from the many photographs taken by Sise, it was later turned into an effective propaganda pamphlet circulated in France and North America.[30]

On Sunday afternoon Bethune, Sise, and Worsley left Almería for Murcia, where they spent the night. Before leaving there on Monday morning, 15 February, Bethune managed to find a couple of journalists and inform them of the disastrous events of the past week.[31] Then he picked up the Ford and, followed by Sise and Worsley in the Renault, set out on the three-hour trip to Albacete. On the way his mind turned to the Instituto and the need for funds to pay the salaries of the Spanish staff and the cost of other medical supplies that they had told him they badly needed. In Albacete he explained to Sise that he had to rush to Paris to get money and buy supplies and told him to go with Worsley to Madrid, asking him to assure the staff of the Instituto that he would be there soon.

But before he left for Paris, he was intent on finding out from Cerrada whether his proposal for a unified blood service had been accepted, so he drove to Valencia on Tuesday. He sent a cable to the CASD in Toronto to request them to transfer money to his American Express account in Paris, then went to the Sanidad Militar. But Cerrada again said no decision had been reached on his proposal. The refusal of the Spanish authorities to give him an answer must have tested Bethune's self-control to the limit, but there was nothing he could do to force them to act.

Late in the evening of 19 February he reached Paris in the Ford and took a room in the Hotel du Quai-Voltaire, where he and Frances had stayed on their honeymoon. On Saturday morning he contacted Peter Rhodes, a United Press International correspondent he knew. After describing the atrocity on the Málaga road, he told Rhodes that he wanted to make a film about the Instituto and needed to find a photographer. Later that day Rhodes arrived at the hotel with a tall, dark-haired young Hungarian whom he introduced as Geza Kárpáthi.[32] Kárpáthi, who worked for a photographer, suggested that he compose a brief scene and film it as a test. Bethune agreed and gave him money to rent a camera and buy film. On Monday, after viewing Kárpáthi's finished product in a projection room, Bethune offered him a position as photographer at a salary of $50 a week. Kárpáthi replied that his interest was in making a contribution against the forces of Franco and that he would accept only $25. Delighted, Bethune gave him 10,000 francs to buy a camera, film, lights, and other equipment. Kárpáthi took his purchases to the Spanish Embassy for shipment to Madrid and left by train for Spain at the end of the week.[33]

Meanwhile, Bethune had been mulling over an idea inspired in him by the plight of Spanish children orphaned and made homeless by the war. He had thought of this earlier and had spoken of it to Sise and Sorensen, but the emotional impact of the Málaga atrocity spurred him into action. He sent a letter to the CASD describing his plan, which was to establish refuges, which he called "children's villages," in areas far from the battle fronts, perhaps in the Pyrenees.[34] Eager to test the official reaction of the government to his idea, he went to the Spanish Embassy in Paris where he had a meeting with Señora Gertrude Araquistain, the wife of the ambassador. She asked him to send her a written outline of his proposal, and he returned to his hotel to do so. Then he dashed off a telegram to Sise, telling him to bring together some architects he knew in Barcelona and put them to work drawing up plans for a refuge for children in the foothills of the Pyrenees.[35]

Over the next few days he collected various supplies and other items to take back to Madrid. With him was Allen May, the CASD representative, who had arrived in Paris two days before Bethune.[36] Having obtained the funds sent by the CASD and bought the necessary supplies in Paris, Bethune and May left for Barcelona, arriving there on Friday, 26 February. At the Hotel

Continental they met Sise and Worsley who had already arrived in response to a cable sent by Bethune from Paris.

From the rage and horror he had felt in Almería, Bethune's mood had now swung to almost feverish enthusiasm. After introducing May to the others, he invited them all to his room where he began to show off his numerous purchases, not all of which had a medical application. First he brought out a portable gramophone which he wound up and placed on a table. From a stack of new records he chose one and played it. Eyeing the gramophone admiringly, he said, "Cute, eh? Nice tone?"[37] He then unpacked various surgical instruments and other supplies before opening another box and pulling out a handful of glossy photographs that he had had taken of himself in Paris. There were one hundred black-and white prints of each of the two poses he had struck for the photographer. Bold and dramatic, they depicted him head-and-shoulders, artistically posed in three-quarter and profile views. Tossing them on his bed, he chose a handful and at once sat down to sign them. He would later inscribe many of them and send them to friends in North America.

His focus suddenly changing, he dropped his pen and asked Sise if he had acted on the telegram he had sent on Wednesday about the children's refuges. Sise replied that he had needed more detail and had decided to wait for Bethune's return. Bethune seized pencil and paper and began to sketch enthusiastically. When he finished, he warned Sise that although the funds for the project would be Canadian, the concept would have to be presented so as to make it appear to be Spanish inspired. He had noted that even though his idea had evoked praise from Señora Araquistain, she seemed sensitive about foreign interference in Spanish affairs. Just like the Sanidad Militar, he added.

This turned his mind to the unresolved question of the unified blood transfusion service. Saying that he was fed up with Cerrada's evasiveness, he announced that he was going to drive to Valencia on Saturday to confront him yet again.[38] Taking a large roll of Spanish money from his suitcase, he waved it in the air. "Money talks, money talks," he chortled, apparently convinced that despite all he had sensed about Spanish reluctance to put a foreigner in charge of the project, this tangible evidence of Canadian funding would buy the acceptance of a unified service with him in charge.[39] However, Sise later took him aside and warned him that he had learned through Sorensen that Duran i Jordà was putting up stiff resistance to the idea of naming Bethune as chief of the proposed service.[40]

Bethune, May, and Antonio Galan, a member of the Instituto staff, arrived in Valencia on Sunday, 28 February. Despite Sise's warning, Bethune, optimistic as ever and keen for publicity, called together several international correspondents in the hotel lounge and announced that he had returned from Paris with a substantial amount of money for a unified blood transfusion service soon to be set up with him in charge. Breezily assuring the reporters that he would sign an agreement with the Sanidad Militar the following morning, he urged them to meet him in the lounge at 11 AM after his meeting with Cerrada, when he would officially break the news. The reporters showed up, but Bethune did not arrive until 11:30. Looking rather subdued, he told them that the agreement had not been signed and asked them to hold the story until he gave the go-ahead.

He was being less than open, for he now knew there would be no go-ahead. Cerrada had told him that the Sanidad Militar would not put him in charge of a unified blood service and that he had also lost autonomous control over the Instituto in Madrid. Two of the Spanish doctors working there would henceforth share full responsibility with him in its operation. Duran i Jordà's objections and the growing opposition of the Spanish government to putting foreigners in positions of responsibility within the military had blocked Bethune's plans. Part of the problem was his inability to speak Spanish, but there was more to the decision. How much Cerrada revealed to Bethune is not clear, but the Sanidad Militar had been informed by one of the Spanish doctors at the Instituto of the problems that had arisen there, and this had convinced them that Bethune's temperament made him unsuitable to administer a large organization.[41] However, although Cerrada had rejected Bethune as the head of the Instituto and of the proposed unified transfusion service, he had made it clear to him that the Sanidad Militar still expected continuing Canadian financial support for the Madrid unit, as well as the additional funds that Bethune had pledged for the new branch of the blood service in Valencia. Canadian money would indeed flow, but it would not buy Bethune what he wanted.[42]

The decision of the Spanish authorities was understandable, but to Bethune it must have seemed immensely unjust. After all, he alone had conceived the Instituto, and it had been his vision of the need for a unified blood transfusion service that propelled the project into existence. Now he saw himself reduced to the level of just another functionary, subject to the orders of others. It was a bitter draught to swallow, for the shadow side of his keen, questing mind was his inability to work with others unless he led. A road of increasing frustration now opened before him.

Clipped Wings

Madrid, Valencia, March–June 1937

The rejection of Bethune's proposal to lead a unified blood transfusion service marked a turning point in his mission to Spain. It seemed to him that blind bureaucracy was hampering the creation of a desperately needed service that would save many lives. The fact that Cerrada had seemed to encourage his proposal in late January and had led him on for five more weeks only deepened his resentment. Since his arrival in Spain the previous November, he had believed fervently that he was part of a truly revolutionary movement free of bourgeois failings. Now he felt that the administrators of the Republican government were no different from the petty bureaucrats he had known and despised all his life in capitalist society. Feeling betrayed, refusing to accept that to some extent his own behaviour had caused the disappointment of his hopes, he burned with anger.

Yet he realized that somehow he had to save face in Canada, for the substantial financial contributions raised by the CASD had been intended to support a unit led and operated by Canadians. It may have been for this reason that on his return to Madrid on Tuesday, 2 March, he concealed the truth from Jean Watts, a *Daily Clarion* reporter who had arrived at the Instituto while he was in Paris.[1] In her front-page story in the 3 March *Daily Clarion*, the first two sentences were: "The Canadian blood transfusion service headed by Dr Norman Bethune was reorganized today to extend to all fronts of the Spanish war with the control board of two Spanish doctors and the medical man. The project, bearing the official stamp of the war ministry, represents a positive achievement in international cooperation."

Still smarting from his rejection by the Sanidad Militar, Bethune now had to turn his full attention to the operation of the Instituto. On 5 February, Franco's forces, attacking from south of Madrid, had launched a major offensive that became known as the Battle of Jarama. Though falling short of their aim of cutting the road to Valencia, the Nationalists inflicted heavy losses on Republican troops over the course of the month. During Bethune's absence the Instituto had been called into action, and although combat had ended during the last week of February, the casualty list approached ten thousand, and the demand for blood continued after his return to Madrid.

On 8 March the Nationalists attacked Madrid again, this time from the north. The offensive was conducted almost entirely by Italians of the Corpe de Truppi Voluntarie. In response to a call from Dr Douglas Jolly, a New Zealander in charge of the International Brigade hospital in Guadalajara, 60 kilometres northeast of Madrid, Bethune set out on Friday morning, 12 March, carrying ten bottles of blood and a refrigerator. With him in the Ford were Sorensen, Antonio Culebras, who was one of the doctors at the Instituto, and Geza Kárpáthi, who had just arrived from Paris. Reaching Guadalajara, Bethune delivered the blood and the refrigerator. Both were desperately needed, and Bethune later wrote, "We feel fine. We feel like a successful salesman who has just placed a big order for goods. This is great! Isn't it grand to be needed, to be wanted!"[2] He performed a transfusion on a badly wounded soldier,[3] and then, looking for an opportunity for Kárpáthi to shoot some action shots of shell explosions for the film, decided to head out toward the front line.

It was early afternoon, and a light rain began to fall as he turned north on N-11, the main highway. They had passed the village of Torija, about twenty kilometres out of Guadalajara, when they saw a series of vehicles moving south on a hill high above the village of Trijueque, some five kilometres to the north. Losing sight of Trijueque at a bend in the highway, they met a long line of Republican soldiers in headlong flight. Those in the lead waved their arms, warning Bethune to turn around. He had driven into a massive retreat, and the vehicles they had seen, Bethune realized, were most likely Italian armoured cars pursuing the Republican forces.

Ignoring his companions' protests, Bethune drove even faster, past dense crowds of fleeing soldiers. A bullet thudded into a front fender and others whined past. Recognizing that they were now under direct enemy fire, he braked, stalling the engine. As he tried to re-start it, two Republican soldiers jumped on the running board; almost immediately one was hit by a bullet and fell onto the pavement. Realizing he had flooded the engine, Bethune shouted, "Out! Everybody out!" and his companions dove into the muddy roadside ditch. Despite the flying bullets, Bethune ran around to the other side of the vehicle to help the unharmed soldier drag his wounded companion to the safety of the ditch. Crouched there, trying to decide what to do next, Bethune glanced up at the Ford. In the middle of the windshield on the driver's side was a bullet hole: had he stayed in his seat, he would have been killed.

Minutes later the firing stopped. Bethune waited a few moments, then ordered his companions across a field to a wood about a hundred metres away. In the scramble to reach cover, the four lost sight of each other; unable to find Sorensen and Kárpáthi, Bethune and Culebras set out through the fields to Torija a short distance to the south. There they reported to a casualty clearing-station where they worked for several hours before being taken back to Madrid in an army truck. As they were arriving in Torija, Republican reinforcements from Madrid were heading north to end the retreat and drive back the Italians. The Ford was picked up the following day and returned to the Instituto. Sorensen and Kárpáthi made their way back to Madrid separately.[4]

For Sorensen, Culebras, and Kárpáthi, the experience on the Guadalajara road – not to mention Bethune's daredevil performance – had been terrifying. But Bethune had been exhilarated. Sise later noted, "He loved getting in danger. He loved the smell of danger ... It was always very exciting being with Bethune ... He needed that adrenalin in the system that comes from a dangerous situation. I got quite frightened with him sometimes, driving blindly into situations. We never knew whether there was a machine gun around the corner, but he would never pause to reconnoitre. He was the cavalry man type."[5] Bethune himself told an American doctor in the International Brigades, "The front is reality. There is the most beautiful detachment there. Every minute is beautiful because it may be the last and so it is enjoyed to the full."[6]

But perhaps it was Bethune's friend Harold Beament who best explained his eagerness to court danger. In doing so, he put his finger on the nexus of narcissism and humanitarianism that lay at the core of Bethune's character. Years later Beament would say of Bethune's risk-taking:

[It] intensified the concept of drama in relation to himself. Beth, more than most men, had a tendency to sit back and look at his own image, not in the mirror, but in the mirror of life and say, "Oh well, gee, I'm quite a guy. Can't take that away from me," [that] sort of thing. That's very important in understanding Beth ... That emerges as extreme dedication, a man who laid his life on the line time and again, persistently trying to aid people in extremely adverse circumstances. That supplied something that Beth's ego needed consistently ... I'm not taking away from the fact that he really wanted to be of some service, some great service within his reach for mankind. I think he was dedicated totally in that way. But this other vanity thing still is in the picture.[7]

The problem was that, although danger thrilled Bethune, routine duties did not, yet on his return from the Guadalajara front he was forced to deal with them. During his absence in southern Spain, complications had arisen in the running of the Instituto. One of them was a crisis in decision-making. For the first five days after he and Sorensen had left Madrid on 11 January, Sise had been in charge of the unit; then Bethune had summoned him to Barcelona and Sise had been absent for a full month. With no official chain of command, Kajsa Rothman took over the running of the Instituto, but she found it difficult to deal with Culebras and Vicente Goyanes, two of the Spanish doctors assigned to the unit.[8] Rothman was efficient, but she won only grudging cooperation from the Spaniards. Irritated by the way she swaggered about wearing the uniform of a *miliciano* and a Sam Browne belt, they were unwilling to be responsible to someone who was not only a foreigner who had turned up at the Instituto by chance but a woman and Bethune's lover into the bargain.

They were also deeply concerned about the questions of their own salary and rank. Goyanes, who had an army rank of lieutenant, had come with the understanding that he would be promoted to captain. Culebras expected to be granted the same rank. So Bethune had promised in late January to pay Culebras a captain's salary and make up the difference between what Goyanes was receiving in army pay as a lieutenant and the salary of captain. However, Bethune's involvement in the Málaga-Almeria tragedy had delayed his departure for Paris to collect money wired to him to cover the Instituto's expenses, so the Spaniards had had to work throughout February without pay. When Bethune returned to Madrid on 2 March, he paid the back salaries of Culebras and Goyanes and also those of two newly appointed doctors, Valentin de la Loma and Andrés Sanz. But this left him with little money to pay for vital equipment needed at the Instituto. As to rank, when Bethune finally had to admit that the Sanidad Militar had rejected his proposal, the Spaniards realized that his promise to arrange the promotion of Goyanes and Culebras meant nothing.

However, the problems in the Instituto ran deeper even than this. On his return, Bethune had seen for himself that the atmosphere there was markedly different from the cheerful bustle of the early days of its existence. The *élan* was gone, and government rules were reducing efficiency. For instance, strict new regulations had been imposed mandating that only union chauffeurs be permitted to drive government vehicles. In a letter to Benjamin Spence,

Bethune pointed out that a high-ranking officer in the Sanidad Militar had actually been arrested for driving the car given to him for his use.[9] Confronted by such triumphs of bureaucratic red tape over common sense, Bethune more and more often gave way to outbursts of temper.

But it was the attitude of the doctors that disturbed him most. Sise had told him that when he returned to Madrid from Almería on 17 February, he had found them in a hostile, almost rebellious mood and openly critical of Bethune's prolonged absence. They also hinted that because Bethune was not a hematologist, he was not competent to head the unit. Now Bethune could see for himself that some of them showed no enthusiasm for their work, treating it as a mere job; he accused them of being "bourgeois loafers." One of them, he told Sorensen, was most certainly a Francoist sympathizer.[10] Softening his tone considerably for CASD reading, he wrote to Spence that "the Spanish doctors who work with us seem to be incapable of accepting responsibility or acting on their own initiative. Consequently, I am forced to attend to every detail myself."[11] As always, his inability to speak Spanish (and his refusal to learn) complicated matters. "If they want to talk to me, they'll have to learn English," he told one of the correspondents he knew.[12]

As it happened, Goyanes and Culebras, the two Spanish doctors appointed by the Sanidad Militar to share management of the Instituto with Bethune, were the ones for whom he had the least respect. Though he was critical of Goyanes, it was Culebras who antagonized him most.[13] When the latter had arrived at the Instituto, Bethune had agreed to hire his wife, Manolita, and three other persons. Only later did he learn that these others were Culebras's sister, her fiancé, and his brother's fiancée. In a staff of fifteen Spaniards, they constituted a powerful nepotistic faction – referred to by Sise as a "family compact" – in conflicts with the others and with the Canadians.[14] To make matters worse, there was an ongoing feud between Culebras and Loma. These internecine struggles poisoned the atmosphere of the Instituto and reduced its efficiency.

After Bethune's return to Madrid in March, the mutual dislike between him and Culebras exploded into open conflict. Neither Loma nor Sanz shared Culebras's loathing of Bethune, but both sympathized with his unwillingness to serve under a foreigner. Culebras resented his subservient role and wanted to replace Bethune as *comandante* of the Instituto. As a member of the Spanish Communist Party he had some influence, and there is little doubt that he had provided information to the Sanidad Militar designed to undermine Bethune. To him it was sweet justice that from now on he and Goyanes would at least share a degree of control over him. To Bethune, on the other hand, it was humiliating that a man whom he despised and considered a slacker would now share in the management of the Instituto. This injustice, as he saw it, confirmed his contempt for the judgment of the Sanidad Militar.

From the point of view of the Spanish, the behaviour of the Canadians also left much to be desired. Many years later Manolita Culebras wrote of them: "They took up space, they ate, they gossiped, they smoked and they drank up to the point that when there was no more whiskey that they had sent from the United States, they drank the laboratory alcohol."[15] It is highly unlikely that the Canadians actually drank the laboratory alcohol, but there is no doubt that a lot of drinking went on at the Instituto – and by Bethune in particular. He always drank heavily when he was frustrated and upset, which he was from March onward, and this affected his work. Sorensen later recalled Bethune's hands shaking badly while he was giving a transfusion after a drinking bout. Alcohol also often fuelled his destructive rages. On one such occasion he picked up a chair and hurled it with such force against a wall that it broke into pieces.[16] In another incident, he returned late to the Instituto from delivering blood; unable to raise a response after repeatedly knocking, he smashed the glass door with his gloved fist.[17]

Unfortunately for his health, his diet was as problematic as his heavy drinking. Because of the severe food shortage, the dishes offered by the Instituto's cook were mostly beans or lentils; only occasionally would there be fish and, very rarely, meat. Rejecting this fare, Bethune went for days eating only black bread and drinking coffee. Another problem was his almost constant insomnia. Unable to sleep at night, he also found it impossible to maintain the practice he had begun at Trudeau of going to bed in the afternoon. Lack of sleep had been a problem for him from the early days of the operation of the blood transfusion service, and exhaustion sometimes overcame him. His response was to lie down wherever he happened to be, even on a train platform, and fall instantly asleep for up to an hour. In the past such random naps would be enough to revive him, and he would forge on with renewed energy; however, this resilience was no longer there. The combination of excessive drinking, inadequate diet, and lack of sleep undoubtedly exacerbated his outbursts of temper.[18]

By mid-March, both the Spaniards and the Canadians in the Instituto had become deeply concerned by Bethune's increasingly erratic behaviour. Two of the Canadians were so alarmed that they decided to take concrete action. One of them, Ted Allan, was the newest arrival at the Instituto. A twenty-one-year-old writer from Montreal, Allan belonged to the CPC; he had left his job as a staff reporter for the *Daily Clarion* to come to Spain in February to join the International Brigades. When Peter Kerrigan, the political commissar of the British Brigade, learned from Allan that he had known Bethune in

Montreal, he sent him to Madrid, where he arrived in late February. Having heard rumours of difficulties in the Instituto, Kerrigan had given Allan the assignment of ferreting out information on Bethune's performance.[19] Bethune liked Allan, invited him to join the growing ranks of the Instituto, and partly in jest, called him the "political commissar" of the blood transfusion service.

The other Canadian determined to do something about Bethune's behaviour was Henning Sorensen, whose disillusionment had been building since December. On their first meeting, Bethune's dynamic personality had had the same impact on Sorensen as it later had on Sise, and what Sorensen witnessed during November and early December of 1936 only confirmed his admiration. He saw Bethune as an ideal communist – intelligent and a tireless worker, courageous to the point of foolhardiness, and compassionate in his treatment of the wounded, especially children – and had felt it was a privilege to be his interpreter. But by mid-December, Bethune's open-door policy at the Instituto and his apparent indifference to the threat of fifth-columnist activity began to change Sorensen's appraisal. Then there was the issue of Kajsa Rothman; Sorensen's initial suspicion and dislike of her had only increased with time. She had begun to act as Bethune's interpreter whenever the two were together, and this upset Sorensen.[20] Sensitive and easily hurt, he felt that her intrusion had distanced Bethune from him and he became jealous of her.

In the end, while giving Bethune credit for many positive qualities such as his courage and his tender treatment of the wounded, Sorensen came to believe that he had feet of clay, that despite his age he behaved "like a gifted youngster who had yet to mature."[21] Sorensen's ideal was that of a "red knight," pure of heart, self-denying, and unfailingly faithful to his beliefs. Bethune's freewheeling and sometimes vulgar ways offended Sorensen's puritanical view of communism. No dedicated party member, he felt, would ever allow his personal interests – especially bourgeois diversions such as sex and partying – to interfere with his commitment to the cause. Sorensen also deplored Bethune's egotism and "unquenchable thirst for attention," which he saw as another bourgeois characteristic.[22] Bethune also tried to pull rank. He often complained that Sorensen failed to give proper credit to his status when he introduced him to Spaniards. On one occasion when they were standing in a queue in a bank, Bethune said, "I'm tired of waiting, Henning. Go up to the teller and tell him who I am." Wincing at this un-proletarian suggestion, Sorensen had a hard time convincing the impatient Bethune that the teller would likely not give him precedence because of who he was.[23] Sorensen was further disturbed by the amount of CASD money Bethune had been spending on expensive hotel accommodations and meals when he went to France, not to mention on his various personal purchases. He was also extremely worried about Bethune's heavy drinking, for he could see that it was affecting his work. Eventually he decided that Bethune's self-indulgence amounted to an abandonment of principle: he was not performing as a loyal party member and must be replaced.[24]

As Sorensen was pondering what action to take, matters came to a head. Possibly to demonstrate his total contempt for the bureaucrats of the Sanidad Militar, Bethune had not sent them the money he had pledged for the establishment of a blood transfusion service in Valencia. When Colonel Cerrada sent a request for the promised funds in March, Bethune refused to answer. Sorensen, who translated Cerrada's message, urged him to send the money but Bethune flew into a rage and refused. Meanwhile Sorensen had just learned from Ted Allan that he had come to the Instituto to investigate Bethune; Allan encouraged Sorensen to try to find some way to control Bethune's behaviour. So the two put their heads together and decided on a course of action. They would write a letter criticizing Bethune's conduct and asking that he be recalled from the Instituto, and they would send it via the Spanish communist party to Tim Buck, secretary of the Communist Party of Canada.[25]

Sorensen then confronted Bethune about the presence of Kajsa Rothman in the Instituto because a recent incident had increased his already deep suspicion of her. After recovering from his illness in Barcelona, he had returned to Madrid in late February to discover that some documents in the Instituto files were missing. Among them was his *salvo conducto*, the document that allowed him to leave and re-enter Spain. He suspected Rothman of stealing the papers. Now he confronted Bethune with an ultimatum: he would leave the Instituto unless she was evicted. Bethune must have either refused to dismiss Rothman or tried to temporize, because Sorensen left Madrid on 19 March for Valencia where, with the assistance of Dr Juan Planelles, medical director of the Fifth Regiment in Madrid, he was given a position in the Sanidad Militar. "I left Bethune in disgust," Sorensen later said.[26]

Events moved quickly over the next few days. Surprised by Sorensen's abrupt departure, Sise, May, and Allan held a meeting to decide what to do. Agreeing that Bethune had to go, they were discussing how to manage this when Bethune stepped out from behind a curtain. "So that's what you're planning to do with me," he said, then stalked out of the Instituto.[27] He stayed away for several days, and on his return he learned that a message had arrived from the Sanidad Militar in Valencia in his absence, ordering him to report there at once. He ignored it as well as a second message that arrived the next day. Only when another telegram informed him that unless he complied with the order he would be placed under military arrest did he leave Madrid for Valencia on Thursday, 1 April.

When he was ushered into Cerrada's office, Bethune found that Sorensen was there to act as interpreter. Sorensen warned him that he was in very hot water, but the ever-cocky Bethune brushed the warning aside, saying that he would not be scalded. The meeting soon escalated into a series of increasingly hostile exchanges between Bethune and Cerrada, with Sorensen having to think fast how to soften Bethune's biting remarks in his translation. When Cerrada demanded to know why he had failed to provide the funds he had promised, Bethune gave the specious excuse that he was unwilling to violate a law about to passed by the Canadian Parliament that would forbid Canadians from serving in foreign military forces.[28] And he pointedly reminded Cerrada that his was not the only broken promise: the Republican government had failed to live up to its agreement to pay the salaries of the Spanish personnel in the Instituto, and Bethune had had to pay them out of CASD funds.

Cerrada then referred to various reports of Bethune's conduct, saying that the Sanidad Militar regarded it as undesirable, and concluded reproachfully, "We don't understand your behaviour, considering you're a communist." He had found the chink in Bethune's armour – his pride in the new faith to which he had committed himself – and Bethune at once changed his tack. Lowering his voice, he maintained that their differences were the result of factors beyond his control: he had not received all the messages sent to him, he had been totally involved in the blood transfusion service during the aftermath of the Battle of the Jarama and during the Battle of Guadalajara, and he had been the victim of the ever-present problem of the language barrier. "It was all a misunderstanding," he insisted.

Tempers cooled somewhat on both sides, and Bethune left the meeting sure that he had got around Cerrada. At the door of the office he grinned at Sorensen and, reminding him of his earlier confidence that he would be able to handle the situation, said, "I told you so, Henning."[29] However, Cerrada was not entirely taken in. After Bethune left, he told Sorensen that the Sanidad Militar had seriously considered ordering Bethune's arrest and court martial. Perhaps because of their hope of future Canadian financial support, they had not done so, but they had called him on the carpet to make it clear that he was in their country and subject to their command. Embarrassed by a fellow-Canadian's bad behaviour, Sorensen was offended by Bethune's haughty indifference to Spanish sensitivities and his refusal to express the slightest regret for his actions.[30] This resentment would have consequences.

Bethune returned to Madrid on Saturday, 3 April. However, Sorensen remained in Valencia at the request of the military police, who interrogated him at length. Some of the information provided by Sorensen was used in a highly condemnatory report of Bethune made by the police on that same date.[31] It referred to the letter that Sorensen and Allan had earlier sent to the Canadian Communist Party requesting Bethune's removal as director of the Instituto. Then, following a brief history of the Instituto from its inception and an account of the meeting between Cerrada and Bethune on Friday, 2 April, the police report stated that there was evidence to suggest that both Kajsa Rothman and Bethune were involved in espionage, and in addition, that Bethune might have stolen jewellery that was in a sealed room of the apartment at Principe de Vergara 36 when he and his companions arrived in December. In fact the supposed "evidence" for these crimes was thin, and the absurd accusation of espionage and theft was no more than the product of the atmosphere of extreme suspicion about foreigners and fear of fifth column activity among the Republicans at this time.[32]

Sorensen returned to Madrid on Monday, 5 April. With him he brought the information that a reorganization of the Sanidad Militar, to be announced within days, would end the autonomy of all foreign units in the Republican sector. The next day, along with May and Sise, he confronted Bethune to try to make him accept that although the Canadian role in managing the Instituto had to end, financial support from Canada was essential if its work were to continue. Bethune had brought the blood transfusion service into being: now he must ensure its survival by returning to Canada to raise the funds to keep it going.

At first Bethune flatly refused. He said that if he could no longer direct the operation of the unit, he would join the International Brigades as he had intended the previous November. He was a surgeon, not a public speaker, and others with greater oratorical skills should act as publicists. The others argued that no one was more qualified than he to tell the story of the blood transfusion service, explain its vital role in the struggle against fascism, and make an appeal to progressive Canadians to continue their generous giving of money to ensure its continued existence. The sometimes heated discussion went on for hours until at last Bethune agreed to return to Canada to undertake a publicity campaign. With him would go the film *Heart of Spain*, which Geza Kárpáthi and Herbert Kline, the photographer and writer, were in the final stage of completing.[33]

The announcement of the change in status of all foreign contingents in Spain was made on Thursday, 8 April 1937.[34] During the next few days

Bethune pondered his promise to return to Canada. It seemed unfair to him that Sorensen, Sise, and May would be remaining behind in his Instituto while he was sent home. He decided to hand the entire operation over to the Spanish authorities at once. Without consulting his comrades, he sent the following cable to the CASD on Monday, 12 April:

> Government decrees all organizations in Spain whether Spanish or foreign must come under control of ministry of War. No independent organizations allowed. The Sanidad Militar have taken over control Canadian unit. Our position now nominal. Fortunately transfusion service is well established and can carry on without us ... Strongly urge you act immediately authorize me by cable as chief to first withdraw Canadian personnel, second hand over to gov't cars, refrigerators and equipment, third agree to provide $200 monthly 6 mos. for maintenance institute, fourth return Canada with such Canadians as desire with film for antifascist propaganda. Our work as Canadians here is finished ... Only future cables signed Beth Bethune are from me ... Continue collection funds many schemes more urgent now than blood transfusion. Will inform you later Salud Beth Bethune.[35]

Bethune's sweeping recommendation that all Canadian participation in the blood transfusion service be terminated astonished the CASD. Benjamin Spence was equally puzzled by Bethune's warning to disregard cables not signed "Beth Bethune." Something was clearly going on behind the scenes at the Instituto, and Spence was determined to find out what it was.

What now ensued was a fencing match by telegram. On 15 April, Spence replied to Bethune's cable, saying that the CASD would prefer that the unit remain intact, even if in future it might take on other duties. He also asked for the input of the other members of the unit about what they wished to see done. Bethune did not reply, so after three days Spence sent another cable addressed to "Bethunit" (not "Beth Bethune") asking for more information. Bethune replied tersely, "Awaiting government decision reorganization next few days till then no fresh news Salud."

On Monday, 19 April, he wrote a letter of resignation to the head of the Sanidad Militar. Perhaps realizing that the CASD would not support pulling all the Canadian personnel out of Madrid, he attempted to define the roles that they would play:

Camarada:
In view of the fact that the Instituto Hispano-Canadiense de Transfusión

de Sangre as conceived by me in January is now operating as an efficient, well-organized institute, and as part of the SM, it is clear to me that my function as chief of the organization here in Spain has come to a natural end. Since I am firmly of the opinion that all services of the Republican Army should be controlled by the Spanish people I hereby offer my resignation as chief of the organization.

If the resignation is accepted I will at once proceed to Canada to carry out propaganda work in connection with the Institute and in support of the Popular Front.

In view of the necessity of the continuation of financial support of the Institute in Spain from the Popular Front in Canada, I hereby delegate my authority as Chief representative of the Canadian Committee to Aid Spanish Democracy to the following members: Allen May, Ted Allan, Hazen Sise and Henning Sorensen. I would also suggest that the functions of the above members of the Committee should be as follows: Allen May, official secretary and responsable [sic] of the Canadian Committee; Ted Allan, political commissar; Hazen Sise, director of transport; Henning Sorensen, liaison officer between Canadian representatives and Sanidad Militar.

Also, in view of the urgency of the situation and the necessity of showing our propaganda film as quickly as possible, I would like my resignation to take effect immediately.

Dr Norman Bethune[36]

Only after he had posted the letter did he show a copy to the other members of the unit. Realizing that officials in the Sanidad Militar would expect a detailed explanation of the situation, Sise, May, and Sorensen hurried to Valencia the following day. Meanwhile, Bethune did not communicate with the CASD again, so one week later, on Tuesday, 27 April, yet another cable arrived from the committee, again addressed to "Bethunit." It expressed concern about what was going on and again asked for the input of the other members of the unit. It is not clear if Bethune showed this cable to Sise, May, and Sorensen when they returned on Wednesday, but on Thursday he replied to the CASD: "No cause anxiety condition unit here cable containing full reorganization information follows in two days."

Seventeen days had now elapsed since Bethune had sent his cable urging termination of the Canadian role in the blood transfusion service, aside from six months' funding. Despite the requests of the CASD for more information and for the input of his companions, the committee had received only two brief replies, both from Bethune, assuring them all was well and that explanations would soon be forthcoming. Increasingly concerned by the lack of information and by rumours about Bethune's personal conduct, Spence decided to call a meeting to discuss how to deal with the crisis.[37] On Tuesday, 4 May, he received the following cable from Bethune, which he read aloud at the CASD meeting:

Relationship with Sanidad Militar clarified and satisfactory. All Spain organization as planned by me now proceeding. Name Hispano-Canadiense being retained for Madrid sector. Bethune unit operating smoothly and efficiently. All here agree Bethune return Canada with wonderful film now finished for propaganda work. Remaining Canadians to direct disposal Canadian funds aid administration along lines my suggestions. All have civil status only. Spanish military medical officers in charge actual operations. During my absence Canadian committee in charge composed May, directing secretary, Sise, in charge transport, Sorensen, liaison with Sanidad ... All representatives content. Signed Bethune, May, Sise, Sorensen. Beth Bethune.[38]

The phrase "during my absence" seems to indicate that despite his letter of resignation to the Sanidad Militar, Bethune had managed to convince himself that he would be able to return to the Instituto after the fundraising tour. In any case, the CASD was not satisfied with his cable. Once again the wording was in Bethune's voice only, despite the multiple signatures. The message merely intensified the committee's suspicion that they were not being given a full account. And they were not, because although Tim Buck was a member of the CASD, he had clearly not revealed to the committee all the contents of the letter of denunciation sent to him by Sorensen and Allan in March. So the committee decided that the only way to learn what was happening was to send A.A. MacLeod as their representative to Madrid to investigate.[39] Spence immediately sent a cable announcing their decision and telling Bethune that he must meet with MacLeod before leaving for Canada. Perhaps assuming that the Canadian funding of the Instituto would be limited now that the blood service would be managed by the Spanish, he also gave Bethune the go-ahead to investigate his idea of child-relief work. MacLeod sailed on 13 May, and on that date Spence cabled Bethune that he and Sorensen should meet him in Paris on 24 May; he added that Bethune should return to Canada as soon as possible with the film, as the committee was planning a rally to welcome him in Toronto on 12 June.[40]

On Sunday, 16 May, Bethune left for Paris. Ignoring Spence's suggestion, he did not take Sorensen along, likely not wishing MacLeod to hear

Sorensen's version of recent developments in the Instituto.[41] While waiting for MacLeod's arrival, Bethune cabled Spence for more funds, but his request was refused. Undeterred, he lived well in Paris, as always. Louis Huot, a friend from Montreal then living in Paris, recalled, "He used to derive the greatest pleasure from staying in the most expensive places ... and ordering ... champagne ... He would go to places like the Tour d'Argent for dinner ... and getting chits ... he would pin all this together and derive great pleasure from the idea of the anguish it would cause when he delivered it."[42] Making the most of his stay, Bethune attended the French tennis championships and shopped for clothing, ordering a number of made-to-measure monogrammed dress shirts, which he paid for with CASD money.[43]

When he met MacLeod on Wednesday, 26 May, Bethune first complained about having been denied further funds for the moment.[44] Then he moved on to his new project to aid Spanish children made homeless by the war. Away from his critics at the Instituto, he felt he had a chance to win over MacLeod and convince him of the urgent need to act. He painted his picture in broad strokes, launching into a description of the desperate plight of thousands of Spanish war orphans. The best way to help them, he told MacLeod, was to create "children's villages" in areas outside the war zone, particularly in northern Spain. As the Instituto's blood transfusion service was in the process of being transferred to Spanish authorities, he argued, it would no longer be necessary to raise funds for it from the Canadian public. The focus of a new appeal could be the children's villages. If the project of supplying blood for the wounded had moved Canadians to donate to the cause, would they not react even more strongly to a request to help children? He did not mention to MacLeod that the Spanish authorities still expected the CASD to fund the Madrid blood transfusion service even after the Sanidad Militar took over the management of it, nor did he mention that they also expected Canadian funding for the unit to be set up in Valencia. Yet he must have known that his new project would either draw funds away from these blood transfusion services or would require twice the amount of fundraising in Canada.

Unaware of these complicating factors, MacLeod was impressed with the idea of the "children's villages." Bethune had already spoken about it to members of a Basque committee in Paris, and they now suggested that the two Canadians fly to Bilbao to discuss the proposal with authorities there. Bedazzled by Bethune's rhetoric, MacLeod took up the duel by telegram with Spence. He cabled him on Thursday, 26 May, agreeing with the decision to delay sending money until he could learn more about the completion of the film and the situation in Madrid. But he added that he was considering flying to Spain with Bethune on a quick visit to investigate his proposal to set up refuges for war orphans there. However, the CASD was not in favour of the Bilbao proposition and was anxious to get Bethune back to Canada. So Spence cabled back the following day, telling MacLeod to arrange for Bethune's immediate return since he was needed for a speaking tour to raise badly needed funds. Spence suggested that if the film were not completed by the time Bethune sailed, MacLeod and one of the members of the Madrid unit could supervise its completion. "Better Bethune without film than both later," he wrote.[45]

But MacLeod was still under Bethune's spell. Ignoring Spence's most recent message, he cabled him on Monday, 31 May, that Bethune needed to remain at least one week longer in order to finish the film. He now asked for $2,000 to cover costs of completing the film, pay Bethune's fare and his other expenses, and launch the new children's project. Bethune could sail on the *Normandie* on 9 June, he wrote. He also recommended that the CASD accept responsibility for maintaining five hundred Spanish war orphans at an annual cost of $50,000. As for the blood transfusion unit, he suggested that he should go to Madrid at once to formally transfer it to the Sanidad Militar.

However, the CASD had already turned down Bethune's request for a similar amount of money for his expenses, and they wanted to know what had happened to the balance of $600 that Bethune had a week earlier told them was in his American Express account. Also, they were not willing to abandon support of the blood transfusion service or to commit themselves to the children's village project without knowing more details. Believing that MacLeod had made his decision in Bethune's favour without getting all the facts, Spence declined to send more money.[46]

Meanwhile, having won over Macleod and confident that things were now going his way, Bethune had not been able to resist tweaking the noses of his less-than-loyal comrades in Madrid. On Saturday, 29 May, he had sent a cable to Sorensen, Sise, and May informing them that he had persuaded MacLeod to withdraw the Canadian staff of the unit from Madrid. He also added that he and MacLeod were going to Bilbao.[47] Thoroughly alarmed at the news, the three Canadians determined to scotch Bethune's plan. They persuaded the military police in Madrid to telegraph the Spanish embassy in Paris with instructions not to allow MacLeod and Bethune to enter Spain. The police invited the Canadians to examine the dossier they kept on Bethune in order to make any necessary corrections of the data they had collected. The dossier revealed that the police had been planning to expel Bethune from Spain if he had not decided to leave voluntarily.[48]

The three next cabled Spence to alert him to the undesirable consequences of withdrawing the transfusion service unit from Madrid; they did not mention Bethune's proposed Bilbao trip nor their conference with the military police. The cable, which the committee received on 31 May, read in part: "Frank expressions withheld to date for obvious reasons. Due to circumstances surrounding Bethune's departure which he doubtless will explain on arrival we advise against his operating further projects in Spain but believe him very valuable in Canada for propaganda. Advise strongly against reducing blood unit support. Withdrawal would have regrettable political consequences. Cable sent about 10 April containing code signature Beth Bethune suggesting withdrawal went without our consent contained misleading information complications of which we repudiate."[49]

At about the same time, out of money and with the CASD refusing to back the children's village project without further information, MacLeod gave in. On 1 June he cabled Spence asking him to rush funds to pay for Bethune's fare to New York and also those of the filmmakers, Geza Kárpáthi and Herbert Kline. Receiving no immediate reply, he borrowed the money to buy third class tickets for them on the *Queen Mary*.[50] On Wednesday, 2 June, Bethune, Kárpáthi, and Kline sailed from Cherbourg for the five-day voyage. Forced out of Spain while the rest of his unit remained in action, frustrated at not being able to carry out his project of establishing children's villages, Bethune fretted his way across the Atlantic. Though it must have galled him to admit it, he was now well aware that his own behaviour had led to his recall. As he would later confess to Sise when they met again in Montreal, "I have blotted my copybook."[51]

✢ 12 ✢

Preaching the Faith

The Speaking Tour, June–October 1937

Bethune arrived in New York on Monday, 7 June 1937, and was met by Benjamin Spence, who shepherded him to a hotel. That afternoon he gave a lengthy press conference, replying in detail to questions on the political and military aspects of the Spanish Civil War and criticizing the failure of the democracies to come to the aid of the Republican government. Pounding fist into palm, he demanded, "What's the matter with England, France, the United States, Canada? Are they afraid that by supplying arms to the Loyalist forces, they'll start a world war? Why, the world war has started. In fact, it's in its third stage – Manchuria, Ethiopia, and now Spain. It's democracy against fascism." Then he added, "We in Madrid cannot understand such timidity, such poltroonery on the part of the democratic nations."[1] Having struck this keynote, he would keep to it: from now on, he would make the threat of international fascism the linchpin of almost every speech he gave. Questioned on the future of the Instituto, he insisted that, following his publicity tour to raise funds, he would return to Spain to resume his role and to set up an organization to aid children orphaned by the war. He apparently still did not believe that he would be permanently excluded from the blood transfusion unit.

For the next five days he stayed in New York, hoping that the film *Heart of Spain* would be completed in time for him to take it to Canada. However, several technical problems caused delays, so it was not yet finished when he left New York by train for Buffalo on Sunday, 13 June. A welcoming committee was waiting to take him to Toronto by automobile. Throughout the week the CASD had been rushing preparations for a reception on the night of Monday, 14 June, at which he would be greeted as a war hero. Front-page stories in the communist *Daily Clarion* focused on him and the parade and rally in his honour. "Let us prepare to welcome one of the greatest Canadians of our time," the paper urged its readers.[2]

En route from Buffalo on Monday afternoon, Bethune and his party stopped briefly in Hamilton to visit with his mother before continuing on to Toronto, arriving shortly before 8 PM at Union Station.[3] Bethune got into an open touring car, and the waiting crowd of more than two thousand people broke into loud applause as he was driven slowly along Front Street, then north on University Avenue. Behind followed two marching bands and a parade of hundreds of placard-bearing marchers that stretched more than two kilometres along the city's widest boulevard.

The parade ended at Queen's Park, where nearly five thousand people enthusiastically welcomed Bethune as he was escorted across the lawn and up the steps of a bandstand. When he stepped to the microphone, the crowd gave him three long cheers. Raising his right hand in a clenched-fist salute, he began, "Friends and comrades, salutations from the anti-fascists of Spain to the anti-fascists of Canada. *Salute* [sic]." The throng roared and raised their fists in response. Bethune spoke briefly, thanking those who had contributed money for the blood transfusion service, praising the courage of the Spanish people, and emphasizing the absolute need of a common front against rising world fascism. The Spanish conflict would lead to a much wider war, he warned, possibly within a year. "The world war is on now," he insisted; "this battle, this world war will mean the end of fascism in world history."[4] At the conclusion of his address, a young girl, one of a group of twelve dressed as Red Cross nurses, crossed the stage to present him with a bouquet. When he kissed her cheek, the eleven others demanded their due, so to the applause of the crowd he went down the line, kissing each of the girls.

The following day, as the featured speaker at a CASD conference held in Carlton United Church in Toronto, he was in a more combative mood. Veering from his previous emphasis on the need to defend democracy against fascism, he came close to revealing his communist faith. "Political democracies," he charged, "are a shell and a sham." England was no more than a handful of capitalists manipulating world events. As for the British Empire, it was only "blocks of gold scattered around the world." He went on to label the coronation of King George VI, which had taken place in Westminster Abbey in May, as "the biggest build-up and advertising stunt for the next war. And we'll be asked to go over there and fight for the Empire." Pausing, he scanned the audience and then continued, "Well, we'll fight, yes, but we want to know what we fight for." These were deliberately provocative words, intended to sting many people in a city where the largest single group was of British origin. The comments were widely and somewhat critically reported in the local press, despite the general admiration for Bethune's achievements.[5]

Bethune next turned to Spain. Knowing that his audience included the leading members of the CASD, he chose to explain in detail his scheme to build a number of children's villages for some of the unfortunate thousands who had become orphans. Back in May, when he had convinced A.A. MacLeod to support his proposal, he had said it would require $50,000 a year. Now he escalated the sum to $1 million, adding, perhaps to his left-wing listeners' surprise, that the best way to raise such a sum was to hire a public-relations expert. "It would be well worth the money," he assured them. "He'll swing it for you!" As a postscript he urged the conference not to consider evacuating orphans from Spain. Children taken from their home-land would "lose that beautiful revolutionary spirit." His sales pitch proved effective. That evening the CASD formally agreed to launch a national fundraising campaign to care for five hundred Spanish children. They also decided to maintain support for the Madrid blood transfusion service, even though it was now controlled by the Republican government of Spain.[6]

Following the conference's afternoon session, Bethune had returned to his hotel to rest before his speech in the evening. Waiting in the lobby was free-lance reporter William Strange, who asked for an interview. "If you don't object to asking your questions while I'm taking a bath and shaving, I'll talk to you," Bethune replied. "Otherwise, no. I've got only a few minutes to spare."[7] Strange agreed. During the interview he made a point of asking, "By the way, doctor, are you a communist?" The question appeared to surprise Bethune, who responded sharply, "Most emphatically, I am not! What makes you ask?"

When Strange mentioned Bethune's clenched-fist salute at Monday night's rally, he retorted, "Look here, let's get this thing straight. You can call me a socialist if you like. I am a socialist in the same way that millions of sane people are socialists. I want to see people getting a square deal, and I hate fas-cism. The clenched fist is used as a 'People's Front' salute. It's used in Spain by everybody who is against the fascists."[8] It was the first time that the ques-tion about Bethune's party membership had been raised, and he responded as he had been told to do. The party line on this matter was absolutely clear: public awareness of his political commitment could alienate potential donors who were as much anti-communist as they were anti-fascist. This was not the last time he would be asked about his political beliefs, and each time he would find it more painful to lie.

After conferring at length with CASD officials on the schedule for the fundraising tour, Bethune left Toronto for Montreal on the afternoon of 17 June for the second stage of his homecoming. As in Toronto, the CASD had carried out an intensive publicity campaign there drawing attention to his arrival. When his train pulled into Windsor Station early that evening, a crowd of a thousand was waiting. CASD members greeted him on the platform, and then supporters lifted him to the shoulders of two men who made their way through a cheering throng to a banner-draped car, one of a cavalcade of automobiles that then paraded through the downtown streets. For two days newspaper advertisements and processions of cars carrying posters had announced his forthcoming appearance at the Mount Royal Arena on Friday night. It was the same meeting place where the scheduled appearance of the three Spanish delegates had been banned by the Montreal City Council nearly seven months earlier. Now municipal authorities chose not to interfere, and the chief of police even provided a squad of twenty-five policemen to prevent interference from any hostile elements.

Bethune arrived at the arena just before 8 PM. More than five hundred people were gathered near the entrance, waiting to hear the speeches that would be broadcast outside by loudspeakers. As he entered the auditorium, a bugle sounded, and the capacity crowd of eight thousand broke into thunderous applause. The bugle sounded again as Bethune joined three others on the speakers' platform. He gazed out over the crowd and raised his fist, and in response people sprang to their feet, cheering, applauding, and returning the salute. When his turn came to move to the microphone, he was cheered wildly again. Speaking slowly and deliberately, he outlined the principles for which the Republicans were fighting and traced the history of the blood transfusion service. When he described the scenes along the Málaga-Almería road, particularly those involving children, he spoke with quivering emotion. He outlined his plan for a "child-city" in Spain, and urged his listeners to find it in their hearts to each support a child for a year, at a cost he estimated at $100.

As he thanked the audience, the band began to play the Popular Front anthem, "No Pasarán." When he returned to his seat, people rushed to the platform with money. Nearly $2,000 was donated on the spot.[9] Dr Gabriel Nadeau, who saw Bethune for the first and last time that night, later remarked: "Tall, pale and thin, he looked ascetic, and with a different garb he would have passed for a friar or a parson. The impression that one got listening to him was that he was sincere and the sincerity of his conviction made his appeal the stronger."[10]

Despite the success of his speeches, Bethune's psychological state was precarious. Although he was lionized daily as a war hero, he knew very well that the CPC was highly critical of his behaviour in Spain, and this ate at his self-esteem. He also soon discovered there was little left of his old life in Montreal. He got away from his CASD duties one day and went out to the Hôpital du Sacré Coeur to visit some former colleagues and patients. After the warm send-off he had received, he was shocked by the staff's hostile reaction to his presence now. Seeing him in the corridor, a group of nursing sisters turned and hurried away. The mother superior refused to see him. He later joked that she had hidden, fearing to meet what she believed was an incarnation of Satan.[11] But the humour barely concealed his hurt and anger that his former associates still believed that God marched with Franco.

Some old social acquaintances avoided him as well. He quarrelled with Fritz and Mieze Brandtner, who were reluctant to give up the lease on the Beaver Hall Square apartment. Other friends simply ignored his presence. When George Holt called, Bethune told him he was the first friend who had done so.[12] Margaret Day was among those who shunned him, though not for political reasons. Despite her having told him their affair was over, he had sent her letters and gifts from Spain, but she had never replied. Now, although he besieged her with phone calls, she refused to meet him.[13] Those who did see him were worried about him. George Mooney later said, "There was less of the sparkle in him. Less of the Beau Brummell. His clothes were cheap and unpressed. He didn't laugh the way he used to. The spring in his step was gone … He was drinking heavily."[14]

Frances Coleman also noted a sharp change. Alarmed by Bethune's worn appearance, she persuaded him to go to the Laurentians with her to escape his political activities for a few days. His debility was apparent even to the CASD officials, who agreed he should avoid public duties for two weeks. So after his weekend with his ex-wife, Bethune went to Ontario for a brief stay with his sister, Janet Stiles, in Kitchener. It was not a successful visit: Bethune and his brother-in-law, a businessman, had several lengthy and heated arguments over politics.[15] Bethune then left for Toronto to visit Paraskeva and Philip Clark. When he admitted he had almost no money, they offered to take him in until the CASD came up with funds they had promised to pay his living expenses. The Clarks also rented a car for him, and he remained with them during the last few days of June.[16] Paraskeva Clark had been fascinated by Bethune since he broke up her dinner party in 1936, and his anti-fascist activities in Spain had added to his appeal. Now, with Bethune as a house guest, their mutual attraction grew. One night as they drove together to a party, he put a hand on her leg and said, "You are like wine." Soon afterward he approached Philip and told him he wanted to make love to Paraskeva but would do so only with Philip's permission. Philip replied that the decision was hers.[17] And so began an affair that would continue off and on until Bethune left for China.

Meanwhile, he was fretting about the upcoming speaking tour. Despite the public accolades his speeches had received, he knew that the tour was in part a face-saving solution imposed upon him by the CPC to get him out of Spain. He believed that by raising needed funds he might atone for aspects of his behaviour he now regretted. But as the day to begin the tour approached, he became more and more convinced that his sins did not merit such a heavy penance. He did not feel qualified for the role, he told the CASD – he was a surgeon, not a travelling publicist. *Heart of Spain*, he felt certain, would tell the story of the transfusion service and reveal the horrors of the war most effectively. Longing to be free to return to Spain, he argued that anyone could present the film to Canadian and American audiences and appeal for financial contributions.

Paraskeva Clark observed him struggling with depression: "Beth had apparently returned from somewhere, sat by this lamp and just emptied a full bottle of rye, and it wouldn't be any effect on him at all, supposedly, only very quiet … Damn it he just … [felt] tremendous melancholy and dis-illusionment, and he felt he, he was disappointed in the sins he found here after Spain, you know … there was no money, everything fell to pieces, the atmosphere fell off, and the communists took him but wanted to hold him and discipline him in a way which you couldn't hold Bethune … and he felt that he cut his bridges from medicine and his great position and comforts and so on … he was kind of just brooding, actually."[18]

But not for long. In the last week of June he marched into the CASD offices in Toronto to announce he was returning to Spain. The CASD officials argued with him, but nothing could deter him. Someone then telephoned CPC headquarters a few blocks away. The only person of authority in the office, Joseph Salsberg, a high-ranking party member, rushed over to try to reason with Bethune. But Bethune was not willing to listen. Seizing a pencil, he slashed bold lines across a map of Spain, indicating Nationalist striking points around Madrid. "Joe, if I don't make it now, I'll never be able to get in," he declared. "I'm needed more there than I am here. You're all here. You can go out and raise money … I must go back." He had made a decision, he said, and it was unalterable.

Recognizing that Bethune's emotions were out of control, Salsberg let him talk himself out and when he finally calmed down, tried again, unsuccess-fully, to reason with him. As a last resort, he warned that Bethune's failure to obey party orders would be a serious breach of discipline and would lead to his disgrace in the eyes of the party. Bethune began to waver. Eventually he backed down and agreed to embark the next week on the first leg of the fundraising tour.[19]

Leaving Toronto by train at the beginning of July, Bethune headed for the Algoma District north of Lake Huron where he had lived during his early teens. On Sunday, 4 July, he made the first speech of his tour in the mining town of Kirkland Lake before an audience of six hundred in the Strand Theatre.[20] More than three months later he would make his last address in Hamilton, Ontario, to eighteen hundred people.[21] In between, with only brief interludes for travel between engagements, he often maintained a daily schedule of two appearances and sometimes as many as four. His itinerary took him from Northern Ontario through the Canadian West to British Columbia, south to California, north again to British Columbia, and back to Central Canada. Then, after brief visits to several American cities, he went east to the Maritimes. Travelling by train, automobile, and ship, he spoke in every large city in Canada before crowds of several thousand and to much smaller groups in many small towns.[22] He appeared in arenas, churches, school auditoriums, and gymnasiums, in Legion, union, and ethnic group halls, and at open-air meetings in parks. He addressed service clubs, Chambers of Commerce, medical conferences, and small gatherings in private homes.

At the beginning of the tour, he was still smarting from having to bow to party discipline. But, he wrote to Frances Coleman on the third day of the tour, "Although this public speaking is not to my liking I will go through with it."[23] Four days later, however, on Sunday, 11 July, he sent a plaintive cable from Sudbury to the Instituto in Madrid: "On trans Canada tour. Can eye [sic] expect from all comrades in Madrid same support as eye am giving unit Wire me committee Winnipeg"[24] It was a plea for backing for his hoped-for return to Spain. On Wednesday, 14 July, Republican forces launched an offensive to the west of Madrid. Bethune eagerly followed daily newspaper reports of what became known as the battle of Brunete, chafing against the heavy schedule of speeches imposed on him, longing to be back in action where he believed he belonged.

Yet he could not help but be moved by the enthusiasm of the crowds wherever he spoke during those first days. Most audiences were made up of workers, many of them unemployed, but there were middle-class men and women among them, and Bethune quickly realized that the majority, whether communists, socialists, or liberals, had come to see, hear, and even touch a man they regarded as a hero. In a world mired in economic depression and in which aggressors were on the march, he was seen by many as a man of principle who had the courage to take a stand. He had always enjoyed performing before an audience, and now, warming to the task and drawing on his natural ability as an actor, he polished his delivery so that he could easily carry his listeners through speeches lasting two hours and more. Speaking into the microphone in an almost conversational tone, he seldom raised his voice, his natural manner convincing those who heard him of the depth of his sincerity. When he described the gradual stirring of a wounded Spanish soldier as colour crept back into his cheeks during a transfusion, they listened in rapt attention. When he lowered his voice to speak about the dead children he had lifted in his arms and carried out of the burning rubble after the bombing of Almería, they hissed and shouted "Shame!" They cheered when he told them about the valiant defence of Madrid by the Republicans and chanted their stirring slogan, "*No pasarán!*"

On most occasions he used the same basic speech. After first outlining the origins of the war and the principles involved, he went on to describe in graphic detail the brutal effect of the military conflict on both combatants and civilians. Then he related the role of the Madrid blood transfusion unit and ended with an appeal for funds to maintain it and to build children's refuges. As he came to feel more at ease on stage, he increasingly addressed another theme: the spread of fascism. Frustrated in his attempts to fight the root causes of tuberculosis, as he had long ago vowed, he now dedicated himself to battling the political disease he believed was threatening the world. He warned his audiences of signs of the emergence of fascism in Canada, bitterly recounting the incident that resulted in his paying duty in France on the Ford ambulance he had bought in London, because the Canadian government was suspicious of the CASD: "I asked Ottawa for permission to recommend the use of a Canadian ambulance," he told his listeners, "and I was refused by Mackenzie King, the same man who a little later was photographed shaking hands with the biggest murderer in the world today – Hitler." He urged his audience to follow the lead of Republican Spain by forming a Canadian united front of liberals, socialists, and communists.[25]

However, straying too far from the theme of aid for Spain was potentially dangerous in the eyes of the CPC. They had made it clear to him that the aim of the tour was to describe the situation in Spain for the purpose of raising funds; he should avoid political rhetoric. Canadian public opinion was fundamentally anti-communist, and Canadian media generally leaned toward the Nationalist cause in Spain, frequently referring to the Republicans as "Reds." As a result, many middle-class liberals who were opposed to the fascist attack on Spain's elected government had become fearful of the degree of communist influence on the Republicans. Bethune understood that, to avoid alienating a large group of potential donors, he must conceal his party membership. In fact, the party had instructed him to deal with the issue in an emphatic manner right at the start. In the town of Timmins, on the third day of the tour, he stated: "I am not a communist. I am an anti-fascist." After telling the audience that the Madrid unit had administered seven hundred transfusions, he added, "They call me a Red. Then if Christianity is Red, I am also a Red. They call me a Red because I have saved some five hundred lives."[26]

For the next two weeks he did not directly raise the issue, though comments he made at a Rotary Club luncheon in Sault Ste Marie on Tuesday, 13 July, clearly revealed where he stood politically. "What side are you on?" he asked his listeners, most of them small businessmen. "Do you feel yourself superior to the man who served you at the table today or the man at work on the streets? If so, then it is wrong. For you and I are not superior in any way to the man who lives by the work of his hands." And he quickly rebutted the words of the Rotarian who introduced him by saying that a desire for adventure had led him to Spain. "I did not go Spain because of any adventurous urge," Bethune insisted, "but because of a very definite principle involved in the conflict there."[27] His position was not lost on his hearers. In the minutes of the meeting, the secretary noted, "Dr Bethune was guest speaker and his talk bordered on communism."[28]

Six days later, on 19 July, came Winnipeg, the first stop on the western leg of the tour. Despite the lateness of the hour – it was 1:30 AM – a band and a jubilant welcoming party of five hundred were waiting on the platform for the train. As the band struck up, Bethune was lifted into the air and carried, clenched fist held high, through the cheering crowd to a waiting taxi which took him to the Hotel Fort Garry. In the afternoon he spoke at the Ukrainian Labour Temple and in the evening in the Walker Theatre, where some of the audience had to be seated on the stage to accommodate the overflow crowd of two thousand.

Bethune, wearing a white suit, was introduced as "the great knight-errant of modern times who had valorously and unselfishly volunteered to help the Spanish people fight for their freedom."[29] Instead of going directly to the situation in Spain as he usually did, he opened his address with a fervent call for the unity of all progressive forces in Canada. He defined these forces by tracing his life from his early years as a worker through university and medical school, and by pointing out that as a doctor, along with white-collar employees, lawyers, teachers, and unskilled labourers, he too was a member of the working class. All of these professions and occupations in Canada should unite as they had in Spain, he said. It was no less important to form a united front here than it was there.

Then he related why he had gone to Spain and outlined the role of the transfusion service. Graphically describing the horrors of the war, his voice rose as he cried that Madrid would never surrender – "Never! Never!! Never!!!"[30] When the applause subsided, he moved to his conclusion with an emotional demand for worker unity in Canada. "Say little, do more. Don't say it, do it! Do it now! Today!" As he stepped back to signal the end of his speech, the crowd was on its feet, cheering and raising clenched fists. It was his most eloquent address to date.

Energized by the emotional response, he felt that the time to speak the truth about his politics had come. The following night he appeared at a banquet in the St Charles Hotel given in his honour by members and supporters of the Winnipeg branch of the CASD. Following a series of eulogies to him, Bethune was invited to speak, and this time he went far beyond his usual text. "I have the honour to be a communist," he began simply. He went on to explain that his conversion had started two years earlier in the Soviet Union where he had contrasted the condition of people he had just seen in the London slums with the healthy citizens of Moscow: "I didn't care then what the system was called," he said, "but I knew that what we wanted was the thing those Russians had got."

Next he turned to another contrast that had impressed him. "The Russian women were not so sex-conscious as Western women. They looked one straight in the face and walked like queens." Then, reprising elements of his speech of 20 December 1935, he went on, "I am reminded of the time when Alice asked if she could be queen and the White Queen answered her: 'Yes, my dear, you'll be queen, but you'll start as a pawn and when we get to the ninth square, we'll all be queens together.' That is the idea of communism. We'll start as pawns and in the end, we'll all be kings and queens together." He then shifted to the theme of male exploitation of women, which he claimed no longer existed in the Soviet Union. "That is why every woman unless she is just a bundle of sensuous nerve-endings, must be either a socialist or a communist," he said. "You women could stop war – just as the clergymen of the last generation could have stopped the Great War – if they had had the courage to say it was against the will of Christ. Why don't you women unite and give up this sense of property?" In conclusion he said, "The men who are fighting in the government forces in Spain are fighting for you, just as much as did the men in the Great War. It is a better thing to fight for democracy than to fight for your king and country. Canada's time of agony has not come yet, but it will come. Do not despair if the bourgeois class will not cooperate with you. When the clash comes, they will melt like snow. We bourgeois must humble ourselves before the workers, not go down to them, but go up to them and ask them if we may help them in their work."[31]

Despite the party's order to remain silent about his political affiliation, it had been only a matter of time before Bethune revealed it. "I wanted to talk," he later explained to his friend George Holt. "I wanted to admit that I am a Communist Party member."[32] His party membership was the badge of the faith to which he had dedicated himself, his white plume; he was proud of it and yearned to flaunt it. As principled as his father, who had also made intemperate public statements, he was fired by the same heartfelt certainty of his beliefs and the same passion to convert others.

But his need to speak out ran even deeper. He had always said that he was an artist, and his conversion to communism had altered his view of what that meant. Just before leaving Spain, in a rambling letter he had sent to Marian Scott and other friends, he had explicitly linked the role of the artist to that of a revolutionary. "The function of the artist is to disturb," he wrote. "His duty is to arouse the sleeper, to shake the complacent pillars of the world. He reminds the world of its dark ancestry, shows the world its present, and points the way to its new birth ... He makes uneasy the static, the set and the still. In a world terrified of change, he preaches revolution – the principle of life. He is an agitator, a disturber of the peace – quick, impatient, positive, restless and disquieting. He is the creative spirit of life working in the soul of man."[33] Bethune had always loved to shock the complacent, but professing his faith in communism now served a purpose that transcended mere provocation – or even politics. In rallying others to the cause, he was avowing a profound sense of who and what he was.

From Winnipeg onward, Bethune's speeches contained increasing amounts of communist rhetoric drawn from the tomes of Marxist theory that filled one of his suitcases and which he pored over at every opportunity. At every stop he bought newspapers and magazines to keep abreast of news from abroad and often stayed up half the night reading them.[34] In Brandon, after his revelation in Winnipeg, he announced, "I am a 'Red' and proud of it." In Saskatoon two days later he spoke at length on the Marxist belief in class struggle.[35]

By openly speaking the truth about his views at last, Bethune felt he was once again in control of his life. But he was still labouring under a heavy physical and emotional burden. The tour was exhausting, and the apathy of many in the audiences he addressed outraged his conviction that Canadians must unite to confront the rising forces of world fascism. A man who heard him speak in Prince Albert, Saskatchewan, remembered: "Certainly the most lasting impression was the sheer driving force of the man ... I have yet to hear another who gave such an irresistible impression of sincerity. But there was another quality ... a sense of something held under control at the cost of supreme effort. I think it was probably a combination of fatigue and anger."[36]

Developments in Spain also fuelled Bethune's rage. The news was bad, for a new Nationalist offensive was again threatening Madrid. Bethune grew ever more frustrated that the party expected him to remain in Canada giving speeches when he should be in Spain where his medical skills were so desperately needed. Perhaps because he had had no reply to his telegram to the Instituto of 11 July, he decided that as soon as the tour ended he would return to Spain to serve in the front lines as a surgeon with the International Brigades. This time, he promised himself, no one would talk him out of it.

Arriving in Regina from Brandon on Thursday, 22 July, he decided to announce his decision to his comrades in Madrid. He had at last received a cable from them, a delayed response to his plea for support. Having wired A.A. MacLeod in Paris for instructions, Sise, Sorensen, and May now replied to Bethune: "Sorry delay reply your wire. Have been at front. Institute working full blast. Over 400 bottles used already during this victorious offensive. Also maintaining transfusion team near front. Have heard glowing reports success your meetings. Bravo. Remember you have *our full support work you are doing in Canada* [authors' italics]. *Salud* to Canadian people plus good luck to yourself."[37] Bethune cabled back that he would be returning to Spain, bringing with him a Ford station wagon donated by a group of farmers in Manitoba and a copy of *Heart of Spain*. After delivering these in Madrid, he would go to Albacete to join the International Brigades as a surgeon.[38] He must have hoped that his former comrades would not attempt to block his returning to Spain if they knew he would not try to return to the Instituto.

Moving ahead with the fundraising tour, Bethune further widened the scope of his speeches. He spoke in greater depth of the changing world order, warning that fascist forces were already at work beyond Spain, feverishly preparing to undermine and destroy democratically elected governments. Even in Canada, he insisted, fascism had "insidiously ... begun to rear its head."[39] He pointed to capitalism as a menace to free societies, speaking more and more of authoritarianism and capitalism as the twin enemies of the common people. He told his listeners that society was made up of two classes: those who believed in special privileges for the few, and those who believed in rewarding individuals who earned their achievements by talent and honest toil.[40] The only way to end this unequal class struggle would be for the common people of Canada to join the struggle for global democracy that would culminate in the establishment of "international socialism."[41]

After two addresses in Regina on Thursday, he left at midnight on a three-day, 1,500 kilometre trip that took him by train west to Saskatoon, north to Edmonton, and south to Calgary. On Monday, 26 July, he went west to British Columbia and changed trains for an even longer journey into the United States to address groups in California. Back in Vancouver on Sunday, 1 August, he appeared before a full house in the Orpheum Theatre, the largest in the city with a seating capacity of just under three thousand. A copy of the completed *Heart of Spain* had at last reached him, and before his address he announced to the audience that they would be the first in Canada to view it. After the showing of the film and Bethune's address, the chairman of the meeting opened the question period that usually followed. When a man stood up and asked if Bethune was a communist, he again professed his faith, replying, "I have the honour to be accepted as a member of the Communist Party."[42]

Rushing to meet schedules, captive to the orders of CASD or party officials who arranged his comings and goings at every stop, Bethune longed for a little time to himself to think and to escape. After the Orpheum engagement, he took the midnight ferry to Vancouver Island. Waiting for him on the dock in Victoria was Nigel Morgan, a prominent CCF official and chairman of the meeting at which Bethune would speak that evening. Morgan took him for breakfast, and then Bethune asked if there was some local spot where he could be alone for awhile.

Morgan drove him to nearby Thetis Lake, where they rented a canoe and paddled to a small island several hundred metres from the shore. "I want to be alone for several hours," Bethune told Morgan. "When I'm ready, I'll whistle and you can come over and get me." As Morgan pushed off in the canoe, he looked at his watch: it was just after 9 AM. It was almost 4 PM before he heard Bethune signal and went to pick him up. Leaving him in the morning, Morgan had thought Bethune to be distant, noticeably tense, and almost uncommunicative. Now his mood had swung to the opposite extreme, and he seemed a different individual, outgoing and chatty. Morgan drove him into the city to the Poodle Dog Café on Yates Street,[43] where Bethune wolfed down a meal, keeping up an animated conversation until they left for the meeting, scheduled for 8:30 PM. There he spoke to a receptive crowd of nearly nine hundred people.[44] From Victoria he travelled north to speak at Cumberland and Nanaimo and then took the ferry south to Seattle, Washington, for a one-day speaking engagement before returning to Vancouver and the Orpheum Theatre for a repeat performance on 7 August.

In all his speeches so far, Bethune had made the point that he would be going back to Spain at the end of the tour. By mid-August, however, he had stopped saying this: at some point he had been told that Spain was closed to him. The truth was that his communist comrades did not want him to return, and in any case the Spanish authorities would not allow him back into the country. Alarmed by Bethune's cable announcing his plan to return to Spain, Sise, Sorensen, and May had reported its contents to A.A. MacLeod. He instructed Rev. A.E. Smith, a Toronto clergyman and prominent CPC member about to leave for Spain, to investigate Bethune's standing there. After Smith conferred with the three Canadians, Sise sent the following message to the local communist organization, the Provincial Committee of Madrid:

Dear comrade Felipe

A.E. Smith, a member of the Central Committee of the Communist Party of Canada was here yesterday. He gave me instructions for you to inform the secret police (Checa) comrade of the Central Committee of Valencia that BETHUNE (in a telegram dated 22 July) announced to us his intention to return to Spain to join the International Brigades.
We would be pleased if the secret police comrade were to send a cablegram to Tim Buck (Secretary-General of the Communist Party of Canada), but only if the secret police is capable of using an indirect method of communication, the word "Noren" must be used instead of BUTHUNE [sic].
If you want to talk about this in more detail, send me a note, telling at what time I may see you,

HAZEN SISE of blood transfusion

The Provincial Committee then prepared a report on Bethune, with a copy of Sise's message attached, and sent it on 17 August to the Central Committee of the Communist Party in Valencia:

This comrade was expelled by the Blood Transfusion Committee and sent back to Canada in a clever manner because he was the one responsible in Madrid for the Canadian Committee for aid to Spain.
For being immoral. Among other things, he was often drunk and never in a condition to carry out a mission as delicate as blood transfusion.
1. He took away jewels with the pretext that he was going to hand them

over to the SRI (Socorro Rojo Internacional) and after declared that he would sell them in Paris to raise funds for the Institute. It's still not known what he did with these objects.

2. He thoughtlessly squandered money without thinking that it came from the solidarity that the Canadian proletariat was showing to Spain and on many occasions this was raised cent by cent.

3. He always showed a great interest in going to the front whenever there were [military] operations; but never with the good intention of performing transfusions.

4. He left Spain taking with him a film that he had made on the various fronts without having it passed by the censors.

5. There are various suspicions that this Bethune may be a spy according to a report now in Central Committee of our Party and in the Headquarters of the Sanidad Militar.

6. He had frequent visits and interviews with a somewhat suspicious woman called "TAJSA" that we believe today is currently in Valencia.

This concrete report shows the most significant things that make us believe that "NOREN" BETHUNE must not come to Spain and for this reason we agree with the Canadian comrades and the Communist Cell of the Madrid Blood Transfusion Institute (located at # 36 Principe de Vergara, telephone 50881.)[45]

As head of the Communist Party of Canada, Tim Buck received a copy of this telegram, and it must have been the final evidence that confirmed the party's decision not to allow Bethune to return to Spain.

It is not possible to know exactly when Bethune finally learned that he could not go back, but the realization must have hit him hard. He had hoped that the speaking tour would atone for his sins. Now his services were again being rejected, and this left him with the serious problem of what to do with his future. He knew that his identification with Republican Spain had closed many doors to him in Montreal, and his outright preaching of communism during the tour had no doubt made matters worse. He had so offended some Catholic authorities in Quebec that they approached owners of newspapers and radio stations and asked them not to publicize his speeches.[46] He could certainly never get his old job at Sacré Coeur back, and he knew his politics would make him *persona non grata* in many other hospitals. On the tour, in addition to confessing he was a communist, he had again raised the question of socialized medicine. "In my practice I hated the two, five and ten-dollar bills that came between me and my patients," he told one audience. "Many other doctors feel the same way. I believe that doctors should be civil servants and that treatment should be free to the public and paid for out of general taxation."[47] Trying to make the point to his audiences that doctors should be no more respected than craftsmen in other occupations, he had on occasion referred to himself as a carpenter, mechanic, or plumber of the human body. Such statements were anathema to most of the Canadian medical establishment. So although he knew that with his skills and experience he could find work somewhere, he also knew that he would never again be a chief of surgery.

His uncertainty about his future went far beyond the loss of his position in his profession. He had become disillusioned with North American society and politics in general. In Spain he had witnessed the weakening of the Republican cause by bitter infighting among communists, socialists, and anarchists, even in the face of enemy attacks. Thus in his speeches he had sought to rally all progressive forces in Canadian society, calling again and again for people to unite against the rising tide of fascism. In small mining towns of the Canadian Rockies and large cities of Canada and the United States, he had warned his listeners that a world war was already going on. He had pointed to the Italian seizure of Abyssinia in 1935, the Nationalist uprising in Spain in 1936, and most recently, the outbreak of the Sino-Japanese War on 7 July 1937.[48] Unless western democracies took immediate action against these aggressors, he warned, a fascist global hegemony would result. But by this point in the tour he realized to his despair that isolationist thinking prevailed in Canada. Most people smugly refused to believe that foreign events could have repercussions in North America; his words fell on deaf ears even among the so-called "progressive" individuals who came to listen to him. Indeed, a member of one of his audiences wrote to the editor of a newspaper demanding to know what possible relationship there was between the battlefields of Spain and the serenity of Northern Ontario.[49]

Such political naiveté exasperated Bethune. He was also outraged by the unwillingness of political leaders to take action to bring the economic depression to an end. Like so many others during the 1930s, he was appalled by what he saw as bourgeois greed, indifference to the plight of the working class, and blind fear of the spread of socialist and communist ideas. This same fear, he believed, had motivated politicians and members of the medical profession to reject his proposals to attack tuberculosis and introduce socialized medicine. Dr Wendell MacLeod, one of his former colleagues in the MGSPH, recalled, "Norman came back from Spain knowing that things were washed up ... because of the same kind of apathy as had washed up the medical care program ... In the mood he was in, he could not have settled down in Montreal to professional practice."[50] His feelings had only grown stronger in the course of his tour. And there was a deeper level to his discontentment. His experience in Spain had changed him forever. He had never lived a conventional life, but in Spain he had been almost constantly on the move, working under crisis conditions and passionately devoted to a cause. Now he found himself permanently uprooted from a normal way of life and alienated from Canadian society.

But as had happened the year before, world events meshed with his personal destiny. Spain had been the focus of his passionate interest; now his attention swung to China. Through newspapers including the *Daily Clarion*, he had been following developments in the Sino-Japanese War, angered at yet another state being attacked by a fascist aggressor. While on tour, he read Agnes Smedley's *China's Red Army Marches*, in which the American left-wing activist told of the heroic struggles of the communist army and of the idealistic new society that Chinese communists were fighting to establish. With the door to Spain barred, it now occurred to him that he might go to China instead, perhaps to establish a blood-transfusion unit there. He mentioned the idea on 12 August at a small afternoon gathering in the home of a CASD official in Salmon Arm, British Columbia, saying that he had been giving thought to a project that would take him to China, where a week earlier Japanese forces had taken control of Beijing. This nugget of news was picked up by a lurking RCMP informer shadowing Bethune and was relayed to headquarters.[51] Whether before this date or later the same month is not clear, but sometime in August Bethune contacted Tim Buck in Toronto and suggested sending a medical unit to China to work with the communist Eighth Route Army.[52] However, as Bethune well knew, all the resources of the CPC and the CASD were currently being poured into Spain; for the moment the party did not give him a definite response.

Mulling over these ideas, for the rest of August he travelled through Alberta, Saskatchewan, and Manitoba, speaking in small towns. He appeared again in Calgary, and from there sent a last wistful appeal to the CASD about Spain. Writing on 16 August, he pleaded, "All engagements assigned to me either by you or the provincial committees since my tour started have been kept by me on time. I have not missed a single date in spite of three and occasionally four speeches a day. Spain will be peaceful after the Canadian publicity tour."[53] There was no reply. From Calgary he went on to Edmonton, Regina, and Saskatoon, reaching Winnipeg, the last stop on his western tour, on Sunday, 29 August. He was in back in Ontario in Windsor on Wednesday, 1 September, and in London the following day.

At a rally in St Catharines on 3 September he gave his last scheduled speech. In a letter published in the *Daily Clarion*, he estimated that thirty thousand people had heard him speak during the two months of the tour.[54] "I have become, for thousands of workers, a symbol – to contemplate this responsibility is terrifying," he wrote. "I feel a tremendous urge to get back into the mass and hide myself from this bright glare. You will know how I feel, I know."[55] For the ebullient individualist and lover of the limelight to write this, he must have been weary indeed. However, the CASD had more plans for him. Impressed by the size of the crowds he was attracting, and in response to requests for him to appear in places where he had not visited, in mid-August it had hastily scheduled a new five-week series of speaking engagements.

Before Bethune began this new tour, the CASD sent him to Detroit where the local committee of the American Medical Bureau to Aid Spanish Democracy had arranged for a meeting in the Detroit Art Institute. On the eve of his departure from Toronto, word reached the CASD that the Detroit police commissioner had warned the local committee that he would not allow them to show *Heart of Spain* unless they removed from the film "uncomplimentary" references to Hitler and Mussolini. Despite a last-minute injunction that prevented the threatened police action, it was clear to both CASD and CPC officials in Toronto that during the Detroit appearance it would be necessary for Bethune to deny emphatically that he had any communist affiliation. For the sake of the cause, he dutifully lied again. During his address he said, "I gave up my hospital. I went to Spain. I did it because I believe in democracy. I am not a socialist or a communist."[56]

The following week he spoke in Niagara Falls, Ontario, on Tuesday, 14 September. Before a gathering in Jubilee Hall, he once more obeyed party orders and told his audience, "I went to Spain last October. I did not represent any political party, just the best people in Canada, the people who believe in democracy."[57] The next evening he appeared before a standing-room crowd of more than three thousand in Toronto's Massey Hall. There he confessed that his political development had begun in Moscow, and that he had gone to Spain because the Spanish Civil War was a class war. But although he ended by calling for the formation of a united front to stop fascism and protect workers' rights, he carefully avoided calling himself a communist. After this engagement he returned to the United States again, addressing audiences in Boston, New York, and Philadelphia before turning north to speak in Halifax and Moncton.[58] Back in Montreal, he appeared in

Strathcona Hall, where almost a year before he had spoken about his trip to the Soviet Union and maintained that he was not ready to become a communist.[59] The political journey he had since made was greater by far than the sum of his travels. Ten days later, with an address in Hamilton, Ontario, on 14 October 1937, the second tour came to an end.[60]

Bethune's extraordinary performance on the tour raised thousands of dollars for the cause of Republican Spain and inspired some young Canadians to volunteer for the Mackenzie-Papineau Battalion, part of the International Brigades fighting there.[61] Yet despite this success and his fervent commitment to communism, the CPC still had reservations about his stability and reliability. A.A. MacLeod later observed, "He could not work with other people; [he was] never a real Party man."[62] Bethune had indulged in creature comforts throughout the tour, and when MacLeod received the bills, "he tore his hair out."[63] And long afterward, Tim Buck commented about Bethune's speaking tour, "Yes, Bethune raised money, but he also spent a lot of money. Norman liked his rye."[64]

Despite the public accolades, Bethune had not yet redeemed himself and in his heart he knew it.

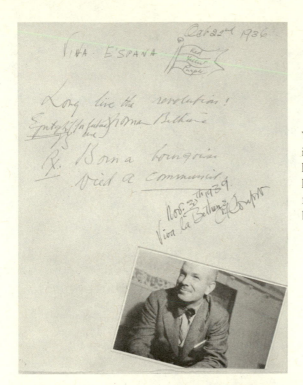

Viva España. In this jaunty inscription Bethune declared his communist faith before he set sail for Spain. LAC C-139723; reproduced by permission

Members of the Canadian blood transfusion unit. Because of the intense fighting in the Madrid sector, Bethune's delivery system brought more blood to battlefronts than any other organization in Spain. NFB/LAC PA-114782; reproduced by permission

The Ford ambulance in front of the Instituto. Sorensen, Sise, and Bethune with two Spanish members of the Instituto. The Spaniards called the Ford *la rubia* (the blond) because of its light-coloured wood panelling. Courtesy BMH

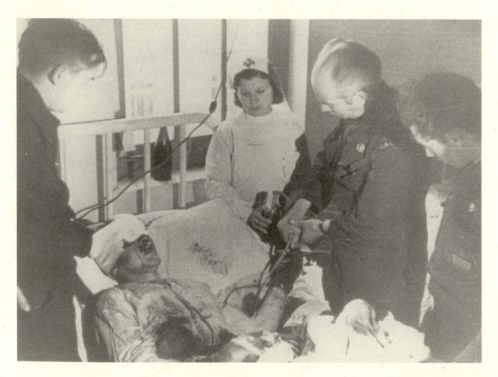

Administering a transfusion. Bethune spoke often of the almost miraculous effect a timely transfusion could have even on badly wounded soldiers. Courtesy BMH

Kajsa Rothman. Bethune's affair with the uninhibited Swede caused tensions within the Instituto. Reproduced by permission of the Labour Movement Archives and Library, Stockholm

Enjoying life in the Sierra de Guadarrama. Bethune spent Christmas 1936 with Loyalist fighters in the mountains northwest of Madrid. Courtesy NFB/Hazen Sise

Bethune in Barcelona. This humorous sketch was done in 1937. Authors' collection

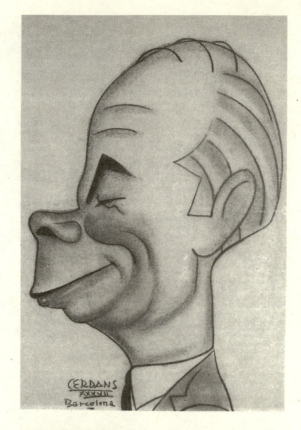

Evacuad Madrid. The menace of the bombing of Madrid by the Nationalists is conveyed in this stunning poster. Authors' collection

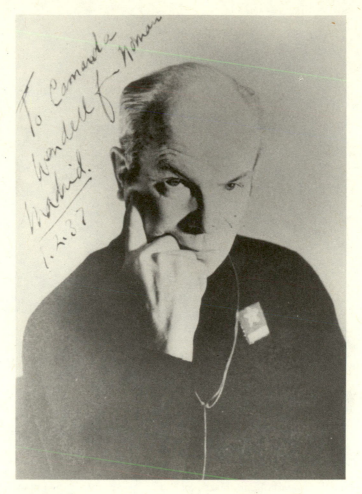

Celebrity photograph. Bethune used CASD funds to have professional photographs taken of himself and ordered many prints to autograph and send to his friends. Courtesy BMH

Mother and child. This photo vividly depicts the misery along the Almería road. Courtesy NFB/Hazen Sise

Refugees along the Almería Road. Hazen Sise's photographs were the only visual record of the sufferings of the thousands of civilians from Málaga who were fired upon by Nationalist forces as they fled to Almería. Courtesy NFB/Hazen Sise

Helping refugees into the ambulance. Horrified by the suffering of the Málaga refugees, Bethune set about rescuing as many children and mothers as he could.
Courtesy NFB/Hazen Sise

Returning from Spain. Bethune's journey home was not a happy one, for he knew that in the eyes of his comrades he had "blotted his copybook."
Courtesy BMH

A hero's welcome. Greeted by enthusiastic crowds, Bethune gave a speech in Toronto that shocked as many as it thrilled because of its criticism of British imperialism.
Courtesy BMH

Paraskeva Clark. Although Bethune had met the Toronto artist in 1936, the two did not become lovers until his return from Spain in 1937. LAC E006078599; reproduced by permission

With children in Sudbury, Ontario. Always at his best with youngsters, Bethune likely enjoyed time out from his speaking tour. Courtesy BMH

A communist in Winnipeg. It was here that Bethune publicly announced his political faith, telling an audience, "I have the honour to be a communist." Courtesy BMH

Raising funds in New York. Many American volunteers who supported Republican Spain also helped Bethune with his preparations for his mission to China. Courtesy BMH

✤ 13 ✤

Entr'acte

Montreal, New York City,
October–December 1937

His hopes of returning to Spain dashed, outraged by the indifference of many Canadians to his impassioned pleas that they address social issues at home and the rise of fascism abroad, Bethune had found the speaking tours a time of lonely frustration. Marian Scott said she only later realized that the tour had been "an unhappy and stormy time in his life."[1] Despite his devotion to communism, he was haunted by feelings that he had not yet accomplished anything great and that time was running out. "In all my life, I have never achieved better than second best," he told his former lover Elizabeth Hurcomb in Montreal in September.[2] He felt personally adrift as well, for Marian Scott remained committed to her marriage and Margaret Day continued to avoid him.[3] His emotional ties to Frances Coleman were, as always, complex and frustrating. Unable to let go of the past, he had written to her occasionally during the tour and as usual could not keep from criticizing her. He went so far as to tell her that he no longer respected her because of the life she was leading. She must have reproached him, because on 14 September he had returned to this theme in a letter written to her from the King Edward Hotel in Niagara Falls:

> Is it not true we might write to each other the remarks of our time and add but little to the poor satisfaction we now possess?
> I regret – it is a constant pain in my heart that I have harmed you. I did not intend to harm you.
> I was ill-educated (sexually) as you, never forget that.
> If I knew how to recompense you I would do so. I do not know that.
> My path is set on a strange road, but as long as I feel it's a good road I will go down it. And you must go down yours.
> When I said I had no longer respect for you – you, who I once respected

– I meant, to me your life was devoid of dignity. But my dignity and your dignity perhaps do not agree.

Mine is uncompromise; hatred of evil and stupidity, personal uncontamination and uncontact; aloneness. That is all I meant. I see now once more, I have made the mistake to suggest to you a course of action.

Forgive me.

Beth[4]

Meanwhile, the CPC had decided to take up the matter of sending a medical unit to China. Because the party lacked funds for such a project, Tim Buck approached Earl Browder, the general secretary of the Communist Party of the United States (CPUSA). At a CPC convention in Toronto on 10 October 1937, Browder agreed that such a unit should be sent, and a joint committee of the two parties was formed.[5] Bethune was asked to be a member of the unit. For him this was a godsend, a way out of the dead end in which he found himself. Eager to prove himself in the party's eyes, he said, "I accept on one condition, that if I don't come back, you will let the world know that Norman Bethune died a Communist Party member."[6]

He was told that funding and organization of the unit would be done in New York and he would have to go there soon. On one level he was elated: he had wanted another chance after Spain, and this was it. Yet he also faced moments of terrifying doubt about what lay ahead. He had been rootless since returning from Spain, and now in his final days in Montreal he said goodbye to the very last of his old life. There is no record of his seeing Frances Coleman or Marian Scott, yet he must have done so. He met Libbie Park for tea, telling her he felt as if he were living in some strange kind of limbo, in an unreal world. Perhaps dreading the isolation he would face, he asked Park to go with him to China, but she said she could not. He also asked Hazen Sise, who was back in Montreal, but Sise too refused.[7] He tried again and again to see Margaret Day, but she kept him at arm's length. Many years later she recalled how a friend finally phoned her saying that Bethune was at her apartment, standing right beside her, and it was Margaret's duty to speak to him. In the end she gave in and saw him. By this time Bethune's mood, ever volatile, had swung from excitement about his new project to depression. "I have burnt my bridges, no hospital will touch me now," he told Day. "The Party's going to send me to China." Then he began to cry, saying, "I'm too old, but there's nothing I can do now. I have no money. I have no job. I have nothing. So I'm going to China." Day thought to herself that he would die there. She felt that he believed that too.[8]

Arriving in New York in late October, he was greeted by a reception committee from the American Medical Bureau to Aid Spanish Democracy.[9] Despite their continuing involvement in the Spanish cause, some members of the organization offered what cash they could for the Chinese project, while others joined in the search for non-medical supplies, ran errands, and provided transportation for Bethune. A few days after his arrival they took him to a Halloween party in the quarters of a little theatre group. It was an evening of dancing, drinking, and socializing with people who treated him as a hero for his commitment to Spain, and Bethune, spirits rising, enjoyed himself thoroughly.

He soon realized, however, that it was one thing for the party to decide to send a medical unit to China and quite another for them to make it happen, for little progress had been made. Among various problems, the most serious was finding enough money for the venture. After his past three months of fundraising, he was well aware that Spain, not China, was the focus of concern for left-wing and liberal elements in North America. Tim Buck had told him frankly that the CPC could offer him no more than best wishes for the China project. The Communist Party of the United States, however, was another matter. It too was fully committed to Spain, but Earl Browder was hopeful that money could also be found for a medical mission to China.

Browder's interest in China dated from his experience as a Comintern agent there during the 1920s. He was also well informed about the most recent political and military developments through reports from his close friend Philip J. Jaffe, who assured him that support could be found for the medical unit. Jaffe was a successful New York businessman and editor of the journal *China Today,* published by the American Friends of the Chinese People, a Communist Party front organization under Comintern control. Jaffe had recently returned from China, where in June he had made the difficult trek to the distant headquarters of the Eighth Route Army at Yan'an, in Shaanxi Province. There he interviewed Mao Zedong and other members of the party hierarchy and spent time with Agnes Smedley, learning her assessment of the deepening military conflict with Japan. Smedley, the American journalist whose book *China's Red Army Marches* Bethune had read on his speaking tour, had been staying in Yan'an since February 1937. Assuring Jaffe that the most urgent need of the embattled Chinese was trained medical personnel, she pressed him to take whatever steps he could to rally American public opinion to the cause. In August she had followed this up with an appeal, made jointly with Mao Zedong, to the American and Canadian Communist parties urging the formation of an organization to send medical supplies and personnel to Yan'an.[10]

Jaffe's response was the formation of the China Aid Council (CAC); its purpose was to focus public interest on China and to appeal for aid to be sent there. The CAC was in fact an outgrowth of the American League for Peace and Democracy (ALPD), a communist front organization. A prominent ALPD figure and Jaffe's close collaborator in launching the CAC was William E. Dodd Jr, son of the American ambassador to Nazi Germany. When Bethune arrived in New York, the CAC had barely begun to function in a small office at 268 Fourth Avenue. Jaffe had provided the money for the rent and office equipment. He also persuaded Corliss Lamont, a wealthy left-wing intellectual, to join him in making a cash donation to a fund to be used to buy supplies for the medical unit to take to China. Each man gave $1,000, and through Dodd's contacts with several affluent New Yorkers sympathetic to the plight of China, additional support was raised.[11] Famous doctors such as Charles Mayo and Wilder Penfield, as well as a large number of celebrities including the dancers Alfred Lunt and Lynn Fontanne and the actors Franchot Tone and Katharine Cornell, also lent their names and help to the enterprise.[12] The mission of the CAC unit would be to proceed to China and there liaise with representatives of the Chinese government in the temporary capital of Hankou, in the hope that they would eventually be sent to serve with the Communist Eighth Route Army.

Not long after his arrival, Bethune learned that another member had been chosen for the unit. After considerable searching, the Communist Party of the United States had persuaded a young doctor to join the mission to China. He was Lewis M. Fraad, a graduate of Downstate Medical College in Brooklyn who was just beginning his internship. As a CPUSA member, he was also trying to organize a union for interns in several Brooklyn hospitals. Despite early misgivings about the venture, which he initially regarded as both romantic and impracticable, Fraad was struck by Bethune's commitment.

At this point the CAC decided that the most useful first step was to introduce Bethune to New Yorkers of substance who were sympathetic to progressive causes. By then an accomplished fundraiser, Bethune skilfully took advantage of this opportunity. By Christmas he, Fraad, and Dodd would manage to raise another $3,500, in addition to the personal donation of $2,000 from Jaffe and Lamont.[13] A huge drawback to their fundraising efforts was the CAC's reluctance to publicize the medical unit's existence until it reached its destination. Fearing that the American government or the

Japanese might try to prevent its arrival in China, they felt it would be unwise to launch a public campaign for money to pay for equipment.

Not knowing their precise destination or the specific role they would play, Bethune and Fraad found it difficult to decide what equipment to take. Influenced partly by information brought back by Jaffe from Yan'an, they began collecting material to outfit a small field hospital. In their appeals for funds, this was their declared objective, and as the money gradually came in, they began making the rounds of medical and surgical supply houses, comparing prices and appealing for discounts. The purchased supplies were stored in a warehouse. Other vital necessities for the unit were suitable clothing and personal items. To endure the rigorous winters in the mountainous regions of northwestern China where the communist forces were operating, Bethune knew that they would require long underwear, socks, sweaters, gloves, and a lined jacket. He bought these in New York, though he waited until his last days in Canada to buy himself a pair of knee-high logger's boots. They also needed a variety of equipment for survival in a mobile guerrilla war. The ideal source for most of these was Abercrombie and Fitch, the renowned New York outfitter, where, among other things, Bethune bought a sleeping bag, canvas water bags, compressed fibre panniers (lighter and more flexible than metal trunks), a Coleman kerosene lamp, an aluminum canteen, and cooking utensils.

His spirits rose as day by day the small mountain of supplies grew. But Fraad complained that what they had collected was ridiculously inadequate. How could they possibly know what they would need? They were setting off into the unknown and had no way of knowing which supplies would be most important. When they ran out of certain medicines, as they surely would, what then? Bethune brushed aside such practical objections, insisting that somehow they would make do. He would have liked to have a greater variety of equipment and supplies to take, but he knew it was not possible given the funds available. What mattered to him was that he was going to China. He said he could no longer tolerate the western decadence that had once seduced him, and found urban life corrupt and boring. In the Chinese hinterland there would be no distracting diversions, only the revolutionary reality of a war in which he could use his surgical skills to make his contribution against a fascist aggressor. Nothing was remotely as important as that. In such upbeat moments, he felt a passionate certainty that China was to be his life's fulfillment.[14]

Bethune's enthusiasm, intense energy, and willingness to give himself unreservedly to something he believed in gradually overcame Fraad's logical pessimism,[15] but that all-consuming dedication made his wife, Irma, shudder. While she shared her husband's commitment to communism, she was absolutely opposed to his decision to accompany Bethune. She and Fraad had been married less than a year, and it was clear to her that in his zeal to get to China, Bethune was trying to take her husband from her. It was of no consequence to him that Fraad might well die there. "He was a rival. As a woman, I saw him as a rival," she later recalled, describing herself as "a ghost at the dinner-party." Bethune's suggestion that she might do a quick study in nursing fundamentals and follow them to China did not relieve her fears.[16]

By this time a third member of the unit had been selected. Although the Canadian Communist Party could not provide financial assistance, it did find a nurse to accompany Bethune and Fraad. She was Jean Ewen, the twenty-six-year-old daughter of Tom McEwen, one of the CPC's founding members. Ewen was neither politically committed nor eager to please her father, with whom she was usually at cross purposes, but she agreed out of humanitarianism and a sincere love for China to join Bethune and Fraad. A graduate of St Joseph's School of Nursing in Winnipeg, she had spent four years in a Roman Catholic mission hospital in the northeastern Chinese province of Shandong, returning to Canada in June 1937. She had found a hospital position in Toronto but yearned to go back to China. She learned of Bethune's mission when Sam Carr, the CPC national organizer, asked her to come to his Toronto office and told her about the formation of the medical unit. As she spoke Chinese and knew something of Chinese culture, he pointed out, she could be invaluable to Bethune and Fraad. There would be no salary, but her expenses would be covered.

Ewen said she was interested but needed time to consider. The next day she telephoned Carr to accept the assignment. Arriving in Manhattan in early December, she was interviewed by a psychologist to determine that she was emotionally fit for such a difficult mission. After being accepted, she met Bethune and joined him for several days in his search for supplies before returning to Toronto to prepare for the trip. He could, she later recalled, "charm a cigar-store Indian right out of his feathers and paint. [He was] witty, sarcastic. Very well educated beyond his profession. He was a ladies' man, and how they threw themselves at him."[17]

Despite his focus on the mission to China and his avowed rejection of bourgeois decadence, Bethune had found time to involve himself in another love affair. At the Halloween party he had attended, he had met Elsie Siff, a pretty young New Yorker of left-wing views.[18] He asked her to dance, and though he was soon whisked away to be introduced to other admirers, he managed to see her again on several occasions. He invited her to the theatre, and during November and December they saw each other often. They first went to see Clifford Odet's *Golden Boy*, starring the ill-fated actress Frances Farmer in her first stage role. Bethune was less impressed by it than by the amateur production *Pins and Needles*, a revue put on at the Labor Stage by union workers in the garment trade. He and Siff went to one of the early performances, and he thoroughly enjoyed the production's ribald thrusts at the establishment in numbers such as "Doing the Reactionary," "Not Cricket to Picket," and "It's Better with a Union Man."

For Siff, who had fallen in love with Bethune, these were joyful days. They danced at house parties, went for Sunday afternoon drives outside the city in a car borrowed for the day, and had coffee and pie at the Manhattan chain of Childs Restaurants, which Bethune liked to frequent – despite complaining that everything tasted like library paste.[19] He was at his best with her, affectionate and caring; when she was suffering from a serious sinus ailment, he insisted on going with her by taxi to Brooklyn to make certain the specialist treated her correctly. The two soon became lovers, but Siff knew from the beginning that she cared far more for him than he did for her. He had mentioned his ex-wife only in passing, but she sensed he was still deeply emotionally involved with her. Despite this, she was so smitten with Bethune that she offered to go to China with him. He refused her, saying that she was too frail for such a difficult mission.[20]

Although he took time off for evening partying and his new affair, Bethune kept busy each day raising funds and visiting medical supply houses. He also had another important task to carry out. Badly in need of a refresher course in general surgery, especially in incisions and sutures, he called on Louis Davidson, assistant professor of thoracic surgery at New York's Columbia University. Davidson, a former fellow patient at Trudeau, was glad to oblige. After bringing Bethune up to date on surgical techniques, he suggested they meet another medical colleague for dinner at Longchamp's Restaurant one evening. Bethune already knew Davidson's other guest, Howard Lilienthal, a distinguished thoracic surgeon and former president of the American Association for Thoracic Surgery. During the dinner Bethune dominated the conversation as usual, holding his listeners rapt as he vividly outlined the horrors of the Japanese invasion of China and explained with deep emotion why he felt compelled to go there. At one point he asked Lilienthal to consider joining him. The incredulous Lilienthal reminded Bethune that he was seventy-six years old. Bethune leaned forward and said, "But, Doctor, we need you and perhaps you might die in China, and what would be more noble than to die in China for your fellow man?" Lilienthal declined the honour.[21]

Shortly after arriving in New York, Bethune had also been in touch with Richard H. Meade, another fellow-member of the AATS who had worked with him in preparing the program of the annual meeting of the Society in Minnesota in 1936. Dr Meade and his wife had been in the audience when Bethune spoke in Philadelphia on the fundraising tour in September, and they had invited him to spend the evening with them. Mary Meade had been much impressed by Bethune's speaking ability and personal charm, so they invited him to Philadelphia to address a meeting of the Foreign Policy Association on Saturday, 20 November. The topic of the address was "Europe: New Forces and Old Tensions." Although he knew little about the subject, Bethune accepted, but he only began to organize his thoughts on the morning train from New York to Philadelphia. He was one of two speakers invited to address the luncheon meeting in the Bellevue Stratford Hotel. The other was Raymond Gram Swing, a popular Mutual Network columnist on the New York station WOR.

Mary Meade later wrote a critique of the speeches for the Foreign Policy Association, stating that Swing's address "was beyond praise" but that Bethune's "was for a variety of reasons perfectly awful. His delivery was execrable and his matter worse. That he apologized and that there were several who had also heard him before – equally dumbfounded – is the coldest comfort. He made a lame emotional plea for Spain which some of the audience were glad to hear as Swing had tossed Spain rather completely aside, but lost his cause by doing it badly."[22] When Bethune met the Meades afterward, he at first seemed downcast by his poor performance but shrugged off his failure and turned the conversation to his belief in communism as the panacea for the world's ills. After dinner his hosts took him to a dance party at a friend's home where he was treated as a guest of honour. He relaxed and enjoyed himself, managing to attract most of the women, who thronged about him throughout the evening. By Monday he was back in Manhattan.[23]

At some point in December, Fraad informed Bethune that he would be unable to accompany him to China because his request for a passport had been turned down. He promised that he would try again and join Bethune later.[24] The CAC managed to find a substitute, Dr Charles Edward Parsons. An American citizen and two years younger than Bethune, he had been medical director and chief surgeon of the Notre Dame Bay Memorial Hospital in Twillingate, Newfoundland, between 1923 and 1934. However, he was an alcoholic and, unable to control his drinking, had left his position and gone to Kingston, New York, to open a private practice. After he agreed to join the unit, Bethune and Fraad visited him at 9:30 one morning to find that Parsons had already been drinking heavily.[25] Despite his alcoholism and the fact that he was not a member of the CPUSA, he was named the head of the medical unit, possibly because he was the only American in the group. This meant he would be responsible for handling the unit's funds and for reporting to the CAC by maintaining contact with Dodd.[26]

Having Parsons put in charge was a blow for Bethune, for he must have thought that, given his experience in Spain, he should have led the unit. It is possible that Tim Buck had informed Earl Browder of Bethune's inability to handle money, his drinking problem, and his tendency to act independently of party orders. Bethune may also have rubbed Jaffe – and possibly Dodd – the wrong way. Jaffe later wrote that Bethune had gotten on his nerves "when on a number of occasions he would come or storm into my office demanding money for a variety of needs."[27] Although his pride was hurt, Bethune tried to convince himself that even the shaky hand of Parsons assisting him would be better than no hand at all. In the remote hinterland of China, he told Fraad, there would be no whisky to tempt Parsons, and he would be able to reform the man's drinking problem.[28] He was perhaps counting on the isolation to keep himself from temptation as well.

Although no longer a member of the unit, Fraad continued to help Bethune, conducting daily telephone canvassing, making visits to potential donors, and checking and rechecking inventory. By this time they had amassed a considerable amount of medical equipment and supplies: scalpels and other surgical instruments, special types of dressings, anaesthesia (local, general, and intravenous), a portable x-ray machine, hypodermic syringes and needles, and surgical gloves. There was also a limited supply of sulfathiazole in ampoules for intramuscular injection and about two thousand sulfa tablets. Yet however much they managed to collect, they knew it would be a drop in the ocean compared to the desperate need that lay ahead in China.[29] But at last the CAC decided that the unit was ready to move, urged on by the impatient Bethune. During these last days he spoke eagerly, almost ecstatically, of the release he would feel when he reached the combat zone, far from the banality and tedium of urban life.[30] He was both fleeing the disappointments of the past and running toward an idealized future.

As the final items were added to the cache of supplies, Bethune's mood fluctuated between this extreme enthusiasm and a darker realization of what going to China meant for him personally. He had eagerly sought the challenge of the mission, but in his more reflective moments he knew only too well the risks involved. He must have asked himself what would happen when the unit's pitifully small amount of supplies was exhausted. If they were having so much trouble raising money now, where would funds come from in the future? He knew that several doctors had been asked by the CPUSA to join the unit but had refused, saying that going to China would be a death sentence.[31] This view was shared by members of the American Medical Bureau to Aid Spanish Democracy who had volunteered time to help Bethune collect and sort supplies throughout November and December. Evelyn Kirkpatrick, one of these volunteers, later recalled the atmosphere in the warehouse where the mission's equipment and supplies were being assembled:

> All of us felt he was going to his death. We knew what conditions were there. He was going to cut himself off at his age from modern medicine. I worked with him in those last months when he would come down and there was no fanfare and he wasn't the hero from Spain and he was sitting around our warehouse and I was putting the stuff together. And the boys were really thinking through with him. What kind of saddle bags? How much medicine? What kind of stuff do you take? What is volatile in this kind of cold? It was grim. He was very business-like, he never showed anything. I would go home and cry … Would anyone have gone to the lengths that he did to go there unless he had already said goodbye to many things here? He was very lonely at the end. The decision put a kind of space around him.[32]

A week before he left New York, Bethune expressed his feeling of apartness in a letter to Elizabeth Hurcomb, to whom he had avoided saying goodbye during his last days in Montreal. He wrote, "My road ahead is a strange and dangerous one … I don't want to attempt at my time – and in my time left – any serious emotional engagement. I am through with such things, I feel myself steeled against them … I loved you once. I have great affection for you now. Remember me with quietness and respect. Beth."[33]

On the following Friday, New Year's Eve, a gala party was held in the same little theatre quarters where Bethune had celebrated Halloween. On this occasion the revellers included most of those who had worked with him during the past two months. Toasts were drunk, hands shaken, and embraces and kisses exchanged. Elsie Siff was there, and Bethune gave her his yellow tartan necktie as a keepsake. As he kissed her farewell, he slipped a note into her hand. In it he tenderly thanked her for her company during his stay in Manhattan.[34] On New Year's Day, 1938, he boarded a train heading west. His first stop was Toronto where he bought a few more supplies. He may have visited his mother in nearby Hamilton, but it seems unlikely, for both she and his sister had been angered and embarrassed by his open avowal of his communist faith. Although he would write many letters from China to friends in North America, he sent none to his family.[35]

During his brief stop in Toronto, Bethune stayed with the Clarks. Paraskeva Clark gave him her set of watercolours in the hope that he might find time in China to paint. "You have so much in your painting," she assured him, and he said, "You know, praise from you means much to me."[36] Then he gathered his luggage and they set off by taxi for Union Station. He reminisced during the ride, and as they passed the University of Toronto mentioned that he had graduated in medicine there. Then a sudden thought struck him: "Oh my God, I've forgotten my surgical instruments!" he exclaimed. In the rush he had left them in his room. With barely time to catch his train, he begged Paraskeva to send the instruments to Vancouver by air freight the following day.[37]

From Toronto he went to Chicago to meet Parsons. If conflict between the two men had not already occurred in New York, it began then, as Parsons mentioned in a letter to Dodd. Writing just a few hours before he, Bethune, and Ewen left Vancouver on the *Empress of Asia*, he informed Dodd, "I had to put up some of our small needs over and above Bethune's 100 – for his equipment which he had not purchased in Toronto as planned. I met him in Chicago and found him broke."[38] Enclosed with the letter was a signed contract that Parsons had just received and was now returning. In it he and Bethune gave their services for a monthly payment of $100, to be paid to a family member. Several months after reaching China, Bethune would direct that his stipend be sent to Frances Coleman.[39] Travel and accommodation costs were to be borne by the CAC. The two doctors and Jean Ewen (who was not paid) had agreed to provide their services for a period of six months.[40]

Having already antagonized Parsons, Bethune also managed to annoy Ewen even before the *Empress of Asia* sailed. On Saturday, 8 January, he and Parsons were leaning over the rail of the ship when they heard the skirl of bagpipes and saw Ewen coming up the gangplank, being played aboard by two pipers in full highland regalia. When she joined them, Bethune demanded, "Who are those oatmeal savages serenading?"

Ewen replied that the pipers were friends who had come to see her off. Bethune sneered, "I don't believe it, Tom's daughter, a damned Scottish nationalist? You should be ashamed of yourself!" Outraged at his rudeness and by his reference to her communist father, with whom she had a stormy relationship, Ewen told him she did not care what he believed.[41]

As the liner glided out of Burrard Inlet into Georgia Strait, Bethune penned notes of farewell to Marian Scott and Frances Coleman. In his letter to Scott he was euphoric: "You see Pony, why I *must* go to China. Please read Edgar Snow's book – *Red Star Over China*. Agnes Smedley – *Red Army Marches*. Bertram's *First Act in China*. I feel so happy & gay now. Happier than since I left Spain. Goodbye & bless you. Beth."[42]

His letter to his ex-wife was very different in tone, revealing as always both his genuine concern and his irresistible urge to criticize and control her. He wrote, "My Dear Frances, I am doing what I can for you, for justice & my former love for you. I am giving you what is due you. Please do not consider it in any other way except as that. It would seem that the time for offering advice is gone but I beg of you to leave Montreal. I feel so unhappy about you & what you have become and will become. Escape for your life or terrible people will kill everything in you that I once loved. Goodbye, Beth."[43]

Frances Coleman later described Bethune's China venture as "his last fling," but it was much more than that. Yearning to overcome his past failures, he had pinned his hopes on this new mission as his last chance to keep the vow he had made so many years before to do something great for humanity. He was fiercely determined that China would be his salvation: this time he would get it right.

Into the Fray

Hankou to Xi'an, 7 February–29 March 1938

Given Bethune's newly minted contempt for bourgeois luxuries, he may not have approved of the comforts of tourist class on his journey to Hong Kong. The ninety passengers aboard the *Empress of Asia* were pampered by a crew of over five hundred. At dinner an orchestra played; gentlemen were expected to wear suits and women evening dresses. The ship's amenities included a swimming pool, shuffleboard, dancing, and movies.[1] Despite the enticement of a well-stocked bar, Bethune seems to have managed to control his drinking, for Jean Ewen later stated that she never saw him drunk or pursuing women.[2] Struggling against temptation probably did not improve his temper, and he chain-smoked in compensation.

The ship's other passengers included several missionaries and their families, the wives of some United States Army servicemen stationed in the Philippines, and a few Chinese businessmen from Hong Kong. Also on board were a number of American pilots en route to join the Flying Tiger squadron that Claire L. Chennault, a retired US Army Air Corps captain, was forming to fight the Japanese. Another passenger was twenty-nine-year-old Michael Lindsay, a graduate of Balliol College, Oxford, where his father was master. Lindsay was on his way to Beijing to teach at Yenching University, an American-sponsored institution. He and Bethune struck up an acquaintance which, against all odds, would be renewed months later in a remote area of northwestern China.

The three weeks' journey did nothing to improve relations among the members of the medical unit. They avoided each other at meals and met only briefly at other times; when they stopped at Yokohama, Kobe, Nagasaki, and Shanghai, each left the ship separately for sightseeing excursions. However, Bethune and Ewen knew that Parsons was drinking heavily and that he spent many hours carousing with the ship's engineers and radio operators. On

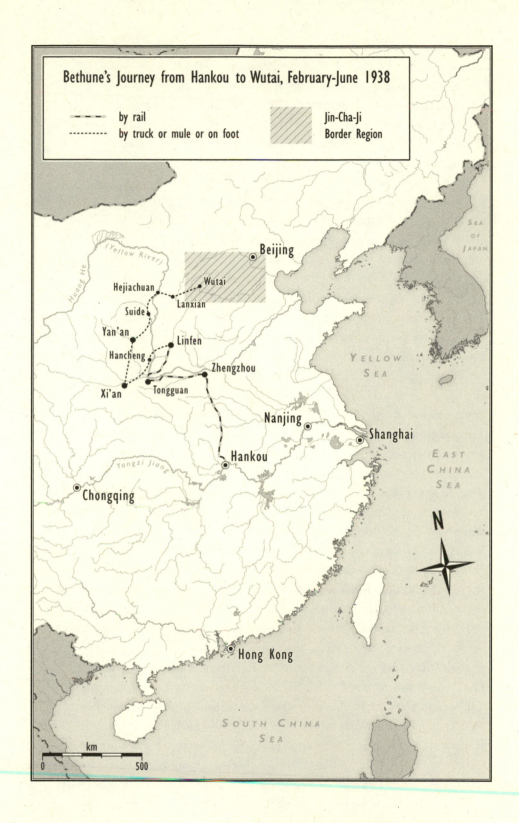

Bethune's Journey from Hankou to Wutai, February–June 1938

--·-- by rail
------- by truck or mule or on foot

Jin-Cha-Ji
Border Region

Beijing

(Yellow River)

Wutai

Hejiachuan

Lanxian

Suide

Yan'an

Linfen

Hancheng

Zhengzhou

Xi'an

Tongguan

Nanjing

Shanghai

YELLOW
SEA

Hankou

EAST
CHINA
SEA

Chongqing

Huang He

Yangzi Jiang

SEA
OF
JAPAN

N

Hong Kong

SOUTH CHINA
SEA

km

0   500

occasion he lost control of himself and once had to be forcibly ejected from the saloon after making a public disturbance.[3]

Bethune was convinced that Parsons was using the unit's money to buy liquor. He also feared that on one of his shore visits Parsons might be mugged and lose their funds as well as the various letters of introduction he carried. Ewen shared Bethune's concern, so they asked Parsons to divide the funds among the three of them and surrender the letters before he went ashore. Parsons refused, saying he was in charge and only he had the right to carry the money and documents. Matters came to a head at Yokohama. When Parsons returned drunk to the ship late at night, Bethune confronted him and demanded an accounting of the unit's finances. When Parsons rebuffed him, Bethune went to Ewen's cabin and described the encounter.[4] Opening his wallet to show her he had only $200 left, he asked her to join him in sending a cable to the China Aid Council asking that Parsons be brought to heel. Reluctant to take sides, Ewen refused, and Bethune stalked out.[5]

Before the *Empress of Asia* reached Shanghai on 24 January, however, Ewen changed her mind. When the ship docked, Bethune went ashore to send a joint cable to Philip Jaffe: "Demand recall drunkard Parsons success already endangered cable Hong Kong."[6] During the final three days of the voyage there was no reply from New York, and Bethune's frustration grew. There was more trouble as soon as they disembarked in Hong Kong. A pre-arranged contact failed to appear, and when they went to the Thomas Cook agency office to collect a money wire Dodd had promised to send, they discovered that it had not arrived. At this point Parsons admitted that he had no more money. According to Ewen, Bethune flew into a rage, "stomping and kicking everything in sight." Parsons suggested they go to the Hotel Sylvia, which was owned by a friend of his, telling them that they would be allowed to sleep in the servants' quarters there. Bethune began to curse Parsons for having drunk away money that was badly needed. But with no other option, he and Ewen paid the taxi fare to the hotel.[7]

Fortunately, funds from New York soon arrived, and they were able to pay for meals and accommodation; their equipment and supplies they deposited in the Canadian Pacific warehouse for later transshipment to the interior. Likely they also received word from the CAC that Agnes Smedley had left Yan'an and was now in Hankou, where she would be able to act as their liaison. They cabled her care of the US Embassy in Hankou, and she arranged for them to fly there on 7 February.[8] Hankou had become the temporary capital of the Chinese Guomindang (Nationalist) government after the Japanese seizure of Nanjing in mid-December 1937 and was being bombed daily by the Japanese. When the unit arrived, they found themselves plunged at once into the atmosphere of war,[9] air raid sirens wailing as an air crew rushed to shroud the plane in camouflage matting. Waiting for them on the tarmac were Smedley and Jack Belden, a young American journalist with United Press International. The vehicle that Smedley had hired was unable to carry their pile of luggage as well as them, so she suggested that they travel by rickshaw. Refusing to be hauled by a human being, Bethune walked behind the others to the docks where they boarded the ferry to cross the Han River to the city centre.[10]

Their destination was an Episcopalian mission compound. Within its walls were a red-brick church, several teachers' bungalows, and the large wooden residence of Bishop Logan H. Roots. Missionaries of other faiths often referred to the compound as the "Moscow-Heaven Axis" or the "Yan'an-Heaven Axis." This was because Roots, known as the "pink bishop," offered hospitality to journalists, diplomats, and officials of both the Guomindang and the Communist Chinese forces. One of the leftists to whom Roots had provided temporary accommodation was Smedley, who had recently arrived from Shanxi Province, where she had spent the last three months of 1937 with the Eighth Route Army.[11] When she told Roots that she had no place to stay and no money for accommodation, he took her in.[12] She had since arranged with him to let the three members of the CAC medical unit stay in the compound until she could find accommodation for them in the city. At dinner that night, Bethune held forth about his experiences and opinions. Smedley also had plenty to say and soon discovered, as Ewen noted, that Bethune had little time for opinionated females.[13]

Shortly after Smedley introduced Bethune and the others to Roots, Zhou Enlai, political director of the Chinese Communist Party, and Bo Gu, coordinator of the Eighth Route Army Medical Service, appeared. Having learned from Smedley of the expected arrival of the medical unit, they were eager to meet them. The two men were acting as liaison officers with the Guomindang government in accordance with the United Front agreement reached between it and the Chinese Communist Party in September 1937.[14] Their advice was that the members of the unit should meet with Dr Robert K.S. Lim, the head of the National Red Cross Society of China.[15]

Late that evening Smedley accompanied Bethune, Ewen, and Parsons to the Lutheran Mission compound where Dr Lim had his office. To their surprise, he addressed them in excellent English delivered in a Scottish accent.[16] Under the terms of the United Front Agreement, Lim was obligated to assist both Communist and Guomindang military forces. He explained that he wanted to coordinate Eighth Route Army hospitals, linking them with ambulances to transport the seriously wounded to the rear. Most doctors and nurses were afraid to go the special area controlled by the Chinese Communists, he said, and he asked Bethune if he would go. Bethune said he had no intention of going anywhere else and asked Ewen if she too was willing. She said she was, but Parsons, clinging to his role as the head of a separate medical unit, turned on them angrily. "I came to China to start a hospital so that the American people would have something they can support and know is their very own," he protested.[17] A prolonged shouting match with Bethune ended with Parsons reluctantly agreeing to surrender to Lim the receipts he carried for the supplies and equipment stored in the warehouse in Hong Kong; these were needed so that Lim could arrange their shipment to Hankou.[18]

Although relieved to learn they would eventually receive the all-important supplies, Bethune hated having to wait for them to arrive. He was also deeply disturbed by the devastation and suffering caused by the enemy attacks on the city. The daily air raids reminded him of the suffering he had witnessed in Madrid and Almería. The aim of the bombing was the same as that of Nationalist attacks in Spain: to slaughter the helpless and inspire terror in civilians. With few Chinese anti-aircraft guns to harass them, the Japanese flew low over the city, choosing their targets at will. Not until a few days before Bethune and Ewen departed did a Chinese fighter squadron, just arrived in Wuhan, take off to harry the enemy.[19]

Moved by the scenes of chaos and destruction around them, Bethune implored Lim to put him and Ewen to work while they waited for their equipment. The following day they went to the sister city of Hanyang to a Presbyterian mission hospital. They found it disorganized and operating with a skeleton staff.[20] There were few beds, and patients lay on the floor, barely attended to. The halls were filled with the wounded, waiting for assistance, some dying before they received it. The hospital had no cleaning staff, so the floors were covered with blood, excrement, and waste from operations; the resulting stench hung in the air.[21] It was far worse than anything Bethune had seen in hospitals in Spain and a total shock for Ewen, who had had no wartime experience.

Meanwhile, Parsons continued to complicate the situation. Although he had turned over the receipts for the medical equipment, he insisted he was still the head of the unit and refused to give up the funds sent to him from New York. The three were now living in a rooming-house Smedley had found for them, but Parsons refused to speak to Bethune and Ewen. While they worked in the Presbyterian hospital, he drank, continuing to draw on the CAC funds. Bethune and Ewen each sent a letter to New York outlining the circumstances and pleading for Parsons's recall. Smedley, who was also concerned, explained the situation to Zhou Enlai and asked him to arrange for a representative from the Chinese Communist Party and also one from the Eighth Route Army to send a cable to the CAC protesting Parsons's behaviour. She sent her own cable demanding that Dodd and Jaffe recall him immediately. Their response was: "Try and smooth out difficulties between Parsons and Bethune. Parsons a first-class surgeon. Bethune, famous blood-transfusion specialist, Spain, fair surgeon."[22] And they sent more money – to Parsons.

Bethune and Smedley were at their wits' end. Bethune was offended because he believed that the CAC thought he and Parsons were engaged in a petty power struggle for control of the unit. Smedley, who had taken on the role of acting as a liaison between New York and the unit, despite not being on the best of terms with the American Communist Party, recognized that the CAC had decided to ignore her assessment of the situation and decided to act. Without explaining her action to the CAC, she dissolved the unit, telling Bethune and Ewen they must now consider themselves members of the Eighth Route Army.[23]

Bethune was angry at the CAC but resented Smedley's arbitrary decision to end the unit's existence. However, he realized that there was nothing he could do: Smedley worked closely with both the Eighth Route Army and Dr Lim, and she knew the military medical conditions in the areas where he and Ewen were heading. She could also provide financial assistance, without which they could do nothing. Since her recent arrival in Hankou, Smedley had formed an organization she named the Northwestern Partisan Relief Committee.[24] Through her many contacts she had already raised a substantial amount intended to aid the families of partisan units fighting alongside the Eighth Route Army, and she told Bethune and Ewen she could draw on these funds to pay for their transportation to the war zone.[25]

Smedley also found another doctor willing to join them. He was Richard Brown, a Canadian Anglican missionary.[26] Having left his mission hospital in Guide in Henan province, he had arrived in Hankou on 15 February to renew his passport, receive dental treatment, and conduct mission business.[27] During a visit to Bishop Roots he learned of the urgent need for medical personnel in the Red Triangle, the northwest region held by Communist forces.[28] When Roots told him that Bethune and Ewen planned to go there, Brown expressed interest. Roots suggested he meet with Smedley to learn more details. After she described the situation, Brown decided to offer his services. He explained that the Japanese, who had already bombed Guide, would soon overrun his area and close the mission hospital. Believing that his commitment was to the Chinese people, he was willing to go where the need was greatest, even if it meant treating communist wounded. On 16 February he met Bethune and Ewen and assured them that as soon as he obtained the permission of his superiors he would follow them to the northwest.[29] On Saturday, 19 February, he sent an airmail letter to Bishop White in Toronto explaining what he proposed to do.[30] Early the following morning he left Hankou to return to his mission at Guide.

Meanwhile, Parsons's behaviour had escalated into crisis. Bethune received a call at the Presbyterian hospital saying that Parsons, in a delirious rage, had threatened some of the residents in his boarding-house. Bethune dashed to the scene, got him into bed, and brought in an English doctor to examine him. The physician gave Bethune a certificate declaring Parsons a chronic alcoholic incapable of caring for himself. With this certificate and the assistance of another doctor, Smedley had Parsons admitted the following day to the Roman Catholic Mission Hospital for treatment. A few weeks later Parsons would agree to return to the United States.[31]

Bethune was relieved to be rid of Parsons at last, but tensions were building between him and Smedley. Their personalities had clashed almost from the beginning: both were strong-willed, outspoken, quick-tempered, and at times self-righteous. Smedley, who was paying for their transport, had her own ideas about how Bethune and Ewen could make themselves most useful to the Eighth Route Army, and at one point she and Bethune argued fiercely. He brought out the instructions he and Parsons had received from the China Aid Council on the eve of their departure from New York and, summoning Ewen, read them aloud. One of them, which he emphasized to Smedley, stated that in the event of a conflict between the instructions of the Eighth Route Army and those of Smedley, he was to accept the decision of the Eighth Route Army.[32]

Bethune's irritation with Smedley was exacerbated by the delay in the arrival of the equipment from Hong Kong. He yearned to be serving at the front with the Eighth Route Army, not floundering in the morass of Hankou. He repeatedly urged Smedley and Lim to allow him and Ewen to leave and to send the equipment after them. James Bertram, a journalist from New Zealand, met Bethune at this time, probably at one of several dinners in Hankou attended by missionary doctors and newspaper men. He later wrote his impression of Bethune's state of mind: "He was then very tense and strung up – smoking heavily and obviously under considerable strain … He wore a small pointed beard *à la* Lenin, and liked to strike a Lenin pose when being photographed … I thought him a very lively and gifted man, but pretty egoistic and certainly driven by a daemon of his own: he wanted to be a hero or a martyr of the Revolution, at any cost."[33] Bethune continued badgering Smedley and Lim, who finally gave in. They could go, they were told, and they would not go empty handed. Lim and Smedley donated money for them to buy enough surgical equipment and medical supplies in Hankou to meet their initial needs.[34] Bethune and Ewen eagerly set about packing the purchases, which, with their personal belongings, filled fifteen pieces of luggage and some cartons.[35]

On Tuesday, 22 February, no doubt to everyone's relief, Bethune and Ewen boarded the 5 AM train bound for Beijing.[36] Accompanying them as their guide was an Eighth Route Army soldier named Zhou Zangzheng who was returning to his unit. Their ultimate destination was the town of Hongtong in the Jin-Cha-Ji Border Region, a political area southwest of Beijing created by the terms of the United Front Agreement and in which the communists had been granted sovereignty.[37] One of the three divisions of the Eighth Route Army was headquartered there. The distance between Hankou and Linfen, the nearest rail terminus to Hongtong, was almost a thousand kilometres. In peacetime it would have been an easy three-day trip, but wartime conditions turned it into an epic journey.

They travelled third class, called "hard seat" because of the uncomfortable wooden benches in the carriages. The spaces beneath the seats and in the racks above were crammed with luggage and personal possessions, and people jammed the narrow aisles. There were no dining facilities in third class, so passengers brought their own food or bought it from the vendors hawking their wares on station platforms. At many stops, boarding passengers lugged with them farm products and livestock such as chickens and goats, and the pungent smells of people and animals in close quarters hung in the humid air. To endure eighteen hours under such conditions was trying even for Ewen and Zhou, who had experience of rail travel in China, but Bethune found it unbearable. Long before the slow-moving train reached the rail-junction city of Zhengzhou, five hundred kilometres north of Hankou, he had decided that he had to find a better way to continue the journey.

They arrived at Zhengzhou at 11 PM. After reclaiming their luggage and equipment and hiring porters to transfer it to a westbound train, they discovered there were no seats available on it. They sent Zhou into the city to find accommodation, but he returned to report that the city's hotels were full of refugees fleeing the Japanese. It was now after midnight and the station was locked, so Zhou suggested they spend the night in a freight shed. As they settled down under their sheepskin coats, a woman carrying a child crept into a corner; there she huddled, trying to protect her wailing baby from the cold. Ewen offered her a quilt that she was carrying and told her Bethune was a doctor. He then brought out a tin of condensed milk and helped the mother spoon-feed the hungry child. The next morning the woman told them she was a soldier's wife and that she had to support herself while her husband was away. Bethune offered her money, which she refused at first. To allow her to save face, he assured her that it was not charity but a loan, and that he would return to collect it at the end of the war.[38]

Shortly before noon they boarded a train bound for Tongguan, nearly three hundred kilometres west of Zhengzhou. By haranguing the conductor and paying him $25 Mex, a rather large sum, Bethune arranged for them to travel second class in a wagon-lit compartment.[39] The journey turned out to be a long one because the engineer kept stopping the train whenever Japanese bombers were sighted. They had travelled for only an hour when alarm bells sounded and the train screeched to a halt. With the other passengers, they ran into a field and threw themselves on the ground. Luckily it was a false alarm: aircraft droned high overhead but were heading for more distant prey. The all-clear soon sounded; however, the engine had been uncoupled and moved several hundred metres down the tracks, and by the time it was again linked to the cars and the passengers had regained their seats, more than an hour had passed. This process would be repeated several times over the course of the next day.

The ancient walled city of Tongguan, where they hoped to transfer to a northbound train to Linfen, is located at the great bend of the Yellow River where it turns eastward toward the sea. There the river cuts through the loess plateau; over the centuries powerful winds from the Gobi Desert have buried a vast region in thick layers of fine silty soil. From the train Bethune and Ewen gazed out at a landscape carved into perfect terraces by wind and water, smooth rounded hills topped by long sharp crests looming above. There were no trees, only scrub dotting the yellowish-brown earth. They arrived at the railway station outside Tongguan at 3 PM on Thursday. Their guide suggested they walk the three kilometres to the south gate of the city while he followed with porters carrying their luggage.

At the city gate they showed their passes, and an Eighth Route Army guard directed them to the barracks, where they were warmly received by the commanding officer. They washed, ate a quick meal, and set to work tending wounded soldiers. Then Bethune was asked to treat a civilian with a gangrenous leg, which he had to amputate. Afterward he was nonplussed to find Ewen in a heated argument with the man's wife, who insisted on taking the maggoty leg so that it could be buried with her husband when he died. "Oh, come on! This is the twentieth century!" Bethune growled and told Ewen not to give it to her. But the woman managed to seize the leg and carry it off.[40]

When they finished surgery, Bethune ordered Ewen to come outside the building with him. She knew from his tone that he was upset, and he soon rounded on her. They had just treated Eighth Route Army patients, the first of many, he said coldly. If she wanted to remain as his assistant, she must understand that the nature of their relationship was entirely professional. Under no circumstances must she ever address him informally: she must always refer to him as "Doctor." And because he was the doctor, it was he and never she who would make every diagnosis and decide the nature of treatment required. Ewen was puzzled. She had never addressed him by his first name during their work together in the hospital in Hanyang and had made no attempt to diagnose a patient's condition. Although angered by his harsh tone and feeling that he was treating her as a servant, she determined to do her best to please him.[41]

Learning to his frustration that they would not be able to make a ferry connection to cross the Yellow River until the following day, Bethune went off on his own to explore the city. He could not resist stopping now and then at vendor's stalls to sample bowls of *bai jiu,* a fiercely potent rice liquor available everywhere in large earthenware vessels. Wandering through the maze of narrow streets, he eventually realized he had lost his way. However, he soon heard his name called and saw a man on a bicycle, a revolver strapped to his waist, pedalling toward him. This turned out to be Dr Robert Mc-Clure, a Canadian medical missionary who was acting field director for the International Red Cross. En route by rail to his headquarters in Zhengzhou, he had stopped at Tongguan station where worried Chinese officials informed him that a Canadian doctor had gone missing.

By this time Bethune had drunk a considerable amount of *bai jiu*. As usual, liquor roused his volatile temper, and he complained bitterly to McClure about the delay in his journey north. As they walked back to the army barracks, McClure tried to turn the conversation to Canada and the practice of medicine there. But Bethune showed no pleasure in meeting another Canadian doctor and fellow graduate of the University of Toronto, even in the unlikely location of northern China in the middle of a war. McClure later said, "He didn't feel himself a Canadian. He felt that he'd given up Canada. He was very critical of the establishment ... They were all money-grubbers, they were status-chasers. Very paranoid about anybody in thoracic surgery, particularly [because] they had ostracized him and had not recognized his ability. They had kept him out of practice, kept him out of the jobs that he wanted to do. They had thwarted him in his efforts to establish his brand of thoracic surgery in Canada. Very bitter ... He was fighting in the world revolution. The Spanish front had closed off and he was going to the China front."[42] McClure warned him that the Japanese were moving rapidly south toward the city of Linfen, but Bethune insisted that he would continue north, Japanese or no Japanese. Back at the barracks McClure wished him luck and left.

The next morning, Bethune, Ewen, and Zhou, followed by ten porters carrying their luggage and equipment in wheelbarrows, set off for the south bank of the Yellow River, Bethune likely nursing a hangover from *bai jiu*. After crossing in a junk, they arrived at the railway station in the town of Fenglingdu on the north side of the river; there they learned that the train leaving for Linfen was already packed with Chinese troops being sent to confront the advancing Japanese. Luckily Zhou noticed an empty boxcar at the end of the train, and the porters helped them haul their fifteen cases and several cartons down the platform and aboard. The three settled in, perched on improvised cushions Zhou had made from bales of hay. A short time later three women in army uniforms climbed in. They identified themselves as teachers en route to Yan'an to enrol in Kangda, the Anti-Japanese Aggression Military and Political University.

Several hours after its scheduled departure time the train at last began its run to the city of Linfen, two hundred kilometres to the north. Like their previous two trains, this one moved agonizingly slowly as it wended its way through the valley of the Fen River. They had gone some distance when one of the teachers began to play a small flute. Another joined her, playing an *er hu*, a traditional Chinese two-stringed violin, and the three teachers sang rousing anti-Japanese songs popular among partisan forces in the north. Bethune dug into his luggage and brought out a ukulele. Twanging away on it, he sang several Spanish tunes. Ewen was astonished, as he seldom let his personal side show. Not to be outdone, Zhou pulled a mouth organ from his pocket. He turned out to be a skilled performer with an extensive repertoire, which to the Canadians' amusement included a lively version of "Yankee Doodle."[43]

During their thirty-hour journey, several trains passed them carrying refugees south to Tongguan. Ominously, each one was packed, with people sitting on the roofs of the cars and even clinging to the engine. But Bethune and Ewen were still unprepared for the chaos they found on reaching Linfen. When the train arrived in mid-afternoon on Saturday, 26 February, the station was in turmoil. Thousands of men, women, and children loaded down with possessions jostled frantically with throngs of soldiers, many of them wounded, all trying to storm the train from Tongguan even before the incoming troops had disembarked. Seemingly unconcerned about their own predicament,

Bethune was outraged that no government agency was attempting to hand out food and medicine to those in need.[44]

There were no porters, but with Zhou's help Bethune and Ewen man-handled their luggage and equipment down the platform, forcing their way through the desperate hordes. Then Zhou went into the city to report to Eighth Route Army Headquarters. Not long after he left, the air-raid siren sounded, and Bethune and Ewen were swept along in the crowd that dashed into trenches dug in the sand near the station. Thirty seconds later, several Japanese planes zoomed in low, strafed the station, then sped on to other targets.

Shortly after the all-clear sounded, Zhou returned with three soldiers to help carry their bags and supplies. He told Ewen that a Japanese force was rapidly bearing down on Linfen and was less than fifteen kilometres away. The headquarters of the Eighth Route Army had been moved, and there was no time to search for it. The only way to avoid capture was to return to Tongguan as soon as possible. When Ewen told Bethune they would have to go back, he lost his temper, blaming the situation on her. "Of all the damned inefficiency I have ever seen!" he shouted. "Where the hell are your brains?" But there was no other option: they were caught between an advancing Japanese army and a retreating Chinese one.[45]

However, the train's engineer, terrified of another Japanese air attack, now refused to leave. As the crowd milled in confusion, Zhou noticed a freight train about to head south. One car, loaded with rice, still had enough room for the three of them and their luggage. They dragged themselves aboard just before the train pulled out. Bethune and Ewen slept intermittently on rock-hard bags of rice and woke in the middle of the night to realize that they were not moving. Angry voices were raised outside, and Zhou went off to find out what was going on. It turned out that they were on a siding in a village called Goasi, only forty kilometres south of Linfen. The engineer had abandoned the train because he was afraid to proceed along the heavily bombed rail line. Bethune and Ewen remained in the car until daylight, when Zhou returned to tell them that an Eighth Route Army officer, Major Li, and a handful of soldiers had decided to carry away the rice, which would otherwise fall into the hands of the advancing enemy. As soon as they could make arrangements to buy mules and carts in nearby villages, they would leave. They would head southwest to the Yellow River and try to cross into the neighbouring province of Shaanxi. Major Li had promised that, after he deposited the rice at an Eighth Route Army depot, he would arrange for the Canadians and their equipment to be taken north to Yan'an.

Resigning themselves to another lengthy wait, Bethune and Ewen sat down under a mulberry tree near the entrance to the village. One on each side of the trunk, they leaned back, exhausted. Suddenly a drop of liquid splashed onto Ewen's hand, and then another. They jumped up to search the tree, and to their horror discovered the body of a child in red trousers suspended upside down from the top branches. "My God! My God!" Bethune muttered as they hurried back to the train.[46]

It was nearly two days before the soldiers found and bought carts and hired mule drivers to carry the two hundred bags of rice, each weighing forty kilos. At noon on 28 February 1938, the caravan of fifty soldiers, drivers, and assistants and forty-two carts, each drawn by three mules, began the trek. It was a warm, sunny day, and at first all went well. About 4 PM Bethune, who was walking beside the lead cart, saw two Japanese planes heading south. The aircraft sighted the caravan and headed in their direction. Major Li shouted a command, and everyone ran away from the mules and carts. There was no shelter, so they threw themselves face down on the sandy ground some fifty metres away. One plane banked and swooped above them to gain a clear sighting of its target. Then it dove, levelling off at no more than sixty metres as it roared toward the caravan. Although Bethune would later estimate that the plane was so low the pilot could have hit the caravan with a baseball, the four bombs it dropped missed the leading carts. However, on the second pass, bombs exploded close to the last carts, spraying deadly shrapnel horizontally at bullet-like speed less than a metre above the ground. The screams of wounded and dying mules filled the air as the plane flew away. Fifteen of the animals were killed in the attack and twelve wounded; four men required medical attention.[47]

Four hours passed during which Bethune treated the wounded, and soldiers transported them to a nearby village. Several carts also had to be repaired and the caravan, now half its original size, was restructured. Ewen, who had been at the rear of the caravan and had narrowly escaped serious injury, was in a state of shock and could barely help Bethune. As he dressed a wound, he said to her, "Every man must have two baptisms in his life, one with water and one with fire. You've just had yours with fire."

"You're nothing but a bloody missionary!" she snapped. The words struck him deeper than she could have known, and he exploded, shouting, "Don't you ever say that again, you fucking son of a bitch!" She ran away in tears.[48]

Travelling all night, sleeping fitfully on the bags of rice, they arrived at dawn on Tuesday at a village on the south bank of the Fen River. They found rooms in a small inn, where, exhausted, they ate the food provided. Then Bethune went off to sleep in the next room while Ewen drowsed where she was. Meanwhile, word of the arrival of a foreign doctor quickly spread through the village and a crowd of people gathered in the front room of the inn waiting for Bethune to awaken. Some began to question a member of the caravan, who was standing guard. He was a young teenager Bethune had nicknamed Buck because of his protruding front teeth, and he launched into a vivid description of the Japanese attack, including a loud rendition of the roars of the Japanese aircraft and the exploding bombs. Suddenly the inner door of the room burst open, and Bethune stalked out "like a thunderstorm in long johns." The Chinese scattered, terrified of the "foreign devil." Picking Buck up by the collar, Bethune carried him outside. "Now for Christ's sake, shut up!" he growled and returned to his room. Ewen, roused by the commotion, heard Buck return and assure his audience, now slowly filtering back, that despite the foreign doctor's bad temper, he had "a good heart and golden hands."[49]

Unable to return to sleep, Bethune and Ewen ordered breakfast, a bowl of sweet fermented rice water containing a beaten egg, and began to examine and treat the patients whom Buck had organized in a long line. A few were soldiers, but most were civilians. During the process Bethune and Ewen several times exchanged sharp words, and she refused to follow the treatment he dictated for a patient suffering from leprosy. Having had considerable experience with the disease during her previous stay in China, she said that vitamin pills and dressings would do nothing for him. Bethune controlled his temper until they had seen the last patient and eaten a meal. Then, as he had done in Tongguan, he suggested they take a walk, and Ewen braced herself for what was coming. Only a few steps from the inn, he burst out, "You are truculent, self-sufficient, overconfident, and absolutely no use to me and you are also a disgrace to your illustrious father!"[50] Ewen shot back, "I always try to be a disgrace to my father." Then, she added, "I will be pleased to leave this bloody unit when we reach Xi'an," and walked off.[51] But this was not the end of Bethune's displeasure with her. When they returned to the inn they found several soldiers, dirty, ragged and covered with lice and blood, waiting for treatment. Bethune demanded dressings and drugs, and Ewen had to tell him they had none left, just a dozen vials of catgut, because Bethune had used up everything else treating people along the way. He refused to believe her, sure the supplies were simply misplaced.[52]

With nothing to do until the carts were transferred to the north side of the Fen River, Bethune explored the city of Xinjiang on the far shore. The river was low for the season, about a metre and a half deep, and Bethune had himself carried across piggyback by a husky Chinese. The twin spires of a Roman Catholic mission church on the city skyline attracted his attention, and he made his way there. The two resident Fransciscan priests greeted him warmly, handing him a cigar and opening a bottle of red wine. They told him they were expecting the Japanese within thirty-six hours. The mayor and the police had already fled, but the parishioners and their families had remained, hoping to find refuge in the church compound. In response to Bethune's question of whether the Japanese would respect the French flag flying above the church, they shrugged and pointed out that the Japanese had killed missionaries in other areas. But, they said, it was their duty to remain to try to protect their parishioners. Bethune relaxed his communist principles so far as to attend an evening service and later wrote of the Franciscans, "I admired their courage ... Their last words to me were, as we parted, 'I hope we meet again on earth, if not, then in Heaven.'"[53]

The following morning the porters hauled the rice across the river, then prepared to carry Bethune and Ewen. She said she would rather swim across in her underwear, but Bethune told her she would scandalize the local population. So she sat on a chair grasped by four porters who lifted it to shoulder height as they waded into the water. Midway, one lost his grip and the chair tipped, plunging Ewen headfirst into the frigid, muddy water. Struggling to her feet, she saw a large group of Chinese on the shore grinning at her mishap. Among them, bent double with laughter, was Bethune. For the next twenty-four hours she refused to speak to him.[54]

The wagon leader, having learned that the Japanese had already captured Linfen and were heading south, was determined to move more rapidly and to travel by night west along the north bank of the Fen River. He was in frequent conflict with Bethune, who insisted on stopping the caravan to treat wounded soldiers along the way. One was a boy of no more than sixteen whose shoulder had been smashed to a pulp by a bullet. Weeping, he cried out, "I don't want to die! I have not lived!" Bethune treated him, as he did all the wounded, "with great tenderness – almost like a nun," Ewen later noted.[55]

To add to their problems, hordes of abandoned, hungry children joined the wagon train every time they stopped. Bethune treated their ailments and often fed them. He also argued the reluctant quartermaster into issuing army trousers and jackets to clothe them, Gleefully putting on as many as three uniforms and caps, the children now considered themselves rich, having so many new clothes and so much rice.[56] Bethune also insisted on treating wounded civilians and refugees who were unconnected with the Eighth Route Army or the communist partisans. Those who had nowhere to go he loaded on the carts. One of these was a woman who had lost her child in a bombing. One night he accompanied some soldiers who went to a village to set booby traps, and he returned with an abandoned baby – a boy – which he gave to the wounded woman. She was overjoyed: kissing his hand, she wished him ten thousand years of life. When Ewen translated, Bethune grinned and replied, "Makes you feel a little like God, don't it?" Ewen brought him back to earth by asking whether there had been a roll of copper coins tied to the baby's rags. Bethune said yes, but that he had given the coins to one of the soldiers. "Then you had better go and get them!" Ewen told him. According to Chinese custom, the coins must be kept as they assured an adoptive parent that the baby would not be claimed by its birth family in the future. Bethune told Ewen she had the mind of a cash register, but he went and fetched the money.[57]

On Thursday, 3 March, they caught up with the retreating Chinese army at the city of Hejin and stayed there overnight. The next day was Bethune's forty-eighth birthday, and after treating some wounded soldiers he marked the occasion by strolling through the market. He was keeping daily notes about the journey, and in a later article he mentioned seeing "live carp in water buckets for sale, black pigs with big floppy ears, barkless dogs, white paper windows, lousy *kangs*."[58] They left Hejin later that day and by mid-evening reached the village of Yumenkou on the east bank of the Yellow River where they found more than five thousand troops of the fleeing Seventy-Sixth Division of the Shanxi Province Army and their military equipment, waiting to be ferried to the opposite side of the broad, swift river.[59] In the same article Bethune described what he saw: "Here was an unforgettable sight. Lit by a dozen fires five thousand men were collected with trucks, carts, mules, horses, artillery and great piles of stores waiting to cross the river into [the province of] Shensi [Shaanxi]. The light of the fires was reflected back from the steep wall-like mountain side. The river rushes between two high cliffs. The swift current (12 miles an hour) carries great floating ice floes which clash against each other far out on the dark surface. The whole scene is wild and fantastic."[60] There were only four junks, and Bethune was told that it might not be possible to get all the men and equipment across before the Japanese arrived. At dawn he and Ewen boarded a junk carrying a hundred soldiers and several pieces of artillery, plus mules and baggage. The officer in charge told them that the Japanese had already entered Hejin. Arriving safely on the west bank, they climbed a hill and were directed to a cave where they could find shelter while their equipment could be brought across the river. Then they returned to the riverbank to watch soldiers setting up artillery pieces and digging trenches. Meanwhile the ferries continued hour after hour transporting men and supplies from the east bank. The mad dash to the Yellow River was over.

Of her experience with Bethune, Ewen later recalled, "no man ever removed so much lead from peoples' bone, flesh, and guts as he did, or set more broken bones or amputated so many extremities. Indeed we had nearly two tons of surgical and medical supplies which we had brought with us – when we got near the Yellow River we didn't have enough to put in a good-sized basket." When the supply of morphine tablets ran out halfway to the Yellow River, Bethune substituted opium dissolved in Chinese whiskey as an anaesthetic, which worked remarkably well.[61]

On Sunday, only hours after the last soldiers and equipment had reached the west bank of the Yellow River, Japanese troops arrived on the opposite shore. The two sides engaged in an intermittent exchange of artillery and machine-gun fire, but fortunately the defences prepared by the Shanxi troops prevented the Japanese from crossing. That evening Bethune and Ewen learned that two soldiers had left for Xi'an, two hundred kilometres to the southwest, to arrange for Eighth Route Army trucks to pick them up. Foraging in a nearby village for medical supplies, they managed to locate some bottles of tincture of camphor, digitalis, and adrenalin as well as silk sutures, syringes, and ampoules of cocaine.[62]

Until the trucks arrived, there was little that they could do to pass the time. Deprived of the opiate of action, Bethune withdrew into himself, often refusing to answer when Ewen spoke to him. When he did talk, he fretted and fumed so much that she compared him to "a bear with a boil in his ear." He criticized everything about her – her lipstick, her frivolities, her playing ball with the young soldiers. At last the fighting ended, and they were able to light a fire outside the cave. Sitting over it, Bethune began to talk for the first time about his life before China. Ewen was surprised that he confided in her because she felt that from the beginning of their journey he had disliked her, considering her unworthy of being the daughter of a distinguished Canadian communist. She observed, "If you weren't sick or wounded he couldn't see you, no matter who you were, except of course for the Party leadership ... He firmly believed the Marxist doctrine alone imbued men with compassion, honesty, and a sense of duty."[63] Now, however, his conversation ranged far beyond matters political, and he talked obsessively about his ex-wife. Ewen later wrote, "It was here I heard about Dr Bethune's wife, Frances, the light of his life. Although I had never met her I learned a great deal about her and how wonderful she was. Dr Bethune blamed himself for the failure of their marriage. He was very unhappy in his personal life and couldn't make the adjustments required for lasting relationships. He did not accept himself or his limitations, was proud to a fault, and his irascibility touched with arrogance made him unapproachable. He lacked understanding of another's point of view, and felt that he was right, or rather that Marx was right."[64]

Finally, unable to endure the forced inactivity any longer, Bethune announced that they must start for Xi'an on foot. On Friday morning he and Ewen set out. With them was a young Eighth Route Army soldier named Li, a replacement for their former guide, for Zhou Zangzheng, to whose quick thinking they owed so much, had left them at Hejin to return to his unit. In the late afternoon of the second day of walking, they passed through the gates of the city of Hancheng. Directed to a base hospital in an abandoned temple, they spent the next seven days treating the sick and wounded. Bethune later wrote that they were "besieged with civilian patients, pulmonary tuberculosis, ovarian cyst, gastric ulcer."[65] On Wednesday, 19 March, an Eighth Route Army truck carrying their luggage and supplies arrived in Hancheng.

Two days later they drove into the ancient walled city of Xi'an.[66] Bethune immediately demanded to be taken to the public baths. He later remarked on the "ineffable bliss of a hot bath," his first since leaving Hankou exactly one month earlier.[67] Ewen, who had been using the ladies' section of the baths, met Bethune in the lobby afterwards. "Well," he said, "you don't look like the person that started out on this junket in Hankou." She replied that he didn't in any way resemble the dude who had stepped off the *Empress of Asia* in Hong Kong. "Jesus!" he said. "It seems a hundred years ago!"[68] A short time later they arrived at the Eighth Route Army barracks, where Lin Beiqu, chairman of the Shan-Gan-Ning Special Regional Government, greeted them and, to their surprise, welcomed them back to the land of the living.[69] He told them that North American newspapers had reported that they had disappeared when Japanese forces overran Linfen and were presumed dead.[70]

Lin Beiqu had reserved rooms for them at the Xi'an Guest House, a small hotel favoured by foreign visitors to the city.[71] He told them that a fine western-style dinner had been ordered for them, and in the spirit of the occasion ordered an old Buick to be brought out of storage to drive them to the hotel in state.[72] After all the two Canadians had been through, it must have been a surreal experience to find themselves seated at a table with a white linen cloth and napkins, eating western cuisine served on fine bone china. While they were eating, other foreigners in the dining room introduced themselves. These included members of the League of Nations Epidemiological Unit stationed in Xi'an: Heinrich von Jettmar, an Austrian, and Hermann Mooser, a Swiss, both medical scientists, and Eric Landauer, a Swiss engineer. Bethune and Ewen lingered over brandy and coffee with them until nearly midnight.

Bethune got on well with the three Europeans. Less than half an hour into the meal, Dr Mooser, the head of the League unit, made him a tentative offer of all the medical equipment and supplies he had brought to Xi'an.[73] The purpose of the League unit, he explained, was to provide services to prevent the outbreak of plague in the region, and in this capacity they had been in Yan'an and knew of the extreme inadequacy of medical facilities there. They had brought from Geneva full equipment for a fifty-bed surgical hospital and were looking for a place to set it up. Yan'an, where they had already established a laboratory to begin testing the population for infectious diseases, would be an ideal location. Mooser said that the offer was tentative only because League regulations specified that that they must provide services solely to civilians and must not side with Chinese or Japanese military forces. A liberal who was clearly opposed to the Japanese, Mooser had no objections to aiding the communists and was eager to find a way around the prohibition. If they could work out what Bethune referred to as a "formula" that would justify the use of the hospital equipment in Yan'an, Mooser would agree to have it transported there in trucks owned by the unit. When the maître d' approached to tell them it was midnight and the dining room was closing, they agreed to consider the matter in more depth and return to their discussions after Bethune and Ewen had had a good night's sleep.

However, on their return to the barracks, they were met by Lin Beiqu and a man in a uniform with no insignia of rank. This was Zhu De, commander in chief of the Eighth Route Army. Having just arrived from Yan'an, he was waiting to see Bethune. While Lin made the introduction, Zhu De shook Bethune's hand and then embraced him. Smiling broadly, each man in his own language said, "Let me have a look at you!" They both laughed as Zhu De walked round and round Bethune, sizing him up. Bethune was thrilled, for he had looked forward to meeting one of the heroes of the Chinese communist revolution. The general greeted Ewen too, and she went to her room to sleep. When she met Bethune for breakfast, she found him as enraptured as a young bride, raving about how wonderful Zhu De was. And no wonder: the renowned military leader had welcomed Bethune as an equal. His discussion with Zhu De and Lin had lasted till early morning. Both of them were receptive to the idea of setting up the League hospital in Yan'an, though final approval, they reminded Bethune, would have to be granted by Mao Zedong and other members of the communist government there.

Despite having had only a couple of hours sleep, Bethune was keen to renew his discussion with Mooser on the hospital scheme. During their next meeting they devised the "formula" for Mooser to present to his superiors in Geneva. He would tell them that a unit of Canadian and American doctors and nurses had arrived in northern Shaanxi province with the purpose of treating people suffering from tuberculosis and other contagious diseases. Though the majority of those treated would be women and children from the civilian population, they would also include wounded soldiers who were diseased. Mooser intended to emphasize Bethune's extensive North American background in tubercular medicine and Ewen's and Richard Brown's medical missionary experience in China.[74]

After the last detail had been worked out, Mooser confessed that the League's permission for the proposal was only a first step, for although he had all the necessary equipment for the hospital, he had no money in his budget to maintain it. As had been the case in Spain, Bethune's response was immediate and typical of his eager optimism. He assured Mooser that he could persuade the organization that had sent him to China to provide the required sum. The following day, Dr Jiang Qixian, chief medical officer of the Eighth Route Army, arrived in Xi'an. After listening to Bethune's summary of his negotiations with Mooser, he immediately agreed in principle. Bethune sent a wire to Agnes Smedley in Hankou asking her to cable New York at once requesting a guaranteed monthly contribution of $1,000.[75]

Meanwhile he continued his discussions with Mooser, and some of these covered more than the matter of the field hospital. Mooser had some experience in hematology, and Bethune discussed with him a matter that had apparently been on his mind since leaving Spain. He was concerned about a number of unexpected deaths that he attributed to transfusions he had given there. The case of the French airmen in Almería was explicable, because the blood with which they were transfused had been carried a long distance over rough roads, likely affecting its quality. But there had been other unexplained deaths following transfusions, and one in particular had continued to trouble him. It was that of a young Norwegian soldier in the International Brigades, whom Bethune described as a mother's dream of a son, just eighteen years old. He said there was no reason for this death except for the transfusion. "It was like I had killed my own son," he told Mooser. And he blamed himself too for not understanding from subsequent unexplained deaths that the transfusions could be deadly for certain patients. At this time the Rh factor had not yet been identified, but Bethune had come to the conclusion that there must be a positive and a negative in blood that needed to be matched between certain donors and recipients. The lack of money for research and a laboratory had prevented him from investigating the problem, but the mystery had continued to haunt him.[76]

However, he had little time to brood over past mistakes. Accompanied by Dr Jiang, he now began to visit various drug and medical supply outlets with money given him by Lin Beiqu to buy materials to take north.[77] He and Ewen also met with members of the League of Nations Epidemiological Unit to discuss the possibility of a unit in the occupied zones and at the front where it was needed.[78] Having attended to business, he found time to poke about in Xi'an. Trying to enter the restricted area that housed government buildings and the residences of political leaders, he was warned off by a Guomindang sentry. Unable to understand Chinese and determined to go where he wanted, Bethune kept walking. He was courteously rounded up by Guomindang soldiers and held incommunicado while word was sent to the authorities. After a few hours' incarceration he was returned to the Xi'an guest house.[79]

He also busied himself with writing. During his stay in Xi'an he first produced a six-thousand word account of the month-long trek there, to which he gave the humorous travelogue title of "See Shensi First."[80] This he sent as a letter to William Dodd Jr of the China Aid Council; he also sent a copy to the Canadian League for Peace and Democracy.[81] In another attempt to mollify the CAC, he prepared a lengthy report explaining his role in the unit after the departure of Parsons and the proposed entry of Brown, and outlining Mooser's offer of the League field hospital. "I am carrying on in the capacity of the head of the unit until I am relieved," he wrote. "My plan is to appoint Dr Brown in charge as soon as he arrives in the north. I will do this on my own responsibility, without waiting for your approval. If you want to send out another man instead of Brown to take charge why that will be OK with me. But consider this seriously – think of the tremendous publicity value of having a medical missionary in charge of a combined Canadian and American Medical unit to the Communist Red Army. The terrible bandits! It's simply perfect."[82]

He also wrote to Smedley, bringing her up to date on the situation with Mooser and telling her that he thought he would need $1,000 (Mex) a month to maintain the proposed field hospital. A lively postscript shows his mind already racing ahead, casting about for ways to make the most of his new situation:

Please send us over books, papers and don't forget to write! Why not send over a Goodwill Delegation! And if they come, to bring with them a Kodak developing outfit for our Rolliflex Camera, more films, printing paper, and a good enlarger. Also a repeating 22 long rifle for shooting ducks, pheasants etc with which the country is filled ... About 2 thousand rounds of ammunition, to go with it. I need some wool socks ... We need coffee too. There's not much to eat here except millet and carrots! We should have a movie done (36 mm. size). But I will write you from Yen-nan [Yan'an] more about our requirements. The coffee and socks can be got in Hong Kong but there is one lesson to be learned – always travel with your luggage in China – never leave it to be sent! Goodbye for the present. We are well and happy.[83]

Bethune had reason to be elated. With his customary luck he had escaped every hazard on his perilous journey, and now Mooser's offer of a fully equipped field hospital had dropped into his lap like a gift of the gods. Despite setbacks such as Parsons's defection and the tension between him and Ewen, he was just one more journey away from where he wanted to be. He had once called Madrid the "centre of gravity of the world," but now he had found a new one – Yan'an, the heart of the Communist Revolution in China.

⊹ 15 ⊹

Mission

Yan'an and Jin-Cha-Ji, 30 March–9 July 1938

Before dawn on Wednesday, 30 March, Bethune and Ewen set off, riding on top of one of a group of Eighth Route Army trucks bound for the city of Yan'an, nearly 250 kilometres to the north. Fine yellow dust raised by the trucks soon coated their faces, hair, and clothing. The rugged road wound through yellowish-brown loess hills carpeted with spring flowers, snaking its way up the sides of plateaus and plunging sharply down into canyons. Flanking the road, tier upon tier of terraced gardens clung to the steep hillsides. The convoy stopped for the night in the town of Sanyuan, and Ewen took Bethune to a performance of Chinese opera, where they were surrounded by people happily munching peanuts and watermelon seeds and quaffing cups of tea. The strange-looking foreigners were a godsend to the comedians warming up the audience before curtain time, and they poked a great deal of fun at them.[1]

After another day of dusty journeying, they stopped to visit the burial ground of Huangdi, the first emperor of China. In his best proletarian mode Bethune made it known that he strongly disapproved of the veneration of ancient kings. However, he made no protest about the marvellous meal they ate that night – mountains of fried noodles accompanied by steamed bread and succulent Shaanxi duck baked in palm leaves in an oven of hot stones.[2] On the third day they emerged into the valley of the Yan River. Ahead of them lay the old walled city of Yan'an, watched over by a lofty eighth-century pagoda on a hill above. Located two hundred kilometres south of the Great Wall, the city had for centuries been the gateway to all who arrived from the north en route to Xi'an. Since January 1937 it had served as the military, medical, and administrative centre of the Eighth Route Army and the Chinese Communist Party.

Just outside the city a young guard stopped them to examine their passes. Gazing at Bethune, he said, "Please let me look at you, for my eyes will perhaps never see such a miracle again. You have come to help us." Ewen translated, and Bethune stepped down from the truck and spoke a few words to the boy before they drove on.[3] The stars were out when they at last drove under the great tower of the city's south gate. The truck stopped in a dingy street, and the driver revved the engine to announce their arrival. Bethune and Ewen got down, while the faithful Buck went off to find out where they were to stay. Then a stocky, dark-haired man tore up to them on a bicycle and after identifying himself as Dr Ma Haide, asked in American-accented English who they were. "Why, the whole town was waiting for you from this morning onward with gongs and drums!" he told Bethune and Ewen. Ma, whose western name was George Hatem, was an American doctor of Lebanese descent who had had arrived in Yan'an in 1936. With him had come the journalist Edgar Snow, to gather information for his book *Red Star over China*. When Snow left the country, Hatem had stayed on to practise medicine in Yan'an.[4]

The authorities were soon notified of the Canadians' arrival, and they were taken to the Yan'an Guest House, a series of caves cut into the hillside. Each had a neatly swept dirt floor, rice-paper windows, whitewashed walls, and a padded drape over the rounded entrance. A *kang* – a heated clay sleeping platform – ran along one wall, and there were a few pieces of crude wooden furniture; a bean-oil lamp provided light. Ewen was discomfited to find that her sleeping area lacked a door. "Never mind, comrade," Bethune teased. "They believe in the open-door policy!"

After the greeting delegation left, Ma invited them to join him for dinner of noodles at a cooperative restaurant, and Bethune peppered him with a thousand questions as they ate. They then went to Ma's cave residence to enjoy the luxury of coffee captured from the Japanese.[5] After they chatted for several hours, Ma escorted them back to the guest house.

They had little time to settle down. Shortly after midnight Ewen came to Bethune's cave to tell him that Mao Zedong had sent a messenger to say he wanted to see him at once. Bethune told her she need not bother coming with him, but she insisted on tagging along. They followed a soldier to Mao's quarters, which were also located in a cave. From a short entrance hall they entered a chamber with a white-vaulted roof and a brick floor. A candle burned on a rough handmade table, and by its flickering light they could see a tall figure in a plain blue cotton uniform awaiting them. Smiling, Mao Zedong walked toward Bethune with arms extended. Grasping Bethune's hands, he repeated "*Huanying*" (welcome) several times in his high-pitched voice. After gazing at Bethune for a long moment, he began to speak while an interpreter, Li Xue, translated into English.[6] Also at the meeting was Dr

Jiang Qixian, the chief medical officer of the Eighth Route Army, who had helped Bethune collect medical supplies in Xi'an.[7]

For Bethune the moment was even more thrilling than his meeting with Zhu De. With childlike pride he presented to Mao a small square of white silk on which had been sewn an inscription certifying him a member of the Communist Party of Canada. To Bethune's delight, Mao responded, "We shall transfer you to the Communist Party of China so that you will be an inalienable part of this country now."[8] To be so accepted and welcomed by the most famous hero of the Chinese revolution was balm to Bethune's self-esteem.

Mao greeted Ewen and asked how it was that she spoke Chinese so fluently. She told him that she had been a missionary. "Oh, yes, aren't we all?" he replied, laughing. Then he invited them to sit down. On the table were small teacups, an open package of cigarettes, and bowls of peanuts and sunflower seeds.[9] As the interpreter poured tea from a large thermos, Mao remarked on Bethune's resemblance to Lenin, and Bethune beamed. The conversation turned to the role that Bethune and Ewen could play in the Eighth Route Army Medical Service. Bethune suggested organizing a transfusion service as he had done in Spain, but on learning that refrigeration, communications, and facilities were lacking, he proposed mobile surgical units instead, insisting he wanted to be near the front. He explained that the sooner medical attention could be given to a wounded soldier, the greater were his chances of recovery. However, Bethune's wish to serve at "the front" created certain problems. It was clear to Mao that Bethune did not understand how guerrillas operated – there was no fixed "front" per se but rather a constantly shifting series of battles and strategic retreats. Discussions on this topic and many others would continue between them over a number of days, for although Mao would later write that he had met Bethune only once, Ewen recalled that Mao in fact walked up the hill to visit Bethune's cave almost every evening.[10]

Bethune also told Mao about Dr Mooser's willingness to offer the League of Nations' fifty-bed surgical hospital for collaborative use with the Eighth Route Army. Mao strongly objected to establishing such a hospital in Yan'an, pointing out that the need of additional medical assistance was greater in Shanxi Province. Bethune replied that perhaps the League facilities could be used to create a mobile field hospital. Maintaining such a unit would depend on financial support from the China Aid Council, he went on, but he said he felt certain that the American organization would agree to his request for a monthly contribution of $1,000. He added that he had already asked Agnes Smedley to transmit his request by cable to New York. The discussion continued until dawn. Mao and Jiang enthusiastically accepted Bethune's proposal that the CAC fund a mobile hospital and agreed to allow Ma Haide to join the unit.[11] Until final arrangements were made, it was decided, Bethune would be assigned to the Border Regional Hospital in Yan'an.

Keyed up by his meeting with Mao, Bethune slept for only a few hours. By 10 AM he was on his way to a series of meetings and interviews, followed by a formal banquet of welcome. Word of his arrival had spread quickly. As an internationally recognized surgeon, a hero in the Spanish Civil War, and the first foreign doctor to arrive in Yan'an since the outbreak of the Sino-Japanese War in July 1937, he was an instant celebrity. Everyone wanted to meet him and hear him speak. His largest audience, several thousand students at Kangda, the Anti-Japanese Aggression Military and Political University, listened to his speech and questioned him about international events, the war in Spain, and the varieties of political opinion in Canada and the United States. More banquets and more invitations to speak followed, but after four days of being lionized, Bethune began to tire of it. By now he and Ewen had been moved to somewhat more humble cave residences at the foot of Phoenix Mountain. They furnished these simply with tables and chairs bought at a market. They also began to do their own cooking. Bethune was determined to pay his own way, believing that he had come to assist the Chinese, not burden them with expenses, which he felt should be covered by the China Aid Council.

He did, however, agree to have a *xiao guei* (little devil) assigned to him as his houseboy. He Zexin, a veteran of the Long March, was little indeed, scarcely more than a metre and a half tall, and weighing less than forty-five kilos; actually twenty years old, he appeared much younger. Terrified by Bethune's looks on their first meeting, he promptly ran away.[12] After being fetched back by an interpreter, he was introduced to Bethune, who showed him where to stow things in the cave and how to arrange his bed. He Zexin also had to prepare Bethune's meals, and as they seldom had an interpreter, he struggled to understand the foreigner's instructions. Bethune was particularly fond of boiled eggs for breakfast and sternly rejected He's many attempts to cook one to his liking. On the day when He finally got it right, Bethune presented him with a book as a reward. Then he had the interpreter take a photograph of him eating the egg, He Zexin beside him.[13]

During these early days in Yan'an, Bethune was pondering the proposed mobile field hospital. Though he was optimistic that the Eighth Route Army and the League Epidemiological Unit would reach some agreement that would allow the equipment to be used, he knew that without the financial support of the China Aid Council, the hospital could not function. Two weeks had passed since he had sent his request for funding via Agnes Smedley to New

York, but he had had no response. He began to wonder if she had received any of the messages that he had sent from Xi'an. On Wednesday, 6 April, he sent another telegram to her in Hankou. Two days later, when he had still received no reply, he asked Dr Robert Lim, who happened to be in Yan'an on a brief visit from Hankou, to deliver a letter to her. In it he wrote,

> This is a desperate effort to contact you and thru [sic] you, the American Committee, of which this Unit is the medical representative. Not having any reply to two letters and two telegrams sent you from Sian [Xi'an], the day before yesterday we sent you another telegram via the commercial telegraph company, from Yennan [Yan'an]. To this telegram, in English, there has also been no reply. The substance of these letters and telegrams has been to report on the medical situation ... I considered it important that you should know and be kept conversant with the particulars ... We regard you, and have given the medical and political authorities of the 8th army the information, as our direct contact with the American Committee, especially for fast relay of news and requests, by cable to America.[14]

He told Smedley of the decisions reached at his first meeting with Mao, emphasizing that he had promised the communist leader that financial support from New York would be forthcoming. Then he added, "Please send us some money. I have 20 dollars left and Jean has a similar amount. We are paying for everything – all our food we buy and cook ourselves, the furniture, etc for our comfortable caves – we don't want to cost the 8th army a cent – but we will if you don't telegraph us some. Yennan [Yan'an] is a very exciting place, but not for surgeons. With comradely greetings, Norman Bethune (temporarily-in-charge-where-the hell-is-Brown), Canadian-American Unit. 8th army."[15]

Four days later, when he and Ewen had used up the last of their money, he had no choice but to approach Dr Jiang Qixian. Asking for financial help was embarrassing, and to make matters worse, Bethune had to confess that since he had not heard from Smedley he was losing hope of support for the mobile field hospital from the China Aid Council. Jiang's immediate response was to arrange for Bethune and Ewen to receive $100.[16]

Meanwhile, Bethune wanted to be put to work, so Dr Nelson Fu invited him to visit the Border Region Hospital, divided between Yan'an and the town of Yanchuan, some forty kilometres away.[17] In Yan'an in the hills on the edge of the city, a row of caves had been cut out to house the hospital wards.[18] Each ward was two metres high by three metres wide. A *kang* along one wall provided space for about eight patients. The only access to the hospital, which was nearly 150 metres above ground level, was by way of a steep, narrow path that became dangerously slippery after rain or snowfall. There were no sheets; patients huddled together on the dirty, matted straw that covered the *kangs*, still clad in the soiled, tattered, and lice-infested remnants of their uniforms. The atmosphere was heavy with the stench of dried pus, blood, urine, and feces. Sanitation measures were almost non-existent, for there was no running water, nor were there latrines. Excrement crawling with flies was left in buckets until they were full; then the waste was taken to the fields to be used as fertilizer. Medicines and instruments were lacking, and electricity was available only in the operating room. Bethune was astounded by what he saw, but when the chief surgeon, Dr Gao, asked him to substitute for him while he went to Hankou, he reluctantly agreed.

However, after only a few days Bethune could no longer put up with the conditions. He went to Dr Fu and demanded a series of changes, only to be told that the medicines and facilities he requested were not available. They were in Yan'an, not Hankou, Fu reminded him. Bethune exploded. Announcing that he would go on strike until the changes were made, he left the hospital and returned to his cave.[19] At this point Dr Ma Haide intervened and persuaded Bethune to discuss his complaints with him and Dr Fu. Over many hours they tried to make Bethune understand that the conditions in the Yan'an hospital were actually superior to those in the battle area to which he was so eager to go. If he could not deal with conditions in the Border Region Hospital, how could he possibly cope in even more extreme situations? Bethune took some convincing, Ma Haide later recalled: "He'd sit down and discuss things and argue things and he'd get awfully impatient. Then he'd have to cool down a little and we'd start all over again ... The realities of the Chinese situation, the political, the material, the medical situation were entirely different than any concepts that he had ... So for us who were here on the spot, he was thinking in terms ... [that] didn't fit and when you'd argue with him, his impatience would get the upper hand."[20] But slowly Bethune's temper cooled. His concern for the sick and wounded overcame his outrage at the conditions in the hospital and he carried out the operations that had been scheduled. He even spoke some kind words to a startled Ewen, saying, "Nurse, I take back everything nasty I have said to you about your work, you are an excellent scrub nurse."[21]

However, a new crisis erupted when the long-awaited reply from Smedley arrived from Hankou, a belated response to Bethune's letter of 26 March in which he had enthusiastically reported the possibility of using the League of Nations hospital and asked for CAC funding. To Bethune's astonishment, her letter oozed venom. She accused him of "bamboozling the American public" by suggesting that for publicity purposes it should be stated that the unit was of substantial size and contained American doctors and nurses when in reality there were only two persons, both of them Canadian. "And so," she said, "I refuse personally to send out reports such as you have suggested." Alleging that Bethune intended to make Brown remain in Yan'an once he arrived, she went on: "If you try to keep him in the rear ... I shall oppose you by every means in this respect. I remind you again that you have no authority over Dr Brown, that he volunteered for the front, that he is needed at the front." She stated that she had not received any money from New York, but that if any arrived, she would let him and Ewen know, and concluded by saying that as the League and the Guomindang authorities in Xi'an had agreed to establish the mobile field hospital in Yan'an, it was up to them to finance it. Bethune should not apply to her for funding.[22]

Nothing since his arrival in China had enraged Bethune as much as did this letter. He told Dr Jiang that he would not work with Smedley in the future.[23] Then he wrote her a searing reply. At first, he said, he had hesitated to respond to her letter, but

the personal vindictiveness of its tone, combined with the calculated inaccuracies of its content, persuaded me of the necessity of taking some definite steps to protect myself against the willful wrongheadedness of the writer. Now, fortunately, I have the honor to belong to the Communist Party, which, I understand, you do not. I, therefore, have laid before the Central Committee, all letters exchanged between you and I; and in addition a full history of our Unit ... I have asked my comrades here to write directly to the Canadian and American Communist Parties and to place before them their findings. I was forced to take this drastic step since the increasingly accusatory tone of your letters to me seemed that you might do me, by your machinations abroad, a mischief.[24]

He then turned to her point that he had no authority over Brown. "Quite so," he answered. "I do not, nor do I wish to. Dr Brown, like myself, is under one authority – and that authority is the 8th Route Army." Then he continued,

In view of such an attitude as yours, the mind of a comparatively calm and sane man, such as mine, is simply staggered and bemused. I ask myself, confused by such obliquity, such as you exhibit – "How in Heaven's Name, does she get that way?"

In conclusion, may I state that it is with extreme reluctance, that I have been forced to write you in such a vein. But I have come to China to help my comrades and I can not afford to stand quietly aside, and perhaps see

my efforts frustrated and come to naught, thru [*sic*] the spiteful intervention of a neurotic personality such as you possess.

Believe that I have the same passionate desire to help our comrades.
Show me that you will work with me collectively towards that end, and
then you will find I will be a good comrade to you. And that is what I
desire to be.

To the 8th Route Army!

Norman Bethune[25]

But Smedley was not Bethune's only problem. He was also angered by the
failure of the China Aid Council to maintain contact with him. After finishing his reply to Smedley, he wrote to the New York committee, enclosing
copies of the letter of 17 April from the "famous trouble-maker," as he called
her, and of his reply to her. Then, clearly hoping to shame them into respond-
ing, he concluded:

To the American Committee, the silent committee, Jean and I say this
– "Friends, we are grateful to you for sending us to China. We are grateful for the beautiful equipment that you have provided us to work with.
We are at work among our comrades. That is what we came for and that
is what we are doing. If you don't want to support us – why that's all right
with us. On our part we will forget your promises to us. We have explained our position to the 8th Army, – how you have left us without
money for so long and the 8th Army has said – "Don't worry, we are not
rich, but you are valuable to us. And, in addition, you are comrades. We
will provide for you." But your silence – so strange!

Sincerely,

Norman Bethune[26]

He next wrote a 4,500-word memorandum outlining the events from the
time of his suggestion to Tim Buck in August 1937 that a unit be sent to
China down to his arrival in Yan'an at the beginning of April 1938.[27] To this
he attached copies of his letter to the China Aid Council and the correspondence between him and Smedley, and presented the report to the Central
Committee of the Communist Party in Yan'an.

Meanwhile, Smedley had received Bethune's letter.[28] She immediately
wrote to the China Aid Council denouncing him and demanding his recall.

She complained that he was not the type of person to be sent to work with the Eighth Route Army, claiming that he insisted on being supplied with American cigarettes and chocolate and that, in a region where most people felt themselves lucky to survive on carrots and millet, he demanded rich food. When there was no reply from the council, she followed up with another letter reiterating her complaints.[29]

The CAC was annoyed by the angry appeals of both Bethune and Smedley regarding the conflict between them as the latest stage in the troubled saga of the medical unit they had sent to China. The council had already made clear its distrust of Bethune by appointing Parsons as the unit head despite their awareness of his alcoholism and then ignoring all complaints against him.[30] Apparently they had no greater respect for Smedley, whom Jaffe considered to be "a neurotic of sorts."[31] So when both Bethune and Smedley began demanding that the committee take sides in their disagreements, its reaction appears to have been "a plague on both your houses."[32] There is no evidence that it ever responded to Smedley's demands for Bethune's recall or Bethune's complaints about her.

The CAC knew that Bethune had reached Yan'an and was under Eighth Route Army jurisdiction; it therefore decided not to send funds directly to him, as it had to Parsons, but instead to remit them to the Medical Relief Commission of the National Red Cross Society of China, directed by Dr Robert Lim, to be disbursed to the Eighth Route Army. In August 1938 they informed Lim that henceforth they would instead be remitting the money they collected to the China Defence League in Hong Kong, for which he also acted as the distributor to the communist forces. Lim later did use some China Aid Council money to send supplies requested by Bethune to the Eighth Route Army.[33] However, there is no indication in Bethune's correspondence or his reports that he knew where CAC funds were being routed or that he ever received any of the supplies Lim sent. If the CAC did inform him of their decision, that letter failed to reach him. He would to the end continue to hope that he would eventually receive direct financial support from New York, but none ever arrived.

Meanwhile, he had had to face another disappointment. Dr Jiang informed him that the negotiations about the League Unit hospital had failed. The Chinese Sanitary Corps, an agency of the Guomindang, had raised objections, and the League Unit had withdrawn its offer: Bethune would not get his mobile field hospital. Jiang therefore decided that Bethune should go to Yanchuan, forty kilometres to the northeast of Yan'an, to serve in a three-hundred bed Eighth Route Army hospital. Bethune refused: Yanchuan was not the front, he protested, insisting he would be of greatest use as close to the fighting as possible. Without the League hospital he would have to rely on the surgical and medical supplies he had brought from New York. These were still en route from Hong Kong, and he demanded that as soon as they reached Yan'an he be allowed to leave for the battle areas. He was determined not to be relegated to some safe backwater.

His heart was set on going to Jin-Ch-Ji, an area made up of parts of three provinces, Shanxi, Chahar, and Hebei. It was one of two areas designated as Border Regions, which had been formed following the United Front agreement reached by the rival Communist and Guomindang factions in September 1937.[34] In order to present a common face against the invading Japanese, they had pledged to end their civil war. The Communists were then given jurisdiction in the Border Regions, Jin-Cha-Ji being the more strategically important. With its northern boundary only fifty kilometres south of Beijing, it was directly in the path of the Japanese Army's planned advance into the Chinese interior.

The task of confronting the invader was given to the newly created Eighth Route Army under the command of General Zhu De. Subordinate to him and in charge of the military forces in Jin-Cha-Ji was General Nie Rongzhen. Although the Communist forces lacked the equipment and trained manpower of the foreign enemy they faced, they had learned much from their years of fighting the Guomindang army. Since early October 1937 they had been conducting a successful campaign of guerrilla warfare against the Japanese.

However, Dr Jiang Qixian was reluctant to grant Bethune's request to go to Jin-Cha-Ji. The chief reason was fear for his safety. In an army in which the average soldier's age was under twenty, the forty-eight-year-old Bethune was considered too old to endure the conditions of guerrilla war; it was believed that his services would be far more useful safely distant from the fighting. When Jiang explained this, saying that it was the considered opinion of the Eighth Route Army Medical Service, Bethune picked up a chair, flung it through a latticed window into a courtyard, and stormed from the room. Ma Haide, also present at the meeting, followed Bethune and told him that his action was discourteous and would be seen as offensive by the Chinese. "I'm willing to apologize to everyone, but you people have to apologize to the amputees with crutches," Bethune retorted.[35] Later, when Bethune had grown calmer, Jiang relented. Yanchuan would not be a permanent posting, he assured Bethune, and when his work was done there, he would be able to move on to the Border Region. Bethune's temper had already made a vivid impression on those around him. Ma Haide would later joke that he was "a dangerous man." Another colleague, Jiang Yizhen, noted that "he loved to kick up a fuss and get into trouble," and still another complained, "A friend like him is really exhausting."[36]

At this point Dr Richard Brown arrived from Xi'an in a League of Nations truck. With him was Dr Robert McClure, who had come for a brief visit.[37] Bethune was relieved to see Brown but berated him taking so long to arrive. Did he not understand that every day of delay meant the loss of anti-Japanese fighters they could have saved? Taken aback by Bethune's tone, Brown explained that he had needed to attend to his mission hospital in Guide before leaving for Xi'an.[38] When he said he was ready to set out at once for the Border Region if Bethune could get permission for them to go, Bethune was somewhat mollified. But he was contemptuous of Brown's Christian convictions, so similar to those of his own parents. Brown conducted a religious service in Chinese two days after his arrival on Good Friday, 15 April, at Mao's request. A Canadian flag was raised, loudspeakers were set up, and Brown gave a sermon based on the parable of the Good Samaritan in which he urged more than two thousand Christian hearers not to oppress the peasants.[39] Bethune listened for a few minutes, then walked out. Later he chided Brown for being so stupid as to believe such Christian myths.[40]

However, on more festive occasions the two men did get along. When the propaganda department of the party sent tickets to Bethune, Brown, and Ewen for an open-air movie, they joined the soldiers and farmers on wooden benches in the courthouse grounds. After the showing of an old Soviet film entitled *Chapiev*, Mao gave a brief speech announcing that two doctors and a nurse had come to help the wounded. The crowd thumped the benches and clapped. Then one *xiao guei* called out that the doctors should sing a song. Bethune got up and sang "The Ballad of Joe Hill," and Brown then translated the words and explained the meaning to the delighted crowd.[41]

Word now reached Bethune that their medical supplies had at last arrived in Xi'an from Hong Kong. On 20 April, he sent Ewen in an Eighth Route Army truck to arrange for their transfer to Yan'an. It was a plan that would inadvertently end Ewen's role in the unit. On the way south, when the driver stopped to assist a northbound Army truck mired in mud, they learned that it was carring their supplies from Hong Kong. Two days later the truck arrived in Yan'an, but without Ewen. She had continued on to Xi'an where, she later claimed, Bethune had sent her to buy more medical materials. After making the required purchases and staying for several days, she returned to Yan'an to find that Bethune and Brown had gone north without her, having stripped her cave of everything including her food. Although she took the first opportunity to follow them, she was prevented from joining them first by the changing military siltuation and then by illness.[42] Bethune, however, maintained that he received no response to two telegrams he sent to Xi'an urging her to return and so decided to leave without her. He told Ma Haide to offer her the option of following or staying in Yan'an.[43] In any case, Bethune's dependence on her knowledge of Chinese had ended with Brown's arrival.[44]

Meanwhile, in the days before leaving for the north, Bethune had turned his mind to trying to establish a blood transfusion service in Yan'an. The main problem was that the Chinese were reluctant to give blood, even the tiny amount necessary to have it typed. He got his chance when an instructor at the Kangda University lost a lot of blood after a bad accident with a grenade. The young man desperately needed a transfusion, and Bethune cajoled the students into allowing themselves to be typed, saying it was just a little prick. Six or seven shamed each other into volunteering. When he got the right blood type, Bethune had the potential donor seized and held down, while he did a direct transfusion to the wounded man. Brown noted wryly that this arbitrary approach did nothing to increase the number of potential blood donors in Yan'an.[45]

On Monday, 2 May, the medical supplies that Bethune and Brown would take north with them were packed into ten metal containers and loaded onto an Eighth Route Army truck. Twelve fully armed soldiers were assigned to go with them. All was in readiness when Bethune noticed that He Zexin, his *xiao guei*, was missing. "Where is He? He must come with me!" he insisted and went to look for him. Finding him back at the cave, he picked up He's knapsack and led him to the truck. Long afterward He recalled with pride, "From that day I remained with him until his death."[46]

The destination of the unit was no longer Yanchuan, for Jiang Qixian had decided that Bethune and Brown should go instead to Shenmu, nearly 150 kilometres north of Yan'an. Plans changed again several hours after they left Yan'an. Jiang met them at Qingjian and told them the need for them was greater at a hospital south of Shenmu at Hejiachuan. The road they followed led north, then east through the barren loess hills along the Yellow River. Rain made the clay surface of the road greasy, and the driver had to reduce speed. Near Suide the road became a quagmire, and the truck ground to a halt. The driver was unable to extricate it, and Bethune and the others got out. The rain quickly soaked his light clothing – a yellow windbreaker, cotton trousers, and yellow sneakers. Hands on hips, he assessed the situation, then got behind the truck and helped push it out of the mud. The soldiers were astonished. As one of his escort said later, "It was so unlike a foreigner to get dirty."[47]

Late Tuesday afternoon, accompanied by Dr Jiang, they arrived in Suide, where they spent the night. Bethune took the opportunity to write letters to

Canada, giving details of the journey and complaining of the lack of support from the CAC.[48] Their next stop was Mizhi, fifteen kilometres to the north. From that point they would have to rely on mules to carry them and the supplies, so they stayed two nights to allow carpenters to make wooden boxes for the supplies to replace the heavier metal ones. When the carpenters said they could not make the round boxes Bethune wanted, he rolled up his sleeves and set to work himself, a task that took all day.[49] On the advice of the guards, he and Brown also equipped themselves better for the trek ahead. As walking was difficult in leather boots, they had flexible straw sandals made, the same type worn by Eighth Route Army soldiers, and each chose a stout walking stick. Bethune also discovered some uniforms in an Eighth Route Army depot in the village and asked permission to wear one. He Zexin set up two mirrors on opposite walls in one of the huts, and Bethune paraded between them, eyeing his reflection and crowing, "Look at me, almost fifty, and I'm a soldier once more!" However, his first attempts to mount a mule the following morning did less for his self-esteem. Chinese guards tried to help him but he waved them off angrily. Only after a series of embarrassing failures did he finally manage to clamber onto one of the beasts, and the caravan of thirteen mules set off.[50]

From Mizhi, the 130-kilometre route wound through a mountain chain that paralleled the Wuding River.[51] They would have to pass through Guomindang territory, so the army commander in Mizhi, uneasy despite the United Front agreement, assigned extra guards to the unit. The going was difficult not only for Bethune and Brown but also for the mules, each burdened with a box on either side of its back. There was the constant risk that one could lose its footing and tumble into the gorge. Whenever the path narrowed, Bethune, Brown, and the guards had to unload the cargo, carry it until the path widened, and then tediously reload the mules.

All along the way Bethune and Brown stopped to treat civilian patients in isolated villages. At night they slept in open courtyards or in peasant homes, where Bethune would set up his folding cot and sleeping bag on top of the clay *kang*. Their food was supplied by the soldiers or by peasants: millet or rice, vegetables, and occasionally eggs, washed down with tea. But at one stop Bethune himself prepared a dish that would become his favourite: steamed potatoes mixed with eggs and sprinkled with sugar.[52]

On Wednesday, 11 May, after five days' walking, they arrived just before dark in the mountain hamlet of Hejiachuan, where the Eighth Route Army hospital that Jiang had asked Bethune to inspect was located. Following the standard Chinese courtesy, the head doctor urged Bethune and Brown to rest and sip a ceremonial cup of tea, but Bethune brushed this suggestion aside, demanding to be taken directly to the wounded. What he saw instantly verified what Nelson Fu and Ma Haide had tried so earnestly to make him understand. The conditions at Hejiachuan were far worse than those that had shocked him in the Yan'an hospital. Led from house to house where the wounded were located, he saw groups of three or four huddled together in lice-ridden clothing, without sheets or blankets. Because the hospital lacked any staff with medical training, many of the wounded had lain on their *kangs* for months without care except for the draining of their wounds and the infrequent changing of their dressings. In all, there were 175 wounded; on closer examination the following day, thirty-five of these required immediate surgical attention.

In his report to Yan'an headquarters, begun on 17 May, Bethune would write: "All [the thirty-five most serious cases] have old neglected wounds of the thigh and leg – most of them incurable except by amputation. Three of the 35 are lying naked on straw-covered *kangs* with only a single cotton quilt. The others are still in their old, unwashed, cotton-padded winter, dirty uniforms. They are, without exception, all anemic, underfed and dehydrated … They are dying of sepsis. These are the cases we are asked to operate on. They are all bad surgical risks."[53] He reacted to the shocking conditions with his usual combination of compassion and rage. After the initial inspection, he stalked off to the quarters assigned to him and Brown, got some of his own clothing and returned to give it to three naked soldiers.[54] He would later refer to the hospital at Hejiachuan as a "pesthole … that should be shut down – lousy position, lousy poverty-stricken area, no food for patients, lousy equipment and a lousy, lazy staff."[55]

But this time he did not go on strike, for the need was too great – far greater than anything he had ever seen before. He and Brown set to work. Before they could begin operating, however, they had to reorganize the hospital in order to provide proper treatment of the wounded. This took three days. In one of the larger houses they prepared two adjacent rooms, one for operating and the other for recovery. They chose several other houses to become post-operative wards. Because there were no hospital materials, they had to create everything they would need. From cotton they had brought they had sheets, gauze squares, masks, and towels made, and also mattress covers, which were then stuffed with straw.[56] As soon as they could, they began a daily round of operations and post-operative care that continued until they left Hejiachuan thirteen days later. Amazingly, despite the poor condition of the patients they operated on, only one died. During one operation, Bethune lay beside the operating table while Brown administered a direct transfusion of his blood to the patient. It was the first of four occasions during his time in China that Bethune would donate his blood to the wounded.[57]

Because the operations were performed in peasant homes, they were sources of public entertainment, and the whole village turned out to watch. Annoyed by heads poking in the windows and door to watch him work, Bethune instructed the orderlies to drive the people away. They scattered only to return as soon as the orderly went inside. One day, losing patience, Bethune charged the crowd himself. With bloodied hands and apron, waving a scalpel, he was a fearsome sight, and the crowd fled screaming from the furious foreign devil. However, it did not take long for their curiosity to overcome their fear, and they soon returned.[58]

In the second section of his report to Mao Zedong, dated 22 May, Bethune presented a detailed critique of conditions in the hospital at Hejiachuan. A primary weakness was the lack of sanitation: "Food is left exposed to flies; dressings, after removal, are thrown on the floor instead of into a receptacle; the patients are not washed; cross infection is the rule not the exception. Two of our cases developed maggots in their wounds within 5 days after operation." He also criticized the improper care of the wounded, the lack of medical training of hospital staff, and the incorrect choices of medicines given to patients.[59] When Dr Jiang Qixian assured him that the conditions at Hejiachuan were representative of those in most Eighth Route Army hospitals, Bethune enlarged his critique of the hospital into a scheme for revamping the entire Eighth Route Army Medical Service. Rapidly reaching a series of conclusions, he outlined these in his report. The Medical Service, he asserted, was deficient in trained medical workers, supplies and equipment, and special hospitals, especially orthopedic facilities, so necessary for the treatment and rehabilitation of the many soldiers suffering from bone damage. To improve in these areas, which would require time and a significant sum of overseas financial support, he offered a series of detailed suggestions.

The lack of competent medical personnel was a critical matter. In the Hejiachuan hospital there was not only no doctor but not even a single trained nurse. "Operations are the least part of the treatment – after-care the most important," he wrote in his report.[60] Knowing that far more than their surgical skill would be required to save the lives of those on whom they would operate, he and Brown were forced to choose only those cases that required a minimum of nursing care. For this reason, he was more than ever determined "to get to the front and, by instruction, to prevent many such cases as we see here from getting into such conditions."[61]

The first step to achieve that aim, he informed Mao, was for him and Brown to make a tour of all the battle areas to assess the number of wounded and the conditions in which they were being treated. At the same time they would give front-line instruction on the treatment of wounds. Another reason for making such a survey was to provide Brown with information he could use as propaganda to raise funds overseas once he returned to his mission duties. As Brown had to return to Guide in July, replacing him was the next vital issue, and his replacement would have to be bilingual. Following the survey tour and Brown's departure, Bethune explained to Mao, he wanted to create an entirely new medical unit: a permanent mobile operating team. It would consist of himself, Brown's replacement, two trained nurses, and ten non-medical personnel. To maintain the unit, he calculated, would require a monthly sum of $1,250 in the Chinese national currency; optimistic as ever, he promised this cost would be "entirely borne by the Canadian and American Committees."[62]

Although Bethune's analysis of the needs of the Eighth Route Army hospitals was keen and detailed, his overall understanding of the military and political facts of the war was still inadequate, and so some of his suggestions simply could not be carried out. For example, he suggested that nurses and doctors be sent to Hankou and other cities not under direct Japanese attack to be trained by mission hospitals and the Chinese Red Cross. The reality was that arranging such transport in wartime was almost impossible. He also insisted on the need for a "tenfold increase of all medical supplies," but there was no money to pay for this, nor for the special hospitals he wanted to see constructed near the front.[63]

Despite his brave words to Mao, Bethune was acutely aware that his promise of foreign financial support depended on help from the China Aid Council, and he had almost lost hope of funding from that quarter. Therefore, along with the report to Mao he sent out a letter and a copy of the report to Earl Browder. "As I have had no reply to a dozen letters and several cables to the American Committee (Wm. Dodd Jr.)," Bethune wrote, "I have come to the conclusion they have ceased to function. So am sending you this material for you to place in the hands of another committee formed in its place."[64]

Bethune also sent copies of the letter and the report to Tim Buck, and for this reason included in the letter an appeal for Canadian aid:

Canada must help these comrades. I know we are poor, I know that Spain needs our help, but Spain never needed our help as these comrades do. They have fought for the salvation of China and the liberation of Asia. They are dying now as they have lived, without complaint.

For 5 months now the American Committee in New York has been completely silent – I have not received a single letter or line from them –

in spite of my urgent appeals, by letter and cable. I can give no explanation to Maotsetung [Mao Zedong]. I am ashamed. If the American Committee has ceased to function, can not another committee be formed? Surely the Canadians can help, in addition to supplying the personnel of the first unit – this, the first mobile operating unit to go to the front in all the armies of China. Cannot Canada alone raise the money to maintain this unit … We must stop being an expence [*sic*] to the 8th Army. It is disgracefull! [*sic*].[65]

After sketching events since he and Brown left Yan'an, Bethune praised the missionary doctor: "Dr. Brown is a grand companion. I am going to make a Communist out of him yet." And he urged Browder to arrange for Brown and his family to receive the same $100 a month that he and Parsons had been promised. He ended wistfully, "Lord, I wish we had a radio and a hamburger sandwich."[66]

Leaving Hejiachuan on Friday, 27 May, Bethune and Brown headed east out of the mountains, descending into valley of the Yellow River. Crossing into the province of Shanxi, they arrived three days later at Lanxian, headquarters of the 120th Division of the Eighth Route Army. Before moving on, they inspected the medical facilities, made suggestions for change, left what medical supplies they could spare, and performed several operations.[67] Learning that a courier was about to leave Lanxian for Yan'an, they took the opportunity to send several messages. In the postscript of a brief report to Mao, Bethune wrote, "I cannot close without telling you how happy we are to be here and to feel that we are of some practical use to our heroic Chinese comrades in their magnificent fight for the salvation of their beautiful country and the emancipation of Asia."[68] To Ma Haide he wrote," We are having a wonderful time … I only wish you were here. I don't know what I shall do without an English-speaking assistant when [Brown] goes."[69] At the same time, Brown wrote to Smedley describing the conditions that he and Bethune had encountered, making an urgent plea for her to redouble her efforts to send aid to the area.[70]

Before leaving Lanxian on 7 June, Bethune and Brown were given Eighth Route Army horses and an escort of twenty-five soldiers armed with captured Japanese machine guns.[71] Three days later, seventy-five partisan fighters joined them as they entered the Japanese-occupied area flanking the railway linking Shanxi's capital city, Taiyuan, in the south to the city of Datong to the north. At midnight on a moonlit night they moved stealthily through enemy lines, first across a road and then the railway tracks, both patrolled by Japanese troops. From there they slipped into the foothills and the relative safety of the

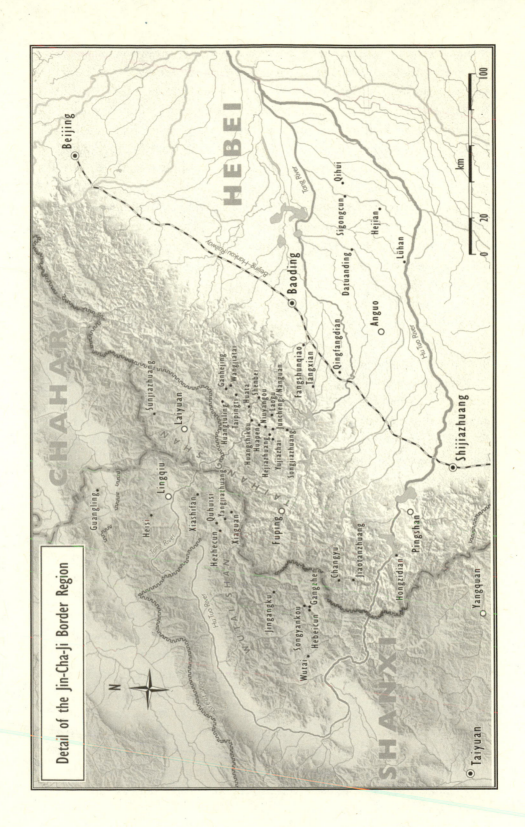

Detail of the Jin-Cha-Ji Border Region

CHAHAR

HEBEI

SHANXI

Beijing

Datuanding

Qihui

Sigongcun

Hejian

Lühan

Baoding

Beijing–Hankou Railway

Tong River

Hu Tuo River

Qingfangdian

Anguo

Fangshunqiao

Tangxian

Shijiazhuang

Sunjiazhuang

Laiyuan

Ganhejing

Wangjiatai

Huata

Shenbei

Laoyu

Juncheng Manguan

Huangtuling

Taipingxi

Huangshikou

Huapen

Niuyangou

Heijiazhuang

Yujiazhai

Songjiazhuang

T A I H A N G   S H A N

Lingqiu

Guangling

Heisi

Xiashifan

Hezhecun

Quhuisi

Yangjiazhuang

Xiaguan

Fuping

Changyu

Jiaotanzhuang

Pingshan

Hongzidian

Yangquan

Jingangku

Songyankou

Gangzhen

Wutai

Hebeicun

WUTAI SHAN

Hu Tuo River

Tong River

N

Taiyuan

km

100

20

0

mountains to the east. The only casualty was Bethune's typewriter, which, to his enraged dismay, went missing.[72] Following dirt trails for the next four days they passed through scenery that variously reminded Bethune of the Canadian Rockies and the west coast of Scotland. "High towering mountains, green fertile valleys make it look a Paradise after the bare, naked hills of Shensi [Shaanxi], treeless and desolate," he wrote. "It was a great relief to be out of the dust storms. Here the air is soft and balmy and filled with the songs of birds and clear running mountain streams."[73]

Nine days after leaving Lanxian, they reached Wutai.[74] With a population of several thousand, it was the largest town in the area, and hundreds of people were waiting to greet them. Bethune and Brown rode down the main street to cheers and applause. Behind the crowds, long banners attached to the sides of buildings welcomed them.[75] After much handshaking with local officials, Bethune asked to be taken to examine the wounded but was told that the nearest base hospital was a two-day ride away.

Leaving Wutai early next morning, they reached the Eighth Route Army headquarters in Jingangku at 6 PM. Located at the base of a steep rock massif, the large white-washed compound with its grey-tiled roofs adorned with dragon finials had been the residence of a wealthy landlord before being confiscated by the army. Awaiting them at the front gate were General Nie Rongzhen, the thirty-nine-year-old commander in chief of the Border Region, and several members of his staff.[76] The general spoke little English, so direct conversation was limited, but Bethune took to him instantly and their relationship would develop into one of mutual respect. After a lengthy discussion about the role he might play in the Border Region, Bethune told Nie he intended to leave early the following morning to travel to the local base hospital. Pointing out that it was a full day's ride from Jingangku, Nie insisted that the doctors rest for a day to recuperate from their trek.[77] Bethune reluctantly agreed and was soon glad he had done so, for in those rare few hours of relaxation he revelled in the use of the landlord's luxurious bathroom. "A hot bath in an immense stone bathtub was Heaven," he wrote.[78]

During his discussion with Nie, Bethune emphasized that his primary aim was to reduce the unnecessarily high mortality rate among the Eighth Route Army wounded. To achieve this, he wanted to set up a mobile team to operate near the battlefronts. There he would be in a position to treat soldiers and partisans soon after they had been wounded. In addition, as he had stated in his report to Mao Zedong, the other two key functions of the team would be to deliver medical supplies and to train medical workers in hospitals throughout Jin-Cha-Ji. Nie accepted Bethune's proposal, but to give him a clear sense of the problems he would have to face, he outlined military-medical conditions in Jin-Cha-Ji. The Border Region contained more than 100,000 Eighth Route Army soldiers and partisan fighters and was divided into ten sub-districts. Each of these had one base hospital and two or three clinics, usually with about fifty medical personnel and one hundred to two hundred patients. The most serious cases were transferred from the clinics to the base hospitals. Nie pointed out that none of the personnel was qualified by western standards and that organizing such an area would be an enormous task. Bethune replied that his first step would be to treat the sick and wounded in the local base hospital; after that he would undertake a survey trip to those of the other sub-districts. After assessing their needs and considering their geographical locations, he would structure a plan of operation to serve the entire Border Region.

The next morning, mounted on large horses captured from the Japanese by Nie's troops, Bethune and Brown set out for the nearest base hospital. There they found that the 350 patients were in fact distributed among three villages.[79] The wounded, numbering about two hundred, were housed in the villages of Hexicun and Songyankou, less than a kilometre apart. Five kilometres away in the village of Hebeicun were soldiers and partisan fighters who were suffering from various illnesses. In each of the three villages the entire population lined the narrow main street when Bethune and Brown arrived, eager to witness the rare sight of a pair of foreigners. As at Wutai, red and green banners bearing messages of welcome draped the sides of houses, and children sang songs to the beating of gongs and drums.

When he visited the wounded, Bethune was for the first time not utterly dismayed by what he found. Though woefully lacking in all categories by western standards, this base hospital was better managed than the four in which he and Brown had previously worked. After requesting that a rather basic operating room be set up in a peasant home in Songyankou, they began examining all the patients, ranking cases according to the severity of their wounds. By the time Brown left twenty-five days later, they had operated on 110 of these patients.[80] Yet already Bethune was growing restless, not convinced that his skills were being put to the best possible use. Songyankou was too peaceful: he wanted the surgical unit to remain mobile and yearned to be working closer to the fighting. He speculated that the need for surgeons might be greater with the 120th Division in western Shanxi or in the south with the 115th and 129th Divisions under Zhu De. And even though his immediate commander, Nie Rongzhen, wished him to remain where he was, Bethune informed Mao Zedong that he would not stay in the Wutaishan area if the military situation remained quiet, adding as if as an afterthought, "I hope you approve of my attitude."[81]

During this period Bethune occasionally rode over to General Nie's headquarters at Jingangku, and on one of these visits he met Captain Evans F. Carlson, an American military attaché assigned to gather information in the Jin-Cha-Ji Border Region. Elated by the success of the work he and Brown were doing in the Base Hospital, Bethune confided to Carlson his dawning sense that he was at last achieving his destiny. "I believe I have found my mission in life, a little late, to be sure, but a tremendous challenge," he said.[82] He was also enthusiastic about an arrangement he believed he had made with the *Manchester Guardian*, to write two articles or more a month for publication. In this way he was hoping to earn an income and so avoid the humiliating need for the Eighth Route Army to pay his personal expenses.[83]

Bethune and Brown maintained a tight operating schedule, averaging six hours daily not counting emergencies. They usually finished work by late afternoon and often relaxed by taking a walk, going for a swim in the nearby Qingshui River, or playing cards. On one occasion they visited the Buddhist monastery of Pusading. Set high on the slope of Mount Wutai, it offered a panoramic view of the surrounding valley. Entering a temple, they came upon an elderly monk prostrating himself before a golden altar, sliding a short distance up its side before returning to the floor. The performance of the ritual over untold years had created a slick patch on the altar. Bethune was disgusted at what he considered a pointless exercise, yelling at the monk, "Silly old fool, what good are you doing there? Why don't you get out and help the wounded or something?"[84] Alarmed and uncomprehending, the monk turned to Brown, who told him that Bethune was only asking him to say a prayer for him. When Brown reported what he had said, Bethune cursed long and explicitly, expressing contempt for religious practices that brought no social benefit.[85]

Living at close quarters as they did, Brown soon became familiar with many of Bethune's traits, including his chronic insomnia. On nights when Bethune was unable to sleep, he thought nothing of waking Brown and talking obsessively for hours. Like McClure before him, Brown noted Bethune's frustration at having failed to receive in Canada the professional recognition he craved. He repeatedly attacked the Canadian medical establishment, saying that many of its members were indifferent to the Hippocratic Oath and motivated solely by greed. Few, he insisted, showed dedication to the sick, especially those who were unable to pay.[86] He also spoke bitterly of his personal life, particularly his childhood, which he said had been unhappy. It seemed to Brown that what Bethune said one night he would contradict the next, alternately blaming each of his parents. Although he was still deeply respectful of his mother, he seemed contemptuous of his father, who he said had had a weak personality, among other faults.[87]

Brown gradually formed an opinion of Bethune, much of it unfavourable. He deprecated Bethune's impulsiveness, feeling that he was "out for the spectacular" and that he was full of criticisms of Chinese conditions and practices but without the means or practical knowledge as to how to improve things: "He wanted to accomplish something, he wanted to do it overnight, he got annoyed with others who he thought probably didn't cooperate sufficiently." Knowledgeable about Chinese customs himself, Brown winced at Bethune's refusal to adjust to cultural differences. For instance, on occasions when care had been taken to prepare special dishes to honour the two foreign doctors, Bethune would often refuse to eat what he was served, letting his hosts see that he disliked the food. Brown came to consider him as "rude and arrogant … very impatient and … quite selfish," noting that much of the load on the long-suffering mules was Bethune's personal equipment such as his camp cot and other items.[88]

Brown had to deal as well with the consequences of Bethune's chronic irritability and frequent explosions of temper. Fortunately for their work together, most of these were not directed against him. He also disapproved of Bethune's habits of drinking a good deal of Chinese wine when he could get it and giving himself shots of morphine to calm his nerves and keep himself going. Noting Bethune's chronic wakefulness and irascibility and his compulsive talking about things that he was going to do but somehow never got around to doing, Brown would later characterize his personality as "psychopathic."[89] Given all of this, their personal relationship cannot have been easy, as Brown's comment to Ewen when he met her months later in Xi'an revealed. When she asked how he had got along with Bethune, she recalled, "[Brown] looked at me and tapped the table with his fingers. 'The Angel Gabriel couldn't get along with Norman Bethune,' he replied. 'He's a horrible man.'"[90]

But despite Bethune's exasperating flaws, Brown respected his deep compulsion to relieve suffering at whatever cost to himself. They would sometimes debate politics and religion, and when Bethune proudly showed Brown his Communist Party membership sewn under his lapel, Brown could not resist saying, "You certainly don't act like a communist. You act more like a monk or a dedicated person who has an interest in the underdog."[91] He was also impressed by Bethune's inventiveness in improvising tools and techniques that aided their work, and praised his efforts to pass on his skills to the Chinese so that they would acquire the knowledge and self-confidence to do the work themselves.[92]

For his part, Bethune kept any personal criticisms of Brown to himself, notwithstanding his contempt for Brown's religion and his belated arrival in Yan'an. In a report to Mao he described Brown as "a real true friend of the 8th Army," and in a letter to a North American friend, wrote: "I am unable to speak of the work of Dr Brown with sufficient praise. He has been of the most invaluable assistance to me. I can say truthfully that the work we have been able to do would not have been possible without him ... Dr Brown speaks Chinese perfectly. His temper is equable. He is kind and considerate and makes a charming travelling companion."[93] Coming from Bethune, who was always critical of other people's failings, this was high praise. The reason was no doubt that despite their personal differences, their twelve-week relationship had been successful professionally. Although Bethune was a dedicated communist and Brown a devout Christian, both shared a profound commitment to serve those in need.[94]

Brown left Songyankou on 13 July.[95] He had been as deeply moved as Bethune by the suffering they had witnessed, and decided that after visiting his mission post he would go to Hankou to try to raise funds to support his and Bethune's work in Jin-Cha-Ji, then rejoin Bethune in three months.[96] Left alone, Bethune measured himself against the desperate conditions in the Eighth Route Army Medical Service in Jin-Cha-Ji. As he wrote to Elsie Siff in New York, "We are completely surrounded by the Japs, north, east, west and south. They hold all the towns on the railways, but we still retain the enclosed country. In this great area of 13,000,000 people and with 15,000 armed troops, I am the only qualified doctor!"[97] Now he was needed as he had never been before. It was overwhelming. It was exhilarating.

⁜ 16 ⁜

Kingly Comrade

Jin-Cha-Chi, July 1938–January 1939

And so Bethune began his second ministry. This time there was no need to preach the communist faith as he had done on the speaking tour: now the focus of his evangelism was to revolutionize the Eighth Route Army Medical Service by spreading the gospel of western medical hygiene and procedure, meanwhile saving as many lives as he could. His goal was that in the shortest possible time Chinese medical personnel would become self-sufficient in the care of the wounded.

However, two factors complicated the mission he had set for himself: his inability to learn Chinese and his chronic irascibility, provoked daily in his dealings with those around him. While Brown was still at Songyankou, the Chinese medical staff had often approached him to ask, "What's wrong with Dr Bethune today? He's throwing his instruments around."[1] Among themselves the staff began to refer to Bethune as "Lao Hu" (Old Tiger).[2] Sometimes, however, his inability to communicate had amusing consequences. One evening, He Zexin, Bethune's *xiao guei*, brought him a basin of water so that he could wash his hands and face. Setting the basin down, He Zexin took a towel from his shoulder and, as was the Chinese custom, put it in the water. Bethune, who wanted his towel dry, shouted "No!" Removing the towel from the basin, he threw it on the floor. Puzzled, the *xiao guei* fetched another towel and again put it in the water. Bethune screamed, "Hey, don't put that goddam towel in the water!" He Zexin scuttled for the door, but from the threshold he shot back, "Goddam towels finished."[3]

At the end of June, Bethune had written hopefully that by the time of Brown's expected return in three months, he might have learned enough Chinese to be on his own.[4] But he must have known that this was wishful thinking, for several paragraphs later he wrote, "General Nie is kindness and consideration itself. He has given orders that anything we want is to be supplied to us. I immediately asked for an interpreter, a radio and a hamburger with a cup of coffee. There seems a reasonable chance that we will get the interpreter."[5]

General Nie was well aware of Bethune's emotional volatility and his over-zealous reaction to the conditions he had discovered in the hospitals of Jin-Cha-Ji. He later wrote, "When Dr Bethune came to this area he and we did not at first understand each other. He went around criticizing this and that. He felt that we were working in an unenlightened way. We felt that he did not appreciate the difficulties under which we laboured. There was a gap between us."[6] Nie also knew that, without Brown, matters might get out of hand. Bethune's inability to communicate would inevitably affect his performance in surgery and also prevent him from introducing the wide-spread medical reforms he planned for the Eighth Route Army. So from the beginning, Nie had been trying to find another interpreter for Bethune, but in remote, mountainous Jin-Cha-Ji this was no easy task. At last, in response to Nie's increasingly urgent requests, the Jin-Cha-Ji government promised to send the chief administrator of Fuping County in Hebei Province to serve as Bethune's interpreter. The twenty-three-year-old Dong Yueqian had gradu-ated in English from Beijing University and spoke the language fluently. How-ever, when he arrived at Nie's headquarters, the general made it clear that his responsibilities would go far beyond those of an ordinary interpreter. His priority must be to foster understanding between Bethune and his colleagues in order to facilitate his work and eliminate future problems. For Bethune to be effective, Nie told Dong, he simply must adjust to Chinese conditions.[7]

As Dong soon discovered, tempering Bethune's fiery nature was no easy task. The revulsion and rage he had felt when he had encountered the poor hospital conditions in Yan'an had only increased as he visited the far worse facilities in Jin-Cha-Ji. He could not – would not – accept that even in such a remote and impoverished area the wounded had to suffer such misery. Although he conceded that the base hospital at Songyankou was better than the others he had visited, he made it clear to the doctors and to General Nie that for it to function efficiently there must be revolutionary changes in how it was run, beginning with the retraining of its entire staff. This suggestion offended the Chinese doctors, and medical workers at all levels found his criticisms severe and his sudden eruptions of anger terrifying.

Undoubtedly this hair-trigger irritability was exacerbated by Bethune's chronic insomnia and reluctance to rest. Life in the remote Border Region placed him under enormous physical and emotional stress, and he over-reacted in many situations. When he found a doctor idly peeling a pear with a scalpel, he shoved him out of the operating room and forbade him to operate again. When he found another doctor improperly using splints on a wound, he slapped his face and upbraided him.[8] Dong Yueqian often had to exercise considerable ingenuity to tone down Bethune's angry rhetoric. After a five-minute dressing-down of a delinquent doctor during which Bethune had cursed him long and explicitly, saying that in Canada he would have been fired at once and his professional career ended, Dong smoothly told the bewildered man, "Dr Bethune is not too satisfied with your behaviour."[9]

Bethune was highly critical of the doctors' tendency to "pass the buck," as he pointed out to Mao and to Nie in a report in early July.[10] They would simply give orders to nurses without following up to ensure that they were carried out. Bethune also complained that staff wasted time in social chatter that made them careless in their work. After writing a stinging critique of such offences at the base hospital, he justified himself by adding, "All the above criticisms are made in a Bolshevist spirit. The only thought behind is the comfort and health of our sick comrades. And that must come first."[11]

At their first meeting Nie had named Bethune "Medical Advisor to the Jin-Cha-Ji Border Region." Acting in this capacity, and without waiting for a response to his initial report to Nie, Bethune began to overhaul the base hospital, and here his analytical skills and ability to improvise came into play.[12] To create conditions to facilitate his work, he designed and supervised construction of a better operating room; he also designed and helped to make a sterilizer, leg and arm splints, and dressing trays. Under his direction an incinerator and stretcher racks were constructed, and a de-lousing sterilizer was planned.

Next he turned to establishing routine. This included defining the duties of all medical workers and posting them on the wall, holding regular staff conferences every Sunday afternoon, making weekly ward rounds, and maintaining patient records. The records were particularly important, as patients were dispersed among various peasant homes in three different villages. So each patient was given a metal disc with his name and number; a master list and a map showing the location of all patients were kept in Bethune's office. To deal with the appalling lack of sanitation, he organized the formation of cleanup squads. He also turned his mind to ways to ease the convalescence of the wounded, ordering the creation of a Patients' Recreation Park with outdoor seating and a hall to be used for reading, games, letter-writing, and listening to lectures. Using a blackboard, he set about improving the standard of medical knowledge, giving the first of a series of lectures with Dong acting as interpreter. He also started to write an illustrated booklet with chapters on anatomy, elementary physiology, treatment of wounds, and the use of drugs. As a result of his efforts, the situation in Songyankou began little by little to improve. "A combination of shouts, tears and smiles has worked wonders here," Bethune wrote to Ma Haide.[13]

In a report to Mao written on 20 July 1938, Bethune described the changes he had made since his arrival in the Wutai area, referring to them as a "Five Weeks Plan" that he had introduced "to make this the finest hospital in the 8th Route Army."[14] It was a first step in the master plan Bethune had begun to develop back in May. The next stage would be to make a survey trip to other subdistricts in the Border Region to assess conditions and offer brief training sessions to personnel in each base hospital. However, he realized that if he undertook such a tour, the wounded who were still arriving at Songyankou would not receive proper care. The solution, he decided, was to create a training school to raise the standard of medical care as quickly as possible, and to construct a hospital where such training could take place.

On Sunday, 7 August, he went to Nie's headquarters in Jingangku to discuss his idea. Nie liked the idea of a training school and said that Bethune should be its principal. But he opposed the construction of a permanent training hospital, as it would provide the Japanese with an inviting target. Every position in guerrilla warfare, he stressed, was temporary, because the location of a battle zone was defined by the often unpredictable movements of the enemy. When Bethune protested that current Japanese troop locations were far to the east and north of Songyankou, Nie warned him that the enemy could easily cross the mountains and penetrate that far. In such a case, he emphasized, his forces could do no more than harass the attackers. The hospital would be destroyed.

Challenged as always by opposition to his ideas by those in authority over him, Bethune refused to give up. He could not believe that within the huge expanse of the Border Region there was not some safe location for a proper training hospital. So on the following Friday, 12 August, he in effect went over Nie's head in a telegram he sent to the Military Council in Yan'an. The pretext for the message was the fact that they had instructed Nie to pay him a monthly sum of $100. Refusing to accept payment for his services, Bethune asked them to take any money designated for his personal use that might arrive from North America and set up a fund to buy tobacco and cigarettes for the wounded. He added that the small amount of money he occasionally needed he would draw from Jin-Cha-Ji headquarters. Then, setting personal matters aside, he detailed the costs of the changes made so far at Songyankou and introduced the matter of the model hospital, for which he said he would submit plans.[15]

Striking on two fronts, he then followed up with a letter to Nie on Saturday, and forwarded a copy of it to Mao Zedong, asking him to present it to the Military Council.[16] He wrote that he would set up a school designed to train all medical workers, but added, "I do not consider the present staff of doctors under Dr Ye sufficiently trained or competent to act as instructors." He identified two other fundamental problems – the lack of textbooks and training facilities – and said he would begin at once to write a textbook, to be translated by Dong Yueqian; he estimated that this could be in print by October.[17] Meanwhile he would continue to treat the wounded arriving from the front and in the process provide on-the-job instruction to the doctors and the nurses at Songyankou. Then he returned to the matter of a permanent hospital. He explained that he had already ordered work to begin on a "model ward" of thirty beds, which he hoped would become the nucleus of a "Demonstration Hospital to be used for training purposes." Finally, he reported that he would try to find time for a flying tour of the other base hospitals.[18]

He followed up by sending Dong to try to persuade Nie to give permission for the construction of the permanent model hospital.[19] Dong discussed Bethune's letter with the general, who reluctantly agreed to submit the proposal to the Military Council in Yan'an. In the end Bethune had his way. Several days later Nie sent word to him that the Military Council had agreed to go along with all of his plans, including the building of the model demonstration hospital in Songyankou. Like Nie, the council recognized the risk, but as Bethune insisted this was the only way to achieve the needed reforms of the medical service, they decided to chance it. Support for Bethune's plan was no doubt also intended as a gesture to demonstrate their gratitude for his extraordinary services to date. But Nie remained pessimistic about Bethune's pet project. "Reality will teach him," he told Dr You Shenghua, the deputy minister of health for Jin-Cha-Ji who was working as Bethune's assistant.[20]

Sure that he would prevail, Bethune had already drawn up plans and ordered construction to begin on the model hospital. He had chosen to locate it in the village of Songyankou, in a grove of willow and pine trees on the site of an abandoned Buddhist temple. The hospital would be built around a fifty-by-thirty metre flagstone courtyard. At one end Bethune planned an operating room flanked by a preparation and a recovery room, at the other end a large covered stage for medical demonstrations. The sides of the courtyard would be occupied by a series of additional rooms, including a thirty-six bed ward.

The task of constructing the buildings and much of the equipment became a massive community effort involving the more than two hundred families of

Songyankou. Work continued through the rest of August and into September. Men lugged stone from the nearby hills and helped masons put up walls. Carpenters built stretchers, beds, and backrests, tinsmiths turned out forceps and tweezers, and blacksmiths crafted metal splints. The village women produced towels, sheets, coverlets, and pillow and mattress covers. Even the older children were organized to gather straw and to perform various tasks. When Bethune finished attending to patients, he frequently joined the work teams, giving directions, answering questions about his plan, and often picking up a tool and using it to demonstrate his intentions.

He was constantly busy. On alternate days in the late afternoon he brought medical workers together in the courtyard, where he conducted classes. On other afternoons and into the evenings, he worked on his textbook, often getting out of his cot at night when he was unable to sleep to spend several hours writing. When there was time for rest, he went for a walk or a swim. There was no radio and he had only a few books and no magazines. No mail had come for him since his arrival in Jin-Cha-Ji. Michael Lindsay, the young Englishman he had met on the *Empress of Asia* on the way to China, visited him in Songyankou in August and found him desperately hungry for conversation and cultural contact.

In the midst of his crowded schedule, Bethune still found time to inspect other hospitals in the area, and despite the squalour of the conditions he found there and the rigours of travel in the mountains, he revelled in the physical beauty around him. In a letter to an unknown friend, written between 15 August and 23 August, he wrote:

You won't find this little village on your map, it's so small – only a few hundred peasants living in their mud huts beside a clear-running green mountain stream, down at the bottom of a deep-cut valley, with steep mountains rising to the north and south ... The hospital is in a Buddhist Temple, among the willow and pine trees, on a little rocky elevation above the road ... The court is filled with flowers in bloom. Huge pink water lilies, like fat slightly breathless dowagers after a good lunch, hang their heavy heads, as big as footballs, over the edges of black earthenware tubs. Geraniums, roses, bluebells, and phlox, provide the colours for the ornately painted doorways. Small gauze squares, washed and now hung out to dry, are spread out on the low orange trees like huge crumpled magnolia blossoms. A few pigs and dogs are asleep. The slightly wounded sit or lie on the temple steps, their bandaged arms and legs in attitudes of awkward repose. Nurses scuttle about in their white aprons. The sun comes down out of a blue sky, warm and beneficent. Across the mountain-tops pass slow, majestic parades of clouds. The golden air is filled with the cooing of doves, the wind in the trees and the murmur of the distant stream.[21]

Clearly, despite his extreme isolation and the daily irritations of his hospital work, Bethune was feeling a deep satisfaction. In the same letter, after detailing the kind of work he did treating the wounded, he went on,

It is true I am tired but I don't think I have been so happy for a long time. I am content. I am doing what I want to do. Why shouldn't I be happy – see what my riches consist of. First I have important work that fully occupies every minute of my time from 5:30 in the morning to 9 at night. I am needed. More than that – to satisfy my bourgeois vanity – the need for me is expressed. I have a cook, a personal servant, my own house, a fine Japanese horse and saddle. I have no money nor the need of it – everything is given me. No wish, no desire is left unfulfilled. I am treated like a kingly comrade, with every kindness, every courtesy imaginable. I have the inestimable fortune to be among, and to work among, comrades to whom communism is a way of life, not merely a way of talking or a way of conscious thinking. Their communism is simple and profound, reflex as a knee jerk, unconscious as the movements of their lungs, automatic as the beating of their hearts.[22]

He had been allowed to build his model hospital with minimal interference from his superiors, and this elated him. But just as important was the respect he was gaining from helping the sick and wounded. "It's a pleasure to work on them," he wrote. "After I dress their wounds they rise and bow profoundly, with an inclination of the body from the waist." He added that the father of a little boy on whom he had operated had knelt on the ground with his head at Bethune's feet to thank him. But the letter also contained an ominous note: "I have an infected finger – it's impossible to avoid them, operating without gloves in these dirty wounds. This is the 3rd in 2 months."[23]

The official opening of the model hospital took place on 15 September 1938. More than two thousand people gathered for the ceremonies, among them the residents of Songyankou, many villagers from the surrounding area, and Eighth Route Army troops and partisan fighters. Propaganda slogans on brightly coloured banners hung above the courtyard, and Bethune had put up several Spanish anti-fascist posters on either side of the stage. Wearing a new grey uniform and white armband around his left sleeve with characters denoting Eighth Route Army, he was the focal point of the ceremonies. Following several addresses, including one from a prominent representative of the Jin-Cha-Ji government, Nie Rongzhen told the crowd that the model hospital was expected to play an important role in the Eighth Route Army Medical Service, and then introduced Bethune. Stepping to the front of the stage, with Dong Yueqian beside him, Bethune saluted smartly. When the enthusiastic applause died down, he took several sheets of paper from his pocket and began to speak.

> Comrades: I thank you for the eight beautiful banners you have given to me and for the kind things you have said about me. I feel, as I know you must feel, that today is an important day in our lives and marks a milestone (I should rather say, a *li* stone), on the path that our hearts and wills are set upon. The eyes of millions of freedom-loving Canadians, Americans and Englishmen are turned to the East and are fixed with admiration on China in her glorious struggle against Japanese Imperialism. This hospital has been equipped by your foreign comrades. I have the honour to have been sent as their representative. Do not consider it strange that people like yourself, thirty thousand *li* away, halfway around the globe, are helping you. You and we are internationalists; we recognize no race, no colour, no language, no national boundaries to separate and divide us. Japan and the war-mongers threaten the peace of the world. They must be defeated. They are obstructing the great historical, progressive movement for a socially organized human society. Because the workers and sympathetic liberals of Canada, England and America know this they are helping China in the defence of this beautiful and beloved country.[24]

The main theme of his address was the importance of technique and leadership in the struggle to defeat death, disease, and deformity, which he defined as the enemies of the Medical Service. His aim, he said, was to encourage the medical workers to develop initiative and self-confidence. This would become a keynote of his policy: throughout his time in China he put pressure on his Chinese associates to make decisions, act upon them, and lead those beneath them to do the same. However he also made another important point: the model hospital – "our hospital" – symbolized for him the bond he was beginning to feel with the Chinese people. "We have changed each other, have we not?" he asked. "We have reacted to each other in a dialectical way ... modified each other ... You have shown me a spirit of selflessness, of working co-operatively, of overcoming great difficulties, and I thank you for those lessons."[25]

The following week an official delegation from Yan'an, accompanied by several journalists, arrived to inspect the model hospital.[26] Afterward, Bethune went with the delegation to Nie's headquarters in Jingangku to join in festivities marking the anniversary of the Eighth Route Army's first victory over the Japanese on 27 September 1937 at the battle of Pingxingguan. Before he left two days later, Bethune received permission from Nie to undertake the long-planned inspection tour of base hospitals in more distant areas of the Border Region.

Riding a large chestnut horse captured from the Japanese and presented to him by Nie during the celebrations, Bethune returned with Dong to Songyankou to make preparations for the extended tour. But he soon received word from Nie that massive Japanese troop formations numbering nearly 25,000 men, including armoured units, were moving westward from neighbouring Hebei Province toward Shanxi. One large column was heading toward the Wutai area. Nie warned Bethune that he had no way to stop such an enemy advance and was preparing to withdraw his forces deeper into the mountains. He sent orders to officials in Songyankou to remove patients from the three hospitals to safety in more distant facilities and to alert the population in the area to the imminent danger. In accordance with the Eighth Route Army policy of leaving nothing for the invader, people in Songyankou and the neighbouring villages hastily packed their belongings, rounded up their animals, and began to move into the mountains. The transfer of the several hundred patients took three days. Led by medical personnel, a long line of stretcher-bearers carrying the more seriously wounded followed the trail south on the week-long journey to hospitals in Pingshan County.[27]

Bethune and his team hastily assembled the equipment for their extended tour of hospitals. The mobile unit included Bethune, Dong Yueqian, Dr Wang Daojian, and Dr You Shenghua on horseback; a nurse, two orderlies, a cook, and two grooms, one of whom was He Zexin, would travel on foot. Their equipment included a collapsible operating table designed by Bethune, surgical instruments, antiseptics, twenty-five wooden leg and arm splints, ten iron leg and arm splints, sterile gauze, and medicines. All this was carried on three mules. After the last of the wounded had been evacuated, the team left the deserted village of Songyankou and the model hospital, which had been in operation for only eighteen days. Bethune was slow to leave and looked back at the hospital again and again.[28] It must have wrenched his heart to abandon his cherished creation, silent and empty, a target for the approaching enemy.

Moving south, they followed the Shibapan path through the Taihang Mountains along the boundary between the provinces of Shanxi and Hebei.

Their destination was the village of Jiaotanzhuang in Pingshan County. As the crow flies, the village was fewer than forty kilometres from Songyankou, but the only route to it lay along narrow, tortuous paths among sharply cleft mountain valleys, so the journey took nearly a week. At Jiaotanzhuang they were surprised to encounter Nie Rongzhen. Japanese units had already driven the general and his staff from their headquarters, forcing them to flee south. The Japanese had entered Jingangku just one day after Nie had left; carrying out the "Three All" policy of "kill all, burn all and take all," they demolished most of the buildings in the village. And there was more bad news, Nie told Bethune. Another enemy unit had entered Songyankou. They had razed the village and completely destroyed the model hospital.[29]

Bethune was overwhelmed by the news. Nie had warned him that this might happen, but driven on by his zeal to bring order to the Eighth Route Army Medical Service, he had insisted on having his own way. Now, after the selfless efforts of the villagers who had built the hospital over a period of several weeks, there was nothing left. Bethune was beginning at last to understand the nature of guerrilla warfare, and now acknowledged that his aim of creating a coherent medical service with trained personnel could not be achieved with a permanent training hospital. He would have to find another way.

Meanwhile, he hoped to inspect every hospital he could and examine the seriously wounded in each of the sub-districts. Nie briefed him about enemy movements to allow him to plan his route, and then Bethune led his team south. Once again they made their way along twisting paths, following the swift-flowing streams that descended to the Hutuo River, the area's main east-west artery. During the next four weeks they covered a distance of 260 kilometres, and Bethune inspected all of the hospitals in the subdistricts. Each was similar to what he had found in Songyankou, a series of tiny peasant houses in which the owners had taken in wounded partisan fighters. After he had examined all the patients, he operated on the serious cases with the assistance of Dr Wang and Dr You.[30] For other patients and those recovering from surgery, he prescribed medicines and explained in detail the nature of the treatment to be administered following the team's departure. When all the fighters had been treated, he examined the villagers who requested attention, always beginning with the children. This was a routine he would continue to follow wherever he went. After dealing with the sick and the wounded, he focused on the organization of each hospital and its personnel. He took over each hospital for as long as a week in an attempt to introduce routine, establish a system of sanitation, and provide brief courses of instruction in the fundamentals of the care of the wounded. He knew this approach was woefully inadequate, but it was all he could do under the circumstances.

Moving from hospital to hospital, the team travelled throughout the month of October, breaking their routine on only one occasion to allow Bethune and Dong to attend a two-day emergency session of the Pingshan County government beginning on 18 October. The meeting took place in Hongzidian, a village that had been attacked and partially destroyed by Japanese troops two weeks earlier. Convened in a warehouse and chaired by a woman, the conference brought together twenty legislators including representatives from several unions such as those of the peasants, the workers, the women, the young men, and the teachers, as well as representatives from the gentry. That they were practising a form of representative government unique in China deeply impressed Bethune. He regarded what he witnessed there as evidence to support his passionately held belief that in the communist region of China a truly democratic society was taking shape.[31] Moved by the warmth of the reception given to him, he felt that he was in some way part of that society, a foreigner but not a stranger.[32] He also felt at ease in the atmosphere of good-natured bantering as the meeting broke for a lunch of cabbage soup and steamed bread. In the late afternoon the chairwoman was persuaded to sing a rousing anti-Japanese song, "The Long Knives Advance," which was followed by others leading the assembly in renditions of "Guard the Yellow River" and "Song of the Guerrillas." Everyone then turned to Bethune, urging him to sing something, so he broke into an International Brigades song. In a long report that he later wrote on the conference, he described his feelings as he sang: "This is a cause worth fighting for, this is the answer to every man's question to himself – 'What shall I do with my life?'" Another incident several hours later deepened this impression. As he and Dong made their way back to their quarters, the beam of Bethune's flashlight picked out some writing on the wall of a partially destroyed house. Dong translated the slogan as "Except by fighting, there is no other Road to Life."[33] It was an apt description of the road that Bethune himself had taken.

On Sunday, 29 October, Bethune and his team returned to Nie's headquarters in Jiaotanzhuang. Having completed his inspection of the hospitals in Pingshan County, he requested and received permission to continue the tour northward to subdistricts in the region of Yanbei. He and his team then went to the nearby village of Changyu to gather supplies from an Eighth Route Army Medical Service depot. There, after completing his detailed monthly report to Nie, Bethune found time to write a letter to Tim Buck outlining the military situation and describing guerrilla tactics used by the Eighth Route Army. "This place is like the Alps, except we have no eidelweiss [sic]," he concluded jauntily. "We even have a few tourists who wander down from Beiping. Why don't you come up and see us some time when you're passing?"[34]

His medical duties had not kept Bethune from turning his mind to propaganda and morale, and on 22 October he wrote to General Nie suggesting various methods to increase recruiting and enhance morale. He recommended, among other things, adopting the practice of awarding service stripes, wound stripes, and medals as well as holding military funerals for the fallen.[35] Ten days later he wrote again from Changyu, reporting the condition of two wounded Japanese prisoners who had received treatment and whom he had photographed. He pointed out that if an interpreter could be found, statements from these men could be used in propaganda leaflets in enemy territory and also abroad.[36] He would continue to take an interest in such details.

The team set out again from Changyu on Sunday, 6 November, all of them heavily garbed against the fierce winter storms in the higher reaches of the Yanbei region. Bethune had an insulated flight suit and hat that Nie's troops had captured from the Japanese, and the rest of the team wore thickly padded uniforms. Their route lay northeastward across mountains to the city of Fuping in the plains below.[37] After pausing there, they continued northward into the mountains again, where they had to struggle along icy paths winding above precipitous valleys. Arriving in the early evening of 19 November at a hospital in the village of Xiaguan, they were greeted by the chief medical officer of the 359th Brigade, Dr Gu Zhengjun.

Bethune brushed aside Gu's suggestion that he rest and have something to eat and insisted on being taken directly to the wounded. A short time later he stomped into Gu's office, anxiously followed by the head doctor who had accompanied him on his round of inspection. Bethune had come across a group of wounded lying huddled on *kangs* without blankets, and the doctor had told him there was none to give them. When Gu admitted that there were no blankets, Bethune cursed and walked out of the office, returning minutes later with one he had taken from his saddle bag. Thrusting it into Gu's hands, he declared that the prime responsibility of all medical workers was to put the interests of their patients above their own, and demanded that he give the blanket to the most seriously wounded soldier. Gu protested that Bethune must not give his own blanket and sent the head doctor to ask the staff members on duty to turn over theirs. Only when the doctor reported that he had found enough blankets did Bethune agree to keep his. He finished examining the wounded before finally sitting down to a meal.[38]

While they ate, Gu explained that as a result of several recent battles against the Japanese, a large number of wounded had been taken by stretcher to hospitals in the villages of Hezhecun and Quhuisi. Told that these villages were less than a day's ride to the northwest, Bethune said that he and his team would be ready to leave by 4:30 AM to treat the wounded there. They arrived on the afternoon of Sunday, 20 November, and by working until late that night and continuing on Monday, Bethune and his two assistants examined 225 wounded and sick soldiers and performed surgery on seven of the most seriously wounded. Shortly after they left the operating room, a courier arrived with a message from Wang Zhen, commander of the 359th Brigade, urgently requesting Bethune to go to Xiashifan to treat his chief of staff, who was badly wounded. Bethune insisted on leaving at once, and as it was dark, Gu agreed to guide him and Dong over the mountain trail on the three-hour ride to the other village. Bethune ordered the rest of his team to follow the next morning.

In the infirmary in Xiashifan, Wang Zhen led Bethune directly to the *kang* where his chief of staff lay. Bethune bent over the twenty-six-year-old soldier and removed the mass of bandages around his bloodied right arm. When he saw what lay underneath, he exclaimed in dismay. Part of the arm was black with gangrene, the result of a tourniquet which, he was told, had been applied when the man had been wounded. Instead of loosening it periodically to allow the flow of blood to continue through the arm, the medical workers had left it tightly fixed throughout the three days that the soldier had been carried from the battle site to Xiashifan. After closer examination, Bethune told Wang Zhen that to prevent blood poisoning he had to amputate the man's right arm. Shortly after midnight he performed the amputation.[39]

Afterwards he vented his fury at the lack of training of the hospital staff, which, he insisted, had caused the unnecessary loss of the soldier's arm. Wang Zhen warned him that he might find similar cases in another group of wounded at the village of Zhuanlinkou, several hours' ride away. Bethune told him he would go there after he had had a few hours of sleep; both Dr Gu and Wang Zhen said they would accompany him. Reaching Zhuanlinkou at midday, he began to examine the twenty-seven patients in the hospital, and in the late afternoon he was joined by Dr Wang and Dr You, who had arrived with the rest of his team.

When they finished, Bethune turned his attention to the wounded who had begun arriving on stretchers. Removing the bandages from the first soldier, he questioned the head of the team of stretcher-bearers, and learned that no one had examined the soldiers' injuries during the three-day trip. As a result, the patient's wound had become infected. Moving to a second soldier, he found another festering injury, and it was the same with a third.

Struggling to contain his anger, Bethune beckoned to Wang Zhen. Pointing to an ugly suppurating wound, and speaking slowly to make certain that Dong did not miss a word, he explained that the hideous infection had been caused by leaving the wound unattended. Then, recognizing that almost all of the thirty-five wounded would be similarly afflicted, he set about the series of operations that would have to be performed.[40]

Even with the help of the two Chinese doctors, the task was daunting. Taking only brief periods of rest, the three worked through the night and into Wednesday morning. After operating on the last soldier, Bethune again made the point to Commander Wang Zhen that many of the operations they had just performed could have been prevented. What was needed was to have the dressings of the wounded changed en route to hospital. Furthermore, he added, the problem could almost be eliminated if a mobile operating team could be sent as close as possible to the field of battle. Wang Zhen was impressed by Bethune's suggestions. He agreed to set up rest stations between the battle area and the hospitals and promised to notify Bethune in advance of the next impending attack so that he could bring his team close to the action. Only then did Bethune agree to go to bed.[41]

On Saturday, 26 November, he led his team westward through a pass among high peaks to the remote village of Yangjiazhuang, the military headquarters and site of the base hospital of the Yanbei district. After examining sixty wounded on Sunday, he decided to begin to operate on forty of them the following day. But late that evening a courier arrived with a message from Wang Zhen informing Bethune that he was planning a large-scale attack against the Japanese on a heavily patrolled highway. He also said that he had chosen a site where Bethune could set up his mobile operating unit near enough to the action to be able to receive soldiers not long after they had been wounded.

The news galvanized Bethune. For the first time since he had come to China, he would be working close to a military action, saving lives that might otherwise be lost to infection. It was his chance to prove to the military command that by treating the wounded early he could significantly reduce the high mortality figures of the Eighth Route Army. He pranced about the room, crowing that at last he would see action. However, Dong brought out their map and showed him the location of the attack, scheduled for Tuesday morning. From Yangjiazhunag they would have to trek more than ninety kilometres over mountain trails, and the temperature had fallen to -25 degrees Celsius. Dong doubted they could make the journey in time, but Bethune told him to have the team ready to leave at 5 AM. The next morning it was still bitterly cold, the mountains sheathed in icy snow. They rode single file, the horses' hoof-beats on the rocky paths echoing back from the valleys below. The trail became increasingly slippery, and they had to dismount and lead the animals. But as darkness fell, they reached the village of Zaijiayou, less than thirty kilometres from their destination, and there they spent the night.[42]

The location chosen for Bethune's unit by Wang Zhen was the mountain hamlet of Heisi, twelve kilometres directly west of the highway where the attack on the Japanese convoy would take place and twenty-three kilometres from the most distant regiment that would be involved in the fighting.[43] The site was the ruins of a small Buddhist temple surrounded by cypress trees. When Bethune and his team arrived in Heisi at 3 PM, they found that soldiers sent to guard the unit had drawn sheets across the crumbling walls of the temple to act as a roof and had built a large fire to provide heat and boil water.

When the first wounded soldier arrived at 5:15 PM, Bethune was relieved to learn that the man had spent only seven hours in his stretcher since receiving his wound. Soon after Bethune began to operate, other stretcher-bearers reached the temple and continued to do so well into the night. When darkness fell, the three doctors had to perform in the dim light supplied by two hurricane lamps and Bethune's flashlight, held for him by an orderly. They continued operating through the night, with the assistant doctors taking only brief periods of rest. Bethune took none. From time to time, he would plunge his head into a bucket of cold water, keeping it there for as long as he could before removing it; then, pacing back and forth, he would rub his hair vigorously with a towel before returning to the operating table. At about 3 AM, he set up the apparatus for an arm-to-arm transfusion to allow Dr Wang to give blood to a wounded soldier.

For hours the only sounds were the clicking of scissors and Bethune's short commands. Then, shortly after daylight on Wednesday morning, Japanese planes attacked, and bombs began to explode near the temple. The sheet over the makeshift operating room flapped crazily, and an exterior wall collapsed, showering the operating area with fragments of stone and wood. Bethune kept working. Luckily, the attack was brief, and no one was injured.[44] But now exhaustion began to dog the members of the operating team. The first to succumb was Dong, who was suffering from a high fever caused by a severe case of tonsillitis. Bethune had trained him as an anaesthetist, and he insisted on continuing to administer anaesthetic until early afternoon when Bethune ordered him to lie down. The three doctors were in only slightly better condition.

Fortunately, at about 3 PM, unexpected help arrived. Two doctors from a medical team from Yan'an, who had arrived in Jin-Cha-Ji only days earlier, had been dispatched to the battle site. One of them was Dr Jiang Yizhen.

When he entered the temple, he found Bethune barely able to stand. He managed to persuade him and the other doctors to rest while he and his comrade took over at the operating tables.

Bethune slept for three hours until Wang Zhen arrived to report that the battle was nearly over. After presenting Bethune with several tins of food and packages of cigarettes found on dead Japanese troops, Wang told him that enemy reinforcements would soon be arriving, so Bethune should prepare his team to leave within the next few hours. Bethune pointed to the more than twenty wounded who still required attention and told Wang Zhen that until every soldier had been examined and treated, he would not go. After wolfing down the contents of one of the tins and smoking a cigarette, he took his place at the operating table beside Dr Jiang. Spelling each other off, the five doctors continued working until 10 AM on Thursday, when the last wounded man was placed on a stretcher to be carried to safety.[45] Bethune, his team, and the two relieving doctors had operated on seventy-one patients over a period of forty hours. By any standards their performance was extraordinary. However, as Bethune pointed out in his report to Nie a week later, the most important thing was that it proved that casualty losses could be reduced significantly by bringing doctors close to the battlefront.

After their operations the patients had been taken by stretcher teams over mountain trails on a trip of nearly three days to the Brigade Hospital in the village of Quhuisi, sixty kilometres to the south. Bethune followed them there, arriving on Friday, 2 December. He at once began examining the wounded he had treated and was delighted to discover that one out of three had survived the rough journey without developing infection, even though their dressings had not been changed along the way. He believed that if they had been changed, the number arriving without infection would have doubled.

These experiences confirmed his opinion that he could save many lives by setting up his team near a battle and arranging for the stretcher-borne wounded to be examined on their way to a base hospital. Such immediate post-operative care would increase the number of patients who would recover completely and be able to return to the ranks fit for combat. If a series of mobile operating units were made available to every commander in Jin-Cha-Ji, that number would be even greater. In his report Bethune wrote triumphantly, "We have demonstrated to our own satisfaction and I hope to the satisfaction of the Army commanders the value of this type of treatment of wounds. It is expected that it will revolutionize our present concepts of the duties of the Sanitary Service. The time is past and gone in which doctors will wait for patients to come to them. Doctors must go to the wounded and the earlier the better. Every Brigade should have at its disposal a Mobile Operating Unit such as ours. It is the connecting link between the Regimental Aid posts and the Base Hospital. In this interval between the Regiment and the Rear, in the past, the wounded have been neglected. This neglect must cease."[46] The operations at Heisi had been the first field test of a system that he had long been urging the leadership to adopt. Now he hoped to be allowed to develop the series of mobile operating units he had proposed. But to do that, he knew he would have to solve the basic problem of finding qualified personnel to serve in the units.[47]

He returned to Yangjiazhuang on 4 December and found that the conditions in the base hospital were still deplorable. Medical workers were incompetent and sometimes lazy; drugs were incorrectly used, sterilization techniques were faulty, and patients were improperly cared for. As a result of these and other problems, the mortality rate was very high. These were similar to his findings in Songyankou, and he came to the same conclusion he had reached there: the only way to eliminate the abuses was by introducing revolutionary changes in the running of hospitals and the training of personnel. His problem was how to institute such changes without a model hospital such as the one lost at Songyankou.

However, the leadership of the Eighth Route Army now offered a suggestion for the needed training facilities. The remoteness of Yangjiazhuang, a village of fewer than two hundred households, made it relatively safe from enemy attack, and this had been the reason for choosing it as the site of the base hospital. As in all Border Region hospitals, almost every peasant family in the village took in wounded Eighth Route Army soldiers or partisan fighters. This arrangement was inconvenient for the residents and the medical workers too. With the influx of the wounded from Heisi, increasing the number of patients in the base hospital to nearly three hundred, the military command decided to invite the residents to a public meeting to deal with what had become a critical situation.

The villagers offered to turn over a group of houses on the east side of the village for use as a hospital.[48] After the completion of structural alterations to the houses, all patients could be transferred there from the villagers' homes. To help carry these out, the villagers would take part in the work to re-plaster and whitewash the donated houses. In addition, they offered to broaden the narrow lanes leading to the new hospital and to loan to it various tables, chairs, and other pieces of furniture. In return they asked for free medical care and drugs, and for as long as it was available, free food for patients who were villagers. The leadership of the Medical Service accepted the proposal. A revamped hospital would allow medical staff to operate with much greater efficiency. For Bethune it provided the setting to begin the reforms that he knew were so desperately required.

Work began immediately on what Bethune named the Special Surgical Hospital. Identical in aim to its forerunner in Songyankou but far less complex and costly, it would serve his purpose, and in the event of a Japanese attack the loss of it would be far less severe than had been the case with the model hospital. Determined to eradicate the many flaws that he had found in Eighth Route Army hospitals, Bethune would later list these weaknesses precisely:

(A) The irresponsibility of certain doctors in the s.s.; their lack of a definite plan of organization and work; their laziness or more commonly, incompetence; their lack of ability to instruct & especially to supervise the work of their juniors such as nurses and orderlies.
(B) The poor standard of nursing among nurses.
(C) The waste of drugs.
(D) Poor sterilization of dressings.
(E) Carelessness and inconsideration towards patients.
(F) Too high a mortality rate among patients.
(G) Patients too long in hospital.
(H) Permanently crippled patients thro [sic] neglect of joints.
(I) Dissatisfaction of nurses – resulting in desertions.
(J) Low standard of education among orderlies and nurses and many others.[49]

The Medical Service officials admitted the validity of this criticism and asked him how to eliminate the problems. In response he set before them a plan modelled on Soviet procedures that incorporated "self-criticism, self-discipline and self-control."[50] He proposed the formation of a Central Committee comprising elected delegates of medical workers, patients, and civilians. This committee would establish a plan of organization for the hospital and standards of performance for all hospital workers. He saw it as a way to replace the system of hierarchical authority with one allowing for truly democratic participation.

Bethune's plan was adopted and went into operation before the end of December. The administrative head of the hospital was a doctor, and his deputy was the village leader. They in turn were responsible to the Hospital Affairs Committee, which included the secretary of the local Communist Party branch, a representative elected by the villagers, and one selected by the patients. Dr You Shenghua, who was deputy minister of health for Jin-Cha-Ji as well as Bethune's assistant, was chosen as general secretary. The role of the Hospital Affairs Committee was to appoint auxiliary hospital workers and to deal with problems raised by patients or villagers. Bethune saw it as a medical organization that was managed in a truly democratic way, and he attended every weekly meeting while he remained in Yangjiazhuang.[51] He would later refer to his plan as "the most important work I have done in the Jin-Cha-Ji military area."[52]

While work was progressing on the new hospital, Bethune and his team were using the existing operating facilities to deal with the 147 sick and wounded they had found in Yangjiazhuang on their return.[53] Meanwhile he sent orders to the various hospitals to send to Yangjiazhuang all wounded with fractures and those with chest, head, and abdominal wounds. Explaining his decision to Nie, he wrote, "Frankly, I cannot trust these types of cases in the hands of doctors and nurses in these Sanitary Services."[54]

Another fundamental problem that had plagued him since his arrival in the Border Region was the lack of blood. He had already learned in Yan'an that the giving of blood was foreign to the experience of most Chinese. By giving his own blood, he was able to overcome the fear of his assistants in Jin-Cha-Ji and encourage them to follow his example. However, some method had to be found to provide a regular and adequate supply of blood. At Yangjiazhuang his growing frustration over this intractable problem led to an emotional scene. Following an operation when he again gave his own blood and then completed the surgery with the help of an assistant, he exploded in anger. "I came to China to help the wounded," he shouted. "I need blood!"[55] Then he launched into a tirade, charging that lives were being lost because of the unwillingness of people to undergo the painless procedure of donating blood.

When at last he grew calmer, he agreed to discuss the question with his assistants and some officials of the Medical Service. Someone then suggested that the matter be placed before the recently formed Central Committee. This was done, and when they learned that both Bethune and the Chinese doctors had donated their blood to save their patients' lives, the village leader and the head of the Women's Rescue Team offered to give blood.[56] After allowing Bethune and You Shenghua to extract a small amount of blood from them before a meeting of the village residents, they then asked for others to do the same. Before the meeting ended, nearly forty persons had stepped forward to become the nucleus of the "Blood Transfusion Volunteers Brigade."[57] After a subsequent analysis of the blood type of each, it was recorded on a piece of cloth that was stitched to each volunteer's clothing.

The plan was that when a blood donation was needed, the volunteer would be called to the hospital, where a direct arm-to-arm transfusion would be performed. Each donor would receive a red cloth strip with the characters "Gave Blood with Glory," which would be sewn over the label indicating the blood type. In addition, every donor would be given five hundred grams of sugar, twenty eggs, and fifty grams of tea.[58] Pleased by the results, Bethune regarded the formation of "the living blood bank" as yet more evidence of a genuine democratic spirit that he believed was developing in the Border Region. It also moved him to apologize for his outburst, admitting that persuasion, not haranguing, had led to the happy result.[59]

Deeply involved as he was in the development of the Special Surgical Hospital during the month of December, Bethune nonetheless managed to complete a short story and a lengthy essay. These marked the culmination of a prolific period of writing, for during 1938 he had produced an amazing number of letters, articles, and reports, not to mention working on textbooks and an extremely detailed sixteen-page constitution for the new hospital at Yangjiazhuang.[60] The short story, entitled "The Dud," was based on a true incident of an illiterate old farmer who discovered in his field a dud shell abandoned by the partisans. The second piece, "Wounds," is a dramatic depiction of the conditions under which Bethune worked and the sufferings of the wounded:

> The kerosene lamp overhead makes a steady buzzing sound like an incandescent hive of bees. Mud walls. Mud floor. Mud bed. White paper windows. Smell of blood and chloroform. Cold. Three o'clock in the morning, Dec. 1, North China, near Ling Chu with the 8th Route Army.
> Men with wounds.
> Wounds like little dried pools, caked with black-brown earth; wounds with torn edges frilled with black gangrene; neat wounds, concealing beneath the abscess in their depths, burrowing into and around the great firm muscles like a dammed-back river, running around and between the muscles like a hot stream; wounds, expanding outward, decaying orchids or crushed carnations, terrible flowers of flesh; wounds from which the dark blood is spewed out in clots, mixed with the ominous gas bubbles, floating on the fresh flood of the still-continuing secondary hemorrhage.[61]

"Wounds" is also a passionate condemnation of wars of aggression and of the roles of capitalism and nationalism in provoking them. Bethune wrote,

Is it possible that a few rich men, a small class of men, have persuaded a million poor men to attack, and attempt to destroy, another million men as poor as they? So that the rich may be richer still? Terrible thought! How did they persuade these poor men to come to China? By telling them the truth? No, they would never have come if they had known the truth. Did they dare to tell these workmen that the rich only wanted cheaper raw materials, more markets and more profit? No, they told them that this brutal war was "The Destiny of the Race," it was for the "Glory of the Emperor," it was for the "Honour of the State," it was for their "King and Country." False. False as Hell![62]

"The Dud" and "Wounds" were both published in left-wing periodicals in North America, of which *The New Masses* was the most widely read.

By the end of December, patients had been moved into the Special Surgical Hospital, and on 4 January 1939 Bethune inaugurated in one of its rooms what he called the Special Surgical Practice School.[63] The class that appeared for "Demonstration Week" was made up of twenty-three doctors from the Yanbei area.[64] None had had formal medical training. Most were peasants in their twenties, some of them barely literate, so teaching them surgery was a truly daunting task. Bethune also wanted to make the doctors familiar with all aspects of hospital organization and with the duties of their co-workers. For this purpose he divided them into groups to carry out the tasks of nurses and orderlies as well as of doctors. Periodically during the course he alternated these to ensure that each doctor performed such lowly tasks as sweeping floors, emptying bedpans, washing patients, and cutting their nails.[65] Not until they became aware of the fundamental routine of every medical worker, Bethune believed, would the doctors be capable of managing a medical unit and training the personnel needed to make it run.

After performing demonstration operations and rehearsing the stages of each one, Bethune observed each doctor performing similar surgical procedures. In addition to the daily clinical sessions, he gave nightly lectures on various aspects of medicine, surgery, and problems associated with the role of mobile units. Already known as a strict disciplinarian, he was extremely demanding throughout the gruelling ten-day course and sharply critical of the errors he noted, often wounding his students' feelings.[66] In his farewell address at the end of the three weeks, he acknowledged his stinging remarks but reminded his audience that his only aim was to reduce carelessness. Then he called forward each member of the class, shook his hand, and presented the proud graduate with a certificate. In contrast to the ad hoc instruction he had given during the building of the model hospital at Songyankou, this was the first time he had held regularly scheduled classes in subjects based on a curriculum, however brief.[67]

For Bethune it was only the beginning, for he intended to hold similar training sessions in each of the other subdistricts. Meanwhile he had to continue his survey of other hospitals. In a letter written several weeks later, he referred to his attempts to train medical workers:

> We travel to one of these "hospitals," inspect the wounded, re-organize the staff (the hospital staff consists of "doctors" of 19 to 22, not one of whom has had a college education or been in a modern hospital or medical school; the nurses who are boys of 14 to 18, just peasants). Imagine the average standard! Imagine their knowledge of hygiene, anatomy, physiology, medicine and surgery! Yet this is the only material we possess and we must make the best of it. They are very eager to learn and to improve themselves and are constantly asking for criticisms of their work. So that although I am often irritable at their ineptitude and ignorance, their lack of order, their carelessness, yet their simplicity and eagerness to learn combined with their true spirit of comradeship and unselfishness, disarms me in the end.[68]

Following the "Demonstration Week," Bethune, Dong Yuequian, and You Shenghua inspected the base hospital in the village of Huata where they introduced Bethune's plan of organization. He later claimed that the hospital "was improved 200 %."[69] At a conference of leading cadres from all parts of Jin-Cha-Ji held three weeks later, You Shenghua reported on the success of Bethune's method in the two hospitals and urged its uniform adoption throughout the Border Region.[70] Meanwhile, in addition to his teaching and surgical duties, Bethune found time to return to writing the medical texts he had begun in Songyankou when he was interrupted at the end of September by the Japanese advance. Recognizing that even the simplest drawings would greatly enhance his manual, he was determined to produce a basic illustrated text for the next course he would offer.[71]

The two months he spent in Yangjiazhuang were relatively quiet, a welcome contrast to the previous weeks of trekking over mountain trails in winter conditions, snatching brief periods of sleep after hours of operating, and inspecting health facilities. The rough life had taken a toll on him, and he now allowed himself a limited amount of badly needed rest. But food was another major problem. The local diet consisted of cabbage, turnip, and other root vegetables stored in underground cellars, along with millet porridge and *mantou* (steamed bread). Pork and chicken were luxuries that only a fortunate few might be able to afford at the New Year or for a wedding feast. Bethune's military superiors tried to provide him with the best food that they could, but he repeatedly refused to accept anything higher in quality than what the common soldier ate.[72] The army commanders recognized the nobility of his motives but feared that he was undermining his health. They routinely sent him most of the tinned food captured from the Japanese, but even this he insisted on sharing with patients. On one of his many stops to perform operations and inspect military hospitals, a cook, concerned about his health, made him a pot of chicken soup – a rare luxury. Bethune accepted a bowl but at once took it to the wounded. Using one of his few Chinese phrases, he asked a soldier how he was, and the moment the man opened his mouth, he popped in a spoonful of soup. The wounded all shouted protests, insisting he eat the soup himself. When Bethune learned what they were saying, he was amused, and for the rest of his stay he made a daily performance of plying them with soup, which they laughingly rejected.

The military and medical authorities responsible for Bethune also worried about his refusal to take adequate rest. When word of this eventually reached General Nie, he spoke to Bethune about it, but Bethune rejected his advice. At this point Nie ordered him into his own room to sleep for six hours. Bethune lay down on the *kang* briefly, then jumped up. Glaring at Nie, he snatched a cigarette from the general's lips and threw it on the ground. "In respect to medical matters, I will not take orders even from you," he told the startled commander. Then he marched out.[73]

Part of Bethune's attitude was true selflessness born of his desire to serve and to be accepted by his comrades. But there was an element of self-will in it too. His experience in Spain had scarred him, not just because of the violence of the war that he had witnessed but also because his uncontrolled behaviour had cost him the respect of his communist comrades; they had removed him from his position at the Instituto and forced him to return to Canada. Now in China he was determined that no one would ever again be able to accuse him of squandering money that was not his or of indulging in bourgeois comforts. As a doctor he must have known that he could not survive long on the diet he was eating – that he would burn himself out. Indeed, he had long since commented that the local diet was seriously deficient in fat and fat-soluble vitamins and protein.[74] Yet his puritanical pride drove him to ignore this. He was running on a combination of adrenalin and nicotine. "I'll be alright as long as I have cigarettes," he wrote to Ma Haide.[75]

He began to lose a great deal of weight. More ominously, despite the basic hardiness of his constitution, the rugged life and inadequate diet were undermining his resistance to disease. It was only with the greatest difficulty that he was able to cure himself of a severe case of tonsillitis that plagued him throughout December. He also had another stubborn infection in one of his fingers.[76] In a letter to a Canadian friend in January 1939 he mentioned the privations he faced: "My life is pretty rough and sometimes tough as well. It reminds me of my early days up in the Northern bush. The village is like all other Chinese villages, made of mud and stone one-story houses, in groups (families) of compounds. Three or four houses are enclosed in a compound facing each other. In the compound are the pigs, dogs, donkeys, etc. Everything is filthy – the people, their houses, etc. I have one house to myself. It has a brick oven running along the single room. In this I have my cot and table. I have made myself a tin stove in which is burnt coal and wood. The windows (one) are papered with white paper. The floor is packed mud, so are the walls."[77] Tellingly, he concluded the letter, "Let me confess that on the 1st of the New Year I had an attack of homesickness. Memories of New York, Montreal and Toronto. If I were not so busy I could find reasons for a holiday."[78]

He needed one badly, for in addition to his physical problems, he was struggling against his growing loneliness. He was cut off from his Chinese colleagues by his inability to speak their language, and except for Richard Brown, he had been in contact with only two other westerners, Michael Lindsay and Lindsay's friend George Taylor, who had visited him at Songyankou the previous August. He had received no more than a handful of letters since arriving in China and had not seen an English-language newspaper in eight months. He had no radio.[79] Used to devouring several daily newspapers and many magazines, he had grown increasingly frustrated by his ignorance of world events. "I would like to know a few facts," he wrote to Ma Haide in Yan'an. "Is Roosevelt still president of the United States? Who is the prime minister of England? Is the communist party in power in France?"[80] He was desperate for books, for it had been his lifelong habit to read several a month. "I am sorry that the books that you sent me have not arrived," he lamented to a Canadian friend. "I am very short of books as I have read and re-read all I have a dozen times."[81] And he pleaded with Ma Haide, "Will you do this for me? Just one thing! Send me three books a month, some newspapers and magazines."[82] Likely Ma had no access to such things either, for there is no evidence that Bethune ever received them.

The isolation in which he found himself was almost unimaginable. Despite the fact that he sometimes described himself as solitary and self-sufficient, Bethune had always needed people around him, and he loved to talk. Now, in all the vast mountain region of northwestern China, there was only one person with whom he could hold a conversation – Dong Yueqian. His relationship with his interpreter was good, for Dong was highly intelligent and also adept at dealing with Bethune's volatile temperament. But although Dong's linguistic skills were excellent, his English was not colloquial and his cultural references were naturally not those of a westerner. Wistfully, Bethune told Dong that since arriving in Jin-Cha-Ji he felt as though he had become deaf and dumb.[83]

So night after night, plagued by insomnia, he spent hours working on his textbook or writing letters home that he feared might never be answered. When all else failed, he shuffled and dealt cards on a table in his room, playing endless games of solitaire by lantern light. Caught up in the sheer intensity of his crusade, the phoenix was burning brightly in the fires of China. But the physical and emotional supports of his being were feeding the flames.

Jean Ewen. After joining the China Aid Council medical unit, the young nurse came to respect Bethune's professional skill but resented his dictatorial ways. Laura Meyer/ Saskatoon Public Library PH-98-111; reproduced by permission

The China Aid Council medical unit (front row). Mutually antipathetic, Bethune, Ewen, and Parson went their separate ways during the voyage to China. Courtesy BMH

In Lenin mode. In China Bethune grew a Lenin-style goatee and enjoyed being told he resembled the leader of the Russian Revolution. Courtesy BMH

Meeting with Mao Zedong. At Yan'an, Bethune and Mao discussed
Bethune's role in the Eighth Route Army Medical Service.
Courtesy BMH

Cave hospital at Yan'an. The loess soil at Yan'an lent itself the
digging of caves which were used as residences and also to house
the local base hospital. Courtesy BMH

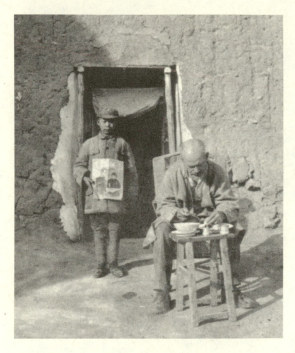

A properly boiled egg. On the first day that He Zexin, Bethune's *xiao guei*, managed to cook a soft-boiled egg to his liking, Bethune rewarded him with a book and had a photograph taken. Courtesy BMH

Bethune, He Long, and Dr Richard Brown. Bethune met General He Long on his way to Jin-Cha-Ji and later in Hebei. Bethune and Brown worked together from May to July 1938. Courtesy BMH

With Nie Rongzhen and Dong Yueqian. General Nie dealt skilfully with Bethune's unpredictable temper. Bethune described Dong Yueqian, his first interpreter, as "my other self." Authors' collection.

Valley in the Wutai Mountains. Despite frustrations and hardships, Bethune rejoiced in the spectacular natural beauty of Shanxi. Courtesy BMH/ Michael Lindsay

Reconstruction of the model hospital, Songyankou. Built at Bethune's insistence despite the warnings of General Nie Rongzhen, the model hospital was destroyed by the Japanese soon after it opened. It was reconstructed in the mid-1970s. Photo: Sharon Stewart

Opening of the model hospital. In his speech Bethune stressed that he and the Chinese had learned much from each other. Courtesy BMH

At the Great Wall.
Bethune's travels took
him to the Great Wall
in August 1938.
Courtesy BMH

Dressed for winter in the mountains. The Eighth Route Army supplied Bethune with winter gear taken from downed Japanese fliers. Courtesy BMH

The mobile surgical unit. On his tours of inspection Bethune sometimes rode on horseback but on narrow mountain trails often had to travel on foot. Courtesy BMH

A teachable moment. Lacking a proper teaching hospital, Bethune never missed an opportunity to demonstrate technique to Chinese medical personnel. Courtesy BMH

Kathleen Hall. The missionary from New Zealand smuggled desperately needed medical supplies through Japanese lines for Bethune.

Cooling off at Shenbei. This image, taken by the famous Chinese photographer Sha Fei, shows Bethune swimming in the Tang River in July 1939. Courtesy BMH/Wang Yan

Writing. Bethune produced an amazing number of letters and reports on his beloved Hermes portable typewriter. He also wrote short stories and essays.
Courtesy BMH

With a young patient.
Bethune spent much
time treating civilians,
especially children.
This photograph,
taken in August 1939,
shows how emaciated
he had become.
Courtesy BMH/
Michael Lindsay

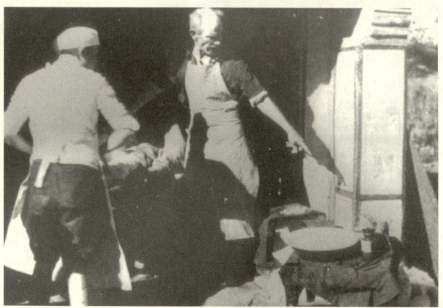

Surgery at Sunjiazhuang. This iconic photograph taken by Wu Yinxian shows
Bethune operating on 29 October 1939. Late that afternoon he sliced his finger
with a scalpel and within days was dead of septicaemia.
Courtesy BMH/Wu Zhuqing

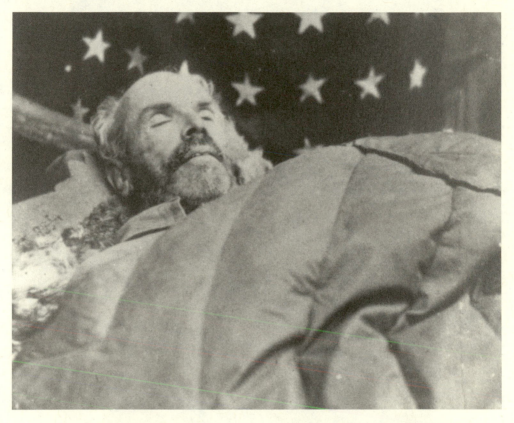

Bethune after death. The Chinese held a memorial ceremony to honour Bethune.
The flag behind him is Chinese. Courtesy BMH

The tomb at Nanguan. This memorial was rebuilt after being destroyed by the Japanese. Bethune was later reinterred in the Martyrs' Cemetery of the Military Region of North China in Shijiazhuang.
Photo: Sharon Stewart

Bethune propaganda graphic book. The smaller characters read: "A proletarian and internationalist fighter." The large ones say, "A Story of Bethune." Courtesy BMH

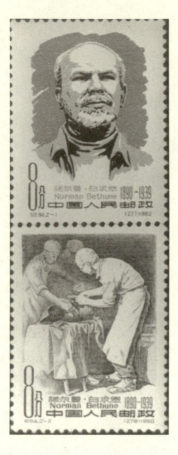

Commemorative stamps, 1960. These stamps reproduced famous photographs of Bethune. In 1990 the Canadian and Chinese governments would jointly issue stamps to mark the centenary of his birth. Courtesy BMH

The Norman Bethune International Peace Hospital. This 800-bed hospital is located in Shijiazhuang, where Bethune is buried in the Martyrs' Cemetery. Photo: Sharon Stewart

Bethune statue, Shijiazhuang. A replica of this statue, a gift of the People's Republic of China, stands in the Place Norman Bethune in Montreal. Photo: Sharon Stewart

Bethune scholars at Huangshikou, 2005. Zhang Yesheng, a Chinese expert on Bethune, with Roderick Stewart in front of the house in which Bethune died. Photo: Sharon Stewart

The Narrow Gate

Jin-Cha-Ji, December 1938–June 1939

One of the problems Bethune was mulling over during those white nights of the winter of 1938–39 was the desperate need of medical supplies in the Jin-Cha-Ji Border Region. He had complained about this constantly since his arrival in the area the previous June, and in a letter to Ma Haide in December 1938 he had again raised the issue: "What is the China Aid Council doing for China, for the 8th Route Army? How much money have they sent? Are they sending more doctors or technicians? Am I to have assistance? Am I to have the medical supplies I have been asking for 5 months? I have exactly 27 tubes of catgut left and ½ lb. of carbolic acid. I have one knife and 6 artery forceps – all the rest I have distributed. There remains 2 ½ lbs. of Chloroform. After that is finished we will operate without anaesthetics."[1]

His was quite literally a voice crying in the wilderness, and he would never learn why there was no reply. Since his arrival in China, he had sent the CAC a copy of each of his monthly reports and detailed copies of his expenditures with receipts, and had made several urgent direct appeals to them for help.[2] In contrast, the CAC sent him only three letters. The first was written in April 1938 and reached him in August in Songyankou. It informed him that they had agreed to his request to send his monthly salary of $100 to Frances Coleman in Montreal but did not mention funds or supplies for China. A second letter asked only for confirmation of Songyankou as his address for correspondence. The third and last was postmarked in New York on 20 September 1938. There is no record of its contents.[3]

Given Bethune's bitter complaints about the CAC, it seems he never learned that it was sending funds raised in New York to the Eighth Route Army via the National Red Cross Society of China and later via the China Defence League in Hong Kong. And although Robert Lim, the agent who disbursed the funds to the Eighth Route Army, had sent supplies directly to Bethune in

1938[4] and would send him more in the spring of 1939, there is no record in Bethune's letters or reports that he ever received them.

The China Defence League had also attempted to assist him. Song Qingling (Madame Sun Yat-sen), the widow of the founder of the Guomindang Party, was the head of the League, and under her leadership the CDL had become the major coordinator of funds and equipment from donors in many parts of the world; the money and supplies collected were then sent on to various locations in China.[5] Song, who was sympathetic to the communist cause, was well aware of Bethune's work for the Eighth Route Army in Jin-Cha-Ji. Between May and October 1938 the CDL received four consignments of drugs, dressings, and clothes sent by the Canadian League for Peace and Democracy, all specifically earmarked for Bethune's unit.[6] In addition, the CDL allocated HK$1,350 from its own treasury for the purchase of supplies to be shipped to him.[7] All these supplies were supposedly sent to Bethune via Yan'an.

And the CDL also received help for Bethune from another source. In July 1938 the International Peace Campaign informed Song Qingling of its wish to found an International Peace Hospital in China; she therefore decided to confer on Bethune's model hospital, then being built in Songyankou, the title of "International Peace Hospital of Wutaishan" and to name Bethune its director.[8] Because of this, an agency of the International Peace Campaign made a substantial financial contribution to the China Defence League, some of it intended for Bethune's work.[9] Yet despite these efforts on his behalf, there is no evidence Bethune received the supplies and money directed to him by Canadian donors and forwarded from Hong Kong by the CDL.[10] In Bethune's correspondence and reports he frequently referred to his desperate need of basic medical supplies and appealed for funds from abroad to meet those needs. At no time did he mention that he had received any response to his pleas.

So the question remains: Why did Bethune not receive the supplies that were supposedly sent to him? Yan'an, the Communist stronghold, was the first stop for all material destined for Jin-Cha-Ji. From there it was transported first by truck and then by mule along the same route taken by Bethune and Brown in May and June of 1938. Maintaining this land transportation and communication lifeline was given highest priority by the Eighth Route Army, and for this purpose General He Long's 120th Division was stationed for some time at Lanxian. When Bethune and Brown arrived there in early June 1938, He Long provided an armed escort to guide them the rest of the way to Wutai.[11] Some of the route lay close to territory held by the Guomindang, and it is possible that government forces might have contravened the United Front Agreement and attacked an Eighth Route Army caravan carrying medical supplies and in this way prevented them from getting through to Bethune. However, had such an attack occurred, General Nie Rongzhen would have been informed by wire or radio, and one would think that he would in turn have notified Bethune about the loss of the supplies. Such speculation would apply only to shipments sent to Bethune in 1938 and the early part of 1939; by mid-1939, despite the terms of the United Front agreement, the Guomindang definitely acted to keep aid from reaching Yan'an, and one of its generals, Hu Zongnan, commander of the 34th Guomindang Army, blockaded the city.[12]

The apportioning of foreign-funded supplies to its forces was decided by the Communist leadership in Yan'an in consultation with the China Defence League before the supplies were sent from Hong Kong. The leadership in Yan'an may have decided to divert some of the supplies funded by foreign donors to the New Fourth Army, at that time operating south of the Yangzi River; it was certainly easier to send supplies there from Hong Kong.[13] Between May and October 1938 the amount of money apportioned to the New Fourth Army by the China Defence League was almost ten times as much as that earmarked for Bethune's unit.[14] Another possibility is that, given the enormous need in the base hospitals located at Yan'an and nearby Yanchuan, supplies that did reach Yan'an may have been assigned there instead of being sent on to Jin-Cha-Ji. However, if a decision was made to divert supplies originally earmarked for Bethune to the base hospitals in Yan'an or to other uses, the Communist authorities did not inform him. Because of this, Bethune became increasingly embittered by what he believed to be the lack of aid from abroad. He had asked Eighth Route Army authorities in Yan'an to notify him as soon as they received foreign money donations for his use, but no such message reached him.

He continued to fret about where he could obtain medical supplies. The remoteness of the Jin-Cha-Ji Border Region contributed greatly to the problem. Supplies could be bought in Xi'an and sent via Yan'an, but it took a mule train as long as six weeks to reach Jin-Cha-Ji from there. Supplies could also be obtained from Beijing, on the northern fringe of the Border Region. Even closer was the city of Baoding, on the Beijing-Hankou rail line several hours south of Beijing. However, both these cities were occupied by the Japanese. Since Michael Lindsay's visit in early August, Bethune had been considering the possibility of using Lindsay's contacts in Beijing. Lindsay had told him that sympathizers in the city had already smuggled supplies out of Beijing and delivered them to partisans. Bethune therefore assumed that the same method could be used to get medical supplies for his use. The question was how to have the supplies transported into the Border Region.[15]

Shortly after his letter to Ma Haide lamenting that he would soon have to operate without anaesthetic, Bethune discovered that there might another way to obtain what he needed from Beijing. Near the end of December 1938, as work was progressing on the Special Surgical Hospital in Yangjiazhuang, he took his unit southeast on an inspection tour into Quyang County in West Hebei. En route he learned from Dong Yueqian that a missionary nurse from New Zealand named Kathleen Hall managed a small "cottage hospital" in the village of Songjiazhuang, not far from the hospital that they were going to inspect. Longing to converse with someone in colloquial English and hoping to hear news of the outside world, Bethune was keen to meet Hall, even though she was a missionary. In general, he disliked missionaries, seeing them as lackeys of the imperialist powers that had invaded China during the nineteenth century and continued to retain control of some areas of the country. He also knew that many missionaries supported the Guomindang, mainly because both Jiang Jieshi and his wife were Christians. Not all took that position, however, for some, like Richard Brown, believed that sincere Christians should ignore the professed atheism of the communists and aid the Eighth Route Army and the partisans in their unequal struggle against the invading Japanese. Dong told him that Hall had been giving medical care to poor people in the region and that Nie Rongzhen spoke highly of her work and was friendly with her.[16]

When Bethune and his team reached the village of Niuzhuang, he learned from local Eighth Route Army officials that Hall made regular trips by train to Beijing to buy supplies for her own hospital and for St Barnabas, the main Anglican hospital in Jin-Cha-Ji, in the city of Anguo thirty kilometres to the southeast. As a foreigner with a British passport she was permitted to do so by the Japanese who controlled the railway. This information made Bethune even more determined to meet her, for he had begun to hope she might be the key to solving his supply problem.

Near the end of December, with an Eighth Route Army soldier guiding him, Bethune walked the short distance to Niuyangou, where Hall ran a small mission, and climbed the hill to the grey-brick Anglican chapel, which was located inside a compound surrounded by a three-metre-high wall.[17] Summoned by a gatekeeper, Hall came out to greet him. In her early forties, she was tall and poised in bearing, with a frank, open expression. She wore a long-sleeved padded gown of plain black silk with a gold cross around her neck.[18] Hall had heard about Bethune and his work several months earlier, and she too was eager to meet someone whose native tongue was English.

Welcoming him warmly, she led him to her three-room apartment at the rear of the church. There they talked for hours, finding that, despite their diametrically different views on organized religion, they shared a deep commitment to helping those in need. When Bethune left, he invited her to visit him in Niuzhuang.

She came the following day, which she spent examining the Eighth Route Army hospital and discussing with him the work of his medical unit.[19] Soon after she left, Bethune reached a decision. The next Sunday morning he returned to Niuyangou and waited at the gate of the compound until Hall emerged with worshippers after conducting morning service. She invited him to join her for a breakfast of small cakes and coffee with goat milk. Then she offered him a glass of red wine.[20] After they raised their glasses, Bethune went directly to the purpose of his visit. In their two previous meetings he had described the scope of his work and told her of his desperate need for medicines. Now he asked her to bring back medical supplies for him from Beijing on some of her trips. Hall hesitated, saying that as a Christian she was a pacifist. To do as he asked would be to take sides and thus participate in the war between China and Japan. Bethune argued passionately that assisting the victims of cruel aggression was not un-Christian, but to no avail. At last, believing that he could still win her over, Bethune for once exercised tact, conceding that for the moment they must agree to disagree. But he suggested that they meet again.

His words had been more convincing than he knew, for the next morning Hall walked back to the hospital in Niuzhuang and told him, "I have decided to help you."[21] They met again to discuss his list of required medicines, and he then raised another matter with her. Dong Yueqian, his interpreter, had been separated from his family for more than a year;[22] Dong's wife, Wang Lanzhen, and their two daughters were in Beijing, where he had left them when he had taken up his position as chief administrator of Fuping County. Bethune asked Hall if she would be willing to bring Dong's family back from Beijing. She could claim that Wang Lanzhen was a nurse who was returning to work in her hospital. Hall agreed at once and suggested that Dong write a note introducing her to his wife and asking her to follow Hall's instructions. She said she would conceal the note from Japanese inspection guards by hiding it at the bottom of a jar of face cream.

Bethune knew how risky it was for Hall to involve herself in Eighth Route Army affairs. Should the Japanese discover what she was doing, her British passport might not protect her from their wrath. This concern may have sparked the next scheme he came up with. When Hall told him in the last week of January that she would soon be going to Beijing, Bethune said he now planned to go with her and buy the medical supplies himself. He explained that Michael Lindsay, who was at Yenching University, had many contacts and could make arrangements to have the supplies filtered through the Japanese blockade. Startled by this idea, Hall asked how he thought he could get through Japanese security en route to Beijing. Bethune replied that he would disguise himself as an Anglican priest. Among the few pieces of Western clothing that he had not given away to Chinese patients was a dark suit. Wearing that, with a cross around his neck and carrying a Bible, he was sure that he could pass surveillance at Japanese checkpoints.[23] Hall doubted that the plan was safe, but he convinced her to go along with it.

Bethune knew he would need the permission of the Eighth Route Army leadership for this adventure and optimistically assumed he could get it. However, when he outlined his idea to Dong Yuequian, his interpreter was aghast. He immediately informed Dr You Shenghua, who was not only the deputy minister of health for the Jin-Cha-Ji Border Region and Bethune's assistant but also the political commissar of the mobile operating unit and therefore directly responsible for Bethune's safety. Horrified by Bethune's scheme, You conferred with the military commander of the subdistrict and then sent a wire to Nie Rongzhen informing him of what Bethune was planning. Within hours Nie sent a wire to Bethune ordering him to return immediately to Eighth Route Army headquarters at Jiaotanzhuang. Bethune probably guessed the unspoken reason. When he told Kathleen Hall of the change in plans, she promised to buy the medical supplies he needed and also try to bring back Wang Lanzhen and her two children from Beijing.

After a three-day journey Bethune and Dong Yueqian reached Jiaotanzhuang on 30 January. The general was waiting for them. More than anyone else associated with Bethune, Nie was the most able to deal with his often unpredictable behaviour and particularly his outbursts of rage. Knowing that Bethune would argue if he forbade him to go to Beijing, Nie likely did not mention the matter directly. Instead, he explained that a Border Region Communist Party assembly was about to be convened in the nearby village of Cangyingou. It was important, he said, that Bethune attend this assembly, where he would be brought up to date on vital strategy in the struggle with the Japanese. After the assembly, Nie added, he would give his permission for Bethune to take his mobile unit on an inspection tour of the hospitals in Central Hebei, a journey he had been asking to make for some time. Nie had withheld authorization until this point because the area, located on the east side of the Beijing-Hankou Railroad, was under Japanese control. Bethune's unit would have to cross the heavily patrolled railway and move into a region where the Japanese occupied all cities and large towns. However, Nie knew the Medical Expedition to the East, as the inspection tour was later called, was necessary and likely regarded it as less dangerous than Bethune's scheme of going to Beijing in disguise. Meanwhile he praised Bethune for persuading Hall to bring medical supplies from Beijing and provided him with money to give to her to pay for them.[24]

Although disappointed that Nie had scotched his plan for a Beijing adventure, Bethune was enthusiastic about the inspection tour. There were many hospitals in Central Hebei, and he was eager to inspect them in order to complete his planned restructuring of the entire Eighth Route Army Medical Service. Although moving about in Japanese-controlled Hebei was not as romantic as risking his neck in Beijing, it would likely provide more than enough excitement. But first there was the Party Congress. As medical adviser to the Border Region and the only foreigner in the Eighth Route Army, Bethune held a place of high honour, and on 3 February he was invited to speak to the assembly. He ended his address, "I must repeat: your war is just, and you are not alone. Our Canada-U.S. medical team is proof that the people of the world support you. Opposition to fascism and imperialism is our common burden. I came to China not just for your sake, but for ours as well; we will fight shoulder-to-shoulder with our Chinese comrades until the War of Resistance is victorious. The Japanese fascists will not be driven from China in a day, and we will not leave in a day; for today we can help you, but after your victory you will be able to help us in just the same way."[25]

Dong's interpretation of these words was greeted with ringing applause. Afterward Bethune asked the conference officials to send a cable to the Communist Party of Canada informing them that its representative had participated in a party congress at which decisions were made that would lead to the eventual defeat of the imperialist invaders.[26] It was a fiercely proud declaration. He believed that he was serving on one front of a world-wide anti-fascist and anti-imperialist conflict that would be won by forces of good against those of evil, and he wanted those back home who had doubted him to know it. The Chinese saw him as the representative of international communism, and he too saw himself in that light. He believed he was the forerunner of many who would come to the aid of China and other victims of imperialism. For one who had been forced out of Spain on CPC orders because of misbehaviour and who had been kept on a short lead thereafter, this was heady stuff. Like his parents, he had discovered his true identity as an evangelist in a cause that he believed would convert the world in his lifetime.

After the conference, Bethune and Dong stopped briefly in the village of Changyu to collect supplies and then moved on to the village of Huata, the staging point for the inspection tour, where they celebrated the Chinese New

Year. On 19 February Bethune led his seventeen-member medical team out of Huata in a blinding snowstorm.[27] The next day they arrived at Song-jiazhuang, where they went to the Anglican mission church to meet Kathleen Hall, who had just returned from Beijing with the medical supplies. To Dong's extreme delight, she had also brought his wife and daughters.[28] However, the reunion was brief, for the following day the unit left Songjiazhuang en route to Central Hebei. Before leaving, Bethune paid Hall with the money given to him by Nie Rongzhen for the medical supplies and her expenses on the Beijing trip.[29] Perhaps not as essential as the supplies, but highly gratifying to Bethune all the same, were the English cigarettes she had smuggled past the Japanese guards for him, sewn inside bed quilts.

Over the next few days Bethune and his team trekked down from the mountains onto the broad plains of Central Hebei. There they followed the Tang River, heading toward the Beijing-Hankou Railroad. Bethune later wrote about his delight in reaching Hebei:

> After a year in the mountains, it was a great pleasure to be on flat ground again. The mountains are very fine but the traveling is arduous – constantly on rough donkey paths along the beds of the swift mountain rivers, then up and over a mountain pass of several thousand feet into another valley and so on. We walk most of the way, although we have horses. Walking is faster. It is very hard on our feet as we wear nothing but cotton slippers. They only last a few days – often less than a week. We average 75 *li* (25 miles) a day. I have been given a fine brown captured Japanese mare, in addition to much other Japanese captured stuff – overcoat, cap, etc. After a week of travel we are dirty, lousy and flea-bitten. We sleep in the villagers' houses on their *kangs*.[30]

Once they had emerged from the relative safety of the high ground, they picked up a military escort of nearly one hundred soldiers, and to avoid detection travelled only at night. On their approach to a village, the order was passed down the line to put out cigarettes, stop talking, and walk in single file as they passed through the narrow main street. To prevent dogs from giving away their presence by barking, peasants had been ordered in advance to remove them to the outskirts of each village along the route.[31]

Nearing the Beijing-Hankou Railroad they were met in the early evening by a partisan leader who led them to a grove of poplars within sight of the tracks. There he ordered them to crouch in silence. Several minutes later they heard the rumbling of an armoured Japanese train approaching from the north. Closer and closer it came, its powerful searchlight swinging from side to side, bathing the limbs of the trees above them in brightness as it thundered by. When the sound of its passing died away, their guide told them to get to their feet. In the moonlight they could see a large dark shape near the tracks less than three kilometres away, and the guide explained that it was the blockhouse of the Japanese garrison. He ordered them to move quickly over the open ground between the trees and the tracks. On the other side they dashed across another open space before reaching cover.

Once through Japanese lines, they were able to travel during the day, although they had to exchange their uniforms for civilian garb. The Japanese controlled only urban areas but because of spies it was unwise for the communist force to draw attention to themselves, even in the countryside. For the next several days they headed southeast toward the Hutuo River where they inspected a rear hospital at the village of Dayi. In a long letter to Tim Buck and other Canadian comrades written from there on 4 March, Bethune described the nature of the guerrilla war against the Japanese, the progress of the Communist Party's work among the people, and his struggles to train medical staff. He concluded by outlining the events of the day:

> Today is my 49th birthday. I have the proud distinction of being the oldest soldier at the front. I spent the day in bed. I went to bed at 6:00 A.M., having operated all night from 7:00 P.M. the day before. We did 19 operations last night on 40 seriously wounded who had arrived from a battle near Hejian. After dressing all the wounded we started to operate on those needing operation. Three fractures of the skull were trephined, 2 amputations of the thigh, 2 suture of perforations of the small intestine, half a dozen bad fractures of arms and legs, and the rest smaller operations. We defeated the enemy. He left 50 dead – a most unusual thing for him to do. We captured 40 rifles. We lost 40 men – a rifle for a life. That is the way we get our guns.[32]

They remained several days in Dayi, treating the wounded and giving instructions on improving the hospital's operation. Then they received an order to move quickly eastward to where a battle was going on with a Japanese force near the village of Lühan. The conflict lasted for five days. Because Bethune and his unit were able to set up an operating theatre less than five kilometres from the centre of the fighting, stretcher-bearers could bring them the wounded in a relatively short period of time. After the enemy withdrew on 19 March, the unit remained in Lühan for nearly a week to provide postoperative treatment to the large number of wounded.

At this time a new interpreter joined the mobile unit. He was Lang Lin, a twenty-six-year-old former clerk in the administration of the Peking Union Medical College in Beijing, who spoke and wrote English. The authorities in Jin-Cha-Ji had long wanted Dong Yueqian to return to his administrative duties in Fuping, so once Nie became convinced that Dong had made some progress in helping Bethune adjust to Chinese conditions and customs, he agreed to replace Dong with another interpreter. Nie told Dong he had a month to break in the new man. Luckily, Bethune took to Lang Lin. Saying he reminded him of a friend in Montreal, he nicknamed him "Bill" and gave him the title of "manager" of the unit.[33]

Lang Lin arrived during a lull in military action that lasted for nearly three weeks. The pause allowed Bethune and the unit to continue the inspection tour of hospitals, and also gave him time to deal with a problem that had cropped up. In a recent engagement with the enemy, the unit had received a belated warning of an approaching Japanese patrol and had had to move quickly to escape capture. They did not have time to secure their equipment properly, and bottles of precious medicines in their cloth saddle-bags had been shattered. Thinking about this problem, Bethune came up with a design for a portable dispensary based on the large wicker baskets that peasants fastened on the backs of mules to carry vegetables and fruit. He purchased a small amount of lumber and nails, and using tools borrowed from a local carpenter spent several days crafting a sturdy container for carrying medical supplies and equipment on mule back. It was a wooden framework roughly shaped like an inverted letter "U" and held together by a horizontal cross-piece; each side of the apparatus contained three drawers divided into compartments large enough to hold medicines, instruments, and material sufficient for one hundred operations and five hundred dressings. He called his portable dispensary the "Marco Polo Bridge" after the site of the opening incident of the Sino-Japanese War on 7 July 1937.[34]

In mid-April the unit was summoned to the village of Datuanding, thirty-five kilometres north of Lühan, on the eve of what turned into a one-day skirmish in which a Japanese force was driven off. This was the first of three encounters that took place over the following four weeks as the Japanese launched a renewed offensive aimed at destroying all partisan and Eighth Route Army elements in Central Hebei. In all of these battles Bethune's unit was never more than five kilometres from the centre of the conflict, and in two of them it came under direct enemy fire.

The focal point of the second battle was Qihui, a large village of more than five hundred households. On Sunday, 23 April, a Japanese force of eight hundred including a light artillery unit had trapped a battalion of five hundred soldiers of the 120th Division of the Eighth Route Army in the village.[35] Following an intense bombardment, Japanese troops equipped with flame-throwers set fire to buildings along three sides of the village, trying to drive the communist forces out. When the Chinese put up an unexpectedly stiff resistance, the Japanese retaliated by spraying poison gas into the openings of tunnels where many of the residents of Qihui had sought refuge.[36] During the next two days, both sides received reinforcements and the battle was fierce, marked by hand-to-hand combat.

The Japanese surprise attack on Qihui had found Bethune and his unit a considerable distance away. When they arrived late at night on Tuesday, 25 April, they set up an operating theatre in a small temple with an adjoining school in the village of Wenjiatun, only four kilometres from Qihui.[37] They began to work just past midnight, and thereafter a continuous flow of wounded on stretchers reached them. Following Bethune's standard rule, medical assistants gave precedence to those with head or abdominal wounds, placing them in a long queue stretching along a path that led to the temple. Inside the building a surgical area had been created by covering the walls with white cotton cloth and improvising rough operating tables, and there Bethune and the two surgeons of his team worked on the wounded. The single oil lamp hanging from the ceiling cast only a dim light, so each of them also had an attendant who focused the beam of a flashlight on the part of the patient's anatomy being operated on.

The trio continued to work throughout the day and into the following night, resting only briefly after each operation. Bethune ordered his two companions to nap in a corner of the room, but he brushed aside their repeated attempts persuade him to do the same. Instead he revived himself, as he had done at Heisi the previous November, by ducking his head into a bucket of cold water. Just before dawn on Thursday morning he began to feel dizzy and finally agreed to lie down. He fell asleep instantly, but in less than two hours he got up and called a nurse to bring him the bucket of water. A few minutes later he was back at the operating table.

In mid-afternoon a Japanese artillery unit began to fire on the village. The walls of the improvised operating room shuddered, and falling tiles shattered on the floor; moments later one wall collapsed with a resounding crash and the ground trembled. Fortunately the bombardment ended without any further damage, and the three doctors resumed their work, which continued until the evening of Friday, 28 April. By taking turns during which each slept for little more than two hours at a time in a corner of the room, they operated on 115 soldiers during a period of sixty-nine consecutive hours. It was an epic performance that surpassed even that of Heisi, and its results again provided proof that Bethune's policy of having doctors go to the wounded near the battlefront could save many lives. The battle was also a great triumph for the Eighth Route Army, which had sent reinforcements to the beleaguered battalion at Qihui. By Thursday the first attacking Japanese force had managed to break out of the trap set for them by the Chinese, but they continued to retreat. The loss of more than 30 per cent of the Japanese contingent was the greatest to date in their conflict with the Eighth Route Army in Jin-Cha-Ji.[38]

After the retreat of the Japanese forces, Bethune accompanied General He Long on a tour of the most hotly contested parts of the battle area.[39] As they picked their way through the ruins of the village of Qihui, smoke was still rising from the crumbled ruins of the shattered houses. Chinese soldiers were picking up Japanese bodies and parts of bodies, but before throwing them on carts to be taken away to be burned, they were stripping the remains of much-needed boots, coats, and all forms of clothing that could be reused. Bethune bent over the body of a lieutenant and with a knife cut off the collar and shoulder insignia of his jacket.[40] At the temporary headquarters of the 120th Division, He Long showed him various spoils left behind by the enemy in its hasty retreat. Among these were several packages of Japanese cigarettes, which he gave to Bethune. Then the two sat down to enjoy cans of Japanese tinned beef and beer. However, the celebration of their victory was brief, for He Long knew that the withdrawal of the Japanese was only a tactical move and that he would have to pull Chinese forces out of the area before the enemy returned with reinforcements.

Their most difficult problem was moving the 280 Chinese wounded.[41] Many were able to walk, but most of the 115 who had been operated on had to be carried by stretcher-bearers. For those who could not survive a long trip, arrangements were being made for them to be hidden in the nearby village of Sigongcun and cared for until they were strong enough to rejoin their unit. On Sunday, 30 April, Bethune and his unit arrived at Sigongcun and found that patients they had operated on during the first two days of the battle of Qihui had already been taken there. They began to change dressings and turn the wounded over to stretcher-bearers who carried them away to peasant homes.

Just after midnight Dong Yueqian woke Bethune with news that a Japanese force of about four hundred had camped seven kilometres to the east and would likely march to Sigongcun at dawn. Bethune and his unit worked non-stop through the night preparing the remaining wounded for transfer. Most were taken to peasants in the village to be concealed in piles of straw until the Japanese had searched the village and moved on. At a few minutes past 5 AM, word came that the Japanese infantry were on the march; even more alarming was the news that a mounted patrol had set out ahead of the main force and would reach the village in less than half an hour. Working at a furious pace, Bethune and his team moved out the last wounded and packed their gear. Then another messenger rushed in to announce that the Japanese cavalry unit was minutes away. Strapping the Marco Polo Bridge to a mule, Bethune seized the beast's tether and mounted his horse. He and the others rode pell-mell out of the western end of the village, but glancing back from the top of a nearby hill, they saw Japanese cavalry galloping after them. They spurred their horses on, but the weight of the supplies slowed the pace of the mules. With the enemy hot on their heels, they dashed out of the hills onto a narrow plain, expecting to be captured at any moment. To their incredulous joy, they saw an Eighth Route Army cavalry unit approaching from the west. The Chinese cavalry swept past them to attack the Japanese while Bethune and his team rode to safety. It was his narrowest escape.

Enraged by their humiliating defeat by the Eighth Route Army at Qihui, the Japanese were now determined to corner and destroy all Chinese forces in the Central Hebei area. Facing overwhelming odds, General He Long prudently decided to withdraw. For the Eighth Route Army Medical Service this meant evacuating all medical personnel from the region and dealing with the logistics of moving all of the wounded soldiers from the various hospitals, many by stretcher, for distances greater than a hundred kilometres. Dressed as civilians, the wounded would have to be slipped through the Japanese blockade to hastily improvised havens in West Hebei.

As the Eighth Route Army units fell back, Dong Yueqian was ordered to return to his duties in Fuping. Bethune must have found it very hard to part with Dong, whom he had called "my other self," saying that without his "patience, good humour and intelligence, I would be lost."[42] They had seen much action together, and Dong, more than anyone, had helped him come to terms with the conditions he had to deal with. But Bethune bade him farewell and moved westward with his team. It was not long before he saw more action, for on 18 May the commander of the army unit that they were accompanying decided to make a stand against pursuing Japanese forces near the town of Songjiazhuang in Hejian County.[43] Bethune had little time to prepare. As had happened so often before, a member of his team selected the ruins of a nearby Buddhist temple as an operating theatre. A short but sharp military encounter followed, but although Bethune's unit came under Japanese artillery fire, no one was injured. The stiff Chinese resistance forced the Japanese to break off the attack, and the Eighth Route Army unit and Bethune's team resumed their retreat before daybreak the following day.

Bethune and his unit now travelled to various hospitals in Hebei, aiding in the mass evacuation of the wounded until the middle of June. Then, in an effort to drive the Eighth Route Army out of Central Hebei before the coming summer rains, the Japanese made a final offensive thrust. On 21 June, in response to an urgent request from a company commander, Bethune led his team to the village of Lianzikou where the Japanese had launched their fiercest attack since the battle of Qihui. During the three-day engagement Bethune and his two assistants performed nearly sixty operations.

Several days later General He Long, foreseeing a renewed Japanese push westward, sent a military escort to guide Bethune and his comrades back to the relative safety of West Hebei. Travelling mostly at night and wearing civilian clothes, the unit recrossed the heavily guarded Beijing-Hankou Railway at Fanshunqiao. They reached Jin-Cha-Ji headquarters at Shenbei on 28 June 1939 and were welcomed by Nie Rongzhen.[44] The Medical Expedition to the East had been a success: Bethune had been able to inspect all of the hospitals in the region, and the unit had had great success in dealing with the wounded after Qihui and other battles. The evacuation of the wounded from Central Hebei, which continued well into June, had also gone amazingly well. Despite the hardships of the journey, not a single soldier of the more than one thousand wounded, some of whom were carried on stretchers for more than a week, had died.[45]

Well before Bethune's journey into Central Hebei, stories about his selflessness and dedication to the wounded of the Eighth Route Army had been spreading among the soldiers of the Jin-Cha-Ji Border Region. They told how he went as close as he could get to the battles to operate instead of staying safely behind the lines, and how he had shared his food and even his clothing with his patients. But after his epic performance operating on the wounded after the battle of Qihui, his exploits became legendary. The Chinese repeated the story of how after the battle he had devoted himself to a soldier with a bad intestinal wound, having him carried everywhere he went and tending to him personally until the man was safely convalescent. And they told how he tenderly addressed the wounded as "my son." They called him Bai Qiuen, a phonetic rendering of his name.[46] Soldiers began to build morale before battles by chanting the slogan, "Attack! If we are wounded, we have Bai Qiuen to treat us!"[47]

Before coming to China, Bethune had feared that he would never achieve more than second best, never reach the goals he had set for himself. Now he was at last receiving the respect, reverence, and unquestioning support that he so deeply craved. From the beginning his physical hardiness, energy, and quick analytical mind had uniquely fitted him for his role in China; even his style of operating, quick, rough, and bold, was suited to battlefield surgery. Now physical and cultural isolation had become his monastery walls, his fortress against himself, shielding him from the temptations of sex and alcohol that had previously undermined his high idealism. Under the conditions of guerrilla warfare, the very flaws that had held him back for a lifetime – his chronic restlessness, his short attention span, his authoritarian nature – became virtues. His fiery temper remained, but the Chinese adapted to it, choosing to see it as an expression of his revolutionary zeal. In the mountain fastnesses of Shanxi and the plains of Hebei, Bethune had entered into his kingdom.

The Celestial City

Jin-Cha-Ji, July–November 1939

Now the rains came, pounding the land into a quagmire and swelling the rivers into raging torrents. Beginning in early July and continuing almost without ceasing into August, the monsoon of 1939 caused the greatest floods known in Hebei Province since the nineteenth century.[1] Whole villages were swept away with great loss of life and property and widespread destruction of crops. And with the drenching rain came intense heat and stifling humidity. The only positive effect was that the weather hampered the movement of Japanese troops, forcing them to discontinue their offensive into West Hebei and to withdraw most of their forces eastward to the safety of the blockaded area along the Beijing-Hankou Railroad.[2]

Photographs of Bethune taken at this time show him working at his typewriter clad only in shorts, or stripped to swim in the river. His feet, which had frequently been immersed in water during the expedition to Central Hebei, had become infected, and the pervading dampness now hindered their healing. However, despite the discomforts of the monsoon season, he took advantage of the lull in military action to turn his attention to organization, planning, and teaching. Soon after his return from Central Hebei he had discovered to his anger and disappointment that his democratic Hospital Central Committee Plan, which he had so proudly seen go into effect at the Special Surgical Hospital at Yangjiazhuang the previous winter and on the constitution of which he had lavished so much of his time, had been allowed to lapse. He had expected to see it put into effect throughout Jin-Cha-Ji, but instead the authorities had decided to move the base hospital from Yangjiazhuang and had dispersed the staff among various other subdistricts; the result was that his idealistic paradigm of hospital committees with representatives democratically elected by staff, patients, and villagers had been completely abandoned. Learning of this, he at once wrote a letter addressed to Ye Qingshan, the minister of health for Jin-Cha-Ji, and You Shenghua, the deputy minister, demanding an explanation. The reasons they offered in their response only increased his indignation. It was the first time since he had come to Jin-Cha-Ji that one of his suggestions had been overruled, and he reacted, as he always had throughout his life when opposed by superior authority, with outrage.

On 12 July he sat down and wrote a truly scorching letter of eight closely typed pages. Although admitting that he was only an advisor whose suggestions might be either accepted or rejected, he proceeded to castigate the two officials who were his nominal superiors for allowing a project he had personally approved to lapse. He told them that as a member of the "International Communist Party" he had been trained to think in general terms, implying that they had not, and criticized both their understanding of a Stalinist slogan they quoted and their failure to think as true revolutionaries. With heavy sarcasm he refuted their arguments against his idea and in a final stinging rebuke warned them of the dangers of bureaucracy.[3] Lang Lin, who had to translate this bombshell of a letter into Chinese, must have struggled to reduce its angry rhetoric into something that he could send to their superiors.[4]

Bethune next turned his mind to the problem of training medical staff. After one year in Jin-Cha-Ji he had inspected every hospital in eight of its ten subdistricts, and throughout the region he had found the same low level of medical and surgical treatment. He had long known that the fundamental problem was the lack of trained medical personnel; he had commented on this as early as the spring of 1938 and had mentioned it again in a report written the following July.[5] "Think of it!" he had written then, "200,000 troops, 2,500 wounded always in hospital, over 1000 battles fought in the past year, and only 5 Chinese graduate doctors, 50 Chinese untrained 'doctors' and one foreigner to do all this work."[6] The situation had not changed much over the last year, and despite his earlier hopes, he had reached the conclusion that it was not likely that other foreign doctors would arrive to help him. The solution to the problem would have to be found within China.

His recent experiences in Central Hebei between February and June had confirmed his original analysis. His own achievements as a battlefield surgeon during the Medical Expedition to the East had been extraordinary, but having witnessed the scope of the conflict against the Japanese and the vast area of territory involved, he knew of the desperate need to train many more surgeons and medical workers of all kinds to staff the Border Region hospitals. To find a way to provide such training was a daunting task, given wartime conditions. He had observed that whenever he had had the opportunity to instruct the Chinese, as he had the members of his mobile unit and later the trainees at Yangjiazhuang, they learned very quickly. But even with that advantage, he knew that creating truly qualified doctors would require a training period far longer than the three-week course he had given at Yangjiazhuang. He now decided to make the training of doctors and other medical staff his priority, even putting it ahead of completing his inspection of hospitals in the remaining two subdistricts. He set about creating a plan for a medical school that would turn out a large number of doctors and nurses with sufficient training to operate in guerrilla warfare.

With this in mind he had begun teaching a new group of students, some of them staff evacuated from Central Hebei, as soon as he arrived in Shenbei. He also drew up a detailed curriculum for a training program for medical workers.[7] Under his plan, all students would take a common course lasting six months. Those hoping to qualify as nurses would take an additional two-month course, and those wanting to become doctors would continue in a six-month course followed by an internship of six months. On completion of that period of training, a doctor wishing to qualify as a surgeon would enter a year-long internship. With painstaking thoroughness Bethune drafted a syllabus providing a description of each course and even made up timetables. He also chose the members of the faculty. Dr Jiang Yizhen, whom he had met in Yan'an and who had arrived to relieve him during the battle of Heisi, would be the director of the school and the instructor in surgery.[8]

To enable the medical students to have practical instruction, Bethune planned for a training hospital with between fifty and one hundred beds to be affiliated to the school. This would be, as he described it in a memorandum, "a Model Hospital in every sense of the word as it sets the example to other hospitals."[9] Although the destruction of the first model hospital at Songyankou had demonstrated the folly of constructing permanent medical facilities in the midst of a guerrilla war, he felt that the desperate need for doctors justified creating a training centre of some kind. Instead of going to the trouble and expense of constructing a new facility, the school and hospital could be housed, as at Yangjiazhung, in remodelled peasant houses, which were relatively easy to replace if destroyed. He also pointed out that in addition to drawing up the plan and syllabus for the new medical school he had written a 150-page textbook entitled *Organization and Technic* [*sic*] *for Divisional Mobile Operating Units;* it was being translated by Lang Lin, and he hoped it would be printed by the beginning of September.[10]

Bethune also prepared a budget that would include the construction of the medical school and hospital and their operating costs. He estimated that the cost of setting up the school would be $2,000 in the Chinese national currency and that a monthly sum of $3,000 would be needed to maintain a student body of two hundred, a staff of eleven instructors, and various support personnel.[11] An additional $1,000 would have to be found to cover the cost of setting up the new model hospital. But it was one thing to draw up a budget and quite another to find the money with which to implement it. Bethune knew that the Eighth Route Army could not fund the proposed medical school and model hospital, so his only hope was to draw on support from abroad.

However, after eighteen months in China, despite his repeated pleas for help, he still had not received any money or medical supplies from foreign donors, a situation that angered him deeply. As has been seen, he was furious at the China Aid Council, from which he had received no aid since reaching Jin-Cha-Ji and no letters since September 1938.[12] But he was also critical of Chinese authorities. He protested against the apparent indifference of the Trustee Committee in Yan'an, which was the parent body of the Eighth Route Army Medical Service.[13] He had routinely sent copies of all his reports to them but had never received a reply. At the bottom of a typed copy of a letter that he wrote to the committee in mid-August 1939, he wrote by hand, "No letter in acknowledgment of reports has ever been received from Trustee Committee by me."[14] Never having received the aid Dr Robert Lim had sent him, he complained in the same report that the National Red Cross Society of China had also ignored his requests for help.[15]

In his frustration at the lack of foreign aid, Bethune turned his mind to Michael Lindsay's connections in the foreign community in Beijing. When Lindsay had visited him nearly a year earlier, he had assured Bethune that there was a good deal of anti-Japanese sentiment among the English and Americans living in the city. Kathleen Hall had told him that her contacts at the Peking Union Medical College said that this sentiment had since grown. Bethune now believed that, if he went to Beijing, Lindsay could introduce him to people in the Anglo-American community who would help him raise enough money to fund the medical school and the new model hospital.

Coincidentally, Kathleen Hall was about to make her second trip to Beijing in less than a month; this was because of a disastrous incident at one of her missions. The Japanese had discovered her role in aiding the Eighth Route Army, possibly through reading articles in the local press that had openly praised her benevolent assistance.[16] During the first week of July, just before the onset of the monsoons, a Japanese force had attacked the village of Songjiazhuang where one of Hall's Anglican missions and a hospital were located. After destroying their contents, they had burnt the buildings to the ground. Fortunately Hall herself was in Beijing at the time, and the villagers of Songjiazhuang, forewarned of the approach of the Japanese, had escaped. Hall was determined to have the mission and hospital rebuilt, and this meant she had to return to Beijing to purchase supplies and medicines to replace those destroyed by the Japanese. When she told Bethune, he outlined his scheme to find money for the medical school. As she had in February, Hall agreed that he could accompany her.

Once again Bethune required the permission of his commander in chief, and this time Nie Rongzhen told Bethune directly that he could not go.[17] He said that the Japanese were aware of sympathy for the Chinese among the missionary communities and had tightened security. For one thing, they were now counting all drugs leaving Beijing and later checking the number of drugs at missions in order to determine whether any had been diverted to the Eighth Route Army. Bethune knew this from his own experience in June when he had sent a note to an American missionary in the city of Baoding asking for ten pounds of chloroform. The missionary had granted Bethune's request but had warned him that because of his fear of Japanese reprisals it was the last time he could do so.[18] The destruction of Hall's mission at Songjiazhuang was an ominous reminder of the lengths to which the Japanese would go to deter missionaries from siding with the Chinese. In addition to such general security problems, Nie warned Bethune, Chinese spies had told the Japanese all about him, and if he fell into their hands, he would certainly be executed.

So when Hall arrived at General Nie's headquarters, Bethune told her "like a shame-faced boy" that he was not allowed to go with her to Beijing. "So I said 'goodbye' to Dr Bethune," she wrote years later. "I can picture him now as he watched me descend the rocky path. He was looking thin and rather worn, but said goodbye with his usual cheerful smile. I did not know it was the last time I would see him."[19] For Hall's own luck had run out. When she arrived in Beijing, mission authorities told her that the Japanese had complained to the British Embassy that she was supporting the Eighth Route Army and had demanded that the British deport her at once. Hall was held under house arrest by the Japanese for several days, then given a special pass and put on the first ship leaving from Tianjin. Before her forced departure she wrote a letter to Nie Rongzhen, hoping that it would somehow make its way to him through Japanese lines. Whether he received her explanation of why she could not return and whether Bethune ever learned what happened to her is not known.[20]

With his hopes of raising funds in Beijing dashed, Bethune decided that there was only one way to fund the development of the medical school and model hospital. He would have to return to North America and conduct a whirlwind speaking tour. On 1 August he wrote a report in which he said, "I have come to the conclusion that I must leave the Region temporarily and go to Yan'an and return to America to raise the guaranteed sum of

$1000 (gold) a month that the Medical School needs. How else can that money be raised except by widespread appeal of one such as myself who knows the needs of this Region thoroughly after spending more than 15 months here?"[21]

Two weeks later he reaffirmed his decision and voiced his frustration in a letter to the Trustee Committee. By this time he had clearly heard that some foreign money was indeed arriving, presumably in Yan'an, because he wrote, "I am leaving this region to return to America about the first week of November if I can clean up my work before ... Then I must make a fast inspection trip of all hospitals (20 now) before leaving ... I plan to be away in America for 3 or 4 months returning next summer. I must have a guaranteed $1000 gold monthly for this region alone, I'm not getting it. I don't know where the money from America is going to. I can get no information from the Trustee Committee or America, so I'm going to find out for myself!"[22]

Other factors also influenced his decision. He knew that his health had declined dramatically in only a matter of months, though he put a brave face on it in a letter to Tim Buck, saying, "I am fairly well. My right ear has gone completely deaf for 3 months. My teeth need a lot of attention and my glasses are giving me trouble. Outside of these minor things and being rather thin, I'm OK."[23] But photographs of him taken in the summer of 1939 by Michael Lindsay and also by the noted Chinese photographer Sha Fei indicate the contrary. They reveal the emaciated frame and gaunt features of a man who looked twenty years older than his actual age.

The inadequacy of his diet had continued to undermine his health. Although he still preferred to eat the same meals as the Chinese soldiers, he had begun do his some of his own cooking in April. But he was unable to find an adequate supply of nutritious food, and his health continued to worsen.[24] His resistance to infection was down; the slight cuts he often suffered when he was operating healed much more slowly than before, and his infected feet continued to trouble him. His Chinese colleagues were convinced that he was suffering from beriberi, a disease of the nervous system now known to be caused by a dietary deficiency of thiamine (vitamin B^1).[25]

Another problem, as Bethune confessed to Lang Lin, was his growing homesickness.[26] Nie Rongzhen noted Bethune's deep loneliness and presented him with a small black dog as a companion.[27] Bethune was delighted; he shared his food with the puppy, which followed him everywhere during the day and curled up beside him at night. But a pet did nothing to assuage his desperate need for English-speaking companionship, which was obvious to Michael Lindsay when he again arrived in Jin-Cha-Ji from Beijing in early August 1939. He remained with Bethune for a week before continuing on his journey to Hong Kong. Shocked by Bethune's wasted appearance, Lindsay thought he badly needed a holiday and a change to foreign food. When Bethune told him of his intention to leave China for fundraising, Lindsay offered to arrange for him to be brought through Japanese lines into Beijing and to be given refuge at Yenching University. There he could receive medical attention and eat properly to make himself fit to travel. Once he had recovered somewhat, Lindsay said, he could be guided either to Shanghai or Hong Kong where he could book ship passage for Canada.[28]

Bethune was grateful for Lindsay's offer but was certain that General Nie would refuse to allow him to leave via Beijing. For this reason, he had already chosen another route, which he outlined in a letter to Tim Buck:

> This is to let you know that I am coming home for a short time. The General did not, at first, want me to go but we must have more money. I don't know where the money from America is going, the only thing is that I am not getting it here for my work ... I have been alone for over a year – no letters, no books, no periodicals, no radio. I must have help to go on. I plan to leave here in November – somewhere about the 1st or 2nd week, go across Shansi [Shanxi] and down to Yenan [Yan'an] and then to Yunnan in the south, arriving at Hong Kong (thru French Indochina) sometime in January. I will take a freighter from there to Hawaii to avoid Japan. I should be in San Francisco about the end of February, '40. I want to stay in Canada about 3 or 4 months to collect more money and supplies – and men if I can – and then come back here next summer ... I have no clothes. My civilian clothes were lost from H.K on the R.R. to Hankow [Hankou] in March last year. Will you please have the China Aid Council send enough money to get me clothes, pay passage to America, pay dentists and doctors in Hong Kong? Perhaps they should send about $1000 to the China Defence Committee in Hong Kong.[29]

On the same day he wrote another letter and made copies of it which he addressed to John Barnwell and several other friends in North America. Lindsay carried these to Hong Kong where he posted them. The letter began:

> It seems such a long time since we last met and so much must have happened to you. It has certainly happened to me. These last (nearly two years) now, have been very full, so full that I hardly know where to start to describe them to you. So this account will be a disconnected one at best. But I am anxious that you should receive one letter at least of those I have written you, for I have written before, but I am supposing that you never

received them as I have had no reply. That is what I have come to accept, more or less resignedly, as part of this life. The mails are very irregular. It takes at least 5 months for any letters to reach me after they have arrived in China. I calculate that I get only 1 in 25. Books and periodicals are even worse. I have received none in one and half years. My reading consists of years old San Francisco papers used as wrappers for sugar, tea and cakes by merchants. I am thoroughly conversant with the doings of the "smart set" and the vagaries of Hollywood, but of anything of importance, I know less than an Arctic explorer. He, at least, has a radio, I have none. It was three months before I knew that Madrid had fallen!

The work that I am trying to do is to take peasant boys and young workers and make doctors out of them. They can read and write and most have a knowledge of arithmetic. None of my doctors have ever been to college or university and none have ever been in a modern hospital (most of them have never been in any hospital) much less a medical school. With this material, I must make doctors and nurses out of them, in 6 months for nurses and 1 year for doctors. We have 2300 wounded in hospital all the time. These hospitals are merely the dirty one-story mud and stone houses of out-of-the-way villages set in deep valleys overhung by mountains, some of which are 10,000 feet high. We have over 20 of these hospitals in our region which stretches from Beiping [Beijing] in the north to Tianjin in the east, south to Shih Chia Chuang [Shijiazhuang], west to Tai Yuan. We are the most active Partisan area in China and engaged in very severe guerrilla warfare all the time.

He described the nature of the Japanese occupation and predicted that the war would be a long one. Then he continued,

We must help these splendid people more than we are doing. We must send them more money and men. Technicians of all kinds are badly needed, doctors, public health workers, engineers, mechanics – everybody that knows some technical specialty well. Last year I travelled 3165 miles, of which 400 miles were marched on foot across Shansi [Shanxi], Shensi [Shaanxi] and Hopei [Hebei] Provinces. 762 operations were performed and 1200 wounded examined. The Sanitary Service of the army was reorganized, 3 textbooks written and translated into Chinese, a Medical Training School established.

It's a fast life. I miss tremendously a comrade to whom I can talk. You know how fond I am of talking! I don't mind the conventional hardships

– heat and bitter cold, dirt, lice, unvaried unfamiliar food, walking in the mountains, no stoves, beds or baths. I find I can get along and operate as well in a dirty Buddhist temple with a 20-foot high statue of the impassive-faced god staring over my shoulder, as in a modern operating room with running water, nice green glazed walls, electric lamps and a thousand other accessories. To dress the wounded we have to climb up on the mud ovens – the *kangs*. They have no mattresses, no sheets. They lie in their old stained uniforms, with their knapsacks as pillows and one padded cotton blanket over them. They are grand. They certainly can take it.

We have had tremendous floods this summer. It's been hellish hot and muggy. Rain for 2 months coming down like a steady shower-bath turned on full. I am planning to return to Canada early next year ... I want to raise a guaranteed $1000 (gold) a month for my work here. I'm not getting it. They need me here. This is "my" Region. I must come back.

I dream of coffee, of rare roast beef, of apple pie and ice cream. Mirages of heavenly food! Books – are books still being written? Is music still being played? Do you dance, drink beer, look at pictures? What do clean white sheets in a soft bed feel like? Do women still love to be loved?

How sad that, even to me once more, all these things may become accepted easily without wonder and amazement at my good fortune ...

Goodbye for the present, dear friend and comrade.

Beth[30]

He planned to begin an inspection tour of the hospitals in West Hebei before setting out for Yan'an but was delayed by illness. One problem was a swollen sore on the middle finger of his right hand that caused him to run a fever and prevented him from typing. Unable to treat it himself, he insisted that Lang Lin lance it for him. At first the interpreter hung back, but a stern glance from Bethune convinced him to go ahead. With the pus released from the wound, it at last began to heal, and Bethune was able to return to his typing. A second ailment, a severely infected foot, was the result of the lingering problems that he had been experiencing since June. His feet had never healed properly and eventually an abscess formed on one of them. He suffered a good deal of pain, and this drove him at last to allow his medical colleagues to put him under a general anesthetic so that they could treat it properly. The operation, performed by Dr Lin Jinliang, was a success. Although Bethune had to hobble about on crutches for weeks, he was able to function normally again by the end of August.[31] But two stubborn infections within such a short period were a sign that his resistance was dangerously low.

In early September he went to treat wounded soldiers at the rear base hospital of the Third Subdistrict.[32] This was located in Huapen, a tiny village nestled in a narrow mountain pass. He and his mobile team remained there for more than a week before making the short trip south to Niuyangou, a village on the banks of the Tang River, the site chosen for the training school and model hospital. Despite the lack of funds, a beginning had been made on the school, and personnel he had taught at Shenbei had already moved to Niuyangou. On 18 September, after ceremonies including speeches by Nie Rongzhen and Bethune and a stage presentation by a drama troupe, the medical school officially began operation.[33] Still only a shell of what Bethune expected it to become, it was housed in a building that linked two large peasant homes.[34] Standing on a broad ledge below the peak of the highest hill in the village, it looked out on a deep valley on the other side of which was the Anglican church where he had first met Kathleen Hall. Hoping to encourage young women to join the Eighth Route Army Medical Service to train as nurses, he had been counting on her to act as director of the training of nurses in the medical school. In her absence he had persuaded Guo Qinglan, a nurse who had joined Hall at Songjiazhuang, to take on the role.[35]

Bethune remained in Niuyangou for only two days before returning to Huapen, where he spent several days making preparations for his planned inspection tour of two subdistricts. The unit was led by Ye Qingshan, the Jin-Cha-Ji minister of health, and included Bethune, his three assistants, doctors Wang Daojian, Lin Jinliang, and Chen Shihua, his interpreter Lang Lin, and several members of the support staff. They left Huapen on 25 September; Bethune's intention was to complete the tour in less than a month and then begin the long journey out of Jin-Cha-Ji en route to Yan'an on Friday, 20 October.[36] Over the next nine days his group visited two army bases and a convalescent centre, examining staff, inspecting facilities, and holding conferences to outline changes he wanted to introduce.

Then misfortune struck. During a heavy rainstorm on Wednesday, 4 October, Lang Lin's horse slipped on a mountain path and ran into Bethune's, which reared and kicked Lang Lin's left leg so hard that he was knocked to the ground.[37] Jumping from his mount, Bethune examined the leg and found that it had been fractured. After applying splints, he assigned several members of the team to carry Lang Lin to a nearby village where he made a plaster cast for the leg. The next morning Bethune and the rest of the team continued on the tour, and Lang Lin was carried by stretcher back to the hospital in Huapen. This left Bethune without an interpreter. Fortunately, Liu Ke, a member of the Jin-Cha-Ji political department who was part of the team, knew some English and was able to replace Lang Lin until Pan Fan, another interpreter, arrived to take over a week later.[38]

Shortly after the unit arrived at the sanatorium in the village of Laogu, they were joined by Nie Rongzhen. He had come to discuss arrangements for Bethune's long journey to Yan'an, scheduled to begin in two weeks. During their meeting Bethune gave Nie the text of a message to be radioed to Yan'an and from there transmitted to the China Aid Council in New York. In the cable, which reached New York several days later, he asked that money be sent to the China Defence League in Hong Kong to pay for his passage across the Pacific.[39] At their meeting Nie introduced two members of a film unit, the director, Yuang Muzhi, and his photographer, Wu Yinxian. When the authorities in Yan'an had learned of Bethune's plan to return to Canada, they decided to obtain footage of him at work for a documentary film that they had been planning on the Eighth Route Army's struggle against the Japanese in the Border Region. The film unit would accompany Bethune's unit until the end of October.[40] Bethune was enthusiastic about the project, hoping that the film would aid fundraising for China as *Heart of Spain* had done for Republican Spain.

For the next ten days he and his team moved deeper into the mountains. On 15 October they received by courier an intelligence report of an expected enemy attack in an area a day's ride away.[41] The report stressed that it appeared that the Japanese would be using poison gas. Bethune immediately suspended the tour and spent several days with health units in the immediate area where the enemy advance would take place, providing instruction on how to treat victims of poison gas.

Assuming that his surgical team might be needed if the Japanese did indeed attack, Bethune delayed his projected departure date to 1 November. However, by the end of the emergency training sessions there was no request from the regional military command for the team's assistance, so they set out on the final stops on the inspection tour. On Friday, 27 October, after visiting the last hospital, they reached the village of Ganhejing, where Bethune began to prepare for his departure for Yan'an the following Wednesday.

Late that evening, word came that an enemy attack was in progress fifty kilometres to the northwest.[42] Before dawn the following morning, the unit set off for Sunjiazhuang, a hamlet of a few households in a narrow mountain pass about ten kilometres from the fighting. When they arrived that evening, an Eighth Route Army officer led them to the ruins of a temple on the side of a hill. The ornate curved roof still stood, and the three remaining walls of the small outbuilding partially enclosed a floor area of fifteen square metres, which Bethune agreed could serve as an operating theatre. Early on the morning of 29 October the team began to set up its equipment. Stretcher-bearers carrying the wounded began to arrive and as usual were told to give precedence to those with abdominal or cranial wounds. Bethune began to operate, assisted by doctors Wang Daojian and Lin Jinliang.[43] The day was sunny and warm, and Bethune wore only a sweater beneath his rubber apron. In the early evening, as he was operating on the last of the wounded, his hand slipped, and the scalpel he was using sliced into the middle finger of his left hand. He stopped while a nurse hurriedly applied iodine and bandaged the finger, and then he resumed his surgery.

The team returned to Ganhejing late on Monday, only to find that wounded soldiers from another engagement with the Japanese had arrived there the day before. On Tuesday Bethune began to examine these cases and operate on the wounded. On Wednesday, 1 November, the date of his planned departure, he was working on a suppurating head wound. He was not wearing gloves because there were none.[44] The injury to his finger had not healed, and infected matter seeped into the open cut.[45] By Friday the finger had begun to swell; Bethune became feverish and was unable to accompany the other members of the unit who were called into action at the scene of a Japanese attack some distance away. The next day the finger had become terribly swollen, and an abscess had appeared inside his left elbow.

Learning of Bethune's injury, Ye Qingshan had sent Dr Chen Shihua to examine him. Bethune at first refused to allow him to do so, but now gave in to his colleagues' pleading. Chen concluded that to remove the source of the infection now spreading through Bethune's veins, he would have to amputate his finger. Bethune refused. Without his finger, how could he function as a surgeon? he demanded.[46] He had had infected fingers several times before and had recovered, and he must have been hoping that would happen again. He told himself that his burning fever might be caused not by septicemia but by typhus, which he might easily have contracted from the lice that infested his clothing and the *kangs* where he slept. So he only allowed the Chinese doctors to lance his finger to release the pus.

On Monday, 6 November, Dr Chen examined him again and found that another abscess had appeared inside Bethune's left elbow and that the lymph gland in his left armpit had become swollen and was intensely painful. The progression of the infection from finger to elbow to armpit was clear, and the Chinese doctors must have known that amputation of the arm was the only chance to save Bethune's life. But they were in too much awe of him to perform the operation without his permission. If they operated and he died, they might be blamed by the authorities. If they operated and Bethune survived, he might blame them for removing his arm unnecessarily. Either way, it was too risky.

But the question remains why Bethune, who was still conscious at times, did not order an amputation himself. He must have known that even without his left arm he could still have been of inestimable use to the Eighth Route Army as an organizer of medical services, instructor, writer of textbooks, and potential fundraiser; it might even have been possible for him to undertake certain medical procedures. But amputation would have meant that he would never again have been able to function as a battlefield surgeon. And surgery was to him more than just a profession; in its drama and incisiveness it was the expression of his way of life, his mode of being. Despite his passionate commitment to communism and to the Chinese struggle against the Japanese, he refused to consent to becoming less than he wanted to be. In his heart of hearts he must have still believed that somehow his luck and his will would carry him through, as they always had before. With the fires of infection raging in his blood, he chose to gamble against the odds.

On Wednesday he heard the rumble of distant artillery fire and started up feverishly. Hoping to calm him, his assistants told him it was only thunder. But he eventually learned from one of his colleagues that a battle was being waged not far away. Over the protests of the other doctors, he insisted that he and the team must go there. "Stop treating me like a Ming vase," he said. "I'm a soldier, not an antique."[47] Getting to his feet, he called for his horse to be brought and made a feeble attempt to mount it. Angered when he could not, he ordered that a walking stick be found for him and led the unit out of Ganhejing on foot.

It was raining most of the time as they made their way to the village of Taipingti, and by the time they arrived, Bethune was trembling with fever and barely able to stand.[48] The next day his colleagues put him on a stretcher and started out on the journey of several hours to the village of Wangjiatai. By then his temperature had reached 40 degrees Celsius. On the morning of Friday, 10 November, the regional commanding officer, Yang Chengwu, arrived in Wangjiatai to determine Bethune's condition.[49] After a brief consultation with the doctors, he ordered them to take Bethune immediately to the base hospital at Huapen, and then dispatched a courier with a message to Nie Rongzhen informing him of the gravity of Bethune's condition. The team put Bethune on a stretcher and set out at once for the base hospital. On the way he complained of a severe headache, then, slipping into delirium, began to vomit as they carried him along the tortuous mountain trail.

Late that afternoon they reached the village of Huangshikou where they planned to stay overnight. They took Bethune to the home of a peasant named Di Junxing, who had offered to provide shelter for him; the small, yellow mud-brick house with a slanting grey tile roof had only a single room. They carried him inside in his sleeping bag in which he had been wrapped on the stretcher and laid him on the *kang*. Then they took turns applying compresses to his burning forehead. By this time, Bethune's face was yellow and his left arm had turned dark.[50] Di's wife insisted on sacrificing a precious chicken to make soup, a cure for illness favoured by the peasants, but Bethune vomited up the broth that she spooned into his mouth. Giving up the idea of trying to feed him orally, Dr Chen Shihua was later able to inject glucose into a vein in his arm. Bethune fell asleep for a short time but woke and complained of feeling cold. Di at once fetched more wood to heat the *kang*, refusing to accept the money that Bethune offered to pay for it. Bethune then sent his interpreter Pan Fan to bring some tins of corned beef captured from the Japanese from his saddlebag to give to Di and his wife.

By late afternoon he was shaking so violently with fever that his teeth rattled. His attendants stoked the fire in the *kang* and piled blankets on him, but nothing helped. They discussed the possibility of carrying him through the night to the hospital in Huapen. But the distance was too great, and they feared that he would not survive the journey. All they could do was apply cold compresses in a futile effort to reduce his suffering. In the evening Dr Lin Jinliang, who had remained behind in Ganhejing, reached Huangshikou. Bethune was barely conscious as Lin began to examine his arm while listening to Chen Shihua's anguished account of his attempt to persuade Bethune to undergo an amputation of his finger. Lin quickly confirmed what the other doctors must have already known: the infection was now so far advanced that Bethune's arm had to be amputated. But Bethune roused enough from his stupor to refuse the operation.[51] The best Lin Jinliang could do under the circumstances was to cross-cut the abscesses inside his left elbow to release the pus and clean the affected area. He and Chen Shihua performed the procedure without resistance from Bethune, who had again become semi-conscious.

Gradually he began to shake less, and finally he drifted off to sleep for several hours. When he awoke early on Saturday morning, he was no longer shaking and seemed more clear-headed. When he said that he felt better, Di's wife suggested that he try to eat a persimmon. Cutting up one of the round, orange-yellow fruits, she spooned the syrupy pieces into his mouth. When he asked for more, she sliced another and he managed to eat some of that too.[52] In the early afternoon He Zexin made some coffee, and Bethune drank a little of it. He then said that he wanted to write some letters, so his comrades propped him against a wooden backrest and set a small table in front of him, placing on it a paper and pencil. Bethune asked to be left alone.

A few minutes after 4 PM, one of his attendants opened the door to look in at him. Bethune had lapsed into unconsciousness, his head drooping on his chest; pieces of paper lay scattered about on the floor. On the *kang* they found a note to Lang Lin, which read:

On the north bank of Tang Ho near Hua Ta, West Hopei [Hebei], 11 November, 1939.

I came back from the front yesterday. There was no good in my being there. I couldn't get out of bed or operate. I left Shih Chia Chuang [Shijiazhuang] (I think) Hospital of Central Hopei [Hebei] troops on 7th. Pan and I went north. I then had infected finger … Reached Tu Ping Ti [Taipingti] late at night … We go over west and joined at 3rd Regiment sanitary service on 8th about 10 *li* east of Yin Fang. Had uncontrolled chills and fever all day. Temp. around 39.6 C., bad. Gave instructions I was to be informed of any abdominal cases of fractured femur or skull cases … Next day (9th), more vomiting all day, high fever. Next day (10th) regiment commander (3rd Regiment) instructed I be sent back, useless for work. Vomiting on stretcher all the day. High fever, over 40° C. I think I have either septicaemia from the gangrenous fever or typhus fever. Can't get to sleep, mentally very bright. Phenacitin and aspirin, woven's powder, antipyrin, caffeine, all useless.

Dr. Ch'en arrived here today. If my stomach settled down will return to Hua Pai Hospital tomorrow. Very rough road over mountain pass.

I feel freely today. Pain over heart – water 120-130. Will see you tomorrow, I expect.[53]

But Bethune must have known that he would not see Lang Lin again, that the rough rafters above the *kang* and the pale light filtering through the small rice-papered window were his last glimpse of the world. For the first two sentences of the unfinished second letter, which was addressed to Nie Rongzhen, were: "I am fatally ill. I am going to die."[54]

During the early evening, between brief periods of restless sleep and delirium, he had moments of partial clarity when he struggled to tell Pan Fan what he wanted to include in his letter to Nie. Before sinking into unconsciousness, he asked the interpreter to accept his watch as a gift. Throughout the night and into Sunday morning, Lin Jinliang, Chen Shihua, Pan Fan, and the faithful He Zexin stood by the *kang* taking turns placing cold compresses on his forehead. In the early hours of the morning Bethune slept fitfully, rousing to ask for news of his mobile unit and trying to give orders to those who stood helplessly by. Shortly after 5 AM he coughed and moved his lips in a vain effort to speak. Then his breathing slowed perceptibly, and at last it stopped. Lin Jinliang checked his pulse and began to weep. Pan Fan glanced at Bethune's watch: the time was twenty minutes past five.

Hearing that a Japanese force was moving toward Huangshikou and reluctant to bury Bethune without official permission, the medical team readied themselves to leave the village by mid-morning. Dr Lin Jinliang was entrusted with transporting the body, and under his supervision it was placed on a stretcher carried by six men. Then the small group set out for the village of Yujiazhai. The narrow trails they followed twisted so much that the stretcher sometimes overturned, pitching the body to the ground, so Lin, who was mounted, for a time carried it before him on his horse.[55] Hoping to prevent the news of Bethune's death from spreading, they concealed his identity by covering his body with a green army coat. To make it appear that they were bearing a wounded soldier, one of his attendants carried a water jug and whenever they passed groups of people he would pretend to ask if the man on the stretcher wanted a drink of water.[56] In the late afternoon they reached the hamlet of Mulan, where one of the villagers offered to conceal the body beneath a pile of firewood; later he agreed to allow them to move it into his cellar until the following morning.

After a gruelling two-day trek along icy trails through the hills, the party reached Yujiazhai on Wednesday. There they washed the body, clothed it in an army uniform, and wrapped it in red cloth. On Friday, 17 November, after a ceremony attended by the few local officials and most of the villagers, they took Bethune's remains to a desolate field at the base of a lonely ridge known as Wolf Mountain Valley Gate. There they dug his grave and the Chinese earth received his body.

Years before, Bethune had written to Marian Scott, "You need an altar to immolate yourself upon – a glad, burning sacrifice to a living God – you ask to be consumed – to rise again like a phoenix from the ashes of your own glad destruction – clean and pure & free – with wings."[57] In China he had found that altar and made that sacrifice.

Epilogue

Bethune's death was announced in a telegram that arrived in Yan'an on 15 November 1939. A four-hour mass meeting was held to mourn him, at which various members of the Central Committee and General Zhu De paid tribute to him. On 21 December Mao Zedong composed a eulogy entitled "In Memory of Norman Bethune." In it he pointed out that Bethune had come to China in its hour of dire peril. Dedicated to his art of healing and with no concern for his own comfort, he had given his life in the service of the Chinese people. "Comrade Bethune's spirit, his utter devotion to others without any thought of self, was shown in his great sense of responsibility in his work and his great warm-heartedness towards all comrades and the people," Mao wrote.

Those people Bethune had served did not forget him in death. In early January the Chinese transported Bethune's body to the village of Juncheng, where an improvised pavilion had been constructed. They placed the body on a funeral bier, laying beside it some of his instruments and a few of his personal effects. On the wall behind they hung a large photograph of him, flanked by commemorative tributes sent from various sectors of the Jin-Cha-Ji Border Region, and draped a Chinese flag above. Wreaths were banked before the bier, and near it on a pedestal burned a circle of candles representing the completeness and light of his life. By 5 January more than ten thousand mourners had shuffled, weeping, past Bethune's frail corpse. On that day Nie Rongzhen and several of Bethune's comrades paid tribute to him at the burial ceremony, and it was announced that the medical school and its affiliated hospital set up by him two months before his death would be named after him.[1] After the funeral, performers staged a play to demonstrate Bethune's service to the people of China.

The villagers of Jun Cheng built a tomb for Bethune, walking thirty miles to a quarry each night through Japanese lines to bring back marble for it.

They carved a statue of him and also a globe, representing his internation-alism, which rested on top of his tomb. Epigraphs were carved on the four sides of the base of the tomb. On the east, "The internationalist spirit of comrade Norman Bethune is worthy to be learned from by all Chinese Com-munists and respected by all Chinese people – The Central Committee of the Chinese Communist Party." On the south, "The scientist and statesman of the masses – Nieh Jung Chen."[2] On the west, "The eternal brilliancy – Shu Tung."[3] On the north, "The Most Valorous Fighter on the Front of the Emancipation of Mankind – Lu Cheng-tsao."[4] The tomb was dedicated on 21 June 1940. Several months later the Japanese invaded the area around Juncheng, so the villagers hid the body and the statue in the surrounding hills. Japanese troops used the globe as a target for machine-gun practice and dynamited it before they left. The Chinese then reconstructed the memorial, set up the statue again, and reinterred the body.

After the establishment of the People's Republic of China in 1949, the tomb was transferred to the large rail junction city of Shijiazhuang, located south of Beijing. In 1952 it was placed near a large statue of Bethune in the Martyrs' Cemetery of the Military Region of North China, a memorial park in Shijiazhuang dedicated to the memory of the 3.2 million Chinese soldiers who died in the region during the struggle against the Japanese and the Guo-mindang. Meanwhile, work had begun on the Bethune Medical School and the Norman Bethune International Peace Hospital. The latter included a small museum containing photographs and line drawings depicting Bethune's work in Jin-Cha-Ji.[5] His Hermes typewriter, some of his instruments, and a few of his personal belongings are on display in a glass case.

Bethune's death was greeted very differently in Canada. News of it reached North America on 26 November 1939 when the China Aid Council in New York released to the press the contents of a cable received from Zhu De, commander in chief of the Eighth Route Army: "Unfortunate injury while operating and resultant septicemia caused the death of Dr Norman Bethune in Wu-t'ai Shan, China. Eighth Route Army mourns medical hero, and conveys deepest condolences to family and friends." Many major Canadian and some American newspapers carried brief reports of the news; the only other references to him appeared in eulogies in the communist press and obit-uaries in medical journals. His passing was barely noticed by the general public in Canada. However, on 20 December 1939, friends, medical col-leagues, and political comrades gathered in the Windsor Hotel in Montreal for a commemorative ceremony. Following brief presentations outlining his achievements in Montreal, Spain, and China, a collection was taken to be sent to China to assist his hospital. Among the tributes that night was a letter from the Communist Party of Canada stating, as Bethune had wished, that he had become a member in 1935.[6]

The official linking of Bethune to the CPC antagonized people who viewed the Canadian party as no more than a pawn of the Soviet Union. Stalin had signed a non-aggression treaty with Hitler in August 1939 and later seized part of Poland after it was overrun by the Nazis; he had also invaded Finland in November and did not intervene when German military forces swiftly overran Western Europe in the spring of 1940. Most Canadians regarded CPC members as supporters of Nazi and Soviet aggression, and the Canadian government declared the CPC an illegal organization by an Order-in-Council in June of that year.[7] Hearing of this, Bethune's sister, Janet Stiles, emptied a trunk containing her brother's possessions which he had left with her on his return from Spain in June 1937. Among them were books and papers related to communism. She burned everything.[8]

In 1952, thirteen years after his death, the first book-length biography of Bethune was published.[9] *The Scalpel, the Sword: The Story of Dr Norman Bethune* was written by two Canadians, Ted Allan and Sydney Gordon, who depicted Bethune as a communist hero. In one sense this accolade could not have been more ill timed, because anti-communist feeling, which had declined after Canada and the Soviet Union became allies in the struggle against Nazi Germany in 1941, had risen again dramatically with the beginning of the Cold War. The testimony of Igor Gouzenko, the cipher clerk in the Soviet Embassy in Ottawa, that a Russian spy network was operating in Canada led to a series of trials. They ended in 1949 with the conviction of several Canadians, two of whom had been CPC comrades of Bethune, on the charge of espionage.[10] One year later, when troops of the communist state of North Korea invaded South Korea, a United Nations force made up of troops from a number of non-communist nations including Canada went to the aid of South Korea. At the time of the release of *The Scalpel, the Sword* in 1952, the Korean War was in its third year, and the stigma of communism limited the appeal of the book to few Canadian readers beyond those on the political left. However, it became popular outside the country; in translation, largely in the languages of nations within the political orbit of the Soviet Union, it would eventually become one of the best-selling Canadian books abroad.

The first honorary recognition of Bethune by his own profession was the result of a tour by the Peking Opera Company in 1960. The company had offered to give a benefit performance in memory of Bethune at the Royal

Victoria Hospital in Montreal. Afterward Dr Ronald Christie, an old friend of Bethune and the physician in chief of the Royal Vic, suggested a Sino-Canadian medical exchange in his honour. This led to the creation of the Norman Bethune Exchange Professorship, an arrangement between McGill University and the Chinese Medical College of Peking. In 1964, Dr K.A.C. Elliott, head of McGill's Department of Biochemistry, became the first Canadian exchange professor to visit China under the program.

That same year, which was the twenty-fifth anniversary of Bethune's death, the Canadian Broadcasting Corporation presented a radio documentary, *Comrade Bethune: A Controversial Hero,* made up largely of interviews with individuals who had known him. Also in 1964, the National Film Board of Canada (NFB) released a documentary film biography entitled *Bethune.* Some Canadians who learned about Bethune from the radio program and the film found him an unusual and admirable individual. Others, outraged by the use of public funds to praise a communist, protested, especially when the film later won first prize at a film festival in the communist German Democratic Republic in 1965.[11] News of the award also reached the American State Department, which persuaded the Canadian government to stop NFB offices in the United States from distributing the film.[12]

Two years later a much more sweeping effort to draw attention to Bethune's achievements got underway in China. In 1966 Mao Zedong set in motion the Great Proletarian Cultural Revolution, and Bethune became part of the propaganda he used to carry out his plan to revive revolutionary spirit in Chinese society. Mao used Bethune as the symbol of the revolutionary zeal, altruism, and absolute dedication to duty that he wanted to promote. Until then relatively few people had known of Mao's brief eulogy of Bethune written in 1939, but it now became one of the "three most-read articles" that all Chinese were urged to study; millions dutifully committed the seven-hundred word essay to memory. Chinese students now learned the story of Bethune's service in their country; statuettes and posters depicted him as a heroic figure; postage stamps bearing his image were issued. In the Martyrs' Cemetery of the Military Region of North China in Shijiazhuang, an impressive museum was opened near his tomb, and in the remote village of Songyankou his first model hospital was reconstructed down to the last detail.[13] Articles about his achievement and memoirs by former colleagues describing his devotion to the wounded were published and widely read. Before the end of the 1960s, through a massive propaganda campaign, virtually every Chinese had become familiar with Bai Qiuen, the heroic Canadian doctor.[14] Because of the enormous population of China, this made Bethune the best-known Canadian in the world.

Shortly after the outbreak of the Cultural Revolution, Pierre Trudeau became prime minister of Canada. One of his principal aims was to bring about a fundamental change in Canada's relationship with the government of the People's Republic of China. After the Communist victory over the Guomindang in 1949, Canada, like most other non-communist states, had refused to recognize Mao Zedong's government in Beijing. Trudeau believed that the lack of normal diplomatic relations with the world's most populous state did not serve the interests of Canada and decided to make an overture to China. The means used to persuade the Chinese to enter into discussions was the NFB film *Bethune*. In the late winter of 1969 a Canadian diplomat in Stockholm extended a dinner invitation to his Chinese counterpart, adding that afterwards he would show a film that he was certain would interest his guest.[15] The result was a series of Sino-Canadian negotiations that culminated in October 1970 with the establishment of full diplomatic relations between the two nations.

One result of Trudeau's manoeuvre was its effect on the reputation of Bethune in Canada. Now that his government had recognized China, Trudeau realized that some form of recognition had to be given to Bethune at home. Not long after the exchange of ambassadors between Canada and China, Bethune's name was placed before the National Historic Sites and Monuments Board, the agency with the responsibility of granting official recognition to Canadians of historical importance. After reviewing the matter, the government-appointed body decided that Bethune did not meet the required standards. However, a little more than a year later, the board reversed its decision, and at a brief ceremony held in Gravenhurst, in the house in which he had been born, Norman Bethune was formally designated a Canadian "of national historic significance." Jean-Luc Pepin, then minister of trade, industry, and commerce, made the announcement before a small group that included his ministerial counterpart from the People's Republic of China. The minister of external affairs, Mitchell Sharp, made the announcement at a Canadian trade fair in Beijing.

The official declaration of Bethune's new status, made on 17 August 1972, ignited a debate that raged for several weeks among editorial writers, columnists, and members of the public. For admirers of Bethune the tribute was welcome, if belated. Other people felt that to honour a communist flew in the face of Canadian democratic values. Still others wondered about the true motives of the Canadian government. A political cartoon summed up these suspicions. It depicted Mitchell Sharp pushing a wheelbarrow labelled "long-term wheat deal" through a Chinese gate. Left outside, an Australian businessman comments to an American, "The password sounds like Bethune."[16]

After Canada officially recognized the People's Republic of China, Chinese delegations began to arrive in Canada on official business, and they invariably asked to visit Bethune's birthplace in Gravenhurst. The house was still, as it had been at Bethune's birth, church property, and for more than two years the resident United Church of Canada minister and his family graciously welcomed an increasing number of Chinese eager to see the room in which Bethune had been born. Eventually church authorities realized they had to find another residence for the minister, and shortly after Prime Minister Trudeau's state visit to China in September 1973, they agreed to terms offered by the Canadian government for the purchase of the manse. Over the next three years a Parks Canada restoration team renovated the building, returning the ground floor and the nursery on the second floor to their approximate structure and appearance at the time the Bethune family lived there. The remainder of the second floor was given over to a series of exhibits outlining Bethune's career and achievements.[17] On 30 August 1976 the Bethune Memorial House was opened to the public as a national museum.[18]

The increased interest in Bethune gave rise to various tributes to him. In 1976 the City of Montreal created Place Norman Bethune at the intersection of Guy Street and De Maisonneuve Boulevard West. The People's Republic of China donated a statue for it, a replica of the Bethune statue that stands before the Norman Bethune International Peace Hospital in Shijiazhuang. In Toronto, York University had already named its newest college after him, and in 1979 a new secondary school would adopt his name.[19] There was also a flurry of books. Roderick Stewart wrote a 1973 biography, *Bethune*, followed four years later by *The Mind of Norman Bethune*, a collection of Bethune's writings and of photographs of him. *Bethune: The Montreal Years*, which includes reminiscences of Bethune by Wendell MacLeod, Libbie Park, and Stanley Ryerson, was published in 1978. Poems and plays followed, along with a movie for television produced by the CBC, *Bethune*, starring Donald Sutherland, who had been fascinated by Bethune since the 1960s.[20] At the end of the decade, to mark the fortieth anniversary of his death, ceremonies were held in both Canada and China. Those in China took place in Beijing and in the areas where Bethune had worked.[21] In Canada, McGill University held a three-day conference sponsored by the Bethune Foundation, an organization originally created in Montreal as the Bethune Memorial Committee.[22] On the centenary of his birth in 1990 the Canadian and Chinese governments jointly issued two postage stamps bearing the image of Bethune. In that same year *Bethune: The Making of a Hero*, touted as the most expensive Canadian feature film made to date, was released. With Donald Sutherland again playing Bethune, it was shot in Spain, China, and Canada.

From the mid-1990s onward, there were more tributes, some of them by Bethune's own profession. In 1998 he was admitted into the Canadian Medical Hall of Fame, and in 2000 the Office of International Surgery established the Bethune Round Table, an annual conference on international surgery in the developing world.[23] More books about him also appeared, first *The Politics of Passion: Norman Bethune's Writing and Art*, by Larry Hannant, and then *Norman Bethune: A Life of Passionate Conviction* by John Wilson. The most recent to date is Adrienne Clarkson's biography, *Norman Bethune*.[24] In October 2008 the Fondation Aubin in Montreal held a colloquium entitled "Norman Bethune, Montreal Internationalist," and in 2009, the seventieth anniversary of his death, the City of Montreal, which is twinned with Shanghai, declared the year to be one of Homage to Norman Bethune. He was also honoured in various ways in Canada, China, and Spain that year.[25]

Even after the opening of the Bethune Memorial House, however, some opposition to the official recognition of Bethune remained, even in Gravenhurst. Bethune was criticized for his communism, and accusations of immorality stemming from often fanciful tales told of his personal behaviour still tainted his memory in some people's minds. To a certain degree such resentment lingers to this day, but with the passage of time much of it has begun to give way to grudging pride. On a warm day in August 2000, Adrienne Clarkson, then governor general of Canada and a Canadian of Chinese ethnicity, officiated at the unveiling of a bronze statue of Bethune erected on the main street of Gravenhurst. The sculptor, Brenda Waiman Goulet, is a resident of the area; the hosts of the event were the mayor and the council of the Town of Gravenhurst. Henry Norman Bethune had at last been formally acknowledged by the place of his birth.

Bethune's life exhibits recurrent cycles of achievement and self-destruction – the pattern of the phoenix. He was a born crusader, and the evangelistic spirit created by his Christian upbringing later informed his developing social consciousness and his ultimate faith in communism. He was driven throughout his life to act as a saviour, not just as a doctor but in his personal relationships and in his developing social commitment. His finest trait was the way he identified with the suffering, the wounded, and the helpless; he often quoted Walt Whitman's lines, "I do not pity the wounded – I become the wounded person." He yearned to achieve, to "live greatly," as Marian Scott said, and to be recognized for his efforts, yet for most of his life his pilgrim spirit measured the progress he had made and found it wanting. In part this was because he often got in his own way and then, impatient at not having reached his goals quickly, burned his bridges behind him. The difficult aspects of his character, his temper and his mood swings, were complicated for much of his life by heavy drinking. Alcohol initially made him gregarious and enabled him to break through the barriers he erected between himself and others, but it often propelled him into violent altercations and offensive behaviour. Whether his abuse of alcohol was a symptom of a borderline mood or personality disorder or was in itself the cause of his instability is impossible to say. He offended many people throughout his life, and there is little doubt that, had he been able to exercise tact and diplomacy, he might have achieved even more than he did. But it was not in his fiery nature to do so. His instinct was to pursue his objectives at all costs and without compromise, and time and again this caused him to crash and burn. Yet one of the most heroic aspects of his personality was his ability to recreate himself after each disaster and climb again.

It is no wonder, then, that the record of his life is uneven. His achievement as a thoracic surgeon, though considerable, was not of the highest calibre. Despite an initial period of productive experimentation and publication, his fundamental restlessness and his growing social consciousness kept him from the reading and research necessary to allow him to publish more and so enhance his professional reputation. He invented various surgical instruments that were widely used in the 1930s and helped make his name; however, technology has changed and only one of his inventions, the Bethune Rib Shears, is still in use today. The social causes he adopted in Canada were not successful in his lifetime. Although a pioneer in proclaiming the need for socialized medicine, he was ultimately frustrated by the obstacles of professional prejudice and public indifference. In the end his most notable achievements were those shaped by his passionate humanitarianism, in Spain and to an even greater degree in China. Although he did not create the first mobile blood transfusion service in Spain (that honour belongs to Dr Frederic Duran i Jordà of Barcelona), his Instituto canadiense de transfusión de sangre did collect and deliver more blood to the active fronts of the fighting in 1936–37 than any other organization. Similarly, despite popular myth, he did not pioneer battlefield surgery or MASH units; mobile surgical teams had been operating close to the action at least since the American Civil War. What he did do was put the concept to work in Jin-Cha-Ji and thus save many lives that would otherwise have been lost.

Bethune's fame is largely the result of one historical event – the ultimate victory of the Chinese communists over the Guodmindang in the Chinese civil war. Had that not occurred, his life would be a footnote, not a chapter in the record of his times. And his reputation has continued to be shaped by politics. The decision of the Trudeau government to grant recognition to him through the establishment of the Bethune Memorial House was an act of opportunism aimed at furthering relations with China. On the other hand, anti-communist critics can argue that during the Cultural Revolution Mao Zedong used Bethune's memory to further his own political agenda.

But it remains true that there was a real basis for Mao's myth-making. During the seventeen months after he arrived in Jin-Cha-Ji, Bethune characteristically made himself a pain in the neck to the Chinese medical authorities. His demands irritated but ultimately heartened and inspired those with whom he worked. He won the admiration of ordinary people by sleeping in their homes, accepting their meagre rations, and suffering hardships alongside them. In the military conflict with the Japanese he and his mobile surgical unit saved many lives, and the belief that Bethune was there to treat the wounded inspired the ranks of the Eighth Route Army. But magnificent as his battlefield achievements were, they ultimately mattered less than his teaching and his personal example of sacrifice. He performed near miracles by teaching peasant boys skills that made them effective medical workers in guerrilla warfare. What most impressed the Chinese, however, was his insistence that by learning the skills he taught, they would be able to carry on without him and pass on their knowledge to others. Although his irascibility hindered him at the beginning of his mission, he learned to adjust to the conditions in which he had to work, and in the end his fierce demands served the cause. General Nie Rongzhen, who knew Bethune's temper well, said of him: "Yes, he was impatient and may have offended some. But during our war this may have had some value. China was then backward ... He was impatient with some who were slow and inefficient." So despite the difficulty of the task he had set himself, Bethune had his reward, for in the eyes of the Chinese he at last saw himself reflected as the hero he had always yearned to be. That regard has stood the test of time: in 2009 Bethune was named one of the ten foreigners who had contributed most to the development of modern China.[26] Each year many thousands of Chinese make the pilgrimage to Gravenhurst to visit the place of his birth.[27]

Bethune has now been dead for more than seventy years, but he still matters because the things he cared about so deeply – social justice and humanitarianism – still matter. For long a "prophet without honour" at home, he was often frustrated by the society of his time and out of step with it. Yet he remained quintessentially Canadian: his family roots, of which he was so proud, struck deep in the history of this country, and he was profoundly shaped by his love of the north woods and the rugged outdoor life he led as a young man. What, then, would this unlikely combination of black sheep and white knight think about his legacy and the rollercoaster ride of his name in Canada from obloquy to veneration? Perhaps, with amusement but also with great pride, he would simply say, "Oh my, oh my, oh my!"

Notes on Sources

The most extensive repository of documentation concerning Norman Bethune is in Library and Archives Canada (LAC). Among its holdings are the Ted Allan fonds R2931-0-4-E, which are the prime source of Bethune's writings. In the early 1940s when Allan was beginning to gather material on Bethune's life, Bethune's former wife, Frances Coleman, allowed him to copy some letters that Bethune had written to her. These are in the fonds. While Allan was in the process of contacting former medical colleagues, friends, and political comrades of Bethune, he also received a trove of documents from the Communist Party of Canada, of which he was then a member. Acting on what they believed to have been the wishes of Bethune, the Communist Party of China sent his papers to their Canadian counterpart; these consisted of copies of most of the letters and reports that he had written in China. These copies were turned over to Allan and are also in his fonds in Library and Archives Canada.

In his later years Allan decided to turn over his personal papers, including his Bethune-related material, to Library and Archives Canada (at that time the National Archives of Canada). Access to Bethune's writings in the Allan fonds is currently open, but restrictions apply to some of Allan's research material on Bethune.

Other Library and Archives Canada fonds containing important information about Bethune include the Norman Bethune fonds R5988-0-6-E, the Hazen Edward Sise fonds R4915-0-7-E, the Marian Scott fonds R2437-0-2-E, and the Frontier College fonds, R3584-0-0-E.

The National Film Board of Canada also has a collection of Bethune-related materials. In the early 1960s when Donald Brittain was gathering data for his National Film Board of Canada documentary *Bethune*, Allan gave him copies of many of Bethune's letters and documents written in China and also his letters to Frances Coleman. These, along with other documents and interviews, are to be found in the National Film Board research file for the film.

There are two other repositories of Bethune's writings in China. Bethune made copies of his personal letters on onionskin paper and sent them to various individuals in Canada and the United States. He also sent copies of reports of his work to Tim Buck of the Communist Party of Canada and to Earl Browder of the Communist Party of the United States. Several letters and reports are in the

Philip J. Jaffe Papers in the Manuscripts, Archives and Rare Book Library of Emory University, Atlanta (Jaffe). There are, in addition, letters and reports from Bethune in the China Aid Council files in the Indusco Incorporated Collection in the Rare Books and Manuscript Library of Columbia University, New York City (Indusco). The Emory and Columbia collections contain copies of letters and reports also in the Allan fonds, as well as letters written by Bethune that are not found elsewhere.

Next to the LAC collection, the largest repositories of documentation and memorabilia related to Bethune are the Osler Library of the History of Medicine Archives at McGill University (OLHMA) and the Bethune Memorial House in Gravenhurst, Ontario (BMH). Another source is the Roderick Stewart Collection of Bethune, MS COLL 34, in the Thomas Fisher Rare Book Library at the University of Toronto. All of these contain some original documents as well as copies of material found in the sources referred to above.

In addition, the authors have a collection of material obtained during their research gathered during the last decade.

Notes

CHAPTER ONE

1 Bethune, letter to Marian Scott, 8 October 1935, MSF, vol. 14, file 20.
2 Béthune is the name of a large town not far from the city of Lille, in the area
  now known as the Pas de Calais. Farther south the Rivière Béthune flows into
  the English Channel near Dieppe in Normandy. For more than a thousand
  years, "Norman" remained a common given name among the Bethunes.
  Among other variants of the surname are Beaton and Beeton.
3 The heraldic meaning of "debonnaire" is "gracious."

4 Reverend John Bethune (1751–1815) arrived in Montreal in 1786 where he formed the St Gabriel Street Presbyterian congregation. The following year, on receiving a grant of land for his loyalty to the British Crown, he went west to settle in Williamstown in what later became the Province of Ontario. There he built a church and attracted a congregation to which he ministered for the remainder of his life. He is considered one of the founders of the Presbyterian Church of Canada.

5 His great-uncle, John Bethune (1791–1872), was dean of the Montreal Anglican cathedral and the second principal of McGill University. Another great-uncle, Alexander Neil (1800–79), was the second Anglican bishop of Toronto.

6 Hilary Russell, "The Chinese Voyages of Angus Bethune," 31. Whether young Norman was ever told of his forebear's adventures in China is not known.

7 Given the prejudice of the day, it is unlikely that Norman's parents told him about his aboriginal heritage. Louisa Mackenzie was believed to be the daughter of Roderick Mackenzie, a trader based in the Athabaska region. He was a relative of the explorer Sir Alexander Mackenzie. The Bethune family referred to Louisa Mackenzie as "Miss Green Blanket;" her aboriginal name is not known.

8 Allan and Gordon, *The Scalpel, the Sword*, 10. Elizabeth Ann Bethune's father was a tool and die maker, and in the British census of 1881 Elizabeth was described as being a machinist by trade and resident in London. The family memories of Janet Cornell and Joan Lindley are not clear about where their grandparents met. A search of the Presbyterian archives in Toronto and Salvation Army records in California and Hawaii revealed no trace of a Hawaiian missionary named Elizabeth Ann Goodwin. However, Hilary Russell's research mentions that in later years the couple enjoyed listening to Hawaiian music on the gramophone and that they possessed some objects supposed to be of Hawaiian origin. See Bethune Memorial House, Janet Cornell to Hilary Russell, Summary of Interviews, BMH, 1975

9 Janet Cornell, daughter of Janet (Bethune) Stiles and niece of Norman Bethune, to Hilary Russell, Summary of Interviews, BMH 1975, 7.

10 Janet Cornell, and Ruth Neilly, also niece of Norman Bethune, to Roderick Stewart (hereafter RS), 1974.

11 It is worth noting that both Malcolm and Elizabeth Bethune were deeply influenced by the revivalist evangelism of Dwight L. Moody (1837–99), an American preacher who, with the gospel singer Ira D. Sankey (1840–1908), attracted a large following in the last quarter of the nineteenth century, not only in the United States but in England, Scotland, and Sweden. It is known that the Bethunes travelled to Toronto on at least one occasion to hear Moody preach at Massey Hall in 1889 (De Zwaan, *The Reverend Malcolm Bethune*, 59, quoting from the *Beaverton Express*, 9 November 1889). They may have heard him again during trips to England in the 1890s during the Moody evangelical crusade there. Moody's tenets were the ruin of mankind by sin, redemption by Christ, and regeneration by the Holy Ghost. An advocate of cross-cultural evangelism, he was a passionate supporter of Christian missions and encouraged members of his congregations to volunteer for service overseas, particularly in China. It is not known whether this might have led Malcolm Bethune to preach on similar themes, which might have provided his son with his first contact with the ideal of service in China.

12 De Zwaan, *The Reverend Malcolm Bethune*, 36, quoting from the *Orillia Packet* of 21 June 1889.

13 Ibid., 156, quoting from the *Orillia Daily Times*, 20 November 1890. During his first year as a preacher, Malcolm Bethune spoke on the evils of alcohol for twelve successive nights at Kennedy's Hall in Orillia.

14 Ibid., 38n93, quoting from the *Orillia Packet*, 27 September 1890.

15 Mrs T.C. McNiece to RS.

16 De Zwaan, *The Reverend Malcolm Bethune*, 37. The observation was made by Rev. W.T. Noble, the Anglican minister in Gravenhurst, after watching Malcolm Bethune deliver an animated sermon.

17 The records of the Town of Gravenhurst indicate that on 6 March 1890 Malcolm reported to Thomas Johnson, the town clerk, that the birth had taken place on 3 March. The *Orillia Packet* of 13 March 1890 reported that as the date, and while it is also the same in the Province of Ontario records, it is certain that Mr Johnson was in error. Bethune always celebrated his birthday on 4 March, and his father confirmed near the end of his life that the birth had taken place on that date (v document in Bethune Memorial House of 16 September 1931).

18 As an adult he usually signed his name H. Norman Bethune.

19 Accounts differ as to the colour of Bethune's eyes, even among those who knew them well. When he joined the army in 1914, his eye colour was recorded as blue, and Dr Aubrey Geddes, with whom he shared a flat for some time, referred to his "fine blue eye." However, Hazen Sise described his eyes as "flecked, greenish-hazel," and Harriet Hammond, a friend of Bethune, referred to them as grey.

20 Janet Cornell to RS.

21 De Zwaan, *The Reverend Malcolm Bethune*, 208, quoting from the *Orillia Packet*, 12 August 1892.

22 BMH, "Outline of Malcolm Bethune's Clerical Career," a summary prepared by Hilary Russell.

23 De Zwaan, *The Reverend Malcolm Bethune*, 212, quoting from the *Beaverton Express*, 3 December 1895.

24 Janet Cornell to RS.

25 De Zwaan, *The Reverend Malcolm Bethune*, 38, quoting from the *Beaverton Express*, 1 November 1895.

26 Janet Cornell to RS.

27 BMH, "Outline of Malcolm Bethune's Clerical Career."

28 Janet Cornell to RS.

29 Ibid.

30 *Aylmer Sun*, 27 July 1900.

31 Janet Cornell to RS.

32 Ibid.

33 Frances (Bethune) Coleman, Alvin and Dolly Gordon interviews, NFB (hereafter cited as NFB, Gordons). The interviews were conducted for Twentieth Century Fox as research for a proposed film on the life of Bethune. The NFB acquired a copy of their research during the preparation for their 1964 documentary film *Bethune*.

34 Janet Cornell to RS.

35 Ibid.
36 Ibid.
37 Bethune, letter to Frances Bethune, 5 January 1929, NFB research file for documentary film *Bethune*.
38 Bethune to Frances Geddes; Frances Geddes to RS, telephone interview, 2004.
39 Joan Lindley, niece of Norman Bethune, to RS, 2006.
40 Allan and Gordon, *The Scalpel, the Sword*, 13. Even when as an adult he made no attempt to conceal his doubts about religion, she was still placing tracts in his books.
41 Janet Cornell to RS.
42 The quotation is from a minister who knew Bethune in his youth. See Ryerson, "Comrade Beth," 158.
43 *Aylmer Express*, 11 July 1901.
44 Janet Cornell to RS.
45 Malcolm Goodwin Bethune interview, NFB, Gordons.
46 Allan and Gordon, *The Scalpel, the Sword*, 12.
47 Janet Cornell to RS.
48 Before the logging boom, the hamlet of Massey Station had been only a stop on a spur of the main line of the CPR. A coincidence that Malcolm likely recognized was that the original settlement of Massey was just a few kilometres north of Fort La Cloche, the Hudson Bay Company's outpost in the Lake Huron District. Malcolm's grandfather Angus had arrived in 1837 to operate the fort for two years as chief factor. Walford, a smaller settlement, was on the rail line thirteen kilometres to the west, and The Mine was ten kilometres to the north.
49 Gutsch, Chisholm, and Floren, *The North Channel and St. Mary's River*, 133–4.
50 Malcolm Goodwin Bethune interview, NFB, Gordons.
51 Margaret Thompson, a schoolmate of Bethune, told Hilary Russell that her cousin let Bethune stay at his home on weekends (BMH, Summary of Interviews, 1975, 222).
52 *Sault Star*, 14 July 1904. A total of 146 had written the examinations. According to the Report of the Board of Examiners to the High School-Collegiate Institute or High School Entrance Examination, 1904, OA, RG2-133, box 4, MS7335, his average was 60 per cent. His highest grade, 76 per cent, was in Writing and Composition. His only failure was History, in which he received 42 per cent. There was no science course.
53 Owen Sound Collegiate and Vocational Institute files, Owen Sound, Ontario.
54 Malcolm Goodwin Bethune, NFB, Gordons.
55 *Sault Star*, 23 February 1905. The elders could not have prevented Malcolm from submitting an application, but their decision to create a competition was in effect a recognition of their dissatisfaction with him.
56 The announcement of his final sermon appeared in the 23 March 1905 edition of the *Sault Star*.
57 The *Owen Sound Sun*, 8 September 1905, reported that he had been given an additional appointment as pastor to Daywood, another rural congregation, which would take effect at the beginning of October.
58 Ibid., 24 April 1905
59 Janet had graduated in Sault Ste Marie.

60 On occasion, when he was in a distant corner of Sydenham Township and was unable to return home at night, Malcolm accepted the offer of an overnight stay and breakfast in the home of a considerate member of his congregation. Once, when he was reluctant to make the long trip into town, his request to be allowed to stay the night was refused. An indignant Malcolm rode his horse home in the dark, and the following Sunday his sermon was entitled "Christian hospitality."

61 The painter Tom Thomson, a member of the Group of Seven, also attended Owen Sound Collegiate, as did the poet William Wilfred Campbell. It is believed that Campbell wrote the following lines about Owen Sound or another nearby bay: "Along the line of smoky hills / The crimson forest stands / And all day long the blue jay calls / Throughout the autumn lands."

62 J.E.C. Smith, a teacher at OSCVI, to RS. Two other prominent Canadians attended the same school during these years. One was Agnes Macphail, who later became the first woman elected to the Legislative Assembly of Ontario in 1921, and still later to the House of Commons. One school year behind Bethune, she too entered in September 1905. The other was W.A. "Billy" Bishop, Canada's most celebrated hero during World War I. Bishop, who was four years younger than Bethune, entered OSCI the year after Bethune's graduation (J.E.C. Smith, ed., *Owen Sound Collegiate and Vocational Institute 125th Anniversary Auditorium, 1981*).

63 BMH, Summaries of Interviews, 1975. The son of one of the members of Malcolm's rural congregation, Ernest S. MacGregor, who boarded with the Bethunes through the 1905–06 school year, saw no evidence of acrimony between father and son. Another witness, a close friend of Janet named Phoebe Ireland who was often in the Bethune home in Owen Sound, was also unaware of any family discord.

64 Janet (Bethune) Stiles interview, NFB, Gordons.

65 University of Toronto Archives, Faculty of Arts, A1989-0011/007. All data regarding Bethune's grades in the Faculty of Arts are from this transcript.

66 Janet Cornell to RS.

67 Ibid.

68 Jean Ewen to RS. After Bethune's death, Ewen, who accompanied Bethune to China, visited Elizabeth Bethune in her retirement home in Toronto. During that visit she used these words to describe her late son.

CHAPTER TWO

1 Janet Cornell to RS. At various times, according to Janet Stiles and Janet Cornell, he worked on boats on Lake Huron and also Lake Ontario, the former likely shortly after graduation from high school, and the latter when he was at university.

2 Two railways were under construction in the Algoma District at the time, the Algoma Central Railway running north from Sault St Marie, and the Manitoulin and North Shore Railway, which ran from Sudbury to Little Current.

3 Janet Cornell to RS.

4 Ibid.

5 The information on Bethune's six months at Edgeley Public School was provided by Elwood Robb, one of Bethune's pupils, in an interview with RS in 1975.

6 Janet Cornell to RS.

7 University of Toronto Archives, A1989-0011/007.

8 Presbytery of Owen Sound Minutes, Victoria College, University of Toronto.

9 The amount was likely about $6,000 (Hilary Russell, "The Bethune Family Finances," BMH).

10 Benjamin Spock, later a famous children's doctor, was another labourer-teacher assigned at the same time by the Reading Camp Association to the Whitefish area, where he worked as a railway track worker. It is not known whether he and Bethune ever encountered each other.

11 Bethune, letter to Frances McMechan, 12 November 1911, LAC, Frontier College fonds, R3584-0-0-E, vol. 6.

12 Ibid.

13 Ibid.

14 H.N. Bethune, letter to A. Fitzpatrick, 31 December 1911, ibid.

15 Janet Cornell to RS.

16 Bethune, letter to A. Fitzpatrick, 4 July 1912, LAC, Frontier College fonds, R3584-0-0-E, vol. 6.

17 Janet Cornell to RS. Because no byline appeared on any articles in microfilm files of *The Telegram* in 1912, and no employee records of the paper have survived, it is impossible to document what he wrote or how long he was employed by the newspaper.

18 Bethune, letter to A. Fitzpatrick, 16 July 1912, LAC Frontier College fonds, R3584-0-0-E, vol. 6.

19 A. Fitzpatrick to Bethune, 20 July 1912, ibid.

20 University of Toronto Archives, A 1973-0026/028(49). All data related to Bethune's Faculty of Medicine record are from this source.

21 Malcolm Goodwin Bethune interview, NFB, Gordons.

22 Miller, *Our Glory and Our Grief*, 16.

23 There is no way to authenticate this allegation. His military service file reveals that his pay began on 24 August (LAC, RG150 accession 1992-93/166, box 705-14). All subsequent data related to his army service are from this source.

24 Ibid. The attestation paper reveals that Bethune already had some military experience, having joined the 31st Regiment of the Grey-Simcoe Militia during his time in Owen Sound.

25 Nicholson *Seventy Years of Service*, 70

26 Dr E.H. Archibald, letter to Dr Gabriel Nadeau, 4 April 1941, Bibliothèque et archives nationales de Québec, Fonds Gabriel Nadeau, MSS177.

27 The German general Max von Fabeck (1854–1916) had predicted before the attack that the Canadians would be "trash, feeble adversaries who [will] surrender in great numbers if attacked in vigour" (Groom, *A Storm in Flanders*, 98).

28 This was a residence for British and imperial non-commissioned servicemen on leave.

29 *President's Report, University of Toronto, for the Year Ending June 30, 1916*, 16, University of Toronto Archives.

30 Dr Charles S. MacDougall to RS, 1970.

31 Ibid.

32 Ibid.

33 Dr William P. Tew to RS, 1970.

34 Janet Stiles interview, NFB, Gordons.

35 One of these classmates was Frederick Banting, later to become one of the co-discoverers of insulin.

36 *Torontensis*, 1917, University of Toronto Archives.

37 Janet Cornell to RS.

38 *Stratford Daily Beacon* 24 April 1917.

39 All data regarding Bethune's experience in the Royal Navy are from the Admiralty Library, Naval Historical Branch, HM Naval Base, Portsmouth, England.

40 Ibid., *Medical Officers' Journal*, HMS *Pegasus*.

41 Bethune, letter to Edward Kupka, 8 November 1926, RSF, 637/1/91.

CHAPTER THREE

1 The current name of the hospital is the Great Ormond Street Hospital for Children.

2 Dr Graham Ross, NFB interview.

3 Mary Larratt Smith, "A Prologue to Norman," copy of original manuscript given to authors by Diana Dodd, daughter of Mary Larratt Smith, 62. The Paterson sisters were the daughters of Bethune's aunt Louisa Bethune, who had married in England. The girls' darkly handsome looks were, according to family gossip, inherited from Louisa Mackenzie, "Miss Green Blanket."

4 Mary Larratt Smith, "Prologue to Norman," 64.

5 His wife later noted his fondness for perfumes, saying that he would sometimes spray himself with them (Frances [Bethune] Coleman, NFB, Gordons).

6 Allan and Gordon, *The Scalpel, the Sword*, 17.

7 Bethune, letter to Marian Scott, 21 November 1935, MSF, vol. 14, file 21.

8 George Holt, a friend of Bethune, to RS, taped interview, RSF 637/2/4.

9 Mary Larratt Smith recalled Bethune's describing to his female relatives how he could deliver a baby using no more equipment than clean newspaper, string, and scissors. Fascinated by her cousin but embarrassed by the topic, she edged away ("Prologue to Norman," 64).

10 Frances (Bethune) Coleman, NFB, Gordons.

11 Dr T. Twistington-Higgins, letter to John Kemeny, NFB research file for the documentary film *Bethune*.

12 Graham Ross, NFB interview.

13 Ibid.

14 Ibid.

15 Ruth Patton, letter to John Kemeny, n.d., NFB research file for documentary film *Bethune*.

16 Ibid.

17 Ellen Stafford, Stratford, ON, to RS. Years after the incident. Bethune's companion of that evening had related it to Ms Stafford.

18 S.W. Rust, a patient of Bethune, to RS.

19 *Stratford Daily Beacon*, 25 November 1919.

20 Dr J.G. McDermott, a resident of Ingersoll, to RS.

21 Mary Sonnenberg to RS.

22 Bonnie Mott to RS.

23 Ibid. Lillian Williams, daughter-in-law of Dr Ralph Williams, related this to Bonnie Mott. From China, Bethune sent his grandfather a sword fashioned of Chinese coins and a small ashtray in the shape of a Buddha (Robin Williams, grandson of Ralph Williams, to RS).

24 The Canadian Air Force was created in February 1920 (Douglas, *Creation of a National Air Force*, 49).

25 In the Admiralty's summary report of Bethune's service aboard HMS *Pegasus*, the concluding notation stated that he had "taken great interest in the general welfare of officers and men also in the study of medical conditions as they affect the R.A.F." C.J. Crocker, the commanding officer who had replaced Phipps, wrote the report.

26 Documentation is sparse on the early history of what became the RCAF. The date of Bethune's enlistment was supplied by S.F. Wise, Directorate of History, Canadian Department of National Defence, Ottawa, in 1971. The admiralty's summary report of Bethune's service includes a notation that he held the rank of captain at Camp Borden.

27 Douglas, *Creation of a National Air Force*, 50.

28 Ibid., 52.

29 Ibid. The admiralty's notation that Bethune held the rank of captain in the CAF at Camp Borden seems to be incorrect.

30 Bethune, postcard to Elizabeth Ann Bethune, undated, NFB research file for documentary film *Bethune*.

31 S.F. Wise to RS. Detailed records were not kept in the first few months of the existence of the RCAF, and there is therefore no record of a discharge subsequently granted to Bethune.

32 Frances (Bethune) Coleman, NFB, Gordons.

33 Frances (Bethune) Coleman, letter to Ted Allan, 29 December 1942, OLHMA, Bethune Collection, P156, accession 443B, folder 5.

34 Fritz Brandtner, NFB, Gordons.

35 Frederick Campbell Penney, brother of Frances, to RS, RSF, 637/2/5.

36 Ibid.

37 Ibid.

38 One day when she was in her early twenties, she invited a friend she had known from schooldays into her room. Carefully closing the door, she brought out a large paper bag and spilled the contents on her bed. They were invoices from her many charge accounts. On the verge of tears, she waved her hand at the paper mound and wailed, "I just don't know where I shall find the money to pay for all these" (T.L. McColl to RS, taped interview, RSF, 637/2/3).

39 Frances (Bethune) Coleman to Ted Allan, 1942 interview, Allan's transcript of his notes, 7 November 1976, OLHMA, Bethune Collection, accession 443B, folder 5.

40 Frederick Campbell Penney to RS, taped interview, RSF, 637/2/5. One of Frances's cousins who met Bethune at this time found him "very amusing, but not the kind of man one marries" (Frances [Bethune] Coleman, letter to Ted Allen, 29 December 1942, OLHMA, Bethune Collection, accession 443B folder 5).

41 Frances (Bethune) Coleman, letter to Ted Allen, 29 December 1942.

42 Anne Wheeldon, Hammersmith and Fulham Archives, London, England, letter to RS, 19 December 2002.

43 Isabelle Rosalind Humphreys-Owen (1884–1965) was the great-granddaughter of David Sassoon (1792–1864), a prosperous Jewish merchant of Baghdad. Sassoon remarried after the death of his first wife and thus founded a dynasty with two branches that flourished in nineteenth and twentieth century England. Humphreys-Owen's brother Sir Victor Sassoon (1881–1961) was a tycoon who managed the extensive family business holdings in India and China. Philip Sassoon (1888–1939), MP and secretary of British Prime Minister David Lloyd George during World War I, and his sister Sybil (1894–1989), the wife of the Marquess of Cholmondesley, both of whom became well-known figures in the European art world during the early decades of the twentieth century, were Humphreys-Owen's first cousins. A contemporary who was a member of the second branch of the family was Siegfried Sassoon (1886–1967), who served in the British Army in France in World War I; his anti-war poetry gained him considerable fame. The mother of Isabelle Humphreys-Owen was Leontine Levy, whose portrait by Bassano hangs in the National Portrait Gallery in London.

44 In the search for her husband Humphreys-Owen had the Serpentine, an eleven-hectare recreational lake in London's Hyde Park, dragged for his body.

45 She graduated in 1926 and went on to a distinguished medical career in London and later in Hampshire.

46 According to Dr D.W. Crombie, a fellow Canadian who in 1923 lived in the Duchess of Connaught hostel at the same time as Bethune, he "went to Portugal and returned with a large packing case full of small tiles, oil paintings, and various other things which he sold at considerable profit in London (D.W. Crombie, letter to Ted Allan, 30 May 1942, LAC, R2931-0-4-E, vol. 24, 38).

47 Frances (Bethune) Coleman to Ted Allan, 1942 interview. Bethune's ex-wife told Allan that Bethune lived with Humphreys-Owen in London; she told the Gordons that the wealthy woman was Bethune's mistress (NFB, Gordons).

48 Lothian Health Services Archive GB239 LHB1/16/60. During this time he lived at Ramsey Lodge on Ramsey Garden (Stephen Kerr, Royal College of Surgeons Library, Edinburgh, letter to RS, 18 December 2002). This was where his Aunt Margaret Alexander had been born in 1868 and his paternal grandmother Janet Anne died of tuberculosis in 1872.

49 The examination period was 9–13 January. He became a fellow of the Royal College of Surgeons (Edinburgh) on 19 May 1922 (Stephen Kerr, Royal College of Surgeons Library, Edinburgh, letter to RS, 18 December 2002).

50 Kevin Brown, Trust Archivist, St Mary's Hospital, London to RS, 11 April 2003. According to Bethune, in a curriculum vitae that he submitted to Dean McCraken of the Detroit College of Medicine in January 1925 (box 18, folder "Norman Bethune," Detroit College of Medicine Office of the Dean 1916–1946, University Archives, Wayne State University, Detroit), he also spent 420 hours in a course in anatomical dissection with Professor Yates of Middlesex Hospital. Libbie Adams, Archivist, UCL Hospitals, NHS Trust, in a letter to RS of 1 January 2003, verifies that there was a Thomas Yeates in the Middlesex Hospital in 1922.

51 B.M. Garton, Royal Free Hospital, Liverpool Road Branch, to RS, 11 May 1972; RSF, 637/1/54. Victoria North, Archivist, Royal Free Hampstead NHS Trust, letter to RS, 7 July 2003.

52 James Sturgis to RS, letter of 9 May 2002. Opened officially on 31 March 1920, its construction was financed by donations of Canadian women to the wife of the Duke of Connaught when he was governor-general of Canada (1911–16). Upon her death her daughter directed that the funds be used to provide quarters for students and other Canadians who required medium-term lodging.

53 Frances (Bethune) Coleman, 1942 interview with Ted Allan. She referred to her workplace as "the Settlement," but research has failed to discover which institution it was. It was not the famous Toynbee House, often referred to as the Settlement House, because female workers were not employed there at that time.

54 Frances (Bethune) Coleman, letter to Ted Allan, 29 December 1942.

55 Frederick Campbell Penney to RS, taped interview, RSF, 637/2/5.

56 Frances (Bethune) Coleman, 1942 interview with Ted Allan.

57 Frances (Bethune) Coleman interview, NFB, Gordons.

58 Frances (Bethune) Coleman, letter to Ted Allan, 29 December 1942.

59 Ibid.

60 Ibid. The ring was of garnets surrounding hair under glass; the name Bethune was engraved inside, with a date in the 1700s. Frances said Isabelle had found it in a junk shop in Barcelona and given it to Bethune. How Fraces made this discovery is not clear, though it seems likely that Bethune must have confessed the truth.

61 Mrs Edward Fitzpatrick, wife of a nephew of Isabelle Humphreys-Owen, to RS, telephone interview, 13 February 2003. No trace was ever found of Arthur Erskine Owen Humphreys-Owen.

62 Frances (Bethune) Coleman, 1942 interview with Ted Allan.

63 The legacy was from her uncle, F.G. Penney (Ian M. Penney, letter to the Superintendent, BMH, 25 April 1993). As far as is known, Frances Penny received no money from her immediate family when she married, which seems unusual given their wealth and social position and likely indicates family disapproval of her match with Bethune. There is no information to indicate whether Norman and Frances ever visited the Penneys in Edinburgh after their marriage.

64 Frances (Bethune) Coleman, letter to Ted Allan, 29 December 1942.

65 Ibid.

66 Ibid.

67 Ibid.

68 Ibid.

69 Ibid.

70 In the curriculum vitae he sent to Dean MacCraken, Bethune claimed to have worked with a Professor Hartman in Paris, but he does not indicate the length of time (Bethune, letter to Dean MacCraken, 26 January 1925, Wayne State University, Detroit, MI, University Archives, Detroit College of Medicine, Office of the Dean, 1916–1946, box 18, folder "Norman Bethune").

71 Frances (Bethune) Coleman, letter to Allan, 29 December 1942.

72 Bethune, letter to Dean MacCraken, 26 January 1925. Bethune told MacCraken that he had spent six months in Vienna doing postgraduate work in cys-

toscopy, gynaecology, and general operative surgery. Numerous attempts to document his Viennese training have failed.

73 Frances (Bethune) Coleman, 1942 interview with Ted Allan. She told Allan that the sum was 3,500, but he could not remember whether the denomination was pounds sterling or dollars. At that time the British pound was worth almost $5 Canadian. Even if the amount were in the much smaller denomination, it would be considerable. Oddly enough, for years afterward, apparently up to the beginning of the Second World War in 1939, Humphreys-Owen sent money and gifts to Bethune's mother in Canada (Janet Cornell to RS).

74 Louis Melzack to RS. Melzack learned this story from Frances Coleman when he purchased the statuette and some of Bethune's books after his death.

75 George Holt to RS, taped interview, RSF, 637/2/4.

CHAPTER FOUR

1 Frances (Bethune) Coleman, NFB, Gordons.

2 Bethune, letter to Frances (Bethune) Coleman, South Porcupine, Ontario, 7 July 1937, NFB research file for documentary film *Bethune*.

3 In the curriculum vitae that Bethune sent to Dean Walter MacCraken in January 1925, he stated that he had spent "two months at the Mayo Clinic with Dr Adson." There is no documentation of his having been there, but a Dr Alfred W. Adson, who later became the head of neurologic surgery, was at the Mayo Clinic in 1924 (Rochester Public Library, Rochester, Minnesota, to RS, 18 February 2006).

4 In a copy of Thomas Hardy's *Jude the Obscure* given by Bethune as a birthday gift to Frances, he wrote "To my darling Frances, Stratford, 11 September 1924."

5 *Detroit This Week*, 3 October 1926.

6 Michigan Historical Center, Lansing, Michigan, Medical Certificate #10116, State of Michigan, dated 5 December 1924. Bethune filed the certificate on 31 December 1924.

7 Frances (Bethune) Coleman, NFB, Gordons.

8 Frances (Bethune) Coleman, letter to Ted Allan, 29 December 1942.

9 Ibid. This quotation is sometimes ascribed to George Bernard Shaw, but most sources consulted attribute it to Oscar Wilde.

10 Bethune, letter to Frances Bethune, 27 March 1927, NFB research file for documentary film *Bethune*.

11 Frances Bethune (Coleman) to Ted Allan, 1942 interview.

12 Eugene Osius to RS.

13 Dr Edward Kupka, a student of Bethune, to RS. Kupka, the son of Czech immigrants to Detroit, said that he was eager to be accepted as Bethune's friend because Bethune was the first man of broader culture that he had met. The older man became "a god" to him, and, he said, "likely enjoyed the fact that I idolized him." Eager to ingratiate himself, Kupka sometimes carried Bethune's medical bag when he did his rounds; he also assisted in the delivery of a baby in a railway car (ibid., taped interview, RSF, 637/2/7).

14 Ibid.

15 Dr J.G. Christopher, a student of Bethune, letter to RS, 9 February 1972, RSF, 637/1/31.

16 Ralph C. Rueger, a student of Bethune, letter to RS, 2 March 1972, RSF, 637/1/31.

17 J.G. Christopher, letter to RS, 9 February 1972.

18 Ibid.

19 Dr H. Shapiro, a student of Bethune, to RS.

20 Dr Edward Kupka to RS, taped interview, RSF.

21 Dr Eugene Osius to RS.

22 Frances (Bethune) Coleman to Ted Allan, letter of 29 December 1942.

23 Ibid.

24 Dr Edward Kupka to RS, taped interview.

25 Ibid.

26 Ibid.

27 Eugene Osius to RS.

28 Bethune, letter to Frances Bethune, Faculty Club, Montreal, undated but probably 1928, attached note by Ted Allan, NFB research file for documentary film *Bethune*.

29 Frederick Campbell Penney to RS, taped interview.

30 France (Bethune) Coleman to Ted Allan, 1942 interview.

31 Ibid.

32 Kathleen McColl to RS, taped interview. Mrs McColl did not give her maiden surname.

33 Bethune, letter to Frances Bethune, Detroit, 20 October 1925, NFB research file for documentary film *Bethune*.

34 Frederick Campbell Penney to RS, taped interview. Meanwhile, missing Frances during her prolonged absence did not prevent Bethune from straying. On one occasion he turned up at a dance held by the medical students. He was a good dancer, although he told Kupka he didn't like dancing because "it was only a faint reflection of the real thing, sexual intercourse." Aggressively on the make, he swept Kupka's date onto the dance floor and did his best to seduce her (Edward Kupka to RS, taped interview).

35 Norah Hume Wright to RS.

36 J. Burns Amberson to RS

37 Frances (Bethune) Coleman, letter to Ted Allan, 29 December 1942.

38 Mary Saghi, a nurse at Calydor, to RS.

39 Bethune, letter to Frances (Bethune) Coleman, Calydor, 1 October 1926, NFB research file for documentary film *Bethune*.

40 Ibid.

41 Bethune, letter to Frances, Calydor, undated, October 1926, NFB research file for documentary film Bethune.

42 Bethune, letter to Edward Kupka, Calydor, 8 November 1926, RSF, 637/1/91.

43 The Trudeau Sanatorium was the creation of Edward Livingston Trudeau (1848–1915), a New York City physician who contracted pulmonary tuberculosis at the age of twenty-five. Acting on medical advice, he went to the Adirondack Mountains in upstate New York, where after a brief period of complete rest in the healthy air of the region, he found that his condition had improved dramatically. Given a new lease on life, he began a medical practice in the village of Saranac Lake, and several years later in 1884 supervised the construction of the first one room-cottage, the "Little Red," which became the

foundation of the Adirondack Cottage Sanatorium, later known as the Trudeau Sanatorium.

44 "The Trudeau Sanatorium," Saranac Lake: Trudeau Institute.

45 Mrs W. Steenken, a student nurse at Trudeau, to RS.

46 Dr John Barnwell, NFB interview. Barnwell recounted how Bethune had borrowed a gun from him and later returned it wrapped in a blood-stained towel. He claimed to have pistol-whipped a man who had offended "a member of his family" and knocked his teeth out. Bethune later repeated a version of the same story to Louis Huot, this time claiming that Frances had worked for the man as a housekeeper and governess and that he had mistreated her. In this version, after pistol-whipping the man, who admitted he deserved it, Bethune had tended his wounds and smuggled him out of the hotel where they had met (Louis Huot to RS, taped interview, RSF, 637/2/6).

47 Dr John Barnwell, NFB interview.

48 Bethune, letter to Frances Bethune, Calydor, undated, October 1926, NFB research file for documentary film *Bethune*. Details of benefits received by Bethune were supplied by J.B. Smith, Equitable Life Assurance Society, to RS, letter of 22 May 1972, RSF, 637/1/128.

49 In a letter to Frances, Bethune mentions not being worried any longer by her dependence on him (27 March 1927, NFB research file for documentary film *Bethune*). Frances mentioned her visit to Trudeau to the Gordons (interview, NFB, Gordons). Dr Henry Leach, a cottage-mate of Bethune, described his treatment of Frances during her visit as "cruel" (interview, NFB, Gordons).

50 Bethune, letter to Frances Bethune, Detroit, 27 March 1927, NFB research file for documentary film *Bethune*.

51 Frances (Bethune) Coleman, letter to Ted Allan, 29 December 1942.

52 Rose Kasner, sister of Dr Wruble, to Professor L.L. Hanawalt, research assistant to RS, 4 April 1972, RSF, 637/1/31.

53 Divorce file #146805, Wayne County, Michigan, RSF, 637/1/31.

54 Mrs W. Steenken to RS.

55 Dr John Barnwell, NFB interview.

56 Dan Boice to RS, taped interview, RSF, 637/2/1; Dr Louis Davidson, NFB, Gordons.

57 Dr Louis Davidson, NFB, Gordons. Davidson was later to become professor of surgery at Columbia University Medical School in New York, where he would meet Bethune when he was preparing for his trip to China. He said that after many hours of drinking beer, Bethune sometimes became fractious. Once when the bartender was slow to respond to his requests, he pushed his way behind the bar and announced that he was taking over. The bartender let him get away with it.

58 Except for some of its more farfetched aspects, few disagreed with Bethune's basic scheme for a "Trudeau University," including his suggestion that part of the staff could be drawn from among the patients. In fact several members of the medical staff were ex-patients. Bethune's professional background had earlier encouraged Dr Lawrason Brown, chairman of the Medical Board, to ask him to give a series of lectures on anatomy in the D. Ogden Mills nursing school that was part of the sanatorium. Thoroughly enjoying his informative and entertaining presentations, the nurses were disappointed to learn on the eve of the

final lecture that it had been cancelled. According to Mrs W. Steenken, Dr Brown was fearful of how the capricious Bethune might treat the subject of human reproduction and therefore announced that the lecture would not be offered.

59 Louise (Guadagni) Vézina to RS, taped interview, RSF 637/2/1.

60 Bethune, "The T.B.'s Progress."

61 Ibid.; Henning Sorensen to RS, taped interview, RSF, 637/2/6; Mieze Brandtner to RS.

62 Dr John Barnwell, NFB interview.

63 Dr Louis Davidson, NFB, Gordons.

64 Dr John Barnwell, NFB interview.

65 In "The T.B.'s Progress" Bethune had written: "Incidentally, this theory of pre-destination is probably a relic of my Scotch ancestors."

66 Bethune, letter to Frances Bethune, Montreal, 5 January 1929, NFB research file for documentary film *Bethune*.

67 Alexander, *The Surgery of Pulmonary Tuberculosis*.

68 Dr John Barnwell, NFB interview.

69 Frances replied that she would love to but it was better that she didn't (John Barnwell, NFB interview).

70 Dr Henry Leach, NFB interview.

71 Alfred Blalock (1889–1964) would later achieve fame for significant contributions in medical research; best known was the "blue-baby" operation.

72 Alfred Blalock, letter to John Kemeny, 7 May 1963, NFB research file for documentary film *Bethune*.

73 Chi Ke, "When the Specter of Death Beckons," 26, in OLHMA, Eugene Perry Link fonds, P121.

74 The vessel bears a remarkable likeness to one in a print that still hangs, as it did in 1926, in the foyer of the Charing Cross apartments.

75 When James McCue, a railway worker from Alabama, discovered that Bethune had chosen 1932 as the year of his probable death, he went into an acute decline. Learning of McCue's reaction, Bethune altered the date to 1940, and McCue swiftly recovered (John Barnwell, letter to Alfred Blalock, 1 June 1963, NFB research file for documentary film *Bethune*).

76 Frances (Bethune) Coleman, NFB, Gordons.

77 For the theme of the mural, he had drawn heavily on John Bunyan's seventeenth-century allegory *The Pilgrim's Progress*, an important source of his childhood religious and moral instruction. Determined to remove his burden of sin and thus escape eternal damnation in Hell, Christian, Bunyan's protagonist, undertakes a tortuous journey on which he is beset by many temptations and lethal pitfalls. Guided by his faith, he overcomes all barriers, enters the Celestial City and is granted eternal life. Bethune knew every obstacle and every fierce monster that Christian faced; all the Bethune children had had to read *The Pilgrim's Progress*, and many Sunday afternoon discussions focused on dangers that they would be likely to face as they matured.

There may have been an additional source of inspiration. In 1842, an American artist named Thomas Cole produced a series of four paintings entitled *Childhood, Youth, Manhood*, and *Old Age*. Known collectively as *The Voyage of Life*, they trace the journey of an individual in a boat through the River of

Life, guided by angels. Cole, who was also undoubtedly influenced by Bunyan, preached the same message: adherence to principles is rewarded by salvation. Widely reproduced in prints and in magazines, *The Voyage of Life* was familiar to most Christians in North America during Bethune's childhood, so it is possible that he had seen it.

78 Daniel Boice, a cottage-mate of Bethune, to RS.

CHAPTER FIVE

1 Dan Boice, a cottage-mate of Bethune, to RS.

2 Dr W. Steenken to RS. While he was receiving one of the first of these, he discovered a way to hasten the process, which he considered tiresomely long. By tinkering with the pressure monometer, he was able to speed up the intake of air. After a nurse discovered his meddling, Dr Warren ordered her to hold a towel over Bethune's eyes in future to prevent him from tampering with the monometer.

3 In the early 1930s the TB mortality rate was 81 per 100,000 in Quebec; in Canada overall it was 53 per 100,000 (address of F. Gurd to the Med Chi Society of Montreal, Med Chi Minutes, 1945, 122, OLHMA).

4 Dr Edward Archibald, letter to Dr Gabriel Nadeau, 27 December 1940, NFB research file for documentary film *Bethune*.

5 Dr David T. Smith to RS, taped interview, RSF, 637/2/4.

6 Ibid.

7 H.N. Bethune, D.T. Smith., and J.L. Wilson, "The Etiology of Spontaneous Pulmonary Disease in the Albino Rat," *Journal of Bacteriology* 20 (November 1930): 361–70. This was Bethune's first piece of medical writing, but before it was published he had already written four other articles, which came out in 1929.

8 Dr David T. Smith to RS, taped interview.

9 Dr Paul Richardson, a staff doctor at Ray Brook, to RS. On other occasions Bethune's heavy drinking proved useful. Throughout his stay at Ray Brook, he had to continue having refills of his pneumothorax, a process he came to dread. Dr Richardson offered to give the refills, but when he was poised to insert the needle containing the anaesthetic, Bethune became agitated. Richardson learned to wait until Bethune returned from a night of partying and would then persuade him to go to his office to receive his refill. In a relaxed state Bethune was less fearful, and Richardson was able to carry out the artificial pneumothorax process successfully.

10 Dr Charles Ryan to RS.

11 Dr John Barnwell, NFB interview.

12 Dr Charles Ryan to RS.

13 Edward William Archibald (1872–1945) was chairman of the Department of Surgery of the Faculty of Medicine at McGill University. Shortly before Bethune's arrival he established the Thoracic-Pulmonary Service at the Royal Victoria Hospital, where several months later he would be named chief of surgery.

14 Pelis, in "Edward Archibald's Notes on Blood Transfusion, 211–14, speculates that Archibald almost certainly influenced Bethune's later transfusion work. Pinkerton, in "Norman Bethune and Transfusion in the Spanish Civil War," 117–20, also raises this question.

15 The technique of adding sodium citrate to blood to prevent clotting was discovered in 1914–15 by several researchers acting independently of each other (Pelis, "Edward Archibald's Notes on Blood Transfusion," 211–12). Among the tiny handful of military doctors who experimented with blood transfusion during the war, it is interesting to note that two Canadians, Dr Archibald of the Royal Victoria and Dr Lawrence Bruce Robertson of the Hospital for Sick Children in Toronto, were the first to make a scientific analysis of the process and submit their findings to learned journals. Commissioned as a major in the Royal Canadian Army Medical Corps, Archibald had carried out transfusions using citrated blood in the No. 1 and No. 3 Casualty Clearing Hospitals during 1915 and 1916. He summarized the result of his work in "The Employment of Blood Transfusion in War Surgery and "A Note upon the Employment of Blood Transfusion in War Surgery." Dr L.B. Robertson described his findings in "The Transfusion of Whole Blood: A Suggestion for Its More Frequent Employment in War Surgery." Among other Canadian pioneers in the field of blood transfusion near the front were Dr Norman M. Guiou and Dr D.E. Robertson. Dr Oswald H. Robertson, an American medical researcher and army doctor in France during World War I, is regarded as the first person to create a cold-storage blood bank. In November 1917 he constructed an ice chest using two ammunition cases and used it to take twenty-two units of blood to a casualty clearing station, where it was used to resuscitate Canadian soldiers. In 1925 in Moscow, Alexander Bogdanov founded the first academic institution specializing in the science of blood transfusion, and in the 1930s the Soviet Union set up a national system for collecting and storing blood in blood banks. The first American blood bank was established in 1937 at Cook's County Hospital in Chicago. The first Canadian blood bank based on volunteer donations was established by James Potter in Ottawa in 1938 (Kapp, "Charles H. Best," 27–46).

16 Delarue, *Thoracic Surgery in Canada*, 553.

17 Bethune, letter to Frances Bethune, probably January 1929, NFB research file for documentary film *Bethune*.

18 Dr Ronald Christie to RS, taped interview, RSF, 637/2/1.

19 *The Royal Victoria Hospital of Montreal, Thirty-Sixth Annual Report for the Year Ended 31 December 1929*, 95.

20 N.D. Johnston, treasurer, McGill University to E.H. Bensley, Department of the History of Medicine, 28 October 1971, RSF, 637/1/43.

21 Bethune, letter to Frances Bethune, Faculty Club, Montreal, undated, attached note by Ted Allan, NFB research file for documentary film *Bethune*.

22 Bethune, letter to Frances Bethune, Montreal, 5 January 1929, NFB research file for documentary film *Bethune*.

23 Bethune, letter to Frances Bethune, likely early 1929, ibid.

24 Dr Arthur Vineberg to RS, taped interview, RSF, 637/2/3.

25 Bethune, letter to Frances Bethune, 1928, most likely late autumn, NFB research file for documentary film *Bethune*.

26 Bethune, letter to Ruth Patton, spring 1929, ibid.

27 Bethune, letter to John Alexander, 22 June 1929, NFB research file for documentary film *Bethune*.

28 Dr Graham Ross, NFB interview.

29 Dr Aubrey Geddes, with whom Bethune shared an apartment in 1934, said Frances was charming (NFB interview). Dr Wendell MacLeod in conversations with Roderick Stewart professed to have admired her, but is nevertheless the source for the negative quote mentioned in the text (MacLeod, Park, and Ryerson, *Bethune, the Montreal Years*, 37).

30 Frances (Bethune) Coleman, interview with Ted Allan, 1942.

31 MacLeod, Park, and Ryerson, *Bethune, the Montreal Years*, 39.

32 Dr Edward Archibald, letter to Ted Allan, 24 April 1942, TAF, vol. 33, file 7.

33 Dr Ronald Christie to RS, taped interview.

34 Dr Arthur Vineberg to RS, taped interview.

35 On one occasion he persuaded a colleague to let him dissect a cadaver that his department had just purchased at some expense, promising to limit his investigations to the chest area. When the colleague returned, he was dismayed to find that Bethune had become so immersed in what he was doing that he had dissected much of the body, leaving it useless for additional research (Beatrice Simon to RS).

36 Diagnosis and Surgical Treatment of Pulmonary and Pleural Disease was a course offered in the 1931–32 and 1932–33 academic years in the McGill University Faculty of Medicine.

37 Dr J.S. Luke to RS, taped interview, RSF, 637/2/3.

38 *The Royal Victoria Hospital of Montreal, Thirty-Sixth Annual Report for the Year Ended December 31, 1929*, 95, 99. Dr Archibald headed the list of surgical staff members who had published a number of papers, but Bethune came second.

39 Various surgeons at the Royal Victoria Hospital told Roderick Stewart that Archibald praised the use of pleural *poudrage* and that it was accepted by other surgeons.

40 Dr Thomas J. Quintin, student of Bethune, to RS, taped interview, RSF, 637/2/4.

41 Henry N. Pilling, letter to Ted Allan, 1 May 1942, TAF vol. 33, file 6.

42 Dr John Barnwell, NFB interview.

43 For various reasons, however, all but one of the numerous surgical instruments that bore his name eventually became obsolete. That he recognized the inevitability of this outcome was revealed in a sentence in "Some New Thoracic Surgical Instruments," his paper published in the *Canadian Medical Association Journal* of December 1936: "The whole backward path of surgery is littered, like the plains of the American desert, with the outworn and clumsy relics of technical advances."

44 Dr Wendell MacLeod, "Dr. Norman Bethune," 39; L.J. Wainer, "Dr. Norman Bethune Remembered," 1; OLHMA, Eugene P. Link fonds, P121, box 263.

45 Dr C.A. Birch, colleague of Bethune, to RS, taped interview, RSF, 637/2/5.

46 Dr T.J. Quintin, student of Bethune, to RS, taped interview.

47 *Montreal Gazette*, 11 April 1934, 15.

48 Bethune, letter to John Alexander, 22 June 1929, NFB research file for documentary film *Bethune*.

49 Bethune henceforth always referred to himself as first assistant to Archibald, but the latter, who subsequently took on other assistants, did not grant them hierarchical status. Bethune was merely the first of several to arrive.

50 This information was found in 1972 by RS in the National Archives of Canada, Department of Pensions and National Health, File #C-144-8-4. However, in 2003 he was informed that there is no record of it in LAC holdings.

51 Norah Hume Wright to RS.

52 Ibid.

53 Frederick Taylor, letter to RS, 12 October 1971, RSF, 637/1/74.

54 This incident was recounted by Fred Taylor to Dr David Mulder and reported by Mulder to RS in a telephone conversation.

55 When Bethune left Ray Brook, it appears that he had persuaded Coleman to leave Detroit and follow him to Montreal; there Coleman had found work with the Bell Telephone Company of Canada. For several weeks in the late spring of 1928 both rented rooms at the McGill Faculty Club before each found an apartment in the city (Grace Reynolds to RS).

56 Harold Beament to RS, taped interview, RSF, 637/2/4.

57 Dr T.J. Quintin, whose wife was a nurse at the Royal Victoria at the time, to RS, taped interview. Dr Arthur Vineberg was then dating a nurse from the hospital. At his request his girlfriend sometimes persuaded another nurse to be Bethune's date and the four would spend an evening together. On one occasion when she was unable to find a companion for Bethune, the three went out together. When they reached Vineberg's car in the hospital parking lot, Vineberg remembered he had left something in the hospital and went back to get it. When he returned a few minutes later, he found Bethune making sexual advances to his girlfriend (Dr Arthur Vineberg to RS, taped interview).

58 Hazen Sise, letter to George Mooney, 4 May 1948, HESF, vol. 15, file Bethune, Norman, George Mooney manuscript 1948.

59 Dorothy Catto, RN, to RS, taped interview, RSF, 637/2/2.

60 Eileen Flanagan, RN, to RS; S.H.D. (pseudonym for Hazen Sise), "Dr Norman Bethune – A Challenge to Mankind," *Canadian Tribune*, Saturday, 23 November 1940; NFB research files for documentary film *Bethune*.

61 H.J. Scott, former cardiothoracic surgeon at McGill University, personal communication to Dr Larry Stephenson; quoted in Stephenson, "Two Stormy Petrels," 70.

62 Dr Aubrey Geddes, NFB interview. Bethune's claim was inaccurate, as was his claim to be descended from the Duc de Sully.

63 Frances (Bethune) Coleman, NFB, Gordons.

64 Louis Huot to RS, taped interview.

65 Dr Eric Richardson, friend of Bethune, to RS; Henning Sorensen, unpublished ms., 163.

66 Dr Edward Kupka to RS, taped interview.

67 Bethune, letter to Frances Bethune, undated, probably autumn 1928, NFB research file for documentary film *Bethune*.

68 National Archives of Canada (now LAC), Department of Pensions and National Health, File # C-144-8-4. See note 50, this chapter.

69 Archibald later wrote in a letter to Ted Allan, 24 April 1942, "In the science of Thoracic Surgery Bethune when he joined my clinic was not well founded. He never did repair that lack properly, as he gave but little time to the study of pathology or of the physiology of the cardio-respiratory system" (NFB research file for documentary film *Bethune*).

70 Ibid. Archibald added, "But his mind was quick in picking up knowledge from our discussions and clinics, though he was never a 'student.' He read little, and mostly about the details of mechanical treatment, such as pneumothorax, and operations and instruments."

71 Dr Arthur Vineberg to RS, taped interview. In contrast to Bethune's style, Archibald's approach to surgery was methodical and cautious. This led to a colleague's quip that once Archibald made the opening incision in an operation, it was time for his assistants to take tea. During his probationary period Bethune frequently became impatient with what he regarded as Archibald's painfully slow movements. Once when he and Dr C.A. McIntosh were assisting, Archibald remained immobile for what seemed to be an inordinately long time. Finally Bethune whispered to Dr McIntosh, "I wonder what the old bugger's going to do next." Without turning his head, Archibald replied, "I wonder." On another occasion Bethune and others watched for two hours while Archibald performed a lobectomy. Afterwards Bethune told an intern that the operation could be done in three-quarters of an hour. A little more than a week later he booked the operating room for the same type of operation and, assisted by the same intern, completed the operation in less than an hour (Dr John V.V. Nichols, the intern who assisted Bethune, to RS).

72 Dr Edward Archibald, letter to Ted Allan, 24 April 1942, NFB research file for documentary film *Bethune*. In 1960, Dr Robert Janes, a classmate of Bethune and later chairman of the Department of Surgery at the University of Toronto, told a young colleague, Dr Irving B. Rosen, of an incident in which Bethune was performing a scalene node biopsy. In performing this relatively simple procedure, Bethune "had injured the subclavian artery … and was compelled to do a forequarter amputation." He then "had the temerity to describe it as an interesting case" (Rosen, "Dr. Norman Bethune as a Surgeon," 73).

73 Delarue, *Thoracic Surgery in Canada*, 36. Archibald later wrote, "In surgical judgment, as to whether the patient had sufficient resistance to stand the proposed operation, I found him really lacking. His mind was set on the mechanical possibility too much, and on the degree and character of the tuberculosis (or other infection) too little" (Rosen, "Dr. Norman Bethune as a Surgeon," 75).

74 Dr V.D. Schaffner, colleague of Bethune, to RS.

75 Entin, *Edward Archibald*, 139.

CHAPTER SIX

1 Curiously, in *The T.B.'s Progress* Bethune had depicted himself heading for Arizona for this purpose. He had also predicted that he would die there. Going to Arizona now may have been his way of defying the destiny he himself had predicted.

2 "Nelson tells me that you are coming on here with a whole caravan of Bethune's latest ingeniosities [*sic*] and I am keen to see them and to hear more about the iron intern, which Nelson speaks highly of. When you come, I wish you would stop with me at home. Will you?" (John Alexander, letter to Dr Norman Bethune, 4 September 1931, Ann Arbor, University of Michigan, Bentley Historical Library, box 1, correspondence "B," 1927–29).

3 Flinn had arrived in the southwest in 1898 in the hope of finding a cure for the pulmonary tuberculosis from which he was suffering, and just as Francis

Trudeau had found the mountain air of the Adirondacks revitalizing, Flinn regained his health in Arizona. Five years later he moved to Prescott and, like Trudeau, began operating a small sanatorium. By the 1920s, Pamsetgaaf was a renowned institution in the field of tubercular treatment.

4 "A Phrenicectomy Necklace," 319–21. Unfortunately, although the operation was a success, Adorée drank heavily, her condition worsened, and she died in October 1933. The decision to write the article resulted from an argument Bethune had had with a colleague in which he had insisted that most editors of medical journals would publish virtually anything without questioning its literary or scientific merits so long as it was written by someone prominent in his field. To prove his case, he bet the colleague $5 that he could find a publisher for an article he would write describing this operation (Sherman Atwell, a laboratory technician with whom Bethune made the wager, to RS). Bethune not only won the wager but took considerable delight several years later in celebrating his little jab against the establishment. Under the heading "Confessional Note," appended to a 1936 article describing some new surgical instruments he had designed, he wrote: "A phrenicectomy necklace described in the *Review of Tuberculosis* ... was abandoned as unnecessary. It was taken, as it was meant to be, as an amusing little trinket" ("Some New Thoracic Surgical Instruments, 656–62).

5 *Tucson Citizen*, 11 April 1932

6 Dr F.R. Harper, Thomas Davis Clinic, to RS.

7 Bethune, letter to Frances Bethune, Grand Canyon National Park, Arizona, 30 November 1931, NFB research file for the documentary film *Bethune*.

8 Ibid.

9 *Minutes of the Seventeenth Annual Session of the Medical and Surgical Association of the Southwest*, Phoenix, Arizona, 3–5 December 1931, National Library of Medicine, Baltimore, Maryland. Bethune's paper was "Some Procedures in Thoracic Surgery." It was published in January 1932.

10 Inez Fisher letter to Ted Allan, 4 June 1942, TAF, vol. 33, file 1.

11 Ibid.

12 Dr John Barnwell, NFB interview. It was published in the *Journal of Thoracic Surgery* 5 (February 1935). Bethune's 1935 Christmas card included a humorous cartoon of a "Filling Station," with a pneumothorax device in front and sign reading, "Can you take it?"

13 Laura Rawlings later wrote: "Dr. Bethune was a guest in our home at Christmas time nine years ago – and having known him very well during a short space of time it was inevitable that he should leave a definite mark upon us" (Laura Bassett Rawlings, letter to Dr Gabriel Nadeau, 5 January 1941, Bibliothèque et archives nationales de Québec, Fonds Gabriel Nadeau, MSS 177).

14 Bethune, letter to Frances Bethune, Mobile, Alabama, 31 December 1931, NFB research file for documentary film *Bethune*. Mrs Rawlings's first name was Laura, so Zarna must have been a nickname.

15 Dr Duane Carr to RS (Dr Carr, a thoracic surgeon, was a resident at the University of Michigan at the time); Clarinda Walker, RN, to RS.

16 In a letter to Archibald, Alexander wrote, "Norman Bethune is spending a month with Hudson in Detroit, watching and doing bronchoscopies and fol-

lowing around with me here" (26 January 1932, Bentley Historical Library, box 2, correspondence "A," 1932). Bethune spent the month of January commuting between Ann Arbor and Detroit.

17 Bethune, letter to John Barnwell, Detroit, 9 January 1931, NFB research file for documentary film *Bethune*.

18 Mrs F. Kerchofer, sister of Dr John Barnwell, to RS.

19 Stephenson, "Two Stormy Petrels," 63.

20 Despite the advice of his colleagues, the flamboyant O'Brien decided to carry out the operations himself. Encased in a body cast that allowed him to move only his head, toes, arms, and hands, he was placed face down on a stretcher that was elevated to a level parallel to the operating table. There, propped up on his left side in a position that allowed him to use his right hand, he performed the four operations, all of them phrenicectomies ("Miracle Man," *Detroit News*, 30 April 1932 ; "Dr. Edward J. O'Brien Dies: Noted Pioneer in TB Surgery," *Detroit Free Press*, 20 October 1959). Various people in the medical world regarded the event, which was widely reported in the press, as sensational and unnecessary (Stephenson, "Two Stormy Petrels," 64).

21 In his famous essay "An Alabama Student," which appeared in the *Johns Hopkins Hospital Bulletin* no. 58 in January 1896, Dr William Osler (1849–1919) had celebrated the professional commitment of Mrs Rawlings's paternal grandfather, Dr John Y. Bassett. During Rawlings's visit, Bethune took her to the Osler Library of the History of Medicine at McGill. Both signed the guest book. Laura Rawlings remained married to J. Mott Rawlings until his death in the 1960s. They had three children.

22 Dr Bruce Douglas, medical director, Herman Kiefer Hospital to RS, taped interview in the authors' possession.

23 Dr Cameron Haight, quoted by Dr Leslie E. Soper in a letter of 8 September 1971 to RS, RSF, 637/1/31. Dr Soper trained in anesthesiology at the University Hospital, University of Michigan, in the early 1960s under Dr Haight, who was then chief of thoracic surgery.

24 Dr Bruce Douglas to RS, taped interview in the authors' possession.

25 Sometimes, however, he confounded his critics by taking an extremely conservative position on a case. On one occasion at a staff conference where the status of patients was being reviewed, not only the surgeons but all of the medical doctors were in favour of surgical intervention in the case of a young boy who was suffering from advanced pulmonary tuberculosis. Bethune, to the surprise of the others, was the only one to oppose the consensus that a thoracoplasty should be performed. He made his argument on a humane, not a clinical basis. Given his condition, Bethune pointed out, the boy had very few years to live. To operate and remove a large number of ribs leaving him bent and misshapen would not be doing him a favour, for he would then suffer through his little remaining time as a grotesque cripple. He refused to operate (ibid.).

26 Ibid. In Walt, "The World's Best-Known Surgeon," 585, Bethune is said to have performed nineteen consecutive lobectomies using mass ligature with only one death. However, Dr Larry W. Stephenson, in an as yet unpublished manuscript, maintains that there is no reference for this claim and that those results would have been exceptional for any surgeon during that period. Stephenson wonders

whether the nineteen lobectormies Walt attributed to Bethune were conflated with the twenty-one lobectomies without a single death perfomed by Dr Pat O'Brien in 1933 ("Detroit Surgeons Then and Now," unpublished ms., chapter 4, appendix 1).

27 Clarinda Walker, RN, to RS, taped interview in the authors' possession. Walker had first met Bethune in Ann Arbor at the University Hospital when Dr Alexander had performed a phrenicectomy on Bethune several months earlier. In Detroit she assisted as nurse-anesthesiologist at the operation in which Bethune's patient died. John Barnwell also referred to this incident in a letter of 25 May 1963 to John Kemeny, NFB research file for the documentary film *Bethune*. Compared to other more complex forms of surgery, such as the thoracoplasty in which several ribs were removed, the phrenicectomy, in which a portion of the phrenic nerve was removed, was a less involved surgical procedure. According to records of several operations performed by Bethune at Kiefer Hospital, he was able to complete a phrenicectomy in less than twenty minutes.

28 Harold Beament to RS.

29 Bethune, letter to Frances Bethune, Detroit, 10 July 1932, NFB research file for documentary film *Bethune*.

30 Bethune, letter to John Barnwell, Montreal, 16 August 1932, ibid.

31 Louis Huot to RS, taped interview.

32 Norah Hume Wright and Dr Graham Ross to RS.

33 Between July 1928 and March 1931 Bethune received a monthly cheque of $125 from the Percy Cowans scholarship fund. He returned cheques that he had received for April and May and no further cheques were issued (N.D. Johnston, McGill University treasurer, to Dr E.H. Bensley, Department of the History of Medicine, 28 October 1971). No reason for his decision to return the cheques is provided in the files, RSF, 637/1/43.

34 He also had an appointment as consultant at Mount Sinai Sanatorium in the town of Ste Agathe, which he probably obtained in 1933. No records exist of his appointment or of his honorarium, but it was not likely substantial.

35 Louis Huot to RS, taped interview.

36 Eloesser, "In Memorium: Norman Bethune, 1890–1939," 461, quoted in Stephenson, "Two Stormy Petrels," 77.

37 Entin, *Edward Archibald*, 138.

38 At the annual convention of the organization in Ann Arbor, the motion to make Bethune a member was put forward by Dr Archibald and seconded by Dr John Alexander (Edward Archibald, letter to John Alexander, 2 February, Bentley Historical Library, box 2, correspondence "A," 1932). In this letter Archibald was replying to a letter from Alexander, who had agreed to second the motion Archibald was planning to make at the convention

39 Dr Arthur Vineberg to RS, taped interview. Vineberg also claimed that Bethune was not above trying out ideas as yet untested in the laboratory directly on patients.

40 Entin, *Edward Archibald*, 139

41 Edward Archibald, letter to Gabriel Nadeau, 27 December 1940, NFB research file for documentary film *Bethune*.

42 Dr C.A. McIntosh to RS.

43 MacLean and Entin, "Norman Bethune and Edward Archibald," 1749.

44 While negotiations continued, Bethune had learned from Barnwell that a sana-torium in South Bend, Indiana, was looking for a superintendent and had sent a letter of application for the position on 14 January. However, when he learned that it had been filled, he decided to come to terms with the religious authori-ties at Sacré Coeur.

45 Bethune, letter to John Barnwell, Montreal, 31 January 1933, NFB research file for documentary film *Bethune*.

46 Bethune, letter to Frances Bethune, Montreal, 12 April 1933, NFB research file for documentary film *Bethune*. Millar, Horne & Hanna was the name of the legal firm that had handled the divorce.

47 Frances (Bethune) Coleman to Ted Allan, interview of 1942.

48 Pierre Beaulieu, Bibliothèque et archives nationales de Quebec, to RS, 6 Janu-ary 2004.

49 A friend of Frances, who requested anonymity, to RS.

50 "Did you know we had a doll-child called Alice, she spent six months with her father and six months with her mother like all good children of divorces. Bethune burnt her up once when he set his room on fire here in Montreal … The pewter was all melted down too" (Frances [Bethune] Coleman, letter to Ted Allan, 29 December 1942).

51 Dr Georges Cousineau to RS.

52 Dr Wendell MacLeod, quoted in *McGill News Alumni Quarterly*, Spring/Sum-mer 1988, 13.

53 Dr Francis MacNaughton, quoted in Entin, *Edward Archibald*, 138.

54 Dr Ronald Christie to RS, taped interview.

55 MacLean and Entin, "Norman Bethune and Edward Archibald," 1749; Frances (Bethune) Coleman, letter to Ted Allan, 29 December 1942; A.A. MacLeod, NFB, Gordons.

56 Sidney Sarkin, a worker-leader of the Communist Party of Canada, quoted in Ryerson, "Comrade Beth," 150.

57 Cyclothemia, like other bipolar syndromes, tends to occur in families. In this context it is interesting to note the depressive illness that afflicted Bethune's father and the instability and alcohol abuse of his grandfather Norman. His great-grandfather Angus, though highly successful as a factor in the fur trade, was aggressive and overbearing, disliked by the men who worked under him, and criticized by his superiors. The governor of the Hudson's Bay Company once said that Angus was "a very poor creature, vain, self-sufficient and tri-fling" (entry by Hilary Russell in the *Canadian Dictionary of National Biog-raphy*, 85). Another possibility is narcissistic personality disorder. Among its symptoms are overweening self-esteem and a penchant for dramatic, emotional behaviour that are similar to the behaviour that characterized Bethune

58 Georges Cousineau to RS.

59 Louise (Guadagni) Vézina to RS, taped interview. Jacques Vézina, who had married Louise in 1929, was in New York City in 1933. Bethune had met the nurse through his colleague Arthur Vineberg at the beginning of the year.

60 Ibid.

61 Ibid. Like Bethune, Pitt was an adventurous, colourful individual who enjoyed risk-taking, and he and Bethune had engaged in friendly competitions before Bethune met Louise. On several occasions the previous winter they attached a

rope several metres long to the rear bumper of Bethune's car. One of them would then drive the vehicle along a winding snow-covered country road, towing the other on skis. The driver would make sharp turns and suddenly vary his speed in an attempt to force the skier to let go of the rope. Bethune held his own in these contests (Hugh MacMillan to RS).

62 Sister Joseph Leon, neé Marguerite Fleury, to RS, taped interview in the authors' possession.

63 Dr Arthur Vineberg to RS, taped interview.

CHAPTER SEVEN

1 Bethune performed seven blood transfusions related to thoracic surgery at Sacré Coeur in 1933 alone (Delva, "Norman Bethune: L'influence de l'Hôpital du Sacré Coeur," 89). Apparently Bethune gave his patients blood transfusions whenever the operation he was to perform was likely to be long and potentially risky (Delva and Fournier, "Norman Bethune – Surgeon Extraordinary," 373–5). One source claims that a blood bank was established at Sacré Coeur in 1933, during Bethune's time at the hospital (Delarue, *Thoracic Surgery in Canada*, 553). If this were the case, it would have been one of the first to exist in a Montreal hospital, and indeed in Canada, antedating by four years the first hospital blood bank established in the United States (see chapter 6, n.15). However, a search of the official archives of the Hôpital du Sacré Coeur has revealed that the first mention of the existence of a blood bank at the hospital was in 1943 (*Rapport général du 1 janvier 1943 au 1 janvier 1944*, Montreal, Archives Providence, M95.34 (41)-AG-Bb3.7; Marie-Claude Béland, archiviste, Archives Providence, to Giovanna Badia, Librarian, Royal Victoria Hospital Medical Library, 13 January 2010).

2 During this time they performed approximately one hundred thoracoplasties each year, an impressive feat (Delarue, *Thoracic Surgery in Canada*, 553–5). And this was not the only surgery Bethune undertook. In early 1934 he also received appointments to perform surgery at the Women's General Hospital and the Royal Edward Institute in Montreal.

3 Fritz Brandtner, NFB, Gordons.

4 Frances Geddes, who married Bethune's flatmate Aubrey Geddes, told Elizabeth Lamont, librarian at the Royal Victoria Hospital in Montreal, that Bethune wanted to be revered (Elizabeth Lamont to RS, telephone interview).

5 Sister Joseph Leon to RS.

6 Delarue, *Thoracic Surgery in Canada*, 555.

7 Louis Huot to RS, taped interview.

8 Delva, "Norman Bethune: L'influence de l'Hôpital du Sacré-Coeur," 89.

9 Marian Scott, NFB interview.

10 Sister Joseph Leon to RS.

11 Delarue, *Thoracic Surgery in Canada*, 37.

12 Bethune, "A Plea for Early Compression" *Canadian Medical Association Journal* 27 (July 1932): 36–42.

13 This play may have been aired on radio, and another of his certainly was. *An Afternoon with a Tuberculosis Patient*, performed by the Montreal Repertory Theatre, with Bethune in the cast, was broadcast on Station CFCF on 9 January 1934 (Rioppel, "Private Viewing," 20).

14 Masson, *Au Service des tuberculeux*.

15 *Montreal Gazette*, 11 April 1934.

16 Dr Arthur Vineberg to RS, taped interview. Vineberg, who as a Jew was firmly anti-fascist, said that Bethune was "a great follower of fascism" until he went to Russia, and that the two of them had had "a big row" about the subject at Vineberg's father's house.

17 The friend was Jean Palardy; his fiancée was the artist Jori Smith, with whom Bethune later became friends (Jean Palardy to RS).

18 Horn, *The Dirty Thirties*, 255.

19 The leading members of the LSR were involved in the founding in 1933 of the Cooperative Commonwealth Federation, the first democratic-socialist party in Canada.

20 Adam Sheriff-Scott to RS.

21 Beginning in 1936, Bethune attended performances of labour theatre productions by Lilian Mendelsohn's New Theatre Group at Victoria Hall in Westmount, joining the cast later at the Samovar Club for drinks and dancing. He spent much of his time in such left-wing artistic circles during his remaining time in Montreal. The New Theatre Group was organized by a member of the Communist Party of Canada's Section 13, the closed group reserved for various professionals whose membership the party wished to conceal. The Artists' Group was another such organization.

22 McMann, *Spring Exhibitions, 1880–1970*, 31.

23 Frances Geddes to RS.

24 Marian Scott, NFB interview.

25 The apartment was at 1947 Bayle Street.

26 F.D. Ackman to RS, taped interview, RSF, 637/2/1.

27 Aubrey Geddes, NFB interview.

28 Ibid.

29 Bethune, letter to Frances Bethune, undated, NFB file for documentary film *Bethune*.

30 Dr Ronald Christie, a professor of medicine at McGill and a friend of Frances and Norman, to RS. The suggestion that Coleman informed the insurance company is in Frances (Bethune) Coleman to Ted Allan, 1942 interview.

31 J.B. Smith, assistant manager, Equitable Assurance Society of North America, letter to RS, 22 May 1972, RSF, 637/1/128.

32 Bethune, letter to Frances (Bethune) Coleman, Montreal, 11 February 1934, NFB research file for documentary film *Bethune*.

33 Bethune, letter to Frances (Bethune) Coleman, 7 June 1934, ibid.

34 Park, "Bethune As I Knew Him," 130. Another piece of evidence of their continuing relationship is a letter Bethune wrote on 31 October 1935 asking his ex-wife to come to Sacré Coeur for lunch (NFB research file for documentary film *Bethune*).

35 Dr Arthur Vineberg to RS, taped interview. Dr Cameron also worked at the Royal Edward Institute where Bethune sometimes performed surgery.

36 Elizabeth Hurcomb (Wallace) to Gabriel Nadeau, letter of 2 June 1941, Bibliothèque et archives nationales du Québec, Fonds Gabriel Nadeau, MSS177.

37 Dr Richard H. Overholt was a pre-eminent thoracic surgeon of the era who operated a well-known clinic in Boston. He had some interest in Bethune and

visited Sacré Coeur to watch him operate (R. Overholt to RS, taped interview, RSF, 637/2/4).

38 Dr Arthur Vineberg to RS, taped interview.

39 Harriet (Hammond) Elliston to RS, taped interview, RSF, 637/2/4.

40 Dr Arthur Vineberg to RS, taped interview.

41 Bethune, letter to John Barnwell, 9 September 1934, NFB research file for documentary film *Bethune*. In a letter to Ewarts Graham, editor of the *Journal of Thoracic Surgery*, Bethune wrote: "I had a spontaneous pneumothorax on my return from Boston and have been laid up since" (26 June 1934, ibid.). He may have remained in bed because of symptoms of shortness of breath until the lung re-expanded or to put less stress on the lung in hope the tiny rupture would heal faster – perhaps for both reasons. Either way it does seem to indicate that he was receiving respiratory benefit from the left lung when it was expanded, despite some scarring in the lung from the previous tuberculosis and the fact that a portion of his phrenic nerve had been removed on that side, which aided his breathing. As he recovered from the pneumothorax, the left lung would presumably have re-inflated gradually. In general Bethune's breathing would likely have improved with exercise, when the intercostal muscles would have contributed to the functioning of his damaged lung. Information for the above passage was supplied by Dr Larry W. Stephenson, professor of surgery and chief of division, Cardiothoracic Surgery, at the Wayne State University School of Medicine, in an email exchange and a telephone conversation with the authors, 23 February 2010.

42 Harriet (Hammond) Elliston to RS, taped interview. Bethune did not see Harriet again until three years later when he was in Boston on his speaking tour following his return from Spain. When they met at a reception, she told him she had married. Her husband was also a doctor. Later, Bethune found her again in the crowd and told her that he had introduced himself to her husband and they had chatted for a while. Reaching for her hand and smiling, he said, "You made the right choice" (Harriet Elliston to RS, taped interview).

43 F.D. Ackman to RS, taped interview.

44 Rioppel, "A Private Viewing," 18.

45 George Mooney, NFB interview. It is alleged that around this time, in the spring of 1935, Bethune's social conscience was stirred by witnessing police repression of a workers' protest march. He is supposed to have given first aid to injured protesters (Allan and Gordon, *The Scalpel, the Sword*, 79).

46 Frances (Bethune) Coleman, NFB, Gordons.

47 Bethune, letter to John Alexander, 11 July 1935, Bentley Historical Library, box 3, correspondence "B," 1935. "I am leaving for a six weeks trip to England, France and Germany tomorrow," he wrote, not mentioning that his trip included the Soviet Union.

48 Marian Scott, NFB interview; also Trépanier, *Marian Dale Scott*, 116.

49 Marian Scott, lecture notes; undated journal entry September 1935, MSF, vol. 14, file 41.

50 Marian Scott, lecture notes, MSF, vols. 14–15, 1979, file 1. By favouring decentralization, Scott tended toward anarchism, an ideology that both social democrats and Marxists abhorred (Trépanier, *Marian Dale Scott*, 115).

51 Ibid., 94

52 Ibid.

53 Marian Scott, fragmentary notes, MSF, vol. 15, file 6.

54 Ibid., vol. 14, file 20.

55 "Reflections on Return from 'Through the Looking Glass,'" address to the Montreal Medico-Chirurgical Society, 20 December 1935, published in the *Bulletin of the Montreal Medico-Chirurgical Society*, March-April 1936.

56 Both the letter and the poem are to be found in MSF, vol. 14, file 20.

57 Marian Scott, journals, 9 and 10 September 1935, MSF, vol.1, file 11; ibid., 10 May 1936, vol.1, file 14.

58 Larry Hannant, interview with Peter Dale Scott, 1995 (Hannant, *Politics of Passion*, 73).

59 Marian Scott, journals, 16 and 21 September 1935, MSF, vol. 1, file 11.

60 Bethune, notes and telegrams to Marian Scott, MSF, vol. 14, file 14-25. Blake's "The Sick Rose" was first published in his *Songs of Experience*. Bethune's use of "Oh my, oh my, oh my!" from Janet Cornell to RS.

61 Marian Scott, journals, 19 October 1936, MSF, vol. 1, file 11.

62 Ibid., 10 January 1936, vol. 1, file 15.

63 Fritz Brandtner (1896–1969), a German born in Danzig (today Gdansk, Poland), emigrated to Canada in 1928 and moved from Winnipeg to Montreal in 1934. Impressed by one of the first of Brandtner's paintings exhibited in Montreal, Bethune bought it. Shortly after making the purchase, he was introduced to the artist by a mutual friend, Robert Ayre, art critic of the *Montreal Gazette*.

64 Park, "Bethune As I Knew Him," 119. A later attempt to do the same thing with a painting of Paraskeva Clark was not appreciated. While he was a house guest of the Clarks, Bethune blithely changed the colour of the puppet stand in her well-known painting *Petrouchka* from red to blue. Annoyed, Clark immediately repainted it red (ibid.).

65 On one occasion, when someone admired them, he took scissors and cut off a substantial swatch of the curtains as a gift (Irene Kon to RS).

66 Fritz Brandtner, NFB, Gordons.

67 Ibid.

68 Louis Huot to RS, taped interview. The vitamin pills are mentioned by Libbie Park, who quoted him as saying, "How valuable they are, what did we ever do without them?" ("Bethune As I Knew Him," 117).

69 Fritz Brandtner, NFB, Gordons.

70 Haze Sise, letter to George Mooney, 4 May 1948.

71 Frances (Bethune) Coleman to Ted Allan, 1942 interview. (Allan's notes indicate that this particular piece of information might have been given him either by Frances Coleman or by Marian Scott.) Some of Bethune's comments about women seem to indicate ambivalence. Libbie Park said, "Norman loved women and said he loved women passionately and made love with some." She pointed out that he was capable of many kinds of relationships with women, not just sexual pursuit ("Bethune As I Knew Him," 99). Frances Coleman said that, whenever they passed a shapely woman on the street, he would ask her, "Did you notice that important structure we just passed?" Then, he would "turn, smile and cock his hat, repeating, 'A very important structure.'" But she also quoted him as saying "Women are beasts" and also "Women are flowers. Get

the fragrance and let them alone" (Frances [Bethune] Coleman to Ted Allan, 1942 interview.

72 Fritz Brandtner, NFB, Gordons.

73 Marian Scott, NFB interview.

74 Marian Scott to RS.

75 Bethune, letter to Marian Scott, Montreal, 8 October 1935, MSF, vol. 14, file 20.

76 The Communist International, known as Comintern, was founded in Moscow in 1919 to overthrow the existing world order by spreading communism abroad.

77 Bethune, letter to Louis Kon, 20 October 1935, NFB research file for documentary film *Bethune*. Bethune's difficult handwriting leaves the exact date of the letter unclear. In *Bethune*, RS gave the date as 28 October. However, David Lethbridge correctly maintains that the date is 20 October (Lethbridge, *Bethune: The Secret Police File*, Commentary on Documents 1-10). A typed version of the letter exists but is undated.

78 Lethbridge, *Bethune: The Secret Police File*, document 4, report of 25 October 1935.

79 This was at 1237 Guy Street. Shortly before leaving Montreal in July, Bethune learned that his landlord had sold the boarding house to a university fraternity, which would take possession while he was away. He therefore decided to store his few possessions and look for a new residence on his return. His friend Harold Beament met him at Windsor Station when he arrived back from the Soviet Union, and he stayed for several days at Beament's residence on Drummond Street before finding a room on Guy Street.

80 Dr Georges Cousineau to RS.

81 Dr John Alexander, letter to Norman Bethune, 15 July 1935, Bentley Historical Library, box 3, correspondence "B," 1935.

82 Marian Scott, NFB interview.

83 Wherrett, "Norman Bethune and Tuberculosis," 68.

84 Bethune, letter to Marian Scott, 8 October 1935, MSF, vol. 14, file 20.

85 Ibid.

86 Bethune, letter to Louis Kon, 20 October 1935, NFB research file for documentary film *Bethune*.

87 Ibid.

88 Bethune, Speech to Friends of the Soviet Union, 30 October 1935, *Montreal Gazette*, 31 Ocober 1935.

89 Bethune, letter to Marian Scott, 6 November 1935, MSF, vol. 14, file 21.

90 Marian Scott, journals, 18 November 1935, MSF, vol. 1 file 11.

91 Bethune, letter to Marian Scott, 21 November 1935, MSF, vol. 14, file 21.

92 Bethune, letter to Marian Scott, 20 December 1935, MSF, vol. 14, file 21. Later that month he wrote to her again, "Pony darling, I adore you. Come & take tea with me on Friday afternoon" (ibid.).

93 The RCMP did not note his CPC membership until 6 October 1936 (Lethbridge, *Bethune: The Secret Police Files*, document 1C, report of 6 October 1936).

CHAPTER EIGHT

1 Bethune, speech to the Friends of the Soviet Union.

2 *Montreal Gazette*, 31 October 1935; Bethune, letter to Marian Scott, 8 October 1935, MSF, vol. 14, file 20.

3 Bethune, letter to Marian Scott, 21 November 1935, MSF, vol. 14, file 21.

4 Park, "Bethune As I Knew Him," 116. No doubt Bethune's loneliness was intensified by his frequent insomnia.

5 Ibid., 117. Stanley Ryerson points out that some of his fellow party members "provided a matrix of warmth and affectionate understanding in his last short but crucial years [*sic*] of a new political experience in Montreal" (Ryerson, "Comrade Beth," 150).

6 Marian Scott Journals, undated entry, September 1935, MSF, vol 1, file 11.

7 Ryerson, "Comrade Beth," 153.

8 Park, "Bethune As I Knew Him," 98.

9 Ibid.

10 Ibid., 107–8

11 F.R. Scott to RS, taped interview, RSF, 637/2/1.

12 This sentence was not in the published version of "Reflections on Return from Through the Looking Glass." Park states that it appeared on the copy of the address from which Bethune read and that he had inserted it in his own handwriting (Park, "Bethune As I Knew Him," 101).

13 Bethune, "Reflections on Return from Through the Looking Glass"; NFB, research file for documentary film *Bethune*.

14 *Memphis Commercial Appeal*, 13 February 1936.

15 Bethune, "Take the Private Profit out of Medicine," Address to the Montreal Medical-Chirugical Society, 17 April 1936, NFB research file for documentary film *Bethune*.

16 Walt, "The World's Best-Known Surgeon," 590. Dr David Mulder from Fred Taylor, related in a telephone conversation with RS. If this meeting were held, no record of its minutes has been discovered.

17 Bethune, letter to Dr Richard Meade, 17 February 1936, BMH.

18 Delarue, *Thoracic Surgery in Canada*, 101.

19 Marian Scott, Journals, 22 March 1936. MSF, vol. 1, file 13

20 Bethune, "A Poem to Pony," 11 March 1936, "Untitled," 20 March 1936; "Remembrance," March 29, 1936; "Encounter, MSF, vol. 14, file "Correspondence to Marian Scott, January 36 to June 36."

21 Marian Scott, Journals, 10 January 1936; 23 March 1936; 2 April 1936, MSF, vol. 1, file 13.

22 Ibid., 10 May, vol. 1, file 13; 4 June, 8 June, 24 September, 24 October, 8 December, vol. 1, file 14.

23 Marian Scott to Esther Trépanier, date unknown, Esther Trépanier to RS, telephone conversation in August 2003.

24 Margaret Day would later marry the artist Philip Surrey. With F.R. Scott and others, she was one of the founding members of the poetry magazine *Preview* in 1942.

25 Margaret Day to Patricia Whitney, taped interview of June 1989. The original tape is in the possession of Les Whitney, Patricia Whitney's husband. A copy of the tape is in the possession of the authors. According to Day, her affair with Bethune continued over the next several months until his departure for Spain.

26 Allan Harrison to RS.

27 Pegi Nicol to Marian Scott; Murray, *Daffodils in Winter*, 123. Events in the Toronto visit are based on Fritz Brandtner's interview by Alvin and Dolly Gordon and an interview with Paraskeva Clark by RS. Bethune's meeting with Paraskeva Clark later led to an affair with her that he maintained until his final few days in Canada before his departure for China.

28 Marian Scott, NFB interview.

29 Park, "Bethune As I Knew Him," 113.

30 Ibid., 116.

31 Art produced by children attending the CCAC won three awards in the children's art section of the Paris World's Fair in 1937 (Trépanier, *Marian Dale Scott*, 103).

32 Bethune, letter to Marian Scott, 13 August 1936, MSF, vol. 14, file 23. Under Duplessis, nothing would be done about public health care for nearly a generation.

33 Ibid.

34 Park, "Bethune As I Knew Him," 130.

35 *Daily Clarion*, 1 August 1936.

36 George Mooney, NFB interview.

37 Margaret Day to Patricia Whitney, taped interview.

38 Mrs F. Kerchofer to RS.

39 Percy Newman to RS.

40 J.L. Biggar, national commissioner of the Canadian Red Cross Society, letter to Norman Bethune, Toronto, 18 September 1936, RSF, 637/1/91.

41 *Daily Clarion*, 16 September 1936. MacLeod was a high-ranking CPC official from Toronto. In early September, he and Tim Buck, the national secretary, had gone to Brussels to attend the Universal Peace Conference. Organized by Lord Cecil of Chelwood, it attracted representatives from thirty-two counties who shared the fear that the Spanish conflict could develop into a far greater one involving much of Europe. From Brussels, after travelling to Madrid to assess the military situation and to offer assistance, MacLeod and Buck learned from Republican government officials that the primary need of the military forces was medical supplies.

42 Hoar, *The MacKenzie-Papineau Battalion*, 10. Hoar, on agreement with MacLeod, used the pseudonym of Allen Dowd. See also A.A. MacLeod, NFB, Gordons.

43 A.A. Macleod, NFB, Gordons

44 Ibid.

45 Larry Hannant, "United Front on the Left: The Committee to Aid Spanish Democracy," unpublished paper, unpaginated.

46 The chairman was the Reverend Benjamin Spence, a prominent Toronto Protestant minister, and while Spry and Rose Henderson, a liberal, were two of the four vice-chairmen, the other two were A.A. MacLeod and Tim Buck. In keeping with Comintern policy, the CPC strategy was to encourage the merging of all progressive forces to create a Popular Front to support the Spanish Republican government. For this reason, the party wished to conceal Bethune's communist allegiance and to depict him as a non-political medical doctor inspired by humanitarian concerns. To the very few CPC members who were aware of

Bethune's party membership, it was ironic that the CCF was unwittingly helping to send a communist to Spain.

47 Elizabeth Smart (1913–86) became a novelist, best known for her novel *In Grand Central Station I Sat Down and Wept*, published in 1945.

48 In his "Memorandum to the Central Committee of the Chinese Communist Party," 20 April 1938, Bethune stated that he resigned from his positions at Sacré Coeur and Women's General Hospitals and the Department of Pensions and National Welfare one week before leaving for Spain (Memorandum Presented to the Central Committee of the Chinese Communist Party, Yennan [Yan'an], 20 April 1938; hereafter cited as Memorandum). Document copy in the possession of the authors.

49 Georges Deshaies, NFB, Gordons.

50 Robert and Thelma Ayre to RS, taped interview, RSF, 637/2/3.

51 Bethune, letter to Marian Scott, 10 October 1936, MSF, vol. 14, file 23.

52 Marian Scott, Journals, 24 October 1936, MSF, vol. 1, file 14

53 Margaret Day to Patricia Whitney, taped interview.

54 Frances (Bethune) Coleman, NFB, Gordons. The date of the will, 28 October, is apparently a typographical error. Bethune had sailed from Quebec four days earlier.

55 *Canadian Forum* 17 (July 1937). Bethune frequently altered his writings. He apparently wrote another version, possibly before the publication of the poem. The differences between the two are insignificant (Petrou, *Renegades*, chapter 13, note 4, 262).

56 Though the *Toronto Star* and the *Daily Clarion* agreed that the crowd was intensely partisan, their estimates of its size differed in their 22 October accounts of the meeting. The *Star* gave a figure of 5,000 and the *Daily Clarion*, 11,000.

57 A final count showed that just under $4,000 in cash, cheques, and amounts pledged had been collected (*Toronto Star*, 22 October 1936).

58 *Montreal Gazette*, 23 October 1936

59 The sources for the banning of the meetings are the *Daily Clarion*, the *Montreal Gazette*, and the *Montreal Herald*. In an address given on Sunday, 25 October, to a gathering of 100,000 in the Craig Street Armory and on the Champ de Mars, Mgr. Charles Gauthier, archbishop co-adjutor of Montreal, warned Roman Catholics against the Spanish Loyalists, whom he described as "those new barbarians who have covered the soil of Spain with ruin and blood." Following the address, which was part of the celebration of the feast of Christ the King, a series of resolutions was passed including one that denounced communist propaganda (*Montreal Gazette*, 26 October 1936).

60 *New York Times*, 27 October 1936

61 F.R. Scott to RS, taped interview.

62 Hannant, *The Politics of Passion*, 116.

CHAPTER NINE

1 There is some evidence that General Queipo de Llano, who was stationed in Seville, may have used the term "fifth column" before Mola.

2 On Saturday morning, 31 October, two prominent fascist leaders and thirty-one others were driven to a cemetery where they were shot. On 2 November and 3 November, a total of seventy-six more fascists met a similar fate.

3 Bethune, letter to Benjamin Spence, 17 December 1936. The money went for the care of miners in Oviedo injured in the abortive uprising in Asturias in 1934 (NFB research files for documentary film *Bethune*).

4 The *Star*, which had given detailed coverage to the Mutual Arena rally of October 21 and was aware of Bethune's plans, likely provided him with Halton's London address and telephone number.

5 *Toronto Star*, 3 November 1936.

6 *New Commonwealth*, 21 November 1936. At this stage of the war the Nationalist forces had not surrounded the entire city, which allowed the airport to operate.

7 Bethune found Hemingway pretentious, and after the writer left the bar, Bethune mockingly imitated his rather stiff gait (Henning Sorensen to RS).

8 The information in the previous three paragraphs was related by Henning Sorensen to RS.

9 Gordon McCutcheon, a member of the same group, to RS.

10 In a letter written in Valencia in 1937 Sorensen stated that he was a member of the Communist Party of Spain. It seems likely that he was also a member of the CPC, which would have known about his plan to go to Spain (Henning Sorensen, letter to the Central Committee of the Communist Party of Spain, Valencia, 4 August 1937; LAC [Moscow Archives], Comintern fonds, MG10-K3, fonds 539, file list 3, file 732).

11 With Spry was Jacques Bieler, who was also a CCF party member. Spry promised to send accreditation documentation to the Canadian Legation in Paris where Sorensen could pick it up en route to Spain (Henning Sorensen, unpublished autobiographical ms. given to RS by Hilda Sorensen, 136). From Copenhagen, Sorensen had travelled via Paris to Spain, arriving in Madrid on 11 October. Two weeks later he went to the British Embassy to collect a cable sent on 23 October from Montreal by the CASD; it informed him that Bethune was sailing the following day from Quebec City and asked him to make contact with him when he reached Madrid. Not knowing the exact date of Bethune's arrival, Sorensen had left the city on a day trip on Sunday and returned to learn that Bethune was registered in the hotel (Henning Sorensen to RS).

12 Henning Sorensen to RS.

13 Hoar, *The Mackenzie-Papineau Battalion*, 50.

14 Henning Sorensen, unpublished ms., 147.

15 Bethune, radio broadcast, "Madrid, Peaceful amid War," 2 January 1937. Bethune's radio broadcasts, along with those of Hazen Sise and J.B.S. Haldane, were later printed as a pamphlet by the CASD: "This Is Station EAQ Madrid, Spain: Hear Dr Norman Bethune, Prof. J.B.S. Hadane, Hazen Sise" (Toronto: Committee to Aid Spanish Democracy, 1936, 1937), OLHMA, Bethune Collection fonds, accession 443B, folder 3.

16 Henning Sorensen, unpublished ms., 148.

17 Contreras was a *nom de guerre*. He was in fact an Italian named Vittorio Vidali (1900–83).

18 Henning Sorensen to RS, taped interview, RSF, 637/2/6.

19 Kléber was a *nom de guerre* used by Lazar Stern, a Hungarian who had served as a captain in the Austrian army in World War I. He had joined the Communist Party in the 1920s and was later appointed to the military section of the

Comintern. Travelling with a Canadian passport fabricated by the NKVD, the Soviet secret police, he had come to Spain to train and lead the International Brigades.

20 Henning Sorensen to RS, taped interview.

21 Ibid.

22 As far as is known, Bethune never fired a gun in a battle, whether during World War I, in Spain, or in China.

23 *New Commonwealth*, 21 November 1936. Another $1,000 was deposited in a bank in Paris.

24 Bethune, postcard to Marian Scott, 11 November 1936, MSF, vol. 14, file 23.

25 Henning Sorensen to RS.

26 Henning Sorensen, unpublished ms., 152.

27 Hazen Sise told RS that they only became aware of Duran i Jordà's work in December, after they had returned to Madrid from London and Paris. It is worth noting that the system invented by Duran i Jordà to transport blood to the front was more sophisticated than the blood service eventually set up by Bethune. The Catalan doctor's service blended blood from different donors, which was enclosed in pressurized ampoules and then transported by refrigerated truck or train to locations near the front. Bethune's service simply bottled blood from individual donors, added sodium citrate as a preservative, and refrigerated it until it could be delivered by ambulance.

28 The fact that they did not mention the work of Duran i Jordà to Bethune at this time would seem to indicate that they, as well as he, were unaware of it.

29 *Daily Clarion*, 20 November 1936.

30 This letter, probably to Benjamin Spence, is quoted in the NFB documentary film *Bethune*.

31 It is likely that it was at this time that Bethune became acquainted with the latest Soviet techniques in blood transfusion including the use of blood from cadavers. Bethune refers to this knowledge in a letter to Benjamin Spence, which appeared in the *Daily Clarion* on 4 December 1936. He may have already have known about the establishment of a national blood bank system in the Soviet Union from his visit there in the summer of 1935; if not, he may have learned about it during his research in London. It is also worth noting that Bethune wrote to Dr Norman M. Guiou, one of the Canadian pioneers in the use of citrated blood, asking him to send him a copy of the Canadian Red Cross pamphlet *Hemorrhage at the Outposts*, which described the freezing test Guiou had developed to cross-match blood quickly. As Bethune was to do later, Guiou had long argued that soldiers in shock "should be handled promptly and not sent back 20 miles to die on the way," and that it was possible to do this (Delarue, *Thoracic Surgery in Canada*, 212).

32 In Ottawa, O.D. Skelton of External Affairs had his staff investigate Bethune's claim. In the report submitted to Skelton, the staff member wrote that the director of Medical Services of the Department of Pensions and National Health had informed him that "besides being a very good surgeon he (Bethune) is a reliable and responsible person." But he added, the CASD "is understood to be a communist organization under the chairmanship of the Reverend Benjamin Spence, and it has been said that Tim Buck is associated with it in some way." On Saturday Massey received the following message from Skelton: "While

Government has full sympathy with any efforts to relieve sufferers on both sides of present Spanish conflict, it would not be possible, in view of what appeared to be political complexion of this mission as indicated … to sponsor it by making a formal request as indicated" (LAC, RG 25M Series G1, vol. 1801, file 631-B).

33 Hazen Sise, NFB interview.

34 In describing his meeting with Sise, Bethune commented to Sorensen, "We'll be lucky to get him. His father is one of the fifty most important men in Canada." Sorensen was upset by this remark, which seemed to him most unfitting for a communist (Sorensen to RS). Bethune's reference to the social status of Sise's father may have reflected his hope that the association of wealthy people with the blood transfusion unit might increase both financial and political support in Canada for the Spanish Republic. Sorensen may also have felt piqued at the intrusion of the *haut bourgeois* Sise into what up to now had been his and Bethune's project.

35 *Mono Azul* (blue overalls) was the name of a Loyalist newspaper.

36 When the International Red Cross later protested, Bethune replaced the red cross with the Maltese Cross set in a wreath, the symbol of the Spanish Army health department, the Sanidad Militar (Hoar, *The Mackenzie-Papineau Battalion*, 53).

37 Sise was taken aback. Many years later he remarked, "That to scoff at a map, to ignore it with bravado was a shocking attitude, a primitive and a disturbing trait to encounter in a man I had come to admire so much" (Hazen Sise, NFB interview).

38 Hazen Sise to RS.

39 In a letter to Benjamin Spence, Bethune states that there were fifteen rooms (Bethune, letter to Benjamin Spence, 17 December 1936, NFB research file for documentary film *Bethune*). Sise and also Sorensen informed RS that the number was eleven.

In *The Forging of a Rebel*, 270–1, Arturo Barea recounts how, not long after moving in, Bethune discovered a trove of hidden documents, some in German. He stalked into the Telefonica building, "with his escort of lumbering, embarrassed young helpers," demanding that the papers be translated. After that was done, "his frizzy grey hair slicked back on his long narrow head, swaying slightly on his feet," he announced that he would drive the documents over to the foreign minister in person.

40 Hazen Sise, NFB interview.

41 She had come to Spain in October with her husband, Morris Greenspan, a writer for the American periodical *New Masses*. Learning that Bethune was looking for a laboratory technician, Greenspan offered her services and he immediately accepted her. The decision to take a partisan role likely made her the first American female volunteer in the Spanish Civil War (New York University, Frances Patai papers, 131, box 2, folder 5, hereafter cited as Frances Patai Papers.)

42 Henning Sorensen told RS that even after several months of using whole blood collected by the unit and treated with sodium citrate, Vicente Goyanes and Antonio Culebras, two Spanish hematologists assigned to the unit by the Socorro Rojo, continued to prefer the traditional method of direct transfusion.

43 Celia Greenspan Seborer to RS, taped interview, RSF, 637/2/1.

44 Hazen Sise interview dated November 1966, OLHMA, Bethune Collection fonds, P156, accession 331.

45 During one of his broadcasts, Bethune mentioned that all the churches in Madrid were open and that he himself had been attending services at a Lutheran church every Sunday. Given that he had stated years before that he had lost his belief in an anthropomorphic god, this was no doubt an attempt to counter the anti-Republican propaganda of the Fascists, who accused the Loyalist forces of viciously persecuting priests, nuns, and the religious faithful.

46 Hazen Sise, OLHMA, Bethune Collection Fonds P156, accession 331. Sise's mother in fact heard one of her son's broadcasts from Spain.

47 Frederick Griffin, "Canadians Lend a Hand," *Toronto Star Weekly*, 27 February 1937. Bethune and the others also visited the remnants of the Thaelmann Brigade (of the International Brigades) on Christmas Eve.

48 CASD, "This Is Station EAQ Madrid, Spain," OLHMA, Bethune Collection fonds, P156 accession 443B, folder 3.

49 *New Commonwealth*, 26 December 1936.

50 Celia Greenspan to Morris Greenspan, 14 January 1937, New York University, Frances Patai Papers.

51 Henning Sorensen to RS.

52 Bethune, letter to Benjamin Spence, 11 January 1937, NFB research file for documentary film *Bethune*.

53 Ibid. Haldane left Madrid early in January but returned later for another brief stay in the Instituto.

54 She planned to use equipment loaned to her by Ivor Montagu, an English filmmaker who had just completed his documentary *Defence of Madrid*, which would be shown in England to raise funds for medical supplies for British aid to Spain (Henning Sorensen to RS, taped interview).

55 Ibid.

56 Viedma, "Everything You Have Done," 37.

57 Allan, "The Sinner Who Became a Saint."

58 Celia Greenspan Seborer to RS.

59 Henning Sorensen to RS.

60 Norman Bethune's personnel file, "Report on the Performance of the Canadian Delegation in Spain," 3 April 1937, LAC (Moscow Archives), Mackenzie-Papineau Battalion fonds, MG10-K2, fond 545, file list 6, file 542, 1937–1940. Sorensen described this incident to RS without indicating that Rothman and Hurtug were present. The "Hurturg" mentioned in the personnel file may in fact have been the Major Hartung mentioned in Barea, *The Forging of a Rebel*, 259.

61 Because the Instituto at this time lacked the clinical equipment to screen the blood for syphilis, the word of the donor had to be accepted. Bethune argued that the need for blood near the front greatly outweighed the risk that some infected blood might be collected. Similarly, they did not screen the blood for malaria, which was endemic in some parts of Spain (Hazen Sise to RS, taped interview, RSF, 637/2/2).

62 The number of registered donors when extractions began in late December is not certain. Bethune and his assistants had not begun to organize the apartment

until 14 December, yet three days later, in a letter to Benjamin Spence, he claimed that there were eight hundred donors. That figure may have been an ambitious estimate of his expectations. Registration of donors, according to Sorensen, did not begin until two days after Bethune had written to Spence. Herbert Matthews, correspondent of the *New York Times*, in a story published on Christmas Day, reported that "A call for volunteer blood donors less than a week ago has brought 2000 offers and donors are coming in at the rate of 50 a day." Coincidentally, Dr R.S. Saxton, a member of British Ambulance Unit, who visited the Instituto in March, wrote in a report on its operation, "There are at present about 800 donors on the books and some 20 more are added every day" ("The Madrid Blood Transfusion Institute," 606–7). Saxton's report, however, refers to conditions nearly three months after the opening of the Instituto. Roderick Stewart tried but failed to find the records of the Instituto canadiense de transfusión de sangre, so it is impossible to provide an accurate figure for the number of donors. In a January letter to Benjamin Spence from Madrid on 11 January 1937, Bethune stated that the amount of extractions was between one-half and three-quarter gallons of blood per day, about two to three litres, which would have been taken from four to six donors (NFB research file for documentary film *Bethune*). These figures indicating the amount of blood taken in the early days of operation of the transfusion service later increased dramatically. Saxton reported the amount "at about 400 litres of preserved blood per month, and is rapidly increasing" ("Madrid Blood Transfusion Institute," 606). Regarding the number of transfusions, Bethune wrote in his 11 January letter to Spence, "Yesterday we did three transfusions – this is about the average daily besides the blood we leave at the hospitals for them to use themselves" (NFB research file for documentary film *Bethune*). At the height of military activity in which the unit provided blood, early in March, Saxton wrote: "As many as 100 transfusions have been given in a day" ("The Madrid Blood Transfusion Institute," 606).

63 Allen May, *New Commonwealth*, 10 April 1937.
64 Bethune, letter to Benjamin Spence, Madrid, 11 January 1937, NFB research file for documentary film *Bethune*.
65 Ibid.
66 Hazen Sise, letter to Kenneth Macgowan, 8 June, 1943, HSEF, vol. 35, file 1. In this letter Sise pointed out that, despite popular myth, Bethune had nothing to do with the discovery or development of the blood plasma technique of transfusion, and that the sodium citrate method of preservation for refrigerated blood had been known and used for some time.

CHAPTER TEN

1 Bethune, letter to Benjamin Spence, Madrid, 17 December 1936, NFB research file for documentary film *Bethune*.
2 Dr José Ramón Navarro Carballo to RS, 2006.
3 Frederic Duran i Jordà (1905–57) had set up the service under the jurisdiction of the Unified Socialist Party of Catalonia (PSUC) in August 1936. To retain the loyalty of the Generalitat, the Government of the Province of Catalonia of which Barcelona is the capital, the Republican government had granted Catalonia a large degree of autonomy in the very early days of the war. The

Socorro Rojo Internacional did not control the health services there as it did in other parts of Republican Spain.

4 See chapter 9, note 27.

5 Bethune, letter to Hazen Sise, Barcelona, 16 January 1937, TAF, vol. 16, file 2.

6 Ibid. "The blood ampules [sic] are OK and since it's a patented and complicated process of putting up the blood, it cannot be reproduced in Madrid, ergo – we must use Barcelona as a collecting centre for this kind of blood."

7 Ibid.

8 Henning Sorensen to RS, Henning Sorensen, unpublished ms., 161–2. This was not Bethune's only known foray into the seamy side of life. Sise recalled an incident in February 1937, in which Antonio Galan, a member of the Instituto, led Bethune, Sise, and Goyanes to a whorehouse in El Barrio Chino of Barcelona. There the madam produced a virgin, "the most enchanting girl I have ever seen in my life," said Sise. "She couldn't have been more than sixteen or seventeen. Beth then went off with her for more than half an hour" (Hazen Sise to RS, taped interview).

9 Thomas Cuthbert Worsley (1907–77), who later became an author and theatre and television critic in England, wrote *Behind the Battle*, published in London in 1939 by Robert Hale Ltd. The book is a *roman à clef* in which Worsley describes his experiences as a driver on the staff of the Instituto. In the book Bethune is portrayed as Rathbone, and Sise as Hesketh, both Americans. Sise told Ted Allan that Worsley's account of the events in which he was involved was accurate.

10 Bethune suggested that the CASD would pay the sum of 25,000 pesetas. Although the agreement was signed by Cerrada, it was not signed by the Spanish minister responsible. Nevertheless, the CASD was obliged to pay salaries until the end of June and also later paid 17,400 pesetas toward the centre in Valencia. This proved to be too great a strain on the resources of the CASD, which was unable to pay the balance of the sum promised (Hazen Sise, "Basis of Agreement with Chief of Blood Transfusion Service, Republican Army," 25 June 1937, TAF, vol. 16, file 3).

11 Bethune, cable to the CASD from Madrid, 27 January 1937, New York University, Fredericka Martin Papers, Bethune, Norman Writings, box 1, folder 54.

12 Celia Greenspan Seborer to RS, taped interview. Uncomfortable with the unevenness of the operation of the Instituto, and eager to be with her husband in Valencia, Greenspan saw Bethune's brief return in late January as an opportunity to leave his staff. Bethune supplied her with a letter of reference, and she left Madrid a few days later.

13 Somehow he had brushed aside the warnings he had already received from officials of the Socorro Rojo Internacional; they had told him clearly that since December all militia units were being stripped of authority as part of the process of creating a unified Republican army.

14 The contents of the cable were published in the 9 February edition of the *Daily Clarion* in a news story headlined, "Bethune Heads All Transfusion Units." In this article the dateline of the cable is given as Madrid, 8 February. In fact Bethune must have sent it before his meeting with Cerrada on 6 February. On 8 February he was on the south coast of Spain, having left Madrid on 31 January to return to Valencia. It seems likely that the CASD did not release the

contents of the cable to the *Clarion* until after they had met to discuss a course of action to follow.

15 The first paragraph of the *Clarion* story, which preceded the text of the cable, was the following: "A medical man to help Dr. Norman Bethune, Chief of the Canadian Medical Unit in Spain, will be sent immediately, the Committee to Aid Spanish Democracy announced last night. The decision was reached after Doctor Bethune informed the Committee that all remaining Spanish blood transfusion stations had been transferred under his direction."

16 Hazen Sise Diary (1937), TAF, vol. 30, file 26.

17 Ibid.

18 Hazan Sise, NFB interview

19 Worsley, *Behind the Battle*, 60

20 Majada Neila and Bueno Perez, *Carretera Málaga-Almería*, 21.

21 Ibid., 50

22 There is a discrepancy about the time. In the description of the events between 10 and 12 February in Bethune's 1937 *The Crime on the Road: Málaga-Almería*, he states that he and his companions arrived in Almería at 5 PM and left an hour later. Worsley claims they arrived at noon, Bethune visited the local hospital, and they later had lunch, activities that would surely have required more than an hour's time. Sise recorded in his diary that they left Almería at 3:30 PM. Worsley claims that they drove fifteen kilometres before they met refugees and only after continuing for several kilometres more did Bethune stop the vehicle to allow Sise the opportunity to take a photograph. If they had left at the hour indicated by Bethune, it would have been close to 7 PM and too dark to take photographs.

23 Worsley, *Behind the Battle*, 185. He named it the "American Blood Transfusion Service."

24 In *The Crime on the Road*, Bethune wrote: "Thousands of children, we counted five thousand under ten years of age and at least one thousand of them barefoot and many of them clad only in a single garment." In *Behind the Battle*, 188, Worsley has Rathbone (Bethune) say: "I've been counting; there must be some twenty thousand kids under ten on this road. Kids only."

25 Sise kept a detailed record of the distance travelled between each point on the trip that he and Worsley took from Barcelona, leaving Thursday, 4 February, and arriving in Madrid on Tuesday, 16 February.

26 He later identified the Republican planes as the two remaining Potez bombers from the España Squadron.

27 Sise later wrote, "Sadly I was right about those ampoules. When I got back to Madrid a few days later, I had the blood tested on a centrifuge and it was badly and dangerously haemolysed [this refers to the destruction of red blood corpuscles caused by agitation]. Of those who had been transfused with it, if they had not died from their wounds, they would have probably been killed by the blood. I think two or three died. If there was not other blood immediately available, I think Bethune took a justifiable chance" (letter to H.S. Thornberry, 2 March 1970, HESF, vol.7, file 22).

28 Hazen Sise, interview of 1966, OLHMA, Bethune Collection fonds, P156, accession 331.

29 Dr Albert B. Byrnne, a member of the American Medical Bureau in Spain, to RS.

30 Bethune, *The Crime on the Road*. Bethune would never know that he had witnessed parts of what would eventually be recognized as perhaps the most heinous atrocity of the Spanish Civil War. During his time in Spain and for many years after, the two-and-one-half-hour carpet-bombing of the undefended Basque town of Guérnica by planes of the German Condor Legion on 26 April 1937, which resulted in the death of between two hundred and three hundred people, was regarded as the most infamous attack on a civilian target in the Spanish Civil War. The name of Guérnica became a symbol of infamy as a result of the painting by that name by Picasso.

   The lack of attention paid to the Málaga-Almería flight can be explained. Bethune's was the only eyewitness account. No journalist, either Spanish or foreign, was there, and the Nationalist victory meant that no reference was made to it during Franco's hold on power, which lasted until his death in 1975. For that reason there is no reliable estimate of the actual number of deaths from bombardment by Nationalist warships and Italian and German airplanes and from exhaustion during the five days of flight. Jesús Majada Neila, a Malagueñan who conducted a series of interviews with survivors of the tragedy, has drawn attention to this lack of reportage (Majada Neila and Bueno Perez, *La Carretera Málaga-Almería*, 10).

31 The first reports of the atrocity were based on Bethune's description, and he gave copies to reporters in Murcia, which were published in European and North American newspapers on Wednesday, 17 February, and Thursday, 18 February.

32 Charles Korvin to RS. Geza Kárpáthi (1907–98) was Hungarian by birth. He later changed his name first to Geza Korvin and then to Charles Korvin, which he used for the rest of his life and by which he became known in the United States as a successful cinema and television actor. Among his many roles were Inspector Duval in the 1960s television series *Interpol Calling*, and Captain Thiele in the 1965 movie *Ship of Fools*.

33 Ibid.

34 This letter, of which there is no extant copy, was referred to in a later letter of 9 March 1937 to Benjamin Spence, OA, Albert Alexander MacLeod fonds, F126 MU7590, file 12.

35 Sise pointed out that although building entire villages for children as Bethune suggested was not really practicable in the desperate situation of wartime Spain, some action was eventually taken on Bethune's idea. Several resort hotels were purchased near the French border in the Pyrenees and used as children's hostels. Sorensen later did work related to them, and Sise believed that at least three of them were set up. He visited one of them on his way out of Spain in August 1937 (Hazen Sise, NFB interview).

36 From Madrid, Sise had sent Bethune a telegram informing him that the CASD had just sent a cable to the Instituto advising them of May's expected arrival in Paris on Wednesday, 17 February. In a letter he sent to Bethune from Barcelona on 25 February, he referred to sending the telegram. Bethune left Paris before the arrival of the letter (HESF, vol. 16, file 2).

37 Worsley, *Behind the Battle*, 270.

38 Ibid., 272.

39 On another occasion when Bethune was talking to the Spanish doctors at the

Instituto, he patted a money belt he was wearing around his waist and assured them that he could get what he wanted with its contents. The Spaniards were not amused (Henning Sorensen to RS).

40 Hazen Sise, letter to Norman Bethune, Barcelona, 25 February 1937, TSF, vol. 16, file 2. In this letter, which Bethune failed to receive, Sise had informed him of information obtained by Sorensen from Antonio Galan. Sise wrote: "Galan said that your agreement was never signed by the minister & that the whole organization was sitting in the air & everything might be wrecked by the row Duran was making etc. etc. Obviously they were all a bit worried about their jobs, especially Galan."

41 Worsely, *Behind the Battle*, 280.

42 The names of the two Spaniards with whom Bethune had the most problems have an ironic meaning in Spanish. Colonel Cerrada's surname means "closed," and Dr Antonio Culebras's means "snakes."

CHAPTER ELEVEN

1 Jean Watts (1910–68) arrived at the Instituto on 21 February and stayed for several months. After graduating with a BA in psychology, she had become active in left-wing groups. She often wore men's clothing and preferred to be addressed as "Jim." Eager to join the Instituto as a truck driver, she had to content herself with writing articles for the *Daily Clarion*. She served in the Canadian Army Women's Corp during World War II. In the 1960s she became active in an organization called the Voice of Women.

2 Norman Bethune, "With the Canadian Blood Transfusion Unit in Guadalajara," *Daily Clarion*, 17 July 1937.

3 After receiving the blood and the refrigerator, Dr Jolly asked Bethune to examine a wounded soldier. He had lost an eye and one hand had been severed; Jolly had had to amputate the other. Even more surgery was required, but Jolly did not want to continue until the soldier had received a transfusion. Another complication, he added, was that despite trying various languages, they had been unable to communicate with the patient. Bethune bent over the man to make the preparations for the transfusion and called Sorensen over. Apparently in response, the man uttered a few halting words. Sorensen at once began to speak to him. Turning to Bethune, he said, "Why he's Swedish. No wonder they can't understand him!" After Bethune administered the transfusion, Sorensen explained to the man what Jolly had done and assured him that he would receive good care. As they left the hospital, Sorensen explained to Bethune that the young Swede had told him that he had been in Spain for only three days, and that the previous day had been his first time in action. "Now I am no more use to my comrades. I have done nothing for the cause," he had lamented to Sorensen (ibid.).

4 Sorensen, unpublished ms., 168.

5 Hazen Sise, NFB interview.

6 Dr Albert B. Byrnne to RS.

7 Harold Beament to RS, taped interview.

8 Goyanes and Culebras had been students of Dr Gustavo Pittaluga of the University of Madrid who had formed the first blood transfusion unit in the city on the third day following the uprising in July 1936. They had performed arm-

to-arm transfusions in the Faculty of Medicine of the university. In early January the Madrid Defence Council ordered them to join the staff of the Instituto. The exact date of their arrival is unclear. Goyanes states, "In February 1937, by order of the Governing Council for the Defence of Madrid The Faculty of Medicine Unit was unified with that sent by the Canadian Committee to Aid Spanish Democracy" (Goyanes Alvarez, "La transfusión de sangre en el sector centro," 163). Goyanes may have been referring to the formal integration of the Faculty of Medicine and the Canadian units in February. It appears most likely that he and Culebras had joined the Instituto in early January. Because Bethune left for Valencia on 11 January 1937, there must have been Spanish doctors already in the unit who could maintain its operation in his absence; Celia Greenspan in a letter to her husband dated 14 January 1937 in fact refers to the presence of two Spanish medical doctors in the Instituto by that date (Celia Greenspan to Morris Greenspan, letter of 14 January 1937, New York University, Francis Patai Papers). Two more doctors, Valentin de la Loma and Andrés Sanz Vilaplana, joined the unit sometime after Goyanes and Culebras had done so. In 1972, RS interviewed Sanz and Loma separately. Sanz told him that he had arrived probably near the end of December, and Loma remembered that he had come in the winter of 1936. However, it seems most likely that they joined the Instituto in early February after Bethune negotiated his agreement with Cerrada.

9 Bethune, letter to Benjamin Spence, 9 March 1937.
10 Henning Sorensen to RS, taped interview.
11 Bethune, letter to Benjamin Spence, 9 March 1937.
12 Ted Farah, *Stratford Beacon Herald*, 27 November 1939. Sorensen also commented on Bethune's refusal to learn Spanish: "He never tried to pick up any Spanish and never learned to say a single sentence in that language" (Sorensen, unpublished ms., 155).
13 Hazen Sise, letter to A.A. MacLeod, 5 August 1937, OA, Albert Alexander MacLeod fonds, Sise referred to Goyanes's "monumental laziness."
14 Hazen Sise, *Aide Memoire to Estellés*, TSF, vol. 16, file 2.
15 Jose Maria Massons, *Historia de la sanidad militar espanola*, vol. 2, 474.
16 Henning Sorensen to RS; Sorensen unpublished ms., 168.
17 Ibid.
18 Henning Sorensen to RS, taped interview.
19 Ted Allan to RS.
20 Henning Sorensen to RS.
21 Henning Sorensen, unpublished ms., 171.
22 Ibid.
23 Henning Sorensen to RS, taped interview.
24 Ibid.
25 Bethune's personnel file, "Report on the Performance of the Canadian Delegation in Spain," 3 April 1937.
26 Henning Sorensen to RS, taped interview. Kajsa Rothman left the Instituto soon afterward.
27 Ted Allan to RS.
28 The excuse was specious because the proposed legislation did not forbid the transfer of funds raised in Canada to foreign organizations. The Foreign Enlist-

ment Act was passed eight days after Bethune spoke to Cerrada. One of its clauses prohibited Canadian citizens from accepting "any commission or engagement in the armed forces of any foreign state at war with a friendly state." On 31 July the act was made applicable to the Spanish Civil War (Hoar, *The Mackenzie-Papineau Battalion*, 103).

29 Henning Sorensen to RS.

30 Ibid.

31 Bethune's personnel file, "Report on the Performance of the Canadian Delegation in Spain," 3 April 1937.

32 Ibid. The report claimed that Bethune had made detailed notes about roads, bridges, and crossings and that Rothman had made detailed road maps. This was taken as evidence of spying, but as has been pointed out by Michel Petrou in *Renegades* (166), it is exactly the kind of information required for the operation of the Instituto's blood service. The report also described the sealed room as belonging to the Chilean Embassy, which once occupied the apartment. Both Sorensen and Sise indicated that when they arrived with Bethune, they found documents belonging to a Spanish lawyer who had acted as legal counsellor to the German Embassy. Neither referred to the Chilean Embassy. The apartment comprised eleven rooms. It is possible, but highly unlikely, that it was divided between the lawyer and the Chilean Embassy. Kajsa Rothman was wrongly suspected of being a fascist sympathizer. She returned to Sweden in 1938 and raised money for an organization she had set up called Kajsa's Milk Fund, the proceeds of which she brought back to Spain to purchase milk for Spanish children. After the victory of the Nationalists she fled to France and eventually went to Mexico, where she died thirty years later in Cuernavaca (Viedma, "Everything You Have Done," 37).

33 Sorensen claimed that the date of the confrontation was Monday, 5 April (Hannant, *The Politics of Passion*, 127); Sise recorded the date as Tuesday, 6 April (TAF, Resource Material, Hazen Sise diary, vol. 30, file 26). *Heart of Spain*, which included scenes of Bethune collecting blood from donors in the Instituto, became one of the classic depictions of the Spanish Civil War. For security the film was smuggled out of Spain in the British diplomatic pouch, and Bethune picked it up in Paris (Hazen Sise to RS, taped interview).

34 The restructuring of the Sanidad Militar began that very day, 8 April, with the appointment of Dr Estellés Salarich as its first chief. The Sanidad began operation as a department under the aegis of the Ministry of War (Carballo, *La Sanidad en Las Brigadas Internacionales*, 108).

35 Bethune, telegram to CASD, 12 April 1937, TAF, vol. 16, file 3. In the same cable Bethune referred to the temporary dismissal in January 1937 of General Kléber of the International Brigades. Apparently Kléber had a conflict with André Marty, the head of the IB. He was also suspected by the Spanish premier Francisco Largo Caballero of wishing to use the Brigades to effect a communist *coup d'état*. Bethune seems to be trying to screen his own partial responsibility for the problems with the Spanish authorities by implying that the takeover of the Instituto by the Sanidad Militar was an anti-communist manoeuvre. It seems more likely that it was part of the Spanish opposition to having foreigners in command of units that were part of the military.

36 NFB research file for documentary film *Bethune*.

37 Benjamin Spence, letter to Dear Comrades, 12 August 1937, TAF, vol. 16, file 3 (hereafter cited as Benjamin Spence, letter to Dear Comrades). In this document Spence sent to Sise, Sorensen, and May a detailed record of the correspondence between himself and Bethune from 1 April 1937 until shortly before Bethune's boarding the *Queen Mary* on 2 June, and of his correspondence with them and with A.A. MacLeod up to the end of June. Spence wrote, "May I say very frankly that reports had been leaking through other channels regarding internal conditions in the Unit which were rather disquieting."

38 Ibid.

39 MacLeod, a high-ranking CPC member who was fully aware of the contents of the Sorensen/Allan letter, was accompanied by William Kashtan, who was also a party member. Kashtan later became the leader of the CPC. Spence later wrote, "During all this time there was not the first intimation of financial stringency as far as the Institute was concerned. We were under the delightful impression that everything was o.k. in Spain and that there was a substantial balance with the American Express Co. in Paris. The extent of this we did not know for financial reports from the very first had been hard to get. We were hoping for an improvement in this regard when Allen May went over there and from reports and records received since can see he did make a very real effort to regularize things and put them into business-like shape. No doubt he, himself, would be the first to admit the difficulties he encountered in his efforts" (Benjamin Spence, letter to Dear Comrades).

40 Ibid.

41 Spence expressed his regret that Bethune had ignored his request to take Sorensen with him to Paris: "It was our thought that Sorensen or one of you men meeting with Mr MacLeod could put him in possession of the facts. This suggestion unfortunately was not followed and you will see how failure to do so caused trouble later" (ibid.).

42 Huot was at this time working as a journalist in Paris and met Bethune there on more than one occasion during his time in Spain (Louis Huot to RS, taped interview).

43 Ted Farah, a journalist in Paris at the time, accompanied Bethune to the Roland Garros stadium to watch tennis one afternoon (Ted Farah to RS, taped interview, RSF, 637/2/1; A.A. MacLeod, NFB, Gordons). In the same interview MacLeod claimed that wherever he and Bethune went in Paris, even a distance as short as a city block, Bethune insisted on taking a taxi. MacLeod also noted that while Bethune revealed little concern for how much money he spent, when he believed that he was being overcharged, he would create a scene. Several days after checking into his hotel he learned that to mark the Paris International Exposition, all hotels were offering room discounts. He therefore went to the front desk to demand a discount. The clerk told him that he was already being given a discounted rate. Bethune argued with him briefly, then began to list various features of the Statler hotels in the United States, pointing out how superior they were to the hotel he was in. Then he turned on his heel and headed for the elevator. When it reached his floor, he thought of something and went back down. Marching to the desk, he informed the clerk, "There is

a little card in every room in all Statler Hotels. And do you know what it says? Well, it says 'The customer is always right.'" Satisfied that he had had the last word, he went back to his room.

44 It was the first rejection that Bethune had received from the CASD. He had cabled the CASD, "Please increase my credit here. Now six hundred, Need two thousand dollars." Spence replied, "Reluctant disappoint you but committee feels situation should be clarified and desires submission definite plans future activities before making remittance" (Benjamin Spence, letter to Dear Comrades).

45 Ibid.

46 Ibid.

47 Hazen Sise Diary, 29 May 1937, TAF, vol. 30, file 26.

48 Ibid.

49 Benjamin Spence, letter to Dear Comrades.

50 On arrival in New York, Bethune told the Canadian Press that he had travelled steerage because "I wasn't spending the unit's money on first-class tickets" (L.S.B. Shapiro, *Montreal Gazette*, 8 June 1937). By the time of Bethune's voyage, steerage accommodation on the *Queen Mary*, which meant staterooms near the bow or at the stern of the ship, had been renamed Third Class.

51 Hazen Sise to RS.

CHAPTER TWELVE

1 L.S.B. Shapiro, Montreal *Gazette*, 8 June 1937.

2 *Daily Clarion*, 9 June 1937.

3 Ted Farah, *Hamilton Spectator*, 28 November 1939.

4 Toronto *Star*, 15 June 1937

5 *Globe and Mail*, 16 June 1937

6 Ibid.

7 William Strange to RS.

8 William Strange, *Toronto Star*, 15 June 1937.

9 *Montreal Gazette*, 19 June 1937.

10 Dr Gabriel Nadeau, "A T.B.'s Progress," 1157.

11 Dr Georges Cousineau to RS.

12 George Holt to RS, taped interview.

13 Margaret Day to Patricia Whitney, taped interview.

14 George Mooney, interview with the CBC, 1939, HESF, vol. 35, file 4.

15 Joan Lindley, daughter of Janet (Bethune) Stiles, to RS.

16 Paraskeva Clark to RS.

17 Philip Clark to RS; Lind, *Perfect Red*, 102.

18 Paraskeva Clark, NFB interview.

19 Zuehlke. *The Gallant Cause*, 129.

20 *Northern Daily News*, 6 July 1937.

21 *Daily Clarion*, 15 October 1937.

22 He went from Sault Ste Marie to Fort William (now Thunder Bay) on board the SS *Hamic* and made several trips by ferry between Vancouver Island and the mainland.

23 Bethune to Frances (Bethune) Coleman, 7 July 1937, NFB, research file for documentary film *Bethune*.

24 Bethune, cable to blood transfusion unit in Madrid, 11 July 1937, HESF, vol. 40, file 8.

25 *Northern Daily News* (Kirkland Lake, ON), 6 July 1937. MacKenzie King, then prime minister of Canada, had visited Hitler in Germany and declared himself to be impressed by him.

26 Lethbridge, *Bethune: The Secret Police File*, documents 22, 65.

27 *Sault Daily Star*, 14 July 1937.

28 James Kelleher to RS, Sault Ste Marie, 8 March 1970, RSF, 637/1/79. James Kelleher's father was then president of the Sault Ste Marie Rotary Club.

29 *Winnipeg Free Press*, 21 July 1937.

30 Lethbridge, *Bethune: The Secret Police File*, document 24.

31 *Winnipeg Free Press*, 22 July 1937.

32 George Holt to RS, taped interview.

33 Bethune, letter, "An Apology for Not Writing Letters," 5 May 1937, NFB research file for documentary film *Bethune*.

34 MacLeod remembers Bethune's buying $12 worth of magazines of all sorts, a very expensive purchase in 1937. Turning the pages rapidly, he would quickly read through each magazine stopping only to write in the margin "Bunk" and "More bunk" when he disagreed. After staying up well into the night to finish reading all of them, he threw them away (A.A. MacLeod, NFB, Gordons).

35 Lethbridge, *Bethune: The Secret Police File*, document 30.

36 Richard Greening to RS, Prince Albert, 18 February 1972, RSF, 637/1/79.

37 HESF, vol. 40, file 8.

38 Ibid.

39 *Edmonton Journal*, 25 July 1937.

40 Lethbridge, *Bethune: The Secret Police File*, document 31.

41 Ibid., Document 34.

42 RCMP files reveal that the questioner, a Communist Party member, later received a severe reprimand from party superiors for "bringing out the face of the party at a most inopportune time." Described as the act of a "provocateur," it lost him his vote in party proceedings for three months (Lethbridge, *Bethune: The Secret Police File*, document 37).

43 Nigel Morgan to RS, taped interview, RSF, 637/2/6.

44 *Victoria Daily Times*, 2 August 1937.

45 Report of the Madrid Provincial Committee to the Central Committee of the Spanish Communist Party, 17 August 1937, RS trans., LAC (Moscow Archives), MG10-K2, fonds 545 file list 6, file 542. "Tajsa" is an incorrect spelling of Kajsa Rothman's name; similarly, "Noren" refers to Norman Bethune. Hazen Sise's letter is in the same file.

46 Jean Hamelin and Nicole Gagnon, *Histoire du catholicisme québécoise*, Montreal: Boréal, 1984, 383, cited in Hannant, *The Politics of Passion*, 169.

47 *Toronto Star*, 16 September 1937. He made this kind of statement often. This was made 15 September in Toronto's Massey Hall.

48 The Japanese had already invaded and occupied the Chinese province of Manchuria in 1931, a fact referred to by Bethune. As a consequence the Chinese government had tolerated the presence of a number of Japanese troops in Beijing. However, on 7 July 1937, Japanese troops opened fire on Chinese forces at the Marco Polo Bridge near Beijing. This led to the outbreak of full-scale

war between China and Japan. Note: Peking ("northern capital") had been for many centuries the capital of China, and was known as such in the English-speaking world. In the late 1920s it was renamed Peiping ("northern peace") when the Guomindang gained control of China and located the capital instead in the southern city of Nanking (present-day Nanjing). In 1949, the Communist government re-established the capital in the north, and the city then reverted to its original name of "northern capital." Under the modern *pinyin* system of romanization of Chinese script, this name is today rendered as Beijing. For purposes of clarity, the modern name of the city is used throughout, with the exception of references in historical documents.

49 A. Brennan, letter to the editor of the *Northern Daily News*, published 13 July 1937, RSF, 637/1/79.

50 Dr Wendell J. MacLeod, NFB interview.

51 Miss E. Stirling to RS; RCMP references is in Lethbridge, *Bethune: The Secret Police File*, document 30.

52 Bethune, Memorandum Presented to the Central Committee of the Chinese Communist Party, Yennan [Yan'an], 20 April 1938. The original of this document was discovered by Dr Gerd Hartmann in the 1980s in the National Archives of Canada. It was then located in the Communist Party of Canada fonds MG 28 IV 4 but can no longer be found. A copy of this document is in the authors' possession.

53 *Daily Clarion*, 6 September 1937.

54 Ibid., 7 September 1937

55 Ibid

56 *Detroit News*, 6 September 1937. While Bethune was in Detroit, John Barnwell called to invite him to Ann Arbor for an overnight visit, and he stayed at the residence of Barnwell's brother. When the maid opened the two Gladstone bags Bethune had brought in order to lay out his pajamas she found nothing but books, two on medicine and the rest on communism. Unconcerned about proprieties, Bethune came down for breakfast in the morning barefoot and in his underwear shorts (Dr John Barnwell, NFB, Gordons).

After Bethune accepted his invitation to go to Ann Arbor, Barnwell called several professors from the Faculty of Medicine at the University of Michigan, to spend a few hours with him and Bethune. During their meeting the doctors persuaded Bethune to outline in some detail the organization and function of the blood transfusion unit. Barnwell rented a Dictaphone machine, which Bethune took up to his room. After spending the entire afternoon recording, he paused for a rest. Then he realized that he had forgotten to turn the machine on and talked for hours without having recorded a word. In fury, he picked up the machine and pitched it out the window of his second-floor room (Dr John Barnwell, NFB research file for documentary film *Bethune*).

57 *Niagara Falls Evening Review*, 15 September 1937

58 *Halifax Chronicle*, 27 September 1937; *Moncton Daily Times*, 30 September 1937. His speeches in Sydney and Halifax, Nova Scotia, were not universally well received. The *Daily Clarion* reported that radio stations refused to advertise his meetings and censored part of his response to questions (Larry Hannant, *The Politics of Passion*, 169).

59 *Montreal Gazette*, 4 October, 1937.

60 *Daily Clarion*, 15 October 1937.

61 Lethbridge, *Bethune: The Secret Police File*, document 38, 9 August 1937; document 38, 18 August 1937.

62 A.A. MacLeod, NFB, Gordons.

63 Jean Ewen to RS, taped interview, RSF, 637/2/6.

64 Tim Buck to RS, Cuernavaca, Mexico, 1973.

CHAPTER THIRTEEN

1 Marian Scott, NFB interview.

2 Elizabeth (Hurcomb) Wallace to RS, 1975. Bethune met her on Tuesday, 21 September, when he was staying at the Hotel de La Salle, 1240 Drummond Street; they had lunch at Café Martin on 1521 Mountain Street and then he went off to New York or Halifax on the speaking tour.

3 Margaret Day to Patricia Whitney, taped interview.

4 Bethune to Frances (Bethune) Coleman, King Edward Hotel, Niagara Falls, 14 September 1937, NFB file for documentary film *Bethune*.

5 Bethune, Memorandum.

6 Earl Browder, quoted in the *Daily Worker*, 11 June 1940.

7 Libbie Park, "Norman Bethune As I Knew Him," 133; Hazen Sise to RS.

8 Margaret Day to Patricia Whitney, taped interview.

9 Evelyn Kirkpatrick to RS, taped interview, RSF, 637/2/4.

10 Price, *The Lives of Agnes Smedley*, 318.

11 Phillip Jaffe to RS, 1975.

12 Jean Ewen to RS, 4 January 1972, RSF, 637/1/108.

13 Lewis Fraad to RS, taped interview, RSF, 637/2/2.

14 Ibid.

15 Ibid.

16 Irma Fraad to RS, taped interview, RSF, 637/2/2.

17 Jean Ewen to RS, 4 January 1972.

18 Elsie Siff to RS, taped interview, RSF, 637/2/2.

19 Ibid., Irma Fraad to RS, taped interview.

20 Else Siff to RS, taped interview.

21 Louis Davidson, NFB, Gordons.

22 Mary Frazier Meade, "Report on Foreign Policy Association meeting of 20 November 1937," Reference Archives, State Historical Society of Wisconsin.

23 Richard Meade to Ted Allan, TAF, vol. 16, file 18.

24 Fraad told RS that the US State Department was reluctant to antagonize Japan by issuing a passport to an American who would be assisting an enemy of Japan. Bethune in his Memorandum referred to the efforts made by him and Fraad to conceal the forming of the unit and its purpose for fear of antagonizing the American and Japanese governments. Parsons, however, was able to obtain a passport. Bethune in the same document states that Fraad was rejected because of his "limited surgical experience." The more likely reason is that Irma Fraad was successful in dissuading her husband from going.

25 Lewis Fraad to RS, 1970.

26 In his Memorandum Bethune stated that Parsons was "appointed 'in-charge' of the Unit."

27 Phillip Jaffe, letter to RS, 8 October 1970, RSF, 637/1/108.

28 Lewis Fraad to RS, taped interview.

29 Ibid.

30 Ibid.

31 Price, *The Lives of Agnes Smedley*, 32.

32 Evelyn Kirkpatrick to RS, 1970, taped interview, RSF.

33 University of Toronto, Thomas Fisher Rare Book Library, RS Collection of Bethune, MS COLL 34.

34 Elsie Siff to RS, taped interview.

35 Jean Ewen told RS that she had visited Bethune's mother in Toronto after his death and learned from Mrs Bethune that he had not written to her. Bethune had long been alienated from his brother, Malcolm. According to his niece Janet Cornell, he did send a telegram sometime in the autumn of 1939 to inform the family that he would be returning briefly to Canada (Janet Cornell to RS).

36 Paraskeva Clark, NFB interview

37 Ibid.

38 Charles Parsons to William Dodd Jr, 8 January 1938, Indusco.

39 Bethune to Oliver Haskell, director, China Aid Council, 19 July 1938. Before asking Haskell to send his monthly payment to Frances Coleman, Bethune thanked him for having already sent to her a sum of $200 (NFB research file for documentary film *Bethune*).

40 Jean Ewen to Edith Sawyer, executive director, China Aid Council, 13 May 1939, Indusco.

41 Jean Ewen, *China Nurse*, 46.

42 Bethune to Marian Scott, 8 January 1938, NFB research file for documentary film *Bethune*.

43 Bethune to Frances (Bethune) Coleman, 8 January 1938, NFB research file for documentary film *Bethune*. His reference to giving her what was due to her apparently referred to having the CAC send her his monthly stipend of $100 (see note 39 above). Frances remained in Bethune's thoughts: he would speak fondly of her to Jean Ewen on the way to Yan'an and in November 1939, in his last hours, he would ask that the CAC send money to her (see chapter 18, note 54). Unfortunately Frances's marriage to A.R.E. Coleman proved to be as unhappy as her marriages to Bethune had been. They divorced, and she returned to Scotland at the end of World War II. There she lived alone in reduced circumstances, supported by her family. Until her death in 1964 she kept a photograph of Bethune on her dresser.

CHAPTER FOURTEEN

1 C.M. Keene, Canadian Pacific Ships, to RS, 15 September 1971, RSF, 637/1/108. The films were *Anna Karenina*, *Wife versus Secretary*, *The Ghost Goes West*, and *Rhodes, the Empire Builder*. One can imagine Bethune's reaction to the last, if he saw it.

2 Jean Ewen to RS, 63, RSF, 637/1/108.

3 Bethune, Memorandum. Bethune stated that he had affidavits made testifying to Parsons's behaviour, which he sent to Dr Chi Chao-ting, a CAC member and editor of *Amerasia*.

4 Bethune, Memorandum.

5 Jean Ewen to RS.
6 Bethune, Memorandum.
7 Ewen, *China Nurse*, 48.
8 Ibid., 49. Ewen claimed that after suggesting they contact Smedley, she took it upon herself to send a cable to which Smedley replied two hours later, informing her that she had paid for and reserved three seats on a China National Airways Corporation flight to Wuhan. Ewen implies that this occurred almost immediately upon their arrival in Hong Kong and that the reservations had been made for two days after her receipt of Smedley's cable. They arrived in Hong Kong on Thursday, 27 January. If she sent the cable on Friday and the reservations were for Sunday, they would have arrived in Wuhan January 30. In his Memorandum Bethune states that they arrived in Wuhan on 7 February. With an occasional exception, he was precise in recording dates. Ewen's memory is surely faulty in this case.
9 Ibid. Bethune and the others waited for several hours at the Hong Kong airport because a Japanese air raid on Wuhan had delayed their flight from taking off. When they were finally on their way, the German pilot announced that he would be flying at a low altitude to avoid a possible attack by Japanese fighter planes, which had occurred on one of his flights a week earlier.
10 Ibid., 48.
11 MacKinnon and MacKinnon, *Agnes Smedley*, 201. Smedley had gone to Hankou at the urging of Zhu De, commander-in-chief of the Eighth Route Army, to raise funds to assist partisan supporters of the Eighth Route Army.
12 Ibid., 325.
13 Ewen, *China Nurse*, 50.
14 Zhang Yesheng, a Chinese expert on Bethune's life in China, told the authors in 2005 that Wang Bingnan, the director of international propaganda and also a liaison officer, attended the meeting, but the evidence is not clear on this.
15 This organization, financed by international contributors sympathetic to China, had no direct connection with the International Red Cross.
16 Born in Singapore, Robert K.S. Lim (1897–1969) had received his secondary school education in Scotland and gone on to graduate in medicine from Edinburgh University. Appointed professor of physiology at Peking Union Medical College in Beijing in 1924, he had remained there until the outbreak of the Sino-Japanese War in July 1937; he then took on the role of director of the Medical Relief Commission of the National Red Cross Society of China.
17 Ewen to RS; Ewen, *China Nurse*, 51–2.
18 Ewen, *China Nurse*, 52.
19 On that day, thirty-eight bombers, the largest Japanese force to date, appeared over the city. The Chinese fighter planes that rose to meet them were piloted mainly by Russians; they destroyed eleven of the attackers while losing four of their own aircraft (Richard Brown, letter to Bishop W.C. White, Hankou, 19 February 1938, GSA).
20 After the fall of the capital city of Nanjing in December 1937, the Guomindang made Hankou the temporary capital; they hoped to hold off the enemy until the move could be made to the new capital city of Chongqing, 1,200 kilometres upstream. Because Hankou was only a temporary stopping point, many

medical personnel and entire hospital staffs had already left for Chongqing. For this reason the medical care available for civilian casualties in Hankou was woefully inadequate.

21 Ewen, *China Nurse*, 53.

22 Bethune, Memorandum.

23 Oliver H. Haskell, director, China Aid Council, Oriental Study Expedition History Project. Oral history interview conducted by Enid Hart Douglass and Arthur L. Rosenbaum, Claremont, California, Claremont Graduate School, 1989.

24 Price, *The Lives of Agnes Smedley*, 325.

25 Bethune, Memorandum.

26 Richard Frederick Brown (1898–1963) was born in Dunstable, England, and immigrated to Canada in 1909. One year after graduation from the Faculty of Medicine at the University of Toronto in 1927, he accepted a position in Henan Province, China, in St Paul's Mission Hospital, built and equipped by the congregation of St Paul's Anglican Church of Toronto.

27 Brown to Bishop W.C. White, Hankou, 19 February 1938, GSA.

28 Brown, NFB interview.

29 Bethune, letter of 16 February to unknown recipient, TAF, vol. 16, file 4. However, in his Memorandum of April 20 Bethune states that the meeting took place on 19 February. In an interview with the National Film Board in 1963, Brown stated that he first met Bethune in Xi'an, not Hankou. As Bethune's letter was written on the day he met Brown, the authors have preferred to accept this as the correct version.

30 He told White that he was going "as a Christian doctor working among the sick of the so-called *Red Triangle* … The need is so great and I hope by my example to influence other Mission doctors to do the same. Poor war-wrecked China. If ever she needs friends it is now. I am not doing this lightly. I feel a definite urge" (Richard Brown to Bishop W.C. White, Hankou, 19 February 1938, GSA).

31 Parsons later had some success in dealing with his alcoholism. In 1940 he was appointed director of the Washingtonian Hospital in Boston, but several months later, on New Year's Eve, he was found dead in a hotel room in New York City. He had gone there to attend sessions of the American Association for the Advancement of Science. Three days earlier he had given a paper entitled, "Problems and Methods in a Hospital for Alcoholics." A brief obituary appeared in the *New York Times* of 31 December 1940.

32 Bethune, Memorandum. Although Smedley had not returned to Hankou until January, 1938, she had met with Phillip Jaffe in Yan'an in June 1937 and discussed the need for medical aid to the Chinese communist forces. It is likely that for this reason she was intended to be the unit's liaison with the Eighth Route Army in Yan'an. Instead she had met Bethune and Ewen in Hankou.

33 James Bertram to RS, 14 January 1971, RSF, 637/1/108. Bertram gave Bethune his sleeping bag, riding boots, and a fur cap, all of which Bethune later found extremely useful.

34 Bethune, Report to the China Aid Council, Xi'an, 24 March 1938, TAF, vol.16, file 5. On the morning of their departure from Hankou, Smedley had given Bethune and Ewen each $200 (Mex) for their expenses on their journey

(Bethune to Agnes Smedley, 26 March 1938, ibid.). Smedley also gave Ewen $200 to be given to Brown when he joined them (Jean Ewen to RS, 1972). It is worth noting that Smedley did not entrust Brown's money to Bethune. The Chinese currency was then based on the national silver dollar, the *yuan*, which was at par with the Mexican peso and was therefore widely referred to as "Mex."

35 Bethune to William Dodd Jr.

36 The description of their journey from Hankou to Xi'an is based on Bethune's letter to William Dodd Jr. Bethune would also humorously retitle the same text "See Shensi First" and send it to the Canadian League for Peace and Democracy, which published a slightly abridged version of it several months later as a pamphlet entitled "From Hankow to Sian." Ewen gives a less detailed account of their eventful trip in *China Nurse*, 56–78. Shensi was the romanized form of the name of the province used at that time; in pinyin, the form of romanization adopted by the People's Republic of China, the name of the province is spelled Shaanxi.

37 Their military forces, under the command of General Zhu De, had been incorporated in the newly formed National Revolutionary Army and were named the Eighth Route Army. Jin, Cha, and Ji are abbreviations that correspond to parts of the provinces of Shanxi, Chahar, and Hebei.

38 Ewen, *China Nurse*, 58.

39 This was probably about $US8. See note 34 for an explanation of Mex currency.

40 Ewen, *China Nurse*, 59–60.

41 Ibid., 60.

42 Dr Robert McClure to RS, taped interview, RSF, 637/2/8. Robert Baird McClure (1900–91) was the son of medical missionaries in China and served as a medical missionary there from 1923 to 1948. He was the moderator of the United Church of Canada from 1968 to 1971. Neither Bethune nor Ewen referred to the meeting with McClure; Bethune likely did not mention it to Ewen. McClure met Bethune again in Yan'an when he arrived with Dr Richard Brown nearly two months later. With the exception of a chronological difference, a similar description of the incident is recorded in Scott, *McClure*, 231.

43 Ewen, *China Nurse*, 61.

44 Ewen, "You Can't Buy It Back" (hereafter YCBIB). This is the original manuscript on which the published version, *China Nurse*, is based. It is in the possession of Ewen's daughter, Laura Meyer. There are minor variations among three versions of the manuscript – a complete handwritten text, a handwritten fragment, and a typed manuscript – and also between them and *China Nurse*. This quote is from the handwritten manuscript, 34–5. Ewen described Bethune's focus on the wounded as an obsession and wondered whether there was a human being underneath it all.

45 The accounts of Bethune and Ewen differ somewhat on circumstances in Linfen. For the most part the authors have based their version on that of Bethune. The quote is from Ewen, *China Nurse*, 63.

46 Ibid., 67.

47 Bethune and Ewen give somewhat different accounts of the attack. Ewen says two drivers were killed (ibid.).

48 Jean Ewen to RS, 8 June 1972, RSF, 637/1/108. Bethune, who did not mention a confrontation, described the incident in his letter to William Dodd Jr: "Jean Ewen showed great pluck and fortitude under her first baptism of fire and immediately after the bomber had passed started to dress the wounded and arrange for their transportation to the nearest village a quarter of a mile away, so that by the time I had walked from the head of the line to the rear where the men had been wounded, she had already applied dressings to the most serious ones" (Bethune to William Dodd Jr).

49 Jean Ewen to RS, letter of 4 January 1972; Ewen, *China Nurse*, 69–70.

50 Ewen, *China Nurse*, 71.

51 Jean Ewen to RS, 1972.

52 Ewen, *China Nurse*, 71–2.

53 Bethune to William Dodd Jr. Jean Ewen states that she accompanied Bethune on this visit to the mission (Ewen, YCBIB, handwritten ms., 49–50). She noted that while they were with the Franciscans, "Dr. Bethune turned on the charm. Even the pictures on the wall looked happy."

54 Ewen, *China Nurse*, 72.

55 Bethune to William Dodd Jr; Jean Ewen to RS, 8 June 1972.

56 Ewen, *China Nurse*, 73–4; Ewen, YCBIB, handwritten ms., 56.

57 Jean Ewen to RS, 8 June 1972.

58 Bethune to William Dodd Jr. A *kang* is a raised sleeping platform made of hardened clay. It was heated from beneath by means of an interior oven.

59 Ibid.; also Ewen, YCBIB, handwritten ms., 56.

60 Bethune to William Dodd Jr.

61 Jean Ewen to RS, 8 June 1972.

62 Bethune letter to William Dodd Jr.

63 Ewen, YCBIB, handwritten ms., 61–2.

64 Ewen, *China Nurse*, 78. After returning to Canada, Ewen visited Bethune's mother, who confirmed that her son was to blame for the failure of the marriage, saying that he had fought with Frances throughout their relationship and that she had been surprised Frances stayed with him as long as she did (Jean Ewen to RS, 8 June 1972). It is also worth noting that in her account of their time living in a cave near the Yellow River, Ewen makes no mention of their walking from there to Hancheng, which Bethune recounts in his letter to William Dodd Jr.

65 Bethune to William Dodd Jr.

66 In his letter to William Dodd Jr., Bethune states that he and Ewen arrived in Xi'an on 21 March, but in his Memorandum of 20 April 1938, he refers to the date as 19 March. March 21 accords with the daily record of his activities as he described them in the letter.

67 Bethune, letter to William Dodd Jr. It was not the first for Ewen, who in *China Nurse*, 73, states that she had bathed in a tub in an abandoned house en route.

68 Ewen, YCBIB, handwritten ms. (fragment), 58.

69 Under the terms of the United Front Agreement, the Communists had been permitted to maintain an administrative unit in Xi'an. Until Jiang Jieshi (Chiang Kai-shek) began to break the spirit and principles of the agreement, Xi'an headquarters remained a vital part of the Eighth Route Army apparatus in its role as a national recruiting centre. Young men and women made their way there

from all parts of China. They were interviewed and informed of the hardships that they would have to face in guerrilla warfare, and then those who were deemed fit received passes and continued north to the central base of all Communist forces in Yan'an.

70 *Ottawa Citizen*, 12 March 1938. Four days later, newspaper reports had them safe in Xi'an. These equally inaccurate reports may have been based on information provided by the Eighth Route Army indicating their arrival in Hancheng and their intended destination of Xi'an.

71 In *China Nurse*, 79, Ewen incorrectly refers to Lin Beiqu as Lin Pai Chen.

72 Jean Ewen, YCBIB, handwritten ms., 57.

73 Bethune to Agnes Smedley, 26 March, 1938, TAF, vol. 16, file 5.

74 Bethune, Report to the Communist Party of the United States and the Communist Party of Canada, 24 March 1938, ibid.

75 Bethune, Memorandum.

76 Jean Ewen to RS, 4 January 1972, RSF.

77 Ewen, *China Nurse*, 83. On the same page she mentions that Bethune questioned Dr Jiang Qixian in depth about Brown. She writes that it was at this point that she and Bethune learned that Brown would become part of the unit. Ewen's memory must have failed here.

78 Ewen, *China Nurse*, 82. She wrote, "For nearly four days we discussed sanitation, delousing, bath houses, and collecting lice, and did surveys on TB and vaccinations with these scientists. It sounded like a bizarre bit of business, but the lice collecting was for serum."

79 Jean Ewen to RS, 1 July 1972, RSF, 637/1/108.

80 This was the same text as the letter to William Dodd Jr. See note 36 for an explanation of the spelling of Shensi/Shaanxi.

81 Bethune to William Dodd Jr. Throughout his remaining time in China he frequently sent summary reports of his activities to Tim Buck of the CPC and on rare occasions to Earl Browder of the CPUSA. He also sent copies of accounts of his work to various persons in Canada and the United States beginning with the salutation "Dear Comrade."

82 Bethune, "Report to the China Aid Council," Xi'an, 24 March 1938, TAF, vol. 16, file 5.

83 Bethune to Agnes Smedley, Xi'an, 26 March 1938, ibid. It is worth noting that Bethune took photographs throughout his time in China and sent them out via Yan'an to be developed, possibly in Hong Kong. The prints were to be sent to Tim Buck in Canada. By September of 1938 the photographer Sha Fei had joined Bethune's unit and photographic materials had been obtained from Tianjin, so Bethune hoped to be able to have prints made on the spot (Bethune to Ma Haide, Songyankou, 30 September 1938, NBF, vol. 1, file 20).

CHAPTER FIFTEEN

1 Ewen, YCBIB, typed ms., 171.

2 Ibid, 174.

3 Ewen, *China Nurse*, 85.

4 George Hatem was born in 1910 to Lebanese immigrant parents in the United States. Brought up in Buffalo, New York, he studied medicine in the United States and Switzerland, then went to Shanghai where he began to practise.

Appalled by the poverty and the incidence of venereal disease in the city and the apparent lack of interest of Jiang Jieshi's Guomindang government in taking steps to eliminate it, he made contact through Agnes Smedley with members of the Chinese Communist Party. Accompanied by the American journalist Edgar Snow, Hatem made his way to Yan'an. There he put his medical training to work while Snow interviewed Mao Zedong and other leading Communist figures. Hatem would stay on in China until his death in 1988. Though very different in personality and temperament from Bethune, his contributions as a foreigner were no less significant. After the Communists came to power in 1949, Ma was an important part of the successful campaigns that significantly reduced the high incidence of venereal disease and helped combat leprosy in China.

5 Ewen, YCBIB, typed ms., 180; YCBIB, handwritten ms., 84. Dr Ma shared his cave residence with Li De (Otto Braun), a Comintern agent who was the only foreigner on the Long March.

6 Ewen, *China Nurse*, 87–8. Li Xue, whom Bethune called "Mike," acted as his interpreter during his stay in Yan'an (Zhang Yesheng to the authors, 2005). The association was an unhappy one: Bethune complained that Li did not have the education to do the job, and Li said that Bethune used too many large words. Ewen wondered why she was not asked to interpret for Bethune but on the whole was relieved to escape such a thankless task (Jean Ewen, YCBIB, handwritten ms., 95).

7 Ewen does not refer to the presence of Jiang Qixian, but Zhang Yesheng assured the authors that Jiang was there.

8 Ewen, *China Nurse*, 88.

9 Ibid.

10 Mao Zedong, "In Memory of Dr Norman Bethune," 338; Jean Ewen, YCBIB, typed ms., 187. In an interview in 1972, Ma Haide told RS that Bethune and Mao had met on several occasions.

11 Bethune to Agnes Smedley, Yan'an, 8 March (likely after 2 April) 1938, TAF, vol. 16, file 4. This letter is mistakenly dated 8 March, when Bethune was still en route to Xi'an from Hankou. The contents of the letter reveal that it was written after 2 April, the date of his meeting with Mao. (Although Bethune refers to the date of his first meeting with Mao as 1 April, the day they had arrived in Yan'an, they did not meet with Mao until after midnight, hence on 2 April.) Despite Mao's initial agreement that Ma Haide could go to Jin-Cha-Ji with Bethune, Ma in fact was never sent there.

12 He Zexin to RS, 1972.

13 Ibid.

14 Bethune, letter to Agnes Smedley, Yan'an, 8 March (likely after 2 April) 1938.

15 Ibid.

16 Bethune, letter to Canada, Suide, 3 May 1938, NFB research file for documentary film *Bethune*.

17 Nelson Fu (1894–1968) was a missionary doctor who had been taken prisoner by the Communists several years earlier and had eventually joined the Chinese Communist Party. He went on the Long March, and though as a Christian he was somewhat an anomaly in the Eighth Route Army, he was highly respected.

18 There are different estimates of the number of caves in the hospital. In *Shark's*

Fins and Millet, 255, Ilona Ralf Sues states that there were seventy. Richard Brown in an interview with the National Film Board claimed that there were "about 30."

19 While Bethune was still sulking, he was visited by Professor Heinrich von Jettmar, whom he had already met in Xi'an. The Viennese microbiologist was in charge of the League of Nations Epidemiological Unit laboratory in Yan'an, and he encouraged Bethune's sense of grievance by agreeing with him about conditions in the hospital, which he described as "a nightmare." He told Bethune that he had already made his criticisms known to the authorities without result (Erich Landauer to RS, 12 October 1970, RSF, 637/1/13).

20 Ma Haide to RS, taped interview, RSF, 637/2/6.

21 Ewen, YCBIB typed ms., 189.

22 Agnes Smedley to Norman Bethune, Hankow (Hankou) 8 April 1938, attachment to Bethune, Memorandum.

23 Bethune, letters to Canada, Suide, 3 May 1938.

24 Bethune to Agnes Smedley, 17 April 1938, attachment to his Memorandum. Although Bethune refers to "letters" from Smedley in this passage, he attached only her letter of 8 April to his Memorandum.

25 Ibid. This letter no doubt provided Bethune with a much-needed emotional release, and it may even have been an honest attempt to set the record straight. But tweaking the tail of the Smedley lion was risky. As the representative of the China Aid Council in Hankou, she was Bethune's lifeline to the outside world. In addition, her organizing of the Northwest Partisan Relief Committee and her close association with Dr Robert Lim of the Medical Relief Commission of the National Red Cross Society of China meant that her name was widely identified in China with the effort to raise funds for Communist partisans fighting behind the lines in the Jin-Cha-Ji Border Region. During the remainder of 1938, Smedley became equally well known abroad. Her articles describing China's heroic resistance against the Japanese and making a fervent plea for the cause of medical relief appeared in newspapers and journals in England, North America, and Hong Kong. See MacKinnon and MacKinnon, *Agnes Smedley*, 204.

26 Bethune to Dear Comrades, Yan'an, 17 April 1938, attachment to Memorandum.

27 Ibid.

28 Smedley later wrote to Eric Landauer, "Did you meet Dr Bethune and hear that I am insane, or half-insane? I am forever meeting men who consider me half-insane or on the verge of a nervous breakdown, that is if I disagree with them or do not sufficiently admire them. Up to the point that I disagree, they consider me one of the sanest and most steady-headed people alive. Bethune thought that until I questioned his superhuman qualities or considered him fallible. Then he told me that I was on the verge of a 'nervous breakdown'" (Erich Landauer to RS).

29 Philip Jaffe to RS, 8 October 1970.

30 Ibid. "Though he was a known alcoholic, we took a calculated risk, but we lost," Jaffe wrote.

31 Ibid.

32 Oliver Haskell, director of the China Aid Council, would later state, "We were dealing with Madame Sun Yat-Sen [Song Qingling] as our representative in

Hong Kong, and with Dr Robert Lim of the Chinese Red Cross in Hankou when the government was there to forward our supplies that we were sending for our medical unit ... Madame Sun ... served as our contact in Hong Kong and Agnes Smedley in Hankou ... She had endless disputes with Dr Bethune. I would get the telegrams. He would send me copies of her telegrams to him and his answers to her" (Oriental Study Expedition History Project, oral history interview conducted by Enid Hart Douglass and Arthur L. Rosenbaum).

33 Robert Lim to Oliver Haskell, director, China Aid Council, 2 October 1938, New York Public Library, Correspondence between Dr Robert Lim and Oliver Haskell of the China Aid Council, United China Relief Collection, box 1, f.b. Chinese Red Cross, 1938–40 (hereafter cited as Robert Lim to Oliver Haskell, 2 October 1938). Lim wrote, "This is to acknowledge your letter of August 23. I note that all funds for the Red Cross will in future be sent to the China Defence League." In the same letter, Lim wrote: "With regard to the US$1500.00 sent by the CAC, I have received monthly remittances up to August. These have been turned over to the Eighth Route Army Reserve Field Hospital, according to the understanding originally reached between Miss Smedley, the Eighth Route Army and myself ... It was also arranged at that time that Dr Bethune and Miss Ewen would work in this hospital. As it took some time before the Hospital could get under way, Dr Bethune left for Shensi [Shaanxi]; consequently he has received no support from the $1500 which you have forwarded." Lim explained to Haskell that although he had not wired money directly to Bethune, he had sent him supplies. "It is difficult for me to consult Dr Bethune concerning his needs, as he is in Wu-Tai-Shan," Lim wrote. "But I have a list of his requirements, and have tried to meet them as far as possible from our Red Cross stores. We have, I think, given him all the important items he asked for. We shall continue to meet all needs of the Northwest, where Dr Bethune is, to the limit of our capacity. Already we have sent over $70,000.00 worth of supplies, and another large consignment is on its way." Lim was likely quoting in the Chinese National Currency, which was then valued at six *yuan* to one American dollar. The list to which he refers was attached to a letter written by Bethune and taken to Lim in Hankou by the Associated Press correspondent Haldore Hanson when he left Songyankou with Richard Brown in July 1938.

34 The formation of the regions was later decided at a conference in the city of Fuping in the province of Hebei between 10 and 15 January 1938.

35 Jiang Yizhen, "Dr Bethune's Spirit Will Live Forever," 24.

36 Ibid.

37 In *Bethune*, 128, RS incorrectly wrote that Richard Brown had arrived in Xi'an and accompanied Bethune on the trip north to Yan'an. However, Min-sun Chen writes that Brown reached Xi'an on 10 April and left one week later on Easter Sunday for Yan'an (Min-sun Chen, "China's Unsung Canadian Hero," 114). Bethune, writing to Agnes Smedley in a letter dated 17 April, stated that Brown was already in Yan'an. During his interview with the National Film Board, Brown claimed that he conducted a Good Friday church service on 15 April in response to a request made by Mao on 13 April. If Chen's claim that Brown arrived in Xi'an on 10 April is correct, Brown must have left for Yan'an the day

of his arrival in Xi'an or no later than 11 April, because the trip by vehicle from Xi'an to Yan'an then took three days.

38 Brown, NFB interview

39 Ibid. Brown claimed that in response to his request the Chinese later gave him the flag, which he had at the time of the interview in 1963. Canada's flag at the time was the Red Ensign.

40 Ibid.

41 Joe Hill was a Swedish-American labour activist who was executed after a controversial murder trial.

42 Bethune to Earl Browder and Tim Buck, Hejiachuan, 23 May 1938, Jaffe, box 4, folder 5; Ewen, *China Nurse*, 95–6.

43 Bethune to Earl Browder and Tim Buck, Hejiachuan, 23 May 1938.

44 Ewen later wrote that she followed Bethune north but that at Suide was given a letter that he had left behind for her, telling her not to try to follow him and Brown to Wutai, because physical conditions there would be too difficult and she was too young for such a mission. He also wrote that she did not understand the gravity or seriousness of the cause they served. Infuriated, she tore the letter into tiny pieces. She later claimed that in spite of his warning she had remained determined to reach Wutai (Ewen, YCBIB, typewritten ms., 217–18). She continued north as far as Lanxian where she helped train nurses, but after that the military situation made it impossible for her to get to Wutai and ill health caught up with her; she suffered severe weight loss and vitamin deficiencies. She left Lanxian on 5 September 1938 and eventually returned to Xi'an, later making her way circuitously to Shanghai. After serving for some months with the New Fourth Army, she returned to Canada in the late spring of 1939 (Ewen to RS, 8 June 1972). Ewen's account of the letter left for her at Suide conflicts with various statements made by Bethune, the latest on 3 July, that he did not know why Ewen had not followed him (Bethune to Ma Haide, Wutaishan, 3 July 1938, Indusco).

45 Brown, NFB interview. Bethune later had considerable success in convincing the Chinese of the safety and efficacy of blood transfusions.

46 He Zexin to RS, 1972.

47 Xue Fang to RS, 1972.

48 Bethune, letters to Canada, Suide, 3 May 1938. The addressees of these letters are not known.

49 Xue Fang to RS, 1972.

50 He Zexin to RS, 1972.

51 Bethune to Earl Browder and Tim Buck, Hejiachuan, 23 May 1938.

52 Xue Fang to RS, 1972.

53 Bethune to Mao Zedong, May 17–22 1938, Jaffe, box 4, folder 5.

54 Xue Fang to RS, 1972.

55 Bethune to Ma Haide, Wutaishan, July 3 1938, Indusco.

56 Bethune to Mao Zedong, Hejiachuan, 17–22 May 1938.

57 Lu and Zou, "Norman Bethune and His Contributions," 2. The article was given as a paper at the International Society of Blood Transfusion (Asia) Conference in 2007.

58 Richard Brown, NFB interview.

59 Bethune, letter to Mao Zedong, Hejiachuan, 17–22 May.

60 Ibid.

61 Ibid.

62 Ibid. See note 33, this chapter, for a discussion of Chinese currency.

63 Ibid.

64 Bethune to Earl Browder and Tim Buck, Hejiachuan, 23 May 1938.

65 Ibid.

66 Ibid.

67 Two of the three days on their trip from the Yellow River to Lanxian were spent at a small hospital in the village of Xingxian.

68 Bethune to Mao Zedong, Lanxian, 6 June 1938, Indusco.

69 Bethune to Ma Haide, Lanxian, 6 June 1938, Indusco.

70 Utley, *China at War*, 137–8.

71 Bethune to Dear Comrade, Jingangku, 30 June 1938, Jaffe, box 4, folder 5.

72 Jean Ewen learned of this incident from Dr Jiang Qixian, whom she met during her travels in Shanxi after she had become separated from Bethune, and who had accompanied Bethune and Brown on their trek to Wutai. "Did he scream?" Ewen asked, laughing, when she heard Bethune's typewriter had vanished. "Did he ever!" replied Dr Jiang, "but it all turned out fine because when they got to headquarters the typewriter was sitting on the table" (Ewen, *China Nurse*, 106).

73 Bethune to Dear Comrade, Jingangku, 30 June 1938.

74 It appears that Bethune miscalculated the length of the journey by a day. Most Chinese sources indicate that Bethune met the military commander General Nie Rongzhen in Jingangku on 17 June. Both Bethune (in his letter to Dear Comrade, 30 June 1938) and Brown (Brown to Agnes Smedley, 6 June 1938, GSA) claim they left Lanxian on June 7. Brown suggested that the trip would take seven days and Bethune states that it did take eight days to reach Wutai. That would date their arrival there as Wednesday, June 15. However, it would seem that the date was actually Thursday, June 16. The following day they made the trip of fifty kilometres from Wutai to General Nie Rongzhen's headquarters in the village of Jingangku.

75 Bethune to Dear Comrade, Jingangku, 30 June 1938.

76 Born in 1899 into a wealthy Sichuan family, Nie Rongzhen (1899–1992) went to France in 1920 to study. There he met Zhou Enlai and joined the Chinese Communist Party. Giving up his intended career in engineering, he returned to China. A veteran of the Long March (1934–35), he had been appointed commander of Eighth Route Army forces in Jin-Cha-Ji in early 1938. Nie achieved the rank of marshal in the People's Liberation Army after the establishment of the People's Republic of China and ultimately became Vice-chairman of the Central Military Commission.

77 Bethune to Dear Comrade, Jingangku, 30 June 1938.

78 Ibid.

79 Many had been wounded ten months earlier at the first Eighth Route Army victory over a Japanese unit in the battle of 25–27 September 1937 in the mountain pass of Pingxingguan in northern Shanxi.

80 Bethune to Elsie Siff, Songyankou, 19 July 1938, RSF, 637/1/120.

81 Bethune to Dear Comrade, Jingangku, 30 June 1938; Bethune to Mao Zedong, Jingangku, 3 July 1938. Both in Jaffe, box 4, folder 5.

82 Jean Ewen to RS, 1972.

83 Bethune to Lilian Goudge, 29 June 1938, TAF, vol. 16, file 6. It is possible that Agnes Smedley, who wrote for the *Guardian*, had provided Bethune with this contact in the days before their bitter quarrel. Bethune did write one long article for the *Guardian*, which he may or may not have sent. It was never published, and the *Guardian* has no record of any correspondence with Bethune.

84 Brown, NFB interview.

85 Hanson, *Humane Endeavour*, 256; Richard Brown, NFB interview.

86 Richard Brown, NFB interview.

87 Ibid.

88 Ibid.

89 Ibid.

90 Jean Ewen to RS, 8 June 1972.

91 Brown, NFB interview.

92 Ibid.

93 Bethune to Mao Zedong, Jingangku, 3 July 1938; Bethune to Dear Comrade, Jingangku, 30 June 1938.

94 As he prepared to leave to set up the hospital in Liaozhou, Brown wrote a letter of resignation from the missionary society saying that he had decided to "throw in my lot with my Chinese brothers and sisters ... The work is full of hardships and bitter sufferings. I am the only foreigner, and as in the past, I shall eat, live and sleep and share my lot with the Chinese. I go, not as a Communist, to the contrary, very anti-Communist, but definitely as a Christian doctor." In commenting on the criticism of his association with communists, he wrote, "May I remind the sub-committee that China is at war, her very entrails ripped and gushing blood and that this is the time for professing Christians to show a little love for her" (Brown to Reverend Canon S. Gould, secretary-treasurer, Missionary Society of Chinese Christians, Xi'an, 24 November 1938, GSA). Brown would later persuade General Zhu De to issue a statement in October to a Mission Leaders' Conference in Xi'an, which assured the Christian missionary community in China that not only was the Eighth Route Army not hostile to its members but it thanked them for the vital medical assistance they had provided to communist troops. Influenced by Guomindang propaganda, most missionaries were strongly anti-communist. To many, Zhu De's conciliatory statement was no more than a ruse designed to achieve temporary gains. Perhaps it was: after the ultimate victory of the Communist side in the second civil war with the Guomindang in the late 1940s, all missionaries were eventually ordered to leave China.

95 With him was Haldore Hanson, a twenty-six-year-old American correspondent for the Associated Press, who spent several days in Songyankou. Hanson, the first foreign newsman to visit Jin-Cha-Ji, later recorded his experiences in China in his book *Humane Endeavour*. He accompanied Brown on his journey to Hankou.

96 Bethune to Dear Comrade, Jingangku, 30 June 1938; Brown to Dr Harold Louckes, Songyankou, 7 July 1938, GSA. Unfortunately for Bethune, Brown

did not return. On the way south, he and Hanson stopped at the general head-quarters of the Eighth Route Army in southeastern Shanxi where General Zhu De pointed out that he needed the same kind of facilities that Brown and Bethune had begun to set up in Songyankou. Brown therefore agreed to come back to the area when he had raised the necessary funds. After persuading the International Red Cross Society in Hankou to provide financial support, he managed to reopen a closed mission hospital in Liaozhou in Shanxi in December 1938. However, he could not remain there long because of his concern for his wife and three children who were in the Japanese-controlled city of Qingdao. He therefore left Liaozhou to be with them. In 1940, Brown made his way from Qingdao to Chonqqing, the wartime capital of China, where he became the medical officer of the British Legation. From there he joined the Royal Army Medial Corps with the rank of major and was assigned to India. In 1944, after his transfer to the Canadian Army, he returned to Toronto. His wife and children, who had left Qingdao on a ship bound for Australia, were at sea when the Japanese attacked Pearl Harbor. When the ship docked in Manila, which had fallen to the Japanese, they were sent to an internment camp. After the Japanese surrender in August 1945, Mrs Brown and the children were reunited with Richard Brown in Toronto. These data come from a number of sources including Chen, "Richard Brown: China's Unsung Hero," 31, and Hanson, *Humane Endeavour*.

97 Bethune to Elsie Siff, Songyankou, 19 July 1938.

CHAPTER SIXTEEN
1 Richard Brown, NFB interview.
2 Ibid.
3 Hanson, *Humane Endeavour*, 355.
4 Bethune to Dear Comrade, Jingangku, 30 June 1938.
5 Ibid.
6 Nie Ronghzhen, "Report at General Headquarters of the Eighth Route Army, October 13, 1944," NFB research file for documentary film *Bethune*.
7 Dong had been appointed to his executive position the previous January. Bethune must have been told that he would be coming, because in a letter to Ma Haide on 13 July, the day Brown left, he wrote that he did not need Ewen to join him because he had a good interpreter (Bethune to Ma Haide, Songyankou, 13 July 1938, NFB research file for documentary film *Bethune*). He also reported that he had trained a first-class staff. This is questionable, given the time it had taken him and Brown to set up a functioning operating room and complete 110 operations in twenty-five days following their arrival on 17 June. Neither of them would have had the time to have undertaken any extensive training of staff. This is confirmed in his letter written to Nie Rongzhen a month later on 13 August in which he says that the present staff of doctors is not "sufficiently trained or competent." He went on, "I have had 2 months' close association with them and am only now beginning to see the results of my instruction to them" (Bethune to Nie Rongzhen, Songyankou, 13 August 1938, Indusco).
8 Jiang Yizhen, "Dr. Bethune's Spirit Will Live Forever," 27.

9 Lindsay, *The Unknown War*, n.p.

10 Bethune to Mao Zedong, Jingangku, 3 July 1938. To this letter Bethune attached a copy of a five-page assessment of conditions at the Base Hospital. The final section reads: "One of my most serious criticisms is against the dilatoriness and inability of doctors to take charge and supervise juniors. A very common fault is to give commands to others but not to see that they are carried out. Important or urgent tasks must be done by the doctor himself. 'Passing the buck' is a common fault. Doctors do not supervise enough. They do not see that orders are carried out promptly. Forgetfullness [*sic*] and carelessness and too many of the staff engaged in a task which only requires half the number, is frequent. Half the time is spent in talk. All work is done very slowly. A new spirit must be put into the staff – of quickness, alertness, and doing work themselves, not leaving it to others. One man – one job. The old saying of Confucius must not be forgotten – "One man can carry 2 buckets of water; 2 men can carry 1 bucket of water, but 3 men can carry no water at all.""

11 Ibid.

12 Zhang Yesheng to the authors, 2005.

13 Bethune to Ma Haide, Songyankou, 19 July 1938, Indusco.

14 Bethune to Mao Zedong, 20 July 1938, Indusco.

15 Bethune, telegram to Military Council at Yan'an, 12 August 1938, Indusco.

16 Bethune to Mao Zedong, Songyankou, 13 August 1938, Indusco.

17 On completing the text, Bethune entitled it "Principles of Organization and Procedure of a Divisional Field Hospital in Guerrilla Warfare."

18 Bethune to Nie Rongzhen, Songyankou, 13 August 1938, Indusco.

19 Dong Chun, daughter of Dong Yueqian, to the authors, 2005.

20 Nie Rongzhen to Dr You Shenghua, deputy minister of health in Jin-Cha-Ji, from the blog of You Liqing, daughter of You Shenghua, trans. Kun Zhang, BMH, 11 March 2009.

21 Bethune, letter to an unidentified recipient, Songyankou, 21 August 1938, Indusco.

22 Ibid.

23 Ibid. These statements are from a brief addendum to the letter, written 23 August.

24 Bethune, speech given at Songyankou, 15 September 1938, Indusco.

25 Ibid.

26 Ye Qingshan, diary, unpublished ms. in the possession of Ye's daughter. A translation of the dates mentioned in this document and a list of the events mentioned in it are in the authors' possession.

27 These were in the villages of Huamu, Qiubudong, and Zhaoti Miao.

28 You Shenghua, "Bethune among the Beacons of Resistance against Japan," in *The Great Internationalist Soldier Bethune*, 11. In a letter to Ma Haide on 30 September, Bethune stated that Japanese forces approaching Songyankou were only 55 li (about 27 kilometres) away and that he would leave the following day (Bethune to Ma Haide, Songyankou, 30 September 1938, NBF, vol. 1, file 20).

29 Only a small pine tree in the courtyard escaped the flames. When in 1974 a complete reconstruction of the model hospital was completed, the pine tree had grown to a substantial height and remains today the symbol of Bethune's doomed venture.

30 In a letter Bethune stated that he had examined 303 patients, of whom he operated on 132 (Bethune to Nie Rongzhen, Changyu, 1 November 1938, TAF, vol. 16, file 7).

31 Two important sources of his understanding of the system of government introduced by the Communists in the areas which they controlled came from Agnes Smedley's *China's Red Army Marches* and Edgar Snow's *Red Star over China*, both of which he had read before leaving for China.

32 Bethune to Nie Rongzhen, Changyu, 1 November 1938.

33 Bethune and Dong Yueqian, "Staff Conference: A Hsien Government at Work in the Fighting Area of North China," TAF, vol. 16, file 7. Bethune appended a copy of this article to his letter of 1 November 1938 to Nie Rongzhen.

34 Lindsay was the "visitor from Beiping." He spent the first week of August in Songyankou with Bethune (Lindsay, *The Unknown War*, n.p.; Bethune to Tim Buck, Changyu, November 1 1938, TAF, vol. 16, file 7).

35 Bethune to Nie Rongzhen, 22 October 1938, ibid.

36 Bethune to Nie Rongzhen, Changyu, 2 November 1938, ibid.

37 There they stayed for several days. When Dong had left his position as chief magistrate of Fuping County to join Bethune in July 1938, he had turned over his responsibilities to another official. Now he wanted to stop at Fuping en route to Yanbei to deal with any questions his successor might have.

38 Zhang Yesheng to the authors, 2005.

39 The date of the operation is in question. Based on Bethune's report of 7 December to Nie Rongzhen, he arrived in Xiashifan on Monday, 21 November (Bethune, report to Nie Rongzhen, Yangjiazhuang, 7 December 1938, Indusco). Zuo Ling, the daughter of Zuo Qi, informed the authors that Bethune amputated her father's right arm in Xiashifan on Sunday, November 20.

40 Bethune, report to Nie Rongzhen, Yangjiazhuang, 7 December 1938; Zhang Yesheng to the authors, 2005.

41 Zhang Yesheng to the authors, 2005.

42 Zhou, *Doctor Norman Bethune*, 54; You Shenghua, "Bethune among the Beacons," in *Great Internationalist Soldier*, 26. Wang Zhen's planned ambush was on the Lingqiu/Guangling highway, the only motor route in the region. The coordinated attack by three Eighth Route Army regiments on a convoy of five trucks carrying a company of two hundred Japanese troops began just after 8 AM on Tuesday, 29 November.

43 Bethune, report to Nie Rongzhen, Yangjiazhuang, 7 December 1938.

44 You Shenghua, "Bethune among the Beacons," in *Great Internationalist Soldier*, 28.

45 Ibid., 53; Jiang Yizhen, "Dr Bethune's Spirit Will Live Forever," 25. In his description of the role of his medical team at Heisi in a report to Nie, Bethune mentions only the arrival "on the 30th day by Dr Lu of the Yan'an medical unit and by another doctor of the Sanitary Service of the 359th Brigade, who relieved us for the evening of that day, permitting Drs You and Wang and myself to take some rest." He makes no reference to Jiang Yizhen (Bethune, report to General Nie, Yangjiazhuang, 7 December 1938).

46 Ibid.

47 On this matter he was pessimistic. He reported to Nie that since his arrival in

Yanbei, he had been extremely disappointed by the performance of the Sanitary Service of the 359th Brigade (ibid.).

48 You Shenghua, "Bethune among the Beacons," in *Great Internationalist Soldier*, 15. The description of the creation of the Special Surgical Hospital is based on data in this essay.

49 Bethune, letter to Ye Qingshan and You Shenghua, Shenbei, 12 July 1939. In his letter to the two doctors, Bethune listed the criticisms that he had placed before them in Yangjiazhuang in December 1938.

50 Ibid.

51 You Shenghua, "Bethune among the Beacons," in *Great Internationalist Soldier*, 20.

52 Bethune, letter to Ye Qingshan and You Shenghua, Shenbei, 12 July 1939, Indusco.

53 Bethune, report to Nie Rongzhen, Yangjiazhuang, 7 December 1938, ibid.

54 Ibid., 172.

55 You Shenghua, interview with Ted Allan, TAF, vol. 3, file 10.

56 You Shenghua, "Bethune among the Beacons," in *Great Internationalist Soldier*, 16.

57 Ibid.

58 Lu and Zou, "Norman Bethune and His Contributions," 3. You Shenghua in "Bethune among the Beacons," in *Great Internationalist Soldier*, 16, indicates that the donor received one hundred eggs. This seems unlikely given the poverty of the area.

59 You Shenghua, interview with Ted Allan, TAF, vol. 3, file 10.

60 The constitution provided for a Central Committee of thirteen to deal with administrative and health-related matters in the hospital. The members of the committee were to be democratically elected by secret ballot by the three sections of staff, patients, and civilians and were to be subject to recall by a democratic vote of their sections. Bethune urged that the civilians of the village should feel themselves to be beholden to the wounded, who had fought to defend them, and must consider themselves a responsible part of the local hospital unit (Bethune, "Constitution of the Special Surgical Hospital [Base District]," Yangjiazhuang, December 1938, NBF, vol. 1, file 15).

61 Bethune, "Wounds," *Daily Worker*, 19 February 1940.

62 Ibid.

63 Bethune to Ye Qingshan and You Shenghua, Shenbei, 12 July 1939. Various Chinese sources fix the date at 3 January 1939.

64 Ibid. They came from the First and Third Subdistricts and the Sanitary Service of the 359th Brigade.

65 The length of the period indicated in most sources is one day. Lu and Zou indicate that it was every three days ("Norman Bethune and His Contributions," 4).

66 On one occasion he noticed that a doctor had stuck his hands in his pockets while watching a colleague operating. Bethune reprimanded the culprit, saying that there was never a moment for relaxation in an operating room because lives depended on alertness (You Shenghua, "Bethune among the Beacons," in *Great Internationalist Soldier*, 23).

67 Zhang Yesheng to the authors, 2005.

68 Bethune to Tim Buck, near Hejian, 4 March 1939, TAF, vol. 16, file 10.

69 Bethune to Ye Qingshan and You Shenghua, Shenbei, 12 July 1939.

70 Ibid.

71 His manual on guerrilla medicine covered the following topics: Brigade Medical Service; Surgery and Medicine; Post-Operative Treatment; General Operating Room Knowledge; Pharmacy; Making of Instruments; General Medicine at the Front.

72 Dong Yueqian, "Throughout the Green Mountains Loyal Bones Lie Buried," in *Great Internationalist Soldier*, 16.

73 George Mooney, diary, 2 April 1946, HSEF, vol. 40, file 20. Mooney met and spoke with Nie Rongzhen while on a mission for United Nations Relief and Rehabilitation Administration (UNRRA).

74 Bethune, "Brief Review of Medical Work in Yan'an," early April 1938, TAF, vol. 16, file 3.

75 Ma Haide to RS, 1972.

76 Zhang Yesheng to the authors, 2005. Zhang stated that none of the written sources or interviewees identified the cause of this finger infection which was likely the result of a scalpel wound during an operation, a not infrequent occurrence owing to Bethune's preference for operating without gloves. In any case, as supplies dwindled during his mission in Jin-Cha-Ji, gloves were no longer available.

77 Bethune to Canada, Yangjiazhuang, 10 January 1939, TAF, vol. 16, file 10.

78 Ibid.

79 Ibid. In another letter to Tim Buck sent two months later, Bethune referred to the correspondence he had received while in China. In addition to "several from Montreal comrades" he listed only ten other letters (including three from the China Aid Council) that he had received since his arrival in China more than a year earlier. (Bethune to Tim Buck, 4 March 1939).

80 Bethune to Ma Haide, Yangjiazhuang, 8 December 1938, TAF, vol. 16, file 7.

81 Bethune, letter to Canada, Yangjiazhuang, 10 January 1939.

82 Bethune to Ma Haide, Yangjiazhuang, 8 December 1938.

83 Zhou, *Doctor Norman Bethune*, 42.

CHAPTER SEVENTEEN

1 Bethune to Ma Haide, Yangjiazhuang, 8 December 1938.

2 In a letter to Ma Haide in Yan'an he enclosed the following text, which Zhou Enlai sent by cable to New York on 3 August: "Canadian-American Medical Unit working for past month in Chin-Cha-Chi [Jin-Cha-Ji] Military District with Partisans in rear of Japanese. One hundred ten operations in twenty-five days. Desperate need money and medical surgical supplies. Cable one thousand dollars gold Maotsesung [Mao Zedong] immediately for use this Region especially" (Bethune to Ma Haide, Songyankou, 19 July 1938, Indusco).

3 Bethune to Tim Buck, near Hejian, 4 March 1939.

4 See chapter 15, note 33. The second consignment sent to Bethune by him is referred to in CDLN, 1 April 1939.

5 She was assisted by Hilda Selwyn-Clark, the wife of the medical director of Hong Kong. Song Qingling was one of three sisters; the other two were Song

Meiling, the wife of Generalissimo Jiang Jieshi [Chiang Kai-shek], and Song Ailing, the wife of H.H. Kung, the minister of finance in Jiang's government. After the defeat of Guomindang forces in the second Chinese civil war (1946–49) and their flight to Taiwan, Song Qingling remained with the victorious Communists. She became a revered figure in the People's Republic of China, living in Beijing until her death in 1981.

6 "China Defence League Financial Report, May to October 1938," NYM. The material was "mainly intended for the Canadian Medical Unit of Dr Bethune."

7 Ibid.

8 "China Defence League Financial Report, October 1938 to April 1939," NYM.

9 The agency was the China Campaign Committee in England. Various sources indicate that the CCC donation was £2,450, but figures in the China Defence League Financial Report of May to October 1938 reveal two CCC donations totaling £625 (about US$3,125) and costs for International Peace Hospital support at HK$5,600 (about US$1,700). It is not clear if this sum was narrowly designed for Bethune or if some of it was intended for Dr Richard Brown who was then making plans to set up another International Peace Hospital in Liaozhou in southern Shanxi. It is also almost certain that news of the destruction of the International Peace Hospital of Wutaishan (Songyankou) had not reached the China Defence League by October 1938.

10 Zhang Yesheng told the authors in 2005 that supplies paid for by the International Peace Campaign did reach the Jin-Cha-Ji Border Region in December 1938. There is no record of this donation in Bethune's reports and correspondence.

11 Bethune to Dear Comrade, 30 June 1938. "Communication [sic] with us are rather limited in the way of mail," Bethune wrote shortly after his arrival in Jin-Cha-Ji, "although we are in contact with the outside by telegraph and telephone and radio (both receiving and sending)." If the Japanese had been able to disrupt telegraph and telephone lines, they could not have prevented radio contact between Jin-Cha-Ji and Yan'an. There was, in addition, a form of courier service that continued to function throughout the time Bethune was in China. It should be noted that Japanese advances far to the east in Hebei Province later in 1938 forced the Eighth Route Army command to move He Long's 120th Division from Lanxian to Central Hebei. It was there in the early spring of 1939 that Bethune and his mobile unit served under He Long's command at the battle of Qihui.

12 Professor Wei Hongyun of Nankai University, Deng Lilan, trans., email to RS, 6 December 2009. It is clear that the Guomindang had no wish to help the Communists. At the invitation of the Eighth Route Army, the US military attaché Captain Evans F. Carlson went to the Wutai area in June 1938 where he met Bethune. When he returned to Hankou, he arranged a meeting with Jiang Jieshi and Madame Jiang at which he described the nature of the struggle of the Eighth Route Army against the Japanese in the northwest and its desperate need for assistance, including medical supplies. Returning from that meeting, he met the journalist Ilona Ralf Sues. "'Let's have a drink in the dining room,' he suggested. 'I'm chilled to the marrow of my bones. He and the Madame listened to me with that impenetrable, icy indifference ... They won't do a thing for Wutaishan'" (Sues, *Shark's Fins and Millet*, 302). Tom Newnham (*Dr.*

Bethune's Angel, 135) asserts that Song Qingling told Kathleen Hall that the Guomindang had blocked supplies destined for Bethune from reaching him. There is, however, no indication of when this occurred or which lots of supplies were involved. Also, any interruption of supply shipments would not affect the sending of funds, which could be wired directly to the Eighth Route Army either at Xi'an or Yan'an. At this period of the war some medical supplies could still be purchased at Xi'an and shipped on to Yan'an, which was three days away by truck.

13 The nucleus of the New Fourth Army was the men and women who had remained behind to guard the Communist base in southern China when the main force began the Long March in 1933.

14 "China Defence League Financial Report, May to October 1938," NYM. The amount for Bethune was HK$1,350; for the New Fourth Army it was HK$12,958.78.

15 Bethune to Nie Rongzhen, 13 August 1938.

16 Newnham, *Dr. Bethune's Angel*, 74.

17 Zhou, *Doctor Norman Bethune*, 88.

18 Newnham, *Dr. Bethune's Angel*, 6.

19 Ibid., 110.

20 Ibid., 247. Kathleen Hall kept two goats for milk. On a later occasion Bethune sent an Eighth Route Army soldier to Songjiazhuang to ask her to provide him with some goat milk.

21 Ibid., 110.

22 A few days earlier Dong had appeared in the morning with a nasty cut on his forehead. Visibly embarrassed, he described to Bethune how he had injured himself. Dreaming about his family the previous night, he had reached out to embrace them and tumbled off the *kang* onto the floor (Dong Chun, a daughter of Dong Yueqian and Wang Lanzhen, to the authors, 2005).

23 Zhou, *Doctor Norman Bethune*, 99.

24 Bethune, report to General Nie Rongzhen, Shenbei, 1 July 1939, Indusco. Bethune wrote that Nie gave him $1,000 (likely National Currency) on 2 February.

25 Dong Yueqian, "Throughout the Green Mountains Loyal Bones Lie Buried," 22.

26 Ibid.

27 Jiang, "Doctor Bethune's Spirit Will Live Forever," 22.

28 Dong Chun to the authors, 2005. Hall had taken the jar of face cream containing Dong's letter to Wang Lanzhen. Wang then quickly made arrangements to leave, and on February 18, she, her two daughters, and Hall boarded a train in the Beijing railway station, bound for Baoding to the south. There Hall had the medical supplies put on mules, and the four of them left on the two day journey on foot to Songjiazhuang.

29 Bethune, report to General Nie Rongzhen, Shenbei, 1 July 1929, Indusco. On 20 February he gave Hall $200 for supplies and on the following day $50 for expenses. He apparently sent her another $500 via General He Long, which she did not receive. He urged that an investigation be conducted to determine what had happened to the money.

30 Bethune to Tim Buck, near Hejian, 4 March 1939.

31 Ibid.

32 Ibid.

33 Lang Lin to RS, 1972.

34 In Chinese the Marco Polo Bridge was called *lugouqiao* (reed village bridge). This is sometimes translated instead as "black moat bridge."

35 Zhang Yesheng to the authors, 2005. In a report to General Nie Rongzhen, Shenbei, 1 July 1939, Bethune states that the Japanese force numbered four hundred.

36 Zhang Yesheng to the authors, 2005.

37 Bethune, report to General Nie Rongzhen, Shenbei, 1 July 1939.

38 More than seven hundred Japanese soldiers were killed (Zhang Yesheng to the authors, 2005).

39 Bethune's tour of the carnage of the battlefield parallels the experience of his grandfather Norman Bethune, who had witnessed the human slaughter on the battlefield of Solferino in 1859 during the Second War of Italian Independence.

40 Zhou, *Doctor Norman Bethune*, 144.

41 Bethune, report to General Nie Rongzhen, Shenbei, 1 July 1939.

42 Bethune, speech given at Songyankou, 15 September 1938. Dong Yueqian (1914–78) would rise in Communist Party ranks. In 1959 he would become the ambassador of the People's Republic of China to Sweden. Like many other faithful party members he suffered persecution during the Cultural Revolution.

43 Songjiazhuang is a not uncommon place name in China. It was also the name of the site of one of Kathleen Hall's missions in Quyang County, Hebei.

44 Zhang Yesheng to the authors, 2005.

45 Ibid.

46 It has been suggested that the Chinese transliteration of Bethune's name means "White Seek Grace" or "White One Sent." These meanings can indeed be attributed to the Chinese characters, but this is entirely coincidental.

47 Zhang Yesheng to the authors, 2005.

CHAPTER EIGHTEEN

1 Zhang Yesheng to the authors, 2005.

2 At the end of July a break in the downpour allowed enemy patrols to move closer to Shenbei, and the villagers began to move their possessions to the far side of the Tang River. Long ladders were placed across the narrowest section of the river to enable people to crawl from one side to the other. Bethune joined the men who went into the swiftly flowing water to assist older persons, children, and women, staying beside them as they made their way across. He had to be physically restrained by the villagers from plunging into the river to try to rescue a horse that was being swept downstream (ibid.).

3 Bethune to Ye Qingshan and You Shenghua, Shenbei, 12 July 1939, Indusco.

4 Ye Qingshan was to receive yet another rocket at the end of the month. Bethune sent his superior a second letter, mainly concerned with the ordering of supplies, which was sharply critical and didactic in tone (Bethune to Dr Ye Qingshan, Shenbei, 31 July 1939, Indusco).

5 Bethune, report to General Nie Rongzhen, Shenbei, 1 July 1939. "I have come back with my mind thoroughly made up that the education of the doctors and nurses of this region is the main task of any foreign unit," he wrote.

6 Ibid.

7 Bethune, A Memoranda [*sic*] on the Medical School of the Chin-Cha-Chi [Jin-Cha-Ji] Military District, 15 July 1939, Indusco.

8 Among the eleven instructors were his nominal superiors Dr Ye Qingshan, director of the Jin-Cha-Ji Medical Service, and Dr You Shenghua, Ye's deputy director, who had also been the director of the model hospital in Songyankou.

9 Bethune, A Memoranda, 15 July 1939.

10 Bethune, Monthly Report of the Canadian-American Mobile Unit to the Military Council, Hejiazhuang, 1 August 1939, Indusco (hereafter cited as Bethune, monthly report, 1 August 1939.)

11 Ibid.

12 Existing records show that from August 1938 until October 1939 the China Aid Council (New York) sent at least US$4,438.28 to the CDL. This figure is derived from amounts published in issues of the *CDLN* dated 15 April 1939, 1 October 1939, and 15 November 1939 (Jaffe, box 18, folder 1) and also on the CDL Financial Report May-October 1938 (NYM). In addition, money from Canada was being sent to the China Defence League. The CDL newsletter of 1 October 1939 stated that in May 1939 the CDL had received a donation of HK$300 from the Canadian League for Peace and Democracy and a second donation from its Toronto branch of NC$6,313.13. The key member in the Canadian League for Peace and Democracy was A.A. MacLeod, and the aim of the CLPD was certainly to assist Bethune. However, there is no evidence that he ever knew of their attempts to fund his medical needs.

13 Bethune, monthly report, 1 August 1939.

14 Bethune to the Trustee Committee, Hejiazhuang, 16 August 1939, Indusco.

15 It has already been noted that by October 1938, Dr Robert Lim of the Chinese National Red Cross had shipped materials intended for Bethune from his Red Cross stores and was about to send another large consignment (see chapter 15, note 33; letter of Dr Robert Lim to Oliver Haskell of the China Aid Council, 2 October 1938). According to the *China Defence League Newsletter* of 1 April 1939, Dr Lim was expected to dispatch more supplies into the battle areas, some of which were to be sent to Bethune. Their transport was made possible by a contribution made in January by the Chinese Patriotic League of Vancouver, which had sent five Studebaker truck chassis to Hong Kong. On 11 March 1939 after the vehicles had been fully assembled, the China Defence League loaded them with various supplies including medical equipment and shipped them to the port of Haiphong in what was then French Indochina. From there they were to travel overland to Guiyang, where the headquarters of the Medical Relief Commission of the National Red Cross Society of China was then located. The report concluded: "They are to proceed to Chongqing, Xi'an & Yan'an, where, with supplies earmarked for the Northwest, they will be handed over to the Eighth Route Army. Some of the supplies are going still further, to Dr Norman Bethune's IPH Hosp. at Wutaishan, Shansi [Shanxi], in the rear of the Japanese. They will accomplish the last leg of their journey by mule-train" (*CDLN*, 1 April 1939). Whether these supplies did reach Jin-Cha-Ji is not known. Because there is no documentary evidence to indicate that either the Japanese or the Guomindang were able to prevent all supplies from reaching Jin-Cha-Ji at this time, it seems likely that this consignment did get through, but given the slow transport methods its arrival there likely occurred after Bethune's death. It is of course

possible that blockade or other interference by Guomindang forces prevented the supplies from arriving in the Border Region.

16 Bethune, report of 1 August 1939

17 Newnham, *Dr. Bethune's Angel*, 132.

18 Bethune, report of 1 August 1939.

19 Newnham, *Dr. Bethune's Angel*, 132.

20 Ibid., 133. Deported from Tianjin in July 1939, Hall went to Hong Kong, where she met Song Qingling. She described Bethune's work and told her that he had received none of the supplies from New York that were supposed to be coming through Hong Kong. Learning that a supply route ran from Haiphong in French Indochina to Sichuan Province, Hall made contact with Dr Robert McClure, who was about to ship two International Red Cross relief trucks containing supplies earmarked for Bethune to Haiphong. Following the Burma Road, McClure and Hall reached Guiyang, China, on 19 November 1939. It was there that they learned of Bethune's death. At this point Dr Jean Jiang of the National Red Cross Society of China joined McClure and Hall, and they went on to Chongqing and then by train via Xi'an to Luoyang. There they were held up by bureaucratic interference by the Guomindang. Hall eventually managed to make her way by mule to Jin-Cha-Ji, taking with her medicines, serum, vaccines, and other supplies, but by then she was suffering from serious health problems, including beriberi. Brought to the Yellow River by a small detachment of the Eighth Route Army, she was taken to Xi'an by train to recuperate and then repatriated to New Zealand, probably sometime in early 1941 (Madgin, "Who Was Kathleen Hall?" 51–2).

21 Bethune, report of 1 August 1939.

22 Bethune, report to Trustee Committee, Hejiazhuang, 16 August 1939.

23 Bethune to Tim Buck, Hejiazhuang, 15 August 1939.

24 Bethune, report to General Nie Rongzhen, Shenbei, 1 July 1939. He listed his personal expenditures for April, May, and June, pointing out that they were for food that he had cooked for himself.

25 Zhang Yesheng to the authors, 2005.

26 Lang Lin, "The Memory Cherished of Dr. Bethune," in *Dr. Norman Bethune in Tangxian County*, 5–6. The source of this material is a partial translation of the Chinese text. The translation is in the possession of the authors.

27 He Zexin to RS, 1972.

28 Lindsay, *The Unknown War*, n.p.

29 Bethune to Tim Buck, Hejiazhuang, 15 August 1939. Despite the loss of his baggage shipped from Hong Kong to Hankou, he had taken clothing with him on the flight to Hankou, and at various times after leaving Yan'an he had given pieces of it to patients. In January, when he planned to accompany Kathleen Hall to Beijing, he still had a suit.

30 Bethune to Dear Comrade, Hejiazhuang, 15 August 1939, NFB research file for documentary film *Bethune*.

31 Ye Qingshan, "Dr Bethune and the Medical School of the Jin-Cha-Ji Military Area," in *Dr. Norman Bethune in Tangxian County*, 2.

32 At this time Bethune purportedly wrote a letter to the Lu Xun Art Academy in Yan'an, which was engaged in training young creative artists in music, literature, art, and drama with the aim of sending them among the masses to spread

propaganda on behalf of the revolution (Bethune to the Lu Xun Art Academy, 2 September 1939, NBF, vol. 1, file 19). Although he may well have viewed art as a powerful means of propaganda, the document displays a detailed knowledge of Chinese art and literature that Bethune was unlikely to have acquired during his brief stay in Yan'an and which he would have had no means of acquiring during his isolation in Jin-Cha-Ji. The document purports to be translated by Ma Haide; however, if Bethune had written it in English, there would be no need for a translation, and if Bethune's original had been for some reason translated into Chinese, it is unlikely that, although Ma Haide spoke Chinese, he would have been able to undertake the translation of a long document from Chinese to English. The authors feel that this document was not in fact written by Bethune.

33 Classes had been held since July 1939.

34 Some staff members came from Yan'an; others had been part of the Special Surgical Hospital that he had set up in Yangjiazhuang in December 1938 but which had since been closed down.

35 Newnham, *Dr. Bethune's Angel*, 121. Guo Qinglan later married Dr Dwarkanath Kotnis (1910–42), an Indian doctor who arrived in Yan'an to serve with the Eighth Route Army and who replaced Bethune after his death.

36 Ye Qingshan, "Dr. Bethune and the Medical School of the Jin-Cha-Ji Military Area," in *Dr. Norman Bethune in Tangxian County*, 3.

37 Zhang Yesheng to RS, 5 March 2009, Dong Chun, trans.

38 Zhang Yesheng letter to RS, 20 August 2008, Dong Chun, trans.

39 Bethune also asked for money to pay for dental treatment and an eye examination in Hong Kong, and for some western clothing for the sea voyage. When Mildred Price, who had replaced Oliver Haskell as director of the China Aid Council, received the cable on 19 October, she sent the following message to A.A. MacLeod in Toronto asking for financial help from the Canadian branch of the League for Peace and Democracy (a communist front organization formerly called the League against War and Fascism): "Dr B. sent us a cable saying that he plans to come the first of the year and he wants the money for his passage. I wrote the China Defence League saying that we would do everything within our power to get it to him as soon as possible. Do you think your organization could help us with the passage money? It will take at least $500 to get him back to the East from the West Coast including his ticket on the boat" (OA, Alexander Albert MacLeod fonds).

40 The decision was in part a belated response to an idea put forward by Song Qingling of the China Defence League. For nearly a year she had been trying to obtain photographs of Bethune and the conditions under which he was operating in the Border Region for use in the *China Defence League Newsletter*. The fortnightly publication was easily the most useful tool in eliciting financial contributions and was circulated throughout Asia, North America, and Europe. It is likely that Bethune himself had a part in the decision of the authorities to make a propaganda film. In a letter to Ma Haide back in September 1938 he had stated that he, Dong Yueqian, and Sha Fei, the well-known photographer, had made plans to buy a movie camera to "take films of the Army and the Partisans" (Bethune to Ma Haide, Songyankou, 30 September 1938, NBF, vol. 1, file 20). Those plans were dashed by the Japanese attack on

Songyankou, but Bethune continued to yearn to have a film made. In his letter to friends on 15 August 1939 he added a postscript to the copy he sent to his acquaintance Eric Adams in New York: "I sent you a cable from Peiping in March thru a friend (Professor M. Lindsay of Yen Ching University) asking you to send me $1000 gold. I wanted you to ask the China Aid Council for it. But I got no reply. Too bad. I could have made a movie to bring back" (Bethune, letter to Dear Comrade, Hejiazhuang, 15 August 1939).

41 Zhang Yesheng to the authors, 2005. At this point Dr Ye Qingshan decided to divide the inspection team into two groups in order to complete their work earlier and therefore left with several members of the team.

42 Zhang Yesheng to the authors, 2005. A group of forty wounded soldiers who were being transported through an area occupied by the enemy to the village of Wangan required medical attention. Bethune decided to go to their assistance.

43 Ibid. One of the most famous photographs of Bethune in China, which shows him operating in the ruins of the Buddhist temple, was taken that day by Wu Yinxian.

44 Richard Brown, NFB interview. Brown stated, "Bethune wouldn't wear gloves." Brown claims he warned him of the danger of operating without gloves, of which at the time there was a supply, but that Bethune ignored his warning and always operated without gloves.

45 According to Lu and Zou, the patient was afflicted with neck erysipelas with cellulitis ("Norman Bethune and His Contributions," 7).

46 "His [Bethune's] chief assistant told us later that he had urged Bethune to have his finger amputated but Bethune refused because it would have crippled him as a surgeon" (Lindsay, *The Unknown War*, n.p.).

47 Dong Yueqian, "Throughout the Green Mountains Loyal Bones Lie Buried," 6.

48 *Jian Kang Bao* (Health Issue), Beijing, 23 January 2009, 6.

49 Yang also presented Bethune with a Japanese sword captured on the field of battle. Ibid.

50 Chen Tongxun, "Around the Days of Dr. Bethune's Passing Away," in *Bethune in Tangxian County*, 8–9.

51 Feng Lin, son of Dr Lin Jinliang, to RS, interview of 5 September 2009.

52 Di Junxing to RS, 1972.

53 Bethune, letter to Lang Lin, 10 November 1939, given by the latter to RS. It is impossible to explain the penultimate sentence. The figures 120–130 may refer to Bethune's pulse rate. His mention of typhus may have been because this disease shares with septicemia some of the symptoms he was experiencing, including fever, nausea and vomiting. However, the formation of the abscess in the arm above the infected finger would seem to make it certain that he died of septicemia contracted via the cut in his finger which became infected from the soldier with the head wound. This is confirmed by Bethune's death certificate, which was prepared and signed by Dr Lin Jinliang. The document, a copy of which is in the possession of the authors, includes a daily record of the treatment of Bethune from 1 November to 12 November 1939, and also a lengthy summary of the attempts made by Bethune's assistants to save his life. In it the cause of death is given as pyaemia, which is a type of septicemia.

54 Zhang Yesheng to RS, 20 August 2008, Dong Chun trans. When Pan Fan tried

to read what Bethune had begun to write to Nie, he found many of the scrawled words indecipherable. So with the help of his colleague Liu Ke and relying heavily on guesswork, he wrote down what he believed Bethune had wanted to say. One page in length, the document is partially a will in which instructions are given for the distribution of Bethune's instruments and personal belongings to Nie Rongzhen and the colleagues in his unit. Among other passages Pan Fan wrote were those in which Bethune bids farewell to his friends in North America, asks for money from the China Aid Council in New York to be sent to his divorced wife in Montreal, and sums up his experience in China, saying, "The last two years have been the most significant, the most meaningful years of my life. Sometimes it has been lonely, but I have found my highest fulfillment here among my beloved comrades." This original text written by Pan Fan in Chinese was translated into English to be sent to North America, and was subsequently re-translated into Chinese after the original was lost.

55 Feng Lin to the authors, interview of 5 September 2009.
56 Chen Tongxun, "Around the Days of Dr. Bethune's Passing Away," *Dr. Norman Bethune in Tangxian County*, 9.
57 Bethune, letter to Marian Scott, Cartierville, 21 November 1935, MSF, vol. 14, file 21.

EPILOGUE

1 The history of the medical college is rather convoluted. After the establishment of the People's Republic of China in 1949, it moved to Shijiazhuang where it merged with the North China Medical College. Through a series of name alterations it became separated from the military and became known as Bethune College of Medical Sciences; since 1978 it has been located in the northern city of Changchun. It is now a college of Ji Lin University in that city. In 1999 the Bethune Military Medical College was established in Shijiazhuang.
2 The inscriptions are written in Wade-Giles, the system of romanization used at the time. Nieh Jung Chen is Nie Rongzhen.
3 Shu Tong was head of the Political Department in Jin-Cha-Ji.
4 Lu Zhengcao was the commander in chief of Eighth Route Army troops in Central Hebei, the area where Bethune served during the Medical Expedition to the East from late February to the end of June 1939.
5 The museum has been considerably enlarged since and is now called the Bethune Memorial Hall of the Bethune International Peace Hospital.
6 *Montreal Star*, 20 December 1939. There were other attempts to honour his memory as well. The *Canadian Tribune*, a communist newspaper in Toronto, donated a mobile blood transfusion unit in his memory to the Ontario Division of the Canadian Red Cross in 1942. And in 1943 the Canadian Congress of Labour passed a motion to "recommend to the Government of Canada that it take the necessary steps to institute a 'living monument' dedicated to the work of Dr Bethune" (Minutes of the 1943 Annual Convention of the Canadian Labour Congress). The government of Mackenzie King chose to ignore this recommendation.
7 With the German invasion of the Soviet Union in June 1941, all of Germany's enemies including Canada immediately pledged support for the besieged communist state.

8   In the 1970s the empty trunk was donated by Janet Stiles's daughters to Parks Canada, the agency responsible for the Bethune Memorial House in Gravenhurst.

9   The first biographical account of Bethune was written by an American, Dr Gabriel Nadeau, a physician from Massachusetts. "A T.B.'s Progress" was published in the *Bulletin of the History of Medicine* 8, no. 8 (October 1940).

10   They were Fred Rose, the party organizer for Quebec, and Sam Carr, the party's national organizer. They were members of the Labour-Progressive Party, the name adopted by the CPC in 1943.

11   The award was granted by the Leipzig International Festival for Documentary and Animated Film on 11 November 1965.

12   In the NFB film *Donald Brittain: Filmmaker* (NFB, 1992), John Kemeny, who did most of the research for the NFB film *Bethune*, including smuggling film from China into Canada, states that after the protest by the US government, *Bethune* was "put on the shelf" in the United States.

13   The museum is named the Norman Bethune and Dwarkanath Kotnis Memorial Hall. Kotnis was the Indian doctor who arrived after Bethune's death to replace him, and who also gave his life in the service of the Eighth Route Army.

14   "What Every Chinese Schoolboy Knows," *Time*, 2 August 1971. *Doctor Bethune*, a major film made in China at the time, was banned by Jiang Qing, Mao's wife. After Mao's death in 1976, she was imprisoned as a member of the infamous Gang of Four, and the film was subsequently released for public showing.

15   MacMillan, *Nixon in China*, 166.

16   *Toronto Star*, 18 August 1972.

17   The historical advisor for the life and career of Bethune was Roderick Stewart.

18   At first it was designated as the Bethune Memorial Home.

19   Norman Bethune College, York University, 1972; Norman Bethune Collegiate Institute, 1979.

20   For his performance in the title role, the Canadian actor Donald Sutherland won the Etrog, awarded for the finest dramatic performance in Canadian television in 1977. The script was based on RS's *Bethune*.

21   The head of the small Canadian delegation invited to attend the ceremonies in China was Dr D. Barootes, the president of the Canadian Medical Association, an organization to which Bethune had not belonged. Other members included Dr Francis McNaughton, a member of the Montreal Group of the Security of the People's Health, and the three daughters of Bethune's sister, Janet. RS, who was then teaching at the Sichuan Institute of Foreign Languages in Chongqing, was also a member.

22   From this successful gathering came the book *Norman Bethune: His Times and His Legacy*, edited by Shephard and Lévesque, which contains the many scholarly papers read at the conference.

23   Beginning in 2002, the Department of Laboratory Medicine and Pathobiology of the University of Toronto instituted the Norman Bethune Award to encourage young talented researchers; one grant is given to a graduate student and one to a resident in microbiology. At the time of the writing of this book, the establishment of a Norman Bethune Chair of Surgery at McGill University is under discussion in Montreal. Plans are also underway to erect a statue of Bethune in

Queen's Park near the University of Toronto and to create a scholarship at the university for surgeons willing to serve abroad. On 21 October 2010, Bethune was inducted into the Canadian Science and Engineering Hall of Fame in Ottawa.

24 Hannant's book is a compilation of most of the writings of Bethune which Ted Allan had collected years earlier and donated as part of his papers to the Library and Archives of Canada in the early 1990s. Wilson's brief biography is part of the Quest Library, and Clarkson's book belongs to the series Extraordinary Canadians.

25 In 2004, a thirteen-hour television series based on Bethune's life was made and shown in China. That same year Bethune also won some recognition in Spain as a result of the efforts of Jesús Majada Neila, a teacher in Málaga who had carried out a successful search for survivors of the tragic flight of refugees from Málaga to Almería in February 1937. Majada Neila combined recorded interviews with some of them and a series of photographs taken by Hazen Sise to mount an exhibition in Málaga in 2004 and in Salamanca in 2006. Under the title of "Norman Bethune: The Trail of Solidarity," the exhibition was brought to Concordia University in Montreal in 2008 as part of a celebration of Bethune and was displayed at the McCord Museum of Canadian History throughout 2009 to mark the seventieth anniversary of Bethune's death. Majada Neila also published a book entitled *Norman Bethune: La huella solidaria* in 2008. He is the co-author, with Roderick Stewart, of *Bethune en España*. Majada Neila's efforts to draw attention to the flight of the refugees from Málaga, a previously little-known episode in Spanish history, and to the even less-known Canadian who became involved in that event, led to a decision by the municipality of Málaga to erect a plaque in honour of Bethune and to name a section of the city's esplanade along the Mediterranean the Paseo de los Canadienses. At the dedication ceremony in 2004, the Canadian ambassador Mark Lortie participated. Since then a street in Málaga and a school for health-care workers located in Almayate, 35 km from Málaga along the Almería road, have been named in honour of Bethune.

26 In a contest held in 2009 by the Chinese newspaper *People's Daily*, Bethune ranked among the top ten of the one hundred foreigners who contributed the most to the establishment of the People's Republic of China. The list appeared on the newspaper's website, http://www.people.com.cn, on 25 May 2009. In a similar contest organized by China Radio International in the same year, 56 million people voted online, ranking Bethune first among the foreign friends of China ("Netizens Honor China's Top Int'l Friends," http://english.cri.cn, 12 October 2009).

27 Some even visit the lonely grave of his great-grandmother, Louisa Mackenzie, on the shores of Lake Superior near Michipicoten (Wawa). See Morrison, "The Fur Trade Heritage of Dr Norman Bethune."

Bibliography

ARCHIVES AND LIBRARIES CONSULTED

Admiralty Library, Naval Historical Branch, Ministry of Defence, HM Naval Base, Portsmouth, UK.

Alan Mason Chesney Medical Archives, Johns Hopkins Medical Institutions, Baltimore, MD.

Alachua County Ancient Records, Alachua County, Gainesville, FL.

Alexander Fleming Laboratory Museum, St Mary's Hospital, London, UK.

American College of Surgeons, Chicago, IL.

Amherst College Archives and Special Collections, Amherst College, Amherst, MA.

Anglican Church of Canada General Synod Archives, Toronto (ACC/GSA) GS75-103, Missionary Society of the Church of England in Canada fonds (MSCC).

Arbetarrörelsens Archiv och Bibliotek (Labour Management Archives and Library), Stockholm.

Archives Nationales du Québec, Montreal.

Archives of the Roman Catholic Archdiocese of Toronto.

Arizona Historical Society Library, Tucson, AZ.

Aylmer & District Library, Aylmer, ON.

Battle Creek Historical Society, Battle Creek, MI.

Becker Medical Library, Washington University School of Medicine, Washington University, St Louis, MO.

Bentley Historical Library, University of Michigan, Ann Arbor, MI, Section of Thoracic Surgery, Records, 1927–1960.

Bethune Memorial House, Gravenhurst, ON.

Bibliotheque et Archives nationales du Québec, Direction du Centre d'archives de Montréal, Fonds Gabriel Nadeau, MSS177.

Billy Bishop Home and Museum, Owen Sound, ON.

Black Creek Pioneer Village, Toronto.

Blind River Public Library, Blind River, ON.

British Library, London, Manuscript Collections.

Burton Historical Collection Edinburgh Academy, Edinburgh.

Camden Local Studies and Archives Centre, Holborn Library, London, UK.

Carleton College, Northfield, MN, Laurence McKinley Gould Library, Digital Collections.

City of Vaughan Archives, Vaughan, ON.

Detroit Public Library, Detroit, MI.

Elgin County Archives, St Thomas, ON.

El Paso County Historical Society, El Paso, TX.

Frontier College, Toronto.

Friends of the Children of Great Ormond Street Library, Institute of Child Health, London, UK.

George Washington University, Special Collections Department, Washington, DC.

Glasgow University Archives, Glasgow.

Greater Sudbury Public Library, Sudbury, ON.

Hammersmith & Fulham Archives and Local History Centre, London, UK.

Hampshire Record Office Enquiry Service, Winchester, Hants, UK.

Health Disciplines Library, West Park Healthcare Centre, Toronto.

Heibei Memorial Institute, Memorial Hall of Dr Bethune and Dr Kotnis, Tangxian, Hebei.

Honnold/Mudd Library of the Claremont Colleges, Claremont, CA: Special Collections, Oriental Study Expedition Oral History Project.

Hoover Institution Library and Archives, Hoover Institution, Stanford University, Stanford, CA, Nym Wales Collection.

Ingersoll and District Historical Society, Ingersoll, ON.

Institute of Naval Medicine, Alverstoke, Gosport, Hants, Historic Collections Library.

King's College London, University of London, London, UK, Information Services and Systems.

Library and Archives of Canada, Ottawa, Hazen Edward Sise fonds R4915-0-7-E; Marian Scott fonds R2437-0-2-E; Norman Bethune fonds, R5988-0-6-E; Ted Allan fonds R2931-0-4-E; Frontier College fonds R3584-0-0-E4; External Affairs, vol. 1801, file 1936-631-B, Activities of Dr H. Sorensen in Spain; also Dr Bethune, RG150 1992-93/166, box 705, file Bethune, Henry Norman Bethune 33018; RG146-A, Registry Records of Canadian Security Intelligence Service, vol. 4680, file Norman Bethune, Moscow Archives MG 10-K2 and MG 10-K3.

London Public Library, London, ON.

Library, New York Academy of Medicine, New York.

Lothian Health Services Archive, Edinburgh University Library, Edinburgh.

Manuscript, Archives and Rare Book Library, Emory University, Atlanta, GA, Philip J. Jaffe papers, Manuscript Collection 605.

Massey Area Museum, Massey, ON.

Matheson Museum Inc., Alachua County, FL.

Mayo Clinic College of Medicine Libraries, Rochester, MN.

McGill University Archives, McLennan Library Building, McGill University, Montreal.

Memphis Public Library, Memphis, TN.

Ministry of Defence, HM Naval Base, Portsmouth, Admiralty Library, Naval Historical Branch (Naval Staff).

Mobile Medical Museum, Mobile, AL.

New York Public Library, New York, Manuscripts and Archives Division, Astor, Lenox and Tilden Foundations, United China Relief Records.

National Archives, Historical Manuscripts Division, London, UK.
National Film Board of Canada, files for the Donald Brittain film, *Bethune*, Montreal.
National Library of Medicine, Baltimore, History of Medicine Division, Lyman H. Brewer III papers MCC553.
National Library of Scotland, Edinburgh.
National Library of Wales, Cardiff, UK.
Newham Archives and Local Studies Library, Stratford Library, London, UK.
Niagara Falls Public Library, Niagara Falls, ON.
Norman Bethune International Peace Hospital, Bethune-Kotnis Memorial Hall, Shijiazhuang, Hebei.
Ontario Archives, Toronto, Alexander Albert MacLeod fonds F126.
Osler Library of the History of Medicine Archives, McGill University, Montreal, Quebec, P89 Roderick Stewart fonds; P121 Eugene Perry Link fonds; P156 Bethune Collection.
Ottawa Public Library, Ottawa.
Owen Sound Public Library, Owen Sound, ON.
Presbyterian Church in Canada Archives, Toronto.
Rare Book and Manuscript Library, Columbia University, New York City, Indusco Incorporated Records, China Aid Council, Dr. Norman Bethune indexed letters and reports.
Reference Research Center, Library of Michigan, Lansing, MI.
Royal Canadian Military Institute, Toronto.
Royal College of Surgeons of Edinburgh, Library, Edinburgh.
Royal College of Surgeons of England, Library and Information Service, London, UK.
Royal Free Hospital Archives Centre, London, UK.
Royal London Hospital Archives and Museum, London, UK.
Royal Victoria Hospital Library, Montreal.
Salvation Army Archives, Canada and Bermuda Territory, Toronto.
St Catharines Public Library, St Catharines, ON.
Saranac Free Library, Saranac Lake, NY.
Sharlot Hall Museum, Prescott, AZ.
Special Collections, University of Edinburgh Library, Edinburgh.
State University of New York, Upstate Medical University, Health Sciences Library, Syracuse, NY.
Stratford-Perth Archives, Stratford, ON.
Stratford Beacon, Stratford, ON.
Tamiment Library and Robert F. Wagner Labor Archives, New York University, New York, Abraham Lincoln Brigade Archives (ALBA) Collections.
Timber Lodge, Blind River, ON.
Toronto District School Board Museum and Archives, Toronto.
Trudeau Institute, Saranac Lake, NY.
United Church of Canada/Victoria University Archives, University of Toronto, Presbyterian Church in Canada Synod of Toronto and Kingston fonds.
University Archives, Alexander A. Walt Collection, Walter P. Reuther Library, Wayne State University, Detroit.
University of Manitoba, Elizabeth Dafoe Library, Winnipeg, MB.

University of Toronto Archives, University of Toronto.

Washington University, Becker Medical Library, St Louis, Missouri.

Wellcome Library for the History and Understanding of Medicine, London, UK.

Windsor Public Library, Windsor, ON.

Vancouver Public Library, Vancouver, History and Government Division, Vancouver.

BOOKS AND ARTICLES

Ai, Wei. *Baiqiuende Daolu* (Bethune's road). Hong Kong: Wenjiao Publishers 1970.

Alexander, John. *The Surgery of Pulmonary Tuberculosis*. Philadelphia and New York: Lea & Febiger 1925.

Allan, Ted. "The Sinner Who Became a Saint." *The Canadian* (supplement to the *Toronto Star*), 6 July 1975.

– "The Making of a Martyr." *The Canadian* (supplement to the *Toronto Star*), 13 July 1975.

Allan, Ted, and Gordon, Sydney. *The Scalpel, the Sword*. Boston: Little, Brown & Co. 1952.

Alley, Rewi. *Six Americans in China*. Beijing: International Culture Publishing Corporation 1985.

Alvarez, Vicente Goyanes. "La Transfusión de sangre en el sector centro." *Revista de Sanidad de Guerra* 2, nos. 11-12 (1938): 159–76.

Archibald, Edward. "The Employment of Blood Transfusion in War Surgery." *Lancet* (September 1916): 439–41.

– "A Note upon Employment of Blood Transfusion in War Surgery." *Journal of the Royal Army Medical Corps* 27 (1916): 636–44.

Baiqiuen zai Zhongguo (Bethune in China). Beijing: People's Publishing House 1977.

Barea, Arturo. *The Forging of a Rebel: The Clash*. Translated by Ilsa Barea. London: Fontana Paperbacks 1984.

Barootes, E.W. "Dr. Norman Bethune: Inspiration for Modern China." *Canadian Medical Journal* 122 (1980): 1176–84.

Bates, Christina. "Norman Bethune, Senior: His Last Years." Parks Canada, April 1991. Bethune Memorial House. Gravenhurst: Parks Canada 1991.

Beevor, Antony. *The Battle for Spain: The Spanish Civil War, 1936–1939*. London: Wiedenfeld & Nicolson 2006.

Bethune, Norman. "Some Procedures in Thoracic Surgery." *Southwestern Medicine* 16, no. 1 (January 1932).

– "A Phrenicectomy Necklace." *American Review of Tuberculosis* 26 (September 1932): 319–21.

– "Reflections on Return from 'Through the Looking Glass.'" *Bulletin of the Montreal Medico-Chirurgical Society* (March-April 1936).

– "Some New Thoracic Surgical Instruments." *Canadian Medical Association Journal* 35 (December 1936): 656–62.

– "The T.B.'s Progress." *The Fluoroscope* 1, no. 7 (15 August 1932).

Braun, Otto. *A Comintern Agent in China*. London: C. Hurst & Co. 1982.

Brewer, Lyman A. "Norman Bethune and China." Paper presented at the

Annual Meeting of the American Association for Thoracic Surgery, 30 April 1985.

Broggi I Vallès, Moises. "Frederic Duran i Jordà." *Gimbernat* 27 (1997): 185–91.

Cam, Sydney. "Playing Politics with the Legacy of Dr. Bethune." *Toronto Star*, 2 March 1990, 23.

Carballo, José Ramon Navarro. *La Sanidad en las Brigadas Internacionales*. Madrid: Colección Adalid 1989.

Carlson, Evans Fordyce. *Twin Stars of China*. New York: Dodd Mead & Co. 1940.

Chen, Min-sun. "Richard Brown: China's Unsung Canadian Hero." *Beijing Review* 11–17 (February 1991): 30–2.

– "China's Unsung Canadian Hero: Dr. Richard F. Brown in North China, 1938–39." In *East Asia Inquiry*, ed. L.N. Shyu et al., 109–37. Montreal: Canadian Asian Studies Association 1991.

– "Ho Lung (1896–1969) and Norman Bethune (1890–1939) in North China, 1938–39." *China Insight* (1985): 71–3.

Clarkson, Adrienne. *Norman Bethune*. Toronto: Penguin Canada 2009.

Cox, Geoffrey. *La Defensa de Madrid*. Madrid: Oberon 2005.

Daniel, Thomas M. *Captain of Death: The Story of Tuberculosis*. Rochester, NY: University of Rochester Press 1997.

Delarue, Norman C. *Thoracic Surgery in Canada*. Toronto: BC Decker 1989.

Delva, Pierre, and Fournier, Pierre. "Norman Bethune – Surgeon Extraordinary." *World Health Forum* 11, no. 4 (1990): 373–5.

De Zwaan, George. *The Reverend Malcolm Bethune: The Early Career of a Presbyterian Minister in Late Victorian Ontario*. Ottawa: Environment Canada, Canadian Parks Service 1988.

Djwa. Sandra. *The Politics of the Imagination: F.R. Scott*. Vancouver: Douglas & McIntyre 1989.

Dr. Norman Bethune in Tang Xian County. Tang Xian: Hebei People's Publishing House 1990.

Dorn, Frank. *The Sino-Japanese War: From Marco Polo Bridge to Pearl Harbor*. New York: Macmillan 1974.

Douglas, W.A.B. *The Creation of a National Air Force*. Toronto: University of Toronto Press 1986.

Duran i Jorda, Frederic. "The Barcelona Blood Transfusion Service." *Lancet* no.1 (1939): 185–91.

Eloesser, Leo. "In Memoriam: Norman Bethune." *Journal of Thoracic Surgery* 10, no. 4 (April 1940).

Entin, Martin A. "The Dynasties of Research at the Royal Victoria Hospital, Montreal." *Canadian Journal of Surgery* 30, no. 6 (November 1987): 449–50.

– "Romance and Tragedy of Tuberculosis: Edward Archibald's Contribution to the Surgical Treatment of Pulmonary Tuberculosis." *Canadian Journal of Plastic Surgery* 3, no. 4 (Winter 1995): 213–16.

– *Edward Archibald: Surgeon of the Royal Vic*. Montreal: McGill University Libraries 2004.

Ewen, Jean. *China Nurse*. Toronto: McClelland & Stewart 1981.

- "You Can't Buy It Back." Unpublished autobiographical manuscript in the possession of Laura Meyer.

Farah, Ted. "Man Who Saved Many Lives Has Died in Service." *Hamilton Spectator*, 27 November 1939.

Fisher, F.H. "Dr. Norman Bethune." *Historical Bulletin* 10, no. 4 (February 1946): 151–9.

Fisher, Lincoln. "Obituary – Norman Bethune, 1890–1939." *American Review of Tuberculosis* 41 (January-June 1940): 820.

Franco, A, J. Cortes, J. Alvarez, and J.C. Diaz. "The Development of Blood Transfusion: The Contributions of Norman Bethune in the Spanish Civil War (1936–1939)." *Canadian Journal of Anaesthesia* 43 no. 10 (1996): 1076–8.

Fransiszyn, Marilyn. "Norman Bethune and His Friends." *Osler Library Newsletter* 10 (June 1972).

Gibson, William C. "Bethune's China Forty Years On." *Journal of the American Medical Association* 242, no. 19 (1979): 2091–2.

The Great Internationalist Soldier Bethune. Translation by Greg Whincup. Beijing: China Youth Publishing House 1972.

Goyanes Alvarez, Vicente. "La Transfusión de sangre en el sector centro." *Revista de Sanidad de Guerra* 2, nos. 11-12 (1938): 159–76.

Groom, Winston. *A Storm in Flanders*. New York: Atlantic Monthly Press 2002.

Grypma, Sonya. "China Nurse Jean Ewen and the Conundrum of Norman Bethune." Unpublished paper.

Gutsch, Andrea, Barbara Chisholm, and Russell Floren. *The North Channel and St. Mary's River*. Toronto: Lynx Images 1975.

Hannant, Larry, ed. "Behind the Legend." *Beaver* 77, no. 4 (1977): 30–5.

- "Doctoring Bethune." *Saturday Night* 113, no. 3 (1998): 75–81.

- "Norman Bethune in China 1938-1939." In *Cardiothoracic Surgery in China: Past, Present, and Future*, edited by Wan Song and Anthony P.C. Kim, 47–72. Beijing: Chinese University Press 2007.

- ed. *The Politics of Passion: Norman Bethune's Writing and Art*. Toronto: University of Toronto Press 1988.

Hanson, Haldore. *Humane Endeavour*. New York: Farrar & Rinehart 1939.

Harmann, W.M. "Famous 'T.B.'s' Henry Norman Bethune, M.D." *Health Rays* (Kemptville, NS): 18, no. 1: 16–19.

Harrison, James Pinckney. *The Long March to Power: A History of the Chinese Communist Party, 1921–1972*. New York: Praeger 1972.

Hazelbaker, L. Edward. *The Pilgrim's Progress in Modern English*. Alachua: Bridge-Logos 1998.

Hoar, Victor. *The MacKenzie-Papineau Battalion*. Toronto: Copp Clark 1969.

Horn, Michiel. *The Dirty Thirties: Canadians in the Great Depression*. Toronto: Copp Clark, 1972.

Horwood, Harold. "Norman Bethune: The Rebel China Reveres." *Reader's Digest*, January 1975, 36–41.

Ibottson, John. "In Remembrance of How Easy It Is to Forget." *Globe and Mail*, 9 November 2002, A21.

Jack, Donald. *Rogues, Rebels and Geniuses: The Story of Canadian Medicine*. Toronto: Doubleday 1981.

Jiang, Yizhen."Dr. Bethune's Spirit Will Live Forever." Beijing: *Beijing Review* 5 (February 1980).

Kapp, Richard W. "Charles H. Best, the Canadian Red Cross Society, and Canada's First National Blood Donation Program." CBMH/BCHM 12 (1995): 27–46.

Ke, Chi. "When the Specter of Death Beckons: An Essay on Bethune's Legacy in Plattsburgh and Saranac Lake." Translation of an article published in *Art* (February 1982) in China.

Larrson, B. Hjalmar. "In Memoriam: Norman Bethune, M.D." *Detroit Medical News*, 4 May 1953, 22–3.

Lerner, Loren. "When the Children Are Sick, So Is Society: Dr. Norman Bethune and the Montreal Circle of Artists." In *Healing the World's Children*, edited by Cynthia Comacchio, Janet Golden, and George Weisz, 253–81. Montreal: McGill-Queen's University Press 2008.

Lethbridge, David, ed. *Bethune: The Secret Police File*. Salmon Arm: Undercurrent Press 2003.

Lindsay, Michael. *The Unknown War: North China, 1937–1945*. London: Bergstrom & Boyle 1973.

Ling Chen, trans. *Doctor Norman Bethune in Tangxian County*. Partial translation of the Chinese text in the possession of the authors. N.d.

Link, Eugene P. The *T.B's Progress: Norman Bethune as Artist*. Plattsburg: Centre for the Study of Canada, SUNY 1991.

Liu, Xiaokang. "Comrade Bethune As I Saw Him." *China Youth* 24 (26 December 1964).

Lozano, Miguel, and Joan Cid. "Frederic Duran-Jorda: A Transfusion Medicine Pioneer." *Transfusion Medicine Reviews* 21 no. 1 (2007): 75–81.

Lu, Y., and Z.R. Zou. "Norman Bethune and His Contribution to Blood Transfusion and Medical Rescue in China." Unpublished paper given at the International Society of Blood Transfusion (Asia) Conference, 2007.

Macintyre, Iain. "Norman Bethune." *Surgeons' News* 8, no. 4 (2009): 82–3.

MacKinnon, Janice R., and MacKinnon, Stephen L. MacKinnon. *Agnes Smedley: The Life and Times of an American Rebel*. London: Virago 1988.

MacLean, Lloyd D., and Martin A. Entin. "Norman Bethune and Edward Archibald: Sung and Unsung Heroes." *Annals of Thoracic Surgery* 70 (2000): 1746–51.

MacLennan, Hugh. *The Watch That Ends the Night*. Toronto: General 1991.

MacLeod, Wendell, Libbie Park, and Stanley Ryerson. *Bethune: The Montreal Years*. Toronto: James Lorimer 1978.

MacMillan, Margaret. *Nixon in China: The Week That Changed the World*. Toronto: Penguin 2006.

Madgin, Diana. "Who Was Kathleen Hall?" Part 1. *Voice of Friendship* 155 (June 2009): 51–2.

– "Who Was Kathleen Hall?" Part 2. *Voice of Friendship* 156 (August 2009): 54–6.

Majada Neila, Jesús. *Norman Bethune: La huella solidaria*. Málaga: Junta de Andalucía 2008.

– ed. *El Crimen de la carretera Málaga-Almería (Febrero de 1937)*. Málaga: Caligrama Ediciones 2005.

Majada Neila, Jesús, and Fernando Bueno Pérez. *Carretera Málaga-Almería*.
  Malaga: Caligrama Ediciones 2006.

Majada Neila, Jesús, and Roderick Stewart. *Bethune en España*. Málaga:
  Fondación Malagón 2009.

Malraux, André. *Man's Hope*. New York: Bantam 1968.

Mao Zedong. "In Memory of Norman Bethune." *Selected Works of Mao
  Tse-tung*. Vol. 2. Beijing: Foreign Languages Press 1965.

Massons, José Maria. *Historia de la Sanidad Militar Española*. Vol. 2.
  Barcelona: Pomares-Corredor D.L. 1994.

McMann, Evelyn de Rostaing. *Montreal Museum of Fine Arts, Formerly Art
  Association of Montreal: Spring Exhibitions, 1880–1970*. Toronto: University of Toronto Press 1988.

Miller, Ian Hugh MacLean. *Our Glory and Our Grief: Torontonians and the
  Great War*. Toronto: University of Toronto Press 2002.

Morrison, Jean. "The Fur Trade Heritage of Dr Norman Bethune." *High-
  Grader Magazine*, Spring 2006.

Murray, Joan, ed. *Daffodils in Winter: The Life and Letters of Pegi Nicol
  MacLeod, 1904–1949*. Moonbeam, ON: Penumbra Press 1984.

Nadeau, Gabriel. "A T.B.'s Progress: The Story of Norman Bethune." *Bulletin
  of the History of Medicine* 7, no. 8 (1940): 1135–71.

Newnham, Tom. *Dr. Bethune's Angel: The Life of Kathleen Hall*. Auckland:
  Graphic Publications 2002.

Nicholson, G.W.L. *Seventy Years of Service: A History of the Royal Canadian
  Army Medical Service*. Ottawa: Borealis Press 1977.

– *Canadian Expeditionary Force, 1914–1919: Official History of the Canadian
  Army in the First World War*. Ottawa: Queen's Printer 1964.

Pan, Fan. "Deep Impression of the Last Seven Days." *A Collection of Medical
  History Records of North China Military Area Command*. Translated by
  Qi Ming, Bethune Military Medical College, Shijiazhuang. Beijing: Medical
  Department of the Logistics Headquarters of North China Military Area
  Command (October 1949).

Paré, Jean. "Le docteur rouge." *Le Maclean*, March 1973, 26, 43–8.

Park, Libbie. "Bethune As I Knew Him." In *Bethune: The Montreal Years*,
  by Wendell MacLeod, Libbie Park, and Stanley Ryerson. Toronto: James
  Lorimer 1978.

Patterson, Robert. "Norman Bethune: His Contributions to Medicine and to
  CMAJ." *CMAJ* 141 (1989): 947–53.

Pelis, Kim. "Edward Archibald's Notes on Blood Transfusion in War Surgery: A
  Commentary." *Wilderness and Environmental Medicine* 13 (2002): 211–14.

Petrou, Michael. *Renegades: Canadians in the Spanish Civil War*. Vancouver
  and Toronto: University of British Columbia Press 2008.

Pinkerton, Peter H. "Norman Bethune, Eccentric, Man of Principle, Man of
  Action, Surgeon, and His Contribution to Blood Transfusion in War." *Transfusion Medicine Reviews* 21, no. 3 (2007): 255–64.

– "Norman Bethune and Transfusion in the Spanish Civil War." Supplement
  to *Vox Sanguinis* 83 (2002): 117–20.

Porter, Edgar A. *The People's Doctor: George Hatem and China's Revoution*.
  Honolulu: University of Hawai'i Press 1997.

Price, Ruth. *The Lives of Agnes Smedley*. New York: Oxford 2005.

Reaman, G.E. *A History of Vaughan Township*. Toronto: George C.H. Snider 1971.

Regler, Gustav. *The Owl of Minerva: The Autobiography of Gustav Regler*. New York: Farrar, Straus and Cudahy 1960.

"Report of the Department of Surgery." *Thirty-Sixth Annual Report for the Year Ended 31st December, 1929*. Royal Victoria Hospital Library, Montreal.

Reverte, Jorge M. *La Batalla de Madrid*. Barcelona: Planeta DeAgostini 2004.

Rioppel, Mary Mason. "A Private Viewing: A Memory of Norman Bethune." *Canadian Forum*, February 1986, 18–4.

Robertson, L.B. "The Transfusion of Whole Blood: A Suggestion for Its More Frequent Employment in War Surgery." *British Medical Journal* (July 1916): 38–40.

Rosen, Irving B. "Dr Norman Bethune as Surgeon." *Canadian Journal of Surgery* 39, no.1 (1996): 72–7.

Russell, Hilary. "Summaries of Interviews re Bethune Memorial." Bethune Memorial House, Gravenhurst. Ottawa: Parks Canada 1975.

– "Norman Bethune's Ancestors and Their Finances." Bethune Memorial House, Gravenhurst. Ottawa: Parks Canada 1976.

– "The Chinese Voyages of Angus Bethune." *The Beaver*, Spring 1977, 22–31.

Ryerson, Stanley Brehaut. "Comrade Beth." In *Bethune: The Montreal Years*, by Wendell MacLeod, Libbie Park, and Stanley Ryerson. Toronto: James Lorimer 1978.

Schiller, Bill. "Comrade Norman Bethune Still a Force in China." *Toronto Star*, 8 November 2009.

Scott, Munroe. *McClure: The China Years of Dr. Bob McClure*. Toronto: Canec Publishing and Supply House 1977.

Shephard, David, and Andrée Lévesque, eds. *Norman Bethune, His Times and Legacy*. Ottawa: Canadian Public Health Association 1982.

Smedley, Agnes. *Battle Hymn of China*. New York: Alfred A Knopf 1945.

Smith, Mary Larratt. *Prologue to Norman: The Canadian Bethunes*. Oakville: Mosaic Press 1976.

Snow, Edgar. *Red Star over China*. New York: Grove Press 1968.

Sorensen, Henning. Unpublished autobiography in the authors' possession.

Stansky, Peter. *Sassoon: The Worlds of Philip and Sybil*. New Haven: Yale University Press 2003.

Stephenson, Larry W. "Two Stormy Petrels: Edward J. O'Brien and Norman Bethune." *Journal of Cardiac Surgery* 18, no. 1 (2003): 59–77.

– "Editorial for 'Two Stormy Petrels.'" *Journal of Cardiac Surgery* 18 (2003): 78–9.

– "The Blalock-Bethune Connection." *Surgery* 130 (April 2001): 882–9.

Stewart, Roderick. *Bethune*. Toronto: New Press 1973.

– *Norman Bethune*. Markham: Fitzhenry & Whiteside 2002.

– *The Mind of Norman Bethune*. Markham: Fitzhenry & Whiteside 2002.

Sues, Ralf Ilona. *Shark's Fins and Millet*. Garden City: Garden City Publishing 1944.

Summers, George V. "Norman Bethune, Canadian Surgeon: His Chinese Connection." *Canadian Journal of Surgery* 26 no. 4 (1983): 379–81.

Taylor, Robert. *Saranac America's Magic Mountain*. New York: Paragon House 1988.

Thomas, Hugh. *The Spanish Civil War*. New York: Modern Library 2001.

Trépanier, Esther. *Marian Dale Scott: Pioneer of Modern Art*. Quebec: Musée du Québec 2000.

Utley, Freda. *China at War*. New York: John Day 1939.

Vanni, Paolo, R. Ottaviani, et al. "Henry Dunant and Norman Bethune." *Vesalius* 8, no. 2 (2002): 30–5.

Viedma, Lucy. "Everything You Have Done For Us Spanish Children Will Live in Our Memories For Ever." *The World in the Basement*. Stockholm: Arbetarrörelsens Arkiv och Bibliotek 2003.

Virtue, John. *Fred Taylor: Brother in the Shadows*. Montreal & Kingston: McGill-Queen's University Press 2008.

Walt, Alexander J. "The World's Best Known Surgeon." *Surgery* 94, no. 4 (1983): 582–90.

Wilson, Dick. *When Tigers Fight: The Story of the Sino-Japanese War, 1937–1945*. New York: Viking Press 1982.

Wilson, Hugh. "From Rebel to Hero." *McGill News Alumni Quarterly* 68, no. 2 (Spring/Summer 1988): 11–13.

Wilson, John. *Norman Bethune: A Life of Passionate Conviction*. Montreal: XYZ Publishers 1999.

Worsley, T.C. *Behind the Battle*. London: Robert Hale 1939.

Wyden, Peter. *The Passionate War: The Narrative History of the Spanish Civil War, 1936–1939*. New York: Simon & Schuster 1983.

Zhang, Xuexin. *Baiqiuen en Zuanle*. (A brief biography of Norman Bethune). Fuzhou: Fuzhou People's Publishing House 1984.

Zhou, Erfu. *Doctor Norman Bethune*. Translated by Alison Bailey. Beijing: Foreign Language Press 1982.

Zuehlke, Mark. *The Gallant Cause: Canadians in the Spanish Civil War, 1936–1939*. Vancouver: Whitecap Books 1996.

Zuidema, George D., and Sloan, Herbert. "Alfred Blalock, Norman Bethune, and the Bethune Murals." *Surgery* 130 (2001): 866–81.

Index

Adorée, Renée, 88–9, 400n4
Albacete, 161, 163, 192, 223
Algoma District, 15, 16, 20, 23, 46
Alexander, Dr John, 60, 88, 114,
123, 399n2, 400n16; backs Bethune
for membership in American Asso-
ciation for Thoracic Surgery,
402n38; performs phrenicectomy
on Bethune, 92–3
Allan, Ted, 201–2, 203, 207, 371
Almería, 184, 185, 186; flight of
refugees toward, 187–8; bombing
of, 189–92
Amberson, Dr J. Burns, 53
American Association for Thoracic
Surgery (AATS), 98, 402n38;
Bethune at 1934 convention of,
112; Bethune on 1934 executive
council of, 105, 114; Bethune at
1936 convention of, 131–2
American League for Peace and
Democracy (ALPD), 243
American Medical Bureau to Aid
Spanish Democracy, 242, 249
Ann Arbor, MI, 88, 93, 139, 402n27,
n38, 426n56. See also University
Hospital, Ann Arbor, MI
Archibald, Dr Edward H., 386n26
Archibald, Dr Edward W., 74, 147,
395n13, n14, 396n15; Bethune as
his assistant, 75–6, 82; critical of
Bethune 79, 86–7, 98–9, 398n69,
399n70; and Percy C. Cowans
scholarship, 76–7, 82; praises
Bethune, 81, 86; recommends

Bethune to the Hôpital du Sacré
Coeur, 99; sponsors Bethune, 80,
81, 93, 98, 402n38; trains Bethune
in blood transfusion techniques, 76
artificial pneumothorax procedure
(collapse therapy): Bethune's advo-
cacy of, 90–1, "Compressionist's
Creed," 91; performed on Bethune,
60, 61–2, 73; refills (repeated treatments) 73, 76, 93
Aylmer, ON, 10, 14

Bai Qiuen (Chinese name for
Bethune) 351, 372, 447n46,
Banting, Dr Frederick, 67, 387n35
Baoding, 340, 357
Barcelona, 164, 179, 193–4, 416n3,
417n8; as centre of proposed unified blood delivery system, 178,
180, 183, 417n6
Barnwell, Dr John B., 71, 81, 88, 91,
128, 394n75; helps Bethune perform abortion on Frances Bethune,
93–4; recounts anecdotes about
Bethune's eccentric behaviour,
393n46, 426n56; socializes with
Bethune, 56, 58, 59, 71, 75; surprised by Bethune's communist
rhetoric, 139
Beament, Harold, 97, 198, 408n79
Beaverton, ON, 8, 17, 64
Beijing (Beiping), 228, 357, 373, 374;
possible source of funds for medical
school, 356; source of medical supplies, 340, 342–3, 345

Davidson, Dr Louis, 58, 59, 246, 393n57

Day, Margaret, 154, 409n25; affair with Bethune, 133–4, 137; becomes pregnant and asks Bethune to perform abortion, 139; ends affair and avoids meeting Bethune, 142, 216, 240; sees Bethune before he goes to China, 241

Dayi, 346

Deshaies, Dr Georges, 104, 105, 123, 141

Detroit: Bethune sells his practice in, 57; Bethune's residences, teaching, and medical-surgical practice in, 47–51; disliked by Bethune and Frances, 48, 52

Doctor Bethune (Chinese film), 453n14

Dodd, William Jr, 243, 248, 250, 257, 272, 432n48

Dong Yueqian, 326, 321, 341, 343, 350, 447n42; Bethune's interpreter, 298, 299, 305, 307; chief administrator of Fuping County, 298, 347, 350; and mobile surgical unit, 305, 310, 311; reunited with his family by Bethune, 342, 345; translates medical textbook by Bethune, 301

Dos Passos, John, 158

Duran i Jordà, Dr Frederic, 164, 176, 178, 179, 376, 413n27; opposes Bethune's leading a unified Spanish blood delivery service, 183, 194, 195

Edgeley, ON, 21–2

Edinburgh, Scotland, 4, 32, 37, 39,

Eighth Route Army: and Agnes Smedley, 242, 255, 429n11; Bethune and Ewen seconded to, 257; Bethune wishes to work with, 228, 256; guerilla warfare and, 283, 300; headquarters at Lanxian, 290; at Jingangku, 292, 306; liaison with Guomindang, 255; Medical Service hospitals of, 278–9, 282, 286–9, 293, 301–2, 313–16; 362; Military Council of, 300–1; military respon-

sibilities of, 283; receives foreign aid, 282, 338–9; victories over Japanese forces, 305, 349, 438n79; at Yan'an, 274. *See also* He Long, General; Nie Rongzhen, General; Zhu De, General

Elkan, Vera, 172

Ellingworth, Dr Clifford, 42

Elliott, Dr K.A.C., 372

evangelism, 5, 6, 382n11; Bethune's evangelistic traits, 13, 123, 127, 297, 344, 375

Ewen, Jean, 245, 252–85 *passim*, 322, 429n8, 431n36, 432n64; admires Bethune 245, 266, 268; Bethune praises, 279, 432n48; difficult relationship with Bethune, 250, 261, 263, 264, 265, 268; left behind by Bethune in Yan'an, 284–5, 437n44; meeting with Mao Zedong, 275–6; notes Bethune's communist fervour, 268, 269, 270; notes Bethune's temper, 254, 263, 264, 265, 268; sides with Bethune against Charles Parsons, 252, 254, 256

Faculty of Medicine, University of Toronto, 22, 25

fascism: Bethune calls for united front against, 213, 222, 227, 229; Bethune mistaken for a fascist in Spain, 158–9; Bethune sees fascism as threat to democracy, 138, 169–70, 212; Bethune sees Spain as significant in the struggle against, 169–70, 182; Bethune shows early enthusiasm for, 107, 405n16; Bethune warns of danger in Canada, 219, 223

Fisher, Dr Lincoln, 56, 71, 90–1

Fraad, Dr Lewis M., 243, 244, 245, 247, 427n24

Franco, Generalissimo Francisco, 138, 419n30

Friends of the Soviet Union (FSU), 122, 124

Frontier College. *See* Reading Camp Association

Fu, Dr Nelson, 278, 434n17

Galan, Antonio, 194, 417n8, 420n40
Ganhejing, 363, 364, 365
Geddes, Dr Aubrey, 85, 109, 113, 383n19
Goyanes, Dr Vicente, 199, 200, 421n13
Graham, Dr Ewarts, 132
Gravenhurst, ON, 373, 374, 375, 377; residence of Bethune family, 5–8, 383n17
Greenspan (Seborer), Celia, 169, 414n41, 420n8; critical of Bethune's running of blood transfusion unit, 172, 173, 181, 417n12
Guadalajara, battle of. *See* Spanish Civil War
Gu Zhengjun, Dr, 308–9

Haldane, J.B.S., 172, 173, 412n15
Hall, Kathleen, 330, 341–2, 445n12, n20, 449n20; buys medical supplies for Bethune, 343, 345, 356–7
Hankou (Hankow), 243; Bethune and Ewen work in hospital in, 256; wartime conditions in, 254–5, 429n19, n20. *See also* Wuhan
Hanson, Haldore, 439n95
Harper Hospital, Detroit, 48, 51
Haskell, Oliver, 428n39, 435n32, 436n33
Hatem, Dr George. See Ma Haide, Dr
Hawaii, 5, 382n8
Heart of Spain (film), 193, 197, 205, 206; delays in completion, 209–10, 212; first showing, 224. *See also* Kárpáthi, Geza
Hebei (Hopei) Province, 283, 305, 341, 353; Bethune in Central Hebei, 343, 345–51. *See also* Medical Expedition to the East
Heise, Dr Frederick, 60
Heisi, battle of, 311–12, 313
Hejiachuan, base hospital at, 286–90
He Long, General, 325, 339, 349–50, 351, 445n11, 446n29
Hemingway, Ernest, 158, 412n7

Herman Kiefer Hospital, Detroit, 94, 95, 96, 402n27
He Zexin, 277, 285, 286, 297, 305, 325; with Bethune in last days, 366, 367
Holt, George, 107, 112, 216, 222
Hôpital du Sacré Coeur: attitudes of staff toward Bethune, 104–5, 138, 140, 141, 216; Bethune appointed head of Pulmonary Surgery and Bronchoscopy at, 99, 100; Bethune gains perspective on social conditions while at, 107; Bethune performs blood transfusions at, 104, 404n1; Bethune trains thoracic surgeons at, 104
Hospital for Sick Children, Great Ormond Street, London, 32, 33, 34–5
Huangshikou, 337; Bethune's death at, 366–8
Huapen, base hospital at, 362, 365, 366
Huata, base hospital at, 318, 344, 345
Huot, Louis, 97, 209, 393n46, 423n42
Humphreys-Owen, Isabelle Rosalind, 38, 389n43, n44, n45; business and personal relationship with Bethune, 38–9, 41, 389n47; ends relationship with Bethune, 44
Hurcomb, Elizabeth, 111–12, 240, 249

influenza epidemic of 1919, 30
Ingersoll, ON, 35
Instituto canadiense de transfusión de sangre: Bethune's erratic behaviour at, 201–3; Bethune resigns from, 206–7; Bethune's temper creates problems at, 200, 201, 203; establishment of, 165, 168–9; functioning of, 173–6, 192, 197, 415n61, n62, 420n8; placed under authority of the Sanidad Militar, 205; tensions within, 171–3, 180–1, 199–201, 417n12
Instituto hispano-canadiense de transfusión de sangre, 181

International Brigades (IB), 161–2, 230; Bethune's intention to return to Spain to join, 205, 223, 225; rejects Bethune's services, 163

International Peace Hospital of Wutaishan, 339, 448n15. *See also* model hospital, Songyankou

Jaffe, Philip J.: dislike of Agnes Smedley, 282; dislike of Bethune, 248; forms China Aid Council, 243; meets with Mao Zedong and Agnes Smedley in Yan'an, 242, 430n32; supports Dr Charles Parsons, 257, 435n30

Jarama, battle of. *See* Spanish Civil War

Jettmar, Heinrich von, 269, 435n19

Jiang, Dr Jean, 449n20

Jiang Jieshi, Generalissimo (Chiang Kai-shek), 341 432n69, 444n5, 445n12

Jiang Qixian, Dr, 271, 278, 433n77, 438n72; conflict with Bethune about where he would be assigned, 282–3; at meeting of Bethune with Mao Zedong, 276–7, 434n7; travels to Hejiachuan with Bethune and Brown, 285, 288

Jiang Yizhen, Dr 284, 311–12, 355, 442n45,

Jiaotanzhuang, 306, 307, 343

Jin-Cha-Ji Border Region (Chin-Ch'a-Chi), 259, 283, 298, 300, 438n76; Bethune plans mobile operating units in, 292; Bethune's fame in, 351; Bethune teaches in, 299–300, 317–18, 329, 354–55, 362, 440n7; communications in, 445n11; defeat of Japanese troops by Eighth Route Army in, 305, 349; democratic hospital reform in, 314–15, 318, 353–4; medical situation in, 293, 296, 312; memorials to Bethune in, 369–70, 372; need for medical supplies in, 338–41, 444n2, 445n10, 448n15; need for medical training

school in, 300–1, 354–6

Jingangku, 292, 294, 300, 305, 438n74; destroyed by Japanese troops, 306

Juncheng, 369–70

Kangda (Anti-Japanese Aggression Military and Political University, Yan'an), 262, 277

Kárpáthi, Geza (Charles Korvin), 193, 211, 419n32; at battle of Guadalajara, 197, 198; and making of film *Heart of Spain*, 205

Kashtan, William, 423n39

Kemeny, John, 453n12

King, William Lyon Mackenzie, 219, 425n25

Kirkpatrick, Evelyn, 249

Kléber, Emilio (Lazar Stern), 162–3, 412n19, 422n35

Kline, Herbert, 205, 211

Kon, Irene, 407n65

Kon, Louis, 122–3, 124, 408n77

Korvin, Charles. *See* Kárpáthi, Geza

Kotnis, Dr Dwarkanath, 450n35, 453n13

Kupka, Dr Edward, 55, 85–6, 128, 391n13, 392n34; Bethune's student and aide, 49, 50–1

Landauer, Eric, 269

Lang Lin, 347, 354, 355, 361, 362–3; Bethune's last letter to, 367

Lanxian, 290, 339, 437n44, 438n74, 445n11

Lawrence, D.H., 59

Lea Cottage, Trudeau Sanatorium, 58, 59, 71; painting of mural *The T.B.'s Progress* at, 61–3, 72

League against War and Fascism (later League for Peace and Democracy), 450n39

League for Socialist Reconstruction (LSR), 108, 114

League of Nations Epidemiological Unit, 269–70, 272

League of Nations field hospital:

Palardy, Jori. *See* Smith, Jori

Pamsetgaaf Sanatorium, Arizona, 88, 399n3,

Pan Fan, 363, 366, 367, 368

Paris, 43, 157; Bethune buys medical equipment and picks up money in, 165, 167, 193; Bethune meets A.A. MacLeod in, 209

Park, Libbie, 129, 241, 374, 407n68, 407n71

Parsons, Dr Charles, 250, 255; abuse of alcohol, 247–8, 252, 254, 258, 428n3, 430n31; appointed head of China Aid Council medical unit instead of Bethune, 247, 282; conflict with Bethune and Ewen over CAC funds, 254, 256–7

partisans in China, 340, 435n25

Pater, Walter, 33

Pearson, Lester B., 166

Penney, Frances Eleanor Campbell, 37–8, 40–2, 70, 388n38. *See also* Bethune, Frances; Coleman, Frances

phrenicectomy, 88, 89, 96, 400n4; and Dr Edward J. (Pat) O'Brien, 401n20; performed on Bethune by Dr John Alexander, 93

Pilling, George, 81

pleural *poudrage* in lung surgery, 80–1, 397n39

Pony. *See* Scott, Marian Dale

Popular Front in Spain, 138, 207

Qihui, battle of, 347–9, 350, 445n11

Queipo de Llano, General, 185, 411n1

Quhuisi, 309, 312

Rawlings, Laura Bassett Boynton, 90, 400n13, n14, 401n21; Bethune falls in love with, 91–2, 93, 95

Reading Camp Association (now Frontier College), 23–5, 67, 386n10

religion: Bethune's attitude toward, 13, 18, 55, 284, 294, 296; Bethune's view of Marxism as a modern religion, 124, 127

Rich, Dr Herbert, 53

Robbins Cottage, Trudeau Sanatorium, 56

Robertson, Dr James A. and Dr Lorne, 29, 35

Roots, Bishop Logan H., 255, 257

Ross, Dr Graham, 32, 34, 78

Rothman, Kajsa, 233; acts as Bethune's interpreter, 202; affair with Bethune, 172–3; leaves the Instituto, 421n26; resented by Henning Sorensen, 173, 202–3; suspected of espionage, 205, 226, 422n32, 425n45; takes over running of the Instituto, 199

Royal Edward Institute, Montreal, 404n2, 405n35

Royal Navy, 387n39; Bethune serves in, 29–30

Royal Victoria Hospital, Montreal, 74, 146; Bethune appointed Dr Archibald's assistant at, 75–6; Bethune asked to resign from, 99; Bethune does research work at, 80–1; Bethune invents surgical instruments at, 81, 309n43; Bethune learns blood transfusion at, 76; Bethune receives Percy P. Cowans fellowship at, 76–7; Bethune's relationship with Archibald at, 79, 86, 87, 98–9; Bethune's reputation at, 80, 86–7; Bethune teaches at, 80, 397n36

Ryerson, Stanley, 374, 409n5

Sacré Coeur Hospital. *See* Hôpital du Sacré Coeur

Sainte Anne de Bellevue Hospital, 82, 98

Salmon Arm, BC, 228

Salsberg, Joseph, 217–18

Sanidad Militar, 209, 210, 226, 422n35; Bethune negotiates with, 178, 179–80, 181, 183, 193; Bethune sends letter of resignation to, 206–7; Bethune's contempt for, 200–1, 203; critical of Bethune's

Zhang Yesheng, 337
Zhou Enlai, 255, 257, 438n76
Zhou Zangzheng, 259, 262, 263, 269
Zhuanlinkou, 309
Zhu De, General, 429n11, 439n94,

n96; meets Bethune in Xi'an; 270,
military command of, 283, 293,
431n37; pays tribute to Bethune,
369; sends cable announcing
Bethune's death, 370